Computer Science

Volume 2

J. Stanley Warford
Pepperdine University

D. C. Heath and Company
Lexington, Massachusetts / Toronto

Address editorial correspondence to:

D. C. Heath
125 Spring Street
Lexington, MA 02173

Acquisitions Editor: Carter Shanklin
Developmental Editor: Katherine Pinard
Production Editor: Jennifer Brett
Designer: Judith Miller
Production Coordinator: Lisa Merrill
Photo Researcher: Ann M. Barnard

Cover Image: Digital Art/Los Angeles

Photo Credits: p. 666—The Bettmann Archive; p. 703—Iowa State University, Public Information Photo Department; p. 757—Ian Yeomans/Susan Griggs Agency Ltd.; p. 825—The Computer Museum; p. 908—The Thinking Machine, Inc.; p. 904—Camermann Inc.

Published simultaneously in Canada.

Printed in the United States of America.

International Standard Book Number: 0-669-24977-7

Library of Congress Catalog Number: 90-84807

10 9 8 7 6 5 4 3 2 1

This book is dedicated to
Ann
(and Moose and Goose).

Preface

This book is the outgrowth of an introductory computer science course taught at Pepperdine University, where the book has been class-tested for five years. The course, as well as the book, is primarily for majors in computer science who intend a more in-depth study later, and secondarily for nonmajors who desire a strong background in computers so that they can deal with them effectively in their chosen fields. The book is designed for a two- or three-semester course.

The Physics Model

The approach taken in this book is unique. The idea is best illustrated by looking at the typical curriculum in physics, a much older discipline. Like computer science, physics is a broad area. Over the years a traditional introductory physics course, which is uniform in content from school to school, has evolved. Physics educators realize that the first course should teach some problem-solving techniques and give the student some laboratory experience. In addition, they realize the importance of introducing the student to all the main areas of study, including mechanics, thermodynamics, electricity, magnetism, and modern physics. In-depth mastery of the subfields of physics is postponed for later courses in which the instructor can assume that the student has already been exposed to the main concepts.

The traditional design of the introductory computer science sequence lacks the breadth of the typical physics sequence. Computer science includes the study of hardware, language theory, algorithms, data structures, architecture, and operating systems. Although the recent trend is to incorporate more topics from data structures into the introductory course, most introductory sequences in computer science neglect hardware, language theory, architecture, and operating systems.

The physics curriculum generally recognizes that the concepts of motion, force, and energy as developed in classical Newtonian mechanics are the foundation on which all the other topics can be presented. However, physics books rarely present just mechanics—they develop the concepts in mechanics first and then move on to the other topics.

Similarly, this introductory computer science text begins with algorithm design in a high-order language, but is not confined to it. Although Pascal programming accounts for much of the content, a substantial portion of the text is devoted to computer organization down to the logic gate level. Students should get an overall picture of the discipline of computer science in their first year of study. Indeed, if they do not get a unified picture of the discipline then, when will they get it later?

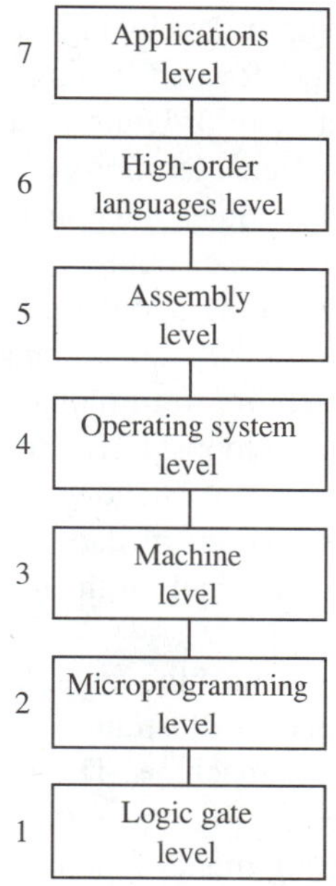

Figure P.1

The level structure of a typical computer system.

Summary of Contents

Computers operate at several levels of abstraction; programming in Pascal at a high level of abstraction is only part of the story. This book presents a unified concept of computer systems based on the level structure of Figure P.1.

The book is divided into six parts corresponding to six of the seven levels of Figure P.1:

Level 7 Applications
Level 6 High-order languages
Level 3 Machine
Level 5 Assembly
Level 4 Operating system
Level 1 Logic gate

Volume 1 of the two-volume edition covers Levels 7 and 6, and Volume 2 covers Levels 3, 5, 4, and 1. Microprogramming, Level 2, is beyond the scope of this book.

The text generally presents the levels top-down, from the highest to the lowest. Level 3, the machine level, is discussed before Level 5, the assembly level, for pedagogical reasons. In this one instance, it is more natural to revert temporarily to a bottom-up approach so that the building blocks of the lower level will be in hand for construction of the higher level.

Level 7 is a single chapter on applications programs. It presents the idea of levels of abstraction and establishes the framework for the remainder of the book. A few concepts of relational databases are presented as an example of a typical computer application. It is assumed that students have experience with text editors or word processors.

Level 6 consists of 10 chapters on algorithm design and data structures in Pascal (Chapters 2–11). The treatment of Pascal is fairly complete and includes separate chapters on recursion and pointers. Some topics, such as passing procedures as parameters, are not included.

Students learn best by studying and imitating complete programs, so the Pascal chapters present the material in a case-study format. Generalizations then follow the examples. As much as possible, Pascal language features are discussed in the context of the specific programs.

Two design methodologies are integrated into the Pascal chapters—stepwise refinement and top-down design. Although these two techniques are closely related (some would say they are identical), they are treated separately. Stepwise refinement is a tool for developing a single main program or a single module. Top-down design is a tool for partitioning a program into modules. (In this book, a module is defined as a main program or a procedure or a function.) The design methodologies and associated terminology are simplified to avoid intimidating the student.

Two other topics integrated throughout the Pascal chapters are assertions and statement execution counts. Assertions are introduced with nested `if` statements as a tool for reasoning about the behavior of executable code. Formal proofs of correctness are left for a later course, but the book lays the groundwork by giving the students the ability to formulate a strong assertion. Statement execution counts are introduced with loops. Given the execution time of a program with a small amount of data, the student is shown how to estimate the execution time of the program with a large amount of data. The numerical exercises included in these chapters give the student a feel for the usefulness of time-complexity results.

Level 3 is the machine level. Its two chapters describe Pep/5, a hypothetical computer designed to illustrate computer concepts. The Pep/5 computer is a classical von Neumann machine. The CPU contains an accumulator, an index register, a base register, a program counter, a stack pointer, and an instruction register. It has four addressing modes—immediate, direct, indexed, and stack relative. The Pep/5 operating system, in simulated read-only memory (ROM), can load and execute programs in hexadecimal format from students' text files. Students run short programs on the Pep/5 simulator and learn that executing a store instruction to ROM does not change the memory value.

Students learn the fundamentals of information representation and computer organization at the bit level. Because a central theme of this book is the relationship of the levels to one another, the Pep/5 chapters show the relationship between the ASCII representation (Level 3) and Pascal variables of type `char` (Level 6). They also show the relationship between two's complement representation (Level 3) and Pascal variables of type `integer` (Level 6).

Level 5 is the assembly level. The text presents the concept of the assembler as a translator between two levels—assembly and machine. It introduces Level 5 symbols and the symbol table.

The unified approach really pays off here. Chapters 14 and 15 present the compiler as a translator from a high-order language to assembly language. In previous chapters students learned a specific Level 6 language, Pascal, and a specific von Neumann machine, Pep/5. These chapters continue the theme of relationships between the levels by showing the correspondence between (a) assignment statements at Level 6 and load/store instructions at Level 5, (b) loops and `if` statements at Level 6 and branching instructions at Level 5, (c) arrays at Level 6 and indexed addressing at Level 5, (d) procedure calls at Level 6 and the run-time stack at Level 5, (e) function and procedure parameters at Level 6 and stack-relative addressing at Level 5, and (f) `case` statements at Level 6 and jump tables at Level 5.

The beauty of the unified approach is that the text can implement many of the examples from the Pascal chapters at this lower level. For example, the run-time stack illustrated in the recursive examples of an earlier chapter corresponds directly to the hardware stack in Pep/5 main memory. Students gain an understanding of the compilation process by translating manually between the two levels.

This approach provides a natural setting for the discussion of central issues in computer science. For example, the book presents structured programming at Level 6 versus the possibility of unstructured programming at Level 5. It discusses the goto controversy and the structured programming/efficiency tradeoff, giving concrete examples from languages at the two levels. As in the Pascal chapters, the style of presentation involves drawing general conclusions from specific examples.

Chapter 16, Language Translation Principles, introduces students to computer science theory. Now that students know intuitively how to translate from a high-level language to assembly language, we pose the fundamental question underlying all of computing, What can be automated? The theory naturally fits in here because students now know what a compiler (an automated translator) must do. They learn about parsing and finite state machines—deterministic and nondeterministic—in the context of recognizing Pascal and Pep/5 assembly language tokens. This chapter includes an automatic translator between two small languages, which illustrates lexical analysis, parsing, and code generation. The lexical analyzer is an implementation of a finite state machine. What could be a more natural setting for the theory?

Level 4 consists of two chapters on operating systems. Chapter 17 is a description of process management. Two sections, one on loaders and another on interrupt handlers, illustrate the concepts with the Pep/5 operating system. Four instructions have unimplemented opcodes that generate software interrupts. The operating system stores the process control block of the user's running process on the system stack while the interrupt service routine interprets the instruction. The classic state transition diagram for running and waiting processes in an operating system is thus reinforced with a specific implementation of a suspended process. The chapter concludes with a description of concurrent processes and deadlocks. Chapter 18 describes storage management, both main memory and disk memory.

Level 1 uses two chapters to present combinational networks and sequential networks. Chapter 19 emphasizes the importance of the mathematical foundation of computer science by starting with the axioms of boolean algebra. It shows the relation between boolean algebra and logic gates, then describes some common SSI and MSI logic devices. Chapter 20 again illustrates the fundamental concept of a finite state machine through the state transition diagrams of sequential circuits. It concludes with the construction of the data section of the Pep/5 computer. The same machine model is thus used from the Pascal level to the logic gate level, providing a complete, unifying picture of the entire system.

Unifying Themes

In physics, fundamental concepts of motion, force, and energy are developed in one area of study and carried over into other areas, thus providing a unifying framework. Unifying themes of this book include abstraction, languages, and finite state machines.

The fundamental space/time tradeoff is another recurring theme. Execution-time analysis begins with the first `while` loop in Chapter 5 and continues throughout the text. The tradeoff occurs in software when the availability of extra memory may permit a faster algorithm, and in hardware when a two-level network may require more gates to implement a binary function than a multilevel one.

The Denning Report

This text reflects the recent recommendations of the Denning Report, "Computing as a Discipline."[1] That report identifies the following nine subareas of computer science on which the introductory sequence should be based:

1. Algorithms and data structures
2. Programming languages
3. Architecture
4. Numeric and symbolic computation
5. Operating systems
6. Software methodology and engineering
7. Databases and information retrieval
8. Artificial intelligence and robotics
9. Human-computer communication

This book emphasizes five areas (1, 2, 3, 5, 6), touches on two others (4, 7), and admits that two areas are beyond its scope (8, 9). Even with the omissions, I believe that this book achieves the goal enunciated in the Denning Report that the "introductory sequence should bring out the underlying unity of the field and should flow from topic to topic in a pedagogically natural way."

Additional Features

Exercises and Programming Assignments In a course based on this book, homework assignments consist of exercises, which are handwritten, and problems, which are programming assignments for computer execution. There are an average of nearly 40 exercises and programming assignments in each chapter. These two types of assignments reflect the difference between analysis and design. Neglecting analysis is like trying to teach children to write (design) before they can read (analyze). At the introductory level, analysis is just as important as design. If students do not get explicit practice in reasoning about control structures, it is more difficult for them to locate logical errors in the loops they write. After all, debugging is analysis, not design.

Software Tools One goal of this text is to give the student useful software tools. Accordingly, I have tried to present the "best" known algorithms. The sequential

1. Peter J. Denning et al., "Computing as a Discipline," *Computer* 22 (February 1989): 63–70. © 1989 by IEEE.

search algorithm installs the search key after the last item in the list, so the loop has only one test. The binary search algorithm is free of the subtle errors described by Pattis.[2] The random number generator is based on that recommended by Park and Miller.[3] The sequential file update algorithm is the balanced-line algorithm as described by Levy.[4] The section on sorting uses the taxonomy of sort algorithms from Merritt.[5] The version of quick sort is one that executes in time $n \log n$ even in the case when the original array is approximately in order.

Use in the Curriculum

With such broad coverage, some instructors may wish to omit some of the material when designing their introductory sequence. To provide maximum flexibility for curriculum design, the model is again the traditional introductory physics textbook, which usually contains many topics and applications that may be omitted depending on the interest of the instructor.

Students are introduced to the concept of an abstract data type as applied to the stack in Chapter 9. Although other data structures topics are normally included in the introductory sequence, it is possible to omit half of Chapter 10 (Dynamic Storage Allocation) and all of Chapter 11 (Data Structures), trading off this depth for the breadth that comes by studying the lower levels. Later material in the book is not dependent on these omitted topics, which can be left to a more advanced data structures course.

In the remainder of the book, Chapters 12–14 must be covered sequentially. Chapters 15 (Compiling to the Assembly Level) and 16 (Language Translation Principles) can be covered in either order. I often skip ahead to Chapter 16 to initiate a large software project, writing an assembler for a subset of Pep/5 assembly language, so students will have sufficient time to complete it during the semester. Chapter 20 (Sequential Networks) is obviously dependent on Chapter 19 (Combinational Networks), but neither depends on Chapter 18 (Storage Management), which may be omitted. Figure P.2, a chapter dependency graph, summarizes the possible chapter omissions.

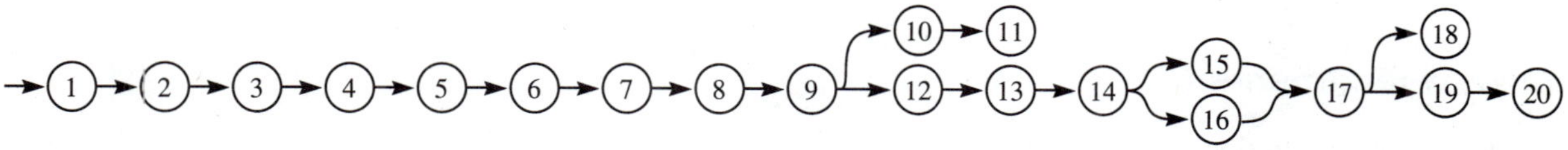

Figure P.2

A chapter dependency graph.

2. Richard E. Pattis, "Textbook Errors in Binary Searching," *ACM SIGCSE Bulletin* 20 (February 1988): 190–94.

3. Stephen K. Park and Keith W. Miller, "Random Number Generators: Good Ones Are Hard to Find," *Communications of the ACM* 31 (October 1988): 1192–1201.

4. Michael R. Levy, "Modularity and the Sequential File Update Problem," *Communications of the ACM* 25 (June 1982): 362–67.

5. Susan M. Merritt, "An Inverted Taxonomy of Sorting Algorithms," *Communications of the ACM* 28 (January 1985): 96–98.

In addition to possible chapter omissions, some sections within chapters may be omitted; examples include sections 6.4 (Scope of Identifiers), 6.5 (Random Numbers), 13.5 (Some Typical Architectures), 15.4 (Data Types at Level 5), 17.3 (Concurrent Processes), and 17.4 (Deadlocks). Selected topics within sections may also be omitted; examples include specific algorithms such as matrix multiplication and recursive merge sort.

Support Materials

Pep/5 Assembler/Simulator Disk Machine-readable source code for the Pep/5 system is available to adopters from the publisher or the author (Bitnet address: warford@pepvax). The package, complete with assembler and trace facilities, is written in Pascal and runs on MS-DOS, MacOS, or UNIX systems. (Please specify which system you use.) The software may be copied freely without express permission.

Instructor's Guide An Instructor's Guide containing solutions to exercises and overhead transparency masters of the figures and program listings is available to adopters. Teaching hints and suggestions on how to structure the course, based on classroom experience teaching computer science from a unified perspective, are also included.

Test Disk The exercises and problems in the book have been combined with additional test items and are available on disk in ASCII format. These can be imported into your word processor to facilitate the printing of exams.

Test Item File A printed Test Item File contains the same questions that are available on the Test Disk.

Program Disk All the programs from the book and the data files necessary to test the programming problems are available on disk.

Acknowledgments

The nroff document-preparation utility on Pepperdine's VAX UNIX system was valuable for preparing early versions of the manuscript. I was able to design most of the figures with MacDraw on a Macintosh. I commend the folks at Apple Computers for such a great desktop graphics system. I believe the quality of the book is significantly better than it would have been without these tools.

Pep/1 had 16 instructions, one accumulator, and one addressing mode. Pep/2 added indexed addressing. John Vannoy wrote both simulators in ALGOL W. Pep/3 had 32 instructions and was written in Pascal as a student software project by Steve Dimse, Russ Hughes, Kazuo Ishikawa, Nancy Brunet, and Yvonne Smith. In an early review Harold Stone suggested many improvements to the Pep/3 architecture that were incorporated into Pep/4 and carried into Pep/5. Pep/4 had special stack instructions, simulated ROM, and software interrupts. Pep/5 is a more orthogonal design, allowing any instruction to use any addressing mode. John Rooker wrote the Pep/4 system and an early version of Pep/5. Gerry St. Romain implemented a MacOS version and an MS-DOS version.

More than any other book, Tanenbaum's *Structured Computer Organization* has influenced this text.[6] This text extends the level structure of Tanenbaum's book by adding the high-order programming level and the applications level at the top.

The following reviewers of the manuscript in its various stages of development shaped the final product significantly: Wayne P. Bailey, Northeast Missouri State University; Fadi Deek, New Jersey Institute of Technology; William Decker, University of Iowa; Gerald S. Eisman, San Francisco State University; Victoria Evans, University of Nevada at Reno; David Garnick, Bowdoin College; Ephraim P. Glinert, Rensselaer Polytechnic Institute; Dave Hanscom, University of Utah; Michael Hennessy, University of Oregon; Michael Johnson, Oregon State University; Robert Martin, Middlebury College; Richard H. Mercer, Pennsylvania State University—Berks Campus; Randy Molmen, Baldwin-Wallace College; Peter Ng, New Jersey Institute of Technology; Bernard Nudel, University of Michigan; Carolyn Oberlink, Western Michigan University; Wolfgang Pelz, University of Akron; James F. Peters III, Kansas State University; James C. Pleasant, East Tennessee State University; Eleanor Quinlan, Ohio State University; Glenn A. Richard, State University of New York at Stony Brook; David Rosser, Ramsey, N.J.; Scott Smith, State University of New York at Plattsburgh; Harold S. Stone, The Interfactor, Inc.; J. Peter Weston, Daniel Webster College; and Norman E. Wright, Brigham Young University.

Don Thompson, Don Hancock, Carol Adjemian, Chelle Boehning, and Janet Davis taught sections of the course on which this book is based. They contributed suggestions and exercises. Thanks especially to Gerry St. Romain, who provided, based on his experience, literally hundreds of ideas that were incorporated into the text. Those who typed early drafts of the manuscript include Julie Teichrow, Russ Hughes, and Janet Davis. Joe Piasentin provided artistic consultation.

It has been a pleasure to work with the publisher of this book, D. C. Heath. Karin Ellison provided constant enthusiasm and encouragement from the beginning. Carter Shanklin guided the project on to completion. Thanks to Kitty Pinard for suggesting the sidebars and to Scott Smith of SUNY Plattsburgh for writing them. Judy Miller did a magnificent job designing the book, and Jennifer Brett did a superb job producing it, no small feat for a technical book of this length.

I am fortunate to be at an institution that is committed to excellence in undergraduate education. Pepperdine University in the person of Ken Perrin provided the creative environment and the professional support in which the idea behind this project was able to evolve. My wife, Ann, provided endless personal support. To her I owe an apology for the time this project has taken, and my greatest thanks.

Stan Warford

6. Andrew S. Tanenbaum, *Structured Computer Organization* (Englewood Cliffs, N.J.: Prentice-Hall, 1984).

Brief Contents

Contents

LEVEL 3

Machine

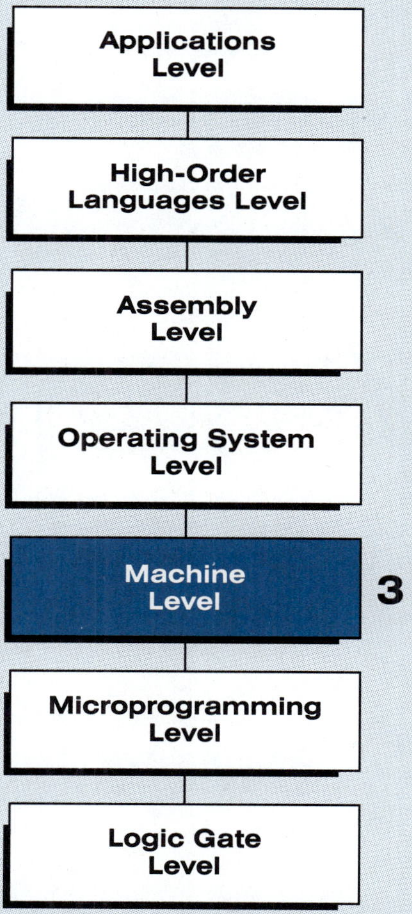

Chapter

12

Information Representation

One of the most significant inventions of mankind is the printed word. The words on this page represent information stored on paper, which is conveyed to you as you read. Like the printed page, computers have memories for storing information. The central processing unit (CPU) has the ability to retrieve information from its memory much like you take information from words on a page.

Reading and writing, words and pages

Some computer terminology is based on this analogy. The CPU *reads* information from memory and *writes* information into memory. The information itself is divided into *words*. In some computer systems large sets of words, usually anywhere from a few hundred to a few thousand, are grouped into *pages*.

Information representation at Level 3

In Pascal, at Level 6, information takes the form of values that you store in a variable in main memory or in a file on disk. This chapter shows how the computer stores that information at Level 3. Information representation at the machine level differs significantly from that at the high-order languages level. At Level 3, information representation is less human-oriented. Later chapters will discuss information representation at the intermediate levels, Levels 5 and 4, and show how they relate to Levels 6 and 3.

12.1 Unsigned Binary Representation

The Mark I computer

Early computers were electromechanical. That is, all their calculations were performed with moving switches called *relays*. The Mark I computer, built in 1944 by Howard H. Aiken of Harvard University, was such a machine. Aiken had procured financial backing for his project from Thomas J. Watson, president of International Business Machines (IBM). The relays in the Mark I computer could compute much faster than the mechanical gears that were used in adding machines at that time.

The ENIAC computer

Even before the completion of Mark I, John V. Atanasoff, working at Iowa State University, had finished the construction of an electronic computer to solve systems of linear equations. In 1941, John W. Mauchly visited Atanasoff's laboratory and in 1946, in collaboration with J. Presper Eckert at the University of Pennsylvania, built the famous Electronic Numerical Integrator and Calculator

(ENIAC). ENIAC's 19,000 vacuum tubes could perform 5000 additions per second compared to 10 additions per second with the relays of the Mark I. Like the ENIAC, present-day computers are electronic, although their calculations are performed with integrated circuits (ICs) instead of with vacuum tubes. Each IC contains thousands of transistors similar to the transistors in radios.

Binary Storage

Electronic computer memories cannot store numbers and letters directly. They can only store electrical signals. When the CPU reads information from memory, it is detecting a signal whose voltage is about equal to that produced by three flashlight batteries.

Computer memories are designed with a most remarkable property. Each storage location contains either a high-voltage signal or a low-voltage signal, never anything in between. The storage location is like being pregnant. Either you are or you are not. There is no halfway.

The word *digital* means that the signal stored in memory can only have a fixed number of values. *Binary* means that only two values are possible. Practically all computers on the market today are binary. Hence, each storage location contains either a high voltage or a low voltage. The state of each location is also described as being either on or off, or, alternatively, as containing either a 1 or a 0.

Each individual storage unit is called a *binary digit* or *bit*. A bit can be only 1 or 0, never anything else, such as 2, 3, A, or Z. This is a fundamental concept. Every piece of information stored in the memory of a computer, whether it is the amount you owe on your credit card or your street address, is stored in binary as 1's and 0's.

In practice, the bits in a computer memory are grouped together into *cells*. A seven-bit computer, for example, would store its information in groups of seven bits, as Figure 12.1 shows. You can think of a cell as a group of boxes, each box containing a 1 or a 0, nothing else. The first two lines in Figure 12.1(c) are impossible because the values in some boxes differ from 0 or 1. The last is impossible because each box must contain a value. A bit of storage cannot contain nothing.

Different computers have different numbers of bits in each cell, although most computers these days have eight bits per cell. This chapter will show examples with several different cell sizes to illustrate the general principle.

Information such as numbers and letters must be represented in binary form to be stored in memory. The representation scheme used to store information is called a *code*. This section examines a code for storing unsigned integers. The remainder of this chapter describes codes for storing other kinds of data. The next chapter examines codes for storing program commands in memory.

(a) A seven-bit cell.

0	1	1	0	1	0	1
1	1	0	1	1	0	0
0	0	0	0	0	0	0

(b) Some possible values in a seven-bit cell.

6	8	0	7	2	5	1
J	A	N	U	A	R	Y
		1	1	0	1	0

(c) Some impossible values in a seven-bit cell.

Figure 12.1

A seven-bit memory cell in main memory.

Integers

Numbers must be represented in binary form to be stored in a computer's memory. The particular code depends on whether the number has a fractional part or is an integer. If the number is an integer, the code depends on whether it is always positive or whether it can be negative as well.

Unsigned binary

The *unsigned binary* representation is for integers that are always positive. Before learning the binary system we will review our own base 10 (*decimal,* or *dec* for short) system, then work our way down to the binary system.

Our decimal system was probably invented because we have 10 fingers with which we count and add. A book of arithmetic using this elegant system was written in India in the eighth century A.D. It was translated into Arabic and was eventually carried by merchants to Europe, where it was translated from Arabic into Latin. The numbers came to be known as Arabic numerals, since at the time it was thought that they originated in Arabia. But Hindu-Arabic numerals would be a more appropriate name because they actually originated in India.

Counting with Arabic numerals in base 10 looks like this (reading down, of course):

Counting in decimal

0	7	14	21	28	35
1	8	15	22	29	36
2	9	16	23	30	37
3	10	17	24	31	38
4	11	18	25	32	.
5	12	19	26	33	.
6	13	20	27	34	.

Starting from "0" the Indians simply invented a symbol for the next number "1," then "2," and so on until they got to the symbol "9." At that point they looked at their hands and thought of a fantastic idea. On their last finger they did not invent a new symbol. Instead they used the first two symbols, "1" and "0," together to represent the next number, "10."

You know the rest of the story. When they got to "19" they saw that the "9" was as high as they could go with the symbols they had invented. So they dropped it down to "0" and increased the "1" to "2," creating "20." They did the same for "29" to "30" and, eventually, "99" to "100." On and on it went.

What if we only had 8 fingers instead of 10? What would have happened? At "7" the next number would be on our last finger, and we would not need to invent a new symbol. The next number would be represented as "10." Counting in base eight (*octal*, or *oct* for short) looks like this:

Counting in octal

0	7	16	25	34	43
1	10	17	26	35	44
2	11	20	27	36	45
3	12	21	30	37	46
4	13	22	31	40	.
5	14	23	32	41	.
6	15	24	33	42	.

The next number after 77 is 100 in octal.

Comparing the decimal and octal schemes, notice that 5 (oct) is the same number as 5 (dec), but that 21 (oct) is not the same number as 21 (dec). Instead, 21 (oct) is the same number as 17 (dec). Numbers have a tendency to look larger than they actually are when written in octal.

But what if we only had 3 fingers instead of 10 or 8? The pattern is the same. Counting in base 3 looks like this:

Counting in base 3

0	21	112	210	1001	1022
1	22	120	211	1002	1100
2	100	121	212	1010	1101
10	101	122	220	1011	1102
11	102	200	221	1012	.
12	110	201	222	1020	.
20	111	202	1000	1021	.

Finally we have arrived at unsigned binary representation. Computers only have 2 fingers. Counting in base 2 (*binary*, or *bin* for short) follows the exact same method.

Counting in binary

0	111	1110	10101	11100	100011
1	1000	1111	10110	11101	100100
10	1001	10000	10111	11110	100101
11	1010	10001	11000	11111	100110
100	1011	10010	11001	100000	.
101	1100	10011	11010	100001	.
110	1101	10100	11011	100010	.

Binary numbers look a lot larger than they actually are. The number 10110 (bin) is only 22 (dec).

Base Conversions

Given a number written in binary, there are several ways to determine its decimal equivalent. One way is to simply count up to the number in binary and in decimal. That method works well for small numbers. Another method is to add up the place values of each 1 bit in the binary number.

Example 12.1 Figure 12.2(a) shows the place values for 10110 (bin). Starting with the 1's place on the right (called the least significant bit), each place

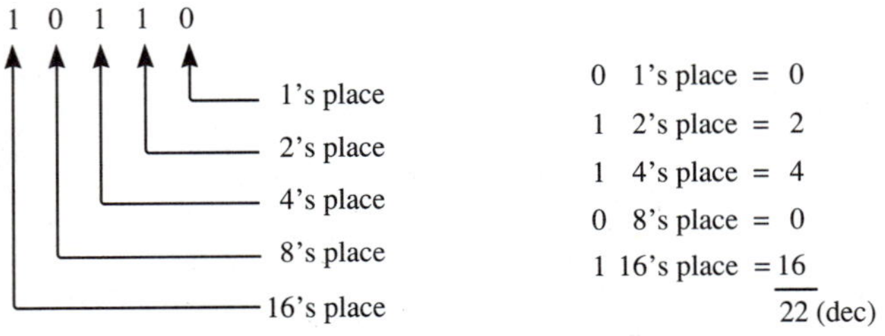

(a) The place values for 10110 (bin).

(b) Converting 10110 (bin) to decimal.

Figure 12.2

Converting from binary to decimal.

has a value twice as great as the previous place value. Figure 12.2(b) shows the addition that produces the 22 (dec) value. ■

Example 12.2 The unsigned binary number system is analogous to our familiar decimal system. Figure 12.3 shows the place values for 58,036 (dec). The figure 58,036 represents six 1's, three 10's, no 100's, eight 1000's, and five 10,000's. Starting with the 1's place from the right, each place value is 10 times greater than the previous place value. In binary, each place value is 2 times greater than the previous place value. ■

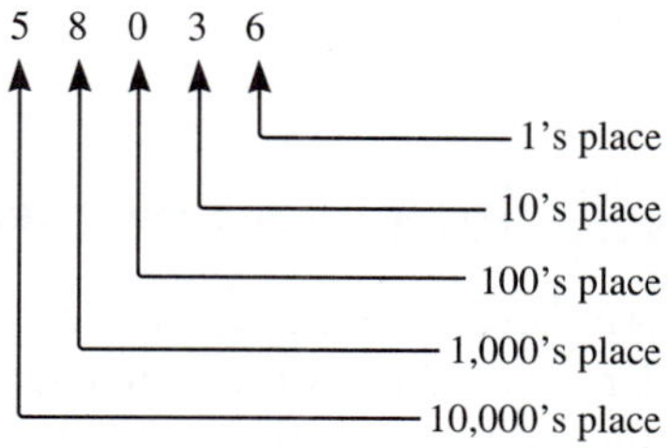

Figure 12.3

The place values for 58,036 (dec).

The value of an unsigned number can be conveniently represented as a polynomial in the base of the number system. (The base is also called the *radix* of the number system.) Figure 12.4 shows the polynomial representation of 10110 (bin) and 58,036 (dec). The value of the least significant place is always the base to the zeroth power, which is always 1. The next significant place is the base to the first power, which is the value of the base itself. You can see from the structure of the polynomial that the value of each place is the base times the value of the previous place.

$$1 \times 2^4 + 0 \times 2^3 + 1 \times 2^2 + 1 \times 2^1 + 0 \times 2^0$$

(a) The binary number 10110.

$$5 \times 10^4 + 8 \times 10^3 + 0 \times 10^2 + 3 \times 10^1 + 6 \times 10^0$$

(b) The decimal number 58,036.

Figure 12.4

The polynomial representation of unsigned numbers.

In binary, the only place with an odd value is the 1's place. All the other places (2's, 4's, 8's, and so on) are even. If there is a 0 in the 1's place, the value of the binary number will come from adding several even numbers, and it will be even, therefore. On the other hand, if there is a 1 in the 1's place of a binary number, its value will come from adding one to several even numbers, and it will be odd. As in the decimal system, you can tell whether a binary number is even or odd simply by inspecting the digit in the 1's place.

To determine the binary equivalent of a number written in decimal is a bit tricky. One method is to successively divide the original number by two, keeping track of the remainders, which will form the binary number when listed in reverse order from which they were obtained.

Example 12.3 Figure 12.5 converts 22 (dec) to binary. The number 22 divided by 2 is 11 with a remainder of 0, which is written in the right column. Then, 11 divided by 2 is 5, with a remainder of 1. Continuing until the number gets down to 0 produces a column of remainders, which, when read from the bottom up, form the binary number 10110. ■

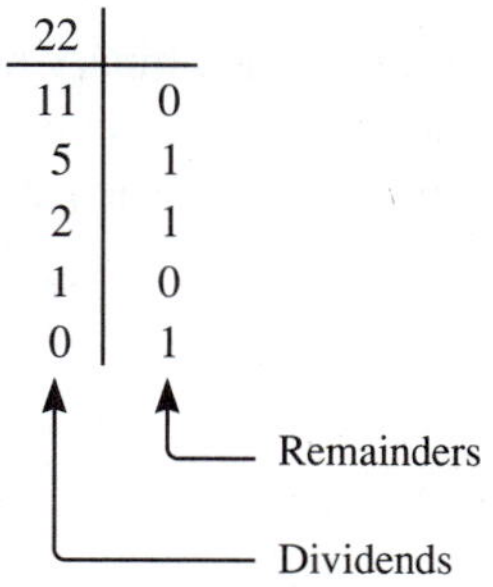

Figure 12.5

Converting from decimal to binary.

Notice that the least significant bit is the remainder when you divide the original value by 2. This fact is consistent with the observation that you can determine whether a binary number is even or odd by inspecting only the least significant bit. If the original value is even, the division will produce a remainder of 0, which will be the least significant bit. Conversely, if the original value is odd, the least significant bit will be 1.

Range for Unsigned Integers

All these counting schemes based on Arabic numerals let you represent arbitrarily large numbers. A real computer, however, has a finite number of bits in each cell. Figure 12.6 shows how a seven-bit computer would store the number 22 (dec). Notice the two leading 0's, which do not affect the value of the number, but which are necessary for specifying the contents of the memory location. In dealing with a seven-bit computer, you should write the number without showing the boxes as

0	0	1	0	1	1	0

Figure 12.6

The number 22 (dec) in a seven-bit computer.

001 0110

The two leading 0's are still necessary. This book displays bit strings with a space for legibility between each group of four bits starting from the right.

The range of unsigned values depends on the number of bits in a cell. A sequence of all 0's represents the smallest unsigned value, and a sequence of all 1's represents the largest.

Example 12.4 The smallest unsigned integer a seven-bit computer can store is

000 0000 (bin)

and the largest is

111 1111 (bin)

The smallest is 0 (dec) and the largest is 127 (dec). A seven-bit computer cannot store an unsigned integer greater than 127. ■

Unsigned Addition

Addition with unsigned binary numbers works like addition with unsigned decimal numbers. But it is easier, since you only need to learn the addition rules for two bits instead of 10 digits. The rules for adding bits are

Binary addition rules

$$0 + 0 = 0$$
$$0 + 1 = 1$$
$$1 + 0 = 1$$
$$1 + 1 = 10$$

The carry technique in binary

The carry technique that you are familiar with in the decimal system also works in the binary system. If two numbers in a column add to a value greater than 1, you must carry 1 to the next column.

Example 12.5 Suppose that you have a six-bit cell. To add the two numbers 01 1010 and 01 0001, simply write one number above the other and start at the least significant column.

	01 1010
ADD	01 0001
	10 1011

Notice that when you get to the fifth column from the right, 1 + 1 equals 10. You must write down the 0 and carry the 1 to the next column, where 1 + 0 + 0 produces the leftmost 1 in the sum.

To verify that this carry technique works in binary, convert the two numbers and their sum to decimal.

01 1010 (bin) = 26 (dec)
01 0001 (bin) = 17 (dec)
10 1011 (bin) = 43 (dec)

Sure enough, 26 + 17 = 43 in decimal. ■

Example 12.6 These examples show how the carry can propagate along several consecutive columns:

	00 0011		00 1111
ADD	01 0001	ADD	00 1001
	01 0100		01 1000

In the second example, when you get to the fourth column from the right, you have a carry from the previous column. Then 1 + 1 + 1 equals 11. You must write down 1 and carry 1 to the next column. ■

The Carry Bit

The range for the six-bit cell of the previous examples is 00 0000 to 11 1111 (bin), or 0 to 63 (dec). It is possible for two numbers to be in range but for their sum to be out of range. In that case the sum is too large to fit into the six bits of the storage cell.

The carry bit in addition

To flag this condition, the CPU contains a special bit called the *carry bit,* denoted by the letter C. When two binary numbers are added, if the sum of the leftmost column (called the *most significant bit*) produces a carry, then C is set to 1. Otherwise C is cleared to 0. In other words, C always contains the carry from the leftmost column of the cell. In all the previous examples, the sum was in range. Hence the carry bit was cleared to 0.

Example 12.7 Here are two examples showing the effect on the carry bit:

	01 0110		10 1010
ADD	10 0010	ADD	01 1010
C = 0	11 1000	C = 1	00 0100

In the second example, the CPU adds 42 + 26. The correct result, which is 68, is too large to fit into the six-bit cell. Remember, the range is from 0 to 63. So the lowest order (that is, the rightmost) six bits are stored, giving an incorrect result of 4. The carry bit is also set to 1 to indicate that a carry occurred from the highest-order column. ■

The carry bit in subtraction

Subtraction is performed with borrows, as in decimal. In unsigned binary representation, if you try to subtract a larger number from a smaller number, the correct answer will be negative, which is out of range. In that case, C is used as a *borrow bit*. When you get to the leftmost column, if you need to borrow again, C gets 1. The result of the subtraction is then stored, but it is not the correct difference. Because C is 1, the value stored is known to be incorrect.

12.2 Two's Complement Binary Representation

The unsigned binary representation works for nonnegative integers only. If a computer is to process negative integers it must use a different representation.

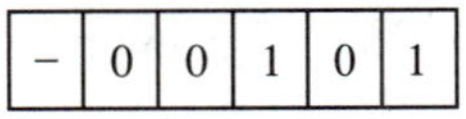

Figure 12.7

An attempt to store a negative number in binary.

Suppose you have a six-bit cell and you want to store the number –5 (dec). Since 5 (dec) is 101 (bin), you might try the pattern shown in Figure 12.7. But this is impossible since all bits, including the first, must be 0 or 1. Remember that computers are binary. The above storage value would require each box to be capable of storing a 0, or a 1, or a dash. Such a computer would have to be ternary instead of binary.

The solution to this problem is to reserve the first box in the cell to indicate the sign. Thus, the six-bit cell will have two parts—a one-bit sign and a five-bit magnitude as Figure 12.8 shows. Since the sign bit must be 0 or 1, one possibility is to let a 0 sign bit indicate a positive number, and a 1 sign bit indicate a negative number. Then +5 could be represented as

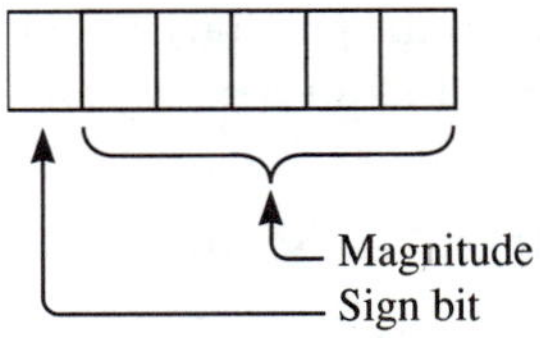

Figure 12.8

The structure of a signed integer.

00 0101

and –5 could be represented as

10 0101

In this code the magnitudes for +5 and –5 would be identical. Only the sign bits would differ.

Few computers use the previous code, however. The problem is that if you add +5 and –5 in decimal you get 0, but if you add 00 0101 and 10 0101 in binary (sign bits and all) you get

	00 0101
ADD	10 0101
C = 0	10 1010

A convenient property of negative numbers

which is definitely not 0. It would be much more convenient if the hardware of the CPU could add the numbers for +5 and –5, complete with sign bits using the ordinary rules for unsigned binary addition, and get 0.

The *two's complement* binary representation has that property. The positive numbers have a 0 sign bit, and a magnitude as in the unsigned binary representation. For example, the number +5 (dec) is still represented as 00 0101.

But the representation of –5 (dec) is not 10 0101. Instead it is 11 1011 since adding +5 and –5 gives

	00 0101
ADD	11 1011
C = 1	00 0000

Note that the six-bit sum is all 0's, as advertised.

Under the rules of binary addition for a six-bit cell, the number 11 1011 is called the *additive inverse* of 00 0101. The operation of finding the additive inverse is referred to as *negation,* abbreviated NEG. To negate a number is also called *taking its two's complement.*

The NEG operation

All we need now is the rule for taking the two's complement of a number. A simple rule is based on the *ones' complement,* which is simply the binary sequence with all the 1's changed to 0's and all the 0's changed to 1's. The ones' complement is also called the NOT operation.

The NOT operation

Example 12.8 The ones' complement of 00 0101 is

NOT 00 0101 = 11 1010

assuming a six-bit cell. ■

A clue to finding the rule for two's complement is to note the effect of adding a number to its ones' complement. Since 1 plus 0 is 1, and 0 plus 1 is 1, any number, when added to its ones' complement, will produce a sequence of all 1's. But then, adding a single 1 to a number of all 1's produces a number of all 0's.

Example 12.9 Adding 00 0101 to its ones' complement produces

	00 0101
ADD	11 1010
C = 0	11 1111

which is all 1's. Adding 1 to this produces

	11 1111
ADD	00 0001
C = 1	00 0000

which is all 0's. ■

In other words, adding a number to its ones' complement plus 1, gives all 0's. So the two's complement of a binary number must be found by adding 1 to its ones' complement.

Example 12.10 To find the two's complement of 00 0101, add 1 to its ones' complement.

NOT 00 0101 = 11 1010

```
      11 1010
ADD   00 0001
-------------
      11 1011
```

The two's complement of 00 0101 is therefore 11 1011. That is,

NEG 00 0101 = 11 1011

Recall that 11 1011 is indeed the negative of 00 0101 since they add to 0 as shown.

■

The general rule for negating a number regardless of how many bits the number contains is

The two's complement rule

- The two's complement of a number is 1 plus its ones' complement.

Or, in terms of the NEG and NOT operations,

- NEG $x = 1 +$ NOT x

In our familiar decimal system, if you take the negative of a value that is already negative, you get a positive value. Algebraically,

$$-(-x) = x$$

where x is some positive value. If the rule for taking the two's complement is to be useful, the two's complement of a negative value should be the corresponding positive value.

Example 12.11 What happens if you take the two's complement of –5 (dec)?

NOT 11 1011 = 00 0100

```
      00 0100
ADD   00 0001
-------------
      00 0101
```

Voila! You get +5 (dec) back again, as you would expect. ■

Two's Complement Range

Suppose you have a four-bit cell to store integers in two's complement representation. What is the range of integers for this cell?

The positive integer with the greatest magnitude is 0111 (bin), which is +7 (dec). It cannot be 1111 as in unsigned binary since the first bit is reserved for the sign and must be 0. In unsigned binary, you can store numbers as high as +15 (dec) with four bits. All four bits are used for the magnitude. In two's complement representation you can only store numbers as high as +7 (dec), because only three bits are reserved for the magnitude.

What is the negative number with the greatest magnitude? The answer to this question might not be obvious. Table 12.1 shows the result of taking the two's complement of each positive number up to +7. What pattern do you see in the table?

Notice that the two's complement operation automatically produces a 1 in the sign bit of the negative numbers, as it should. Even numbers still end in 0, and odd numbers end in 1.

Also, –5 is obtained from –6 by adding 1 to –6 in binary, as you would expect. Similarly, –6 is obtained from –7 by adding 1 to –7 in binary. We can squeeze one more negative integer out of our four bits by including –8. When you add 1 to –8 in binary, you get –7. The number –8 should therefore be represented as 1000. Table 12.2 shows the complete table for signed integers assuming a four-bit memory cell.

The number –8 (dec) has a peculiar property not shared by any of the other negative integers. If you take the two's complement of –7 you get +7 as follows:

```
NOT  1001 = 0110

     0110
ADD  0001
---------
     0111
```

But if you take the two's complement of –8, you get –8 back again.

```
NOT  1000 = 0111

     0111
ADD  0001
---------
     1000
```

This property exists because there is no way to represent +8 with only four bits.

We have determined the range of numbers for a four-bit cell with two's complement binary representation. It is

1000 to 0111

as written in binary, or

–8 to +7

as written in decimal.

The same patterns hold regardless of how many bits are contained in the cell. The largest positive integer is a single 0 followed by all 1's. The negative integer with the largest magnitude is a single 1 followed by all 0's. Its magnitude is 1 greater than the magnitude of the largest positive integer. The number –1 (dec) is represented as all 1's.

Decimal	Binary
–7	1001
–6	1010
–5	1011
–4	1100
–3	1101
–2	1110
–1	1111

Table 12.1

The result of taking the two's complement in a four-bit computer.

Decimal	Binary
–8	1000
–7	1001
–6	1010
–5	1011
–4	1100
–3	1101
–2	1110
–1	1111
0	0000
1	0001
2	0010
3	0011
4	0100
5	0101
6	0110
7	0111

Table 12.2

The signed integers for a four-bit cell.

Example 12.12 The range for six-bit two's complement representation is

10 0000 to 01 1111

as written in binary, or

–32 to 31

as written in decimal. Unlike all the other negative integers, the two's complement of 10 0000 is itself, 10 0000. Also notice that –1 (dec) = 11 1111 (bin). ■

Base Conversions

Converting from decimal to binary

To convert a negative number from decimal to binary is a two-step process. First, convert its magnitude from decimal to binary as in unsigned binary representation. Then negate it by taking the two's complement.

Example 12.13 For –7 (dec) in a ten-bit cell

+7 (dec) = 00 0000 0111 (bin)

NOT 00 0000 0111 = 11 1111 1000

```
     11 1111 1000
ADD  00 0000 0001
-----------------
     11 1111 1001
```

So –7 (dec) is 11 1111 1001 (bin). ■

Converting from binary to decimal

To convert a number from binary to decimal in a computer that uses two's complement representation, always check the sign bit first. If it is 0, the number is positive and you may convert as in unsigned representation. If it is 1, the number is negative and you can choose one of two methods. One method is to make the number positive by negating it. Then convert to decimal as in unsigned representation.

Example 12.14 Say you have a 10-bit cell that contains 11 1101 1010. What decimal number does it represent? The sign bit is 1, so the number is negative. First negate the number.

NOT 11 1101 1010 = 00 0010 0101

```
     00 0010 0101
ADD  00 0000 0001
-----------------
     00 0010 0110
```

00 0010 0110 (bin) = 32 + 4 + 2 = 38 (dec)

So the original binary number must have been the negative of 38. That is,

11 1101 1010 (bin) = –38 (dec) ■

Another method is to convert directly without taking the two's complement. Simply add 1 to the sum of the place values of the 0's in the original binary number. This method works because the first step in taking the two's complement of a positive integer is to invert the bits. Those bits that were 1's, and thus contributed to the magnitude of the positive integer, become 0's. The 0's, not the 1's, of a negative integer contribute to its magnitude.

Example 12.15 Figure 12.9 shows the place values of the 0's in 11 1101 1010 (bin). Adding 1 to their sum gives

11 1101 1010 (bin) = –(1 + 32 + 4 + 1) = –38 (dec)

which is the same result as with the previous method. ■

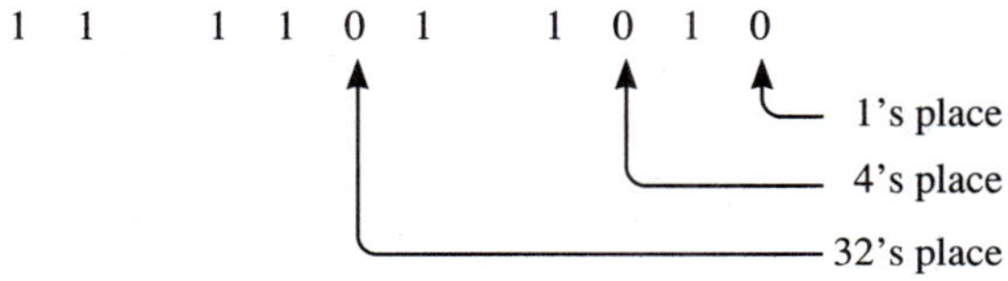

Figure 12.9

The place values of the 0's in 11 1101 1010 (bin).

The Number Line

Another way of viewing binary representation is with the number line. Figure 12.10 shows the number line for a three-bit cell with unsigned binary representation. A total of eight numbers are represented.

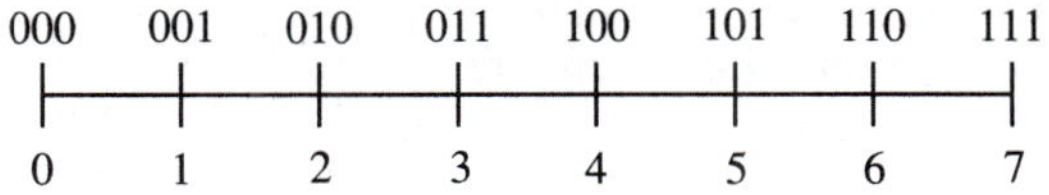

Figure 12.10

The number line for a three-bit unsigned system.

You add by moving to the right on the number line. For example, to add 4 and 3, start with 4 and move three positions to the right to get 7. If you try to add 6 and 3 on the number line, you will fall off the right end. If you do it in binary, you will get an incorrect result, because the answer is out of range.

	110
ADD	011
C = 1	001

The two's complement number line comes from the unsigned number line by breaking it between 3 and 4 and shifting the right part to the left side. Figure 12.11 shows that the binary number 111 is now adjacent to 000, and what used to be +7 (dec) is now –1 (dec).

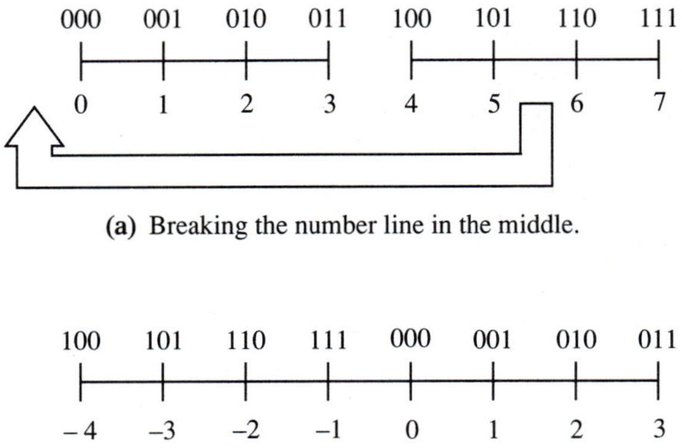

(a) Breaking the number line in the middle.

(b) Shifting the right part to the left side.

Figure 12.11

The number line for a three-bit two's complement system.

Addition is still performed by moving to the right on the number line, even if you pass through 0. To add –2 and 3, start with –2 and move three positions to the right to get 1. If you do it in binary, the answer is in range and correct.

	110
ADD	011
C = 1	001

These bits are identical to those for 6 + 3 in unsigned binary. Notice that the carry bit is 1, even though the answer is in range. With two's complement representation, the carry bit no longer indicates whether the result of the addition is in range.

Sometimes you can avoid the binary representation altogether by considering the shifted number line entirely in decimal. Figure 12.12 shows the two's complement number line with the binary number replaced by its unsigned decimal equivalent. In this example, there are three bits in each memory location. Thus, there are 2^3, or 8, possible numbers.

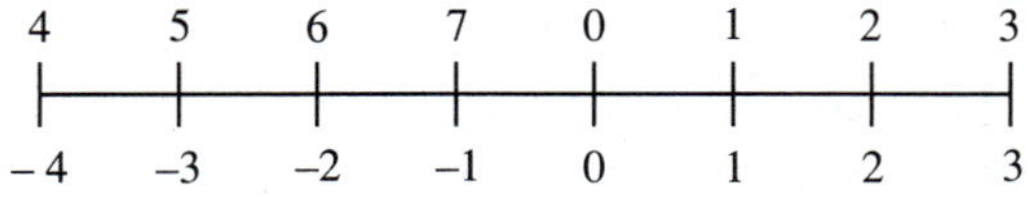

Figure 12.12

The two's complement number line with unsigned decimals.

Now the unsigned and signed numbers are the same from 0 up to 3. Furthermore, you can get the signed negative numbers from the unsigned numbers by subtracting 8.

$7 - 8 = -1$
$6 - 8 = -2$
$5 - 8 = -3$
$4 - 8 = -4$

Example 12.16 Suppose you have an eight-bit computer. There are 2^8, or 256, possible integer values. The nonnegative numbers go from 0 to 127. Assuming two's complement binary representation, what do you get if you add 97 and 45? In unsigned binary the sum is

97 + 45 = 142 (dec, unsigned)

But in two's complement binary the sum is

142 – 256 = –114 (dec, signed)

Notice that we get this result by avoiding the binary representation altogether. To verify the result, first convert 97 and 45 to binary and add.

97 (dec) = 0110 0001 (bin)
45 (dec) = 0010 1101 (bin)

	0110 0001
ADD	0010 1101
C = 0	1000 1110

which is a negative number because of the 1 in the sign bit. And now, to determine its magnitude

NEG 1000 1110 = 0111 0010 (bin)
= 114 (dec)

This produces the expected result. ■

The Overflow Bit

An important characteristic of binary storage at Level 3 is the absence of a type associated with a value. In the previous example, the sum 1000 1110 when interpreted as an unsigned number is 142 (dec), but when interpreted in two's complement representation is –114 (dec). Although the value of the bit pattern depends on its type, whether unsigned or two's complement, the hardware makes no distinction between the two types. It only stores the bit pattern.

When the CPU adds the contents of two memory cells, it uses the rules for binary addition on the bit sequences, regardless of their types. In unsigned binary, if the sum is out of range the hardware simply stores the (incorrect) result, sets the C bit accordingly, and goes on. It is up to the software to examine the C bit after the addition to see if a carry out occurred from the most significant column and to take appropriate action if necessary.

The C bit detects overflow for unsigned integers.

We noted above that in two's complement binary representation, the carry bit no longer indicates whether a sum is in range or out of range. An *overflow condition* occurs when the result of an operation is out of range. To flag this condition for signed numbers, the CPU contains another special bit called the *overflow bit* denoted by the letter V. When the CPU adds two binary integers, if their sum is out

The V bit detects overflow for signed integers.

of range when interpreted in the two's complement representation, then V is set to 1. Otherwise V is cleared to 0.

The CPU performs the same addition operation regardless of the interpretation of the bit pattern. As with the C bit, the CPU does not stop if a two's complement overflow occurs. It sets the V bit and continues with its next task. It is up to the software to examine the V bit after the addition.

Example 12.17 Here are some examples with a six-bit cell showing the effects on the carry bit and on the overflow bit:

Adding two positives:		00 0011		01 0110
	ADD	01 0101	ADD	00 1100
	C = 0	01 1000	C = 0	10 0010
	V = 0		V = 1	
Adding a positive and a negative:		00 0101		00 1000
	ADD	11 0111	ADD	11 1010
	C = 0	11 1100	C = 1	00 0010
	V = 0		V = 0	
Adding two negatives:		11 1010		10 0110
	ADD	11 0111	ADD	10 0010
	C = 1	11 0001	C = 1	00 1000
	V = 0		V = 1	

Notice that all combinations of values are possible for C and V. ■

How can you tell if an overflow condition will occur? One way would be to convert the two numbers to decimal, add them, and see if their sum is outside the range as written in decimal. If so, an overflow has occurred.

The hardware detects an overflow by comparing the carry into the sign bit with the C bit. If they are different, an overflow has occurred, and V gets 1. If they are the same, V gets 0.

Instead of comparing the carry into the sign bit with C, you can tell directly by inspecting the signs of the numbers and the sum. If you add two positive numbers and get a negative sum or if you add two negative numbers and get a positive sum, then an overflow occurred. Is an overflow possible by adding a positive number and a negative number?

12.3 Operations in Binary

Since all information in a computer is stored in binary form, the CPU processes it with binary operations. The previous sections presented the binary operations NOT, ADD, and NEG. NOT is a logical operator, the ADD and NEG are arithmetic operators. This section describes some other logical and arithmetic operators that are available in the CPU of the computer.

Logical Operators

One interesting property of binary digits is that you can interpret them as logical quantities. At Level 3 (machine level), a 1 bit can represent true, and a 0 bit can represent false. Tables 12.3(a) and (b) are the truth tables for the AND and the OR operators at Level 3.

p	*q*	*p* AND *q*
0	0	0
0	1	0
1	0	0
1	1	1

(a)

p	*q*	*p* OR *q*
0	0	0
0	1	1
1	0	1
1	1	1

(b)

Table 12.3

The truth tables for the AND and OR operators at Level 3.

At Level 6 (high-order languages level), AND and OR operate on boolean expressions, whose values are either true or false. They are used in `if` statements and loops to test conditions that control the execution of statements. An example of the AND operator is the Pascal phrase

```
if (Ch >= 'a') and (Ch <= 'z') then
```

Tables 12.4(a) and (b) are the truth tables for AND and OR at Level 6. They are identical to Tables 12.3(a) and (b) with 1 at Level 3 corresponding to true at Level 6, and 0 at Level 3 corresponding to false at Level 6.

p	*q*	*p* AND *q*
true	true	true
true	false	false
false	true	false
false	false	false

(a)

p	*q*	*p* OR *q*
true	true	true
true	false	true
false	true	true
false	false	false

(b)

Table 12.4

The truth tables for the AND and OR operators at Level 6.

Logical operations are easier to perform than addition because no carries are involved. The operation is applied bit-wise to the corresponding bits in the sequence. Neither the carry bit nor the overflow bit is affected by logical operations.

Example 12.18 Some examples for a six-bit cell are

	01 1010		01 1010
AND	01 0001	OR	01 0001
	01 0000		01 1011

Note than when you take the AND of 1 and 1, the result is 1 with no carry. ■

Each of the operations AND and OR combines two groups of bits to produce its result. But NEG operates on only a single group of bits. It is, therefore, called a *unary operation.*

Arithmetic Operators

Two other unary operations are ASL, which stands for *arithmetic shift left,* and ASR, which stands for *arithmetic shift right.* As the name ASL implies, each bit in the cell shifts one place to the left. The bit that was on the leftmost end shifts into the carry bit. The rightmost bit gets 0. Figure 12.13 shows the action of the ASL operator for a six-bit cell.

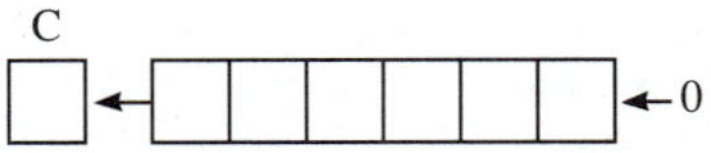

Figure 12.13

The action of the ASL operator for a six-bit computer.

Example 12.19 Three examples of the arithmetic shift left operation are

ASL 11 1100 = 11 1000, C = 1
ASL 00 0011 = 00 0110, C = 0
ASL 01 0110 = 10 1100, C = 0 ■

The operation is called an arithmetic shift because of the effect it has when the bits represent an integer. Assuming unsigned binary representation, the three integers in the previous example before the shift are

60 3 22 (dec, unsigned)

After the shift they are

56 6 44 (dec, unsigned)

ASL doubles the number.

The effect of ASL is to double the number. ASL could not double the 60 because 120 is out of range for a six-bit unsigned integer. If the carry bit is 1 after the shift, an overflow has occurred when you interpret the binary sequence as an unsigned integer.

In the decimal system, a left shift produces the same effect, but the integer is multiplied by 10 instead of by 2. For example, a decimal ASL applied to 356 would give 3560, which is 10 times the original value.

What if you interpret the numbers in two's complement representation? Then the three integers before the shift are

–4 3 22 (dec, signed)

After the shift they are

–8 6 –20 (dec, signed)

Again, the effect of the ASL is to double the number, even if it is negative. This time ASL could not double the 22 because 44 is out of range when you assume two's complement representation. This overflow condition causes the V bit to be set to 1. The situation is similar to the ADD operation where the C bit detects overflow of unsigned values, but the V bit is necessary to detect overflow of signed values.

In the ASR operation, each bit in the group shifts one place to the right. The least significant bit shifts into the carry bit, and the most significant bit remains unchanged. Figure 12.14 shows the action of the ASR operation for a six-bit cell.

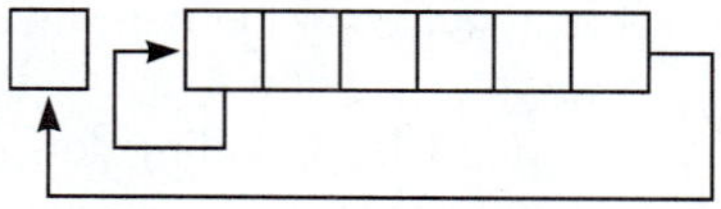

Figure 12.14

The action of the ASR operator for a six-bit computer.

Example 12.20 Four examples of the arithmetic shift right operation are

ASR 01 0100 = 00 1010, C = 0
ASR 01 0111 = 00 1011, C = 1
ASR 11 0010 = 11 1001, C = 0
ASR 11 0101 = 11 1010, C = 1 ■

The ASR operation is designed specifically for the two's complement representation. Since the sign bit does not change, negative numbers remain negative, and positive numbers remain positive.

ASR halves the number.

Shifting to the left multiplies an integer by 2, whereas shifting to the right divides it by 2. Before the shift, the four integers in the previous example are

20 23 –14 –11 (dec, signed)

After the shift they are

10 11 –7 –6 (dec, signed)

The even integers can be divided by 2 exactly, so there is no question about the effect of ASR on them. When odd integers are divided by 2, the result is always rounded down. For example, $23 \div 2 = 11.5$, and 11.5 rounded down is 11. Similarly, $-11 \div 2 = -5.5$, and –5.5 rounded down is –6. Note that –6 is less than –5.5 since it lies to the left of –5.5 on the number line.

Neural Networking

Prompted by advancements in the development of expert systems, and by studies in psychology and neurophysiology, considerable interest has developed in a specialized kind of computing known as *neural networking* (also referred to as *parallel distributed processing* [PDP] or *connectionism*).

The study of neural networking is based upon fundamental knowledge of the structure of the human brain and upon the performance of everyday cognitive tasks—such as walking without falling down, identifying objects we see, and understanding this sentence—which we all do quickly and efficiently. It has been ascertained that however we perform these tasks, we don't perform them sequentially. In terms of switching speed, the basic circuitry of the brain is slower than today's computers. Yet despite the computer's ability to beat us at a narrow range of arithmetic problems, humans, dogs, and even laboratory rats are better suited to quickly perform many general-purpose cognitive tasks. The obvious conclusion is that if we're not accomplishing this with fast circuitry, the circuitry we do have must be very cleverly organized.

The architectural components of a neural network are modeled on the neurological structure of the brain; the networks contain correlates of the axons, dendrites, and synapses of the brain. But no attempt at completeness in modeling the brain is near at hand, since neural networking is still a young research area. Current work is at the level of postulating what the basic components are, how they are interconnected, and how to interpret them. The problems that neural networking can now solve are relatively limited; two examples are spell-checking a work within a highly restricted context and driving the vision component of an industrial robot that decides which of a handful of objects is the next one on the conveyor belt.

A neural network doesn't compute an output as a whole as much as it changes its overall activation state in response to both its environment and its prior programming and wiring (connectivity pattern). For example, the industrial robot mentioned above is programmed to recognize a certain number and specific types of objects. If an object on the conveyor belt does not meet the exact description of any of the objects the robot is programmed to recognize, the robot will classify the object according to its size, shape, and features. When that object appears again, the robot will recognize the object because it has programmed itself—it learned how—to classify the new object.

Neural networking is an extremely active area of research right now. Contributors to the body of research and literature include psychologists, computer scientists, neurologists, linguists, and other members of the cognitive science community. The researchers' diverse, and sometimes overlapping, goals range from seeking a theoretical understanding of the human mind, all the way to applying the research to the building of parallel computers that work faster than the ones we currently have. The experts often disagree on how our understanding of computer science may change to accommodate the new ways of thinking about computing. Some argue that neural networks are simply a natural progression toward more efficient architectures for some tasks and are theoretically equivalent to current designs. Others contend that we are on the edge of a breakthrough in computing not unlike the revolution in physics that occurred when Einstein upset the Newtonian apple cart.

Regardless of who turns out to be right, computer science students in the nineties should recognize that the concept of the computer is a bit of a moving target. Computing is such a young field now that today's students will do much to define its future.

12.4 Hexadecimal and Character Representations

The binary representations in the previous sections are integer representations. This section deals with yet another number base, which will be used with the computer introduced in the next chapter. It also shows how that computer stores alphabetic information.

Hexadecimal

Suppose humans had 16 fingers instead of 10. What would have happened when Arabic numerals were invented? Remember the pattern. With 10 fingers, you start from "0" and keep inventing new symbols, "1," "2," and so on until you get to your penultimate finger, "9." Then on your last finger you combine "1" and "0" to represent the next number, "10."

With 16 fingers, when you get to "9" you still have plenty of fingers left. You must go on inventing new symbols. These extra symbols are usually represented by the letters at the beginning of the English alphabet. So counting in base 16 (*hexadecimal*, or *hex* for short) looks like this:

Counting in hexadecimal

0	7	E	15	1C	23
1	8	F	16	1D	24
2	9	10	17	1E	25
3	A	11	18	1F	26
4	B	12	19	20	.
5	C	13	1A	21	.
6	D	14	1B	22	.

When the hexadecimal number contains many digits, counting can be a bit tricky. Consider counting the next five numbers in hexadecimal starting with 8BE7, C9D, or 9FFE.

8BE7	C9D	9FFE
8BE8	C9E	9FFF
8BE9	C9F	A000
8BEA	CA0	A001
8BEB	CA1	A002
8BEC	CA2	A003

When written in octal, numbers have a tendency to look larger than they actually are. In hexadecimal, the effect is the opposite. Numbers have a tendency to look smaller than they actually are. Comparing the list of hexadecimal numbers with the list of decimal numbers shows that 18 (hex) is 24 (dec).

Base Conversions

In hexadecimal, each place value is 16 times greater than the previous place value. To convert from hexadecimal to decimal simply multiply the place value by its digit and add.

Example 12.21 Figure 12.15 shows how to convert 8BE7 from hexadecimal to decimal. The decimal value of B is 11, and the decimal value of E is 14. ■

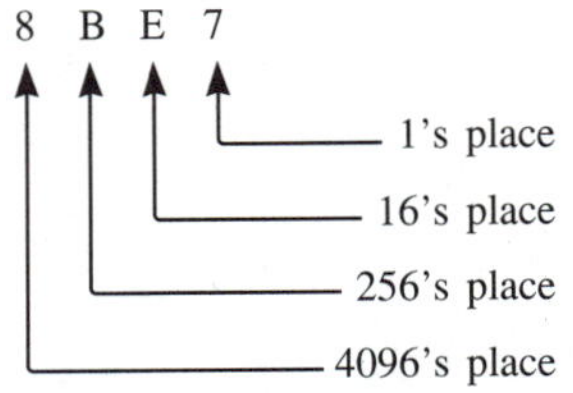

(a) The place values for 8BE7.

$$\begin{array}{rrr} 7 \times & 1 = & 7 \\ 14 \times & 16 = & 224 \\ 11 \times & 256 = & 2{,}816 \\ 8 \times & 4096 = & 32{,}768 \\ \hline & & 35{,}815 \end{array}$$

(b) Converting 8BE7 to decimal.

Figure 12.15

Converting from hexadecimal to decimal.

The procedure for converting from decimal to hexadecimal is analogous to the procedure for converting from decimal to binary. Instead of successively dividing the number by 2, you divide it by 16 and keep track of the remainders, which are the hexadecimal digits of the converted number.

For numbers up to 255 (dec) or FF (hex), converting either way is easily done with the chart of Table 12.5. The body of the table contains decimal numbers. The left column and top row contain hexadecimal digits.

	0	1	2	3	4	5	6	7	8	9	A	B	C	D	E	F
0_	0	1	2	3	4	5	6	7	8	9	10	11	12	13	14	15
1_	16	17	18	19	20	21	22	23	24	25	26	27	28	29	30	31
2_	32	33	34	35	36	37	38	39	40	41	42	43	44	45	46	47
3_	48	49	50	51	52	53	54	55	56	57	58	59	60	61	62	63
4_	64	65	66	67	68	69	70	71	72	73	74	75	76	77	78	79
5_	80	81	82	83	84	85	86	87	88	89	90	91	92	93	94	95
6_	96	97	98	99	100	101	102	103	104	105	106	107	108	109	110	111
7_	112	113	114	115	116	117	118	119	120	121	122	123	124	125	126	127
8_	128	129	130	131	132	133	134	135	136	137	138	139	140	141	142	143
9_	144	145	146	147	148	149	150	151	152	153	154	155	156	157	158	159
A_	160	161	162	163	164	165	166	167	168	169	170	171	172	173	174	175
B_	176	177	178	179	180	181	182	183	184	185	186	187	188	189	190	191
C_	192	193	194	195	196	197	198	199	200	201	202	203	204	205	206	207
D_	208	209	210	211	212	213	214	215	216	217	218	219	220	221	222	223
E_	224	225	226	227	228	229	230	231	232	233	234	235	236	237	238	239
F_	240	241	242	243	244	245	246	247	248	249	250	251	252	253	254	255

Table 12.5

The hexadecimal conversion chart.

Example 12.22 To convert 9C (hex) to decimal, look up row 9 and column C to find 156 (dec). To convert 125 (dec), look it up in the body of the table and read off 7D (hex) from the left column and top row. ■

If computers store information in binary format, why learn the hexadecimal system? The answer lies in the special relationship between hexadecimal and binary, as Table 12.6 shows. There are 16 possible combinations of four bits, and there are exactly 16 hexadecimal digits. Each hexadecimal digit, therefore, represents four bits.

Hexadecimal as a shorthand for binary

Bit patterns are often written in hexadecimal notation to save space on the printed page. A computer manual for a 16-bit machine might state that a memory location contains 01D3. That is shorter than saying it contains 0000 0001 1101 0011.

To convert from unsigned binary to hexadecimal, partition the bits into groups of four starting from the rightmost end, and use the hexadecimal from Table 12.6 for each group. To convert from hexadecimal to unsigned binary, simply reverse the procedure.

Example 12.23 To write the 10-bit unsigned binary number 1010011100 in hexadecimal, start with the rightmost four bits, 1100.

10 1001 1100 (bin) = 29C (hex)

Since 10 bits cannot be partitioned into groups of four exactly, you must assume two additional leading 0's when looking up the leftmost digit in Table 12.6. The leftmost hexadecimal digit comes from

10 (bin) = 0010 (bin) = 2 (hex)

in this example. ■

Example 12.24 For a 14-bit cell,

0D60 (hex) = 00 1101 0110 0000 (bin)

Note that the last hexadecimal 0 represents four binary 0's, but the first hexadecimal 0 only represents two binary 0's. ■

To convert from decimal to unsigned binary, you may prefer to use the hexadecimal table as an intermediate step. You can avoid any computation by looking up the hexadecimal value in Table 12.5, then converting each digit to binary according to Table 12.6.

Example 12.25 For a six-bit cell,

29 (dec) = 1D (hex) = 01 1101 (bin)

where each step in the conversion is a simple table lookup. ■

Hexadecimal	Binary
0	0000
1	0001
2	0010
3	0011
4	0100
5	0101
6	0110
7	0111
8	1000
9	1001
A	1010
B	1011
C	1100
D	1101
E	1110
F	1111

Table 12.6

The relation between hexadecimal and binary.

In machine language program listings or program traces, numbers are rarely written in hexadecimal notation with negative signs. Instead, the sign bit is implicit in the bit pattern represented by the hexadecimal digits. You must always remember that hexadecimal is only a convenient shorthand for a binary sequence. The hardware only stores binary values.

Example 12.26 If a 12-bit memory location contains F7A (hex), then the number in decimal is found by considering the following bit pattern:

F7A (hex) = 1111 0111 1010 (bin)

The sign bit is 1, so the number is negative. Converting to decimal gives

F7A (hex) = –134 (dec)

Notice that the hexadecimal number is not written with a negative sign, even though it may be interpreted as a negative number. ■

Characters

Since computer memories are binary, alphabetic characters must be coded to be stored in memory. A widespread binary code for alphabetic characters is the *American Standard Code for Information Interchange,* also known as ASCII (pronounced *as–key*). *ASCII*

ASCII contains all the uppercase and lowercase English letters, the 10 numeric digits, and special characters such as punctuation signs. Some of its symbols are nonprintable and are used mainly to transmit information between computers or to control peripheral devices.

ASCII is a seven-bit code. Since there are $2^7 = 128$ possible combinations of seven bits, there are 128 ASCII characters. Table 12.7 shows all these characters. The first column of the table shows the nonprintable characters, whose meanings are listed at the bottom. The rest of the table lists the printable characters.

Example 12.27 The sequence 000 0111, which stands for *bell,* causes a terminal to beep. Another example is the set of commands necessary for a paper printer to begin printing at the start of a new line. The computer sends a carriage return character (CR, which is 000 1101) followed by a line feed character (LF, which is 000 1010). CR makes the print carriage return to the left side of the page, and LF advances the paper by one line. ■

Example 12.28 The name

```
Tom
```

would be stored in ASCII as

101 0100
110 1111
110 1101

Char	Bin	Hex	Char	Bin	Hex	Char	Bin	Hex	Char	Bin	Hex
NUL	000 0000	00	SP	010 0000	20	@	100 0000	40	`	110 0000	60
SOH	000 0001	01	!	010 0001	21	A	100 0001	41	a	110 0001	61
STX	000 0010	02	"	010 0010	22	B	100 0010	42	b	110 0010	62
ETX	000 0011	03	#	010 0011	23	C	100 0011	43	c	110 0011	63
EOT	000 0100	04	$	010 0100	24	D	100 0100	44	d	110 0100	64
ENQ	000 0101	05	%	010 0101	25	E	100 0101	45	e	110 0101	65
ACK	000 0110	06	&	010 0110	26	F	100 0110	46	f	110 0110	66
BEL	000 0111	07	'	010 0111	27	G	100 0111	47	g	110 0111	67
BS	000 1000	08	(	010 1000	28	H	100 1000	48	h	110 1000	68
HT	000 1001	09	)	010 1001	29	I	100 1001	49	i	110 1001	69
LF	000 1010	0A	*	010 1010	2A	J	100 1010	4A	j	110 1010	6A
VT	000 1011	0B	+	010 1011	2B	K	100 1011	4B	k	110 1011	6B
FF	000 1100	0C	,	010 1100	2C	L	100 1100	4C	l	110 1100	6C
CR	000 1101	0D	-	010 1101	2D	M	100 1101	4D	m	110 1101	6D
SO	000 1110	0E	.	010 1110	2E	N	100 1110	4E	n	110 1110	6E
SI	000 1111	0F	/	010 1111	2F	O	100 1111	4F	o	110 1111	6F
DLE	001 0000	10	0	011 0000	30	P	101 0000	50	p	111 0000	70
DC1	001 0001	11	1	011 0001	31	Q	101 0001	51	q	111 0001	71
DC2	001 0010	12	2	011 0010	32	R	101 0010	52	r	111 0010	72
DC3	001 0011	13	3	011 0011	33	S	101 0011	53	s	111 0011	73
DC4	001 0100	14	4	011 0100	34	T	101 0100	54	t	111 0100	74
NAK	001 0101	15	5	011 0101	35	U	101 0101	55	u	111 0101	75
SYN	001 0110	16	6	011 0110	36	V	101 0110	56	v	111 0110	76
ETB	001 0111	17	7	011 0111	37	W	101 0111	57	w	111 0111	77
CAN	001 1000	18	8	011 1000	38	X	101 1000	58	x	111 1000	78
EM	001 1001	19	9	011 1001	39	Y	101 1001	59	y	111 1001	79
SUB	001 1010	1A	:	011 1010	3A	Z	101 1010	5A	z	111 1010	7A
ESC	001 1011	1B	;	011 1011	3B	[	101 1011	5B	{	111 1011	7B
FS	001 1100	1C	<	011 1100	3C	\	101 1100	5C	|	111 1100	7C
GS	001 1101	1D	=	011 1101	3D	]	101 1101	5D	}	111 1101	7D
RS	001 1110	1E	>	011 1110	3E	^	101 1110	5E	~	111 1110	7E
US	001 1111	1F	?	011 1111	3F	_	101 1111	5F	DEL	111 1111	7F

Abbreviations for Control Characters

NUL null, or all zeros
SOH start of heading
STX start of text
ETX end of text

EOT end of transmission
ENQ enquiry
ACK acknowledge
BEL bell

BS backspace
HT horizontal tabulation
LF line feed
VT vertical tabulation

FF form feed
CR carriage return
SO shift out
SI shift in

DLE data link escape
DC1 device control 1
DC2 device control 2
DC3 device control 3

DC4 device control 4
NAK negative acknowledge
SYN synchronous idle
ETB end of transmission block

CAN cancel
EM end of medium
SUB substitute
ESC escape

FS file separator
GS group separator
RS record separator
US unit separator

SP space
DEL delete

Table 12.7

The American Standard Code for Information Interchange (ASCII).

If that sequence of bits is sent to an output terminal the word "Tom" would be printed. ■

Example 12.29 The street address

```
52 Elm
```

would be stored in ASCII as

011 0101
011 0010
010 0000
100 0101
110 1100
110 1101

The blank space between `2` and `E` is a separate ASCII character. ■

EBCDIC	Binary
A	1100 0001
B	1100 0010
C	1100 0011
.	.
.	.
.	.
0	1111 0000
1	1111 0001
2	1111 0010
.	.
.	.
.	.

Table 12.8

Some representatives EBCDIC values.

Although ASCII is widespread, it is by no means the only code possible for representing string characters. Another popular code used mostly in IBM mainframes is the *Extended Binary Coded Decimal Interchange Code,* also known as EBCDIC (pronounced *ebbseedick*). It is an eight-bit code with 256 possible combinations of bits, although not all combinations are used. Table 12.8 shows some representative EBCDIC examples.

To a certain extent, the code for representing character information is arbitrary and can be designed for a specific application. The New York Stock Exchange (NYSE) has a six-bit code that includes fractions for price quotations on the stock market. Table 12.9 shows some representative NYSE code values.

NYSE	Binary
A	00 0011
B	01 1001
C	00 1110
D	00 1001
.	.
.	.
.	.
1	10 0011
2	11 1001
$\frac{1}{8}$	11 0000
$\frac{1}{4}$	11 0111
.	.
.	.
.	.

Table 12.9

Some representative values from the NYSE code.

Relation to Level 6

Pascal is a Level 6 language. When programmers declare variables in Pascal, they must specify the type of values that the variables can have. At Level 3, the values are binary.

Suppose you declare

```
var
   I, J:     integer;
   Ch1, Ch2: char
```

in a Pascal program and run it on a seven-bit computer. At Level 3, values of type `integer` are stored in two's complement binary representation. If the values of `I` and `J` are 8 and –2, respectively, and the program contains the expression

```
I + J
```

then the expression is evaluated at Level 3 as

```
      000 1000
ADD   111 1110
C = 1 000 0110
V = 0
```

At Level 3, values of type `char` are stored in ASCII or some other character code. If `Ch1` has the value '-' and `Ch2` has the value '2', then at Level 3 these values are stored as

010 1101   011 0010

This bit pattern is certainly different from the integer value for `J`, which is 111 1110.

In Pascal, at Level 6, each character has a position on the number line with an ordinal value, which can be accessed with the `ord` function. At Level 3, the machine level, the ordinal value is simply the binary value of the character code interpreted as an unsigned integer. Since different computers may choose to use different binary character codes, the ordinal values of their characters may differ.

Example 12.30 From the ASCII table, `D` is represented as 100 0100. Furthermore, 100 0100 (bin) = 68 (dec). On a computer that uses the ASCII code, `ord ('D')` will be 68, therefore. ■

Example 12.31 To ring the bell on your output device, you can execute the Pascal statement

```
write (chr (7))
```

The `chr` function converts 7 (dec) to 000 0111 (bin) and sends it to the output device, which makes the bell ring. ■

At Level 6, a typical statement in a high-order language is

```
write ('Tom')
```

where the string constant 'Tom' is sent to the output device. This statement is not so simple at Level 3. In machine language you cannot "write Tom." Instead you must send the sequence of bits

101 0100
110 1111
110 1101

to the output device.

The reason for binary

Why must we deal with bits instead of the English letters and decimal digits that we are accustomed to? Because computers are electronic. The cheapest, most reliable way to manufacture the electronic parts that make up a computer is to make them binary.

So we are stuck with binary machines with which to process our information. The problem at Level 3 is that the information we want to process is in the form of decimal numbers and English letters, while the machine language to represent it is in the form of 1's and 0's. Hence the need for codes, such as two's complement binary representation and ASCII.

A basic problem at all levels

This mismatch between the form of the information to be processed and the language to represent it is not unique to Level 3. It is the major area of concern at all the higher levels as well.

The situation can be illustrated for Level 6 by the traveling-salesman problem. A salesman is responsible for accounts in 8 different cities, which he visits by commercial airline. The cities are connected by 14 airline routes. The data to be processed is in the form of a map supplied by the airline showing the routes of all the flights connecting the cities in the salesman's territory. The map, Figure 12.16, also shows the cost of the flight along each route.

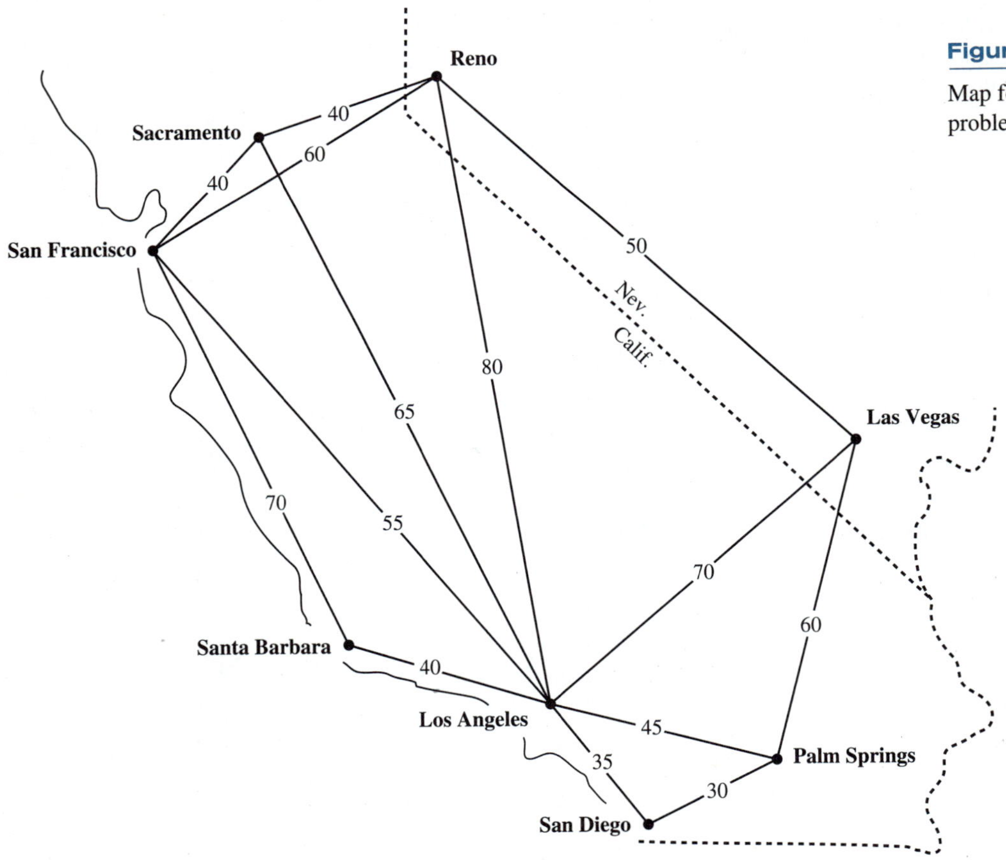

Figure 12.16

Map for the traveling-salesman problem.

The salesman must start from Los Angeles, visit every city in his territory, then return to Los Angeles. Naturally, he wants to plan his trip to minimize the total cost.

Determining the optimum itinerary sounds like a perfect job for a computer. The salesman gives the map to a programmer who knows how to speak in some Level 6 language such as Pascal.

But now the programmer faces this fundamental problem of computer science. There is a mismatch between the data, which is in the form of a map, and the Level 6 language. Pascal does not understand maps. It only understands things such as real numbers, integers, and arrays.

The programmer must decide how to represent the data in a form that Pascal can process. For example, she might represent the map as a two-dimensional array of real numbers as shown in Table 12.10. In this scheme, the integers in the top row and left column represent the cities in the salesman's territory. Each real number represents the cost in dollars to travel from the city indicated by the row index to the city indicated by the column index. If the name of the two-dimensional array is `Cost`, then

```
Cost [1, 6] = 65
```

represents the fact that to fly from city 1 (Los Angeles) to city 6 (Sacramento) costs $65. The fact that

```
Cost [2, 8] = 1e30
```

indicates that there is no airline route between city 2 (San Diego) and city 8 (Las Vegas).

After the original data is transformed into a representation that Pascal can handle, the Level 6 programmer can proceed with her algorithm design and eventually solve the problem. But the first step is to represent the data in a form that the language can deal with.

At Level 3 the problem was how to represent numbers and letters with machine language bits. At Level 6 the problem was how to represent a map of cities, routes, and airline costs with Pascal integers, real numbers, and arrays. At both levels it was the fundamental data representation problem.

	1	2	3	4	5	6	7	8
1	1e30	35	45	40	55	65	80	70
2	35	1e30	30	1e30	1e30	1e30	1e30	1e30
3	45	30	1e30	1e30	1e30	1e30	1e30	60
4	40	1e30	1e30	1e30	70	1e30	1e30	1e30
5	55	1e30	1e30	70	1e30	40	60	1e30
6	65	1e30	1e30	1e30	40	1e30	40	1e30
7	80	1e30	1e30	1e30	60	40	1e30	50
8	70	1e30	60	1e30	1e30	1e30	50	1e30

City Numbers

1 Los Angeles
2 San Diego
3 Palm Springs
4 Santa Barbara
5 San Francisco
6 Sacramento
7 Reno
8 Las Vegas

Table 12.10

One array representation of the airline map of Figure 12.16.

Alternative Representations

One challenging aspect of the representation problem is that usually there are several different ways to represent the data. The particular representation selected depends on how the data is to be processed.

An example at Level 3 is an alternative representation for positive integers. Although this chapter presented the unsigned binary representation for positive numeric values, it is not the only possibility. Positive integers can also be stored in *binary coded decimal* (BCD) representation.

Binary coded decimal (BCD)

In BCD, each decimal digit requires exactly 4 bits. The decimal number 142 would be stored in binary as

0001 0100 0010

Since there are only 10 decimal digits, a group of 4 BCD bits is only allowed to be 0000, 0001, 0010, 0011, 0100, 0101, 0110, 0111, 1000, or 1001. The bit patterns 1010 through 1111 are unused.

Unsigned binary is usually chosen when the data is subjected more to arithmetic operations within the computer, as opposed to I/O operations. BCD is frequently chosen when the data is financial in nature and is subjected to many I/O operations. BCD is easier to convert to decimal for printed reports. The circuitry for BCD arithmetic operations is usually slower than the circuitry for unsigned binary arithmetic operations, however.

The same kind of option is available in the traveling-salesman problem. For example, airlines do not offer a flight between all possible pairs of cities, especially small ones. To get from Palm Springs to Reno, you must first fly from Palm Springs to Los Angeles and then from Los Angeles to Reno. In Table 12.10, `Cost` has 64 elements even though there are only 14 routes. Most of the elements are 1e30, and of the 28 that are not 1e30, only 14 are really necessary.

For example, the two entries

```
Cost [1, 6] = 65
Cost [6, 1] = 65
```

represent the fact that there is a single route between Los Angeles and Sacramento. Assuming the air fares are equal in both directions, only one entry is really necessary. The other is redundant.

The programmer may therefore opt to represent the map as in Table 12.11. In a Level 6 language, the list of routes can be implemented as an array, `Route`, of records with three fields—`From`, `To`, and `Cost`. Then

```
Route [3].From = 1
Route [3].To = 6
Route [3].Cost = 65
```

represents the fact that to fly between Los Angeles and Sacramento costs $65.

With this representation of the map, no storage is wasted on nonexistent routes. If there is no air route from city 9 to city 11 it is simply not stored in the list.

Route number	From	To	Cost
1	1	2	35
2	1	3	45
3	1	4	40
4	1	5	55
5	1	6	65
6	1	7	80
7	1	8	70
8	2	3	30
9	3	8	60
10	4	5	70
11	5	6	40
12	5	7	60
13	6	7	40
14	7	8	50

Table 12.11

Another representative of the airline map of Figure 12.16.

Having an alternate representation of the map at Level 6 is just like having an alternate representation of unsigned integers at Level 3. At any level, you may have several methods to represent the data, any one of which can produce correct results.

It is often difficult to determine which representation is best. Indeed, it is often difficult even to define what "best" means. If your computer has a great deal of memory, the best representation for you might be one that is a bit wasteful of storage, since you have plenty to spare. If memory is scarce, on the other hand, the best representation for you might take less storage, even though the algorithm to process the data in that representation is slow. This space/time tradeoff applies at all levels of abstraction in a computer system. As with any creative endeavor, the choice is not always clear-cut.

What is "best"?

Models

A model is a simplified representation of some physical system. Workers in every scientific discipline, including computer science, construct models and investigate their properties. Consider some models of the solar system that astronomers have constructed and investigated.

Aristotle, who lived in Greece about 350 B.C., proposed a model in which the earth was at the center of the universe. Surrounding the earth were 55 celestial spheres. The sun, moon, planets, and stars were each carried around the heavens on one of these spheres.

How well did this model match reality? It was successful in explaining the appearance of the sky, which looks like the top half of a sphere. It was also successful in explaining the approximate motion of the planets. Aristotle's model was accepted as accurate for hundreds of years.

Then in 1543 the Polish astronomer Copernicus published *De Revolutionibus*. In it he modeled the solar system with the sun at the center. The planets revolved around the sun in circles. This model was a better approximation to the physical system than the earth-centered model.

In the latter part of the sixteenth century the Danish astronomer Tycho Brahe made a series of precise astronomical observations that showed a discrepancy in Copernicus's model. Then in 1609 Johannes Kepler proposed a model in which the earth and all the planets revolved around the sun not in circles, but in flattened circles called ellipses. This model was successful in explaining in detail the intricate motion of the planets as observed by Tycho Brahe.

Each of these models is a simplified representation of the solar system. None of the models is a completely accurate description of the real physical world. We know now that even Kepler's model is an approximation, in light of Einstein's theories of relativity. No model is perfect. Every model is an approximation to the real world.

When information is represented in a computer's memory, that representation is only a model as well. Just as each model of the solar system describes some aspects of the underlying real system more accurately than other aspects, so does a

Models as approximations of reality

representation scheme describe some property of the information more accurately than other properties.

For example, one property of positive integers is that there is an infinite number of them. No matter how large an integer you write down, someone else can always write down a larger integer. The unsigned binary representation in a computer does not describe that property very accurately. There is a limit to the size of the integer when stored in memory.

You may be aware that the square root of 2 is

$$\sqrt{2} = 1.4142136\ldots$$

The digits go on forever, never repeating. The representation scheme for storing real numbers is a model that only approximates numbers such as the square root of 2. It cannot represent the square root of 2 exactly.

Solving a problem at any level involves constructing an imperfect model and investigating its properties. The traveling salesman problem at Level 6 was to determine the itinerary that minimized his cost. His expenses were modeled by the airline map. The model did not include the fact that some hotels in some cities may charge a different rate on weekends than on weekdays. Taking a more realistic model of expenses may change the optimum itinerary.

Two sources of approximations in computer-based models

The previous examples illustrate that any time a computer solves a problem, approximations are always involved because of limitations in the models. These approximations can arise from limitations in the representation scheme, such as the limited precision of real numbers in trying to store the square root of 2, or from simplifications of the problem, such as failing to take into account different hotel rates.

Modeling the computer itself

All sorts of physical systems are commonly modeled with computers—inventories, national economies, accounting systems, and biological population systems to name a few. In computer science, it is often the computer itself that is modeled.

The only physically real part of the computer is at Level 1. Ultimately, a computer is just a complicated, organized mass of circuits and electrical signals. At Level 3 the high signals are modeled as 1's and the low signals as 0's. The programmer at Level 3 does not need to know anything about electrical circuits and signals to work with his model. Remember that at Level 3 the 1's and 0's represent the word `Tom` as

101 0100
110 1111
110 1101

The programmer at Level 6 does not need to know anything about bits to work with his model. In fact, programming the computer at any level requires only a knowledge of the model of the computer at that level.

A programmer at Level 6 can model the computer as a Pascal machine. This model accepts Pascal programs and uses them to process data. When the programmer instructs the machine to

```
write ('Tom')
```

he need not be concerned with how the computer is modeled as a binary machine at Level 3. Similarly, when a programmer at Level 3 writes a sequence of bits he need not be concerned with how the computer is modeled as a combination of circuits at Level 1.

This modeling of computer systems at successively higher levels is an idea that is not unique to computer science. Consider a large corporation with six divisions throughout the country. The president's model of the corporation is six divisions, with a vice president of each division reporting to him. He views the overall performance of the company in terms of the performance of each of the divisions. When he tells the vice president of the Widget Division to increase earnings, he does not need to be concerned with the vice president's model of the Widget Division.

And when the vice president goes to each department manager within the Widget Division with an order, she does not need to be concerned with the department manager's model of his department. To have the president himself deal with the organization at the department level would be just about impossible. There are simply too many details at the department level of the entire corporation for one person to manage.

The computer user at Level 7 is like the president. He gives an instruction such as "compute the grade point average of all the sophomores" to a program originally written by a programmer at Level 6. He need not be concerned with the Level 6 model to issue the instruction. Eventually this command at Level 7 is transformed through successively lower levels to Level 1. The end result is that the user at Level 7 can control the mass of electrical circuitry and signals with a very simplified model of the computer.

SUMMARY

A binary quantity is restricted to one of two values. At the machine level, computers store information in binary. A bit is a binary digit whose value can be either 0 or 1. Nonnegative integers use unsigned binary representation. The rightmost bit is in the 1's place, the next bit to the left is in the 2's place, the next bit to the left is in the 4's place, and so on with each place value double the preceding place value. Signed integers use two's complement binary representation in which the first bit is the sign bit and the remaining bits determine the magnitude. For positive numbers, the two's complement representation is identical to the unsigned representation. For negative numbers, however, the two's complement of a number is obtained by taking 1 plus the ones' complement of the corresponding positive number.

Every binary integer, signed or unsigned, has a range that is determined by the number of bits in the memory cell. The smaller the number of bits in the cell, the more limited the range. The carry bit, C, is used to flag an out-of-range condition for an unsigned integer, and the overflow bit, V, is used to flag an out-of-range condition for an integer in two's complement representation. Operations on binary integers include ADD, AND, OR, and NOT. ASL, which stands for arithmetic shift left, multiplies a binary value by 2, and ASR, which stands for arithmetic shift right, divides a binary value by 2.

The hexadecimal number system, which is a base 16 system, provides a compact notation for expressing bit patterns. The 16 hexadecimal digits are 0, 1, 2, 3, 4, 5, 6, 7, 8, 9, A, B, C, D, E, and F. One hexadecimal digit represents four bits. The American Standard Code for Information Interchange, abbreviated ASCII, is a common code for storing characters. It is a seven-bit code with 128 characters including the uppercase and lowercase letters of the English alphabet, the decimal digits, punctuation marks, and nonprintable control characters.

A basic problem at all levels of abstraction is the mismatch between the form of the information to be processed and the language to represent it. A program in machine language processes bits. A program in a high-order language processes items like arrays and records. Regardless of the level in which the program is written, the information must be cast into a format that the language can recognize. Matching the information to the language is a basic problem at all levels of abstraction and is a source of approximation in the modeling process of problem solving.

EXERCISES

At the end of each chapter in this book is a set of exercises and problems. Work the exercises on paper by hand. Answers to the starred exercises are in the back of the book. (For some multipart exercises, answers are only supplied for selected parts.) The problems are programs to be entered into the computer.

Section 12.1

*1. Count the next 10 numbers (a) in octal starting from 267, (b) in base 3 starting from 2102, (c) in binary starting from 10101, and (d) in base 5 starting from 2433.

2. Count the next 10 numbers (a) in octal starting from 466, (b) in base 3 starting from 1201, (c) in binary starting from 11011, and (d) in base 5 starting from 3434.

*3. Convert the following numbers from binary to decimal, assuming unsigned binary representation.

(a) 10010 (b) 110 (c) 1011
(d) 1000 (e) 11111 (f) 1010101

4. Convert the following numbers from binary to decimal, assuming unsigned binary representation.

(a) 10110 (b) 10 (c) 10101
(d) 10000 (e) 1111 (f) 11110000

*5. Convert the following numbers from decimal to binary, assuming unsigned binary representation.

(a) 25 (b) 16 (c) 1 (d) 14 (e) 5 (f) 41

6. Convert the followng numbers from decimal to binary, assuming unsigned binary representation.

(a) 12 (b) 35 (c) 3 (d) 0 (e) 27 (f) 16

7. With unsigned binary representation, what is the range of numbers as written in binary and in decimal for the following cells?

*(a) a two-bit cell *(b) a three-bit cell (c) a four-bit cell
(d) a five-bit cell (e) an n-bit cell in general

*8. Perform the following additions on unsigned integers assuming a seven-bit cell. Show the effect on the carry bit.

(a)
```
     010 1011
ADD  100 1001
C =
```
(b)
```
     101 1001
ADD  011 0111
C =
```
(c)
```
     111 1111
ADD  111 1111
C =
```
(d)
```
     111 1111
ADD  000 0001
C =
```

9. Perform the following additions on unsigned integers assuming a nine-bit cell. Show the effect on the carry bit.

(a)
```
     0 0100 1011
ADD  0 1101 0001
C =
```
(b)
```
     1 0001 1101
ADD  0 1110 1000
C =
```
(c)
```
     1 1111 1111
ADD  0 0000 0001
C =
```
(d)
```
     1 1111 1111
ADD  1 1111 1111
C =
```

10. Suppose you have a 12-bit cell. Find a binary number such that when you add it to 0110 0101 0111 the sum is all 0's. That is, find the missing number in the following operation:

```
     0110 0101 0111
ADD  ???? ???? ????
     0000 0000 0000
```

The number you find might set the carry bit to 1. Without reading Section 12.2, can you determine the rule for finding the missing number from any number in general? Hint: A simple rule involves the NOT operation.

11. This section stated that you can tell whether a binary number is even or odd only by inspecting the digit in the 1's place. Is that always possible for an arbitrary base? Explain.

12. Converting between octal and decimal is analogous to the technique of converting between binary and decimal. *__(a)__ Write the polynomial representation of the octal number 70146 as in Figure 12.4. **(b)** Use the technique of Figure 12.5 to convert 7291 (dec) to octal.

13. Fractional numbers in binary are analogous to fractional numbers in decimal. Instead of a decimal point, however, a binary fraction contains a binary point. *__(a)__ Write the polynomial representation of the decimal number 29.458 as in Figure 12.4. **(b)** Write the polynomial representation of the binary number 1011.100101 as in Figure 12.4. **(c)** What is the decimal value of the binary number in (b)?

14. Why do programmers at Level 3 confuse Halloween and Christmas? Hint: What does 31 (oct) equal?

Section 12.2

***15.** Convert the following numbers from decimal to binary, assuming seven-bit two's complement binary representation.

(a) 49 **(b)** –27 **(c)** 0
(d) –64 **(e)** –1 **(f)** –2
(g) What is the range for this computer as written in binary and in decimal?

16. Convert the following numbers from decimal to binary, assuming nine-bit two's complement binary representation.

(a) 51 (b) –29 (c) –2
(d) 0 (e) –256 (f) –1
(g) What is the range for this cell as written in binary and in decimal?

*17. Convert the following numbers from binary to decimal, assuming seven-bit two's complement binary representation.

(a) 001 1101 (b) 101 0101 (c) 111 1100
(d) 000 0001 (e) 100 0000 (f) 100 0001

18. Convert the following numbers from binary to decimal, assuming nine-bit two's complement binary representation.

(a) 0 0001 1010 (b) 1 0110 1010 (c) 1 1111 1100
(d) 0 0000 0001 (e) 1 0000 0000 (f) 1 0000 0001

*19. Perform the following additions assuming seven-bit two's complement binary representation. Show the effect on the carry and overflow bits.

```
(a)        010 1011     (b)        111 1001
     ADD   000 1110          ADD   000 1101
     C =                     C =
     V =                     V =

(c)        100 0110     (d)        110 0001
     ADD   101 0101          ADD   111 0101
     C =                     C =
     V =                     V =

(e)        000 1101     (f)        100 1001
     ADD   011 0100          ADD   010 1011
     C =                     C =
     V =                     V =
```

20. Perform the following additions assuming nine-bit two's complement binary representation. Show the effect on the carry and overflow bits.

```
(a)        0 1010 1100     (b)        1 1110 0101
     ADD   0 0011 1010          ADD   0 0011 0101
     C =                        C =
     V =                        V =

(c)        1 0001 1011     (d)        1 1000 0101
     ADD   1 0101 0100          ADD   1 1101 0110
     C =                        C =
     V =                        V =

(e)        0 0011 0100     (f)        1 0010 0111
     ADD   0 1101 0010          ADD   0 1010 0111
     C =                        C =
     V =                        V =
```

21. With two's complement binary representation, what is the range of numbers as written in binary and in decimal notation for the following cells?

*(a) a two-bit cell *(b) a three-bit cell (c) a four-bit cell
(d) a five-bit cell (e) an n-bit cell in general

Section 12.3

*22. Perform the following logical operations, assuming a seven-bit cell.

```
(a)       010 1100        (b)       000 1111
      AND 110 1010              AND 101 0101
      ------------              ------------

(c)       010 1100        (d)       000 1111
       OR 110 1010               OR 101 0101
      ------------              ------------

(e) NEG 010 1100
    NOT 110 1010
```

23. Perform the following logical operations, assuming a nine-bit cell.

```
(a)       1 1001 0011     (b)       0 0000 1111
      AND 1 0111 0101           AND 1 0111 0101
      ---------------           ---------------

(c)         1001 0011     (d)       0 0000 1111
       OR 1 0111 0101            OR 1 0111 0101
      ---------------           ---------------

(e) NEG 1 1001 0011
    NOT 1 0111 0101
```

*24. Assuming seven-bit two's complement representation, convert each of the following decimal numbers to binary, show the effect of the ASL operation on it, then convert the result back to decimal. Repeat with the ASR operation.

(a) 24 (b) 37 (c) –26
(d) 1 (e) 0 (f) –1

25. Assuming nine-bit two's complement representation, convert each of the following decimal numbers to binary, show the effect of the ASL operation on it, then convert the result back to decimal. Repeat with the ASR operation.

(a) 94 (b) 135 (c) –62
(d) 1 (e) 0 (f) –1

Section 12.4

26. Count the next five numbers in hexadecimal, starting with the following:

*(a) 3AB7 (b) 6FD (c) B9E

27. Convert the following numbers from hexadecimal to decimal.

*(a) 2D5E (b) 2F (c) 7

28. This chapter mentioned the method of converting from decimal to hexadecimal but gave no examples. Use the method to convert the following decimal numbers to hexadecimal.

*(a) 26,831 (b) 4096 (c) 9

29. The technique for converting from decimal to any base will work for bases other than binary with some modification. **(a)** Explain the method to convert from decimal to octal. **(b)** Explain the method to convert from decimal to base n in general.

*30. Assuming seven-bit two's complement binary representation, convert the following numbers from hexadecimal to decimal. Remember to check the sign bit.

(a) 5D (b) 2F (c) 40

31. Assuming nine-bit two's complement binary representation, convert the following numbers from hexadecimal to decimal. Remember to check the sign bit.

(a) 1B4 (b) 0F5 (c) 100

*32. Assuming seven-bit two's complement binary representation, write the bit patterns for the following decimal numbers in hexadecimal.

(a) –27 (b) 63 (c) –1

33. Assuming nine-bit two's complement binary representation, write the bit patterns for the following decimal numbers in hexadecimal.

(a) –73 (b) –1 (c) 94

*34. Decode the following secret ASCII message (reading across).

100 1000	110 0001	111 0110	110 0101
010 0000	110 0001	010 0000	110 1110
110 1001	110 0011	110 0101	010 0000
110 0100	110 0001	111 1001	010 0001

35. Decode the following secret ASCII message (reading across).

100 1101	110 0101	110 0101	111 0100
010 0000	110 0001	111 0100	010 0000
110 1101	110 1001	110 0100	110 1110
110 1001	110 0111	110 1000	111 0100
010 1110			

*36. How is the following string of 9 characters stored in ASCII?

```
Pay $0.92
```

37. How is the following string of 13 characters stored in ASCII?

```
(321)497-0015
```

38. You are the chief communications officer for the Lower Slobovian army at war with the Upper Slobovians. Your spies will infiltrate the enemy's command headquarters in an attempt to gain the "upper" hand. You know the Uppers are planning a major assault, and you also know the following: (1) It will be at either sunrise or sunset. (2) It will come by land, air, or sea. (3) It will occur on March 28, 29, 30 or 31, or on April 1. Your spies must communicate with you in binary. Devise a suitable binary code for transmitting the information. Try to use the fewest number of bits possible.

39. Based on the EBCDIC bit pattern for A, B, and C in Table 12.8, what do you think the EBCDIC bit pattern for Z is? Look up the complete EBCDIC code in another book or computer manual and see if your educated guess is correct.

40. Octal numbers are sometimes used instead of hexadecimal numbers to represent bit sequences. *(a) How many bits does one octal number represent? How would you represent the decimal number –13 in octal with the following cells?

(b) a 15-bit cell (c) a 16-bit cell (d) an 8-bit cell

PROBLEMS

Section 12.1

41. Write a program in Pascal that takes as input a three-digit octal number and prints the next 10 octal numbers. Define an octal number as

```
type
   OctDigType = 0..7;
   OctNumType = array [1..3] of OctDigType;
```

42. Write a program in Pascal that takes as input an eight-bit binary number and prints the next 10 binary numbers. Define a binary number as:

```
type
   BitType    = 0..1;
   BinNumType = array [1..8] of BitType;
```

43. Write a function in Pascal to convert an eight-bit unsigned binary number to a positive decimal integer. Use the definition of a binary number as given in Problem 42. Test your function with interactive input.

44. Write a procedure in Pascal to convert a positive decimal integer to an eight-bit unsigned binary number. Use the definition of a binary number as given in Problem 42. Test your procedure with interactive input.

45. Defining a binary number as in Problem 42, write the procedure

```
procedure BinaryAdd (var Sum:  BinNumType;
                     var CBit: BitType;
                         Bin1: BinNumType;
                         Bin2: BinNumType)
```

to compute `Sum` as the sum of the two binary numbers, `Bin1` and `Bin2`. `CBit` should be the value of the carry bit after the addition. Test your procedure with interactive input.

Section 12.2

46. Write a function in Pascal to convert an eight-bit two's complement binary number to a decimal integer. Use the definition of a binary number as given in Problem 42. Test your function with interactive input.

47. Write a procedure in Pascal to convert a decimal integer to an eight-bit two's complement binary number. Use the definition of a binary number as given in Problem 42. Test your procedure with interactive input.

Section 12.3

48. Defining a binary number as in Problem 42, write the procedure

```
procedure BinaryAnd (var BAnd: BinNumType;
                         Bin1: BinNumType;
                         Bin2: BinNumType)
```

to compute `BAnd` as the AND of the two binary numbers `Bin1` and `Bin2`. Test your procedure with interactive input.

49. Write the procedure for Problem 48, using the OR operation.

50. Defining a binary number as in Problem 42, write the procedure

```
procedure ShiftLeft (var BinNum: BinNumType; var CBit: BitType)
```

to perform an arithmetic shift left on `BinNum`. `CBit` should be the value of the carry bit after the shift. Test your procedure with interactive input.

51. Write the procedure for Problem 50, using the arithmetic shift right operation.

Section 12.4

52. Write a program in Pascal that takes as input a three-digit hexadecimal number and prints the next 10 hexadecimal numbers. Define a hexadecimal number as

```
type
   HexType    = 0..15;
   HexNumType = array [1..3] of HexType;
```

Use the uppercase letters of the alphabet for the hexadecimal I/O. For example, 3C6 should be valid input.

53. Write a function in Pascal to convert a three-digit hexadecimal number to a positive decimal integer. Use the definition of a hexadecimal number as given in Problem 52. Test your function with interactive input. Use the uppercase letters of the alphabet for the hexadecimal input.

54. Write a procedure in Pascal to convert a positive decimal integer to a three-digit hexadecimal number. Use the definition of a hexadecimal number as given in Problem 52. Test your procedure with interactive input. Use the uppercase letters of the alphabet for the hexadecimal output.

55. Write a function in Pascal to convert a three-digit hexadecimal number to a possibly negative decimal integer. Use the definition of a hexadecimal number as given in Problem 52. Assume the hexadecimal value represents the bits of a 12-bit cell with two's complement representation. Test your function with interactive input. Use the uppercase letters of the alphabet for the hexadecimal input.

56. Write a procedure in Pascal to convert a possibly negative decimal integer to a three-digit hexadecimal number. Use the definition of a hexadecimal number as given in Problem 52. Assume the hexadecimal value represents the bits of a 12-bit cell with two's complement representation. Test your procedure with interactive input. Use the uppercase letters of the alphabet for the hexadecimal output.

57. Write a function in Pascal to convert a positive number in an arbitrary base to decimal. For four-digit base 6 numbers, for example, declare

```
const
   Base         = 6;
   BaseMinusOne = 5;
   NumDigits    = 4;
type
   BaseType    = 0..BaseMinusOne;
   BaseNumType = array [1..NumDigits] of BaseType;
```

Test your function with interactive input. Read the number to be converted into a variable of type `StrType` with procedure `GetString`. Use the uppercase letters of the alphabet for input if required by the value of `Base`. Write a procedure to convert it to the proper value of type `BaseNumType` before converting it to decimal.

You must be able to modify your program for operation with a different base by changing only `Base` and `BaseMinusOne` in the constant definition part. You must be able to modify the program for a different number of digits by changing only `NumDigits` in the constant definition part.

58. Write a procedure in Pascal to convert a positive decimal integer to a number in an arbitrary base. Declare `BaseNumType` as in Problem 57. Test your procedure with interactive input. Use the uppercase letters of the alphabet for output if required by the value of `Base`.

You must be able to modify your program for operation with a different base by changing only `Base` and `BaseMinusOne` in the constant definition part. You must be able to modify the program for a different number of digits by changing only `NumDigits` in the constant definition part.

Chapter

13

Computer Architecture

An architect takes components such as walls, doors, and ceilings and arranges them together to form a building. Similarly, the computer architect takes components such as input devices, memories, and CPU registers and arranges them together to form a computer.

Buildings come in all shapes and sizes, and so do computers. This fact raises a problem. If we select one computer to study out of the dozens of popular models that are available, then our knowledge will be somewhat obsolete when that model is inevitably discontinued by its manufacturer. Also, this book would be less valuable to people who use the computers we chose not to study.

A hypothetical computer

But there is another possibility. In the same way that a book on architecture could examine a hypothetical building, this book can explore a hypothetical computer that contains important features similar to those found on all real computers. This approach has its advantages and disadvantages.

Advantages and disadvantages of a hypothetical computer

One advantage is that the hypothetical computer can be designed to illustrate only the fundamental concepts that apply to most computer systems. We can then concentrate on the important points and not have to deal with the individual quirks that are present on all real machines. Concentrating on the fundamentals is also a hedge against obsolete knowledge. The fundamentals will continue to apply even as individual computers come and go in the marketplace.

The primary disadvantage of studying a hypothetical computer is that some of its details will be irrelevant to those who need to work with a specific real machine at the assembly language level or at the machine level. If you understand the fundamental concepts, however, then you will easily be able to learn the details of any specific machine.

The Pep/5 computer

There is no 100% satisfactory solution to this dilemma. We have chosen the hypothetical computer approach mainly for its advantages in illustrating fundamental concepts. Our hypothetical machine is called the Pep/5 computer. This chapter will make comparisons of Pep/5 with several physical machines to give a flavor of what computers are like out there in the "real world."

13.1 Hardware

The Pep/5 hardware consists of four major components at the machine level (Level 3). They are

- The central processing unit (CPU)
- The main memory
- The input device
- The output device

The block diagram of Figure 13.1 shows each of these components as a rectangular block. The *bus* is simply a group of wires that connects the four major components. It carries the data signals and control signals sent between the blocks.

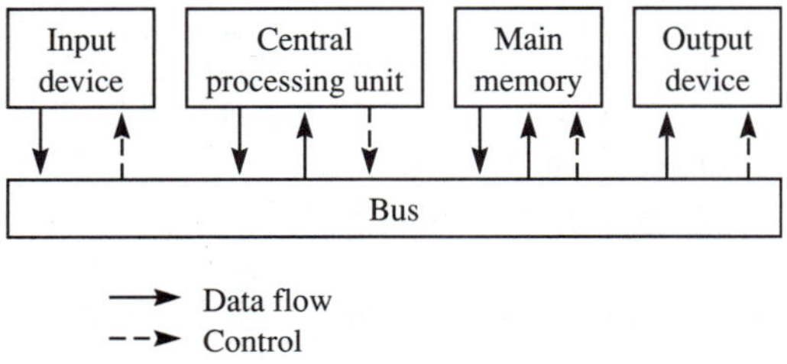

Figure 13.1

Block diagram of the Pep/5 computer.

Central Processing Unit (CPU)

The CPU contains seven specialized memory locations called *registers*. As shown in Figure 13.2, they are

- The 4-bit status register (`NZVC`)
- The 16-bit accumulator (`A`)
- The 16-bit index register (`X`)
- The 16-bit base register (`B`)
- The 16-bit program counter (`PC`)
- The 16-bit stack pointer (`SP`)
- The 24-bit instruction register (`IR`)

The `V` and `C` bits in the *status register* are the overflow and carry bits as discussed in Sections 12.1 and 12.2. The `N` and `Z` bits indicate whether the result of an operation is negative (`N`), and whether it is zero (`Z`). The *accumulator* is the register that contains the result of an operation. The next four registers—`X`, `B`, `PC`, and `SP`—help the CPU access information in main memory. The *index* and *base registers* are for accessing elements of an array. The *program counter* is for accessing instructions. Next, the *stack pointer* is for accessing elements on the run-time

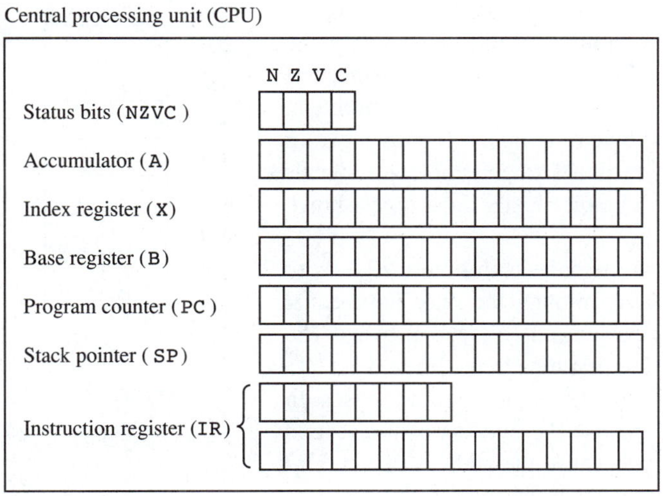

Figure 13.2

The central processing unit of the Pep/5 computer.

stack. The *instruction register* holds an instruction after it has been accessed from memory.

In addition to these seven registers, the CPU contains all the electronics (not shown in Figure 13.2) to execute the Pep/5 instructions.

Main Memory

Figure 13.3 shows the main memory of the Pep/5 computer. It contains 4096 eight-bit storage locations. A group of eight bits is called a *byte* (pronounced *bite*). Each byte has an address similar to the number address on a mail box. In decimal the addresses range from 0 to 4095, in hexadecimal from 0000 to 0FFF. Main memory is sometimes called *core memory*.

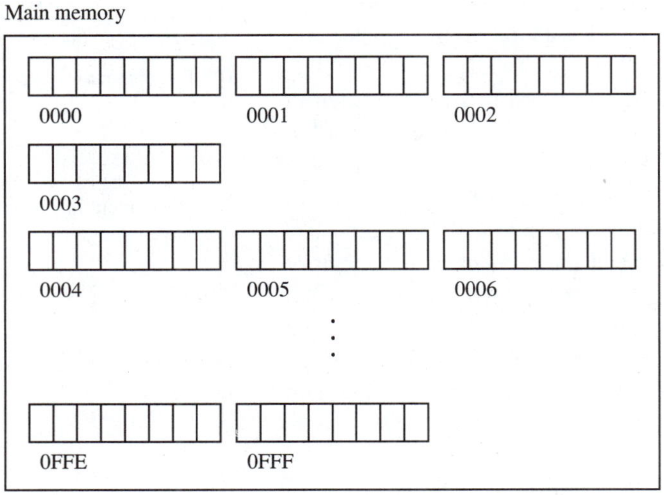

Figure 13.3

The main memory of the Pep/5 computer.

Figure 13.3 shows the first three bytes of main memory on the first line, the next byte on the second line, the next three bytes on the next line, and, finally, the last two bytes on the last line. Whether you should visualize a line of memory as containing one, two, or three bytes depends on the context of the problem. Sometimes it is more convenient to visualize one byte on a line, sometimes two or three. Of course, in the physical computer a byte is a sequence of eight signals stored in an electrical circuit. The bytes would not be physically lined up as shown in the figure.

Frequently it will be convenient to draw main memory as in Figure 13.4, with the addresses along the left side of the block. Even though the lines have equal widths visually in the block, a single line may represent one or several bytes. The address on the side of the block is the address of the first byte in the line.

You can tell how many bytes the line contains by the sequence of addresses. In the figure, the first line must have three bytes because the address of the second line is 0003. The second line must have one byte because the address of the third line is 0004, which is one more than 0003. Similarly, the third and fourth lines each have three bytes, the fifth has one, and the sixth has two. From the figure, it is impossible to tell how many bytes the seventh line has. The first three lines of Figure 13.4 correspond to the first six bytes in Figure 13.3.

Regardless of the way the bytes of main memory are laid out on paper, the bytes with small addresses are referred to as the "top" of memory, and those with large addresses are referred to as the "bottom."

Most computer manufacturers specify a word to be a certain number of bytes. In the Pep/5 computer a word is two adjacent bytes. A word, therefore, contains 16 bits. Most of the registers in the Pep/5 CPU are word registers. In main memory, the address of a word is the address of the first byte of the word. For example, Figure 13.5(a) shows two adjacent bytes at addresses 000B and 000C. The address of the 16-bit word is 000B.

It is important to distinguish between the content of a memory location and its address. Memory addresses in the Pep/5 computer are 16 bits long. Hence, the memory address of the word in Figure 13.5(a) could be written in binary as 0000 0000 0000 1011. The content of the word at this address, however, is 0000 0010 1101 0001. Do not confuse the content of the word with its address. They are different.

To save space on the page, the content of a byte or word is usually written in hexadecimal. Figure 13.5(b) shows the content in hexadecimal of the same word at address 000B. In a machine language listing, the address of the first byte of a group is printed followed by the content in hexadecimal as in Figure 13.5(c). In this format, it is especially easy to confuse the address of a byte with its content.

In the example of Figure 13.5, you can interpret the content of the memory location several ways. If you consider the bit sequence 0000 0010 1101 0001 as an integer in two's complement representation, then the first bit is the sign bit, and the binary sequence represents decimal 721. If you consider the rightmost seven bits as an ASCII character, then the binary sequence represents the character Q. The main

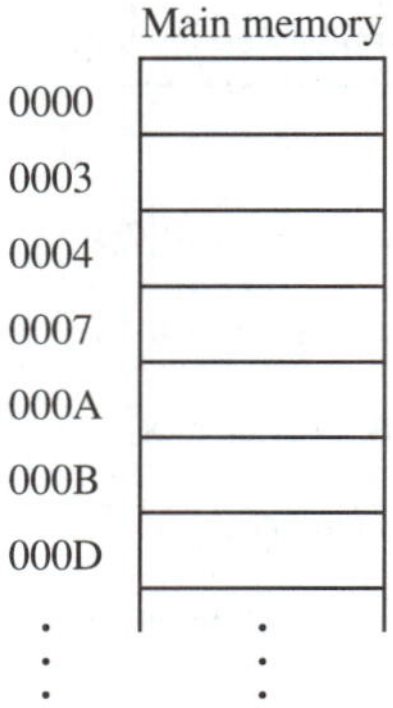

Figure 13.4

Another style for depicting main memory.

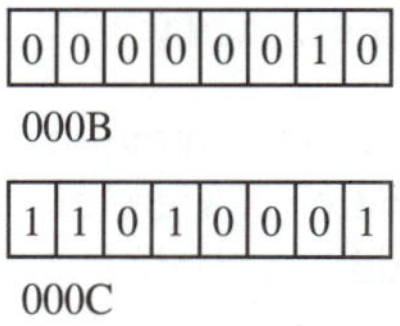

(a) The content in binary.

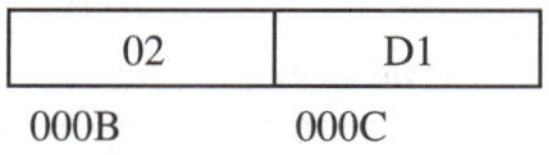

(b) The content in hexadecimal.

000B 02D1

(c) The content in a machine language listing.

Figure 13.5

The distinction between the content of a memory location and its address.

memory cannot determine which way the byte will be interpreted. It simply remembers the binary sequence 0000 0010 1101 0001.

Input Device

You may be wondering where this Pep/5 hardware is located and if you will ever be able to get your hands on it. The answer is, the hardware does not exist! At least it does not exist as a physical machine. Instead, it exists as a set of programs that you can execute on your computer system. The programs simulate the behavior of the Pep/5 machine described in these chapters.

Text file or keyboard as input

The Pep/5 system simulates two input devices—a text file and the keyboard. You cannot specify both in a single Pep/5 program. Before executing a program, you must specify whether you want the input to come from a file or the keyboard. If you specify a text file, the system will ask you from which file the input is to come. As in the Pascal `reset` statement, this file must have been previously created with a text editor.

Output Device

Text file or screen as output

The Pep/5 system also simulates two output devices—a text file and the screen. As with input, you cannot specify both in one program. If you specify a text file as output, the system will ask you for the name you want to give the file that the program will create. When you give this specification, the program will execute the equivalent of the Pascal `rewrite` statement.

Data and Control

The solid lines connecting the blocks of Figure 13.1 are data flow lines. Data can flow from the input device on the bus to main memory. It can also flow from main memory on the bus to the CPU. It cannot flow directly from the input device to the CPU.

Similarly, data cannot flow directly from the CPU to the output device. If you want to transfer data from the CPU to the output device you must send it to main memory first. It can then go from main memory to the output device.

The dashed lines are control lines. Control signals all originate from the CPU, which means that the CPU controls all the other parts of the computer. For example, to make data flow from the memory to the output device along the solid data flow lines, the CPU must transmit a send signal along the dashed control line to the memory, and a receive signal along the dashed control line to the output device. The important point is that the processor really is central. It controls all the other parts of the computer.

Table 13.1

The Pep/5 instruction set at Level 3.

Opcode	Instruction
00000	Stop execution.
00001	Load operand into register *R*.
00010	Store register *R* to operand.
00011	Add operand to register *R*.
00100	Subtract operand from register *R*.
00101	AND operand to register *R*.
00110	OR operand to register *R*.
00111	Ones' complement of register *R*.
01000	Arithmetic shift left register *R*.
01001	Arithmetic shift right register *R*.
01010	Load byte operand into register *R*.
01011	Store byte from register *R* to operand.
01100	Load operand into register `B`.
01101	Add operand to register `B`.
01110	Branch to different instruction.
01111	Branch if the `N` bit is 1.
10000	Branch if the `Z` bit is 1.
10001	Branch if the `V` bit is 1.
10010	Branch if the `C` bit is 1.
10011	Branch if the `N` bit or the `Z` bit is 1.
10100	Compare register *R* with operand.
10101	Add operand to register `SP`.
10110	Subtract operand from register `SP`.
10111	Jump to a subroutine.
11000	Return from a subroutine.
11001	Return from an interrupt.
11010	Character input to operand.
11011	Character output from operand.
11100	Unimplemented opcode, interrupt.
11101	Unimplemented opcode, interrupt.
11110	Unimplemented opcode, interrupt.
11111	Unimplemented opcode, interrupt.

Instruction Format

Each computer has its own set of instructions wired into its CPU. The instruction set varies from manufacturer to manufacturer. It often varies among computers made by the same company, although many manufacturers produce a family of models, each one of which contains the same instruction set as the other models in that family.

The Pep/5 computer has 32 instructions in its instruction set shown in Table 13.1. Each instruction consists of either a single byte called the *instruction specifier*, or the instruction specifier followed immediately by a word called the *operand specifier*. Instructions that do not have an operand specifier are called *unary instructions*. Figure 13.6(a) shows the structure of the instruction specifier and the operand specifier.

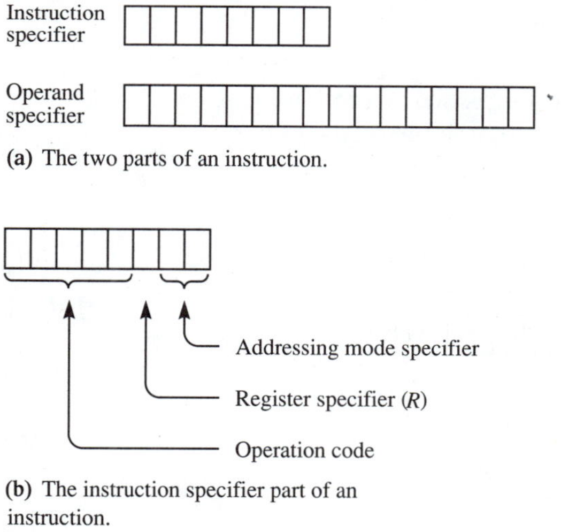

Figure 13.6

The Pep/5 instruction format.

Figure 13.6(b) shows the instruction specifier divided into the following three fields:

- The five-bit operation code
- The one-bit register specifier
- The two-bit addressing mode specifier

The five bits of the operation code, often referred to as the *opcode*, determine which of the 32 instructions in the instruction set is to be executed. The register specifier indicates whether the instruction will affect the accumulator or the index register, as shown in Table 13.2.

Register specifier	Register specified (*R*)
0	Accumulator (A)
1	Index register (X)

Table 13.2

The register specified by the register specifier part of the opcode.

Example 13.1 Suppose the opcode field contains 00101, which is the opcode for the AND operation. If the register specifier contains 0, then the CPU takes the AND of the operand and the accumulator and places the result in the accumulator. If it contains 1, the CPU ANDs the operand to the index register. ■

Addr. mode specifier	Addr. mode specified
00	Immediate (`i`)
01	Direct (`d`)
10	Indexed (`x`)
11	Stack relative (`s`)

Table 13.3

The addressing mode specified by the addressing mode specifier part of the opcode.

Pep/5 executes each instruction in one of four addressing modes—immediate, direct, indexed, or stack relative. The two addressing mode specifier bits determine the addressing mode, as Table 13.3 shows.

The operand specifier, for those instructions that are not unary, indicates the operand to be processed by the instruction. The CPU can interpret the operand specifier several different ways, depending on the bits in the instruction specifier. For example, it may interpret the operand specifier as an ASCII character, as an integer in two's complement representation, or as an address in main memory where the operand is stored.

Instructions are stored in main memory. The address of an instruction in main memory is the address of the first byte of the instruction.

Example 13.2 Figure 13.7 shows two adjacent instructions stored in main memory at locations 01A3 and 01A6. The instruction at 01A6 is unary; the instruction at 01A3 is not.

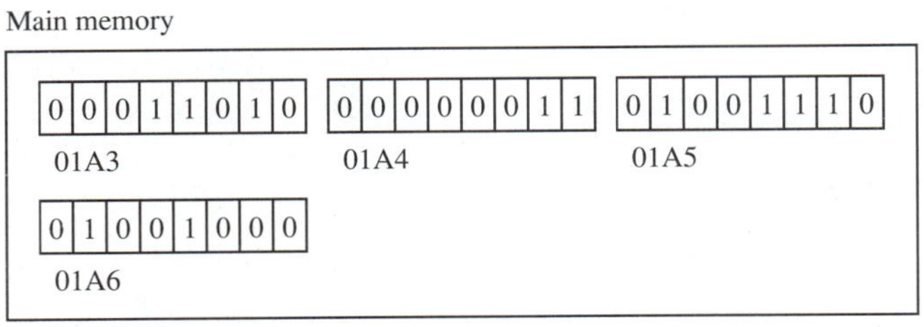

Figure 13.7

Two instructions in main memory.

In this example, the instruction at 01A3 has

Opcode: 00011

Register specifier: 0

Addressing mode specifier: 10

Operand specifier: 0000 0011 0100 1110

where all the quantities are written in binary. According to the opcode chart of Table 13.1, this is an add instruction. The register specifier indicates that the accumulator is affected, as opposed to the index register. So this instruction adds the operand to the accumulator. The addressing mode specifier indicates indexed addressing, so the operand specifier is interpreted accordingly. In this chapter, we will confine our study to the direct addressing mode. The other modes will be taken up in later chapters.

The unary instruction at 01A6 has

Opcode: 01001

Register specifier: 0

Addressing mode specifier: 00

The opcode indicates that the instruction will do an arithmetic shift right. The register specifier indicates that the accumulator is the register in which the shift will take place. Since this is a unary instruction, the addressing mode specifier is ignored. The CPU would not execute this instruction any differently if the addressing mode bits had some other value. ■

In the previous example, the following form of the instructions is called machine language:

0001 1010 0000 0011 0100 1110
0100 1000

Machine language is a binary sequence, that is, a sequence of ones and zeros, that the CPU interprets according to the opcodes of its instruction set. A machine language listing would show these two instructions in hexadecimal preceded by their memory addresses as follows:

Machine language

```
01A3  1A034E
01A6  48
```

If you have only the hexadecimal listing of an instruction, you must convert it to binary and examine the three fields in the instruction specifier to determine what the instruction will do.

13.2 Character I/O and Direct Addressing

The Pep/5 system can take its input from the keyboard and send its output to the screen. These I/O devices are based on the ASCII character set. When you press a key, a byte of information representing a single ASCII character goes from the keyboard along the bus to main memory. When the CPU sends a byte to the screen along the bus, the screen interprets the byte as an ASCII character, which it displays.

At Level 3, the machine level, computers usually have no input or output instructions for any type of data except bytes. The interpretation of the byte occurs in the input or output device, not in main memory. Pep/5's only input instruction transfers a byte from the input device to main memory, and its only output instruction transfers a byte from main memory to the output device. Since these bytes are usually interpreted as ASCII characters, the I/O at Level 3 of the Pep/5 system is called *character I/O*.

This section describes the operation of some of the Pep/5 instructions at Level 3, including the character I/O instructions. It describes how they operate in conjunction with the direct addressing mode.

Direct Addressing

The addressing mode specifier determines how the CPU interprets the operand specifier. An addressing mode specifier of 01 indicates direct addressing. With direct addressing, the CPU interprets the operand specifier as the address in main memory of the cell that contains the operand. In mathematical notation

The relation between the operand and the operand specifier in direct addressing

```
Oprnd = Mem [OprndSpec]
```

where `Oprnd` stands for "operand," `OprndSpec` stands for "operand specifier," and `Mem` stands for main memory.

The bracket notation indicates that you can think of main memory as an array and the operand specifier as the index of the array. In Pascal, if `V` is an array and `I` is an integer, `V [I]` is the "cell" in the array that is determined by the value of the integer `I`. Similarly, the operand specifier in the instruction identifies the cell in main memory that contains the operand.

The cells in memory are like elements of an array.

What follows is a description of 12 instructions from the Pep/5 instruction set. Each description lists the opcode and gives an example of the operation of the instruction when used with the direct addressing mode. Values of `N`, `Z`, `V`, and `C` are always given in binary. Values of other registers and of memory cells are given in various representations. At the machine level, all values are ultimately binary. After describing the individual instructions, this chapter will conclude by showing how you can put them together to construct a machine language program.

00000 Stop Execution When this instruction is executed it simply makes the computer stop. Since Pep/5 is a simulated computer, you execute it by running the Pep/5 simulator on your computer. The simulator has a menu of command options for you to choose from. One of those options is to execute your Pep/5 program. When your Pep/5 program is executing, if it encounters this instruction it will stop and return the simulator to the menu of command options.

The stop execution instruction is unary. It ignores the addressing mode specifier bits and has no operand specifier. It also ignores the register specifier bit.

00001 Load Operand into Register R This instruction loads one word (two bytes) from a memory location into either the index register or the accumulator. It affects the `N` and `Z` bits. If the operand is negative, it sets the `N` bit to 1; otherwise it clears the `N` bit to 0. If the operand consists of 16 0's, it sets the `Z` bit to 1; otherwise it clears the `Z` bit to 0.

Example 13.3 Suppose the instruction to be executed is 09004A in hexadecimal, which is

0000 1001 0000 0000 0100 1010

in binary. (In these examples we will bracket the bits in the opcode and the addressing mode specifier as a reminder of the instruction format.) Notice that the register specifier in this example is 0, which indicates a load to the accumulator instead of the index register. The addressing mode specifier is 01, which indicates direct addressing. If the contents of the accumulator and of memory location 004A are

Before a load instruction

`A:`	036D (hex)
`Mem [004A]:`	92EF (hex)

to begin with, and the instruction 09004A is executed, then the contents after the instruction is executed are

After a load instruction

`A:`	92EF (hex)
`Mem [004A]:`	92EF (hex)
`NZ:`	10 (bin)

The load instruction does not change the content of the memory location. It sends a copy of the memory cell to the register. Whatever was in the register before the instruction was executed, in this case 036D, is destroyed. The `N` bit is set to 1 because the bit pattern loaded has 1 in the sign bit. The `Z` bit is set to 0 because the bit pattern is not all 0's. The `V` and `C` bits are unaffected by the load instruction. ■

Figure 13.8 shows the data flow lines and control lines that the load instruction activates. As indicated by the solid lines, data flows from the main memory on the bus to the CPU, then into the register.

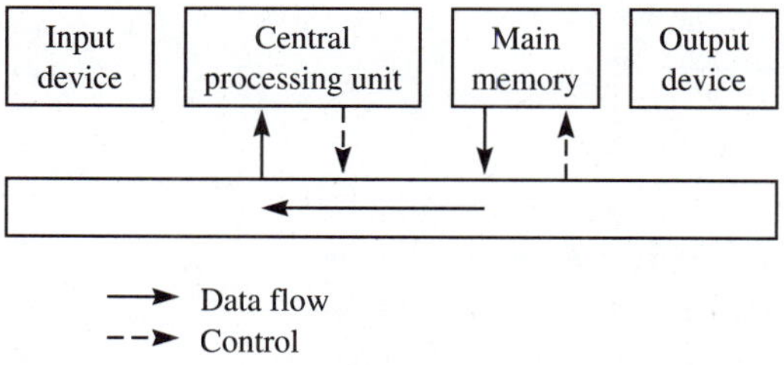

Figure 13.8
The data flow and control lines activated by the load instruction.

For this data transfer to take place the CPU must send a control signal, as indicated by the dashed lines, to main memory telling it to put the data on the bus. The CPU also tells main memory the address from which to fetch the data.

00010 Store Register R to Operand This instruction stores one word (two bytes) from either the accumulator or the index register to a memory location. The operand specifies the memory location in which the information is stored.

Example 13.4 Suppose that the instruction to be executed is 15004A in hexadecimal, which is

0001 0101 0000 0000 0100 1010

in binary. This time, the register specifier indicates that the instruction will affect the index register. The addressing mode specifier, 01, indicates direct addressing. If the contents of the index register and of memory location 004A are

Before a store instruction

```
X:          92BC (hex)
Mem [004A]: F082 (hex)
```

to begin with and instruction 15004A is executed, then the contents after the instruction is executed are

After a store instruction

```
X:          92BC (hex)
Mem [004A]: 92BC (hex)
```

The store register instruction does the opposite of the load register instruction. It sends a copy of the register to the memory cell. Whatever was in the memory cell before the instruction was executed, in this case F082, is destroyed. This instruction affects none of the status bits. ■

Figure 13.9 shows the data flow lines and control lines that the store register instruction activates. As indicated by the solid lines, data flows from the CPU on the bus to main memory. As before, the CPU must send a control signal to memory so that it will receive the data correctly.

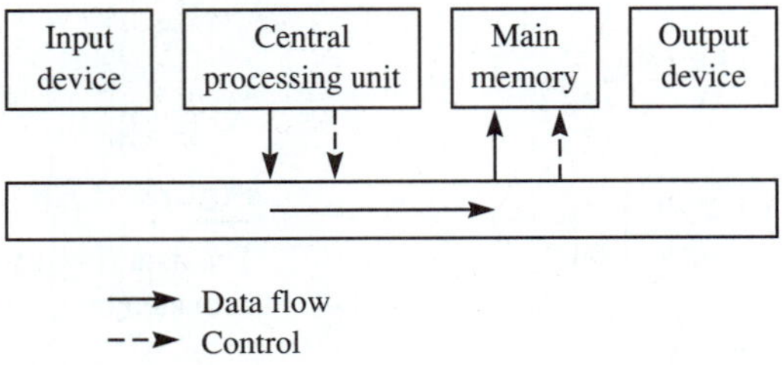

Figure 13.9

The data flow and control lines activated by the store instruction.

00011 Add Operand to Register R The add register *R* instruction is similar to the load register *R* instruction in that data is transferred from main memory to register *R* in the CPU. But with the add register R instruction, the original content of the register is not just written over by the content of the word from main memory. Instead, the content of the word from main memory is added to the content of the register. The sum is placed in the register, and the status bits are set accordingly. As with the load accumulator instruction, a copy of the memory word is sent to the CPU. The original content of the memory word is unchanged.

Example 13.5 Suppose that before the instruction executes, the computer has

Before an add instruction

```
A:          1111 1111 1011 0110 (bin)
Mem [004A]: 0000 0000 0010 0011 (bin)
```

Then the instruction 19004A executes, which is

0001 1001 0000 0000 0100 1010

in binary. The contents after the instruction executes are

After an add instruction

`A:`	1111 1111 1101 1001 (bin)
`Mem [004A]:`	0000 0000 0010 0011 (bin)
`NZVC:`	1000 (bin)

The `N` bit is 1 because the sum is negative. The `Z` bit is 0 because the sum is not all 0's. The `V` bit is 0 because an overflow did not occur, and the `C` bit is 0 because a carry did not occur out of the most significant bit. ■

The data flow lines and control lines that the add instruction activates are identical to those activated by the load instruction as shown in Figure 13.8.

00100 Subtract Operand from Register R This instruction is similar to the add instruction, except that the operand is subtracted from the register. The result is placed in the register, and the operand is unchanged.

Example 13.6 Suppose that before the instruction executes, the computer has

Before a subtract instruction

`X:`	13 (dec)
`Mem [004A]:`	15 (dec)

Then the instruction 25004A executes, which is

0010 0101 0000 0000 0100 1010

in binary. Note that the register specifier is 1, which indicates that the instruction affects the index register, not the accumulator. The contents after the instruction executes are

After a subtract instruction

`X:`	–2 (dec)
`Mem [004A]:`	15 (dec)
`NZVC:`	1001 (bin)

The `C` bit is 1 because of the borrow in the most significant column during the subtraction. ■

00101 AND Operand to Register R The AND instruction is also similar to the add instruction. Rather than add the operand to the register, the instruction performs the AND operation to the register. The AND operation is useful for masking out undesired 1 bits in a bit pattern.

Example 13.7 Suppose you have the bit pattern

0110 1011 0101 1101 (bin)

in the index register and you want to strip away all the 1 bits in the leftmost 12 places. To do that, you can AND the index register with a bit pattern called a *mask*. In this case, the mask would have 0's in the leftmost 12 places and 1's in the rightmost 4 places. Specifically, suppose that before the instruction executes, the computer has

Before an AND instruction

`X:`	6B5D (hex)
`Mem [004A]:`	000F (hex)

Then the instruction 2D004A executes, which is

0010 1101 0000 0000 0100 1010

in binary. The contents after the instruction executes are then

After an AND instruction

`X:`	000D (hex)
`Mem [004A]:`	000F (hex)
`NZ:`	00 (bin)

The bits that you AND with the 0's in the mask become 0's, and the bits that you AND with the 1's in the mask remain unchanged. The AND instruction does not affect the `V` and `C` bits. ■

00110 OR Operand to Register R This instruction is similar to the AND instruction, except that the OR operation is applied to the register. The OR operation is useful for inserting one bits into a bit pattern.

Example 13.8 Suppose you have the bit pattern

0000 1100 0100 1101

in the accumulator and you want to change all the bits in the leftmost 12 places to 1's without changing the bits in the rightmost 4 places. To do that, OR the accumulator with a mask that has 1's in the leftmost 12 places and 0's in the rightmost 4 places. Specifically, suppose that before the instruction executes the computer has

Before an OR instruction

`A:`	0C4D (hex)
`Mem [004A]:`	FFF0 (hex)

Then the instruction 31004A executes, which is

0011 0001 0000 0000 0100 1010

in binary. The contents after the instruction executes are

After an OR instruction

`A:`	FFFD (hex)
`Mem [004A]:`	FFF0 (hex)
`NZ:`	10 (bin)

The bits that you OR with the 1's in the mask become 1's, and the bits that you OR with the 0's in the mask remain unchanged. The `N` bit is 1 because there is a 1 in the sign bit of the accumulator after the instruction executes. As with the AND instruction, the OR instruction does not affect the `V` or `C` bits. ■

00111 Ones' Complement of Register R This instruction is unary. It ignores the addressing mode specifier bits and has no operand specifier. It performs the NOT operation on either the accumulator or the index register.

Example 13.9 Suppose that before the instruction executes, the accumulator has

`A:` 0000 1111 0110 0011 (bin)

Before a NOT instruction

Then the instruction 39 (hex) executes, which is

0011 1001

in binary. After the instruction executes, the accumulator contains

`A:` 1111 0000 1001 1100 (bin)
`NZ:` 10 (bin)

After a NOT instruction

The ones' complement instruction affects the `N` and `Z` bits as usual, and does not affect the `V` or `C` bits. ■

01010 Load Byte Operand into Register R This instruction, along with the next three, is a byte instruction. *Byte instructions* operate on a single byte of information, instead of a word. The load byte instruction loads the operand into the right half of either the accumulator or the index register. It leaves the left half of the register unchanged.

Example 13.10 Suppose the instruction to be executed is 51004A in hexadecimal, which is

0101 0001 0000 0000 0100 1010

in binary. If the contents of the accumulator and of memory location 004A are

`A:` 036D (hex)
`Mem [004A]:` E2 (hex)

Before a load byte instruction

to begin with and the instruction 51004A is executed, then the contents after the instruction is executed are

`A:` 03E2 (hex)
`Mem [004A]:` E2 (hex)
`NZ:` 00 (bin)

After a load byte instruction

When the load instruction executes with an operand at `Mem [004A]`, it loads the two bytes at locations 004A and 004B into the specified register. When this load byte instruction executes with an operand at `Mem [004A]`, it loads only the byte at location 004A. ■

01011 Store Byte from Register R to Operand The store byte instruction stores the right half from either the accumulator or the index register to a memory location. It ignores the left half of the register.

Example 13.11 Suppose that the instruction to be executed is 5D004A in hexadecimal, which is

0101 1101 0000 0000 0100 1010

in binary. If the contents of the index register and of memory location 004A are

Before a store byte instruction

`X:` 92BC (hex)

`Mem [004A]:` F0 (hex)

to begin with, and instruction 5D004A is executed, then the contents after the instruction is executed are

After a store byte instruction

`X:` 92BC (hex)

`Mem [004A]:` BC (hex)

The byte at `Mem [004B]` is not affected as it would be if the instruction executed were the store register instruction. ■

11010 Character Input to Operand The character input instruction takes the next ASCII character from the input device and stores the corresponding binary code for that character in a byte in main memory. It ignores the register specifier bit.

Example 13.12 Consider the instruction D1004A, which is

1101 0001 0000 0000 0100 1010

in binary. Suppose the content of a byte in memory is

Before a character input instruction

`Mem [004A]:` 1111 1010 (bin)

and the next ASCII character from the input device is `W`. After the instruction D1004A executes, the memory location gets the value

After a character input instruction

`Mem [004A]:` 0101 0111 (bin)

where the byte stored at 004A in main memory is the binary code for `W`.

Notice that ASCII is a seven-bit code, but a byte is eight bits. The character input instruction stores the bit pattern in the rightmost seven bits of the byte and sets the leftmost bit to 0. The input instruction does not affect the status bits. ■

The character input instruction activates the data flow and control lines shown in Figure 13.10. Even though data does not flow to or from the CPU, the CPU must still issue the control signals to the input device and to main memory. It issues a command to the input device to put the next character on the bus and a command to main memory to get the data from the bus.

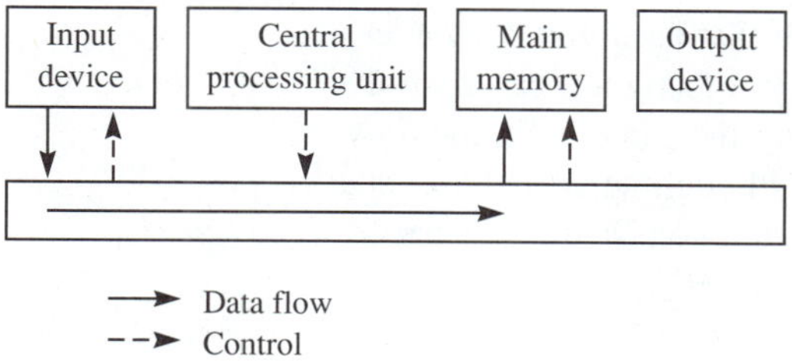

Figure 13.10

The data flow and control lines activated by the character input instruction.

11011 Character Output from Operand The character output instruction sends the content of a byte in memory to the output device, which prints the corresponding ASCII character. The CPU ignores the register specifier bit in the instruction specifier.

Example 13.13 Consider the instruction D9004A, which is

1101 1001 0000 0000 0100 1010

in binary. If the content of a byte in memory is

`Mem [004A]:` 0010 0101 (bin)

and the instruction D9004A executes, the CPU will send the byte to the output device, which will print the `%` character. As with the character input instruction, the character output instruction does not affect the status bits. ■

Figure 13.11 shows the data flow lines and control lines activated by the character output instruction.

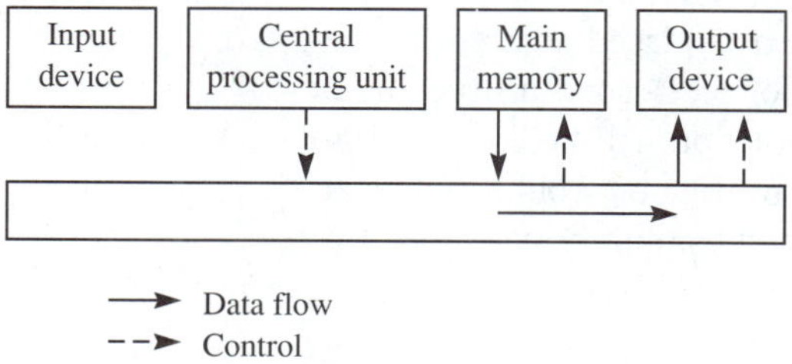

Figure 13.11

The data flow and control lines activated by the character output instruction.

13.3 Von Neumann Machines

In the earliest electronic computers, each program was hand wired. To change the program, the wires had to be manually reconnected, a tedious and time-consuming process. The ENIAC computer described in Section 12.1 was an example of this kind of machine. Its memory was used only to store data.

In 1945, John von Neumann had proposed in a report from the University of Pennsylvania that the United States Ordnance Department build a computer that would store not only the data in main memory, but the program as well. The stored program concept was a radical idea at the time. Maurice V. Wilkes built the Electronic Delay Storage Automatic Calculator (EDSAC) at Cambridge University in England in 1949. It was the first computer to be built that used von Neumann's stored program idea. Practically all commercial computers today are based on the stored program concept, with programs and data sharing the same main memory. Such computers are called von Neumann machines, although some believe that J. Presper Eckert, Jr., originated the idea several years before von Neumann's paper.

The von Neumann Execution Cycle

The Pep/5 computer is a classical von Neumann machine. The following pseudocode describes the steps required to execute a program.

A pseudocode description of the von Neumann execution cycle

```
Load the machine language program.
Initialize PC and SP
repeat
    Fetch the next instruction.
    Increment PC
    Execute the instruction fetched.
until the stop instruction executes
```

The `repeat` loop is called the *von Neumann execution cycle*. The cycle consists of the four operations—fetch, increment, execute, and repeat. What follows is a more detailed description of the steps in the execution process.

Load the program

To load the machine language program into main memory, the first instruction is placed at address 0000 (hex). The second instruction is placed adjacent to the first. If the first instruction is unary, then the address of the second instruction is 0001. Otherwise the operand specifier of the first instruction will be contained in the bytes at 0001 and 0002. The address of the second instruction would then be at 0003. The third instruction is placed adjacent to the second similarly, and so on for the entire machine language program.

Initialize PC and SP

To initialize the program counter and stack pointer, `PC` is set to 0000 (hex), and `SP` is set to `Mem [0FF8]`. The purpose of the program counter is to hold the address of the next instruction to be executed. Since the first instruction was loaded into main memory at address 0000, the `PC` must be set initially to 0000. The purpose of the stack pointer is to hold the address of the top of the run-time stack. The next section will explain why `SP` is set to `Mem [0FF8]`.

Fetch instruction

The first operation in the von Neumann execution cycle is *fetch*. To fetch an instruction, the CPU examines the 16 bits in the `PC` and interprets them as an address. It then goes to that address in main memory to fetch the instruction specifier (one byte) of the next instruction. The eight bits of the instruction specifier are brought to the CPU and held there in the first byte of the instruction register (`IR`). The CPU then examines the opcode to determine if the instruction is unary. If it is not unary, the CPU fetches the operand specifier (one word) from memory and stores it in the last two bytes of the `IR`.

Increment PC

The second operation in the von Neumann execution cycle is *increment*. The CPU adds 0001 to the `PC` if the instruction was unary. Otherwise it adds 0003. Regardless of which number is added to the `PC`, its value after the addition will be the address of the following instruction, since the instructions are loaded adjacent to one another in main memory.

Execute instruction fetched

The third operation in the von Neumann execution cycle is *execute*. The CPU executes the instruction that is stored in the `IR`. The five-bit opcode tells the CPU which of the 32 instructions to execute.

Repeat the cycle

The fourth operation in the von Neumann execution cycle is *repeat*. The CPU returns to the fetch operation unless the instruction just executed was the stop instruction. Pep/5 will also terminate at this point if the instruction attempts an illegal operation. Some instructions are not allowed to use certain addressing modes. The most common illegal operation that makes Pep/5 terminate is attempting execution of an instruction with a forbidden addressing mode.

The following pseudocode is a more detailed description of the steps to execute a program on the Pep/5 computer. We will present four examples of machine language programs that use the instructions described previously.

A more detailed pseudocode description of the von Newman execution cycle

```
Load the machine language program into memory
   starting at address 0000.
PC := 0000
SP := Mem [0FF8]
repeat
   Fetch the next instruction specified by PC
   if the instruction is unary then
      PC := PC + 1
   else
      PC := PC + 3
   Execute the instruction fetched
until (the stop instruction executes)
or (an illegal operation is attempted)
```

Program 13.1

Program 13.1 is a simple machine language program that outputs the characters `Hi` on the output device. It uses two instructions: 11011, which is the character output instruction, and 00000, which is the stop instruction. The first listing shows the machine language program in binary. Main memory stores this sequence of ones and zeros. The first column gives the address in hex of the first byte of the bit pattern on each line.

Program 13.1

A machine language program to output `Hi`.

Addr. Machine Language (bin)

```
0000   1101 1001 0000 0000 0000 0111
0003   1101 1001 0000 0000 0000 1000
0006   0000 0000
0007   0100 1000
0008   0110 1001
```

Addr. Machine Language (hex)

```
0000   D90007   ;Character output
0003   D90008   ;Character output
0006   00       ;Stop
0007   48       ;ASCII H character
0008   69       ;ASCII i character
```

Output

```
Hi
```

The second listing shows the same program abbreviated to hexadecimal. Even though this format is slightly easier to read, remember that memory stores bits, not literal hexadecimal characters as in this listing. Each line in the second listing has a comment that begins with a semicolon to separate it from the machine language. The comments are not loaded into memory with the program.

Figure 13.12 (pp. 662–63) shows each step the computer takes to execute the program. Figure 13.12(a) is the initial state of the Pep/5 computer. The input device is not shown. Several of the CPU registers not used by this program are also omitted. Each question mark indicates four bits. Initially, the contents of the main memory cells and the CPU registers are unknown.

Figure 13.12(b) shows the first step of the process. The program is loaded into main memory starting at address 0000. The details of where the program comes from and what puts it into memory will be described in later chapters.

Figure 13.12(c) shows the second step of the process. The program counter is cleared to 0000 (hex). The figure does not show the initialization of `SP`, since this program does not use the stack pointer.

Figure 13.12(d) shows the fetch part of the execution cycle. The CPU examines the bits in the `PC` and finds 0000 (hex). It signals the main memory to send the byte at that address to the CPU. When the CPU gets the byte, it stuffs it into the first part of the instruction register. Then it determines from the opcode that the instruction is not unary and brings the operand specifier into the `IR` as well. The original bits at addresses 0000, 0001, and 0002 are not changed by the fetch. Main memory has sent a copy of the 24 bits to the CPU.

Figure 13.12(e) shows the increment part of the execution cycle. The CPU adds 0003 to the `PC`.

Figure 13.12(f) shows the execute part of the execution cycle. The CPU examines the first five bits of the `IR` and finds 11011. This opcode signals the circuitry to execute the character output instruction.

Consequently, the CPU examines the addressing mode bits and finds 01, which indicates direct addressing. It then examines the operand specifier and finds 0007 (hex). It sends a control signal back to main memory to go directly to address 0007 and put the byte at that address on the bus. Simultaneously, it sends a control signal to the output device to get the byte from the bus. The output device interprets the byte as an ASCII character and displays it, ignoring the leftmost bit since ASCII is a seven-bit code. If the addressing mode had not been direct, the CPU would not have signaled main memory to go directly to address 0007 for the byte.

Figure 13.12(g) shows the fetch part of the execution cycle. This time the CPU finds 0003 (hex) in the `PC`. It fetches a copy of the byte at address 0003, determines that the instruction is not unary, then fetches the word at 0004. As a result, the original content of the `IR` is destroyed.

Figure 13.12(h) shows the increment part of the execution cycle. The CPU adds 0003 to the `PC`, making it 0006 (hex).

Figure 13.12(i) shows the execute part of the execution cycle. As in part (f), the CPU finds the opcode for the character output instruction and the addressing mode bits for direct addressing. But this time the operand specifier is 0008 (hex). The byte at address 0008 is 69 (hex), which is 0110 1001 (bin). Since the rightmost seven bits are 110 1001, the output device displays the ASCII character `i`.

Figure 13.12(j) shows the fetch part of the execute cycle. The PC contains 0006 (hex), so the byte at that address comes to the CPU. This time when the CPU examines the opcode, it discovers that the instruction is unary. So, the CPU does not fetch the word at address 0007.

Figure 13.12(k) shows the increment part of the execution cycle. The CPU adds 0001 to the `PC`, making it 0007 (hex).

Figure 13.12(l) shows the execute part of the execution cycle. This time the CPU finds the opcode for the halt instruction in the `IR`. Therefore, it ignores the addressing mode bits and simply stops the execution cycle.

Just outputing a couple of characters may seem a rather involved process, but it all happens rather quickly in human terms. The fetch part of the execution cycle

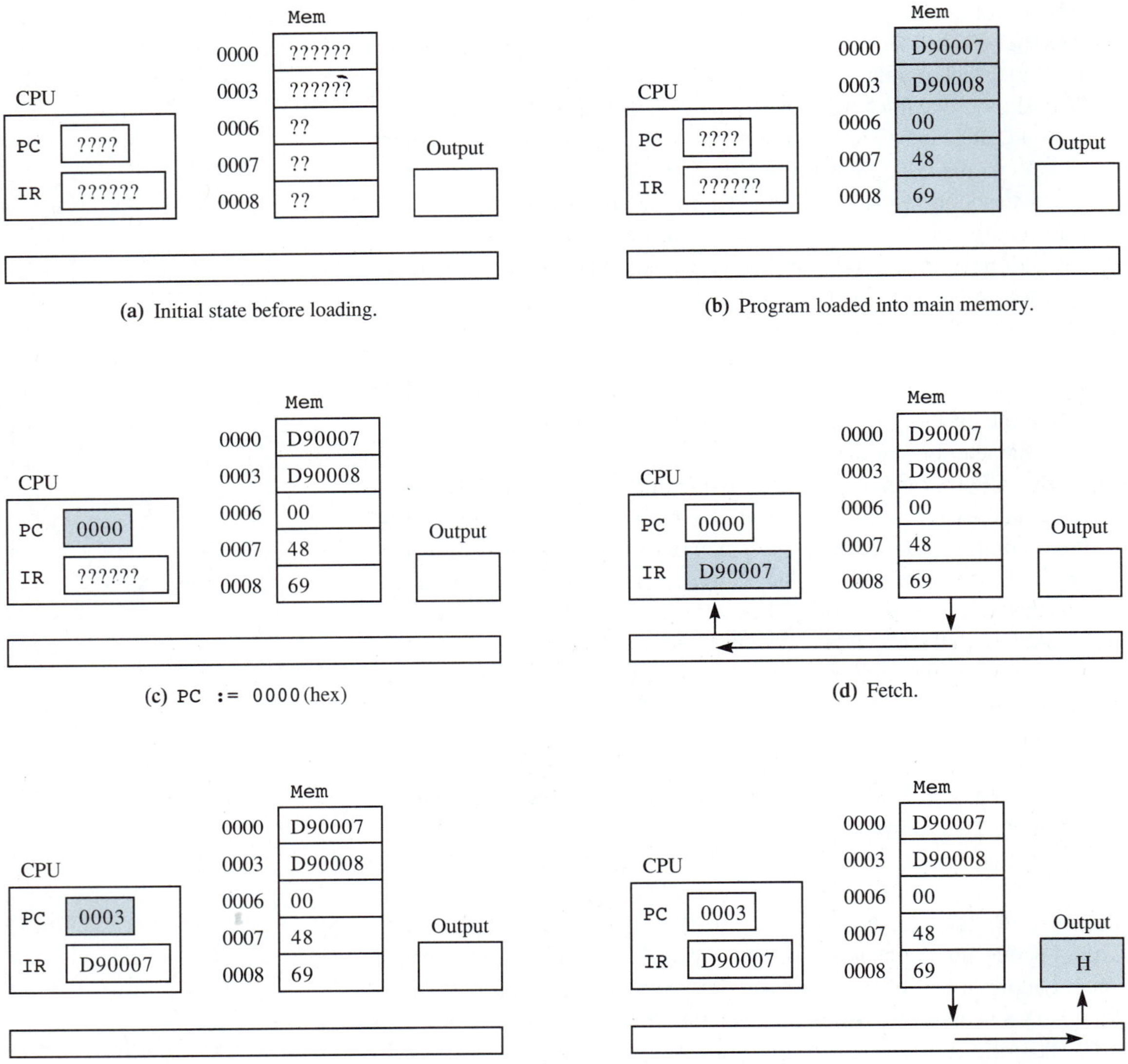

(a) Initial state before loading.

(b) Program loaded into main memory.

(c) PC := 0000 (hex)

(d) Fetch.

(e) Increment PC.

(f) Execute. Character H sent to output device.

Figure 13.12

The von Neumann execution cycle of Program 13.1

takes less than a microsecond on many computers. Since the execution part of the execution cycle depends on the particular instruction, a complex instruction may take many microseconds to execute, whereas a simple instruction may take less than a microsecond.

The computer does not attach any meaning to the electrical signals in its circuitry. Specifically, main memory does not know whether the bits at a particular address represent data or an instruction. It remembers only individual ones and zeros.

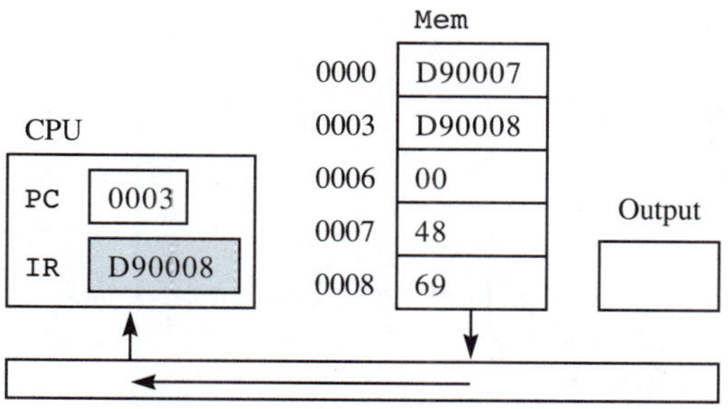

(g) Fetch.

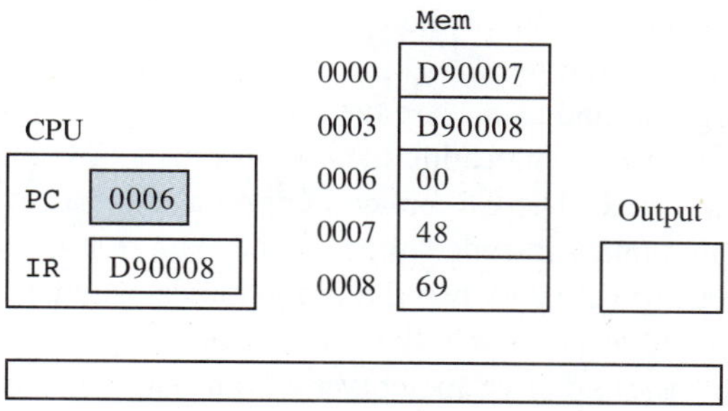

(h) Increment PC.

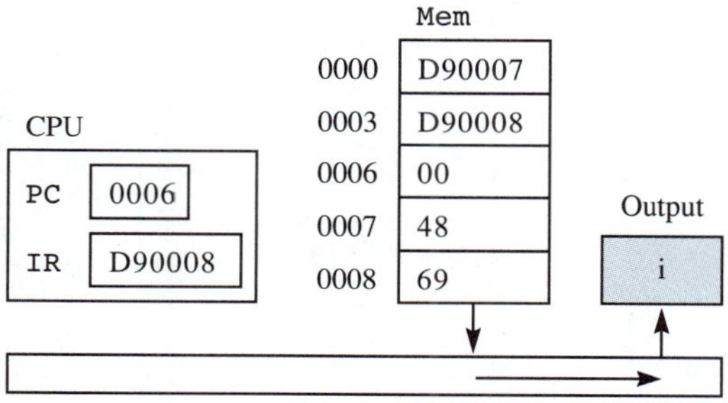

(i) Execute. Character `i` sent to output device.

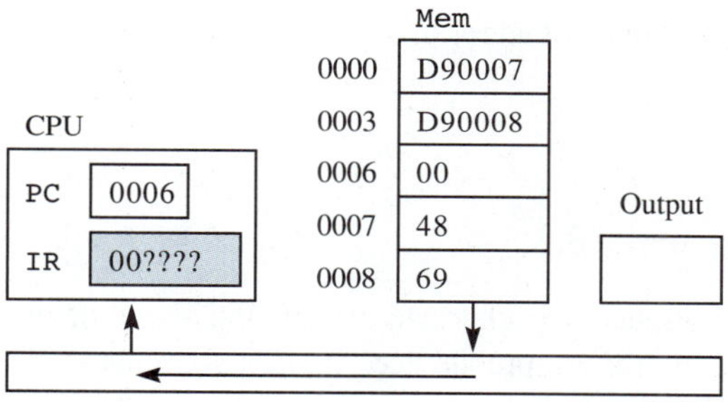

(j) Fetch.

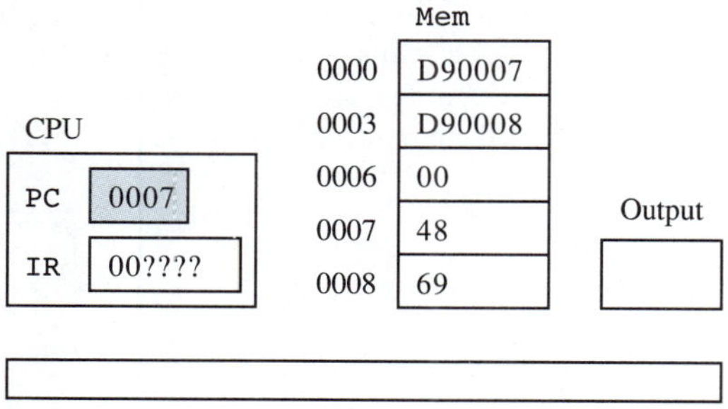

(k) Increment PC.

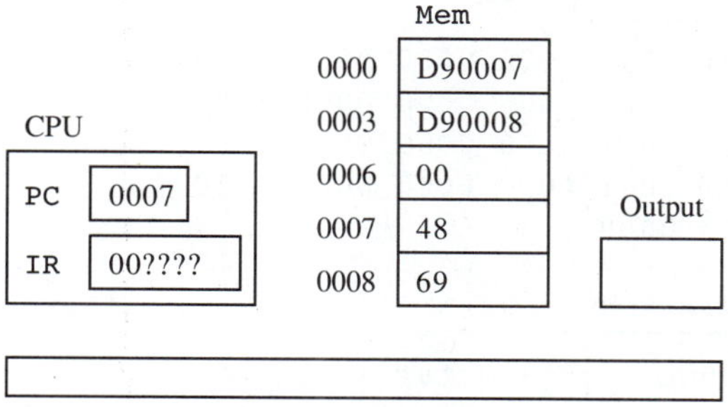

(l) Execute. The computer halts.

Figure 13.12, continued

Von Neumann Bugs

Executing data as instructions

In Program 13.1, the bits at addresses 0000 to 0006 were used by the CPU as instructions, and the bits at 0007 and 0008 were used as data. The programmer placed the instruction bits at the beginning because she knew the PC would be initially cleared to 0000 and would be incremented by 0001 or by 0003 on each iteration of the execution cycle. If the stop instruction (opcode 00000) were omitted by mistake, the execution cycle would continue to fetch the next byte and interpret it as the instruction specifier of the next instruction, even though the programmer intended to have it interpreted as data.

Since programs and data share the same memory, programmers at the machine level must be careful in allocating memory for each of them. Otherwise two types of problems can arise. The CPU may interpret a sequence of bits as an instruction when the programmer intended them to be data. Or the CPU may interpret a sequence of bits to be data when the programmer intended them to be an instruction. Both types of bugs occur at the machine level.

Interpreting instructions as data

Although the sharing of memory by both data and instructions can produce bugs if the programmer is not careful, it also presents an exciting possibility. A program is simply a set of instructions that are stored in memory. The programmer, therefore, can view the program as data for yet another program. It becomes possible to write programs that process other programs. Compilers, assemblers, and loaders are programs that adopt this viewpoint of treating other programs as data.

Program 13.2

Program 13.2 inputs two characters from the input device and outputs them in reverse order on the output device. It uses the character input instruction with direct addressing to get the characters from the input device.

Program 13.2

A machine language program to input two characters and output them in reverse order.

Addr.	Machine Language (bin)
0000	1101 0001 0000 0000 0000 1110
0003	1101 0001 0000 0000 0000 1101
0006	1101 1001 0000 0000 0000 1101
0009	1101 1001 0000 0000 0000 1110
000C	0000 0000

Addr.	Machine Language (hex)	
0000	D1000E	;Character input
0003	D1000D	;Character input
0006	D9000D	;Character output
0009	D9000E	;Character output
000C	00	;Stop

Input

```
up
```

Output

```
pu
```

The first instruction, D1000E, has an opcode that specifies the character input instruction and addressing mode bits that specify direct addressing. It puts the first character from the input device into the byte at `Mem [000E]`. Although this byte is not shown on the listing, it is surely available since memory goes all the way up to address 0FFF. The second instruction, D1000D, also specifies character input, but to `Mem [000D]`.

The third instruction, D9000D, has an opcode that specifies the character output instruction. It outputs the byte that was previously stored at `Mem [000D]`. The fourth instruction, D9000E, outputs the byte that was previously stored at `Mem [000E]`.

Program 13.3

Program 13.3 adds two single-digit numbers and outputs their single-digit sum. It illustrates the inconvenience of dealing with output at the machine level.

Program 13.3

A machine language program to add 5 and 3 and output the single character result.

Addr. Machine Language (bin)

```
0000  0000 1001 0000 0000 0001 0001
0003  0001 1001 0000 0000 0001 0011
0006  0011 0001 0000 0000 0001 0101
0009  0101 1001 0000 0000 0001 0000
000C  1101 1001 0000 0000 0001 0000
000F  0000 0000
0010  0000 0000
0011  0000 0000 0000 0101
0013  0000 0000 0000 0011
0015  0000 0000 0011 0000
```

Addr. Machine Language (hex)

```
0000  090011  ;Load accumulator
0003  190013  ;Add accumulator
0006  310015  ;OR accumulator
0009  590010  ;Store byte accumulator
000C  D90010  ;Character output
000F  00      ;Stop
0010  00      ;Character to output
0011  0005    ;Decimal 5
0013  0003    ;Decimal 3
0015  0030    ;Mask for ASCII char
```

Output

```
8
```

John von Neumann

John von Neumann was a brilliant mathematician, physicist, logician, and computer scientist. Legends have been passed down about the phenomenal speed at which von Neumann solved problems and of his astonishing memory. He used his talents not only for furthering his mathematical theories, but also for memorizing entire books and reciting them years after he had read them. But ask a highway patrolman about von Neumann's driving ability and he would be liable to throw up his hands in despair; behind the wheel, the mathematical genius was as reckless as a rebel teenager.

John von Neumann was born in Hungary in 1903, the oldest son of a wealthy Jewish banker. He entered high school by the time he was 11, and it wasn't long before his math teachers recommended he be tutored by university professors. At only 19, with the publication of his first paper, he was recognized as a professional mathematician. Von Neumann went on to become a brilliant mathematician—one of the last great universal mathematicians—who was as comfortable with applied work as he was with theory. It would be hard to choose his most valuable contribution to mathematics during the 1930s because he played an important role in every aspect in which he was involved.

Von Neumann left Nazi Germany for the United States before the outbreak of World War II. During the war, von Neumann was hired as a consultant for the U.S. armed forces and related civilian agencies because of his knowledge of hydrodynamics. He was also called upon to participate in the construction of the atomic bomb in 1943. It was not surprising that, following this work, President Eisenhower appointed him to the Atomic Energy Commission in 1955.

Even though bombs and their performance fascinated von Neumann for many years, a fortuitous meeting in 1944 with Herbert Goldstine, a pioneer of one of the first operational electronic digital computers, introduced the scientist to something more important than bombs—computers. Von Neumann's chance conversation in a train station with Goldstine sparked the beginning of a new fascination for him. He started working on the stored program concept and concluded that by internally storing a program, the hours of tedious labor required to reprogram computers in those days could be eliminated. He also developed a new computer architecture to perform this storage task. In fact, today's computers are often referred to as von Neumann machines because the architectural principles he described have proven so tremendously successful. Changes in computers over the last 40 years have been primarily in terms of the speed and composition of the fundamental circuits, but the basic architecture designed by von Neumann has persisted.

In 1957 von Neumann died of bone cancer in Washington, D.C., at the age of 54. Perhaps his work with the atomic bomb resulted in the bone cancer that caused the death of one of the most brilliant minds of the twentieth century.

During his lifetime, von Neumann taught at many respected institutions, including Berlin, Hamburg, and Princeton Universities. (While at Princeton, he worked with the talented and as yet unknown British student Alan Turing.) He received many awards, including honorary Ph.D.'s from Princeton, Harvard, and Istanbul Universities. Von Neumann was also a member of the American Mathematical Society and the U.S. National Academy of Sciences.

The two numbers to be added are 5 and 3. The program stores them at `Mem [0011]` and `Mem [0013]`. The first instruction loads the 5 into the accumulator, then the second instruction adds the 3. At this point the sum is in the accumulator.

Now a problem arises. We want to output this result, but the only output instruction for this Level 3 machine is the character output instruction. The problem is that our result is 0000 1000 (bin). If the character output instruction tries to output that, it will be interpreted as the backspace character, BS, as shown on the ASCII chart of Table 12.7.

So the program must convert the decimal number 8, 0000 1000 (bin), to the ASCII character '8', 0011 1000 (bin). The ASCII bits differ from the unsigned binary bits by the two extra 1's in the third and fourth bits. To do the conversion, the program inserts those two extra 1's into the result by ORing the accumulator, with the mask 0000 0000 0011 0000 using the OR register instruction.

Converting integer to ASCII with the OR operation

```
     0000 0000 0000 1000
OR   0000 0000 0011 0000
------------------------
     0000 0000 0011 1000
```

The accumulator now contains the correct sum in ASCII form. The store byte instruction stores the character in `Mem [0010]`, and the character output instruction outputs it.

If you replace the word at `Mem [0013]` with 0009, what does this program output? Unfortunately, it does not output `14` even though the sum in the accumulator is

14 (dec) = 0000 0000 0000 1110 (bin)

after the add accumulator instruction executes. The OR instruction changes this bit pattern to 0000 0000 0011 1110 (bin), producing an output of >. Since the only output instruction at Level 3 is one that outputs a single byte, the program cannot output a result that should contain more than one character. We will see in the next chapter how to remedy this shortcoming.

Program 13.4

Program 13.4 illustrates a curious possibility based on the von Neumann design principle. Notice that the program from 0006 to 001D is identical to Program 13.3 from 0000 to 0015. This program has two instructions at the beginning that are not in Program 13.3, however. Since the instructions are shifted down six bytes, their operand specifiers are all greater by six than the operand specifiers of the previous program. Other than the adjustment by six bytes, however, the instructions beginning at 0006 would appear to duplicate the processing of Program 13.3.

In particular, it appears that the load accumulator instruction would load the 5 into the accumulator, the add instruction would add the 3, the OR instruction would change the 8 (dec) to ASCII '8', the store byte accumulator instruction

Program 13.4

A machine language program that modifies itself. The add accumulator instruction changes to a subtract instruction.

Addr.	Machine Language (bin)
0000	0101 0001 0000 0000 0001 1101
0003	0101 1001 0000 0000 0000 1001
0006	0000 1001 0000 0000 0001 0111
0009	0001 1001 0000 0000 0001 1001
000C	0011 0001 0000 0000 0001 1011
000F	0101 1001 0000 0000 0001 0110
0012	1101 1001 0000 0000 0001 0110
0015	0000 0000
0016	0000 0000
0017	0000 0000 0000 0101
0019	0000 0000 0000 0011
001B	0000 0000 0011 0000
001D	0010 0001

Addr.	Machine Language (hex)	
0000	51001D	;Load byte accumulator
0003	590009	;Store byte accumulator
0006	090017	;Load accumulator
0009	190019	;Add accumulator
000C	31001B	;OR accumulator
000F	590016	;Store byte accumulator
0012	D90016	;Character output
0015	00	;Stop
0016	00	;Character to output
0017	0005	;Decimal 5
0019	0003	;Decimal 3
001B	0030	;Mask for ASCII char
001D	21	;Byte to modify instruction

Output

```
2
```

would put the '8' in `Mem [0016]`, and the character output instruction would print the 8. Instead, the output is 2.

Since program and data share the same memory in a von Neumann machine, it is possible for a program to treat itself as data and modify itself. The first instruction loads the byte 21 (hex) into the right half of the accumulator, and the second instruction puts it in `Mem [0009]`. What was at `Mem [0009]` before this change? The instruction specifier of the add accumulator instruction. Now the bits at `Mem [0009]` are 0010 0001. When the computer gets these bits in the fetch part of the von Neumann execution cycle, the CPU detects the opcode as 00100, the opcode for the subtract register instruction. The register specifier indicates the accumulator, and the addressing mode bits indicate direct addressing. The instruction subtracts 3 from 5 instead of adding it.

Of course, this is not a very practical program. If you wanted to subtract the two numbers, you would simply write Program 13.3 with the subtract instruction in place of the add instruction. But it does show that in a von Neumann machine, main memory places no significance on the bits it is storing. It simply remembers ones and zeros and has no idea which are program bits, which are data bits, which are ASCII characters, and so on. Furthermore, the CPU cranks out the von Neumann execution cycle and interprets the bits accordingly with no idea of their history. When it fetches the bits at `Mem [0009]` it does not know, or care, how they got there in the first place. It simply repeats the fetch, increment, execute cycle over and over again.

13.4 Programming at Level 3

To program at Level 3, is to write a set of instructions in binary. To execute the binary sequence, first you must load it into main memory. The operating system is responsible for loading the binary sequence into main memory.

An operating system is a program. Like any other program, a software engineer must design, write, test, and debug it. Most operating systems are so large and complex that teams of engineers must write them.

The primary function of an operating system is to control the execution of applications programs on the computer. Since the operating system is itself a program, it must reside in main memory in order to be executed. So main memory must store not only the applications programs, but also the operating system.

In the Pep/5 computer, the bottom part of main memory is reserved for the operating system. The top part is reserved for the applications program. Figure 13.13 shows the place of the operating system in main memory. It starts at memory location 0BC1 and occupies the rest of main memory. That leaves memory locations 0000 to 0BC0 for the applications program.

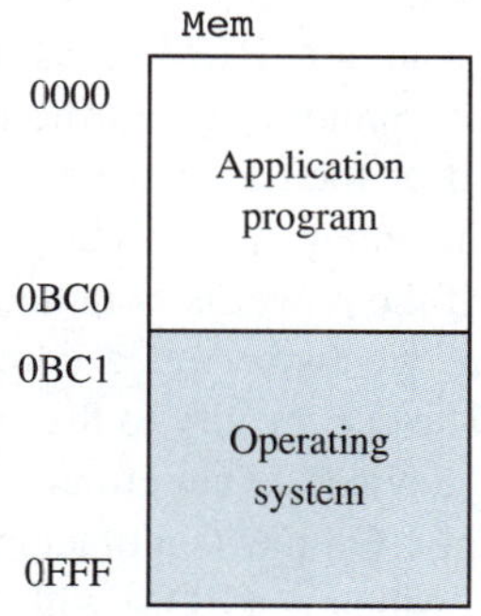

Figure 13.13

The location of the Pep/5 operating system in main memory.

The *loader* is that part of the operating system that loads the applications program into main memory so it can be executed. What loads the loader? The answer is that the Pep/5 loader, along with many other parts of the operating system, is permanently stored in main memory.

Read-Only Memory

There are two types of electronic circuit elements from which memory devices are manufactured—read/write circuit elements and read-only circuit elements.

In Program 13.4, when the store byte instruction, 590016, executed, the CPU transferred the content of the right half of the accumulator to `Mem [0016]`. The original content of `Mem [0016]` was destroyed, and the memory location then contained 0011 0010 (bin). When the character output instruction was executed next, the bits at location 0016 were sent to the output device.

The circuit element at memory location 0016 is a read/write circuit. The store instruction did a write operation on it, which changed its content. The character output instruction did a read operation on it, which sent a copy of its content to the output device. If the circuit element at location 0016 were a read-only circuit, the store instruction would not have changed its content.

Both types of main memory circuit elements, read/write and read-only, are random-access devices, as opposed to serial devices. When the character output instruction does a read from memory location 0016, it does not need to start at location 0000 and sequentially go through 0001, 0002, 0003, and so on until it gets to 0016. Instead, it can go directly to location 0016. Since it can go to a random location in memory directly, the circuit element is called a *random-access device.*

Read-only memory devices are known as ROM. *Read/write memory devices* should be known as RWM. Unfortunately, they are known as RAM, which stands for random-access memory. That name is unfortunate because both read-only and read/write devices are random-access devices. The characteristic that distinguishes a read-only memory device from a read/write memory device, is that the content of a read-only device cannot be changed by a store instruction. Since use of the term RAM is so pervasive in the computer industry, we also will use it to refer to read/write devices. But in our hearts we will know that ROMs are random also.

RAM should be called RWM.

Main memory usually contains some ROM devices. Those parts of main memory that are ROM contain permanent binary sequences, which the store instruction cannot alter. Furthermore, when power to the computer is switched off at the end of the day and then switched on at the beginning of the next day, the ROM will retain those binary sequences in its circuitry. RAM will not retain its memory if the power is switched off. It is therefore called *volatile.*

There are two ways a computer manufacturer can buy ROM for a memory system. She can specify to the circuit manufacturer the bit sequences desired in the memory devices. The circuit manufacturer then can manufacture the devices accordingly. Or the manufacturer can order a *programmable read-only memory* (PROM), which is a ROM with all zeros. The computer manufacturer then can permanently change any desired location to a one, in such a way that the device will contain the proper bit sequence. This process is called "burning in" the bit pattern.

The Pep/5 Operating System

Most of the Pep/5 operating system has been burned into ROM. Figure 13.14 shows the ROM part of the operating system. It begins at location 0C29 and continues down to 0FFF. That part of main memory is permanent. A store instruction cannot change it. If the power is ever turned off, when it is turned on again, that part of the operating system will still be there. The region from 0BC1 to 0C28 is the RAM part of the operating system for our computer.

The RAM part of the operating system is for storing the system variables. Their values will change while the operating system program is executing. The ROM part of the operating system contains the loader, which is a permanent fixture. Its job is to load the application program into RAM starting at address 0000.

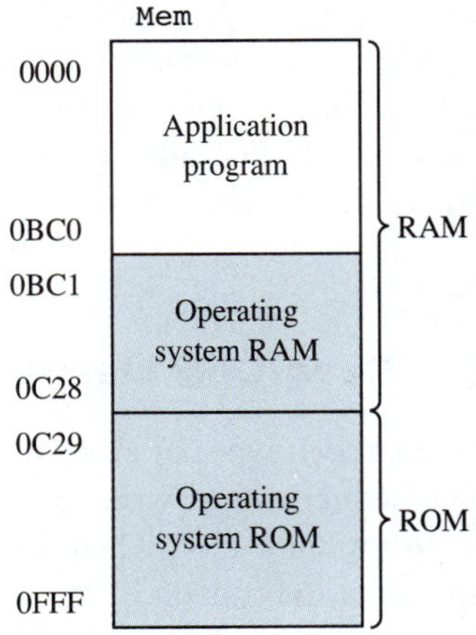

Figure 13.14

The read-only memory in the Pep/5 system.

On the Pep/5 machine, you invoke the loader by choosing the loader option from the menu of the simulator program.

Figure 13.15 is a more detailed memory map of the Pep/5 system. As in the previous figure, the shaded area represents the operating system region, and the clear area represents the application region.

The run-time stack for the application program, called the *user stack,* begins at memory location 0BC1, just above the operating system. The stack pointer register in the CPU contains the address of the top of the stack. When procedures are called, storage for the parameters, the return address, and the local variables are allocated on the stack at successively lower addresses. Hence the stack "grows upwards" in memory.

The run-time stack for the operating system begins at memory location 0C25, which is 100 bytes below the start of the user stack. When the operating system executes, the stack pointer in the CPU contains the address of the top of the system stack. Like the user stack, the system stack grows upward in memory. The operating system never needs more than 100 bytes on its stack, so there is no possibility that the system stack will try to store its data in the user stack region.

The Pep/5 operating system consists of two programs—the loader, which begins at address 0C29, and the interrupt service routine, which begins at address 0C70. You will recall from Table 13.1 that the last four instructions of the instruction set are unimplemented at Level 3. The interrupt service routine implements these four instructions for the assembly language programmer. Chapter 14 describes the instructions at Level 5, the assembly level, while Chapter 17 shows how they are implemented at Level 4, the operating system level.

Associated with these two parts of the operating system are four words at the very bottom of ROM that are reserved for special use by the operating system. They are called *machine vectors* and are at addresses 0FF8, 0FFA, 0FFC, and 0FFE, as shown in Figure 13.15.

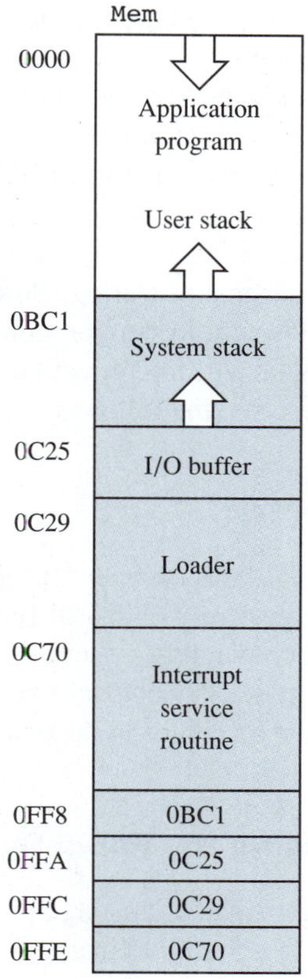

Figure 13.15

A memory map of the Pep/5 system.

When you choose the loader option from the Pep/5 simulator menu, the following two events occur:

Selecting the load option

```
SP := Mem [0FFA]
PC := Mem [0FFC]
```

In words, the content of memory location 0FFA is copied into the stack pointer, and the content of memory location 0FFC is copied into the program counter. After these events occur the execution cycle begins. Figure 13.16 illustrates these two events.

Selecting the load option in effect initializes the stack pointer and program counter to the predetermined values stored at 0FFA and 0FFC. It just so happens that the value at address 0FFA is 0C25, the bottom of the system stack. 0C25 is the value the stack pointer should have when the system stack is empty. It also happens that the value at address 0FFC is 0C29. In fact, 0C29 is the address of the first instruction to be executed in the loader.

The system programmer who wrote the operating system decided where the system stack and the loader should be located. Realizing that the Pep/5 computer would fetch the vectors from locations 0FFA and 0FFC when the load option is selected, she placed the appropriate values in those locations. Since the first step in the execution cycle is fetch, the first instruction to be executed after selecting the load option is the first instruction of the loader program.

If you wish to revise the operating system, your loader might not begin at 0C29. Suppose it begins at 0BD6 instead. When the user selects the load option, the computer will still go to location 0FFC to fetch the vector. So you would need to place 0BD6 in the word at address 0FFC.

This scheme of storing addresses at special reserved memory locations is flexible. It allows the system programmer to place the loader anywhere in memory that is convenient. A more direct but less flexible scheme would be to design the computer to execute the following operations when the user selects the load option.

```
SP := 0C25
PC := 0C29
```

If selecting the load option produced these two events, the loader of the current operating system would still function correctly. However, it would be difficult to modify the operating system. The loader would always have to start at 0C29, and the system stack would always have to start at 0C25. The system programmer would have no choice in the placement of the various parts of the system.

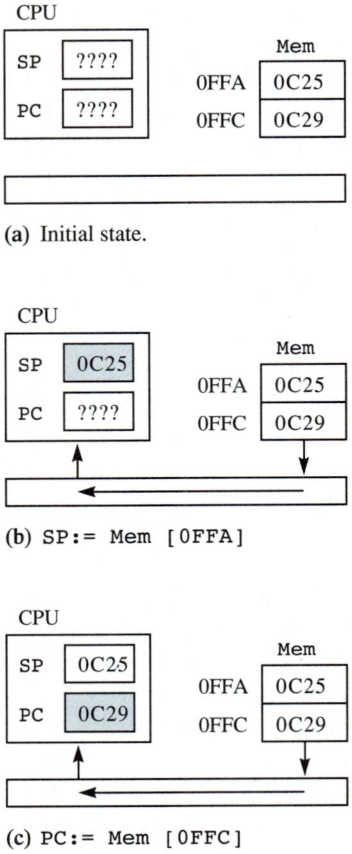

Figure 13.16

The Pep/5 load option.

Using the Pep/5 System

To load a machine language program on the Pep/5 computer, you fortunately do not need to write it in binary. You may write it with ASCII hexadecimal characters in a text file. The loader will convert from ASCII to binary for you when it loads the program.

The following listing shows how to prepare a machine language program for loading. It is Program 13.1, which outputs `Hi`. You simply write in a text file the binary sequence in hexadecimal without any addresses or comments. Terminate the list of bytes with lowercase `zz`, which the loader detects as a sentinel. The loader will put the bytes in memory one after the other, starting at address 0000 (hex).

Program 13.1 prepared as input to the loader

Addr.	Machine Language (hex)	
0000	D90007	;Character output
0003	D90008	;Character output
0006	00	;Stop
0007	48	;ASCII H character
0008	69	;ASCII i character

Hex Version for the Loader

```
D9 00 07 D9 00 08 00 48 69 zz
```

Output

```
Hi
```

The Pep/5 loader is extremely particular about the format of your machine language program. To work correctly, the very first character in your text file must be a hexadecimal character. No leading blank lines or spaces are allowed. There must be exactly one space between bytes. If you wish to continue your byte stream on another line, you must not leave trailing spaces on the preceding line. The reason for these user-unfriendly restrictions is to maximize the loader execution speed.

After you write your machine language program and load it with the loader option, you must select the execute option to run it. The following two events occur when you select the execute option.

Selecting the execute option

```
SP := Mem [0FF8]
PC := 0000
```

Then the von Neumann execution cycle begins. Since `PC` has the value 0000, the CPU will fetch the first instruction from `Mem [0000]`. Fortunately, that is where the loader put the first instruction of the applications program.

Figure 13.15 shows that `Mem [0FF8]` contains 0BC1, the address of the bottom of the user stack. The applications program in this example does not use the run-time stack. If it did, the applications program could access the stack correctly because `SP` would be initialized to the address of the bottom of the user stack.

Enjoy!

13.5 Some Typical Architectures

This section describes the architecture of computers from two different manufacturers—International Business Machines (IBM) and Digital Equipment Corporation (DEC). Both of these manufacturers use their architectures in a family of models that span a price and performance range. IBM produces the 370 family and DEC the VAX family. Some models are slower but less expensive than other models in a given family. Even though the families overlap somewhat in performance, generally the 370 family is faster, larger, and more expensive than the VAX family. The section concludes with a brief discussion of several popular microprocessors.

The 370 Family

In 1964 IBM announced the System/360 family of computers, which went on to become probably the most successful system in the marketplace. The system popularized the concept of levels of abstraction for hardware. From the largest model in the family to the smallest, each could be programmed with the same instruction set at Level 3, the machine level. The models differed significantly at Levels 1 and 2, but the differences were transparent to the programmer at Level 3.

Levels of abstraction in System/360

This situation is analogous to the machine independence of Pascal at Level 6. Regardless of the machine on which you run your Pascal program, the compiler translates it to the machine language of that machine. To run it on a different machine, you do not need to rewrite your Pascal program. You simply compile it with a compiler for the different machine. The advantage is that you do not need to rewrite your program, since Pascal is machine independent.

With System/360, the concept was similar but a language translator was not necessary to produce the machine independence. The hardware of each model in the System/360 family appeared identical. The registers in the CPU were identical, and a binary machine language instruction on one model would produce the same effect as the binary instruction on another model in the family. The only perceptible differences between models were the speed of execution, the amount of main memory available, and the peripheral devices that could be attached.

In 1970 IBM introduced the System/370, which retained the same System/360 architecture but had a number of performance improvements. IBM introduced new families again later—the 4300 series in 1979 and the 3090 series in 1985—that had the identical structure at Level 3. This section refers to all these series as the 370 family.

The CPU of a 370 processor has

- Sixteen 32-bit general purpose registers
- Four 64-bit floating-point registers
- One 64-bit program status word (`PSW`)

as Figure 13.17 shows. IBM defines a word on a 370 machine as 32 bits. The general-purpose registers contain values of integers and characters. The floating-point registers contain real values.

The `PSW` is divided into eight fields, two of which are shown in the figure. The last field of the `PSW` is the *program counter*. Another field, two bits wide, is the

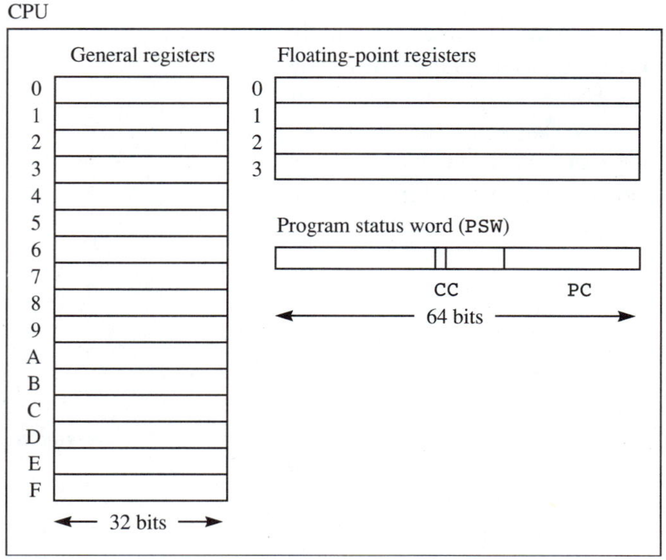

Figure 13.17

The central processing unit of the IBM 370.

condition code (`CC`). These bits are similar to `NZVC` in Pep/5. For arithmetic instructions, they are set to

- 00 if the result is zero
- 01 if the result is less than zero
- 10 if the result is greater than zero
- 11 if the result caused overflow

Where Pep/5 has two instruction formats, one for unary and one for nonunary instructions, 370 has five instruction formats, as Figure 13.18 shows. They are called the RR, RX, RS, SI and SS formats. Each instruction has an eight-bit opcode, regardless of its format.

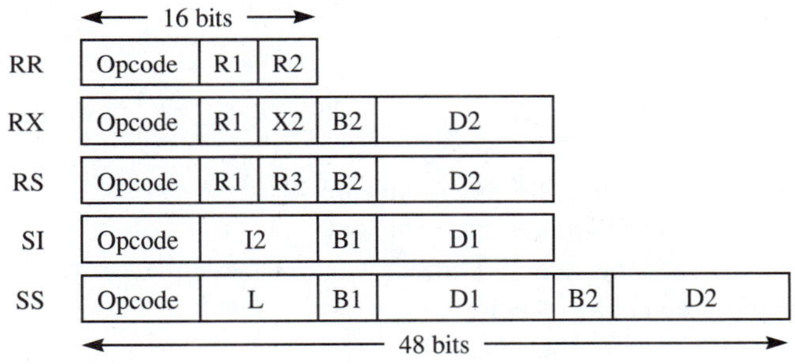

Figure 13.18

The five IBM 370 instruction formats.

The fields labeled R1, R2, and R3 are four-bit register fields that specify one of the 16 general-purpose registers. For example, a register field that contains 0101 specifies register number 5 in the CPU. Pep/5's CPU has two special-purpose registers designated as the base and index registers. By contrast, the 370 CPU allows any of its 16 general-purpose registers to be a base register or an index register. The four-bit fields labeled B1 and B2 specify which of the general registers is to be the base, and the field labeled X2 specifies which is to be the index. The D1 and D2 fields are called *displacement fields*.

Some 370 add instructions

Example 13.14 An example of the add instruction is 1A63 (hex). The opcode, 1A, specifies addition in the RR format. The R1 field has value 6 (hex), and the R2 field has the value 3 (hex). This instruction would add the content of register 6 to register 3 and put the sum in register 6. ■

Example 13.15 Another example of an add instruction is 5A624F0D. The opcode, 5A, specifies addition in the RX format. The R1 field has the value 6, X2 has the value 2, B2 has the value 4, and D2 has the value F0D. The RX format is roughly equivalent to Pep/5's indexed addressing mode to be described in the next chapter. This instruction uses register 2 as the index register and register 4 as the base register along with the displacement F0D, to define the second operand. It adds the second operand to the content of register 6, which is the first operand, and places the result in register 6. ■

The five-bit opcode of the Pep/5 architecture allows $2^5 = 32$ instructions in its instruction set. The eight-bit opcode of the 370 architecture allows $2^8 = 256$ instructions. Only about 170 of these instructions are used, the rest being unimplemented. Many of the instructions are similar to those in Pep/5. There are instructions to shift left and right, add, subtract, multiply, and divide both integer and real values. A set of branching instructions is also included.

The 370 instruction set

An example of an instruction in the SS format is the one to move a sequence of bytes from one memory location to another. The L field tells the CPU how many bytes to move. Pep/5 does not have this type of instruction. To move data from one main memory location to another, you must execute a load followed by a store.

The VAX family

In 1978 DEC announced the VAX-11/780 computer, which was the beginning of an extensive family of machines that are based, as is the 370 family, on the concept of levels of abstraction. Although it is no longer manufactured, the 780 model was so successful in the marketplace that it has become a standard of comparison for machines from DEC and from other manufacturers. VAX series that share the same basic Level 3 architecture as the 780 include the 6200 series, with up to 11 times the power of the 780; the 8800 and 8900 series, with up to 48 times the power; and the MicroVAX series, which is less powerful than the 780 but small enough to fit on a desktop.

Levels of abstraction in the VAX family

The CPU of a VAX processor has

- Sixteen 32-bit general-purpose registers
- One 32-bit program status longword (`PSL`)

as Figure 13.19 shows. DEC defines a word on a VAX machine as 16 bits even though its general-purpose registers contain 32 bits. Unlike the 370, the VAX does not have special registers to hold 64-bit real values. Instead, it stores real values in two consecutive general-purpose registers.

The `PSL`, like the `PSW` of the IBM 370, is divided into numerous fields. The last four bits of the `PSL` are the `NZVC` bits, which function identically to the `NZVC` bits of Pep/5. Unlike the 370, the program counter is not contained in the `PSL`.

The 16 registers in the CPU are not quite as general-purpose as the registers in the 370. Register R12 is called the *argument pointer* (`AP`), R13 is the *frame pointer* (`FP`), R14 is the *stack pointer* (`SP`), and R15 is the program counter (`PC`). These registers are reserved for special use by the VAX hardware and software. The `SP` and `PC` function the same as the `SP` and `PC` of Pep/5. The parameters, return address, and local variables on the run-time stack constitute the stack frame when a

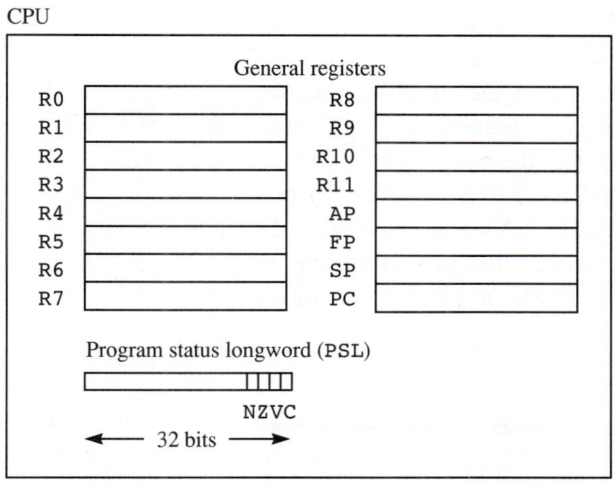

Figure 13.19

The central processing unit of the VAX.

procedure is called. The FP in the VAX is for accessing these quantities in the stack frame.

Figure 13.20 shows the VAX instruction formats. An instruction can have an opcode of one or two bytes. It is also possible for an instruction to have one or several operand specifiers. There are more than 300 instructions in the VAX instruction set.

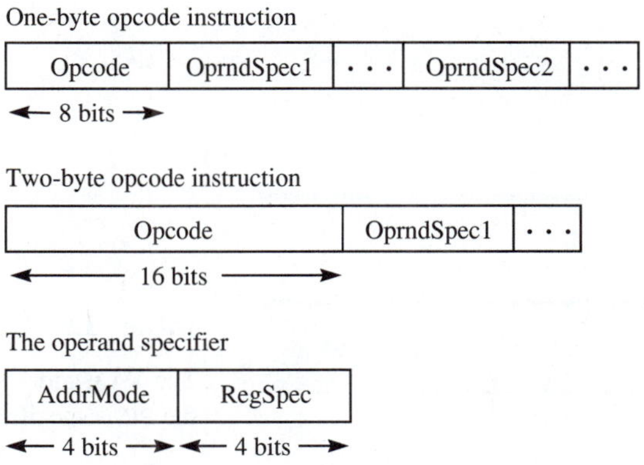

Figure 13.20

The VAX instruction formats.

The first four bits of an operand specifier specify an addressing mode. Since there are four bits, there are $2^4 = 16$ addressing modes. The second four bits specify one of the 16 registers in the CPU. The Pep/5 was modeled after this format, except that its two-bit addressing mode allows for only $2^2 = 4$ addressing modes. Also, the single register specifier bit in Pep/5 can specify one of only two registers instead of 16.

Any of the 16 addressing modes can be used with just about any register. The only exception is when you specify R15, the program counter. In that case, only addressing modes 8 through F are allowed. Table 13.4 lists the addressing modes when the register specifier does not specify the program counter. Table 13.5 lists the addressing modes when the register specifier specifies the program counter.

Compared with Pep/5's 4 addressing modes and the 370's 5 instruction formats (each equivalent to a separate addressing mode), the VAX has a rich set of 21 different addressing modes. The VAX addressing modes that are equivalent to Pep/5's immediate, direct, indexed, and stack-relative modes are immediate, absolute, indexed, and word displacement, respectively.

Addressing mode specifier	Addressing mode
0–3	Literal
4	Indexed
5	Register
6	Register deferred
7	Autodecrement
8	Autoincrement
9	Autoincrement deferred
A	Byte displacement
B	Byte displacement deferred
C	Word displacement
D	Word displacement deferred
E	Longword displacement
F	Longword displacement deferred

Table 13.4

The VAX addressing modes when the `PC` is not specified.

Addressing mode specifier	Addressing mode
8	Immediate
9	Absolute
A	Byte relative
B	Byte relative deferred
C	Word relative
D	Word relative deferred
E	Longword relative
F	Longword relative deferred

Table 13.5

The VAX addressing modes when the `PC` is specified.

Microprocessors

It is remarkable that practically all commercial computers today share the same basic von Neumann design. From the largest supercomputer to the smallest microcomputer, each has a binary main memory and a CPU that cranks out the fetch, increment, execute cycle. The only conceptual difference between machines at Level 3 is the organization of their CPUs; that is, the number of registers they contain, the instruction formats, and the instruction sets.

The 8086/8088 processor

For example, the 8086/8088 microprocessor manufactured by Intel and used in the popular IBM PC is such a device. The CPU has 12 16-bit registers divided into three groups. The registers in the data group are the accumulator, the base register, the count register, and the data register. The pointer and index group registers are the stack pointer, the base pointer, the source index, and the destination index. In the segment group, the registers are the code segment register, the data segment register, the stack segment register, and the extra segment register. In addition, there are the usual program counter and status bits.

The M68000 processor

Another example of a microprocessor at Level 3 is the M68000 manufactured by Motorola and used in the Macintosh computer produced by Apple. Its CPU has eight 32-bit address registers, one of which is the stack pointer, and eight 32-bit data registers. It has the obligatory program counter because it is a von Neumann machine.

You can see from these examples of actual machines that Pep/5 shares many of their features. It is a von Neumann machine whose program and data share the same memory. It has a program counter to keep track of which instruction will be fetched next. It has a specific instruction format and instruction set, and several addressing modes. If you ever need to deal with a real machine at Level 3, these features will all be present. Only the details will differ and should be easy to learn if you master the concepts inherent in Pep/5.

SUMMARY

Virtually all commercial computers are based on the von Neumann design principle in which main memory stores both data and instructions. The four components of a von Neumann machine are input devices, the central processing unit (CPU), main memory, and output devices. The CPU contains a set of registers, one of which is the program counter (`PC`), which stores the address of the instruction to be executed next.

The CPU has an instruction set wired into it. An instruction consists of an instruction specifier and an operand specifier. The instruction specifier, in turn, consists of an opcode, a register specifier, and an addressing mode specifier. The opcode determines which instruction in the instruction set is to be executed. An n-bit opcode allows 2^n instructions in the instruction set. The register specifier determines which register participates in the operation. The addressing mode specifier determines which addressing mode is used for the source or destination of the data.

Each addressing mode corresponds to a relationship between the operand specifier, (`OprndSpec`) and the operand (`Oprnd`). In the direct addressing mode, the operand specifier is the address in main memory of the operand. In mathematical notation, `Oprnd = Mem [OprndSpec]`.

To execute a program, a group of instructions and data are loaded into main memory and then the von Neumann execution cycle begins. The von Neumann execution cycle consists of the following steps: (1) fetch the instruction specified by PC, (2) increment PC, (3) execute the instruction fetched, and (4) repeat by going to Step (1). Since main memory stores instructions as well as data, two types of errors at the machine level are possible. You may interpret data bits as instructions, or you may interpret instruction bits as data. Another possibility that is a direct result of storing instructions in main memory is that a program may be processed as if it were data. Loaders and compilers are important programs that take the viewpoint of treating instruction bits as data.

The operating system is a program that controls the execution of application programs. It must reside in main memory along with the application programs and data. On some computers, a portion of the operating system is burned into read-only memory (ROM). One characteristic of ROM is that a store instruction cannot change the content of a memory cell. The run-time stack for the operating system is located in random-access memory (RAM). A machine vector is an address of an operating system component, such as a stack or a program, used to access that component. Two important functions of an operating system are the loader and the interrupt service routines.

EXERCISES

Section 13.1

* **1.** **(a)** How many bytes are in the main memory of the Pep/5 computer? **(b)** How many words are in it? **(c)** How many bits are in it? **(d)** How many total bits are in the Pep/5 CPU? **(e)** How many times bigger in terms of bits is the main memory than the CPU?

2. **(a)** Suppose the main memory of the Pep/5 was completely filled with unary instructions. How many instructions would it contain? **(b)** What is the maximum number of instructions that would fit in the main memory if none of the instructions is unary? **(c)** Suppose the main memory is completely filled with an equal number of unary and nonunary instructions. How many total instructions would it contain?

* **3.** Answer the following questions for the machine language instructions 54F82C and 3223D0. **(a)** What is the opcode in binary? **(b)** What does the instruction do? **(c)** What is the register specifier in binary? **(d)** Which register does it specify? **(e)** What is the addressing mode specifier in binary? **(f)** Which addressing mode does it specify? **(g)** What is the operand specifier in hexadecimal?

4. Answer the questions in Exercise 3 for the machine language instructions 1B00AC and 0D0BD3.

Section 13.2

* **5.** Suppose Pep/5 contains the following four hexadecimal values.

A:	19AC
X:	FE20
Mem [0A3F]:	FF00
Mem [0A41]:	103D

If it has these values before each of the following statements executes, what are the four hexadecimal values after each statement executes?

(a) 090A3F	(b) 510A3F	(c) 5D0A41
(d) 150A41	(e) 190A3F	(f) 250A41
(g) 290A3F	(h) 310A3F	(i) 3C

6. Repeat Exercise 5 for the following statements.

(a) 0D0A3F	(b) 550A3F	(c) 590A41
(d) 110A41	(e) 1D0A3F	(f) 210A41
(g) 2D0A3F	(h) 350A3F	(i) 38

Section 13.3

*7. Determine the output of the following Pep/5 machine language program. The left column is the memory address of the first byte on the line.

```
0000  D9000A
0003  D9000B
0006  D9000C
0009  00
000A  4A6F
000C  79
```

8. Determine the output of the following Pep/5 machine language program if the input is 'tab'. The left column is the memory address of the first byte on the line.

```
0000  D10010
0003  D10011
0006  D10012
0009  D90011
000C  D90010
000F  00
```

9. Determine the output of the following Pep/5 machine language program. The left column in each part is the memory address of the first byte on the line.

*(a)

```
0000  09000E
0003  290010
0006  59000D
0009  D9000D
000C  00
000D  00
000E  A94F
0010  FFFD
```

(b)

```
0000  09000C
0003  38
0004  59000B
0007  D9000B
000A  00
000B  00
000C  F0D4
```

Section 13.4

10. Suppose you need to process a list of 800 integers contained in Pep/5 memory at one integer per word. You estimate that 20% of the instructions in a typical program are unary instructions. What is the maximum number of instructions you can expect to be able to use in the program that processes the data? Keep in mind that your application program must share memory with the operating system and with your data.

Section 13.5

11. **(a)** What company manufactured the computer you are using? **(b)** How many bytes are in its main memory? **(c)** How many registers are in its CPU? How many bits are in each register? **(d)** How many bits are contained in a single instruction? **(e)** How many bits of the instruction are reserved for the opcode?

PROBLEMS

Section 13.4

12. Write a machine language program to output your first name on the output device. Write it in a format suitable for the loader and execute it on the Pep/5 simulator.

13. Write a machine language program to output the four characters `Frog` on the output device. Write it in a format suitable for the loader and execute it on the Pep/5 simulator.

14. Write a machine language program to output the three characters `Cat` on the output device. Write it in a format suitable for the loader and execute it on the Pep/5 simulator.

15. Write a machine language program to add the three numbers 2, –3, and 6 and output the sum on the output device. Write it in a format suitable for the loader and execute it on the Pep/5 simulator.

16. Write a machine language program to input two one-digit numbers, add them and output the one-digit sum. Write it in a format suitable for the loader and execute it on the Pep/5 simulator.

17. Write Program 13.3 in hexadecimal format for input to the loader. Verify that it works correctly by running it on the Pep/5 simulator. Then modify the store byte instruction and the character output instruction so that the result is stored at `Mem [0E06]` and the character output is also from `Mem [0E06]`. What is the output? Explain.

LEVEL 5

Assembly

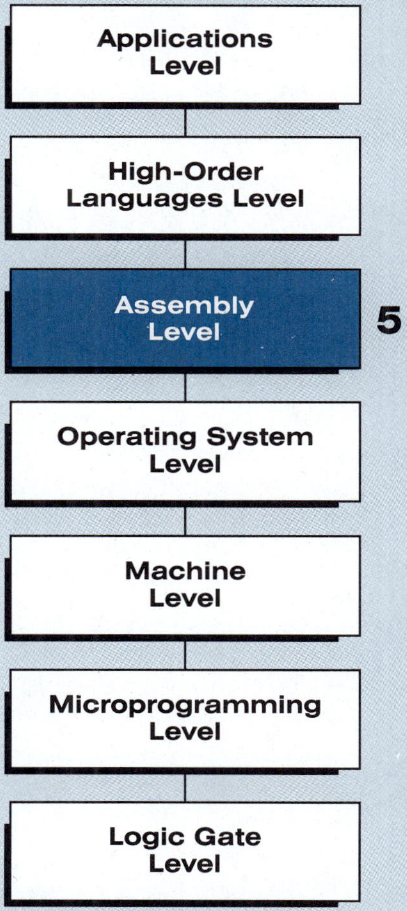

Chapter

14 Assembly Language

The Level 3 language is machine language, sequences of ones and zeros sometimes abbreviated to hexadecimal. Although the computer pioneers had to program in machine language, they soon revolted against such an indignity. Memorizing the opcodes of the machine and having to continually refer to ASCII charts and hexadecimal tables to get their programs into binary was no fun. The assembly level was invented to relieve programmers of the tedium of programming in binary.

The previous chapter described the Pep/5 computer at Level 3, the machine level. This chapter describes Level 5, the assembly level. Between these two levels lies the operating system. Remember that the purpose of levels of abstraction is to hide the details of the system at the lower levels. This chapter illustrates that principle of information hiding. You will use the interrupt service routine of the operating system without knowing the details of its operation. That is, you will learn what the interrupt service routine does without learning how the routine does it. A later chapter will reveal the inner workings of the interrupt service routine.

The assembly level uses the operating system below it.

14.1 Assemblers

The language at Level 5 is called *assembly language.* It provides a more convenient way of writing machine language programs than binary does. Program 13.1, which outputs `Hi`, contained two types of bit patterns, one for instructions and one for data. These two types are a direct consequence of the von Neumann design, where program and data share the same memory with a binary representation for each.

The two types of bit patterns at Level 3

Assembly language contains two types of statements that correspond to these two types of bit patterns. *Mnemonic statements* correspond to the instruction bit patterns, and *pseudo-operations* correspond to the data bit patterns.

The two types of statements at Level 5

Instruction Mnemonics

Suppose the machine language instruction

0000 1000 0000 0000 1001 1010

is stored at some memory location. This is the load register *R* instruction. The register specifier bit is 0, which indicates the accumulator and not the index register. The addressing mode bits are 00, which specify immediate addressing.

This instruction is written in the Pep/5 assembly language as

```
LOADA h#009A,i
```

A mnemonic for the opcode

The mnemonic `LOADA`, which stands for *load accumulator,* is written in place of the opcode, 00001, and the register specifier, 0. A *mnemonic* is a memory aid. It is easier to remember that `LOADA` stands for the load accumulator instruction instead of having to remember that opcode 00001 and register specifier 0 stands for the load accumulator instruction. The operand specifier is written in hexadecimal, `009A`, preceded by `h#`, which stands for hexadecimal constant.

The letter i, d, x, or s for the addressing mode

In Pep/5 assembly language, you specify the addressing mode by placing the letter `i` (for immediate addressing), `d` (for direct addressing), `x` (for indexed addressing), or `s` (for stack relative addressing) after the operand, with a comma between them.

Table 14.1 shows more examples of the load register *R* instruction written in binary machine language and in assembly language. `LOADX` corresponds to the same machine language statement as `LOADA`, except that the register specifier bit for `LOADX` is 1 instead of 0.

Table 14.1

Examples of the `LOAD`*R* instruction.

Machine language	Assembly language
0000 1000 0000 0000 1001 1010	LOADA h#009A,i
0000 1001 0000 0000 1001 1010	LOADA h#009A,d
0000 1010 0000 0000 1001 1010	LOADA h#009A,x
0000 1011 0000 0000 1001 1010	LOADA h#009A,s
0000 1100 0000 0000 1001 1010	LOADX h#009A,i
0000 1101 0000 0000 1001 1010	LOADX h#009A,d
0000 1110 0000 0000 1001 1010	LOADX h#009A,x
0000 1111 0000 0000 1001 1010	LOADX h#009A,s

Table 14.2 summarizes the 32 instructions of the Pep/5 instruction set at Level 5. It shows the mnemonic that goes with each opcode and the meaning of each instruction. The addressing mode column tells the addressing modes allowed (`i`, `d`, `x`, or `s`) or whether the instruction is unary (*U*). The status bits column lists the status bits the instruction affects when it executes.

Opcode	Mnemonic	Meaning	Addr. modes	Status bits
00000	STOP	stop execution	*U*	
00001	LOAD*R*	*R* := Oprnd	idxs	NZ
00010	STORE*R*	Oprnd := *R*	dxs	
00011	ADD*R*	*R* := *R* + Oprnd	idxs	NZVC
00100	SUB*R*	*R* := *R* - Oprnd	idxs	NZVC
00101	AND*R*	*R* := *R* AND Oprnd	idxs	NZ
00110	OR*R*	*R* := *R* OR Oprnd	idxs	NZ
00111	NOT*R*	*R* := NOT *R*	*U*	NZ
01000	ASL*R*	C := most significant bit; *R* := arithmetic shift left *R*	*U*	NZVC
01001	ASR*R*	C := least significant bit; *R* := arithmetic shift right *R*	*U*	NZC
01010	LDBYT*R*	*R* := byte Oprnd	idxs	NZ
01011	STBYT*R*	byte Oprnd := *R*	dxs	
01100	LOADB	B := Oprnd	idxs	NZ
01101	ADDB	B := B + Oprnd	idxs	NZVC
01110	BR	PC := Oprnd	ix	
01111	BRN	if N=1 then PC := Oprnd	ix	
10000	BRZ	if Z=1 then PC := Oprnd	ix	
10001	BRV	if V=1 then PC := Oprnd	ix	
10010	BRC	if C=1 then PC := Oprnd	ix	
10011	BRNZ	if N=1 or Z=1 then PC := Oprnd	ix	
10100	COMP*R*	*R* - Oprnd	idxs	NZVC
10101	ADDSP	SP := SP + Oprnd	i	NZVC
10110	SUBSP	SP := SP - Oprnd	i	NZVC
10111	JSR	SP := Sp - 2; Mem [SP] := PC; PC := Oprnd	ix	
11000	RTS	PC := Mem [SP]; SP := SP + 2	*U*	
11001	RTI	not used at Level 5	*U*	
11010	CHARI	byte Oprnd := input	dxs	
11011	CHARO	output := byte Oprnd	idxs	
11100	DECI	Oprnd := input	dxs	NZV
11101	DECO	output := Oprnd	idxs	
11110	HEXO	output := Oprnd	idxs	
11111	NOP	no operation	*U*	

Table 14.2

The Pep/5 instruction set at Level 5.

Table 14.2 shows the unimplemented opcode instructions replaced by four new instructions:

The unimplemented opcode instructions at Level 5

`DECI`	decimal input
`DECO`	decimal output
`HEXO`	hexadecimal output
`NOP`	no operation

These new instructions are available to the assembly language programmer at Level 5, but they are not part of the instruction set at Level 3. The operating system at Level 4 provides them with its interrupt service routine. At the assembly level you may simply program with them as if they were part of the Level 3 instruction set, even though they are not. At Level 3 these instructions are always unary, but at Level 5 they may or may not be unary. The interrupt service routine of the operating system makes the first three nonunary and the last instruction unary. Chapter 17 shows in detail how the operating system provides these instructions. You do not need to know the details of how they are implemented to program with them.

Pseudo-Operations

Pseudo-operations (pseudo-ops) are assembly language statements. Pseudo-ops do not have opcodes and do not correspond to any of the 32 instructions in the Pep/5 instruction set. Pep/5 assembly language has eight pseudo-ops:

The eight pseudo-ops of Pep/5 assembly language

`.ADDRSS`	the address of a symbol
`.ASCII`	a string of ASCII bytes
`.BLOCK`	a block of bytes
`.BURN`	initiate ROM burn
`.BYTE`	a byte value
`.END`	the sentinel for the assembler
`.EQUATE`	equate a symbol to a constant value
`.WORD`	a word value

All the pseudo-ops except `.BURN`, `.END`, and `.EQUATE` insert data bits into the machine language program. Pseudo means false. They are called pseudo-ops because the statements that generate data bits do not generate patterns whose first five bits correspond to the opcodes of any of the 32 instructions in the instruction set. They are also called *assembler directives* or *dot commands* because each must be preceded by a '.' in assembly language.

The following three programs will show how to use the `.ASCII`, `.BLOCK`, `.BYTE`, `.END`, and `.WORD` pseudo-ops. The other pseudo-ops will be described later.

Program 14.1

Program 14.1 is Program 13.1 written in assembly language instead of machine language.

Assembler Input

```
;Stan Warford
;June 3, 1989
;A program to output 'Hi'
;
CHARO   h#0007,d    ;Output 'H'
CHARO   h#0008,d    ;Output 'i'
STOP
.ASCII  /Hi/
.END
```

Assembler Output

```
D9 00 07 D9 00 08 00 48 69 zz
```

Program Output

```
Hi
```

Program 14.1

An assembly language program to output `Hi`. It is the assembly language version of Program 13.1.

The line-oriented nature of assembly language

Pep/5 assembly language, unlike Pascal, is line oriented. That is, each assembly language statement must be contained on one and only one line. You cannot continue a statement onto another line, nor can you place two statements on the same line.

Assembly language comments

Comments begin with a semicolon `;` and continue until the end of the line. It is permissible to have a line with only a comment on it, but it must begin with a semicolon. The first four lines of this program are comment lines. The `CHARO` instructions also contain comments, but only after the assembly language statements. As in Pascal, your assembly language programs should contain, at a minimum, your name, the date, and a description of the program. To conserve space in this book, however, the rest of the programs will not contain such a heading.

`CHARO` is the mnemonic for the character output instruction. The statement

```
CHARO   h#0007,d
```

means "Output one character from `Mem [0007]` using the direct addressing mode."

The .ASCII pseudo-op

The `.ASCII` pseudo-op generates contiguous bytes of ASCII characters. In assembly language, you simply write `.ASCII` followed by a string of ASCII characters enclosed by an arbitrary string delimiter. In this program, the string delimiter was a slash `/`, but in general it can be any printable character. The first printable character after `.ASCII` is assumed to be the delimiter, with which you must terminate the ASCII sequence.

Example 14.1 If you want to include in your program a sequence of ASCII characters that contains the slash, you may choose the single quote character as the delimiter and write it as

```
.ASCII 'Circumference / Pi = '
```

Or you may prefer to use % as the delimiter and write

```
.ASCII %Circumference / Pi = %
```

■

You must end your assembly language program with the `.END` command. It does not insert data bits into the program the way the `.ASCII` command does. It simply indicates the end of the assembly language program.

Assemblers

Compare this program written in assembly language with the same program written in machine language. Assembly language is much easier to understand because of the mnemonics in place of the opcodes. Also, the characters `H` and `i` written directly as ASCII characters are easier to read.

Unfortunately, you cannot simply write a program in assembly language and expect the computer to understand it. The computer can only execute programs by performing its von Neumann execution cycle (fetch, increment, execute, repeat), which is wired into the CPU. As shown in the previous chapter, the program must be stored in binary in main memory starting at address 0000 for the execution cycle to process it correctly. The assembly language statements must somehow be translated into machine language before they are loaded and executed.

In the early days, programmers wrote in assembly language and then translated each statement into machine language by hand. The translation part was straightforward. It only involved looking up the binary opcodes for the instructions and the binary codes for the ASCII characters in the ASCII table. The hexadecimal operands could similarly be converted to binary with hexadecimal conversion tables. Only after the program was translated could it be loaded and executed.

The translation of a long program was a routine and tedious job. Soon programmers realized that a computer program could be written to do the translation. Such a program is called an *assembler,* and Figure 14.1 illustrates how it functions.

An assembler is a program whose input is an assembly language program, and whose output is that same program translated into machine language in a format suitable for a loader. Input to the assembler is called the *source program.* Output from the assembler is called the *object program.* Figure 14.2 shows the effect of the Pep/5 assembler on the assembly language of Program 14.1.

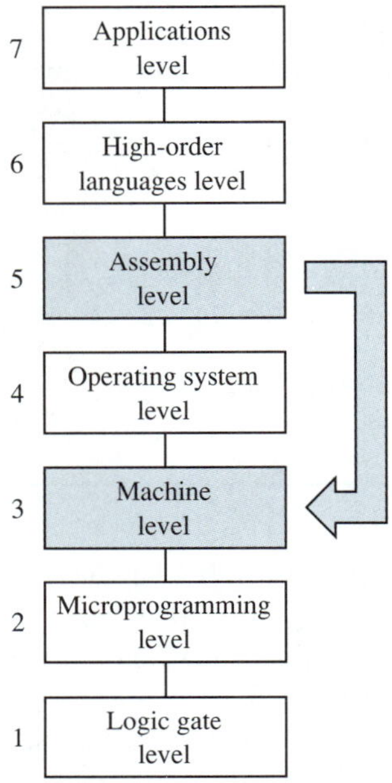

Figure 14.1

The function of an assembler. It translates a program in a Level 5 language to an equivalent program in a Level 3 language.

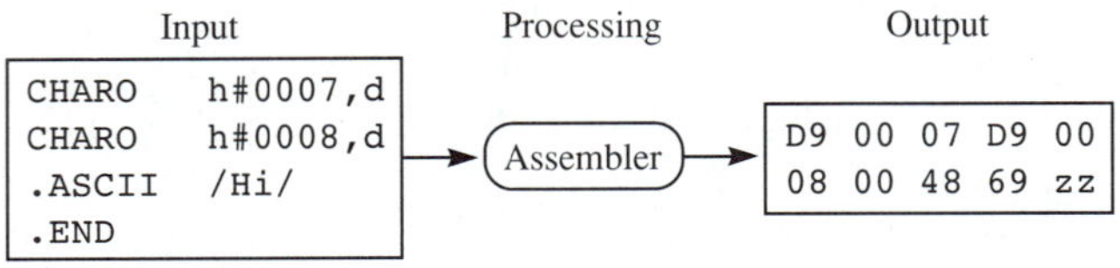

Figure 14.2

The action of the Pep/5 assembler on Program 14.1.

It is important to realize that an assembler merely translates a program into a format suitable for a loader. It does not execute the program. Translation and execution are separate processes, and translation always occurs first.

Since the assembler is itself a program, it must be written in some programming language. The computer pioneers who wrote the first assemblers had to write them in machine language. Or, if they wrote them in assembly language, they had to translate them into machine language by hand since no assemblers were available at the time. The point is that a machine can only execute programs that are written in machine language.

Program 14.2

Program 14.2 is the assembly language version of Program 13.2. It inputs two characters and outputs them in reverse order.

Assembler Input

```
CHARI   h#000E,d    ;Input first character
CHARI   h#000D,d    ;Input second character
CHARO   h#000D,d    ;Output second character
CHARO   h#000E,d    ;Output first character
STOP
.BLOCK  d#1         ;Storage for first char
.BLOCK  d#1         ;Storage for second char
.END
```

Assembler Output

```
D1 00 0E D1 00 0D D9 00 0D D9 00 0E 00 00 00 zz
```

Program Input

```
up
```

Program Output

```
pu
```

Program 14.2

An assembly language program to input two characters and output them in reverse order. It is the assembly language version of Program 13.2.

You can see from the assembler output that the first input statement, `CHARI h#000E,d`, translates to D1000E, and the last output statement, `CHARO h#000E,d`, translates to D9000E. After that, the `STOP` statement translates to 00.

The .BLOCK pseudo-op

The `.BLOCK` pseudo-ops generate the next two bytes of zeros. The dot command

```
.BLOCK  d#1
```

means "Generate a block of one byte of storage." The notation `d#` means decimal number. The assembler expects a decimal number after `d#` and will generate that number of bytes of storage, setting them to zeros. In the program, you could replace both `.BLOCK` commands by a single

```
.BLOCK  d#2
```

which means "Generate a block of two bytes of storage." Although the assembler output would be the same, you could not write the two separate comments on the `.BLOCK` lines in the assembly language program.

Program 14.3

Program 14.3 is the same as Program 13.3 to compute 5 plus 3. It illustrates the `.WORD` pseudo-op.

Program 14.3

An assembly language program to add 3 and 5 and output the single character result. It is the assembly language version of Program 13.3.

Assembler Input

```
LOADA   h#0011,d    ;A := first number
ADDA    h#0013,d    ;Add the two numbers
ORA     h#0015,d    ;Convert sum to character
STBYTA  h#0010,d    ;Store the character
CHARO   h#0010,d    ;Output the character
STOP
.BLOCK  d#1         ;Character to output
.WORD   d#5         ;Decimal 5
.WORD   d#3         ;Decimal 3
.WORD   h#0030      ;Mask for ASCII char
.END
```

Assembler Output

```
09 00 11 19 00 13 31 00 15 59 00 10 D9 00 10 00
00 00 05 00 03 00 30 zz
```

Program Output

```
8
```

The .WORD pseudo-op

Like the `.BLOCK` command, the `.WORD` command generates code for the loader, but with two differences. First, it always generates one word (two bytes) of code, not an arbitrary number of bytes. Second, the programmer can specify the content of the word. The dot command

```
.WORD   d#5
```

means "Generate one word with a value of 5 (dec)." The dot command

```
.WORD   h#0030
```

means "Generate one word with a value of 0030 (hex)."

The .BYTE pseudo-op

The `.BYTE` command works like the `.WORD` command, except that it generates a byte value instead of a word value. In this program, you could replace

```
.WORD   h#0030
```

with

```
.BYTE   h#00
.BYTE   h#30
```

and generate the same machine language.

You can compare the assembler output of this assembly language program with the hexadecimal machine language of Program 13.3 to see that they are identical. The assembler was designed to generate output that carefully follows the format expected by the loader. There are no leading blank lines or spaces. There is exactly one space between bytes, with no trailing spaces on a line. The byte sequence terminates with `zz`.

Using the Pep/5 Assembler

Execution of Program 14.2, the application program that outputs the two input characters in reverse order, requires the computer runs shown in Figure 14.3.

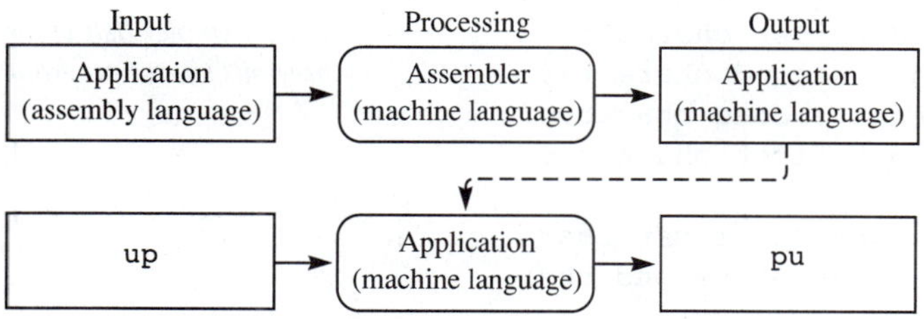

Figure 14.3

Two computer runs necessary for execution of Program 14.2.

First the assembler is loaded into main memory and the applications program is taken as the input file. The output from this run is the machine language version of the applications program. It is then loaded into main memory for the second run. All the programs in the center boxes must be in machine language.

The Pep/5 system comes with an assembler as well as the simulator. When you execute the assembler, it will ask you to name the file that contains your assembly language program, previously created with a text editor. If you have made no errors in your program, the assembler will generate the object code in a format suitable for the loader. Otherwise it will protest with one or more error messages and state that no code was generated. After you generate code from an error-free program, you can use it with the simulator as described in the previous chapter.

When writing an assembly language program, you must place at least one space after the mnemonic or dot command. Other than that, there are no restrictions on spacing. Your source program may be in any combination of uppercase or lowercase letters. For example, you could write your source of Program 14.2 as follows, and the assembler would accept it as valid and generate the correct code.

A valid source program

```
chari h#000E,d    ;Input first character
CHARI h#000D,d    ;Input second character
charo     H#    000D,d    ;Output second character
charo   h#   E   ,   d;Output first character
stop
.bloCK  d#1          ;Storage for first char
.BLOCK  d#1          ;Storage for second char
.END
```

In addition to generating object code for the loader, the assembler gives you the option of requesting a program listing, either on the screen, in a text file, or both. The assembler listing converts the source program to a consistent format of uppercase and lowercase letters and spacing. The following is an assembler listing from the source program of the previous paragraph.

The assembler listing for the previous source program

```
-----------------------------------------------------------------
      Object
Addr  code    Mnemon  Operand    Comment
-----------------------------------------------------------------
0000  D1000E  CHARI   h#000E,d   ;Input first character
0003  D1000D  CHARI   h#000D,d   ;Input second character
0006  D9000D  CHARO   h#000D,d   ;Output second character
0009  D9000E  CHARO   h#000E,d   ;Output first character
000C  00      STOP
000D  00      .BLOCK  d#1        ;Storage for first char
000E  00      .BLOCK  d#1        ;Storage for second char
000F          .END
-----------------------------------------------------------------
```

The listing also shows the hexadecimal object code that each line generates and the address of the first byte where it will be loaded by the loader. Note that the `.END` command did not generate any object code.

This book will present the rest of the assembly language programs as assembler listings, but without the column headings produced by the assembler, which are shown in the previous listing. The second column will be the machine language object code, and the first column will be the address of where the loader will place it in main memory. This layout is typical of most assemblers. It is a vivid presentation of the correspondence between machine language at Level 3 and assembly language at Level 5.

Cross Assemblers

Machines built by one manufacturer generally have different instruction sets from those in machines built by another manufacturer. Hence, a program in machine language for one brand of computer will not run on another machine.

If you write an application in assembly language for a personal computer, you will probably assemble it on the same computer. An assembler written in the same language as the language to which it translates, is called a *resident assembler.* The assembler resides on the same machine as the application program. The two runs of Figure 14.3 are on the same machine.

Resident assemblers

However, it is possible for the assembler to be written in Brand X machine language, but to translate the application program into Brand Y machine language for a different machine. Then the application program cannot be executed on the same machine on which it was translated. It must first be moved from Brand X machine to Brand Y machine.

A *cross assembler* is an assembler that produces an object program for a different machine from the one that runs the assembler. Moving the machine language version of the application program from the output file of Brand X to the main memory of Brand Y is called *downloading*. Brand X is called the *host machine* and Brand Y is called the *target machine*. In Figure 14.3, the first run would be on the host and the second run would be on the target.

Cross assemblers

This situation often occurs when the target machine is a small special-purpose computer, such as the computer that controls the cooking cycles in a microwave oven. Assemblers are large programs that require significant main memory, as well as input and output peripheral devices. The processor that controls a microwave oven has a very small main memory. Its input is simply the buttons on the control panel and perhaps the input signal from the temperature probe. Its output includes the digital display and the signals to control the cooking element. Since it has no input/output files, it cannot be used to run an assembler for itself. Its program must be downloaded from a larger host machine that has previously assembled the program into the target language.

14.2 Decimal I/O and Immediate Addressing

With direct addressing, the operand specifier is the address in main memory of the operand. Mathematically,

```
Oprnd = Mem [OprndSpec]
```

But with *immediate addressing*, the operand specifier is the operand.

Immediate addressing

```
Oprnd = OprndSpec
```

An instruction that uses direct addressing contains the address of the operand. But an instruction that uses immediate addressing contains the operand itself.

Program 14.4

Program 14.4 shows how to write Program 14.1 with immediate addressing. It outputs the message `Hi`.

Program 14.4

A program to output `Hi` using immediate addressing.

```
0000   D80048 CHARO    c#/H/,i     ;Output 'H'
0003   D80069 CHARO    c#/i/,i     ;Output 'i'
0006   00     STOP
0007          .END
```

Output

```
Hi
```

The assembler translates the character output instruction

```
CHARO   c#/H/,i
```

into object code D80048 (hex), which is

1101 1000 0000 0000 0100 1000

in binary. A check of Table 14.2 verifies that 11011 is the correct opcode for the `CHARO` instruction. Also, the addressing mode bits are 00 (bin), which indicates immediate addressing.

The notation `c#` stands for *character constant.* You must always follow it by a one- or two-character string, enclosed by arbitrary delimiters. The character constant always generates one word of binary. If one character is enclosed by delimiters, there are nine leading 0's, as shown in this program. If two characters are enclosed, one word is still generated with one ASCII character per byte, right-justified in each byte. For example, the statement

```
COMPA  c#/XY/,i
```

would generate the object code

1010 0000 0101 1000 0101 1001

where 10100 is the opcode for `COMPA`, `X` has the ASCII representation 101 1000, and Y has the ASCII representation 101 1001.

That is how the assembler translates the statement to binary. But what happens when the loader loads the program and the first instruction executes? If the addressing mode were direct, the CPU would interpret 0048 as an address and it would instruct main memory to put Mem [0048] on the bus for the output device. Since the addressing mode is immediate, the CPU interprets 0048 as the operand itself (not the address of the operand) and puts 48 on the bus for the output device. The second instruction does likewise with 0069.

Two advantages of immediate addressing over direct addressing

Immediate addressing has two advantages over direct addressing. The program is shorter because the ASCII string does not need to be stored separately from the instruction. Program 14.1 has nine bytes compared with this program, which has seven bytes. The instruction also executes faster because the operand is immediately available to the CPU in the instruction register.

Program 14.5

Although the assembly language features we have learned so far are a big improvement over machine language, several irritating aspects remain. They are illustrated in Program 14.3, which adds 3 and 5, converts the sum to a single ASCII character and outputs it.

The first instruction of Program 14.3,

```
LOADA   h#0011,d   ;A := first number
```

puts the content of Mem [0011] into the accumulator. To write this instruction, the programmer had to know that the first number would be stored at address 0011 (hex) after the instruction part of the program. The problem with placing the data at the end of the program is that you do not know exactly how long the instruction part of the program will be until you have finished it. Therefore, you do not know the address of the data while writing the instructions that require that address.

The problem of address computation

Another problem is program modification. Suppose you want to insert an extra statement in your program. That one modification will change the addresses of the data, and every instruction that refers to the data will need to be modified to reflect the new addresses.

It would be easier to program at Level 5 if you could place the data at the top of the program. Then you would know the address of the data when you write a statement that refers to that data.

The problem of restricting numeric operations to a single character

Another irritating aspect of Program 14.3 is the restriction to single character results because of the limitations of CHARO. Since CHARO can only output one byte as a single ASCII character, it is difficult to perform I/O on decimal values that require more than one digit for their ASCII representation.

Program 14.5 alleviates both of these irritations. It is a program to input an integer, add 1 to it, and output the sum. It stores the data at the beginning of the program and permits large decimal values.

Program 14.5

A program to add 1 to a decimal value. It illustrates decimal I/O.

```
0000  700005 BR      h#0005     ;Branch around data
0003  0000   .BLOCK  d#2        ;Storage for one integer
             ;
0005  E10003 DECI    h#0003,d   ;Get the number
0008  E90003 DECO    h#0003,d   ;and output it
000B  D80020 CHARO   c#/ /,i    ;Output ' + 1 = '
000E  D8002B CHARO   c#/+/,i
0011  D80020 CHARO   c#/ /,i
0014  D80031 CHARO   c#/1/,i
0017  D80020 CHARO   c#/ /,i
001A  D8003D CHARO   c#/=/,i
001D  D80020 CHARO   c#/ /,i
0020  090003 LOADA   h#0003,d   ;A := the number
0023  180001 ADDA    d#1,i      ;Add one to it
0026  110003 STOREA  h#0003,d   ;Store the sum
0029  E90003 DECO    h#0003,d   ;Output the sum
002C  00     STOP
002D         .END
```

Input

```
-479
```

Output

```
-479 + 1 = -478
```

When you select the execute option in the Pep/5 simulator, PC gets the value 0000 (hex). The CPU will interpret the bytes at `Mem [0000]` as the first instruction to execute. To place data at the top of the program, we need an instruction that will cause the CPU to skip the data bytes when it fetches the next instruction.

The unconditional branch, BR

The unconditional branch, BR, is such an instruction. It simply places the operand of the instruction in the PC. In this program,

```
BR      h#0005     ;Branch around data
```

places 0005 in the PC. In mathematical notation, the BR instruction executes

```
PC := Oprnd
```

During the fetch part of the next execution cycle, the CPU will get the instruction at 0005 instead of the instruction at 0003, which it would have gotten if the PC were not altered.

Since the branch instructions nearly always use immediate addressing, the Pep/5 assembler does not require that the addressing mode be specified. If you do not specify the addressing mode for a branch instruction, the assembler will assume immediate addressing and generate 00 for the addressing mode bits.

The correct operation of the BR instruction depends on the details of the von Neumann execution cycle. For example, you may have wondered why the cycle is fetch, increment, execute, repeat instead of fetch, execute, increment, repeat. Figure 13.12(f) showed the execution of instruction D90007 to output H while the value of PC is 0003, the address of instruction D90008. If the execute part of the von Neumann execution cycle had been before the increment part, then PC would have had the value 0000 when the instruction at address 0000, which was D90007, executed. It seems to make more sense to have the PC correspond to the executing instruction. Why doesn't the von Neumann execution cycle have the execute part before the increment part?

Because then BR would not work properly. In Program 14.5, PC would get 0000, the CPU would fetch the BR instruction, 700005, and BR would execute, placing 0005 in PC. Then PC would increment to 0008. Instead of branching to 0005, your program would branch to 0008. Since the instruction set contains branching instructions, the increment part of the von Neumann execution cycle must be before the execute part.

The reason increment must come before execute in the von Neumann execution cycle

DECI and DECO are two of the instructions the operating system provides to the assembly level, which the Pep/5 hardware does not provide at the machine level. DECI, which stands for decimal input, converts a sequence of ASCII digit characters to a single word that corresponds to the two's complement representation of the value. DECO, decimal output, does the opposite conversion, from the two's complement value in a word to a sequence of ASCII characters.

The DECI instruction

DECI permits any number of leading spaces or line feeds on input. The first printable character must be a decimal digit, a +, or a -. The following characters must be decimal digits. DECI sets Z to 1 if you input 0 and N to 1 if you input a negative value. It sets V to 1 if you enter a value that is out of range. Since a word is 16 bits and 2^{16} = 32768, the range is –32768 to 32767 (dec). DECI does not affect the C bit.

The DECO instruction

DECO prints a - if the value is negative but does not print + if it is positive. It does not print leading zeros and outputs the minimum number of characters possible to properly represent the value. You cannot specify the field width as you can with a Pascal write statement. DECO does not affect the NZVC bits.

In Program 14.5, the statement

```
DECI    h#0003,d    ;Get the number
```

when confronted with input sequence -479, converts it to 1111 1110 0010 0001 (bin) and stores it in Mem [0003]. DECO converts the binary sequence to a string of ASCII characters and outputs them.

Program 14.6

Program 14.6 illustrates HEXO, which means *hexadecimal output*, and NOP, which means *no operation*. They are two of the instructions that trigger an interrupt at the machine level but are bona fide instructions at the assembly level. The program

```
0000  700007 BR      h#0007      ;Branch around data
0003  0100   .WORD   d#256       ;First
0005  8000   .WORD   h#8000      ;Second
             ;
0007  E90003 DECO    h#0003,d    ;Interpret first as dec
000A  D8000A CHARO   h#000A,i    ;Output linefeed
000D  F10003 HEXO    h#0003,d    ;Interpret first as hex
0010  D8000A CHARO   h#000A,i    ;Output linefeed
0013  F8     NOP
0014  E90005 DECO    h#0005,d    ;Interpret second as dec
0017  D8000A CHARO   h#000A,i    ;Output linefeed
001A  F10005 HEXO    h#0005,d    ;Interpret second as hex
001D  00     STOP
001E         .END
```

Output

```
256
0100
-32768
8000
```

Program 14.6

A program that interprets a value as decimal and as hexadecimal.

stores two bit patterns with `.WORD` commands and outputs each twice with `DECO` and `HEXO`.

The HEXO instruction

`HEXO` outputs one word of information as four hexadecimal digits. It always outputs four characters with no leading, embedded, or trailing spaces. Like `DECO`, it does not affect the `NZVC` bits.

The NOP instruction

`NOP` is an instruction that does nothing; well, almost nothing. It does take some time to do nothing, however, and that is its main use on a computer. Programmers can use `NOP`s when they need to have the computer pause briefly because of timing requirements in their applications. The Pep/5 operating system includes `NOP` as a convenient opcode for programming assignments. In Chapter 17 you will learn how to program the interrupt handler to change `NOP` into a useful new instruction.

To display each value on a separate line, the program outputs a line feed character after each `DECO` and `HEXO`. According to the ASCII code in Table 12.7, 0A (hex) is line feed. When you execute

```
CHARO   h#000A,i
```

the screen cursor returns to the left margin for the start of a new line.

It does not matter to the `CHARO` instruction that the operand specifier uses the `h#` hexadecimal constant instead of the `c#` character constant. In fact, it would be impossible to type a line feed character between the delimiters of a `c#` specifier, since the act of typing <return> just before the delimiter would cause the delimiter to be on the next line of the assembly language program.

Program 14.6 emphasizes the difference between translation and execution. Once the assembler translates the bit patterns from the `.WORD` command and the loader loads the program, the CPU has no knowledge of the history of the patterns. It is perfectly legal to execute a `DECO` from a location whose storage value you set with `h#`, and vice versa. The dot command

```
.WORD    h#8000       ;Second
```

generates 1000 0000 0000 0000 during translation, which `DECO` dutifully outputs as `-32768` during execution.

Disassemblers

The one-to-one mapping of an assembler

An assembler translates each assembly language statement into exactly one machine language statement. Such a transformation is called a *one-to-one mapping*. One assembly language statement maps to one machine language statement. This is in contrast to a compiler, which, as we shall see later, produces a one-to-many mapping.

Given a single assembly language statement, you can always determine the corresponding machine language statement. But can you do the inverse? That is, given a bit sequence in a machine language program, can you determine the original assembly language statement from which the machine language came?

The nonunique nature of the inverse mapping of an assembler

No, you cannot. Even though the transformation is one-to-one, the inverse transformation is not unique. Given the binary machine language sequence

0101 0111

you cannot tell if the assembly language programmer originally used an ASCII assembler directive for the ASCII character `W`, or if she wrote the `LDBYTX` mnemonic with stack relative addressing. The assembler would have produced the exact same sequence of bits regardless of which of these two assembly language statements was in the original program.

Furthermore, during execution main memory does not know what the original assembly language statements were. It only remembers the ones and zeros that the CPU processes via its execution cycle.

The following listing shows two assembly language programs that produce the same machine language, and so produce identical output. Of course, a serious programmer would not write the second program, because it is more difficult to understand than the first program.

```
0000  D9000A CHARO   h#000A,d
0003  D9000B CHARO   h#000B,d
0006  D9000C CHARO   h#000C,d
0009  00     STOP
000A  50756E .ASCII  /Pun/
000D         .END

0000  D9000A CHARO   h#000A,d
0003  D9000B CHARO   h#000B,d
0006  D9000C CHARO   h#000C,d
0009  00     STOP
000A  50756E LDBYTA  h#756E,i
000D         .END
```

Two assembly language programs that produce the same object code and, therefore, the same output

Output

```
Pun
```

Because of pseudo-ops, the inverse assembler mapping is not unique. If there were no pseudo-ops, there would be only one possible way to recover the original assembly language statements from binary object code. Pseudo-ops are for inserting data bits, as opposed to instruction bits, into memory. The fact that data and programs share the same memory is a major cause of the nonunique nature of the inverse assembler mapping.

The cause of the nonunique nature of the inverse mapping

The difficulty of recovering the source program from the object program can be a marketing benefit to the software developer. If you write an applications program in assembly language, there are two ways you can sell it. You can sell the source program and let your customer assemble it. Your customer would then have both the source program and the object program. Or you could assemble it yourself and only sell the object program.

The advantage of object code for software distribution

In both cases, the customer has the object program necessary for executing the application program. But if he has the source program as well, he can easily modify it to suit his own purposes. He may even enhance it and then try to sell it as an improved version in direct competition with you, with little effort on his part. Modifying a machine language program would be much more difficult.

Most software products are sold only in object form to prevent the customer from tampering with the program. Sometimes the source program is sold as well, but usually at a much higher price.

Disassemblers

A *disassembler* is a program that tries to recover the source program from the object program. It can never be one hundred percent successful because of the nonunique nature of the inverse assembler mapping. The programs in this chapter place the data either before or after the instructions. In a large program, sections of data are typically placed throughout the program, making it difficult to distinguish data bits from instruction bits in the object code. A disassembler can read each byte and print it out several times—once interpreted as an instruction specifier, once interpreted as an ASCII character, once interpreted as an integer with two's complement binary representation, and so on. A person then can attempt to reconstruct the source program, but the process is tedious.

Who Gets Credit for the First Computer?

Determining the founder of the modern computer is a complex problem. We must acknowledge contributions such as the ancient Chinese abacus, Charles Babbage's analytical engine of the 1800s, and Lady Lovelace's musings on computation, but the real objects of our search are the immediate inventors of electronic digital computers. Candidates include John Atanasoff, Clifford Berry, John Mauchly, J. Presper Eckert, Konrad Zuse, and John von Neumann; each of these men actively pursued the research and development of electronic computing devices during the late 1930s and early 1940s. The history of modern computing was largely oversimplified until a lawsuit between Sperry Rand Corporation and Honeywell, Inc., in the late 1960s focused attention on it.

Throughout the 1950s and 1960s, it was generally accepted that Mauchly and Eckert were the fathers of the electronic computer, and that the ENIAC (Electronic Numerical Integrator and Calculator), completed in 1945, was the first electronic computer. Mauchly's and Eckert's successful work on the ENIAC attracted grant money, then spun off into commercial ventures. Their work also became very high profile when the U.S. military decided to use the ENIAC to help compute ballistics tables quickly and accurately.

Sperry Rand bought the patent for the ENIAC and its underlying concepts in 1951. Subsequently, the company required other computer manufacturers to pay royalties to use the important concepts that they owned—in particular, the fundamental architectural structures found in all modern computers, such as circuitry for doing arithmetic via logical switching and memory refresh circuits to prevent the decay of electronically represented information. Honeywell did not want to get into the expensive bind of paying royalties for every computer they would build and sell, so they sent their lawyers to research the history of modern computers.

The lawyers from Honeywell presented evidence that John Atanasoff and Clifford Berry of Iowa State College had beaten Mauchly and Eckert to the punch by several years. ENIAC was not operational until 1945; however Atanasoff had working prototypes by 1939 and a special-purpose computer by 1942. Atanasoff's machine contained the memory refresh circuitry and electronic adder/subtractor circuits that were used in ENIAC and in almost all other commercially successful machines. Also, the Honeywell lawyers discovered that Mauchly visited Atanasoff for several days during June of 1941 and that some of Atanasoff's ideas appeared in Mauchly's project after that time. All of this information strongly suggested that Atanasoff's work directly influenced the development of the ENIAC. In the end, the courts invalidated the ENIAC patent in 1973, declaring that Atanasoff's contributions were significant and that Mauchly borrowed on those ideas.

John Atanasoff.

Of course, part of academic scholarship includes discussing research projects; there is no implied accusation that Mauchly was out to steal Atanasoff's ideas. Atanasoff could have applied for a patent if he had wanted to protect himself. But Atanasoff and Berry didn't market their research very aggressively, and their project fell into stagnation when they had to serve in World War II. Mauchly, however, pushed his project forward by promoting its use to the War Department. Consequently, he received the early credit for the electronic computer.

We should point out that Konrad Zuse also had a general-purpose computer in mind at about the same time as Atanasoff, Berry, Mauchly, and Eckert did. Unfortunately, Zuse lived and worked in Nazi Germany, where academic pursuits lost out to warmongering, so the seeds of his ideas never bore fruit. Likewise, von Neumann's contribution of the stored program concept, which was adopted by Mauchly and Eckert, cannot be overemphasized for its importance in lifting their design to another level of elegance.

14.3 Symbols

The previous section introduced BR as an instruction to branch around the data at the beginning of the program. Although this technique alleviates the problem of manually determining the address of the data cells, it does not eliminate the problem. You must still determine the addresses by counting in hexadecimal, and if the number of data cells is large, mistakes are likely. Also, if you want to modify the data section, say by removing a .WORD command, the addresses of all the data cells following the deletion will change. You must modify any instructions that refer to the modified addresses.

Assembly language symbols eliminate the problem of manually determining addresses. The assembler lets you associate a *symbol,* similar to a Pascal identifier, with a *memory address.* Anywhere in the program you need to refer to the address, you can refer to the symbol instead. If you ever modify a program by adding or removing statements, when you reassemble the program the assembler will calculate the new address associated with the symbol. You do not need to rewrite the statements that refer to the changed addresses via the symbols.

The purpose of assembly language symbols

Program 14.7

The assembly language of Program 14.7 produces object code identical to that of Program 14.5. It uses two symbols, Num and Main.

The syntax rules for symbols are similar to the syntax rules for Pascal identifiers. The first character must be a letter, and the following characters must be letters or digits. Symbols can be a maximum of only eight characters long. The characters are case sensitive. For example, Number would be a different symbol from number because of the uppercase N.

You can define a symbol on any assembly language line by placing it at the beginning of the line. When you define a symbol, you must terminate it with a colon, :. No spaces are allowed between the last character of the symbol and the colon. In this program, the statement

```
Num:      .BLOCK   d#2
```

defines the symbol Num, in addition to allocating a block of two bytes. Although this line has spaces between the colon and the pseudo-op, the assembler does not require them.

When the assembler detects a symbol definition, it stores the symbol and its value in a symbol table. The value is the address in memory of where the first byte of the object code generated from that line will be loaded. If you define any symbols in your program, the assembler listing will include a printout of the symbol table with the values in hexadecimal. Table 14.3 is the symbol table printout from the listing of this program.

The value of a symbol is an address.

When you refer to the symbol, you cannot include the colon. The statement

```
LOADA   Num,d
```

```
0000  700005            BR      Main        ;Branch around data
0003  0000    Num       .BLOCK  d#2         ;Storage for one integer
              ;
0005  E1003   Main      DECI    Num,d       ;Get the number
0008  E90003            DECO    Num,d       ;and output it
000B  D80020            CHARO   c#/ /,i     ;Output ' + 1 = '
000E  D8002B            CHARO   c#/+/,i
0011  D80020            CHARO   c#/ /,i
0014  D80031            CHARO   c#/1/,i
0017  D80020            CHARO   c#/ /,i
001A  D8003D            CHARO   c#/=/,i
001D  D80020            CHARO   c#/ /,i
0020  090003            LOADA   Num,d       ;A := the number
0023  180001            ADDA    d#1,i       ;Add one to it
0026  110003            STOREA  Num,d       ;Store the sum
0029  E90003            DECO    Num,d       ;Output the sum
002C  00                STOP
002D                    .END
```

Input

```
-479
```

Output

```
-479 + 1 = -478
```

Program 14.7

A program to add 1 to a decimal value. It is identical to Program 14.5 except that it uses symbols.

refers to the symbol `Num`. Since `Num` has the value 0003 (hex), this statement generates the same code as

```
LOADA   h#0003,d
```

Similarly, the statement

```
BR      Main
```

generates the same code as

```
BR      h#0005
```

since the value of `Main` is 0005 (hex).

Symbol	Value	Symbol	Value
Main	0005	Num	0003

Table 14.3

The symbol table listing for Program 14.7.

Note that the value of a symbol is an address, not the content of the cell at that address. When this program executes, `Mem [0003]` will contain –479 (dec), which it gets from the input device. The value of `Num` will still be 0003 (hex), not –479 (dec), which is different. It might help you to visualize the value of a symbol as coming from the address column on the assembler listing in the line that contains the symbol definition.

Symbols not only relieve you of the burden of calculating addresses manually, they also make your programs easier to read. `Num` is easier on the eyes than `h#0003`. Good programmers are careful to select meaningful symbols for their programs to enhance readability.

Program 14.8

Program 14.8 is equivalent to Program 14.6, except for its symbols. It also illustrates the `.EQUATE` command.

```
0000  700007           BR       Main        ;Branch around data
0003  0100    First:   .WORD    d#256
0005  8000    Second:  .WORD    h#8000
              LineFeed:.EQUATE  h#000A      ;ASCII line feed
              ;
0007  E90003  Main:    DECO     First,d     ;Interpret first as dec
000A  D8000A           CHARO    LineFeed,i
000D  F10003           HEXO     First,d     ;Interpret first as hex
0010  D8000A           CHARO    LineFeed,i
0013  E90005           DECO     Second,d    ;Interpret second as dec
0016  D8000A           CHARO    LineFeed,i
0019  F10005           HEXO     Second,d    ;Interpret second as hex
001C  00               STOP
001D                   .END
```

Output

```
256
0100
-32768
8000
```

Program 14.8

A program that interprets a value as decimal and as hexadecimal. It is identical to Program 14.6 except that it uses symbols.

The program defines symbols `First`, `Second`, and `Main` with the technique of the previous program. However, it defines `LineFeed` differently, since this symbol precedes an `.EQUATE` command. The `.EQUATE` command does not generate object code. Notice the gap in the object code column of the assembler listing

The value of an .EQUATE symbol is not an address.

on the .EQUATE line. Instead, .EQUATE lets the programmer equate a value to a symbol.

In this program, the statement

```
LineFeed:.EQUATE h#000A
```

equates the value 000A (hex) to the symbol LineFeed. The normal mechanism of taking the value of a symbol from the address of the object code does not apply. Indeed, there is no object code to associate with an address. Table 14.4 is the symbol table printout for this program.

Symbol	Value	Symbol	Value
First	0003	LineFeed	000A
Main	0007	Second	0005

Table 14.4

The symbol table listing for Program 14.8.

Roughly speaking, the .EQUATE command at the assembly level functions like a constant definition at the Pascal level. In Pascal, if you define

```
const
   LineFeed = 10;
```

then anywhere you use LineFeed in your program, it is equivalent to using the constant 10.

The primary use of .EQUATE in assembly language is for readability. The statement

```
CHARO   LineFeed,i
```

is easier to read than

```
CHARO   h#000A,i
```

Program 14.9

When you program with symbols at Level 5, it is easy to lose sight of the von Neumann nature of the computer. The two classic von Neumann bugs—manipulating instructions as if they were data and attempting to execute data as if they were instructions—are still possible.

For example, consider the following assembly language program:

```
This: DECO This,d
      STOP
      .END
```

You might think that the assembler would object to the first statement, since it appears to be referring to itself as data in a nonsensical way. But the assembler does not look ahead to the ramifications of execution. Since the syntax is correct, it translates accordingly as shown in the following assembler listing for Program 14.9.

```
0000  E90000 This:    DECO    This,d
0003  00              STOP
0004                  .END
```

Output

```
-5888
```

Program 14.9

A nonsense program that illustrates the underlying von Neumann nature of the machine.

During execution, the CPU interprets E9 as the opcode for the decimal output instruction with direct addressing. It interprets the word at `Mem [0000]`, which is E900 (hex), as a decimal number and outputs its value, `-5888`.

It is important to realize that computer hardware has no innate intelligence or reasoning power. The execution cycle and the instruction set are wired into the CPU. As this program illustrates, the CPU has no knowledge of the history of the bits it processes. It has no overall picture. It simply grinds though the execution cycle over and over again. The same thing is true of main memory, which has no knowledge of the history of the bits it remembers. It simply stores ones and zeros as commanded by the CPU. Any intelligence or reasoning power must come from software, which is written by humans.

14.4 Assignment Statements

A compiler translates a program in a high-order language (Level 6) into a lower level language, so eventually it can be executed by the machine. Some compilers translate directly into machine language (Level 3) as shown in Figure 14.4(a). Then the program can be loaded into memory and executed. Other compilers translate into assembly language (Level 5) as shown in 14.4(b). An assembler then must translate the assembly language program into machine language before it can be loaded and executed.

Like an assembler, a compiler is a program. It must be written and debugged as any other program must be. The input to a compiler is called the source program, and the output from a compiler is called the object program, whether it is machine language or assembly language. This terminology is identical to that for the input and output of an assembler.

Compilers and assemblers are programs.

This section describes the translation process from Pascal to Pep/5 assembly language. It shows how a compiler translates `read`, `write`, and assignment statements, and how it enforces the concept of type at the Pascal level. The next chapter continues the discussion of the relationship between the high-order languages level (Level 6) and the assembly level (Level 5).

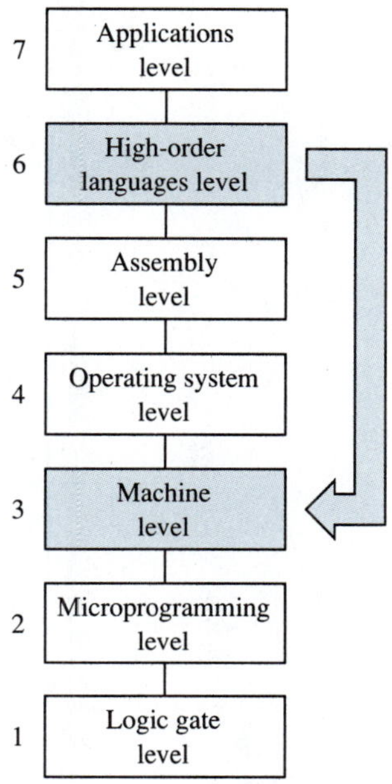

(a) Translation directly to machine language.

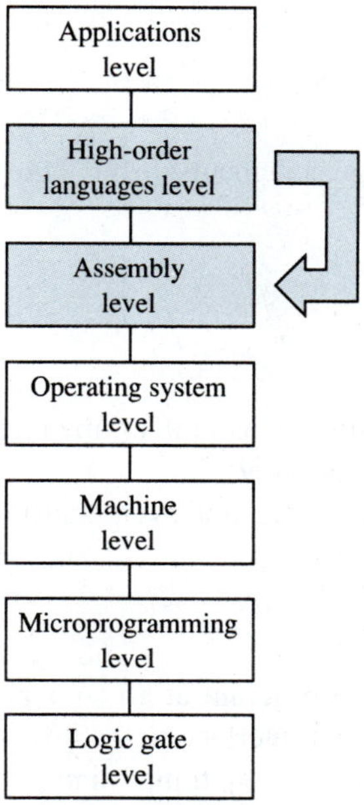

(b) Translation to assembly language.

Figure 14.4

The function of a compiler.

Program 14.10

Program 14.10 shows how a compiler would translate a simple Pascal program with one output statement into assembly language.

Program 14.10

The `write` statement at Level 6 and Level 5.

High-Order Language

```
program Message (output);
   begin
   write ('Love')
   end.
```

Assembly Language

```
0000  D8004C CHARO    c#/L/,i
0003  D8006F CHARO    c#/o/,i
0006  D80076 CHARO    c#/v/,i
0009  D80065 CHARO    c#/e/,i
000C  00     STOP
000D         .END
```

Output

```
Love
```

The single Pascal statement

```
write ('Love')
```

gets translated into four assembly language statements:

```
CHARO   c#/L/,i
CHARO   c#/o/,i
CHARO   c#/v/,i
CHARO   c#/e/,i
```

This is a one-to-four mapping. In contrast to an assembler, the mapping for a compiler generally is not one-to-one, but one-to-many.

Other elements of the Pascal program are not even translated directly. For example,

```
program Message (output);
```

does not appear in the assembly language program at all. A real compiler would use the program heading to make the correct interface to the operating system. The Pep/5 system ignores these kinds of details to keep things simple at the introductory level.

This is not the only possible translation of the `write` statement. The next chapter will show a different translation based on a loop. It is common for two different compilers to translate the same source program into different object programs. Even though the object programs are not identical, their differences are not in what they do, but how they do it. For example, if the source is a program to compute the payroll of a company, both object programs would produce identical payrolls. However, one object program might execute faster or use more memory than the other.

Figure 14.5 shows the input and output of a compiler with this program. Part (a) is a compiler that translates directly into machine language. The object program

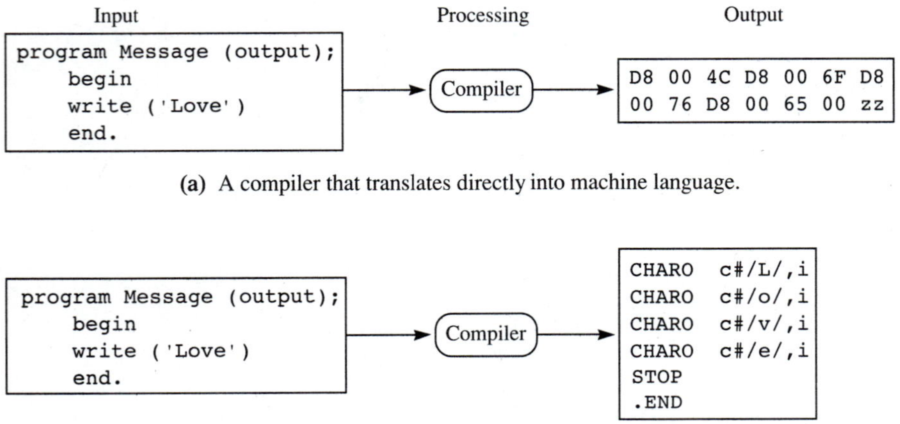

(a) A compiler that translates directly into machine language.

(b) A compiler that translates into assembly language.

Figure 14.5 The action of a compiler on Program 14.10.

could be loaded and executed. Part (b) is a compiler that translates to assembly language at Level 5. The object program would need to be assembled before it could be loaded and executed.

Variables and Types

Recall the three attributes of a Pascal variable—name, type, and value. For each variable in the variable declaration part, the compiler reserves one or more memory cells in the machine language program. A variable in a high-order language is simply a memory location in a low-level language. Level 6 programs refer to variables by names, which are Pascal identifiers. Level 3 programs refer to them by addresses. The value of the variable is the value in the memory cell at the address associated with the Pascal identifier.

The compiler must remember which address corresponds to which variable name in the Level 6 program. It uses a symbol table to make the connection between variable names and addresses.

The symbol table for a compiler

The symbol table for a compiler is similar to, but inherently more complicated than, the symbol table for an assembler. A variable name in Pascal is not limited to eight characters, as is a symbol in Pep/5. In addition, the symbol table for a compiler must store the variable's type as well as its associated address.

A compiler that translates directly to machine language does not require a second translation with an assembler. Figure 14.6(a) shows the mapping produced by the symbol table for such a compiler. The programs in this book illustrate the translation process for a hypothetical compiler that translates to assembly language, however, because assembly language is easier to read than machine language. Variable names in Pascal will correspond to symbols in Pep/5 assembly language, as Figure 14.6(b) shows.

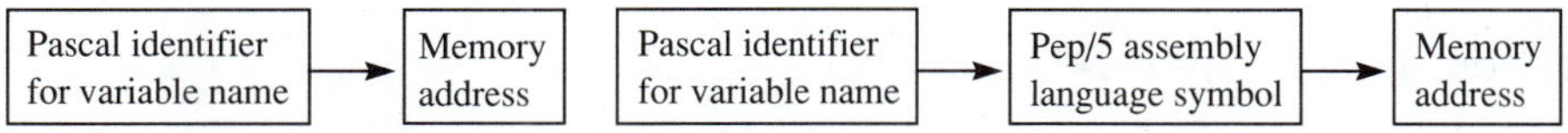

(a) A compiler that translates to machine language.

(b) A hypothetical compiler for illustrative purposes.

Figure 14.6

The mapping a compiler makes between a Level 6 variable and a Level 3 storage location.

The correspondence in 14.6(b) is unrealistic for compilers that translate to assembly language. Consider the problem of a Pascal program that has two variables named `DiscountRate1` and `DiscountRate2`. Since they are longer than eight characters, the compiler would have a difficult time mapping the identifiers to unique Pep/5 symbols. Our examples will limit the Pascal identifiers to, at most, eight characters to make clear the correspondence between Pascal and assembly language. Real compilers that translate to assembly language typically do not use assembly language symbols for the variable names.

Program 14.11

Program 14.11 shows assignment statements at Level 6 and the corresponding assembly language program, which the compiler produces. The object program contains comments. Real compilers do not generate comments, since human programmers usually do not need to read the object program.

Program 14.11

The assignment statement at Level 6 and Level 5.

High-Order Language

```
program Test (input, output);
   var
      Ch: char;
      I:  integer;
   begin
   read (Ch, I);
   I := I + 1;
   Ch := succ (Ch);
   writeln (Ch);
   write (I: 1)
   end.
```

Assembly Language

```
0000  700006           BR      Test
0003  00      Ch:      .BLOCK  d#1
0004  0000    I:       .BLOCK  d#2
              LineFeed:.EQUATE h#000A
              ;
0006  D10003  Test:    CHARI   Ch,d        ;read (Ch, I)
0009  E10004           DECI    I,d
000C  090004           LOADA   I,d         ;I := I + 1
000F  180001           ADDA    d#1,i
0012  110004           STOREA  I,d
0015  510003           LDBYTA  Ch,d        ;Ch := succ (Ch)
0018  180001           ADDA    d#1,i
001B  590003           STBYTA  Ch,d
001E  D90003           CHARO   Ch,d        ;writeln (Ch)
0021  D8000A           CHARO   LineFeed,i
0024  E90004           DECO    I,d         ;write (I: 1)
0027  00               STOP
0028                   .END
```

Input

```
M  419
```

Output

```
N
420
```

Remember that a compiler is a program. It must be written and debugged just like any other program. A compiler to translate Pascal programs can be written in any language—even Pascal! The following program segment illustrates some details of this incestuous state of affairs. It is part of a simplified compiler that translates Pascal source programs into assembly language object programs.

A symbol table definition for a hypothetical compiler

```
program PascalCompiler (input, output);
   type
      NameType      = packed array [1..32] of char;
      HexDigitType = 0..15;
      HexNumType    = array [1..4] of HexDigitType;
      KindType      = (PInteger, PBoolean, PChar, PReal);
      SymbolTableEntry  =
         record
         Symbol: NameType;
         Value:  HexNumType;
         Kind:   KindType
         end;
   var
      SymbolTable: array [1..100] of SymbolTableEntry;
```

An entry in a symbol table contains three parts—the symbol itself; its value, which is the address in Pep/5 memory where the value of the variable will be stored; and the kind of value that is stored, that is, the variable's type.

Figure 14.7 shows the entries in the symbol table for this program. The first variable has the symbolic name `Ch`. The compiler allocates the byte at `Mem [0003]` by generating the `.BLOCK` command and stores its type as `PChar` in the symbol table, an indication that the variable is a Pascal character. The second variable has the symbolic name `I`. The compiler allocates two bytes at `Mem [0004]` for its value and stores its type as `PInteger`, indicating a Pascal integer. It gets the types from the variable declaration part of the Pascal program.

	Symbol	Value	Kind
[1]	Ch	0003	PChar
[2]	I	0004	PInteger
[3]	⋮	⋮	⋮

Figure 14.7

The symbol table for a hypothetical compiler that translates Program 14.11.

During the code generation phase, the compiler translates

```
read (Ch, I)
```

into

```
CHARI   h#0003,d
DECI    h#0004,d
```

It consults the symbol table, which was filled at an earlier phase of compilation, to determine the addresses for the operands of the `CHARI` and `DECI` instructions. As explained previously, our listing shows the generated instructions as

```
CHARI   Ch,d
DECI    I,d
```

for readability.

Note that the value stored in the symbol table is not the value of the variable during execution. It is the memory address of where that value will be stored. If the user enters `419` for `I` during execution, then the value stored at `Mem [0004]` will be 01A3 (hex), which is the binary representation of 419 (dec). The symbol table contains 0004, not 01A3, as the value of the symbol `I` at translation time. Values of Pascal variables do not exist at translation time. They exist at execution time.

Assigning a value to a variable at Level 6 corresponds to storing a value in memory at Level 5. The compiler translates the assignment statement

```
I := I + 1
```

into

An assignment statement at Level 5

```
LOADA   I,d
ADDA    d#1,i
STOREA  I,d
```

`LOADA` and `ADDA` perform the computation on the right hand side of the assignment statement, leaving the result of the computation in the accumulator. `STOREA` assigns the result back to `I`.

Similarly, the compiler translates

```
Ch := succ (Ch)
```

into

The succ function at Level 5

```
LDBYTA  Ch,d
ADDA    d#1,i
STBYTA  Ch,d
```

The same instruction that adds 1 to `I`, `ADDA`, performs the `succ` function to `Ch`.

The compiler translates

```
writeln (Ch)
```

into

```
CHARO   Ch,d
CHARO   LineFeed,i
```

and translates

```
write (I: 1)
```

into

```
DECO    I,d
```

The compiler generates a line feed output as the last object code statement for a `writeln`. A Pascal field width specification of 1 corresponds to the output format of a `DECO` instruction.

Again the compiler must search its symbol table to make the connection between a symbol such as Ch and its address, 0003. The symbol table is an array. If it is not maintained in alphabetical order by symbolic name, a sequential search would be necessary to locate Ch in the table. If the symbolic names are in alphabetical order, a binary search is possible.

Type Compatibility

The Kind part of the symbol table allows the Pascal compiler to check for type compatibility. If the source program contained an assignment statement such as

Illegal at Level 6

```
Ch := I + 7
```

and there were no type checking, the following code would be generated:

Legal at Level 5

```
LOADA   I,d     ;Get I
ADDA    d#7,i   ;Add 7 to it
STBYTA  Ch,d    ;Assign sum to Ch
```

These statements are perfectly legal in assembly language. All assembly language statements operate at the bit level and attach no meaning to the bits on which they operate.

The Pascal compiler checks for type compatibility, on the other hand. To evaluate the right-hand side of the assignment statement, it would look up the address for I in the symbol table, generate

```
LOADA   I,d
```

and note from the Kind part of the symbol table that I is an integer. The compiler would then recognize that 7 is an integer, which is compatible with I, and generate

```
ADDA    d#7,i
```

Type compatibility enforced by the compiler

When it looks up Ch, it sees from the Kind part of the symbol table that Ch has type char, which is not compatible with type integer. So it issues the message

```
Syntax error
Type conflict of operands
```

and refuses to generate code for the assignment statement. The programmer must correct the syntax error before attempting another compile.

Having the compiler check for type compatibility is a tremendous help. It keeps you from writing meaningless statements, such as assigning an integer value to a character variable. When you program directly in assembly language at Level 5, there are no type compatibility checks. All data consists of bits. When bugs occur due to incorrect data movements, they can only be detected at run time, not at translation time. That is, they are logical errors instead of syntax errors. Logical errors are notoriously more difficult to locate than syntax errors.

Program 14.12

A program translating a Pascal constant to machine language and illustrating the `ASRR` statement.

High-Order Language

```
program Grade (input, output);
   const
      Bonus = 5;
   var
      Exam1: integer;
      Exam2: integer;
      Score: integer;
   begin
   read (Exam1, Exam2);
   Score := (Exam1 + Exam2) div 2 + Bonus;
   write ('Score = ', Score: 1)
   end.
```

Assembly Language

```
0000  700009          BR      Grade
              Bonus:  .EQUATE d#5
0003  0000    Exam1:  .BLOCK  d#2
0005  0000    Exam2:  .BLOCK  d#2
0007  0000    Score:  .BLOCK  d#2
              ;
0009  E10003  Grade:  DECI    Exam1,d    ;read (Exam1,
000C  E10005          DECI    Exam2,d    ;   Exam2)
000F  090003          LOADA   Exam1,d    ;Score := (Exam1
0012  190005          ADDA    Exam2,d    ;   + Exam2)
0015  48              ASRA               ;   div 2
0016  180005          ADDA    Bonus,i    ;   + Bonus
0019  110007          STOREA  Score,d
001C  D80053          CHARO   c#/S/,i    ;write ('Score = ',
001F  D80063          CHARO   c#/c/,i
0022  D8006F          CHARO   c#/o/,i
0025  D80072          CHARO   c#/r/,i
0028  D80065          CHARO   c#/e/,i
002B  D80020          CHARO   c#/ /,i
002E  D8003D          CHARO   c#/=/,i
0031  D80020          CHARO   c#/ /,i
0034  E90007          DECO    Score,d    ;   Score: 1)
0037  00              STOP
0038                  .END
```

Input

```
68  84
```

Output

```
Score = 81
```

Program 14.12

Program 14.12 shows how to translate a Pascal constant to machine language. It also illustrates the `ASRR` assembly language statement. The program calculates a value for `Score` as the average of two exam grades plus a five-point bonus.

The I/O and assignment statements are similar to previous programs. `read` translates to `DECI` or `CHARI` as required, and `write` to `DECO` or `CHARO`. In general, assignment statements translate to (a) load register, (b) evaluate expression if necessary, and (c) store register.

You do not need to allocate storage with the `.BLOCK` command for the integer constant `Bonus`. Since its value will never change during execution, a separate memory cell to hold its value is not required. Instead, you can equate the symbol `Bonus` to the value 5 with the `.EQUATE` command. Note that when you add `Bonus` in the evaluation of the right side of the assignment statement, you must use immediate addressing.

Immediate addressing for constants

In a more realistic program, `Score` would have type `real`, and you would compute the average with the real division operator. Pep/5 does not have hardware support for real numbers. Nor does its instruction set contain instructions for multiplying or dividing integers. These operations must be programmed with the shift left and shift right instructions.

Recall from Chapter 13 that an arithmetic shift right corresponds to division by 2. The compiler translates the `div 2` operation into the `ASRA` instruction. You can see from the listing that `ASRA` is unary. The assembler generates only one byte of object code.

The ASRR instruction

`ASRA` does the arithmetic shift right operation on the 16-bit accumulator. It shifts the least significant bit into `C` and replicates the sign bit. If the remaining bits in the accumulator are all 0's, then the CPU sets `Z` to 1. Otherwise, it clears `Z` to 0. If the result is a negative number (which it will be if the accumulator originally contains a negative number), then it sets `N` to 1. `ASRA` does not affect the `V` bit, since dividing a number by 2 can never produce a value that is out of range. `ASRX` behaves similarly, except that it performs the operation on the index register.

`ASLA` performs the arithmetic shift left operation on the accumulator. It shifts the most significant bit into `C` and 0 into the least significant bit. In addition to affecting `N` and `Z` as `ASRA` does, `ASLA` affects the `V` bit. Since an arithmetic shift right corresponds to a multiplication by 2, the result can be out of range. `ASLX` behaves similarly, except that it performs the operation on the index register.

The ASLR instruction

SUMMARY

An assembler is a program that translates a program in assembly language into the equivalent program in machine language. The von Neumann design principle calls for instructions as well as data to be stored in main memory. Corresponding to each of these bit sequences are two types of assembly language statements. For program statements, assembly language uses mnemonics in place of opcodes and register specifiers, hexadecimal instead of binary for the operand specifiers, and mnemonic letters for the addressing modes. For data statements, assembly language uses pseudo-ops, also called dot commands.

With direct addressing, the operand specifier is the address in main memory of the operand. But with immediate addressing, the operand specifier is the operand. In mathematical notation, `Oprnd = OprndSpec`. Immediate addressing is preferable to direct addressing because the operand does not need to be stored separately from the instruction. Such instructions execute faster because the operand is immediately available to the CPU in the instruction register.

Assembly language symbols eliminate the problem of manually determining the addresses of data and instructions in a program. The value of a symbol is an address. When the assembler detects a symbol definition, it stores the symbol and its value in a symbol table. When the symbol is used, the assembler substitutes its value in place of the symbol.

A variable at the high-order languages level (Level 6) corresponds to a memory location at the assembly level (Level 5). An assignment statement at Level 6 that assigns an expression to a variable, translates to a load, followed by an expression evaluation, followed by a store at Level 5. Type compatibility at Level 6 is enforced by the compiler with the help of its symbol table, which is more complex than the symbol table of an assembler. At Level 5, the only type is bit, and any operation can be performed on any bit pattern.

EXERCISES

Section 14.1

*1. Convert the following machine language instructions into assembly language assuming they were not generated by pseudo-ops.

(a) 080D4E
(b) 48
(c) 11014B

2. Convert the following machine language instructions into assembly language assuming they were not generated by pseudo-ops.

(a) 0C09A3
(b) 44
(c) 150F47

*3. Convert the following assembly language instructions into hexadecimal machine language.

(a) `ASLA`
(b) `CHARI h#000F,s`
(c) `BRN h#01E6,x`

4. Convert the following assembly language instructions into hexadecimal machine language.

   (a) `ADDA h#01FE,i`
   (b) `HEXO h#000D,x`
   (c) `LOADX h#01FF,s`

*5. Convert the following assembly language pseudo-ops into hexadecimal machine language.

   (a) `.ASCII /Bear/`
   (b) `.BYTE h#F8`
   (c) `.WORD d#790`

6. Convert the following assembly language pseudo-ops into hexadecimal machine language.

   (a) `.BYTE d#13`
   (b) `.ASCII /Frog/`
   (c) `.WORD h#FFE0`

*7. Predict the output of the following assembly language program.

```
CHARO   h#000C,d
CHARO   h#000B,d
CHARO   h#000A,d
STOP
.ASCII  /gum/
.END
```

8. Predict the output of the following assembly language program.

```
CHARO   h#0008,d
CHARO   h#0007,d
STOP
.ASCII  /is/
.END
```

9. Predict the output of the following assembly language program if the input is `g`. Predict the output if the input is `A`. Explain the difference between the two results.

```
CHARI   h#0010,d
LDBYTA  h#0010,d
ANDA    h#0011,d
STBYTA  h#0010,d
CHARO   h#0010,d
STOP
.BLOCK  d#1
.WORD   h#00DF
.END
```

Section 14.2

*10. Predict the output of Program 14.6 if the `.WORD` commands are changed to

```
.WORD    d#129        ;First
.WORD    h#FFFE       ;Second
```

11. Predict the output of Program 14.6 if the `.WORD` commands are changed to

```
.WORD    d#-16        ;First
.WORD    h#7FFE       ;Second
```

12. Determine the object code and predict the output of the following assembly language programs.

*(a)

```
DECO     c#/m/,i
CHARO    h#000A,i
DECO     c#/mm/,i
CHARO    h#000A,i
HEXO     d#-456,i
CHARO    h#000A,i
CHARO    h#0026,i
STOP
.END
```

(b)

```
DECO     c#/Q/,i
CHARO    h#000A,i
HEXO     d#880,i
CHARO    h#000A,i
CHARO    h#007D,i
STOP
.END
```

Section 14.3

*13. In the following code, determine the values of the symbols `Here` and `There`. Write the object code in hexadecimal.

```
         BR       There
Here:    .WORD    d#9
There:   DECO     Here,d
         STOP
         .END
```

14. In the following code, determine the values of the symbols `This`, `That`, and `TheOther`. Write the object code in hexadecimal.

```
         BR       TheOther
This:    .WORD    d#17
That:    .WORD    d#19
TheOther:DECO     This,d
         DECO     That,d
         STOP
         .END
```

*15. In the following code, determine the value of the symbol `This`. Predict the output of the assembly language program.

```
This:    HEXO     This,d
         STOP
         .END
```

16. In the following code, determine the value of the symbol `This`. Predict the output of the assembly language program.

```
This:     CHARO    This,d
          STOP
          .END
```

Section 14.4

17. How are the symbol table of an assembler and a compiler similar? How do they differ?

*18. How does a Pascal compiler enforce type compatibility?

19. Assume that you have a Pep/5 type computer and the following disk files.

- File A: a Pep/5 assembly language assembler written in machine language
- File B: a Pascal-to-assembly-language compiler written in assembly language
- File C: a Pascal program that will read numbers from a data file and print their median
- File D: a data file for the median program of file C

To compute the median, you must make the four computer runs described schematically in Figure 14.8. Each run involves an input file that will be operated on by a program to produce an output file. The output file produced by one run may be used either as the input file or as the program of a subsequent run. Describe the content of files E, F, G, and H, and label the empty blocks in Figure 14.8 with the appropriate file letter.

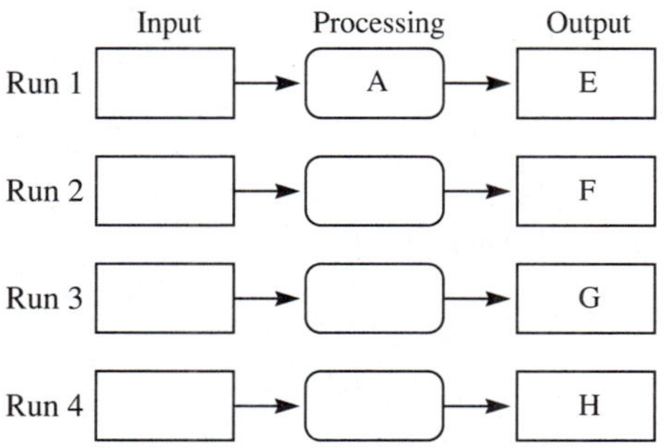

Figure 14.8

The computer runs for Exercise 19.

PROBLEMS

Section 14.1

20. Write an assembly language program that prints your first name on the screen. Use the `.ASCII` pseudo-op to store the characters at the bottom of your program. Use the `CHARO` instruction to output the characters.

Section 14.2

21. Write an assembly language program that prints your first name on the screen. Use immediate addressing with `c#` to designate the operand of `CHARO`.

22. Write an assembly language program that prints your first name on the screen. Use immediate addressing with `d#` to designate the operand of `CHARO`.

23. Write an assembly language program that prints your first name on the screen. Use immediate addressing with `h#` to designate the operand of `CHARO`.

24. Write an assembly language program that corresponds to the following Pascal program.

```
program Prob24 (input, output);
   var
      Num1: integer;
      Num2: integer;
   begin
   read (Num1, Num2);
   writeln (Num2: 1);
   writeln (Num1: 1)
   end.
```

25. Write an assembly language program that corresponds to the following Pascal program.

```
program Prob25 (input, output);
   const
      ChConst = 'a';
   var
      Ch1: char;
      Ch2: char;
   begin
   read (Ch1, Ch2);
   writeln;
   writeln (Ch1, ChConst, Ch2)
   end.
```

26. Write an assembly language program that corresponds to the following Pascal program.

```
program Prob26 (input, output);
   const
      Amount = 20000;
   var
      Num: integer;
      Sum: integer;
   begin
   read (Num);
   Sum := Num + Amount;
   writeln ('Sum = ', Sum: 1)
   end.
```

Test your program twice. The first time, enter a value for `Num` to make the sum within the allowed range for the Pep/5 computer. The second time, enter a value that is in range, but that makes `Sum` outside the range. Note that the out-of-range condition does not cause an error message, it just gives an incorrect value. Explain the value.

27. Write an assembly language program that corresponds to the following Pascal program.

```
program Rect (input, output);
   var
      Width:  integer;
      Length: integer;
      Perim:  integer;
   begin
   read (Width, Length);
   Perim := (Width + Length) * 2;
   writeln ('W = ', Width: 1);
   writeln ('L = ', Length: 1);
   writeln;
   writeln ('P = ', Perim: 1)
   end.
```

28. Write an assembly language program that corresponds to the following Pascal program.

```
program Before (input, output);
   var
      Ch: char;
   begin
   read (Ch);
   Ch := pred (Ch);
   writeln (Ch)
   end.
```

29. Write an assembly language program that corresponds to the following Pascal program.

```
program Negate (input, output);
   var
      Num1: integer;
      Num2: integer;
   begin
   read (Num1);
   Num2 := -Num1;
   writeln ('Num1 = ', Num1: 1);
   writeln ('Num2 = ', Num2: 1)
   end.
```

30. Write an assembly language program that corresponds to the following Pascal program.

```
program Div8 (input, output);
   var
      Num: integer;
   begin
   read (Num);
   Num := Num div 8;
   writeln ('Num = ', Num: 1)
   end.
```

Chapter

15 Compiling to the Assembly Level

The theme of this book is that the concept of levels of abstraction applies to computer science. This chapter continues the theme by showing the relationship between the high-order languages level and the assembly level. It examines features of the Pascal language at Level 6 and shows how a compiler might translate programs that use those features to the equivalent program at Level 5.

Data abstraction

One major difference between Level 6 languages and Level 5 languages is the absence of extensive data types at Level 5. In Pascal, you can define integers, reals, arrays, booleans, and records in almost any combination. But assembly language has only bits and bytes. If you want to define an array of records in assembly language, you must partition the bits and bytes accordingly. The compiler does that job automatically when you program at Level 6.

Program abstraction

Another difference between the levels concerns the flow of control. Pascal has `if`, `while`, `repeat`, `for`, `case`, and `procedure` statements to alter the normal sequential flow of control. You will see that assembly language is limited by the basic von Neumann design to more primitive control statements. This chapter shows how the compiler must combine several primitive Level 5 control statements to execute a single, more powerful Level 6 control statement.

15.1 Branching Instructions and Flow of Control

The Pep/5 instruction set has five conditional branches:

The conditional branch instructions at Level 5

`BRN`	branch on `N`
`BRZ`	branch on `Z`
`BRV`	branch on `V`
`BRC`	branch on `C`
`BRNZ`	branch on `N` or `Z`

The first four conditional branches test a status bit. If the status bit is 1, the operand is placed in the `PC`, causing the branch. If the status bit is 0, the operand is not placed in the `PC`, and the instruction following the conditional branch executes normally. The fifth conditional branch instruction, BRNZ, operates similarly except that the branch occurs if the N bit is 1 or if the Z bit is 1.

Whether a branch occurs depends on the value of the status bits. The status bits are in turn affected by the results of other instructions. For example,

```
LOADA   Num,d
BRN     Place
```

causes the content of Num to be loaded into the accumulator. If the word represents a negative number, that is, if its sign bit is 1, then the N bit is set to one. BRN tests the N bit and causes a branch to the instruction at Place. On the other hand, if the word loaded into the accumulator is not negative, then the N bit is cleared to 0. When BRN tests the N bit the branch does not occur and the instruction after BRN executes next.

Program 15.1

Program 15.1 shows how a compiler would translate an if/then statement from Pascal to assembly language. The program computes the absolute value of an integer.

Program 15.1

The if/then statement at Level 6 and Level 5.

High-Order Language

```
program AbsVal (input, output);
   var
      Number: integer;
   begin
   read (Number);
   if Number < 0 then
      Number := -Number;
   write (Number: 1)
   end.
```

Assembly Language

```
0000  700005                BR      AbsVal
0003  0000    Number:       .BLOCK  d#2
              ;
0005  E10003  AbsVal:       DECI    Number,d    ;read (Number)
0008  090003  If:           LOADA   Number,d    ;if Number < 0 then
000B  780011                BRN     Then
000E  70001B                BR      EndIf
0011  090003  Then:         LOADA   Number,d    ;Number := -Number
0014  38                    NOTA
0015  180001                ADDA    d#1,i
0018  110003                STOREA  Number,d
001B  E90003  EndIf:        DECO    Number,d    ;write (Number: 1)
001E  00                    STOP
001F                        .END
```

The assembly language comments show the statements that correspond to the high-level program. The `read` statement translates to `DECI` and the `write` statement translates to `DECO`. The assignment statement translates to the sequence `LOADA`, `NOTA`, `ADDA`, `STOREA`. `NOTA` and `ADDA` compute the two's complement of the value.

The compiler translates the `if` statement into the sequence `LOADA`, `BRN`, `BR`. When `LOADA` executes, if the value loaded into the accumulator is negative, the `N` bit is set to 1. That condition calls for executing the body of the `if` statement. `BRN` following the `LOADA` branches to the body of the `if` statement under that condition. The unconditional branch skips the body if the condition is not satisfied.

Figure 15.1(a) shows the structure of the `if/then` statement at Level 6. S1 represents the statement `read (Number)`, C1 represents the condition `Number < 0`, S2 represents the statement `Number := -Number`, and S3 represents the statement `write (Number: 1)`. Figure 15.1(b) shows the structure with the more primitive branching instructions at Level 5. The first dot following C1 represents the conditional branch, `BRN`, and the second dot represents `BR`.

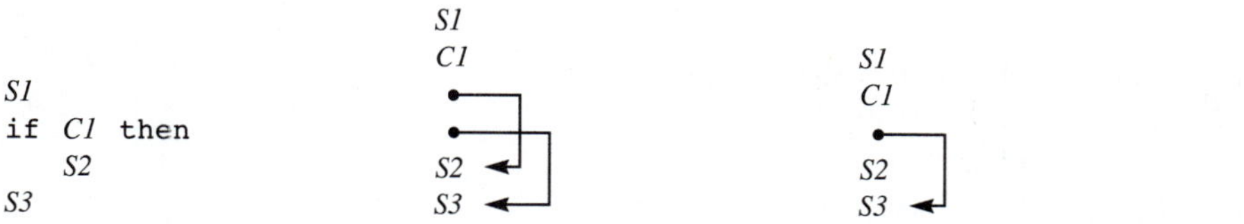

(a) The structure at Level 6.

(b) The structure at Level 5 for Program 15.1.

(c) Another possible structure at Level 5.

Figure 15.1

The `if/then` statement at Level 6 and Level 5.

The compiler in this program had to generate both a `BRN` and a `BR` to translate the `if` statement. Sometimes the compiler can translate an `if` statement with only a conditional branch. For example, the sequence

```
Statement 1
if Number >= 0 then
   Statement 2
Statement 3
```

allows the translation

```
         Statement 1
If:      LOADA   Number,d
         BRN     EndIf
Then:    Statement 2
EndIf:   Statement 3
```

Figure 15.1(c) shows this structure. If `N` is 0 from the load, the branch will not take place, and Statement 2 will execute.

The `begin/end` pair for delimiting a compound statement has no counterpart in assembly language. The sequence

```
Statement 1
if Number >= 0 then
   begin
   Statement 2
   Statement 3
   end
Statement 4
```

translates to

```
        Statement 1
If:     LOADA    Number,d
        BRN      EndIf
Then:   Statement 2
        Statement 3
EndIf:  Statement 4
```

Optimizing Compilers

You may have noticed an extra load statement that was not strictly required in Program 15.1. You can eliminate the `LOADA` at 0011, since the value of `Number` will still be in the accumulator from the previous load at 0008.

The question is, what would a compiler do? The answer is that it depends on the compiler. A compiler is a program that must be written and debugged. Imagine that you must design a compiler to translate from Pascal to assembly language. When the compiler detects an assignment statement, you program it to generate the following sequence: (a) load accumulator, (b) evaluate expression if necessary, (c) store result to variable. Such a compiler would generate the code of Program 15.1, with the `LOADA` at 0011.

Imagine how difficult your compiler program would be if you wanted it to eliminate the unnecessary load. When your compiler detected an assignment statement, it would not always generate the initial load. Instead, it would analyze the previous instructions generated and remember the content of the accumulator. If it determined that the value in the accumulator was the same as the value that the initial load put there, it would not generate the initial load. In Program 15.1, the compiler would need to remember that the value of `Number` was still in the accumulator from the code generated for the `if` statement.

Purpose of an optimizing compiler

A compiler that expends extra effort to make the object program shorter and faster is called an *optimizing compiler.* You can imagine how much more difficult an optimizing compiler is to design than a nonoptimizing one. Not only are optimizing compilers more difficult to write, they also take longer to compile, because they must analyze the source program in much greater detail.

Advantages and disadvantages of an optimizing compiler

Which is better, an optimizing or a nonoptimizing compiler? That depends on the use to which you put the compiler. If you are developing software, a process that requires many compiles for testing and debugging, then you would want a compiler that translates quickly, that is, a nonoptimizing compiler. If you have a large fixed program that will be executed repeatedly by many users, you would want fast execution of the object program, hence, an optimizing compiler.

Frequently, software is developed and debugged with a nonoptimizing compiler then translated one last time with an optimizing compiler for the users.

Real compilers come in all shades of gray between these two extremes. The examples in this chapter will occasionally present object code that is partially optimized. Most assignment statements, such as the one in Program 15.1, will be presented in nonoptimized form.

Program 15.2

Program 15.2 illustrates the translation of the `if/then/else` statement. The `then` part requires an extra unconditional branch around the `else` body. If the compiler omitted the `BR` at 001D and the input were 127, the output would be `highlow`.

Program 15.2

The `if/then/else` statement at Level 6 and Level 5.

High-Order Language

```
program HighLow (input, output);
   const
      Limit = 100;
   var
      Num: integer;
   begin
   read (Num);
   if Num >= Limit then
      write ('high')
   else
      write ('low')
   end.
```

Assembly Language

```
0000  700005            BR       HighLow
                Limit:  .EQUATE  d#100
0003  0000      Num:    .BLOCK   d#2
                ;
0005  E10003 HighLow:   DECI     Num,d      ;read (Num)
0008  090003 If:        LOADA    Num,d      ;if Num >= Limit then
000B  A00064            COMPA    Limit,i
000E  780020            BRN      Else
0011  D80068 Then:      CHARO    c#/h/,i    ;write ('high')
0014  D80069            CHARO    c#/i/,i
0017  D80067            CHARO    c#/g/,i
001A  D80068            CHARO    c#/h/,i
001D  700029            BR       EndIf      ;else
0020  D8006C Else:      CHARO    c#/l/,i    ;write ('low')
0023  D8006F            CHARO    c#/o/,i
0026  D80077            CHARO    c#/w/,i
0029  00     EndIf:     STOP
002A                    .END
```

Unlike the previous program, the `if` statement in this program does not compare a variable's value with zero. It compares it with another nonzero value using `COMPA`, which stands for *compare accumulator*. `COMPA` subtracts the operand from the accumulator and sets the `NZVC` status bits accordingly. `COMPR` is identical to `SUBR` except that `SUBR` stores the result of the subtraction in register *R* (accumulator or index register), while `COMPR` ignores the result of the subtraction.

This program computes `Num - Limit` and sets the `NZVC` bits. `BRN` tests the `N` bit, which is set if

```
Num - Limit < 0
```

that is, if

```
Num < Limit
```

That is the condition under which the `else` part must execute.

Figure 15.2 shows the structure of the control statements at the two levels. Part (a) shows the Level 6 control statement, and part (b) shows the Level 5 translation for this program. As with the previous program, an alternate structure may be required for the Pep/5 assembler code, depending on the `if` test, as part (c) shows.

Figure 15.2

The `if/then/else` statement at Level 6 and Level 5.

```
S1
if C1 then
    S2
else
    S3
S4
```

(a) The structure at Level 6.

(b) The structure at Level 5 for Program 15.2.

(c) Another possible structure at Level 5.

Some architectures, such as the IBM 370 and VAX families, provide conditional branch instructions for all possible ordinal tests, namely <, <=, >, >=, =, and <>. Compilers for these architectures would never need to generate the more complex control structures of Figures 15.1(b) or 15.2(c). In Program 15.1, they would generate a "branch on positive" instruction to implement the structure of Figure 15.1(c). Such an instruction would branch if the `N` bit were zero.

Program 15.3

Translating a loop requires branches to previous instructions. Program 15.3 shows the translation of a `while` statement. The program echos ASCII input characters to the output using the sentinel technique with `*` as the sentinel. If the input is `Goodbye*`, the output is `Goodbye`.

Program 15.3

The `while` statement at Level 6 and Level 5.

High-Order Language

```
program Echo (input, output);
   var
      Letter: char;
   begin
   read (Letter);
   while Letter <> '*' do
      begin
      write (Letter);
      read (Letter)
      end
   end.
```

Assembly Language

```
0000  700004          BR      Echo
0003  00     Letter:  .BLOCK  d#1
             ;
0004  D10003 Echo:    CHARI   Letter,d   ;read (Letter)
0007  080000          LOADA   h#0000,i
000A  510003 While:   LDBYTA  Letter,d   ;while Letter <> '*'
000D  A0002A          COMPA   c#/*/,i
0010  80001C          BRZ     EndWh
0013  D90003          CHARO   Letter,d   ;write (Letter)
0016  D10003          CHARI   Letter,d   ;read (Letter)
0019  70000A          BR      While
001C  00     EndWh:   STOP
001D                  .END
```

The test for a `while` statement is made with a conditional branch at the top of the loop. This program tests a character value, which is a byte quantity. The load instruction at 0007 clears both bytes in the accumulator, so the most significant byte will be 00 (hex) after the load byte instruction at 000A executes. You must guarantee that the most significant byte is 0, since the compare instruction compares a whole word.

Every `while` loop ends with an unconditional branch to the test at the top of the loop. The branch at 0019 brings control back to the initial test. Figure 15.3 shows the structure of the `while` statement at the two levels. This program does not require the more complex structure of Figure 15.3(c).

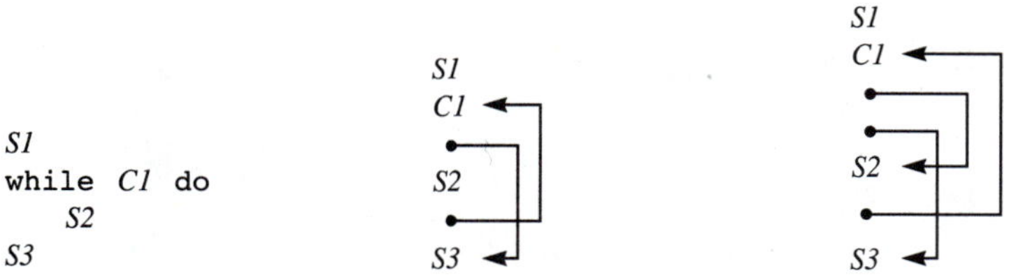

(a) The structure at Level 6. **(b)** The structure at Level 5 for Program 15.3. **(c)** Another possible structure at Level 5.

Figure 15.3

The `while` statement at Level 6 and Level 5.

Program 15.4

A highway patrol officer parks behind a sign. A driver passes by traveling 20 meters per second, which is faster than the speed limit. When the driver is 40 meters down the road, the officer gets his car up to 25 meters per second to pursue the offender. How far from the sign does the officer catch up to the speeder?

Program 15.4 solves the problem by simulation. The values of `Cop` and `Driver` are the positions of the two motorists, initialized to 0 and 40 respectively

Program 15.4

The `repeat` statement at Level 6 and Level 5.

High-Order Language

```
program Catch (output);
   var
      Cop:    integer;
      Driver: integer;
   begin
   Cop := 0;
   Driver := 40;
   repeat
      Cop := Cop + 25;
      Driver := Driver + 20
   until Cop >= Driver;
   write (Cop: 1)
   end.
```

Assembly Language

```
0000  700007          BR      Catch
0003  0000   Cop:     .BLOCK  d#2
0005  0000   Driver:  .BLOCK  d#2
             ;
0007  080000 Catch:   LOADA   d#0,i        ;Cop := 0
000A  110003          STOREA  Cop,d
000D  080028          LOADA   d#40,i       ;Driver := 40
0010  110005          STOREA  Driver,d
0013  090003 Repeat:  LOADA   Cop,d        ;Cop := Cop + 25
0016  180019          ADDA    d#25,i
0019  110003          STOREA  Cop,d
001C  090005          LOADA   Driver,d     ;Driver := Driver + 20
001F  180014          ADDA    d#20,i
0022  110005          STOREA  Driver,d
0025  090003 Until:   LOADA   Cop,d        ;until Cop >= Driver
0028  A10005          COMPA   Driver,d
002B  780013          BRN     Repeat
002E  E90003          DECO    Cop,d        ;write (Cop)
0031  00              STOP
0032                  .END
```

Each execution of the `repeat` loop represents one second of elapsed time, during which the officer travels 25 meters and the driver 20, until the officer catches the driver.

A `repeat` statement has its test at the bottom of the loop. In this program, the compiler translates the `until` test to the sequence, `LOADA`, `COMPA`, `BRN`. `BRN` executes the branch if `N` is set to 1. Since `COMPA` computes the difference, `Cop - Driver`, `N` will be 1 if

```
Cop - Driver < 0
```

that is, if

```
Cop < Driver
```

That is the condition under which the loop should repeat.

Figure 15.4 shows the structure of the `repeat` statement at Levels 6 and 5. A more complex structure at Level 5, not shown in the figure but analogous to the structures of the previous programs, may be necessary for translation to Pep/5 object code.

```
S1
repeat
   S2
until C1
S3
```

(a) The structure at Level 6.

```
S1
S2 <-+
C1   |
 •---+
S3
```

(b) The structure at Level 5 for Program 15.4.

Figure 15.4

The `repeat` statement at Level 6 and Level 5.

Program 15.5

`for` statements are similar to `while` statements in that the test is at the top of the loop. The compiler must generate code to initialize and to increment the control variable. Program 15.5 shows two ways that two different compilers might generate code for the `for` statement. In both versions, the body of the loop executes exactly the same way. The difference is the value the control variable has after the loop terminates. Since different compilers use different code-generation techniques with the `for` statement, you should always treat the value of the control variable as undefined after the loop terminates.

The first version translates the `for` statement into the following sequence:

One version of the for statement at Level 5

- Initialize the control variable.
- Test the control variable.
- Execute the loop body.
- Increment the control variable.
- Branch to the test.

The test compares the value of the control variable with its upper bound. If the control variable is less than or equal to its upper bound, the body executes.

Program 15.5

The `for` statement at Level 6 and Level 5.

High-Order Language

```
program TestFor (output);
   var
      I: integer;
   begin
   for I := 1 to 3 do
      writeln ('I = ', I: 1);
   writeln ('I = ', I: 1)
   end.
```

Assembly Language—Version 1

```
0000  700005           BR      TestFor
0003  0000   I:        .BLOCK  d#2
             LineFeed:.EQUATE h#000A
             ;
0005  080001 TestFor: LOADA   d#1,i       ;initialize I := 1
0008  110003           STOREA  I,d
000B  A00003 For:      COMPA   d#3,i       ;test for I <= 3
000E  980014           BRNZ    Body
0011  700032           BR      EndFor
0014  D80049 Body:     CHARO   c#/I/,i     ;writeln ('I = ', I: 1)
0017  D80020           CHARO   c#/ /,i
001A  D8003D           CHARO   c#/=/,i
001D  D80020           CHARO   c#/ /,i
0020  E90003           DECO    I,d
0023  D8000A           CHARO   LineFeed,i
0026  090003           LOADA   I,d         ;increment I := I + 1
0029  180001           ADDA    d#1,i
002C  110003           STOREA  I,d
002F  70000B           BR      For
0032  D80049 EndFor:   CHARO   c#/I/,i     ;writeln ('I = ', I: 1)
0035  D80020           CHARO   c#/ /,i
0038  D8003D           CHARO   c#/=/,i
003B  D80020           CHARO   c#/ /,i
003E  E90003           DECO    I,d
0041  D8000A           CHARO   LineFeed,i
0044  00               STOP
0045                   .END
```

Output

```
I = 1
I = 2
I = 3
I = 4
```

Assembly Language—Version 2

Program 15.5, continued

```
0000  700005           BR       TestFor
0003  0000    I:       .BLOCK   d#2
              LineFeed:.EQUATE  h#000A
              ;
0005  080000  TestFor: LOADA    d#0,i        ;initialize I := 0
0008  110003           STOREA   I,d
000B  A00003  For:     COMPA    d#3,i        ;test for I < 3
000E  780014           BRN      Incr
0011  700032           BR       EndFor
0014  090003  Incr:    LOADA    I,d          ;increment I := I + 1
0017  180001           ADDA     d#1,i
001A  110003           STOREA   I,d
001D  D80049  Body:    CHARO    c#/I/,i      ;writeln ('I = ', I: 1)
0020  D80020           CHARO    c#/ /,i
0023  D8003D           CHARO    c#/=/,i
0026  D80020           CHARO    c#/ /,i
0029  E90003           DECO     I,d
002C  D8000A           CHARO    LineFeed,i
002F  70000B           BR       For
0032  D80049  EndFor:  CHARO    c#/I/,i      ;writeln ('I = ', I: 1)
0035  D80020           CHARO    c#/ /,i
0038  D8003D           CHARO    c#/=/,i
003B  D80020           CHARO    c#/ /,i
003E  E90003           DECO     I,d
0041  D8000A           CHARO    LineFeed,i
0044  00               STOP
0045                   .END
```

Output

```
I = 1
I = 2
I = 3
I = 3
```

In this program, `COMPA` computes the difference, `I - 3`. `BRNZ` branches to the body if `N` or `Z` is 1, that is, if

```
I - 3 <= 0
```

or, equivalently,

```
I <= 3
```

The body executes once each for `I` having the values 1, 2, and 3. The last time through the loop, `I` increments to 4, which is the value written by the output statement following the loop.

Another version of the for statement at Level 5

The second version translates the `for` statement into the following sequence:

- Initialize the control variable.
- Test the control variable.
- Increment the control variable.
- Execute the loop body.
- Branch to the test.

Since the increment step precedes the body of the loop, the initialization is to a value one less than the initial value in the Pascal code. The test compares the value of the control variable with its upper bound. If the control variable is strictly less than its upper bound, the body executes.

The terminating value of the control variable

Compare the output of this version with the previous version. The control variable has the upper bound value on termination in this version, but one more than the upper bound value in the previous version. The version a compiler chooses depends in part on the architecture of the machine on which the object code will run.

For example, Table 13.4 showed the addressing modes of the VAX architecture, one of which is the autoincrement mode. This mode increments a register automatically when it is used as part of the operand specifier. A compiler might translate a `for` statement into Level 5 instructions, one of which uses this addressing mode to take advantage of the automatic increment of the control variable. A particular machine may not have an autoincrement addressing mode or, even if it does, the compiler may not be designed to take advantage of it.

Standard Pascal does not specify the terminating value of the control variable, so compiler writers can choose a translation that is the most convenient for the machine that will execute the object code. You cannot know how your compiler treats the terminating value without experimentation. It would be interesting to run the Pascal program of this program with your compiler to discover the terminating value of the control variable.

Program 15.6

At the assembly level, a programmer can write control structures that do not correspond to the control structures in Pascal. For example, you can construct a loop that is neither a `while` loop nor a `repeat` loop. A `while` statement tests for loop termination at the top of the loop, and a `repeat` tests at the bottom. Program 15.6 tests in the middle of the loop.

In fact, this program does exactly the same thing as Program 15.3. It even uses one less instruction, because `CHARI` is not duplicated. Since the original program contains a total of 29 bytes and this contains 26 bytes, the amount of memory required to store the program has been reduced by more than 10%. In a large program, a 10% savings in memory could be substantial.

```
0000  700004          BR      Echo
0003  00      Letter: .BLOCK  d#1
              ;
0004  080000  Echo:   LOADA   h#0000,i
0007  D10003  Loop:   CHARI   Letter,d    ;read (Letter)
000A  510003          LDBYTA  Letter,d    ;compare Letter with '*'
000D  A0002A          COMPA   c#/*/,i
0010  800019          BRZ     Exit        ;exit loop if '*'
0013  D90003          CHARO   Letter,d    ;write (Letter)
0016  700007          BR      Loop
0019  00      Exit:   STOP
001A                  .END
```

Program 15.6

A loop at Level 5 that cannot be written directly in Pascal.

Advantages and disadvantages of programming at Level 5

This is a general phenomenon. Assembly language programs generated by a compiler, such as the one in Program 15.3, are usually longer than programs written by humans directly in assembly language. Not only that, but they often execute slower as well, although in this particular case both programs execute equally fast. If human programmers can write shorter, faster assembly language programs than compilers, why does anyone program in a high-order language?

One reason is the ability of the compiler to perform type checking, as mentioned in the previous chapter. Another is the additional burden of responsibility that is placed on the programmer when given the freedom of using primitive branching instructions. If you are not careful when you write programs at Level 5, the branching instructions can get way out of hand, as the next program shows.

Program 15.7

Program 15.7 is an extreme example of the problem that can occur with unbridled use of primitive branching instructions. It is difficult to understand because of its lack of comments and indentation and its inconsistent branching style. Actually the program performs a very simple task. Can you discover what it does?

The body of an `if` statement or a loop in Pascal is a block of statements, sometimes contained in a compound statement delimited by a `begin/end` pair. Additional `if` statements and loops can be nested entirely within these blocks. Figure 15.5(a) pictures this situation schematically. A flow of control that is limited to nestings of the `if/then/else`, `case`, `while`, `repeat`, and `for` statements is called *structured flow of control*.

The branches in the mystery program do not correspond to the structured control constructs of Pascal. Although the program's logic is correct for performing its intended task, it is difficult to decipher because the branching statements branch all over the place. This kind of program is called *spaghetti code*. If you draw an arrow from each branch statement to the statement to which it branches, the picture looks rather like a bowl of spaghetti, as shown in Figure 15.5(b).

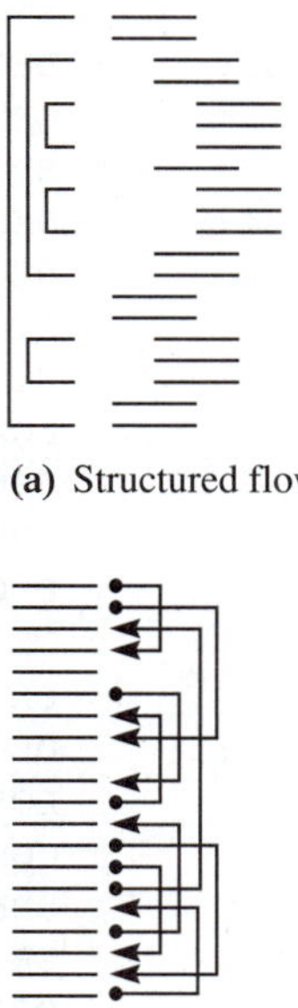

(a) Structured flow.

(b) Spaghetti code.

Figure 15.5

Two different styles of flow of control.

Program 15.7

A mystery program.

```
0000  700009           BR      Mystery
0003  0000   N1:       .BLOCK  d#2
0005  0000   N2:       .BLOCK  d#2
0007  0000   N3:       .BLOCK  d#2
             ;
0009  E10005 Mystery:  DECI    N2,d
000C  E10007           DECI    N3,d
000F  090005           LOADA   N2,d
0012  A10007           COMPA   N3,d
0015  78002A           BRN     L1
0018  E10003           DECI    N1,d
001B  090003           LOADA   N1,d
001E  A10007           COMPA   N3,d
0021  780074           BRN     L7
0024  700065           BR      L6
0027  110007           STOREA  N3,d
002A  E10003 L1:       DECI    N1,d
002D  090005           LOADA   N2,d
0030  A10003           COMPA   N1,d
0033  780053           BRN     L5
0036  E90003           DECO    N1,d
0039  E90005           DECO    N2,d
003C  E90007 L2:       DECO    N3,d
003F  00               STOP
0040  E90005 L3:       DECO    N2,d
0043  E90007           DECO    N3,d
0046  700081           BR      L9
0049  E90003 L4:       DECO    N1,d
004C  E90005           DECO    N2,d
004F  00               STOP
0050  110003           STOREA  N1,d
0053  090007 L5:       LOADA   N3,d
0056  A10003           COMPA   N1,d
0059  780040           BRN     L3
005C  E90005           DECO    N2,d
005F  E90003           DECO    N1,d
0062  70003C           BR      L2
0065  E90007 L6:       DECO    N3,d
0068  090003           LOADA   N1,d
006B  A10005           COMPA   N2,d
006E  780049           BRN     L4
0071  70007E           BR      L8
0074  E90003 L7:       DECO    N1,d
0077  E90007           DECO    N3,d
007A  E90005           DECO    N2,d
007D  00               STOP
007E  E90005 L8:       DECO    N2,d
0081  E90003 L9:       DECO    N1,d
0084  00               STOP
0085                   .END
```

It is often possible to write efficient programs with unstructured branches. Such programs execute faster and require less memory for storage than if they were written in a high-order language with structured flow of control. Some specialized applications require this extra measure of efficiency and are therefore written directly in assembly language.

Balanced against this savings in execution time and memory space is difficulty in comprehension. When programs are hard to understand they are hard to write, debug, and modify. The problem is economic. Writing, debugging, and modifying are all human activities, which are labor intensive. They are, therefore, expensive. The question you must ask is whether the extra efficiency justifies the additional expense.

Flow of Control in Early Languages

Computers had been around for many years before structured flow of control was discovered. In the early days there were no high-order languages. Everyone programmed in assembly language. Computer memories were expensive, and CPUs were slow by today's standards. Efficiency was all-important. Since a large body of software had not yet been generated, the problem of program maintenance was not appreciated.

The first widespread high-order language was FORTRAN, developed in the 1950s. Since people were used to dealing with branch instructions, they included them in the language. An unconditional branch in FORTRAN is

```
GOTO 260
```

where 260 is the statement number of another statement. It is called a *goto statement*. A conditional branch is

The goto statement in Level 6 languages

```
IF (NUMBER .GE. 100) GOTO 500
```

where `.GE.` means "is greater than or equal to." This statement compares the value of variable `NUMBER` with 100. If it is greater than or equal to 100, the next statement executed is the one with a statement number of 500. Otherwise the statement after the `IF` is executed.

FORTRAN'S conditional `IF` is a big improvement over Level 5 branch instructions. It does not require a separate compare instruction to set the status bits. But notice how the flow of control is similar to Level 5 branching: If the test is true, do the `GOTO`. Otherwise continue to the next statement.

As people developed more software, they noticed that it would be convenient to group statements into blocks for use in `if` statements and loops. The most notable language to make this advance was ALGOL-60, developed in 1960. It was the first widespread block-structured language, although its popularity was confined mainly to Europe.

The Structured Programming Theorem

This section has shown how high-level structured control statements translate into primitive branch statements at a lower level. It also has shown how you can write branches at the lower level that do not correspond to the structured constructs. That raises an interesting and practical question: Is it possible to write an algorithm with goto statements that will perform some processing that is impossible to perform with structured constructs? That is, if you limit yourself to structured flow of control, are there some problems you will not be able to solve that you could solve if unstructured goto's were allowed?

Corrado Bohm and Guiseppe Jacopini answered this important question in a computer science journal article in 1966.[1] They proved mathematically that any algorithm containing goto's, no matter how complicated or unstructured, can be written with only nested `if` statements and `while` loops. Their result is called the *structured programming theorem.*

The structured programming theorem

Bohm's and Jacopini's paper was highly theoretical. It did not attract much attention at first because programmers generally had no desire to limit their freedom with goto statements. Bohm and Jacopini showed what could be done with nested `if` statements and `while` loops, but left unanswered why programmers would want to limit themselves that way.

People experimented with the concept anyway. They would take an algorithm in spaghetti code and try to rewrite it using structured flow of control without goto statements. Usually the new program was much clearer than the original. Occasionally it was even more efficient.

The Goto Controversy

Two years after Bohm and Jacopini's paper appeared, Edsger W. Dijkstra of the Technological University at Eindhoven, the Netherlands, wrote a letter to the editor of the same journal in which he stated his personal observation that good programmers used fewer goto's than poor programmers.[2] In his opinion, a high density of goto's in a program indicated poor quality. He stated in part:

An excerpt from Dijkstra's famous letter

> For a number of years I have been familiar with the observation that the quality of programmers is a decreasing function of the density of goto statements in the programs they produce. More recently I discovered why the use of the goto statement has such disastrous effects, and I became convinced that the goto statement should be abolished from all "higher level" programming languages

1. Corrado Bohm and Guiseppe Jacopini, "Flow-diagrams, Turing Machines and Languages with Only Two Formation Rules," *Communications of the ACM* 9 (May 1966): 366–71.
2. Edsger W. Dijkstra, "Goto Statement Considered Harmful," *Communications of the ACM* 11 (March 1968): 147–48. Reprinted by permission.

> (i.e., everything except, perhaps, plain machine code). . . . The goto statement as it stands is just too primitive; it is too much an invitation to make a mess of one's program.

To justify these statements, Dijkstra developed the idea of a set of coordinates that are necessary to describe the progress of the program. When a human tries to understand a program, he must maintain this set of coordinates mentally, perhaps unconsciously. Dijkstra showed that the coordinates to be maintained with structured flow of control were vastly simpler than those with unstructured goto's. Thus he was able to pinpoint the reason that structured flow of control is easier to understand.

Dijkstra acknowledged that the idea of eliminating goto's was not new. He mentioned several people who influenced him on the subject, one of whom was Niklaus Wirth, who had worked on the ALGOL-60 language.

Dijkstra's letter set off a storm of protest, now known as the famous *goto controversy.* To theoretically be able to program without goto was one thing. But to advocate that goto be abolished from high-order languages such as FORTRAN was altogether something else.

The impact of the goto controversy

Old ideas die hard. However, the controversy has died down and it is now generally recognized that Dijkstra was, in fact, correct. The reason is cost. When software managers began to apply the structured flow of control discipline, along with other structured design concepts, they found the resulting software was much less expensive to develop, debug, and maintain. It was usually well worth the additional memory requirements and extra execution time.

FORTRAN 77 is a more recent version of FORTRAN standardized in 1977. The goto controversy influenced its design. It contains a block style `IF` statement with an `ELSE` part similar to Pascal. For example,

```
IF (NUMBER .GE. 100) THEN
   Statement 1
ELSE
   Statement 2
ENDIF
```

You can write the `IF` statement in FORTRAN 77 without goto.

Niklaus Wirth designed Pascal from the beginning to take full advantage of the structured flow of control concept. He included the goto statement for those rare occasions where efficiency might demand it. None of the Pascal programs in this book, however, use the goto statement. Modula-2, a newer Level 6 language also designed by Wirth, has no goto statement.

One point to bear in mind is that the absence of goto's in a program does not guarantee that the program is well structured. It is possible to write a program with three or four nested `if` statements and `while` loops when only one or two are necessary. Also, if a language at any level contains only goto statements to alter the flow of control, they can always be used in a structured way to implement `if` statements and `while` loops. That is precisely what a Pascal compiler does when it translates a program from Level 6 to Level 5.

15.2 Stack-Relative Addressing and Procedure Calls

A Pascal procedure call changes the flow of control to the first executable statement in the procedure. At the end of the procedure, control returns to the statement following the procedure call. In assembly language, the code that corresponds to a procedure or function body is a *subroutine*. The compiler implements procedure calls with `JSR`, which stands for *jump to subroutine*. It implements the return to the calling statement with `RTS`, which stands for *return from subroutine*.

The `JSR` instruction pushes the content of the program counter onto the run-time stack, then loads the operand into the program counter. One implementation of a stack is with an array and an integer variable that points to the top of the stack. In the Pep/5 run-time stack, main memory corresponds to the array and the stack pointer corresponds to the integer that points to the top of the stack. The CPU implements `JSR` accordingly as

The JSR instruction

```
SP := SP - 2;
Mem [SP] := PC;
PC := Oprnd
```

In effect, the return address for the procedure call is pushed onto the stack and a branch to the procedure is executed.

The operation of `JSR` crucially depends on the von Neumann execution cycle of fetch, increment, execute, repeat. The three-step sequence just presented is the execute part of `JSR`. Since the program counter increments before the execute part, the value of the program counter that is saved on the stack is the address of the instruction immediately following the `JSR`. Notice that the CPU implements the branch by replacing the content of the program counter after saving its old value on the stack.

As with the branch instructions, `JSR` usually executes in the immediate addressing mode, in which case the operand is the operand specifier. If you do not specify the addressing mode, the Pep/5 assembler will assume immediate addressing.

The `RTS` instruction pops the return address off the stack into the program counter.

The RTS instruction

```
PC := Mem [SP]
SP := SP + 2
```

The next instruction to execute, therefore, is the one specified by the address on top of the stack. If that address was put there by a previously executed `JSR` instruction, then the next instruction to execute will be the one immediately following the `JSR`. `RTS` is a unary instruction.

Program 15.8

Program 15.8 shows how a compiler implements a procedure call without parameters. The program outputs three triangles of asterisks.

Program 15.8

A procedure call at Level 6 and Level 5.

High-Order Language

```
program Pattern (output);
   procedure PrintTri;
      begin
      writeln ('*');
      writeln ('**');
      writeln ('***');
      writeln ('****')
      end;
   begin
   PrintTri;
   PrintTri;
   PrintTri
   end.
```

Assembly Language

```
0000  70002E          BR      Pattern
             LineFeed:.EQUATE h#000A
             ;
             ;------- procedure PrintTri -------
0003  D8002A PrintTri:CHARO   c#/*/,i     ;writeln ('*')
0006  D8000A          CHARO   LineFeed,i
0009  D8002A          CHARO   c#/*/,i     ;writeln ('**')
000C  D8002A          CHARO   c#/*/,i
000F  D8000A          CHARO   LineFeed,i
0012  D8002A          CHARO   c#/*/,i     ;writeln ('***')
0015  D8002A          CHARO   c#/*/,i
0018  D8002A          CHARO   c#/*/,i
001B  D8000A          CHARO   LineFeed,i
001E  D8002A          CHARO   c#/*/,i     ;writeln ('****')
0021  D8002A          CHARO   c#/*/,i
0024  D8002A          CHARO   c#/*/,i
0027  D8002A          CHARO   c#/*/,i
002A  D8000A          CHARO   LineFeed,i
002D  C0              RTS
             ;
             ;------- main program -------
002E  B80003 Pattern: JSR     PrintTri    ;PrintTri
0031  B80003          JSR     PrintTri    ;PrintTri
0034  B80003          JSR     PrintTri    ;PrintTri
0037  00              STOP
0038                  .END
```

Chapter 13 described the execute option of the Pep/5 simulator as

```
SP := Mem [0FF8];
PC := 0000
```

where `Mem [0FF8]` contains 0BC1, the machine vector that initializes the stack pointer when you run a program, as shown in Figure 13.15. Consequently, just before the `JSR` at 002E executes, the program counter and stack pointer have the values shown in Figure 15.6(a).

The increment step of the von Neumann execution cycle changes the program counter to 0031. The three steps in the `JSR` instruction,

```
SP := SP - 2;
Mem [SP] := PC;
PC := Oprnd
```

change the stack pointer to 0BBF, put the current value of the program counter in `Mem [0BBF]`, and put the operand, 0003, in the program counter. Figure 15.6(b) shows the result after execution of the first `JSR`. The instruction at 0003, the first instruction of the procedure, executes next.

The last instruction in the procedure, `RTS`, pops the top of the stack, 0031, into the program counter. The next instruction to execute is at 0031, the second instruction in the main program.

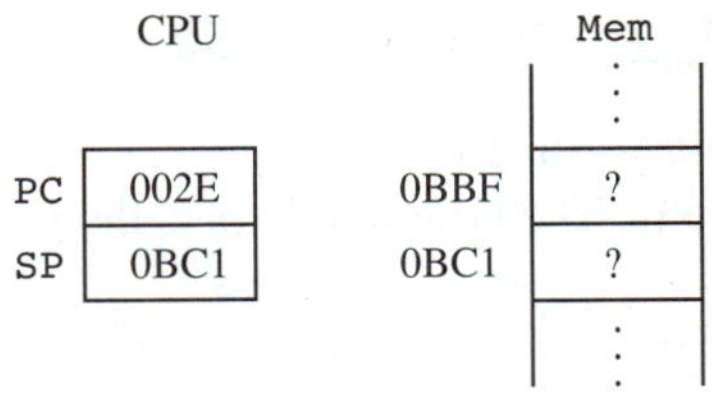

(a) Before execution of the first `JSR`.

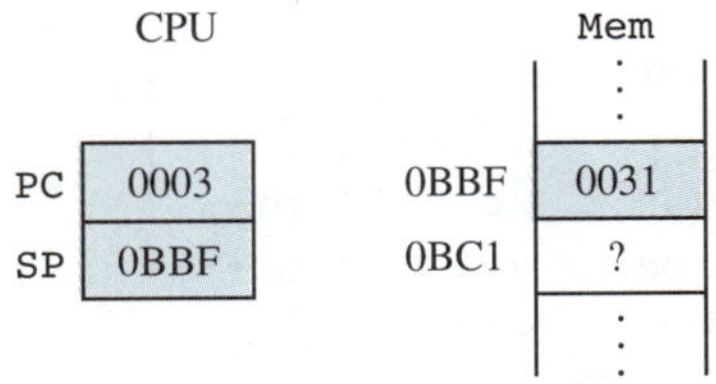

(b) After execution of the first `JSR`.

Figure 15.6

Execution of `JSR` in Program 15.8.

Stack-Relative Addressing

When a program calls a procedure, it allocates storage on the run-time stack for the parameters and the return address. Then the procedure allocates storage for its local variables. Stack-relative addressing allows the procedure to access the information that was pushed onto the stack.

The relationship between the operand and the operand specifier in stack-relative addressing

In *stack-relative addressing,* the relationship between the operand and the operand specifier is

```
Oprnd = Mem [SP + OprndSpec]
```

The stack pointer acts as a memory address to which the operand specifier is added.

You can think of the operand specifier as the offset from the top of the stack. If the operand specifier is 0, the instruction accesses `Mem [SP]`, the value on top of the stack. If the operand specifier is 2, it accesses `Mem [SP + 2]`, the value two bytes below the top of the stack.

The ADDSP and SUBSP instructions

The Pep/5 instruction set has two instructions for manipulating the stack pointer directly, `ADDSP` and `SUBSP`, both of which are restricted to the immediate addressing mode. (`JSR` and `RTS` manipulate the stack pointer indirectly.) `ADDSP` adds a value to the stack pointer, and `SUBSP` subtracts a value. Figure 13.15

showed the user stack growing toward low addresses. Therefore, to allocate storage on the stack you subtract a positive value with `SUBSP`, and to deallocate storage you add with `ADDSP`.

Program 15.9

Program 15.9 shows how to push data onto the stack, access it with stack-relative addressing, and pop it off the stack. The program pushes the string 'real' onto the stack, then accesses the three characters 'e', 'a', and 'r' and, finally, deallocates 'real'.

Figure 15.7(a) shows the values in the stack pointer and main memory before the program executes. As in the previous program, the machine initializes the stack pointer to 0BC1 from the vector at `Mem [0FF8]`.

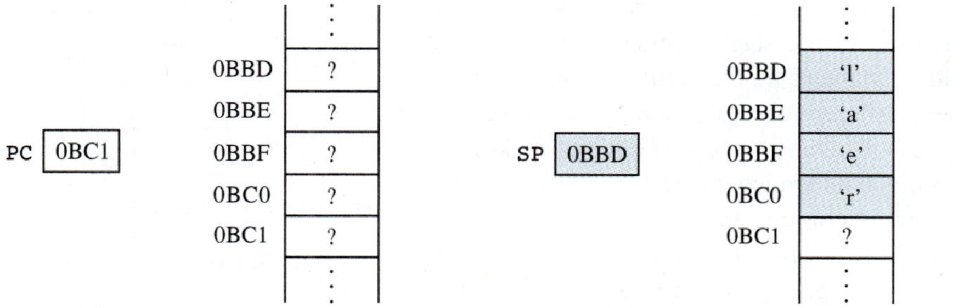

(a) Before the program executes. (b) After `SUBSP` executes.

Figure 15.7

Pushing 'real' onto the stack in Program 15.9.

Program 15.9

Stack-relative addressing.

```
0000  080072 LOADA   c#/r/,i    ;put 'r' on stack
0003  5BFFFF STBYTA  d#-1,s
0006  080065 LOADA   c#/e/,i    ;put 'e' on stack
0009  5BFFFE STBYTA  d#-2,s
000C  080061 LOADA   c#/a/,i    ;put 'a' on stack
000F  5BFFFD STBYTA  d#-3,s
0012  08006C LOADA   c#/l/,i    ;put 'l' on stack
0015  5BFFFC STBYTA  d#-4,s
0018  B00004 SUBSP   d#4,i      ;push 'real'
001B  DB0002 CHARO   d#2,s      ;output 'e'
001E  DB0001 CHARO   d#1,s      ;output 'a'
0021  DB0003 CHARO   d#3,s      ;output 'r'
0024  A80004 ADDSP   d#4,i      ;pop 'real'
0027  00     STOP
0028         .END
```

Output

```
ear
```

The first two instructions,

```
LOADA   c#/r/,i
STBYTA  d#-1,s
```

put an ASCII 'r' character just above the top of the stack. LOADA puts the 'r' byte in the right half of the accumulator, and STBYTA puts it above the stack. The store instruction uses stack-relative addressing with an operand specifier of –1 (dec) = FFFF (hex). Since the stack pointer has the value 0BC1, the 'r' is stored at `Mem [0BC1 + FFFF] = Mem [0BC0]`.

The next six instructions put 'e', 'a', and 'l' at `Mem [0BBF]`, `Mem [0BBE]`, and `Mem [0BBD]` respectively. The SUBSP instruction subtracts 4 from the stack pointer, as shown in Figure 15.7(b). That completes the push operation.

Tracing a program that uses stack-relative addressing does not require you to know the absolute value in the stack pointer. The push operation would work the same if the stack pointer were initialized to some other value, say 0A18. In that case, 'r', 'e', 'a', and 'l' would be at `Mem [0A17]`, `Mem [0A16]`, `Mem [0A15]`, and `Mem [0A14]` respectively, and the stack pointer would wind up with a value of 0A14. The values would be at the same locations relative to the top of the stack, even though they would be at different absolute memory locations.

Figure 15.8 is a more convenient way of tracing the operation and makes use of the fact that the value in the stack pointer is irrelevant. Rather than show the value in the stack pointer, it shows an arrow pointing to the memory cell whose address is contained in the stack pointer. Rather than show the address of the cells in memory, it shows their offsets from the stack pointer. Figures depicting the state of the run-time stack will use this drawing convention from now on.

Note that the stack-relative address of 'r' before SUBSP executes is –1, but its address after SUBSP executes is 3. Its stack relative address is different because the stack pointer has changed. Both instructions

```
STBYTA  d#-1,s
```

and

```
CHARO   d#3,s
```

access the same memory cell.

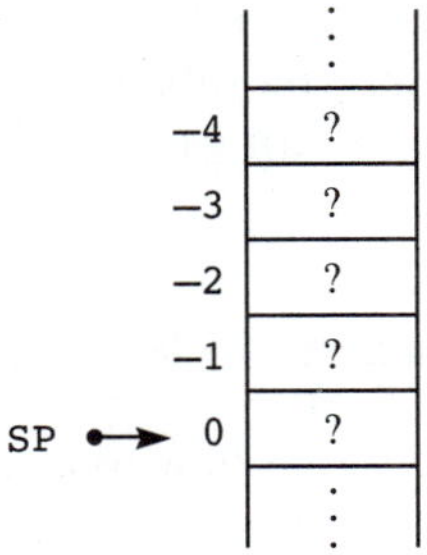

(a) Before the program executes.

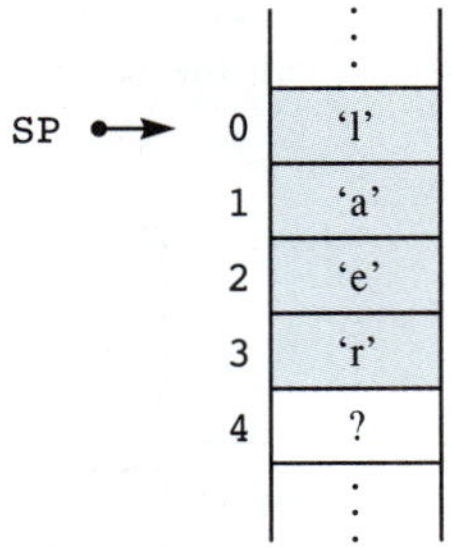

(b) After SUBSP executes.

Figure 15.8

A simplified diagram of the stack in Program 15.7.

Program 15.10

The allocation process when you call a procedure is

- Push the actual parameters.
- Push the return address.
- Push storage for the local variables.

At the high-order language level, the instructions that perform these operations on the stack are hidden. The programmer simply writes the procedure call, and during execution the stack allocation occurs automatically.

At the assembly level, however, the translated program must contain explicit instructions for the allocation. Program 15.10 (pp. 748–49) shows a Level 6 program that prints a bar chart, and the program's corresponding Level 5 translation. It shows the Level 5 statements, not explicit at Level 6, that are required to push the parameters and local variables.

The calling routine is responsible for pushing the actual parameters and executing `JSR`, which pushes the return address onto the stack. The called routine is responsible for allocating storage on the stack for the local variables. After the called routine executes, it must deallocate the storage for the local variables, then pop the return address by executing `RTS`. Before the calling routine can continue, it must deallocate the storage for the actual parameters.

In summary, the calling and called routines do the following:

The calling sequence for a procedure

- Calling pushes actual parameters.
- Calling executes `JSR`.
- Called allocates local variables.
- Called executes its body.
- Called deallocates local variables.
- Called executes `RTS`.
- Calling pops actual parameters.

Note the symmetry of the operations. The last three operations undo the first three operations in reverse order. That order is a consequence of the last in, first out property of the stack.

The variables in the Level 6 main program—`NumPts`, `Value`, and `I`—correspond to the identical Level 5 symbols, whose symbol values are 0003, 0005, and 0007 respectively. These are the addresses of the memory cells that will hold the run-time values of the variables.

What do the formal parameter, `N`, and the local variable, `J`, correspond to at Level 5? Not absolute addresses, but stack-relative addresses. The procedure defines them with

```
N: .EQUATE d#4
J: .EQUATE d#0
```

Remember that `.EQUATE` does not generate object code. The assembler does not reserve storage for them at translation time. Instead, storage for `N` and `J` is allocated on the stack at run time. The decimal numbers 4 and 0 are the stack offsets appropriate for `N` and `J` during execution of the procedure. The procedure refers to them with stack-relative addressing.

The statements that correspond to the procedure call in the calling routine are

```
LOADA   Value,d     ;call by value
STOREA  d#-2,s
SUBSP   d#2,i       ;push parameter
JSR     PrintBar    ;push RetAddr
ADDSP   d#2,i       ;pop parameter
```

Program 15.10

A procedure call with a parameter at Level 6 and Level 5.

High-Order Language

```
program BarChart (input, output);
   var
      NumPts: integer;
      Value:  integer;
      I:      integer;

   procedure PrintBar (N: integer);
      var
         J: integer;
      begin
      for J := 1 to N do
         write ('*');
      writeln
      end;

   begin
   read (NumPts);
   for I := 1 to NumPts do
      begin
      read (Value);
      PrintBar (Value)
      end
   end.
```

Input

```
12   3 13 17 34 27 23 25 29 16 10 0 2
```

Output

```
***
*************
*****************
**********************************
***************************
***********************
*************************
*****************************
****************
**********

**
```

Assembly Language

```
0000  700031           BR       BarChart
0003  0000   NumPts:  .BLOCK   d#2
0005  0000   Value:   .BLOCK   d#2
0007  0000   I:       .BLOCK   d#2
             LineFeed:.EQUATE  h#000A
```

Program 15.10, continued

```
                ;
                ;------- procedure PrintBar -------
                N:        .EQUATE d#4        ;formal parameter
                J:        .EQUATE d#0        ;local variable
0009   B00002 PrintBar:SUBSP    d#2,i        ;allocate local
000C   080001           LOADA   d#1,i        ;initialize J := 1
000F   130000           STOREA  J,s
0012   A30004 For1:     COMPA   N,s          ;test for J <= N
0015   98001B           BRNZ    Body1
0018   70002A           BR      EndFor1
001B   D8002A Body1:    CHARO   c#/*/,i      ;write ('*')
001E   0B0000           LOADA   J,s          ;increment J := J + 1
0021   180001           ADDA    d#1,i
0024   130000           STOREA  J,s
0027   700012           BR      For1
002A   D8000A EndFor1:  CHARO   LineFeed,i ;writeln
002D   A80002           ADDSP   d#2,i        ;deallocate local
0030   C0               RTS                  ;pop RetAddr
                ;
                ;------- main program -------
0031   E10003 BarChart:DECI     NumPts,d     ;read (NumPts)
0034   080001           LOADA   d#1,i        ;initialize I := 1
0037   110007           STOREA  I,d
003A   A10003 For2:     COMPA   NumPts,d     ;test for I <= NumPts
003D   980043           BRNZ    Body2
0040   700061           BR      EndFor2
0043   E10005 Body2:    DECI    Value,d      ;read (Value)
0046   090005           LOADA   Value,d      ;call by value
0049   13FFFE           STOREA  d#-2,s
004C   B00002           SUBSP   d#2,i        ;push parameter
004F   B80009           JSR     PrintBar     ;push RetAddr
0052   A80002           ADDSP   d#2,i        ;pop parameter
0055   090007           LOADA   I,d          ;I := I + 1
0058   180001           ADDA    d#1,i
005B   110007           STOREA  I,d
005E   70003A           BR      For2
0061   00     EndFor2:  STOP
0062                    .END
```

Since the parameter is called by value, LOADA uses direct addressing. That puts the run-time value of Value in the accumulator, which STOREA pushes onto the stack. The offset is –2 because Value is a two-byte integer quantity.

The statements that correspond to the procedure call in the called routine are

```
SUBSP    d#2,i        ;allocate local
.
.
.
ADDSP    d#2,i        ;deallocate local
RTS                   ;pop RetAddr
```

`SUBSP` subtracts 2 because the local variable, `J`, is a two-byte integer quantity. Figure 15.9 shows the run-time stack before and after the procedure call.

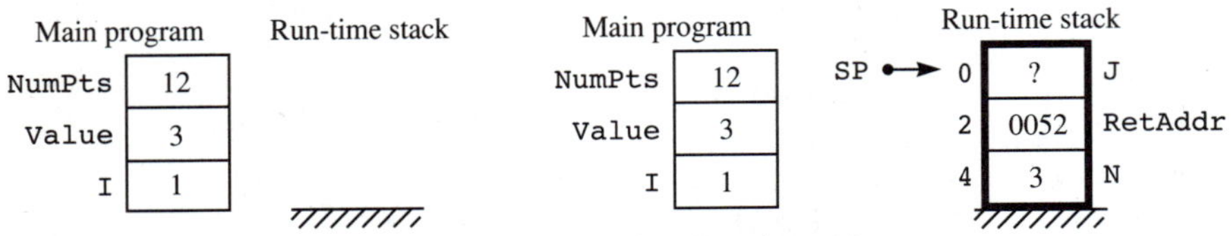

(a) After `read (Value).`

(b) After allocation with `SUBSP` in procedure PrintBar.

Figure 15.9

The run-time stack for Program 15.10.

The stack address of `N` is 4 because both `J` and the return address occupy two bytes on the stack. If there were more local variables, the stack address of `N` would be correspondingly greater. The compiler must compute the stack addresses from the number and size of the quantities on the stack.

Program 15.11

The allocation process when you call a function is

- Push storage for the returned value.
- Push the actual parameters.
- Push the return address.
- Push storage for the local variables.

Allocation for a function call differs from that for a procedure call by the extra value that you must allocate for the returned function value.

Program 15.11 (pp. 752–53) computes the binomial coefficient recursively and is based on Pascal's triangle of coefficients.[3] The recursive definition of the binomial coefficient is

$$b(n, k) = b(n-1, k) + b(n-1, k-1) \qquad \text{for } 0 \le k \le n$$

The basis of the recursion is

$$b(n, 0) = 1$$
$$b(k, k) = 1$$

3. Program 15.11 is identical to Program 9.5 in Volume 1 and the combined edition of this book. You may refer to Figure 9.10 for a complete trace of the run-time stack. Note that Figure 15.10 corresponds to Figure 9.10(g).

The function tests for the basis with an `if` statement, using the OR boolean operator. If neither condition is satisfied, it calls itself recursively twice—once to compute $b(n - 1, k)$ and once to compute $b(n - 1, k - 1)$. Figure 15.10 shows the run-time stack produced by a call from the main program with actual parameters (3, 1). The function is called twice more with parameters (2, 1) and (1, 1), followed by a return. Then a call with parameters (1, 0) is executed, followed by a second return, and so on. Figure 15.10 shows the run-time stack at the assembly level immediately after the second return.

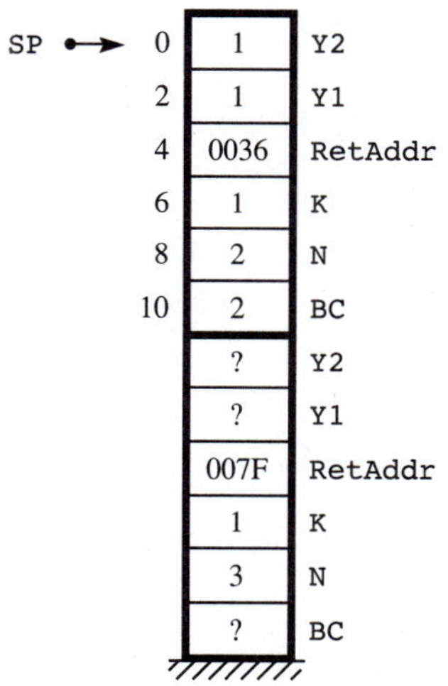

Figure 15.10

The run-time stack of Program 15.11 immediately after the second return.

At the start of the main program when the stack pointer has its initial value, the first actual parameter has a stack offset of –4, and the second has a stack offset of –6. In a procedure call, these offsets would be –2 and –4 respectively. Their magnitudes are greater by 2 because of the two-byte value returned on the stack by the function. The `SUBSP` instruction at 0079 allocates six bytes, two each for the actual parameters and two for the returned value.

When the function returns control to `ADDSP` at 007F, the value it returns will be on the stack below the two actual parameters. `ADDSP` pops the parameters and returned value by adding 6 to the stack pointer, after which it points to the cell directly below the returned value. So `DECO` outputs the value with stack-relative addressing and an offset of –2.

The `if` statement in the function must analyze a compound boolean expression containing the OR operation. If `K` is 0, it branches directly to `Then`, avoiding the test, `N = K`. This is the short-circuit evaluation compiler technique.

The function calls itself by allocating actual parameters according to the standard technique. For the first recursive call, it computes `N - 1` and `K` and pushes those values onto the stack along with storage for the returned value. After the return, the sequence

```
ADDSP   d#6,i       ;pop params and ret val
LOADA   d#-2,s      ;Y1 := ret val
STOREA  Y1,s
```

pops the two actual parameters and returned value and assigns the returned value to `Y1`. For the second call, it pushes `N - 1` and `K - 1` similarly.

Program 15.11

A recursive function at Level 6 and Level 5.

High-Level Language

```
program Binomial (output);

   function BinCoeff (N, K: integer): integer;
      var
         Y1, Y2: integer;
      begin
      if (K = 0) or (N = K) then
         BinCoeff := 1
      else
         begin
         Y1 := BinCoeff (N - 1, K);
         Y2 := BinCoeff (N - 1, K - 1);
         BinCoeff := Y1 + Y2
         end
      end;

   begin
   write (BinCoeff (3, 1): 1)
   end.
```

Assembly Language

```
0000  70006D           BR       Binomial
             ;
             ;------- function BinCoeff -------
             BC:       .EQUATE d#10       ;returned value
             N:        .EQUATE d#8        ;formal parameter
             K:        .EQUATE d#6        ;formal parameter
             Y1:       .EQUATE d#2        ;local variable
             Y2:       .EQUATE d#0        ;local variable
0003  B00004 BinCoeff:SUBSP    d#4,i      ;allocate locals
0006  0B0006 If:       LOADA   K,s        ;if (K = 0)
0009  800018           BRZ     Then
000C  0B0008           LOADA   N,s        ;or (N = K)
000F  A30006           COMPA   K,s
0012  800018           BRZ     Then
0015  700021           BR      Else
0018  080001 Then:     LOADA   d#1,i      ;BinCoeff := 1
001B  13000A           STOREA  BC,s
001E  700069           BR      EndIf
```

Program 15.11, continued

```
0021  0B0008 Else:    LOADA   N,s         ;push N - 1
0024  200001          SUBA    d#1,i
0027  13FFFC          STOREA  d#-4,s
002A  0B0006          LOADA   K,s         ;push K
002D  13FFFA          STOREA  d#-6,s
0030  B00006          SUBSP   d#6,i       ;push params and ret val
0033  B80003          JSR     BinCoeff    ;BinCoeff (N - 1, K)
0036  A80006          ADDSP   d#6,i       ;pop params and ret val
0039  0BFFFE          LOADA   d#-2,s      ;Y1 := ret val
003C  130002          STOREA  Y1,s
003F  0B0008          LOADA   N,s         ;push N - 1
0042  200001          SUBA    d#1,i
0045  13FFFC          STOREA  d#-4,s
0048  0B0006          LOADA   K,s         ;push K - 1
004B  200001          SUBA    d#1,i
004E  13FFFA          STOREA  d#-6,s
0051  B00006          SUBSP   d#6,i       ;push params and ret val
0054  B80003          JSR     BinCoeff    ;BinomCoeff (N - 1, K - 1)
0057  A80006          ADDSP   d#6,i       ;pop params and ret val
005A  0BFFFE          LOADA   d#-2,s      ;Y2 := ret val
005D  130000          STOREA  Y2,s
0060  0B0002          LOADA   Y1,s        ;BinCoeff := Y1 + Y2
0063  1B0000          ADDA    Y2,s
0066  13000A          STOREA  BC,s
0069  A80004 EndIf:   ADDSP   d#4,i       ;pop locals
006C  C0              RTS
             ;
             ;------- main program -------
006D  080003 Binomial:LOADA   d#3,i       ;push 3
0070  13FFFC          STOREA  d#-4,s
0073  080001          LOADA   d#1,i       ;push 1
0076  13FFFA          STOREA  d#-6,s
0079  B00006          SUBSP   d#6,i       ;push params and ret val
007C  B80003          JSR     BinCoeff    ;BinomCoeff (3, 1)
007F  A80006          ADDSP   d#6,i       ;pop params and ret val
0082  EBFFFE          DECO    d#-2,s      ;output ret val
0085  00              STOP
0086                  .END
```

15.3 Indexed Addressing and Arrays

A variable at Level 6 is a memory cell at Level 3. At Level 6, a variable is referred to by its name, at Level 3 by its address. At Level 5, a variable can be referred to by its symbolic name, but the value of that symbol is the address of the cell in memory.

What about an array of values? An array contains many elements, and so consists of many memory cells. The memory cells of the elements are contiguous, that is, they are adjacent to one another. This section will show how to access the individual components of an array.

Program 15.12

The problem that Program 15.12 solves is to write 'A long message.' to the output device. A straightforward, brute force approach would be to write 15 CHARO instructions, one for each character in the message. This approach does not have much appeal for long messages, however.

Program 15.12 stores the message as an array of contiguous characters with .ASCII and appends the message with a null character (eight zeros) to act as a sentinel. It outputs the character with one CHARO in a loop.

Program 15.12

Outputting a string with an impure program at Level 5. This is a bad programming technique.

High-Order Language

```
program StringOut (output);
   begin
   write ('A long message.')
   end.
```

Assembly Language

```
0000  080000           LOADA   d#0,i       ;A := 0
0003  51001C PrntMore:LDBYTA  Msg,d       ;test char
0006  80001B           BRZ     Halt        ;if null then exit
0009  D9001C           CHARO   Msg,d       ;output next char
000C  090004           LOADA   h#0004,d    ;get LDBYTA OprndSpec
000F  180001           ADDA    d#1,i       ;increment it
0012  110004           STOREA  h#0004,d    ;modify LDBYTA OprndSpec
0015  11000A           STOREA  h#000A,d    ;modify CHARO OprndSpec
0018  700003           BR      PrntMore    ;repeat the loop
001B  00     Halt:     STOP
001C  41206C Msg:      .ASCII  /A long message./
      6F6E67
      206D65
      737361
      67652E
002B  00               .BYTE   h#00
002C                   .END
```

If the CHARO uses direct addressing, what should its operand specifier be? It starts with an operand specifier of Msg, which is 001C, the address of the first character in the array. Each time the loop is repeated, the program modifies the operand of the CHARO instruction by adding 1 to it. Although the program listing says that the output instruction is D9001C, which will output the `A`, the program soon modifies the instruction itself to D9001D, which outputs the space.

The program uses the null byte as a sentinel to test for loop termination. It tests for null by loading the character into the accumulator. The operand of `LDBYTA`, therefore, must be incremented along with the operand of `CHARO`. The instructions at 0012 and 0015 perform the modification.

Impure Programs

Program 15.12 illustrates an important property of von Neumann machines. Since programs as well as data are stored in main memory, they can be altered just as data can be altered. When von Neumann machines were invented, many programmers were fascinated by the idea. To write a program that modified itself was considered clever, and the technique was common.

Disadvantages of self-modifying programs

After the novelty wore off, people began to realize that self-modifying programs were difficult to understand. For example, just by looking at the `CHARO` and `LDBYTA` instructions in this program, you cannot tell that eventually they will be modified by the program. Impure programs are especially difficult to decipher when they are large and the modifying part of the program is located far from the instructions it modifies.

Programs that modify themselves are called *impure,* while programs that do not are called *pure*. Impure programs are now widely regarded as inferior to pure programs, at least when they are written at the assembly level. A notable exception to this general philosophy is the LISP language. LISP is a high-order language, whose self-modifying capability is recognized as a powerful feature for solving problems in artificial intelligence. Indexed addressing will let us write a pure program to output the long message.

Indexed Addressing

Here is a summary of the relationship between the operand specifier and the operand for each addressing mode:

The relationship between the operand and the operand specifier for all the addressing modes

- Immediate addressing:
  `Oprnd = OprndSpec`
- Direct addressing:
  `Oprnd = Mem [OprndSpec]`
- Indexed addressing:
  ```
  if byte instruction then
     Oprnd = Mem [B + X + OprndSpec]
  else
     Oprnd = Mem [B + 2*X + OprndSpec]
  ```
- Stack-relative addressing:
  `Oprnd = Mem [SP + OprndSpec]`

Indexed addressing is commonly used for accessing the elements of an array. The operand depends on whether the instruction is accessing an array of bytes or an array of words. Of the 32 instructions in the Pep/5 instruction set, only `LDBYTR`, `STBYTR`, `CHARI`, and `CHARO` are byte instructions. The rest are word instructions.

Regardless of whether the instruction is a byte or word instruction, an element of an array is accessed, and the values of both the base register and the index register affect the calculation of the operand. For byte instructions, the operand is in the memory cell whose address is the sum of the base register, index register, and operand specifier. For word instructions, its address is the sum of the base register, twice the index register, and the operand specifier.

The idea is that the index register will contain the index of the array. Instead of modifying the operand specifier, as the previous impure program did, you can leave the operand specifier unchanged and modify the index register instead.

Program 15.13

Program 15.13 outputs 'A long message.' without modifying itself. The `CHARO` and `LDBYTA` instructions use indexed addressing. To conserve space, the listings for this program and the rest that follow show only the first three ASCII characters in the object code.

Program 15.13

Outputting a string at Level 6 and Level 5 without an impure program.

High-Order Language

```
program StringOut (output);
   begin
   write ('A long message.')
   end.
```

Assembly Language

```
0000  600000           LOADB   d#0,i      ;B := 0
0003  0C0000           LOADX   d#0,i      ;X := 0
0006  080000           LOADA   d#0,i      ;A := 0
0009  520019 PrntMore:LDBYTA   Msg,x      ;test Mem [Msg + X]
000C  800018           BRZ     Halt       ;if null then exit
000F  DA0019           CHARO   Msg,x      ;output next char
0012  1C0001           ADDX    d#1,i      ;X := X + 1
0015  700009           BR      PrntMore   ;repeat the loop
0018  00     Halt:     STOP
0019  41206C Msg:      .ASCII  /A long message./
0028  00               .BYTE   h#00
0029                   .END
```

Edsger Dijkstra

Every field of human endeavor has its leading contributors who are acclaimed for their theoretical insights, extensions of fundamental ideas, or innovative changes that redefined the subject. Just as Beethoven, Shubert, Mozart, and Hayden ring true in the world of classical music, while the Beatles, Rolling Stones, and the Who stand out in rock 'n' roll, Edsger Dijkstra has a place reserved for him in the computer language hall of fame.

Born to a Dutch chemist in Rotterdam in 1930, Dijkstra grew up with a formalist predilection toward the world. While studying at the University of Leiden in the Netherlands, Dijkstra planned to take up physics as his career. But his father heard about a summer course on computing in Cambridge, England, and Dijkstra jumped aboard the computing bandwagon just as it was gathering speed around 1950. He has been a leading contributor to the programming language field ever since.

One of Dijkstra's most famous contributions to programming was his strong advocacy of structured programming principles. Dijkstra observed that programs written with goto statements often turned into a rat's nest of jumping back and forth among disorganized, ad hoc sections of programs, making the programs difficult to understand even for the authors—not to mention the colleagues who might be asked later to maintain the program. Dijkstra argued that the goto was not the be-all and end-all of control structures, and he strongly encouraged the use of iterative, or looping, constructs that clearly bracket the scope of branching in a program and effectively self-document the program. By adhering to these structured programming principles, Dijkstra claimed that programs would be far easier to understand and maintain and would be less likely to contain errors.

Beyond his clear theoretical contributions, Dijkstra is an interesting character in the computing world. He has developed a reputation for speaking his mind, often in inflammatory or dramatic ways that most of us couldn't get away with. For example, Dijkstra once remarked that "the use of COBOL cripples the mind; its teaching should therefore be regarded as a criminal offence." Not one to single out only one language for his criticism, he also said that "it is practically impossible to teach good programming to students that have had a prior exposure to BASIC; as potential programmers they are mentally mutilated beyond hope of regeneration." Some people find his message cogent and feel that his manner is politically necessary to make his point. Others, aware of the historical development of languages and the contexts in which they were designed, appreciate his message but find his manner a bit strident.

Besides his work in language design, Dijkstra is also noted for his work in proofs of program correctness. The field of program correctness is an application of mathematics to computer programming. Researchers are trying to construct a language and proof technique that might be used to certify unconditionally that a program will perform according to its specifications—entirely free of bugs. Needless to say, whether your application is customer billing or flight control systems, this would be an extremely valuable claim to make about a program.

In 1972 the Association for Computing Machinery acknowledged Dijkstra's rich contributions to the field by awarding him the distinguished Turing Award.

The first two instructions clear the base and index registers to 0. When

```
LDBYTA  Msg,x
```

executes, the operand is calculated as

Oprnd = Mem [B + X + OprndSpec]
= Mem [0 + 0 + 0019]
= Mem [0019]

The byte at 0019 is sent to the accumulator, and the NZVC bits are set accordingly. Similarly, LOADA sends the same byte to the output device, which interprets the byte as a character and writes it.

Then ADDX increments the index register to 1. So the next time LOADA executes, the operand is

Oprnd = Mem [B + X + OprndSpec]
= Mem [0 + 1 + 0019]
= Mem [001A]

The byte at 001A is sent to the accumulator for testing and then to the output device.

Each time around the loop, the index register is one greater than its previous value, and the next byte in the ASCII array is tested and output. When the index register contains 15 (dec), the null byte is tested and the loop terminates.

Program 15.14

Program 15.14 shows an array of integers at Level 6, and the corresponding program at Level 5. If the starting index of the array is 0, the base register should contain 0 when accessing an element of the array.

Program 15.14

Accessing an array whose starting index is 0 at Level 6 and Level 5.

High-Level Language

```
program Reverse (input, output);
   var
      I: integer;
      V: array [0..3] of integer;
   begin
   for I := 0 to 3 do
      read (V [I]);
   for I := 3 downto 0 do
      begin
      write (I: 1, '  ');
      writeln (V [I]: 1)
      end
   end.
```

Input

Program 15.14, continued

```
558   -32   781   440
```

Output

```
3  440
2  781
1  -32
0  558
```

Assembly Language

```
0000  70000D          BR      Reverse
0003  0000   I:       .BLOCK  d#2
0005  000000 V:       .BLOCK  d#8
      000000
      0000
             LineFeed:.EQUATE h#000A
             ;
000D  600000 Reverse: LOADB   d#0,i        ;B := 0
0010  0C0000          LOADX   d#0,i        ;initialize I := 0
0013  150003          STOREX  I,d
0016  A40003 For1:    COMPX   d#3,i        ;test for I <= 3
0019  98001F          BRNZ    Body1
001C  70002E          BR      EndFor1
001F  E20005 Body1:   DECI    V,x          ;read (V [I])
0022  0D0003          LOADX   I,d          ;increment I := I + 1
0025  1C0001          ADDX    d#1,i
0028  150003          STOREX  I,d
002B  700016          BR      For1
002E  0C0003 EndFor1: LOADX   d#3,i        ;initialize I := 3
0031  150003          STOREX  I,d
0034  A40000 For2:    COMPX   d#0,i        ;test for I >= 0
0037  780055          BRN     EndFor2
003A  E90003 Body2:   DECO    I,d          ;write (I: 1, '  ')
003D  D80020          CHARO   c#/ /,i
0040  D80020          CHARO   c#/ /,i
0043  EA0005          DECO    V,x          ;writeln (V [I]: 1)
0046  D8000A          CHARO   LineFeed,i
0049  0D0003          LOADX   I,d          ;decrement I := I - 1
004C  240001          SUBX    d#1,i
004F  150003          STOREX  I,d
0052  700034          BR      For2
0055  00     EndFor2: STOP
0056                  .END
```

Since V has four elements, the compiler allocates a block of four words (eight bytes) for it. The value of symbol V is the address of the first word in the block. The first instruction initializes the base register to 0. It remains 0 throughout the program.

Variable `I` is initialized, tested, and incremented via the index register instead of the accumulator. The Level 6 statement

```
read (V [I])
```

translates to

```
DECI    V,x
```

because the current value of `I` is in the index register. The first time `DECI` executes, its operand is

$$\begin{aligned} \texttt{Oprnd} &= \text{Mem}\,[B + 2 \times X + \text{OprndSpec}] \\ &= \text{Mem}\,[0 + 2 \times 0 + 0005] \\ &= \text{Mem}\,[0005] \end{aligned}$$

which is the first word in the block reserved for `V`. The second time it is

$$\begin{aligned} \texttt{Oprnd} &= \text{Mem}\,[B + 2 \times X + \text{OprndSpec}] \\ &= \text{Mem}\,[0 + 2 \times 1 + 0005] \\ &= \text{Mem}\,[0007] \end{aligned}$$

which is the second word in the block. Each time `I` and, therefore, the index register increase by 1, the operand increases by 2, accessing the next two-byte word in the block.

Program 15.15

The first element in the array of the previous program had an index of 0. If the first index is not 0, you can adjust the base register so that the assembly language instruction will still access element `V [I]` when the index register contains the current value of `I`. Program 15.15 is identical to the previous program, except that the index of the first element of `V` is 5.

Since `V` has four elements, `.BLOCK` still allocates eight bytes of storage. The code for initializing, testing, and incrementing `I` is unchanged from the previous program, except that the bounds are 5 and 8, instead of 0 and 3.

Program 15.15

Accessing an array whose starting index is not zero at Level 6 and Level 5.

High-Level Language

```
program Reverse (input, output);
   var
      I: integer;
      V: array [5..8] of integer;
   begin
   for I := 5 to 8 do
      read (V [I]);
   for I := 8 downto 5 do
      begin
      write (I: 1, '  ');
      writeln (V [I]: 1)
      end
   end.
```

Program 15.15, continued

Input

```
558  -32  781  440
```

Output

```
8  440
7  781
6  -32
5  558
```

Assembly Language

```
0000  70000D           BR       Reverse
0003  0000   I:        .BLOCK   d#2
0005  000000 V:        .BLOCK   d#8
      000000
      0000
             LineFeed:.EQUATE h#000A
             ;
000D  60FFF6 Reverse:  LOADB    d#-10,i       ;offset for V array
0010  0C0005           LOADX    d#5,i         ;initialize I := 5
0013  150003           STOREX   I,d
0016  A40008 For1:     COMPX    d#8,i         ;test for I <= 8
0019  98001F           BRNZ     Body1
001C  70002E           BR       EndFor1
001F  E20005 Body1:    DECI     V,x           ;read (V [I])
0022  0D0003           LOADX    I,d           ;increment I := I + 1
0025  1C0001           ADDX     d#1,i
0028  150003           STOREX   I,d
002B  700016           BR       For1
002E  0C0008 EndFor1:  LOADX    d#8,i         ;initialize I := 8
0031  150003           STOREX   I,d
0034  A40005 For2:     COMPX    d#5,i         ;test for I >= 5
0037  780055           BRN      EndFor2
003A  E90003 Body2:    DECO     I,d           ;write (I: 1, '  ')
003D  D80020           CHARO    c#/ /,i
0040  D80020           CHARO    c#/ /,i
0043  EA0005           DECO     V,x           ;writeln (V [I]: 1)
0046  D8000A           CHARO    LineFeed,i
0049  0D0003           LOADX    I,d           ;decrement I := I - 1
004C  240001           SUBX     d#1,i
004F  150003           STOREX   I,d
0052  700034           BR       For2
0055  00     EndFor2:  STOP
0056                   .END
```

Program 15.15 initializes the base register to –10 (dec). The first time the input loop executes, the index register has the value 5. The operand is calculated as

$$\begin{aligned} \texttt{Oprnd} &= \text{Mem}\,[\text{B} + 2 \times \text{X} + \text{OprndSpec}] \\ &= \text{Mem}\,[-10 + 2 \times 5 + 0005] \\ &= \text{Mem}\,[0005] \end{aligned}$$

which is the first word in the block reserved for V. The second time through the loop it is

$$\begin{aligned}\texttt{Oprnd} &= \text{Mem}\,[B + 2 \times X + \text{OprndSpec}] \\ &= \text{Mem}\,[-10 + 2 \times 6 + 0005] \\ &= \text{Mem}\,[0007]\end{aligned}$$

which is the second word in the block.

The compiler must produce code to set the base register to an offset value that will cancel the effect of the index register when the index register contains the starting index value. In this program, the base offset of –10 cancels 2 × 5, where 5 is the starting index value. In general, for byte instructions the offset is

Base offset = –(initial index)

and for word instructions it is

Base offset = –2 × (initial index)

Program 15.16

The Pep/5 system also uses indexed addressing to implement call by reference. Program 15.16 computes the perimeter of a rectangle and shows how a variable parameter translates to assembly language.

Variable parameters differ from value parameters in Pascal because the actual parameter provides a reference to a variable in the calling routine instead of a value. At the assembly level, the code that pushes the actual parameter onto the stack pushes the address of the actual parameter. The code in the called routine knows that the corresponding formal parameter is an address and uses it accordingly.

Program 15.16

A procedure call with an integer variable parameter at Level 6 and Level 5.

High-Order Language

```
program Rect (input, output);
   var
      Width:  integer;
      Height: integer;
      Perim:  integer;

   procedure CalcRect (var Per: integer;
                           Wid: integer;
                           Ht:  integer);
      begin
      Per := 2 * (Wid + Ht)
      end;

   begin
   read (Width, Height);
   CalcRect (Perim, Width, Height);
   write (Perim: 1)
   end.
```

Assembly Language

Program 15.16, continued

```
0000  70001A           BR       Rect
0003  0000    Width:   .BLOCK   d#2
0005  0000    Height:  .BLOCK   d#2
0007  0000    Perim:   .BLOCK   d#2
              ;
              ;------- procedure CalcRect -------
              Per:     .EQUATE d#6        ;formal parameter
              Wid:     .EQUATE d#4        ;formal parameter
              Ht:      .EQUATE d#2        ;formal parameter
0009  0B0004 CalcRect:LOADA   Wid,s      ;2 * (Width + Height)
000C  1B0002           ADDA     Ht,s
000F  40               ASLA
0010  630006           LOADB    Per,s      ;assign to Per
0013  0C0000           LOADX    d#0,i
0016  120000           STOREA   d#0,x
0019  C0               RTS                 ;pop RetAddr
              ;
              ;------- main program -------
001A  E10003 Rect:     DECI     Width,d    ;read (Width, Height)
001D  E10005           DECI     Height,d
0020  080007           LOADA    Perim,i    ;call by reference
0023  13FFFE           STOREA   d#-2,s
0026  090003           LOADA    Width,d    ;call by value
0029  13FFFC           STOREA   d#-4,s
002C  090005           LOADA    Height,d   ;call by value
002F  13FFFA           STOREA   d#-6,s
0032  B00006           SUBSP    d#6,i      ;push parameters
0035  B80009           JSR      CalcRect   ;push RetAddr
0038  A80006           ADDSP    d#6,i      ;pop parameters
003B  E90007           DECO     Perim,d    ;write (Perim: 1)
003E  00               STOP
003F                   .END
```

In this program, the statements

```
LOADA   Perim,i
STOREA  d#-2,s
```

push `Perim` onto the stack. `LOADA` puts `Perim` in the accumulator with immediate addressing, and `STOREA` puts it on the stack. Had `LOADA` used direct addressing, the run-time value of `Perim`, namely `Mem [0007]`, would be pushed. Since `LOADA` uses immediate addressing, the symbol value of `Perim`, which is 0007, is pushed. Figure 15.11 shows the run-time stack.

In the called routine, the statements

```
LOADB   Per,s
LOADX   d#0,i
STOREA  d#0,x
```

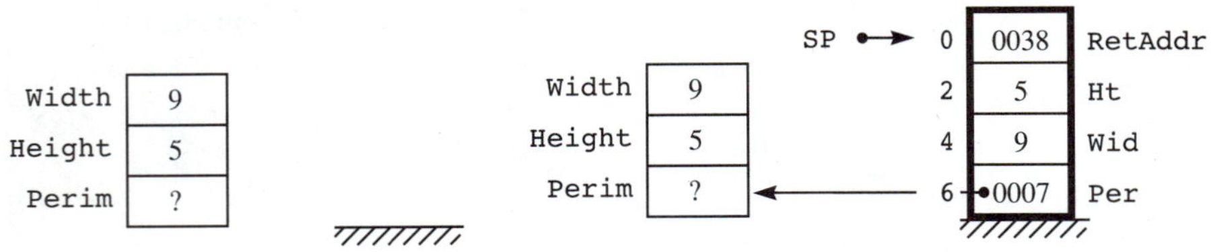

(a) After `read (Width, Height)`.

(b) After allocation with `SUBSP` in procedure `CalcRect`.

Figure 15.11 The run-time stack for Program 15.16.

assign the content of the accumulator to formal parameter `Per`. `LOADB` puts the content of the formal parameter, `Per`, in the base register. It is the address, 0007, of the actual parameter. `LOADX` clears the index register to 0. `STOREA` has an operand specifier of 0 and uses indexed addressing. So its operand is

`Oprnd` = Mem [B + 2 × X + OprndSpec]
= Mem [0007 + 2 × 0 + 0]
= Mem [0007]

The computed value of the perimeter is assigned to variable `Perim` in the main program.

In general, to access a formal variable parameter in a called routine, place the content of the formal parameter in the base register. Set the index register to 0, and access the formal parameter with an instruction whose operand specifier is 0. The operand will be the actual parameter from the calling routine.

Indirect Addressing

Some machines have an indirect addressing mode that facilitates accessing parameters called by reference. With direct addressing, the operand specifier is the address of the operand. With *indirect addressing,* the operand specifier is the address of the memory cell that contains the address of the operand. That is, the operand specifier is the address of the address of the operand. There is a natural progression from immediate to direct to indirect addressing.

The indirect addressing concept

- Immediate addressing:
  `Oprnd = OprndSpec`
- Direct addressing:
  `Oprnd = Mem [OprndSpec]`
- Indirect addressing:
  `Oprnd = Mem [Mem [OprndSpec]]`

Some machines even have a double indirect mode that would be one more level of indirection beyond indirect addressing. Can you guess how it is defined?

The VAX deferred addressing modes listed in Tables 14.4 and 14.5 are a variation on this theme of indirection. In Pep/5, a stack–relative deferred mode would be convenient for implementing call by reference. Compared to stack-relative addressing, such a mode would define the operand as

- Stack-relative addressing:
  `Oprnd = Mem [SP + OprndSpec]`
- Stack-relative deferred addressing:
  `Oprnd = Mem [Mem [SP + OprndSpec]]`

A proposed stack-relative deferred addressing mode for Pep/5

If Pep/5 had such an addressing mode, you could shorten the code from the previous program that assigns the value in the accumulator to variable parameter `Per`. Instead of

```
LOADB   Per,s
LOADX   d#0,i
STOREA  d#0,x
```

you could write a single

```
STOREA  Per,f
```

where `f` would indicate stack-relative deferred addressing.

So why does Pep/5 not have a stack-relative deferred addressing mode? As with most issues in computer science, it is a tradeoff. Pep/5 was designed for teaching fundamental computer science concepts at the introductory level. Overriding goals were simplicity and small size to make the machine easy to understand, while at the same time maintaining a certain level of realism.

To keep the machine small, it was desirable for the operand specifier to occupy only one byte, as shown in Figure 14.6. The operand specifier requires five bits for the opcode to allow for $2^5 = 32$ instructions. It requires one bit for the register specifier, which leaves two bits to specify the addressing mode. Two bits implies $2^2 = 4$ addressing modes. To include more addressing modes would either require more addressing mode bits, which would result in a shorter opcode and fewer instructions, or it would necessitate the sacrifice of another addressing mode.

Design tradeoffs at the machine level

These tradeoffs are typical in computer design. Each design goal has a corresponding cost. In the foregoing considerations, the cost of including a desirable addressing mode was a decrease in the number of instructions in the instruction set or the sacrifice of another addressing mode. Computer architects continually weigh design goals, many of which are conflicting and each one of which has a cost. Their job is to make the tradeoffs to produce a machine that satisfies the design goals within the cost constraints.

You are familiar with the tradeoff principle in software design. Some programs sacrifice program portability for program size, and numerical algorithms typically trade off accuracy for execution time. The space/time tradeoff is fundamental to computer science. This is a hardware manifestation of the same principle, which applies at all levels of a computer system.

Program 15.17

Program 15.17 shows how to pass an array as a reference parameter. Procedure `GetStr` has one formal parameter, `S`, which is called by reference. Although the Pascal source program contains only one explicit procedure, the compiler generates an implicit procedure, `PrntMsg`, for outputting strings.

The compiler allocates three bytes for variable `Name` in the main program. It also appends a null byte as a sentinel, so the packed array of characters can be output with the same routine that outputs the strings.

The first `write` statement in the main program translates to a procedure call to `PrntMsg`. Pascal's `write` statement is a standard procedure that, in this case, has an actual parameter of 'Enter name: '. Logically, the parameter should be called by value, since the purpose of the procedure is not to change the actual parameter in the calling routine. To push all the characters of the string onto the stack, however, would be unnecessarily expensive both in space and in time. Instead, the compiler collects all the strings in the program and groups them into an area below the main program, appending a null byte to each. It passes the address of the first byte of the string to print. Note the immediate addressing of `LOADA` at 0032.

Program 15.17

A procedure call with an array variable parameter at Level 6 and Level 5.

High-Order Language

```
program StrIn (input, output);
   type
      StrType = packed array [1..3] of char;
   var
      Name: StrType;

   procedure GetStr (var S: StrType);
      var
         I: integer;
      begin
      for I := 1 to 3 do
         read (S [I]);
      readln
      end;

   begin
   write ('Enter name: ');
   GetStr (Name);
   write ('Hello ');
   write (Name);
   write ('. How are you?')
   end.
```

Interactive Input/Output

```
Enter name: Sue
Hello Sue. How are you?
```

Assembly Language

```
0000  700032                BR      StrIn
0003  000000 Name:          .BLOCK  d#3
0006  00                    .BYTE   h#00
```

Program 15.17, continued

```
                 ;
                 ;------- procedure GetStr -------
                 S:       .EQUATE d#4          ;formal parameter
                 I:       .EQUATE d#0          ;local variable
0007  B00002 GetStr:  SUBSP    d#2,i        ;allocate local
000A  630004          LOADB    S,s          ;B := S (an address)
000D  68FFFF          ADDB     d#-1,i       ;offset for S array
0010  0C0001          LOADX    d#1,i        ;initialize I := 1
0013  170000          STOREX   I,s
0016  A40003 For:     COMPX    d#3,i        ;test for I <= 3
0019  98001F          BRNZ     Body
001C  70002E          BR       EndFor
001F  D20000 Body:    CHARI    h#0000,x     ;read (S [I])
0022  0F0000          LOADX    I,s          ;increment I := I + 1
0025  1C0001          ADDX     d#1,i
0028  170000          STOREX   I,s
002B  700016          BR       For
002E  A80002 EndFor:  ADDSP    d#2,i        ;deallocate local
0031  C0              RTS
                 ;
                 ;------- main program -------
0032  08007E StrIn:   LOADA    Msg1,i       ;write ('Enter name: ')
0035  13FFFE          STOREA   d#-2,s
0038  B00002          SUBSP    d#2,i
003B  B800A1          JSR      PrntMsg
003E  A80002          ADDSP    d#2,i
                 ;
0041  080003          LOADA    Name,i       ;GetStr (Name)
0044  13FFFE          STOREA   d#-2,s
0047  B00002          SUBSP    d#2,i
004A  B80007          JSR      GetStr
004D  A80002          ADDSP    d#2,i
                 ;
0050  08008B          LOADA    Msg2,i       ;write ('Hello ')
0053  13FFFE          STOREA   d#-2,s
0056  B00002          SUBSP    d#2,i
0059  B800A1          JSR      PrntMsg
005C  A80002          ADDSP    d#2,i
                 ;
005F  080003          LOADA    Name,i       ;write (Name)
0062  13FFFE          STOREA   d#-2,s
0065  B00002          SUBSP    d#2,i
0068  B800A1          JSR      PrntMsg

                 ;
006E  080092          LOADA    Msg3,i       ;write ('. How are you?')
006B  A80002          ADDSP    d#2,i
0071  13FFFE          STOREA   d#-2,s
0074  B00002          SUBSP    d#2,i
0077  B800A1          JSR      PrntMsg
007A  A80002          ADDSP    d#2,i
007D  00              STOP
```

Program 15.17, continued

```
007E  456E74 Msg1:     .ASCII  /Enter name: /
008A  00               .BYTE   h#00
008B  48656C Msg2:     .ASCII  /Hello /
0091  00               .BYTE   h#00
0092  2E2048 Msg3:     .ASCII  /. How are you?/
00A0  00               .BYTE   h#00
             ;
             ;------- Print subroutine -------
             ;Prints a string of ASCII bytes until it encounters a null
             ;byte (eight zero bits).  Assumes one parameter, which
             ;contains the address of the message.
             ;
             MsgAddr: .EQUATE d#2          ;Address of message to print
             ;
00A1  630002 PrntMsg: LOADB    MsgAddr,s   ;B := address of message
00A4  0C0000          LOADX    d#0,i       ;X := 0
00A7  080000          LOADA    d#0,i       ;A := 0
00AA  520000 PrntMore:LDBYTA   h#0000,x    ;Test next char from Mem [B + X]
00AD  8000B9          BRZ      StopPrnt    ;If null then exit
00B0  DA0000          CHARO    h#0000,x    ;else print
00B3  1C0001          ADDX     d#1,i       ;X := X + 1 for next character
00B6  7000AA          BR       PrntMore
00B9  C0     StopPrnt:RTS
00BA                  .END
```

Procedure `PrntMsg` has logic similar to the program of Program 15.13, except that it takes the address of the string as a parameter on the stack. `LOADB` at 00A1 puts the address of `Msg1`, which is 007E, into the base register. `LOADX` clears the index register to 0. `LDBYTA` and `CHARO` access a character with indexed addressing using the familiar scheme of incrementing the index register by 1 each time around the loop. For example, the third time through the loop the index register contains 2, and the operand is

```
Oprnd = Mem [B + X + OprndSpec]
      = Mem [007E + 2 + 0]
      = Mem [0080]
```

the ‘t’ in ‘Enter name: ’.

In Program 15.13, the operand specifier was the address of the string to print and the base register was 0. In this subroutine, the operand specifier is 0 and the address of the string to print is in the base register. In both cases the index register is added and the effect is the same.

The call to procedure `GetStr` passes the address of `Name` because it is called by reference. The first index of `Name` is 1, not 0, so the program must include an offset to access an element. `LOADB` at 000A puts the formal parameter in the base register, in this case 0003, since that is the symbol value of `Name`. `ADDB` adds the proper offset to the address. `CHARI` at 001F accesses the element of the array using indexed addressing with the current value of `I` in the index register.

Program 15.18

Program 15.18 shows how a compiler implements the `case` statement. It uses an interesting combination of indexed addressing with the unconditional branch, BR. Subroutine `PrntMsg` is identical to the print subroutine of the previous program and is not shown in this listing.

Program 15.18

A case statement at Level 6 and Level 5.

High-Order Language

```
program Question (input, output);
   var
      Guess: integer;
   begin
   write ('Pick a number: ');
   readln (Guess);
   case Guess of
      1: write ('Not close');
      2: write ('Close');
      3: write ('Right on');
      4: write ('Too high')
   end {case}
   end.
```

Assembly Language

```
0000  700005            BR      Question
0003  0000    Guess:    .BLOCK  d#2
              ;
              ;------- main program -------
0005  08006E Question:LOADA   Msg0,i      ;write ('Pick a number: ')
0008  13FFFE            STOREA  d#-2,s
000B  B00002            SUBSP   d#2,i
000E  B800A0            JSR     PrntMsg
0011  A80002            ADDSP   d#2,i
0014  E10003            DECI    Guess,d     ;readln (Guess)
0017  60FFFE            LOADB   d#-2,i      ;offset for JTable
001A  0D0003            LOADX   Guess,d     ;case Guess of
001D  720020            BR      JTable,x
0020  0028    JTable:   .ADDRSS Case1
0022  003A              .ADDRSS Case2
0024  004C              .ADDRSS Case3
0026  005E              .ADDRSS Case4
0028  08007E  Case1:    LOADA   Msg1,i      ;write ('Not close')
002B  13FFFE            STOREA  d#-2,s
002E  B00002            SUBSP   d#2,i
0031  B800A0            JSR     PrntMsg
0034  A80002            ADDSP   d#2,i
0037  70006D            BR      EndCase
```

Program 15.18, continued

```
003A  080088 Case2:   LOADA   Msg2,i      ;write ('Close')
003D  13FFFE          STOREA  d#-2,s
0040  B00002          SUBSP   d#2,i
0043  B800A0          JSR     PrntMsg
0046  A80002          ADDSP   d#2,i
0049  70006D          BR      EndCase
004C  08008E Case3:   LOADA   Msg3,i      ;write ('Right on')
004F  13FFFE          STOREA  d#-2,s
0052  B00002          SUBSP   d#2,i
0055  B800A0          JSR     PrntMsg
0058  A80002          ADDSP   d#2,i
005B  70006D          BR      EndCase
005E  080097 Case4:   LOADA   Msg4,i      ;write ('Too high')
0061  13FFFE          STOREA  d#-2,s
0064  B00002          SUBSP   d#2,i
0067  B800A0          JSR     PrntMsg
006A  A80002          ADDSP   d#2,i
006D  00     EndCase: STOP
006E  506963 Msg0:    .ASCII  /Pick a number: /
007D  00              .BYTE   h#00
007E  4E6F74 Msg1:    .ASCII  /Not close/
0087  00              .BYTE   h#00
0088  436C6F Msg2:    .ASCII  /Close/
008D  00              .BYTE   h#00
008E  526967 Msg3:    .ASCII  /Right on/
0096  00              .BYTE   h#00
0097  546F6F Msg4:    .ASCII  /Too high/
009F  00              .BYTE   h#00
```

At the Pascal level, if a user enters 3 for `Guess`, the case statement branches directly to the third alternative without comparing `Guess` to 1 or 2. At the assembly level, the `case` statement is implemented with a jump table defined at 0020 in this program. The *jump table* is an array of addresses. Each entry in the table is the address of the code to be executed for one of the cases.

The .ADDRSS pseudo-op

The compiler generates a jump table with `.ADDRSS` pseudo-ops. Every `.ADDRSS` command must be followed by a symbol. The code generated by `.ADDRSS` is the value of the symbol. For example, `Case3` is a symbol whose value is 004C, the address of the code to be executed if `Guess` has a value of 3. Therefore, the object code generated by `.ADDRSS` at 0024 is 004C.

In this program, `Guess` is in the range `1..4`, so you can think of the jump table as an array of words whose first index is 1. The appropriate offset for the base register of such an array is –2, loaded by `LOADB` at 001A.

Suppose the user enters 3 for `Guess`. `LOADX` puts 3 in the index register, after which

```
BR  JTable,x
```

executes. Indexed addressing means that the operand is computed as

Indexed addressing with a branch instruction

```
Oprnd = Mem [B + 2 × X + OprndSpec]
      = Mem [–2 + 2 × 3 + 0020]
      = Mem [4 + 0020]
      = Mem [0024]
      = 004C
```

What does the unconditional branch do with the operand? It puts it in the program counter.

```
PC := Oprnd
```

Because of the von Neumann cycle, the next instruction to execute is at 004C. This is precisely the code that should execute when `Guess` has the value 3.

`BR` branched directly to `Case3` without first comparing the value of `Guess` with 1 or 2. Had the user entered 4, the operand would be `Mem [0026]`, which is 005E. `BR` would branch directly to `Case4`. Also note the unconditional branch at the end of each `case` part to skip to the end of the `case` statement.

If the user enters a number not in the range `1..4`, a run-time error will occur. For example, if the user enters 5 for `Guess`, the operand will be computed as

```
Oprnd = Mem [B + 2 × X + OprndSpec]
      = Mem [–2 + 2 × 5 + 0020]
      = Mem [8 + 0020]
      = Mem [0028]
      = 0800
```

so the branch will be to memory location 0800 (hex). The problem is that the bits 0800 were generated by the assembler for the `LOADA` instruction and were never meant to be interpreted as a branch address.

15.4 Data Types at Level 5

The purpose of a compiler is to create a high level of abstraction for the programmer. For example, it lets the programmer think in terms of a single `while` loop instead of the detailed conditional branches at the assembly level that are necessary to implement the loop on the machine. Hiding the details of a lower level is the essence of abstraction.

But abstraction of program control is only one side of the coin. The other side is abstraction of data. At the assembly and machine levels, the only data types are bits and bytes. The compiler provides enumerated, boolean, set, record, and pointer types in addition to integer and character types of the previous programs.

Data abstraction provided by the compiler with its symbol table

As you recall, the compiler uses its symbol table to provide the higher level of data abstraction. As it scans the variable declaration part, it stores the type of each variable in the `Kind` part of the symbol table. When it encounters a variable in the executable part of the program, it consults its symbol table to see if the program statement adheres to the allowed operations for that type and generates the proper object code.

The net effect is that the Pascal programmer is shielded from the complexity inherent in data representation at the machine level. This section shows how the compiler hides the lower-level details by describing implementation techniques that it uses to generate object code for some Pascal data types.

Enumerated Types

An enumerated type lets the programmer give a name to a nonnegative integer value. The compiler stores these names in a table. When it encounters the name later in the program, it substitutes the corresponding value. The following code fragment shows an equivalent enumerated type at the assembly level.

Enumerated types at Level 6 and Level 5

High-Order Language

```
type
   ErrType = (None, Warning, Fatal);
var
   Error: ErrType;

Error := Warning
```

Assembly Language

```
                None:     .EQUATE d#0
                Warning:  .EQUATE d#1
                Fatal:    .EQUATE d#2
                ;
0000   0000     Error:    .BLOCK  d#2
                ;
0002   080001             LOADA   Warning,i   ;Error := Warning
0005   110000             STOREA  Error,d
0008                      .END
```

The names `None`, `Warning`, and `Fatal` correspond to the values 0, 1, and 2. An assembly language program connects the names to the values with `.EQUATE` commands, which do not generate object code. At the Pascal level, the only values `Error` can have are `None`, `Warning`, or `Fatal`. At the assembly level, allocation for `Error` is identical to allocation for an integer. Note from the object code at 0002 that assigning `Warning` to `Error` is equivalent to assigning a value of 1 to an integer variable.

This representation of enumerated types means that there is no run-time execution penalty for the `ord` function. For example, if `I` is an integer, the compiler translates the Pascal statement

```
I := ord (Error)
```

to a simple

```
LOADA   Error,d
STOREA  I,d
```

with no function call. The object program does not push the formal parameter onto the stack or execute a `JSR`. The `ord` function is only necessary for type compatibility. You need not worry that, because it looks like a function call, it will consume an inordinate amount of execution time. The same principle holds with the `chr` function, which provides type conversion from `integer` to `char` with no function call at the assembly level.

Subrange Types

In contrast to enumerated types, which engender no run-time penalty, subrange types have an execution cost. When the value of a subrange variable changes, whether by assignment or by input, the program must verify that it is within its specified range. The following code fragment shows the object code generated by an input to a subrange variable.

Subrange types at Level 6 and Level 5

High-Order Language

```
type
   GuessType = 1..4;
var
   Guess: GuessType;

readln (Guess);
```

Statement 1

Assembly Language

```
0000  0000    Guess:   .BLOCK  d#2
              ;
0002  E10000           DECI    Guess,d     ;readln (Guess)
0005  090000           LOADA   Guess,d     ;A := Guess
0008  A00001           COMPA   d#1,i       ;if Guess < 1
000B  7801F8           BRN     RangeErr
000E  A00004           COMPA   d#4,i       ;or Guess > 4 then
0011  980017           BRNZ    S1
0014  7001F8           BR      RangeErr    ;branch to range error
0017  F8      S1:      NOP                 ;Statement 1
```

Contrast this code with the code generated for the same input statement in Program 15.18. Not only must the compiler generate `DECI` to input the value, it must verify that the value is in the range `1..4`. If it is not in range, the program branches to an error routine not shown in the fragment (at 01F8), which outputs a range error message and stops the program prematurely. That is, the program crashes.

The compiler must generate this range check code for every input and assignment to a subrange variable. The extra code makes the object program bigger and execute slower. On the other hand, if a value is ever out of range, the error message can tell the user the cause of the problem and perhaps the source line on which it occurred. If the user is a programmer and has access to the source code, that can be valuable information for correcting the problem. To the user who is not a programmer or who does not have the source code, however, such crashes are anathema. It would be better to declare the variable an integer and program the range check into the source code for more user-friendly treatment.

Boolean Types

Pascal classifies boolean and enumerated types as ordinals. Several schemes exist for storing boolean values at the assembly level. The one most appropriate for Pascal is to treat the values false and true as enumerated values of a built-in boolean enumerated type. The ordinal values are

```
ord (false) = 0
ord (true)  = 1
```

The following code adheres to this convention at the assembly level.

Boolean types at Level 6 and Level 5

High-Order Language

```
const
   RtrmtAge = 65;
var
   Age:      integer;
   Retired: boolean;

Retired := (Age >= RtrmtAge)
```

Assembly Language

```
              RtrmtAge:.EQUATE d#65
              False:    .EQUATE d#0
              True:     .EQUATE d#1
              ;
0000   0000   Age:      .BLOCK  d#2
0002   0000   Retired: .BLOCK  d#2
              ;
```

```
0004  090000           LOADA   Age,d
0007  A00041           COMPA   RtrmtAge,i
000A  780013           BRN     SetFalse
000D  080001           LOADA   True,i
0010  700016           BR      Continue
0013  080000 SetFalse:LOADA    False,i
0016  110002 Continue:STOREA   Retired,d
```

The object code must compare `Age` with the constant `RtrmtAge`, which stands for retirement age. It uses primitive branches to load the accumulator with the proper boolean value before assigning the value to `Retired`.

Representing false and true at the bit level as 0000 and 0001 (hex) has advantages and disadvantages. Consider the logical operations on boolean quantities and the corresponding assembly instructions AND*R*, OR*R*, and NOT*R*. If `P` and `Q` are boolean variables, then

```
P and Q
```

translates to

```
LOADA P,d
ANDA  Q,d
```

If you AND 0000 and 0001 with this object code you get 0000 as desired. The OR operation also works as desired.

The NOT operation is a problem, however, because if you apply NOT to 0000 you get FFFF instead of 0001. Also, applying NOT to 0001 gives FFFE instead of 0000. If you were designing a compiler with 0000 and 0001 representing false and true, what object code would you need to generate for the Pascal statement `P := not Q`?

To avoid this problem, you could design the representation of boolean values with FFFF for true and 0000 for false. Then the assembly instructions AND*R*, OR*R*, and NOT*R* would produce straightforward object code. The exercises at the end of the chapter explore some of the ramifications of alternate boolean representations.

Set Types

The following code fragment shows an implementation of a set at the assembly level. The basic idea is to store a set as a sequence of bits, one for each element of the base type. If the bit is 1, that element is in the set, otherwise it is not.

Testing a constant for set membership at Level 6 and Level 5

High-Order Language

```
type
   DayType    = (Mon, Tue, Wed, Thu, Fri);
   DaySetType = set of DayType;
var
   UserPref: DaySetType;

if Thu in UserPref then
   Statement 1
Statement 2
```

Assembly Language

```
                Mon:     .EQUATE d#0
                Tue:     .EQUATE d#1
                Wed:     .EQUATE d#2
                Thu:     .EQUATE d#3
                Fri:     .EQUATE d#4
                ;
                SetMon:  .EQUATE d#1
                SetTue:  .EQUATE d#2
                SetWed:  .EQUATE d#4
                SetThu:  .EQUATE d#8
                SetFri:  .EQUATE d#16
                ;
0000  0000      UserPref:.BLOCK  d#2
                ;
0002  080008             LOADA   SetThu,i    ;if Thu in UserPref then
0005  290000    TestIn:  ANDA    UserPref,d
0008  80000C             BRZ     S2
000B  F8        S1:      NOP                 ;Statement 1
000C  F8        S2:      NOP                 ;Statement 2
```

Level 6	Level 5
`[]`	00000
`[Mon]`	00001
`[Tue]`	00010
`[Wed]`	00100
`[Mon, Tue]`	00011
`[Mon, Wed]`	00101
`[Mon..Fri]`	11111

Table 15.1

Some representations for set values of `UserPref`. Only the rightmost five bits of the word allocated for `UserPref` are shown.

This code has five elements in the base type `DayType`, so the set uses the five rightmost bits of the word reserved for `UserPref` to indicate set membership. Table 15.1 shows some representative values of the set, and Figure 15.12 shows the bit positions in the set for the base elements with `[Mon, Wed]`.

This representation for set values is convenient for the union and intersection operations. If you perform the OR operation between two words that represent sets, the result is a word that will correctly represent the union of the sets. Similarly, the AND operation corresponds to the intersection.

One way to test a value for membership in set `UserPref` is to compute the intersection of `UserPref` with another set having the value as its only member. To test if element `Thu` is in `UserPref`, the object code needs a representation for the set `[Thu]`. The assembler notation for `[Thu]` is `SetThu`, with a binary value of 01000 for the rightmost five bits. The code performs the AND operation of `SetThu` with `UserPref`. If `UserPref` is, say, `[Tue, Thu]` = 01010, the code produces

```
      01000
AND   01010
      -----
      01000
```

The conditional branch tests `Z`. Since the result of the `AND` is not 0, `Thu` is in `UserPref`, and Statement 1 executes as desired.

The situation is more complicated if you have a variable whose type is the base type and you need to test it for membership in the set. The next code fragment shows one translation for such a statement.

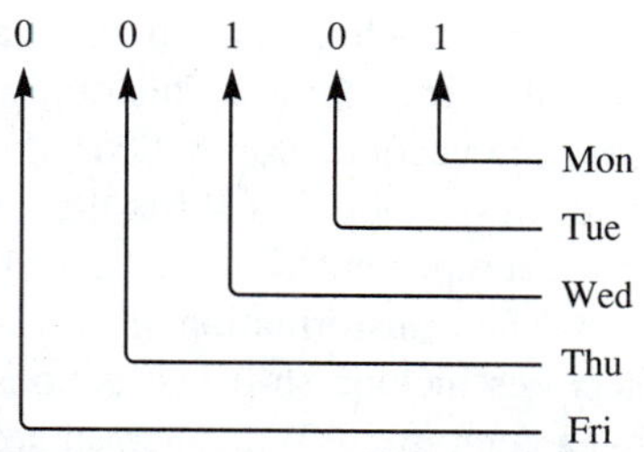

Figure 15.12

The bit positions for the rightmost five bits in `UserPref`.

Testing a variable for set membership at Level 6 and Level 5

High-Order Language

```
type
   DayType     = (Mon, Tue, Wed, Thu, Fri);
   DaySetType = set of DayType;
var
   Day:       DayType;
   UserPref: DaySetType;

if Day in UserPref then
   Statement 1
Statement 2
```

Assembly Language

```
             Mon:      .EQUATE d#0
             Tue:      .EQUATE d#1
             Wed:      .EQUATE d#2
             Thu:      .EQUATE d#3
             Fri:      .EQUATE d#4
             ;
0000  0000   Day:      .BLOCK  d#2
0002  0000   UserPref:.BLOCK  d#2
             ;
0004  080001           LOADA   h#0001,i    ;A := 0001 (hex)
0007  0D0000           LOADX   Day,d       ;X := Day
000A  800014 Loop:     BRZ     TestIn      ;Quit if X = 0
000D  40               ASLA                ;All zeros except one 1
000E  240001           SUBX    d#1,i       ;X := X - 1
0011  70000A           BR      Loop
0014  290002 TestIn:   ANDA    UserPref,d ;If Day in UserPref then
0017  80001B           BRZ     S2
001A  F8     S1:       NOP                 ;Statement 1
001B  F8     S2:       NOP                 ;Statement 2
```

The problem is to compute a representation for `[Day]` given a value of `Day`, as Table 15.2 shows. This object code computes the set value in a loop. It initializes the accumulator to 0001 (hex) and the index register to the value of `Day`. It executes a loop that shifts the single 1 bit to the left enough times to produce the correct representation for `[Day]`.

The transformation shown in Table 15.2 is common enough that some architectures include shift instructions to shift an arbitrary number of times depending on a count field. With such an architecture, the transformation from `Day` to `[Day]` could be done with a single assembly language instruction. That instruction would transfer the details of the shift to a lower level in the system, either Level 2 or Level 1.

Day	[Day]
0	00001
1	00010
2	00100
3	01000
4	10000

Table 15.2

Values for the set `[Day]` that the object code must produce from the value for `Day` to test for set membership.

Record Types

Records are the key to data abstraction at Level 6, the high-order languages level. They let the programmer consolidate variables with primitive types into a single abstract data type. The compiler provides the record construct at Level 6. At Level 5, the assembly level, a record is a contiguous group of bytes, as the following code fragment illustrates.

Records at Level 6 and Level 5

High-Order Language

```
type
   NameType     = packed array [1..20] of char;
   NumberType   = packed array [1..10] of char;
   CustomerType =
      record
      Name:   NameType;
      Age:    integer;
      Salary: integer;
      Number: NumberType
      end;
var
   Customer: CustomerType;

read (Customer.Salary);
```

Assembly Language

```
             Name:    .EQUATE d#0
             Age:     .EQUATE d#20
             Salary:  .EQUATE d#22
             Number:  .EQUATE d#24
             ;
0000  000000 Customer:.BLOCK  d#34
             ;
0022  600016          LOADB   Salary,i
0025  0C0000          LOADX   d#0,i
0028  E20000          DECI    Customer,x
```

`Customer` is a record with four fields. At the assembly level, enough storage must be allocated for all the fields in the record, 34 bytes in this program. To conserve space in the listing, only the first three bytes of the object code for `.BLOCK` are shown. Figure 15.13 shows the structure of record `Customer`.

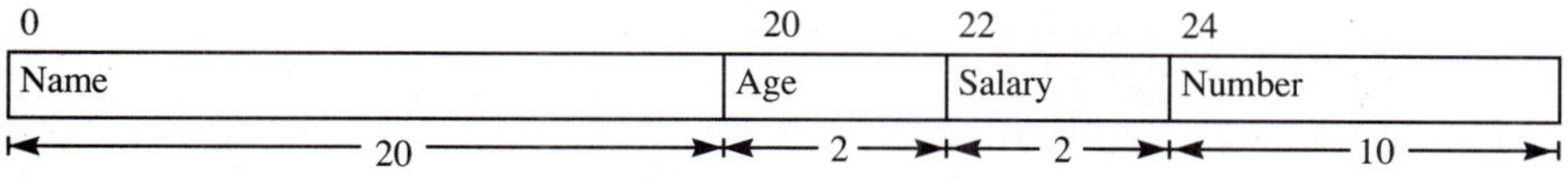

Figure 15.13

The structure of record `Customer`. The widths below the record are the number of bytes in the field. The numbers above are byte offsets from the first byte of the first field.

The compiler computes the offset of each field from the first byte of the record and stores that information in its symbol table. In this program, it computes the offset for `Name`, `Age`, `Salary`, and `Number` as 0, 20, 22, and 24 (dec) respectively. It looks up these offsets for generating object code that accesses a field in a record. The example program shows access to the salary field with indexed addressing. The assembly language program puts the offset for the salary field into the base register and 0 into the index register. `DECI` computes the operand as

$$\begin{aligned}\texttt{Oprnd} &= \text{Mem}\,[\text{B} + 2 \times \text{X} + \text{OprndSpec}]\\ &= \text{Mem}\,[0016 + 2 \times 0 + 0000]\\ &= \text{Mem}\,[0016]\end{aligned}$$

where the value of the base register is 22 (dec) = 0016 (hex). Had an access to an array within the record been required, the index value would be loaded into the index register.

Pointer Types

A pointer at Level 6 is a memory address at Level 5. If `P` is a variable of type pointer, `new (P)` allocates storage from the heap and sets `P` to the address of the cell allocated, and `dispose (P)` deallocates the cell whose address `P` contains.

The heap is a region of memory different from the stack. The compiler, in cooperation with the operating system under which it runs, must generate code to perform the allocation and deallocation. Unfortunately, there is no simple way for Pep/5 to illustrate the operation of procedures `new` and `dispose`. The following code, however, shows how to access a value via a pointer, assuming it has been previously allocated with `new`.

Pointers at Level 6 and Level 5

High-Order Language

```
var
   P: ^char;

write (P^)
```

Assembly Language

```
0000  0000    P:      .BLOCK  d#2
              ;
0002  610000          LOADB   P,d
0005  0C0000          LOADX   d#0,i
0008  DA0000          CHARO   d#0,x
```

Since `P` is a pointer and memory addresses in Pep/5 are two bytes, storage for `P` is always two bytes regardless of the number of bytes allocated with `new`. In this example program, `P` points to an ASCII character that occupies one byte in the heap (not shown in the listing). Even so, storage for `P` is two bytes. Had `P` been defined to point to a 100-byte record in the heap, `P` itself would still consist of only two bytes.

Since `P` is an address, to access the cell pointed to by `P`, the assembly language program puts the value of `P` in the base register and sets the index register to 0. `CHARO` accesses the cell with a 0 operand specifier with indexed addressing.

SUMMARY

A compiler uses conditional branch instructions at the machine level to translate `if` statements and loops at the high-order languages level. An `if/then/else` statement requires a conditional branch instruction to test the `if` condition, and an unconditional branch instruction to branch around the `else` part. The translation of a `while` or `repeat` loop requires a branch to a previous instruction. The `for` loop requires, in addition, instructions to initialize and increment the control variable.

The structured programming theorem, proved by Bohm and Jacopini, states that any algorithm containing goto's, no matter how complicated or unstructured, can be written with only nested `if` statements and `while` loops. The goto controversy was sparked by Dijkstra's famous letter, which stated that programs without goto's were not only possible but desirable.

Procedures and functions allocate parameters and local variables on the run-time stack. Values are pushed onto the stack by incrementing the stack pointer (`SP`) and popped off the stack by decrementing `SP`. The subroutine call instruction pushes the contents of the program counter (`PC`), which acts as the return address, onto the stack. The subroutine return instruction pops the return address off the stack into the `PC`. Instructions access values on the run-time stack with stack-relative addressing. In stack-relative addressing, the address of the operand is computed as the contents of the stack pointer plus the operand specifier. In mathematical notation, `Oprnd = Mem [SP + OprndSpec]`.

Array values are stored in consecutive main memory cells and are accessed with indexed addressing. In indexed addressing, the address of the operand is computed as `Oprnd = Mem [B + X + OprndSpec]` for byte instructions and as `Oprnd = Mem [B + 2*X + OprndSpec]` for all other instructions. `X` is the index register and contains the index value of the array element. `B` is the base register and contains a value determined by the first index value in the array declaration. In call by reference, the address of the actual parameter is pushed onto the run-time stack; this is conveniently accomplished with immediate addressing.

The compiler implements the primitive Pascal types by combinations of assembly language statements and dot commands. Enumerated types translate into `.EQUATE` commands. Subrange types require code for checking out-of-range conditions at run-time. Several techniques are possible for translating boolean types, including 0 for false and 1 for true. A set is a sequence of bits, one for each element of the base type. A pointer is an address of a memory location in the heap.

EXERCISES

Section 15.1

1. Draw flowcharts for the following Programs.

*(a) 15.1	(b) 15.2	(c) 15.3
(d) 15.4	(e) 15.5, both versions	(f) 15.6

2. What is an optimizing compiler? When would you want to use one? When would you not want to use one? Explain.

*3. The object code for Program 15.5 has a `COMPA` at 000B to test the value of `I`. Since the program branches to that instruction from the bottom of the loop, why doesn't the compiler generate a `LOADA I,d` at that point before `COMPA`?

4. Discover the function of the mystery program of Program 15.7, and state in one short sentence what it does.

5. Read the papers by Bohm and Jacopini and by Dijkstra that are referred to in this chapter and write a summary of them.

Section 15.2

*6. Draw the values just before and just after the `JSR` at 0031 of Program 15.8 executes as they are drawn in Figure 15.6.

7. Draw the run-time stack, as in 15.10, that corresponds to the time just before the second return.[4]

Section 15.3

*8. In the object code of Program 15.18, if you enter 0 for `Guess`, the following statements execute: `LOADB`, `LOADX`, `BR`, `STOP`. Why?

9. Section 15.3 did not show how to access an element from a two-dimensional array. **(a)** Describe how a two-dimensional array might be stored and the assembly language object code that would be necessary to access an element from it. Consider the case where the starting index of both dimensions is 0. **(b)** Repeat the exercise for the case where the starting indexes are not 0.

---

4. The run-time stack at the Pascal level is shown in Figure 9.10(f) in Volume 1 and the combined edition of this book.

Section 15.4

* **10.** Write the assembly language object code for the following Pascal fragment.

```
type
   AnimalType = (Tiger, Lion, Bear);
var
   Animal: AnimalType;

Animal := Lion
```

11. Write the assembly language object code for the following Pascal fragment.

```
type
   DegreeType = 0..359;
var
   Degree: DegreeType;

readln (Degree);
```
Statement 1

12. Write the assembly language object code for the following Pascal fragment.

```
const
   BCutOff = 89;
   CCutOff = 79;
var
   Grade:  integer;
   GradeB: boolean;

GradeB := ((Grade > CCutOff) and (Grade <= BCutOff))
```

13. If you were designing a compiler with 0000 (hex) and 0001 (hex) representing false and true, what object code would you need to generate for the Pascal statement `P := not Q`?

14. Suppose you are designing a compiler that represents boolean values with FFFF (hex) for true and 0000 (hex) for false. Write the object code for the following expressions with this representation. The object code should leave the value of the expression in the accumulator.

* (a) `P and Q` (b) `P or Q` (c) `not P`
* (d) `ord (P)` (e) `succ (P)` (f) `pred (P)`

* **15.** Repeat Exercise 14 for a compiler that represents false as 0000 (hex) and true as any bit pattern that is not 0000 (hex).

16. Assuming `DayType` and `DaySetType` are defined as in the program of Section 15.4, and `Pref1` and `Pref2` are defined as `UserPref`, write the assembly language object code for the following Pascal set expressions. The object code should leave the value of the expression in the accumulator.

* (a) `Pref1 + Pref2` (b) `Pref1 * Pref2` (c) `Pref1 - Pref2`
* (d) `Pref1 <= Pref2` (e) `Pref1 >= Pref2` (f) `Pref1 = []`

17. Write the assembly language object code for the following Pascal fragment.

```
type
   NameType     = packed array [1..15] of char;
   EmployeeType =
      record
      EmplNum: integer;
      Name:    NameType;
      Salary:  integer;
      end;
var
   Employee: EmployeeType;

read (Employee.Salary)
```

*18. Write the assembly language object code for the following Pascal fragment where `EmployeeType` is defined as in Exercise 17.

```
var
P: ^EmployeeType;

write (P^.Name [6])
```

19. Write the assembly language object code for the following Pascal fragment where `EmployeeType` is defined as in Exercise 17.

```
var
I, J:  integer
Table: array [0..100] of EmployeeType;

read (Table [I].Name [J])
```

You will need to compute the address of the first byte of the `I`th record with a loop and put it in the base register.

PROBLEMS

Section 15.1

20. Write an assembly language program that corresponds to the following Pascal program.

```
program OddEven (input, output);
   var
      Num: integer;
   begin
   read (Num);
   if odd (Num) then
      write ('Odd')
   else
      write ('Even')
   end.
```

21. Write an assembly language program that corresponds to the following Pascal program.

```
program TstWhile (input, output);
   const
      Limit = 5;
   var
      Num: integer;
   begin
   read (Num);
   while Num < Limit do
      begin
      Num := Num + 1;
      writeln (Num)
      end
   end.
```

22. Write an assembly language program that corresponds to the following Pascal program.

```
program NestedIf (input, output);
   var
      Ch: char;
   begin
   read (Ch);
   if (Ch >= 'A') and (Ch <= 'Z') then
      write ('A')
   else if (Ch >= 'a') and (Ch <= 'z') then
      write ('a')
   else
      write ('$')
   end.
```

23. Write the object code for Program 15.4 with the repeat test changed to

```
until Cop > Driver;
```

24. Write an assembly language program that corresponds to the following Pascal program.

```
program TestFor (input, output);
   var
      Num: integer;
      I:   integer;
      X:   integer;
      Sum: integer;
   begin
   read (Num);
   Sum := 0;
   for I := 1 to Num do
      begin
      read (X);
      Sum := Sum + X
      end;
   write ('Sum: ', Sum: 1)
   end.
```

Sample Input

```
4     8 -3 7 6
```

Sample Output

```
Sum: 18
```

Section 15.2

25. **(a)** Write a Pascal program that converts a lowercase character to an uppercase character. Declare

```
function Uppercase (Ch: char): char
```

to do the conversion. If the actual parameter is not a lowercase character, the function should return that character value unchanged. Test your function in a main program with interactive I/O. **(b)** Write the corresponding assembly language program.

26. Write an assembly language program that corresponds to the following Pascal program.

```
program Arrange3 (input, output);
   var
      A, B: integer;

   procedure Swap (var R, S: integer);
      var
         Temp: integer;
      begin
      Temp := R;
      R := S;
      S := Temp
      end;

   procedure Order3 (var X, Y: integer);
      begin
      if X > Y then
         Swap (X, Y)
      end;

   begin {Arrange3}
   readln (A);
   readln (B);
   Order3 (A, B);
   writeln (A: 1, B: 1)
   end.
```

27. **(a)** Write a Pascal program that defines

```
function Minimum (I1, I2: integer): integer
```

and test it with interactive input. **(b)** Write the corresponding assembly language program.

28. The Fibonacci sequence is

0 1 1 2 3 5 8 13 21 ···

Each Fibonacci number is the sum of the preceding two Fibonacci numbers. The sequence starts with the first two Fibonacci numbers defined as

$$\text{Fib}(0) = 0$$
$$\text{Fib}(1) = 1$$
$$\text{Fib}(n) = \text{Fib}(n-1) + \text{Fib}(n-2) \quad \text{for } n > 1$$

(a) Write a program in Pascal that inputs a small integer, n, uses a recursive function to compute Fib (n), and outputs it. **(b)** Write the corresponding assembly language program.

29. **(a)** Write a program in Pascal that prints the solution to the Towers of Hanoi puzzle.[5] It should input the number of disks in the puzzle, the peg to which all of the disks are placed initially, and the peg to which the disks are to be moved.

Sample Input

```
3 3 2
```

Sample Output

```
Move a disk from peg 3 to peg 2.
Move a disk from peg 3 to peg 1.
Move a disk from peg 2 to peg 1.
Move a disk from peg 3 to peg 2.
Move a disk from peg 1 to peg 3.
Move a disk from peg 1 to peg 2.
Move a disk from peg 3 to peg 2.
```

(b) Write the corresponding assembly language program.

30. The recursive binomial coefficient function in Program 15.11 can be simplified by omitting `Y1` and `Y2` as follows:

```
function BinCoeff (N, K: integer): integer;
   begin
   if (K = 0) or (N = K) then
      BinCoeff := 1
   else
      BinCoeff := BinCoeff (N - 1, K) + BinCoeff (N - 1, K - 1)
   end;
```

Write an assembly language program that calls this procedure. Keep the value returned from the `BinCoeff (N - 1, K)` call on the stack and allocate the actual parameters for the `BinCoeff (N - 1, K - 1)` call on top of it. Figure 15.14 shows a trace of the run-time stack where the stack frame contains four words (for `BC`, `N`, `K`, and `RetAddr`) and the shaded word is the value returned by a function call. The trace is for a call of `BinCoeff (3,1)` from the main program.

5. The Towers of Hanoi problem is explained in Section 9.3 of Volume 1 and the combined edition of this book.

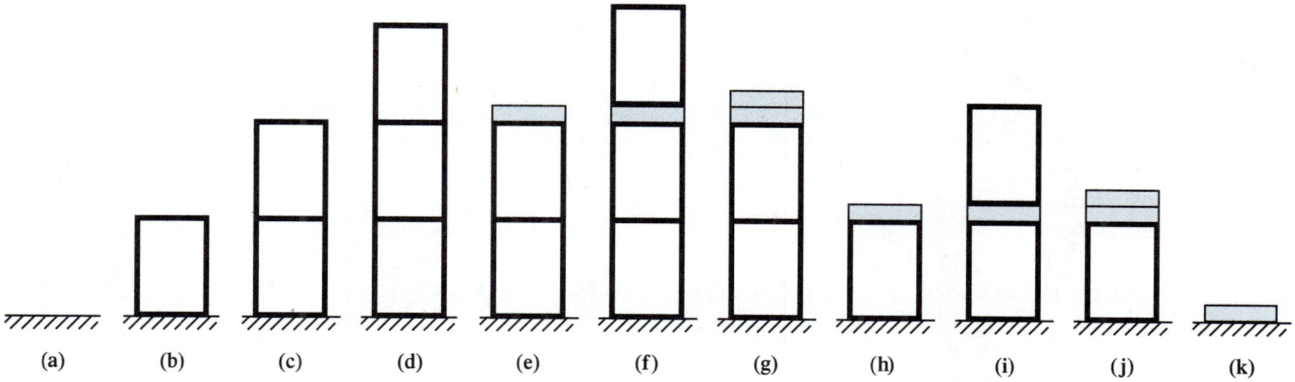

Figure 15.14

Trace of the run-time stack for Problem 30.

31. The instruction, `DECO X,d` corresponds to `write (X: 1)`. Write a procedure in Pascal

```
procedure Print (X: integer; FWid: integer)
```

that formats the output as `write (X: FWid)` does, but that only uses `write (X: 1)` to do it. Translate the procedure and a main program to test it into assembly language. Assume the value of `X` may be negative, but that its magnitude will be less than 10,000.

Section 15.3

32. Program 15.15 accessed an element of `V` by putting the offset for the starting index in the base register and the symbol value of `V` in the operand specifier. **(a)** Write the object code for this program with the symbol value of `V` in the base register and the starting index offset in the operand specifier. **(b)** Write the object code with the symbol value of `V` added to the starting index offset in the base register and zero in the operand specifier.

33. Write an assembly language program that corresponds to the following Pascal program.

```
program Rotate (input, output);
   const
      MaxLength = 10;
   type
      ListType = array [1..MaxLength] of integer;
   var
      NumItems: integer;
      List:     ListType;

   procedure GetList (var L:      ListType;
                      var NumItm: integer);
      var
         I: integer;
      begin
      read (NumItm);
      for I := 1 to NumItm do
         read (L [I])
      end;
```

```
procedure PutList (L: ListType; NumItm: integer);
   var
      I: integer;
   begin
   for I := 1 to NumItm do
      write (L [I]: 1, ' ');
   writeln
   end;

procedure RotateLeft (var L: ListType; NumItm: integer);
   var
      I:    integer;
      Temp: integer;
   begin
   Temp := L [1];
   for I := 1 to NumItm - 1 do
      L [I] := L [I + 1];
   L [NumItm] := Temp
   end;

begin
GetList (List, NumItems);
PutList (List, NumItems);
RotateLeft (List, NumItems);
writeln;
PutList (List, NumItems)
end.
```

34. Write an assembly language program that corresponds to the following Pascal program.

```
program SelectionSort (input, output);
   const
      MaxLength = 10;
   type
      ListType = array [1..MaxLength] of integer;
   var
      List:     ListType;
      NumItems: integer;

   procedure GetList (var NumItm: integer;
                      var L:      ListType);
      var
         I: integer;
      begin
      read (NumItm);
      for I := 1 to NumItm do
         read (L [I])
      end;
```

```
procedure PutList (NumItm: integer; L: ListType);
   var
      I: integer;
   begin
   for I := 1 to NumItm do
      write (L [I]: 1, ' ');
   writeln
   end;

procedure SortList (NumItm: integer; var L: ListType);
   var
      Temp:     integer;
      MaxIndex: integer;
      I, N:     integer;
   begin
   for N := NumItm downto 2 do
      begin
      MaxIndex := 1;
      for I := 2 to N do
         if L [I] > L [MaxIndex] then
            MaxIndex := I;
      Temp := L [N];
      L [N] := L [MaxIndex];
      L [MaxIndex] := Temp
      end
   end;

begin
GetList (NumItems, List);
PutList (NumItems, List);
SortList (NumItems, List);
writeln;
PutList (NumItems, List)
end.
```

All Sections

35. Code generators for compilers sometimes generate `NOP` instructions whose sole purpose is to serve as a place to which another statement will branch. An example is

```
    STOREA J,d
L1: NOP
L2: NOP
    LOADA  I,d
```

where `L1` and `L2` are labels for the `NOP` instructions and occur in branch instructions elsewhere in the program. An optimizing phase of the compiler can shorten the code to

```
    STOREA J,d
L1: LOADA  I,d
```

provided that it also changes all other occurrences of `L2` to `L1`.

Write a procedure that performs this optimization on a code array declared as follows:

```
type
   CodeRecType =
      record
      Label: integer;
      Instr: char
      end;
   CodeArrType = array [0..100] of CodeRecType

procedure OptimizeCode (var Code:      CodeArrType;
                        var NumInstr: integer)
```

Each record represents an object code instruction with `NumInstr` the number of records in the array. A `Label` value of 0 means the instruction has no label, otherwise the value represents the label. An `Instr` value of 'N' stands for the `NOP` instruction, otherwise it represents some other instruction in the instruction set. Corresponding to the previous example, `OptimizeCode` should change

```
0  S
1  N
2  N
0  L
```

to

```
0  S
1  L
```

Assume that every `NOP` will have a label and that other instructions will not. Test your procedure in a main program.

36. Add an integer field called `OprndSpec` to the record of Problem 35 that represents the operand specifier of the instruction. When `OptimizeCode` consolidates `L1` and `L2` into `L1` in the example, it should also change every occurrence of 2 to 1 in the `OprndSpec` fields of all instructions in the program.

Chapter

16

Language Translation Principles

You are now multilingual because you understand at least four languages—English, Pascal, Pep/5 assembly language, and machine language. The first is a natural language, while the other three are artificial languages.

The fundamental question of computer science

Keeping that in mind, let's turn to the fundamental question of computer science, which is, What can be automated? We use computers to automate everything from writing payroll checks to correcting spelling errors in manuscripts. Although computer science has not yet been very successful in automating the translation of natural languages, say from German to English, it has been successful in translating artificial languages. You have already learned how to translate between the three artificial languages of Pascal, Pep/5 assembly language, and machine language. Compilers and assemblers automate this translation process for artificial languages.

Automatic translation

Since each level of a computer system has its own artificial language, the automatic translation between these languages is at the very heart of computer science. Computer scientists have developed a rich body of theory about artificial languages and the automation of the translation process. This chapter introduces the theory and shows how it applies to the translation of Pascal and Pep/5 assembly language.

Syntax and semantics

Two attributes of an artificial language are its syntax and semantics. A computer language's *syntax* is the set of rules that a program listing must obey to be declared a valid program of the language. Its *semantics* is the meaning or logic behind the valid program. Operationally, a syntactically correct program will be successfully translated by a translator program. The semantics of the language determine the result produced by the translated program when the object program is executed.

The part of an automatic translator that compares the source program with the language's syntax is called the *parser*. The part that assigns meaning to the source program is called the *code generator*. Most computer science theory applies to the syntactic rather than the semantic part of the translation process.

Four common techniques to describe a language's syntax are

Techniques to specify syntax

- Syntax charts
- Grammars
- Finite state machines
- Regular expressions

You are already familiar with the syntax charts of the Pascal language. This chapter introduces grammars and finite state machines. It shows how to construct a software finite state machine to aid in the parsing process. The last section shows a complete program, including code generation, that automatically translates between two languages. Space limitations preclude a presentation of regular expressions.

16.1 Languages, Grammars, and Parsing

Every language has an alphabet. Formally, an *alphabet* is a finite, nonempty set of characters. For example, the Pascal alphabet is the nonempty set

The Pascal alphabet

```
{a, b, c, d, e, f, g, h, i, j, k, l, m, n,
 o, p, q, r, s, t, u, v, w, x, y, z, A, B,
 C, D, E, F, G, H, I, J, K, L, M, N, O, P,
 Q, R, S, T, U, V, W, X, Y, Z, 0, 1, 2, 3,
 4, 5, 6, 7, 8, 9, +, -, *, /, =, <, >, [,
 ], (, ), {, }, ., ,, :, ;, ^}
```

The alphabet for Pep/5 assembly language is similar except for the punctuation characters, as shown in the following set:

The Pep/5 assembly language alphabet

```
{a, b, c, d, e, f, g, h, i, j, k, l, m, n,
 o, p, q, r, s, t, u, v, w, x, y, z, A, B,
 C, D, E, F, G, H, I, J, K, L, M, N, O, P,
 Q, R, S, T, U, V, W, X, Y, Z, 0, 1, 2, 3,
 4, 5, 6, 7, 8, 9, #, ., ,, :, ;}
```

For example, the # character is not in the Pascal alphabet, but it is required in an assembly language program to represent constants, as in `d#` for decimal constant.

Another example of an alphabet is the alphabet for the language of real numbers, not in scientific notation. It is the set

```
{0, 1, 2, 3, 4, 5, 6, 7, 8, 9, +, -, .}
```

Concatenation

An abstract data type is a set of possible values together with a set of operations on the values. Notice that an alphabet is a set of values. The pertinent operation on this set of values is *concatenation*, which is simply the joining of two or more characters to form a string. An example from the Pascal alphabet is the concatenation of `:` and `=` to form the string `:=`. In the Pep/5 assembly alphabet you can concatenate `d` and `#` to make `d#`, and in the language of real numbers `-`, `2`, `3`, `.`, and `7` to make `-23.7`.

Concatenation applies not only to individual characters in an alphabet to construct a string, but also to strings to construct bigger strings. From the Pascal alphabet, you can concatenate `program`, `Correct`, and `(output)` to produce the program heading

```
program Correct (output)
```

The length of a string is the number of characters in the string. The string `program` has a length of seven. The string of length zero, called the empty string, is denoted by the Greek letter ε to distinguish it from the English characters in an alphabet. Its concatenation properties are

The empty string

$$\varepsilon x = x\varepsilon = x$$

where x is a string. The empty string is useful for describing syntax rules.

In mathematics terminology, ε is the identity element for the concatenation operation. In general, an *identity element*, i, for an operation is one that does not change a value, x, when x is operated on by i.

Identity elements

Example 16.1 One is the identity element for multiplication since

$$1 \cdot x = x \cdot 1 = x$$

and true is the identity element for the AND operation since

$$\text{true AND } q = q \text{ AND true} = q$$

■

Languages

The closure of an alphabet

If T is an alphabet, the closure of T, denoted T^*, is the set of all possible strings formed by concatenating elements from T. T^* is extremely large. For example, if T is the set of characters and punctuation marks of the English alphabet, T^* includes all the sentences in the collected works of Shakespeare, in the English Bible, and in all the English encyclopedias ever published. It includes all strings of those characters ever printed in all the libraries in all the world throughout history, and then some.

Not only does it include all those meaningful strings, it includes meaningless ones as well. Here are some elements of T^* for the English alphabet:

```
To be or not to be, that is the question.
Go fly a kite.
Here over highly toward?
alkeu jfoj ,9nm20mfq23jk l?x!jeo
```

Some elements of T^* where T is the alphabet of the language for real numbers are

```
-2894.01
24
+78.3.80
--234--
6
```

You can easily construct many other elements of T^* with the two alphabets just mentioned. Since strings can be infinitely long, the closure of any alphabet has an infinite number of elements.

What is a language? In the examples of T^* that were just presented, some of the strings are in the language and some are not. In the English example, the first two strings are valid English sentences; that is, they are in the language. The last two strings are not in the language. A *language* is a subset of the closure of its alphabet. Of the infinite number of strings you can construct from concatenating strings of characters from its alphabet, only some will be in the language.

The definition of a language

Example 16.2 Consider the following two elements of T^* where T is the alphabet for the Pascal language.

```
program Correct (output);
   begin
   write ('Valid')
   end.

program Correct (output)
   begin
   write ('Valid')
   end.
```

The first element of T^* is in the Pascal language, but the second is not, since it has a syntax error. ■

Grammars

To define a language, you need a way to specify which of the many elements of T^* are in the language and which are not. The Pascal syntax charts are one way of specifying a valid Pascal program. By tracing through a chart, you can determine the strings to concatenate to form a valid program. A *grammar* is another system that specifies how you can concatenate the characters of alphabet T to form a legal string in a language. Formally, a grammar contains four parts:

The four parts of a grammar

- N, a nonterminal alphabet
- T, a terminal alphabet
- P, a set of rules of production
- S, the start symbol, an element of N

An element from the nonterminal alphabet, *N*, represents a group of characters from the terminal alphabet, *T*. A nonterminal symbol is frequently enclosed in angle brackets, <>. You see the terminals when you read the language. The rules of production use the nonterminals to describe the structure of the language, which may not be readily apparent when you read the language.

Example 16.3 In the Pascal grammar, the nonterminal <compound-statement> might represent the following group of terminals:

```
begin
read (I);
I := I + 1;
write (I)
end
```

The listing of a Pascal program always contains terminals, never nonterminals. You would never see a Pascal listing such as

```
program Test (input);
   var
      I: integer;
   <compound-statement>.
```

The nonterminal symbol, <compound-statement>, is useful for describing the structure of a Pascal program. ■

Every grammar has a special nonterminal called the *start symbol*, *S*. Notice that *N* is a set, but *S* is not. *S* is one of the elements of set *N*. The start symbol, along with the rules of production, *P*, enables you to decide whether a string of terminals is a valid sentence in the language. If, starting from *S*, you can generate the string of terminals using the rules of production, then the string is a valid sentence.

Grammar 16.1

Grammar 16.1 specifies a Pascal identifier. Even though a Pascal identifier can use any uppercase or lowercase letter or digit, to keep the example small this grammar permits only the letters `a`, `b`, and `c` and the digits `1`, `2`, and `3`. You know the rules for constructing an identifier. The first character must be a letter and the remaining characters, if any, can be letters or digits in any combination.

This grammar has three nonterminals, namely, <identifier>, <letter>, and <digit>. The start symbol is <identifier>, one of the elements from the set of nonterminals.

The rules of production are of the form

$$A \rightarrow w$$ *Productions*

Grammar 16.1

A grammar for Pascal identifiers.

N = {<identifier>, <letter>, <digit>}
T = {a, b, c, 1, 2, 3}
P = the productions

1. < identifier> → <letter>
2. < identifier> → <identifier> <letter>
3. < identifier> → <identifier> <digit>
4. < letter> → a
5. < letter> → b
6. < letter> → c
7. < digit> → 1
8. < digit> → 2
9. < digit> → 3

S = <identifier>

where *A* is a nonterminal and *w* is a string of terminals and nonterminals. The symbol → means "produces." You should read production rule number 3 in this grammar as, "An identifier produces an identifier followed by a digit."

Derivations

The grammar specifies the language by a process called a *derivation*. To derive a valid sentence in the language, you begin with the start symbol and substitute for nonterminals from the rules of production until you get a string of terminals. Here is a derivation of the identifier `cab3` from this grammar:

<identifier>	⇒ <identifier> <digit>	Rule 3
	⇒ <identifier> 3	Rule 9
	⇒ <identifier> <letter> 3	Rule 2
	⇒ <identifier> b 3	Rule 5
	⇒ <identifier> <letter> b 3	Rule 2
	⇒ <identifier> a b 3	Rule 4
	⇒ <letter> a b 3	Rule 1
	⇒ c a b 3	Rule 6

Next to each derivation step is the production rule on which the substitution is based. For example, Rule 2,

<identifier> → <identifier> <letter>

was used to substitute for <identifier> in the derivation step

<identifier> 3 ⇒ <identifier> <letter> 3

The symbol ⇒ means "derives in one step." You should read this derivation step as "Identifier followed by 3 derives in one step identifier followed by letter followed by 3."

Analogous to the closure operation on an alphabet is the closure of the derivation operation. The symbol ⇒* means "derives in zero or more steps." You can summarize the previous eight derivation steps as

<identifier> ⇒* c a b 3

This derivation proves that cab3 is a valid identifier, since it can be derived from the start symbol, <identifier>. A language specified by a grammar consists of all the strings derivable from the start symbol using the rules of production. The grammar provides an operational test for membership in the language. If it is impossible to derive a string, the string is not in the language.

Grammar 16.2

Grammar 16.2 defines the language of signed integers, where d represents a decimal digit. The start symbol is I, which stands for integer. F is the first character, which is an optional sign, and M is the magnitude.

Sometimes the rules of production are not numbered and are combined on one line to conserve space on the printed page. You can write the rules of production for this grammar as

I ⇒ FM
F ⇒ + | - | ε
M ⇒ d | dM

where the vertical bar, |, is the alternation operator and is read as "or." Read the last line as "M produces d, or d followed by M."

Here are some derivations of valid signed integers in this grammar:

I ⇒ FM	I ⇒ FM	I ⇒ FM
⇒ FdM	⇒ FdM	⇒ FdM
⇒ FddM	⇒ Fdd	⇒ FddM
⇒ Fddd	⇒ dd	⇒ FdddM
⇒ -ddd		⇒ Fdddd
		⇒ +dddd

Note how the last step of the second derivation used the empty string to derive dd from Fdd. It used the production F → ε and the fact that εd = d. This production rule with the empty string is a convenient way to express the fact that a positive or negative sign in front of the magnitude is optional.

Some illegal strings from this grammar are ddd+, +-ddd, and ddd+dd. Try to derive these strings from the grammar to convince yourself that they are not in the language. Can you informally prove from the rules of production that each of these strings is not in the language?

The productions in both of the example grammars have recursive rules in which a nonterminal is defined in terms of itself. Rule 3 of Grammar 16.1 defines an <identifier> in terms of an <identifier> as

Recursive productions

<identifier> → <identifier> <digit>

and Rule 5 of Grammar 16.2 defines M in terms of M as

M → dM

N = {I, F, M}
T = {+, -, d}
P = the productions
1. I → FM
2. F → +
3. F → -
4. F → ε
5. M → dM
6. M → d

S = I

Grammar 16.2

A grammar for signed integers.

Recursive rules produce languages with an infinite number of legal sentences. To derive an identifier, you can keep substituting <identifier> <digit> for <identifier> as long as you like to produce an arbitrarily long identifier.

Like all recursive definitions, there must be an escape hatch to provide the basis for the definition. Otherwise the sequence of substitutions for the nonterminal could never stop. The rule M → d provides the basis for M in Grammar 16.2.

Grammar 16.3

N = {A, B, C}
T = {a, b, c}
P = the productions
1. A → aABC
2. A → abC
3. CB → BC
4. bB → bb
5. bC → bc
6. cC → cc

S = A

Grammar 16.3

A context sensitive grammar.

The production rules for the previous grammars always contained a single nonterminal on the left side. Grammar 16.3 has some production rules with both a terminal and nonterminal on the left side.

Here is a derivation of a string of terminals with this grammar:

A ⇒ aABC	Rule 1
⇒ aaABCBC	Rule 1
⇒ aaabCBCBC	Rule 2
⇒ aaabBCCBC	Rule 3
⇒ aaabBCBCC	Rule 3
⇒ aaabBBCCC	Rule 3
⇒ aaabbBCCC	Rule 4
⇒ aaabbbCCC	Rule 4
⇒ aaabbbcCC	Rule 5
⇒ aaabbbccC	Rule 6
⇒ aaabbbccc	Rule 6

An example of a substitution in this derivation is using Rule 5 in the step aaabbbCCC ⇒ aaabbbcCC. Rule 5 says that you can substitute c for C, but only if the C has a b to the left of it.

In the English language, to quote a phrase out of context means to quote it without regard to the other phrases that surround it. Rule 5 is an example of a context-sensitive rule. It does not permit the substitution of C by c unless C is in the proper context, namely, immediately to the right of a b.

Context-sensitive grammars

Loosely speaking, a *context-sensitive grammar* is one in which the production rules may contain more than just a single nonterminal on the left side. In contrast, grammars that are restricted to a single nonterminal on the left side of every production rule are called *context-free*. (The precise theoretical definitions of context-sensitive and context-free grammars are more restrictive than these definitions. For the sake of simplicity, this chapter will use the previous definitions, although you should be aware that a more rigorous description of the theory would not define them as we have here.)

Some other examples of valid strings in the language specified by this grammar are abc, aabbcc, and aaaabbbbcccc. Two examples of invalid strings are aabc and cba. You should derive these valid strings and also try to derive the invalid strings to prove their invalidity to yourself. Some experimentation with the rules should convince you that the language is the set of strings that begins with one or more a's, followed by an equal number of b's, followed by the same number of c's. Mathematically, this language, L, can be written

$$L = \{a^n b^n c^n \mid n > 0\}$$

which you should read as "The language L is the set of strings $a^n b^n c^n$ such that n is greater than 0." The notation a^n means the concatenation of n a's.

The Parsing Problem

Deriving valid strings from a grammar is fairly straightforward. You can arbitrarily pick some nonterminal on the right side of the current intermediate string and select rules for the substitution repeatedly until you get a string of terminals. Such random derivations can give you many sample strings from the language.

An automatic translator, however, has a more difficult task. You give a translator a string of terminals that is supposed to be a valid sentence in an artificial language. Before the translator can produce the object code, it must determine if the string of terminals is indeed valid. The only way to determine if a string is valid is to derive it from the start symbol of the grammar. The translator must attempt such a derivation. If it succeeds, it knows the string is a valid sentence. The problem of determining whether or not a given string of terminal characters is valid for a specific grammar is called *parsing*, and is illustrated schematically in Figure 16.1.

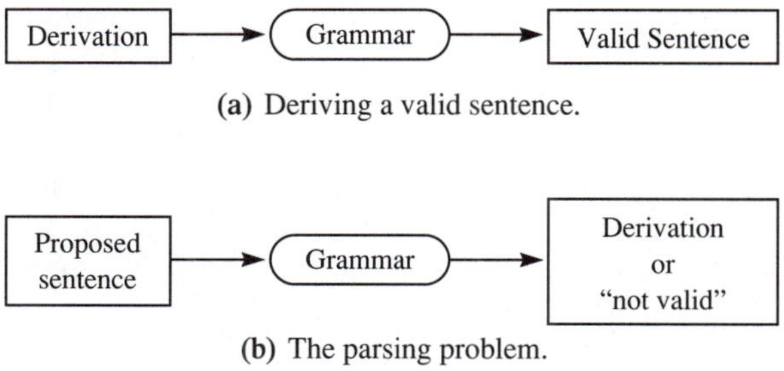

Figure 16.1

The difference between deriving an arbitrary sentence and parsing a proposed sentence.

Parsing a given string is more difficult than deriving an arbitrary valid string. The parsing problem is a form of searching. The parsing algorithm must search for just the right sequence of substitutions to derive the proposed string. Not only must it find the derivation if the proposed string is valid, but it must also admit the possibility that the proposed string may not be valid. If you look for a lost diamond ring in your room and do not find it, that does not mean the ring is not in your room. It may simply mean that you did not look in the right place. Similarly, if you try to find a derivation for a proposed string and do not find it, how do you know that such a derivation does not exist? A translator must be able to prove that no derivation exists if the proposed string is not valid.

Grammar 16.4

To see some of the difficulty a parser may encounter, consider Grammar 16.4, which describes an arithmetic infix expression. Suppose you are given the string of terminals

```
( a * a ) + a
```

and the production rules of this grammar and are asked to parse the proposed string. The correct parse is

E ⇒ E + T	Rule 1
⇒ T + T	Rule 2
⇒ F + T	Rule 4
⇒ (E) + T	Rule 5
⇒ (T) + T	Rule 2
⇒ (T * F) + T	Rule 3
⇒ (F * F) + T	Rule 4
⇒ (a * F) + T	Rule 6
⇒ (a * a) + T	Rule 6
⇒ (a * a) + F	Rule 4
⇒ (a * a) + a	Rule 6

N = {E, T, F}
T = {+, *, (,), a}
P = the productions
1. E → E + T
2. E → T
3. T → T * F
4. T → F
5. F → (E)
6. F → a

S = E

Grammar 16.4

A grammar for expressions. Nonterminal E represents the expression. T represents a term and F a factor in the expression.

The reason this could be difficult is that you might make a bad decision early in the parse that looks plausible at the time, but which leads to a dead end. For example, you might spot the "(" in the string that you were given and choose Rule 5 immediately. Your attempted parse might be

E ⇒ T	Rule 2
⇒ F	Rule 4
⇒ (E)	Rule 5
⇒ (T)	Rule 2
⇒ (T * F)	Rule 3
⇒ (F * F)	Rule 4
⇒ (a * F)	Rule 6
⇒ (a * a)	Rule 6

Until now, you have seemingly made progress toward your goal of parsing the original expression, since the intermediate string looks more like the original string at each successive step of the derivation. Unfortunately, now you are stuck, since there is no way to get the + a part of the original string.

After reaching this dead end, you may be tempted to conclude that the proposed string is invalid, but that would be a mistake. Just because you cannot find a derivation, does not mean that such a derivation does not exist.

One interesting aspect of a parse is that it can be represented as a tree. The start symbol is the root of the tree. Each interior node of the tree is a nonterminal, and each leaf is a terminal. The children of an interior node are the symbols from the right side of the production rule substituted for the parent node in the derivation. The tree is called a *syntax tree*, for obvious reasons. Figure 16.2 shows the syntax tree for `(a * a) + a` with Grammar 16.4, and Figure 16.3 shows it for `dd` with Grammar 16.2.

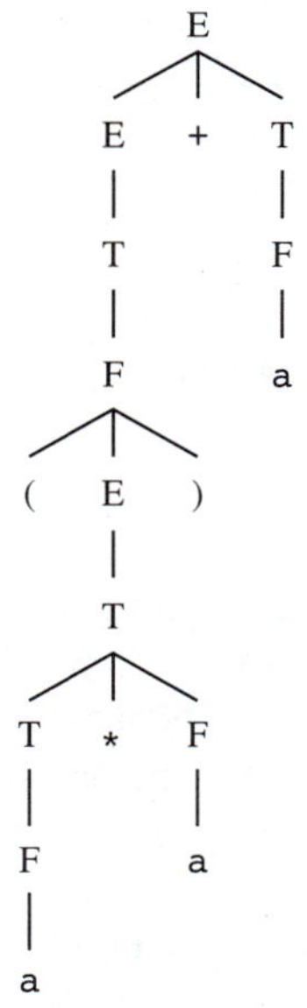

Figure 16.2

The syntax tree for the parse of `(a * a) + a` in Grammar 16.4.

Grammar 16.5

The rules of production for Grammar 16.5 (pp. 802–3) specify a small subset of the Pascal language. The only primitive types in this language are integer and boolean. The language has no provision for constant or type declarations and does not permit functions or reference parameters. It also omits `case`, `repeat`, and `for` statements. Despite these limitations, it gives an idea of how the syntax for a real language is formally defined.

The nonterminals for this grammar are enclosed in angle brackets, <>. Any symbol not in brackets is in the terminal alphabet and may literally appear in a Pascal program listing. <relop> means relational operator, <addop> means addition operator, and <mulop> means multiplication operator. The meaning of the other nonterminals should be obvious. The start symbol for this grammar is the nonterminal <program>.

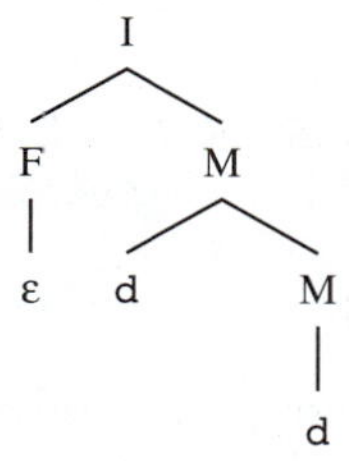

Figure 16.3

The syntax tree for the parse of `dd` in Grammar 16.2.

Backus Naur Form (BNF)

The specification of a programming language by the rules of production of its grammar is called *Backus Naur Form*, abbreviated BNF. In BNF, the production symbol → is sometimes written `::=`. The AGOL-60 language, designed in 1960, popularized BNF.

The following example of a parse with this grammar shows that

```
while A <= 9 do
   S1
```

is a valid <statement>, assuming that S1 is a valid <statement>. The parse consists of the following derivation:

<statement>
⇒ `while` <expression> do <statement>
⇒ `while` <simple-expression> <relop> <simple-expression> do <statement>
⇒ `while` <term> <relop> <simple-expression> do <statement>
⇒ `while` <factor> <relop> <simple-expression> do <statement>
⇒ `while` <variable> <relop> <simple-expression> do <statement>
⇒ `while` <identifier> <relop> <simple-expression> do <statement>
⇒ `while` <letter> <relop> <simple-expression> do <statement>
⇒ `while A` <relop> <simple-expression> do <statement>
⇒ `while A <=` <simple-expression> do <statement>
⇒ `while A <=` <term> do <statement>
⇒ `while A <=` <factor> do <statement>
⇒ `while A <=` <constant> do <statement>
⇒ `while A <=` <integer> do <statement>
⇒ `while A <=` <digit> do <statement>
⇒ `while A <= 9` do <statement>
⇒ `while A <= 9` do *S1*

Figure 16.4 (p. 804) shows the corresponding syntax tree for this parse. The nonterminal <statement> is the root of the tree, because the purpose of the parse is to show that the string is a valid <statement>.

With this example in mind, consider the task of a Pascal compiler. The compiler has programmed into it a set of production rules similar to the rules of Grammar 16.5. A programmer submits a text file containing the source program, a long

```
<program> →
      program <identifier> ; <declarations>
      <procedure-declarations> <compound-statement> .

<identifier-list> →
      <identifier>
      | <identifier-list> , <identifier>

<declarations> →
      var <declaration-list>
      | ε

<declaration-list> →
      <identifier-list> : <type> ;
      | <declaration-list> <identifier-list> : <type> ;

<type> →
      integer
      | boolean

<procedure-declarations> →
      <procedure-declarations> <procedure-declaration>
      | ε

<procedure-declaration> →
      <procedure-head> <declarations> <compound-statement> ;

<procedure-head> →
      procedure <identifier> <arguments> ;

<arguments> →
      ( <parameter-list> )
      | ε

<parameter-list> →
      <identifier-list> : <type>
      | <parameter-list> ; <identifier-list> : <type>

<compound-statement> →
      begin <statement-list> end

<statement-list> →
      <statement>
      | <statement-list> ; <statement>

<statement> →
      <elementary-statement>
      | if <expression> then <statement> else <statement>
      | if <expression> then <statement>
      | while <expression> do <statement>

<elementary-statement> →
      <variable> <assignop> <expression>
      | <procedure-statement>
      | <compound-statement>
```

Grammar 16.5

A grammar for a subset of the Pascal language.

Grammar 16.5, continued

<variable> →
    <identifier>

<procedure-statement> →
    <identifier>
    | <identifier> `(` <expression-list> `)`

<expression-list> →
    <expression>
    | <expression-list> `,` <expression>

<expression> →
    <simple-expression>
    | <simple-expression> <relop> <simple-expression>

<simple-expression> →
    <term>
    | <simple-expression> <addop> <term>

<term> →
    <factor>
    | <term> <mulop> <factor>

<factor> →
    <variable>
    | <constant>
    | `(` <expression> `)`
    | `not` <factor>

<identifier> →
    <letter>
    | <identifier> <letter>
    | <identifier> <digit>

<integer> →
    <digit>
    | <integer> <digit>

<constant> → <integer> | `true` | `false`

<relop> → = | <> | < | <= | >= | >

<addop> → + | - | `or`

<mulop> → * | `div` | `mod` | `and`

<assignop> → `:=`

<letter> →
    a | b | c | d | e | f | g | h | i | j | k | l | m |
    n | o | p | q | r | s | t | u | v | w | x | y | z |
    A | B | C | D | E | F | G | H | I | J | K | L | M |
    N | O | P | Q | R | S | T | U | V | W | X | Y | Z

<digit> →
    0 | 1 | 2 | 3 | 4 | 5 | 6 | 7 | 8 | 9

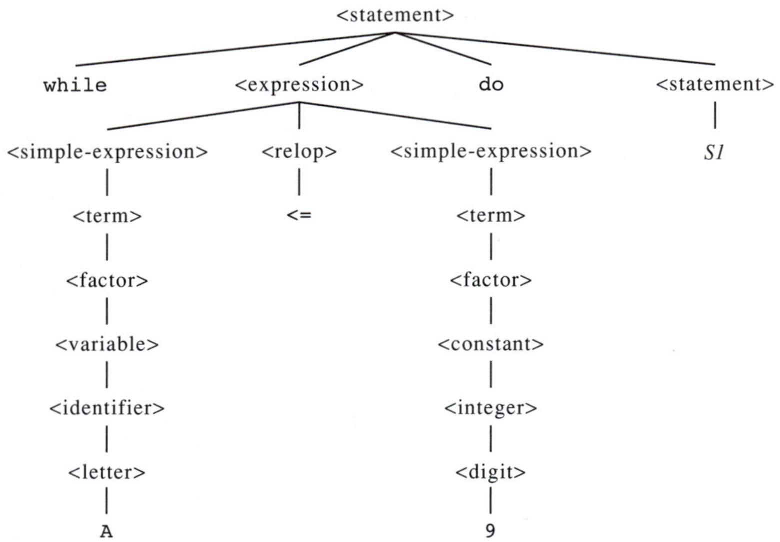

Figure 16.4

The syntax tree for a parse of the <statement>

`while A <= 9 do`
    S1

in Grammar 16.5.

string of terminals, to the compiler. First, the compiler must determine if the string of terminal characters represents a valid Pascal program. If the string is a valid <program>, then the compiler must generate the corresponding object code in a lower-level language. If it is not, the compiler must issue an appropriate syntax error.

There are more than 200 rules of production in the standard Pascal grammar. Imagine what a job the Pascal compiler has, sorting through those rules every time you submit a program to it! Fortunately, computer science theory has developed to the point where parsing is not difficult for a compiler. When designed using the theory, Pascal compilers can parse a program in a way that guarantees they will correctly decide which production to use for the substitution at every step of the derivation. If their parsing algorithm does not find the derivation of <program> to match the source, they can prove that such a derivation does not exist and that the proposed source program must have a syntax error.

Code generation is more difficult than parsing for compilers. The reason is that the object code must run on a specific machine produced by a specific manufacturer. Since every manufacturer's machine has a different architecture with different instruction sets, code-generation techniques for one machine may not be appropriate for another. A single, standard von Neumann architecture based on theoretical concepts does not exist. Consequently, not as much theory for code generation has been developed to guide compiler designers in their compiler construction efforts.

Context Sensitivity of Pascal

It appears from Grammar 16.5 that the Pascal language is context-free. Every production rule has only a single nonterminal on the left side. This is in contrast to a context-sensitive grammar, which can have more than a single nonterminal on the left as in Grammar 16.3. Appearances are deceiving. Even though the grammar for this subset of Pascal, as well as the full standard Pascal language, is context-free, the language itself has some context-sensitive aspects.

Consider Grammar 16.3. How do its rules of production guarantee that the number of `c`'s at the end of a string must equal the number of `a`'s at the beginning of the string? Rules 1 and 2 guarantee that for each `a` generated, exactly one C will be generated. Rule 3 lets the C commute to the right of B. Finally, Rule 5 lets you substitute `c` for C in the context of having a `b` to the left of C. The language could not be specified by a context-free grammar, because it needs Rules 3 and 5 to get the C's to the end of the string.

There are context-sensitive aspects of the Pascal language that Grammar 16.5 does not specify. For example, the definition of <parameter-list> allows any number of formal parameters, and the definition of <expression-list> allows any number of actual parameters. You could write a Pascal program containing a procedure with three formal parameters and a procedure call with two actual parameters that is derivable from <program> with Grammar 16.5. If you try to compile the program, however, the compiler will declare a syntax error.

The fact that the number of formal parameters must equal the number of actual parameters in Pascal is similar to the fact that the number of `a`'s at the beginning of the string must equal the number of `c`'s at the end of the string in the language defined by Grammar 16.3. The only way to put that restriction in Pascal's grammar would be to include many complicated context-sensitive rules. It is easier for the compiler to parse the program with a context-free grammar and check for any violations after the parse, usually with the help of its symbol table, that the grammar cannot specify.

16.2 Finite State Machines

Finite state machines are another way to specify the syntax of a sentence in a language. In diagram form, a *finite state machine* is a finite set of states represented by circles called *nodes* and transitions between the states represented by *arcs* between the circles. Each arc begins at one state and ends at another, and contains an arrowhead at the ending state. Each arc is also labeled with a character from the terminal alphabet of the language.

One state of the finite state machine (FSM) is designated as the start state and at least one, possibly more, is designated a final state. On a diagram, the start state has an incoming arrow and a final state is indicated by a double circle.

Mathematically, such a collection of nodes connected by arcs is called a *graph*. When the arcs are directed, as they are in an FSM, the structure is called a *directed graph* or *digraph*.

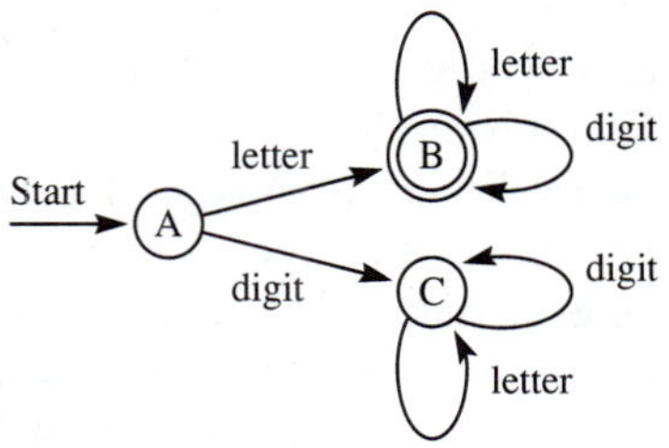

Figure 16.5

A finite state machine (FSM) to parse an identifier.

An FSM to Parse an Identifier

Figure 16.5 shows an FSM that parses an identifier as defined by Grammar 16.1. The set of states is {A, B, C}. A is the start state, and B is the final state. There is a transition from A to B on a letter, from A to C on a digit, from B to B on a letter or a digit, and from C to C on a letter or a digit.

To use the FSM, imagine that the input string is written on a piece of paper tape. Start in the start state, and scan the characters on the input tape from left to right. Each time you scan the next character on the tape, make a transition to another state of the finite state machine. Use only the transition that is allowed by the arc corresponding to the character you have just scanned. After scanning all the input characters, if you are in a final state the characters are a valid identifier. Otherwise they are not.

Current state	Next state	
	letter	digit
A	B	C
B	B	B
C	C	C

Table 16.1

The state transition table for the FSM of Figure 16.5.

Example 16.4 To parse the string `cab3`, you would make the following transitions:

Current state: A	Input: `cab3`	Scan `c` and go to B.
Current state: B	Input: `ab3`	Scan `a` and go to B.
Current state: B	Input: `b3`	Scan `b` and go to B.
Current state: B	Input: `3`	Scan `3` and go to B.
Current state: B	Input:	Check for final state.

Since there is no more input and the last state is B, a final state, `cab3` is a valid identifier. ■

You can also represent an FSM by its state transition table. Table 16.1 is the state transition table for the FSM of Figure 16.5. The table lists the next state reached by the transition from a given current state on a given input symbol.

Finite state machines are similar to syntax diagrams. With both structures you traverse a diagram while scanning the characters from an input alphabet. The difference is that a syntax diagram has the characters on the nodes, while an FSM is a graph with the characters on the transitions.

Simplified Finite State Machines

It is frequently convenient to simplify the diagram for an FSM by eliminating the state whose sole purpose is to provide transitions for illegal input characters. State C in this machine is such a state. If the first character is a digit, the string will not be a valid identifier regardless of the following characters. State C acts like a failure state. Once you make a transition to C you can never make a transition to another state, and you know the input string eventually will be declared invalid. Figure 16.6 shows the simplified FSM of Figure 16.5 without the failure state.

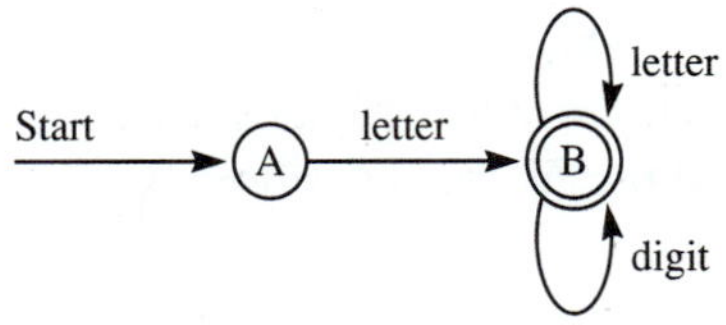

Figure 16.6

The FSM of Figure 16.5 without the failure state.

When you parse a string with this simplified machine, you will not be able to make a transition when you encounter an illegal character in the input string. There are two ways to detect an illegal sentence in a simplified FSM:

- You may run out of input, and not be in a final state.
- You may be in some state, and the next input character does not correspond to any of the transitions from that state.

Table 16.2 is the corresponding state transition table for Figure 16.6. The state transition table for a simplified machine has no entry for a missing transition. Note that this table has no entry under the digit column for the current state of A. The remaining machines in this chapter will be written in simplified form.

Current state	Next state: letter	Next state: digit
A	B	
B	B	B

Table 16.2

The state transition table for the FSM of Figure 16.6.

Nondeterministic Finite State Machines

When you parse a sentence using a grammar, frequently you must choose between several production rules for substitution in a derivation step. Similarly, nondeterministic finite state machines require you to decide between more than one transition when parsing the input string. Figure 16.7 is a nondeterministic FSM to parse a signed integer. It is nondeterministic because there is at least one state that has more than one transition from it on the same character. For example, state A has a transition to both B and C on a digit. There is also some nondeterminism at state B because, given that the next input character is a digit, a transition both to B and to C is possible.

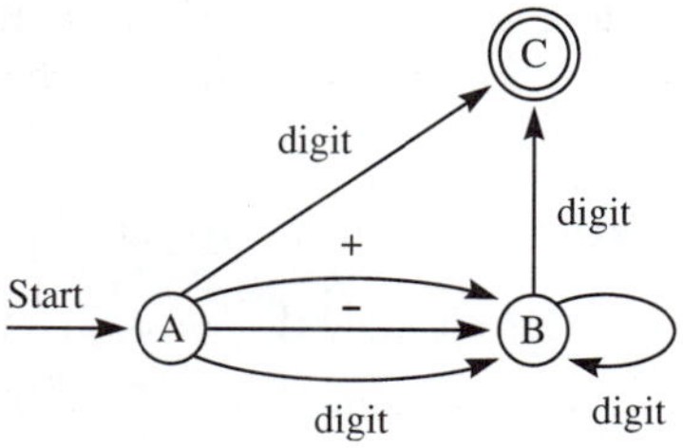

Figure 16.7

A nondeterministic FSM to parse a signed integer.

Example 16.5 You must make the following decisions to parse `+203` with this nondeterministic FSM.

Current state: A	Input: `+203`	Scan + and go to B.
Current state: B	Input: `203`	Scan `2` and go to B.
Current state: B	Input: `03`	Scan `0` and go to B.
Current state: B	Input: `3`	Scan `3` and go to C.
Current state: C	Input:	Check for final state.

Since there is no more input and you are in the final state C, you have proven that the input string `+203` is a valid signed integer. ■

When parsing with rules of production, you run the risk of making an incorrect choice early in the parse. You may reach a dead end where no substitution will get your intermediate string of terminals and nonterminals closer to the given string. Just because you reach such a dead end does not necessarily mean that the string is invalid. All invalid strings will produce dead ends in an attempted parse. But even valid strings have the potential for producing dead ends if you make a wrong decision early in the derivation.

The same principle applies with nondeterministic finite state machines. With the machine of Figure 16.7, if you are in the start state, A, and the next input character is 7, you must choose between the transitions to B and to C. Suppose you choose the transition to C and then find that there is another input character to scan. Since there are no transitions from C, you have reached a dead end in your attempted parse. You must conclude, therefore, that either the input string was invalid or it was valid and you made an incorrect choice at an earlier point.

Table 16.3 is the state transition table for the machine of Figure 16.7. The nondeterminism is evident from the multiple entries (B, C) in the digit column. They represent a choice that must be made when attempting a parse.

Current state	Next state		
	+	–	digit
A	B	B	B, C
B			B, C
C			

Table 16.3

The state transition table for the FSM of Figure 16.7.

Machines with Empty Transitions

In the same way that it is convenient to incorporate the empty string into production rules, it is sometimes convenient to construct finite state machines with transitions on the empty string. Such transitions are called *empty transitions*. Figure 16.8 is an FSM that corresponds closely to Grammar 16.2 to parse a signed integer.

In the figure, F is the state after the first character, and M is the magnitude state analogous to the F and M nonterminals of the grammar. In the same way that a sign can be +, –, or neither, the transition from A to S can be on +, –, or ε.

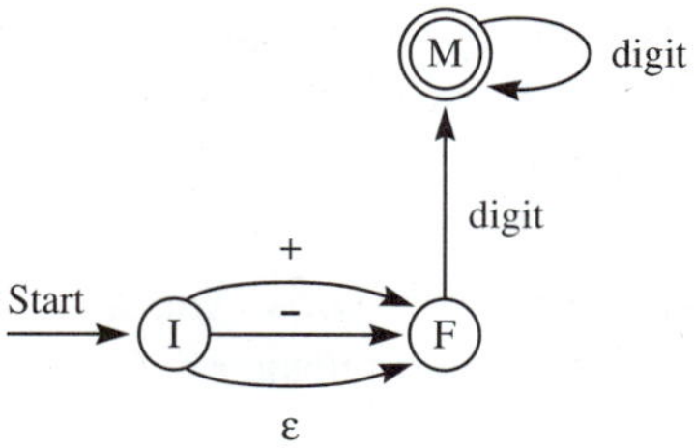

Figure 16.8

An FSM with an empty transition to parse a signed integer.

Example 16.6 To parse `32` requires the following decisions:

Current state: I	Input: `32`	Scan ε and go to F.
Current state: F	Input: `32`	Scan `3` and go to M.
Current state: M	Input: `2`	Scan `2` and go to M.
Current state: M	Input:	Check for final state.

The transition from I to F on ε does not consume an input character. When you are in state I, you can do one of three things: (a) scan + and go to F, (b) scan – and go to F, or (c) scan nothing (that is, the empty string) and go to F. ■

Machines with empty transitions considered nondeterministic

Machines with empty transitions are always considered nondeterministic. In the previous example, the nondeterminism comes from the decision you must make when you are in state I and the next character is +. You must decide whether to go from I to S on + or from I to S on ε. These are different transitions, since they leave you with different input strings, even though they are transitions to the same state.

Given an FSM with empty transitions, it is always possible to transform it to an equivalent machine without the empty transitions. Figure 16.9 shows how to remove an empty transition. If you have a transition from state X to state Y on ε,

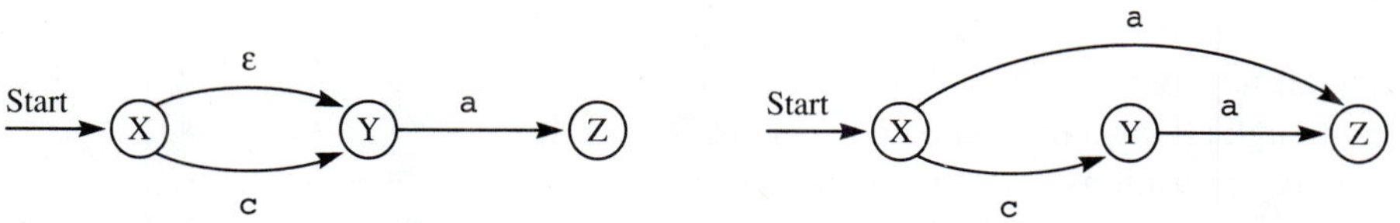

(a) The original FSM.

(b) The equivalent FSM without an empty transition.

Figure 16.9

Removing an empty transition.

and from state Y to state Z on a, you can eliminate the empty transition if you construct a transition from state X to state Z on a.

This procedure follows from the concatenation property of ε.

εa = a

If you are in X, you might just as well go to Z directly on a. The state and remaining input will be the same as if you went from X to Z via Y on ε.

Figure 16.10 shows this transformation on the FSM of Figure 16.8. The empty transition from I to F is replaced by the transition from I to M on digit, because there is a transition from F to M on digit.

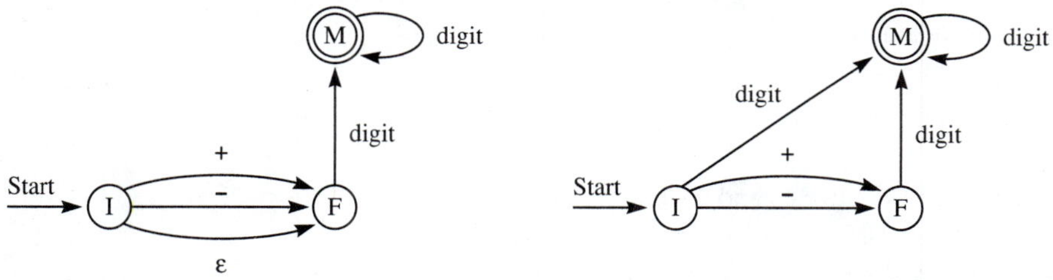

(a) The original FSM.

(b) The empty transition removed.

Figure 16.10

Removing the empty transition from the FSM of Figure 16.8.

In this case, there was only one transition from F to M, so the empty transition from I to F was replaced by only one transition from I to M. If an FSM had, for example, transitions from X to Y on a and X to Z on b, as in Figure 16.11, then you would need to replace an empty transition from W to X on ε by two transitions, one from W to Y on a and one from W to Z on b.

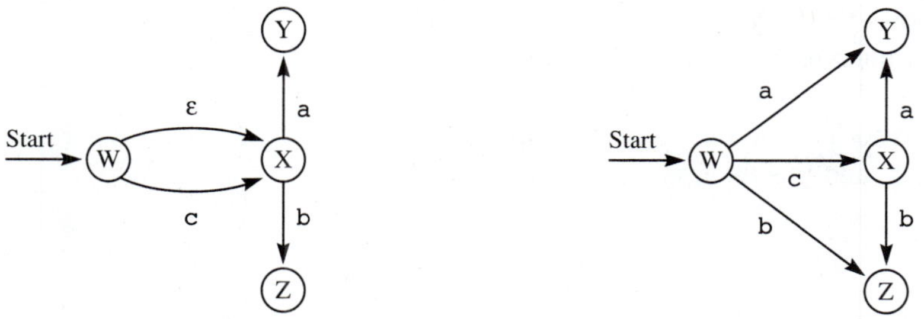

(a) The original FSM.

(b) The equivalent FSM without an empty transition.

Figure 16.11

Removing an empty transition.

Removing the empty transition from Figure 16.8 produced a deterministic machine. In general, however, removing all the empty transitions does not guarantee that the FSM is deterministic. Even though all machines with empty transitions are nondeterministic, an FSM with no empty transitions may still be nondeterministic. Figure 16.7 is such a machine, for example.

The advantage of a deterministic FSM

Given the choice, you are always better off parsing with a deterministic rather than a nondeterministic FSM. With a deterministic machine there is no possibility of making a wrong choice with a valid input string and terminating in a dead end. If you ever terminate at a dead end you can conclude with certainty that the input string is invalid.

Computer scientists have been able to prove that for every nondeterministic FSM there is an equivalent deterministic FSM. That is, there is a deterministic machine that recognizes exactly the same language. Unfortunately, the proof of this useful result is beyond the scope of this book. The proof consists of a recipe that tells how to construct the deterministic machine from the nondeterministic one.

Multiple Token Recognizers

The definition of a token

A *token* is a set of terminal characters that has meaning as a group. The characters usually correspond to some nonterminal in a language's grammar. For example, consider the Pep/5 assembly language statement

```
Number: .BLOCK d#2
```

The tokens in this statement are `Number:`, `.BLOCK`, `d#`, and `2`. Each is a set of characters from the assembly language alphabet and has meaning as a group. Their individual meanings are a symbol definition, a dot command, a decimal number specification, and a decimal value, respectively.

To a certain extent, the particular grouping of characters that you choose to form one token is arbitrary. For example, you could choose the string of characters `d#2` to be a single decimal number token. You would normally choose the characters of a token to be those that make the implementation of the FSM as simple as possible.

A common use of an FSM in a translator is to detect the tokens in the source string. Consider the assembler's job when confronted with this source line. Suppose the assembler has already determined that `Number:` is a symbol definition and `.BLOCK` is a dot command. It knows that either an `h#` specifier or a `d#` specifier can follow the dot command, so it must be programmed to accept either. It needs an FSM that recognizes both.

Figure 16.12(a) shows the two machines for parsing the `h#` and `d#` specifiers. C is the final state in the first machine for `h#`, and F is the final state in the second machine for `d#`.

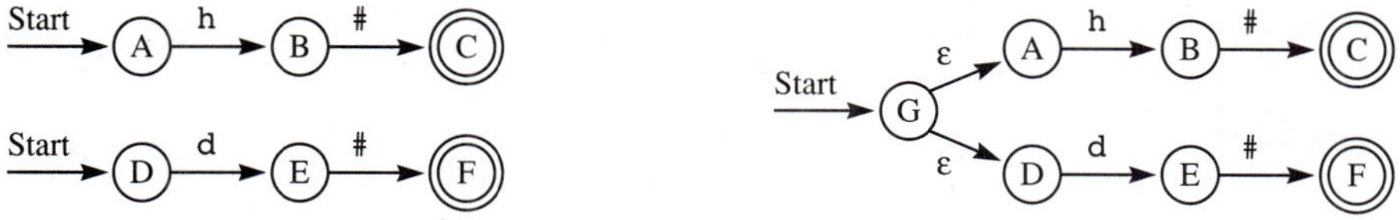

(a) Separate machines for the `h#` and `d#` tokens.

(b) One nondeterministic FSM that recognizes the `h#` or `d#` token.

Figure 16.12

Combining two machines to construct one FSM that recognizes both tokens.

To construct an FSM that will recognize both `h#` and `d#`, draw a new start state for the combined machine, in this example state G. Then draw empty transitions from the new start state to the start state of each individual machine, in this example from G to A and G to D. The result is one nondeterministic FSM that will recognize either token. The final state on termination tells you what token you have recognized. After the parse, if you terminate in state C you have detected `h#` and if you terminate in state F you have detected `d#`.

To get the machine into a more useful form you should eliminate the empty transitions. Figure 16.13(a) shows removal of the empty transitions for the FSM of Figure 16.12(b). After their removal, states A and D are inaccessible; that is, you can never reach them starting from the start state regardless of the input string. Consequently, they can never affect the parse and can be eliminated from the machine, as shown in Figure 16.12(b).

(a) Removing the empty transitions.

(b) Removing the inaccessible states.

Figure 16.13

Transforming the FSM of Figure 16.12(b).

As another example of when the translator needs to recognize multiple tokens, consider the assembler's job when confronted with the following two source lines:

```
NOTE: LOADA This,d ;comment 1
      NOTA         ;comment 2
```

The first token on the first line is a symbol definition. The first token on the second line is a mnemonic for a unary instruction. At the beginning of each line the translator needs an FSM to recognize a symbol definition, which is in the form of an identifier followed immediately by a colon, or a mnemonic, which is in the form of an identifier. Figure 16.14 shows the appropriate multiple token FSM.

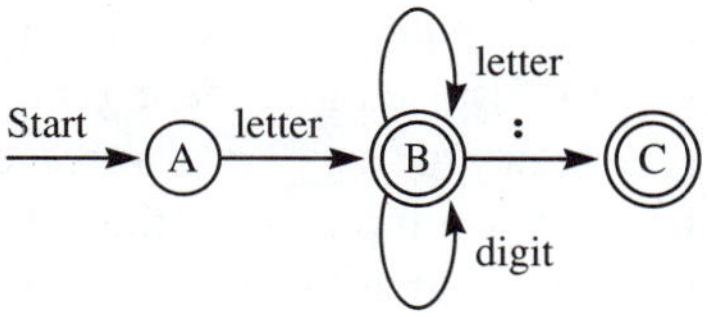

Figure 16.14

An FSM to parse a Pep/5 assembly language identifier or symbol definition.

In the first line this machine makes the following transitions:

A to B on `N`

B to B on `O`

B to B on `T`

B to B on `E`

B to C on `:`

after which the translator knows it has detected a symbol definition. In the second line it makes transitions

A to B on `N`

B to B on `O`

B to B on `T`

B to B on `A`

Since the next input character is not a colon, the FSM does not make the transition to state C. The translator knows it has detected an identifier because the terminal state is B.

16.3 Implementing Finite State Machines

The syntax of a programming language is usually specified by a formal grammar, which forms the basis of the parsing algorithm for the translator. Rather than specifying all the syntax, as Grammar 16.5 does, the formal grammar frequently specifies an upper level of abstraction and leaves the lower level to be specified by regular expressions, finite state machines, or syntax diagrams.

Figure 16.15 shows the steps in a typical compilation process. The low-level syntax analysis is called *lexical analysis*, and the high-level syntax analysis is called *parsing*. (This is a more specialized meaning of the word "parse." It is sometimes used in a more general sense to include all of syntax analysis.) In most translators for artificial languages, the lexical analyzer is based on a deterministic FSM whose input is a string of characters. The parser is usually based on a grammar whose input is the sequence of tokens taken from the lexical analyzer.

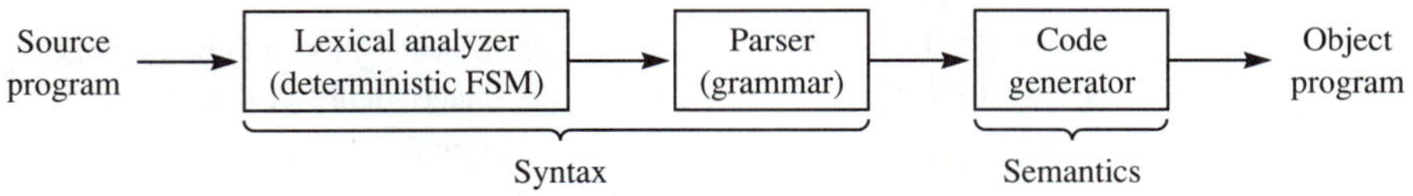

Figure 16.15
Steps in the compilation process.

A nonterminal symbol for the lexical analyzer becomes a terminal symbol for the parser. A common example of such a symbol is an identifier. The FSM has individual letters and digits as its terminal alphabet and inputs a string of them as it makes its state transitions. If the string `abc3` is input, the FSM declares that an identifier has been detected and passes that information on to the parser. The parser uses <identifier> as a terminal symbol in its parse of the sentence from the language.

When you design software that requires a parse of the input, the specification is sometimes not given in the form of an FSM and a grammar. If the structure of the input is not too complex, however, you may be able to combine the lexical analysis and parsing, and draw an FSM directly from the specification of the problem in order to analyze the syntax. If the FSM is nondeterministic you would need to convert it to an equivalent deterministic FSM. After you draw a deterministic FSM, you can implement it with a program.

More complex structures, such as those encountered by compilers that translate high-order languages, are usually specified with a formal grammar. Typically, you cannot analyze the syntax for such a language with just one FSM. Instead, you must use both stages for the syntax analysis, as shown in Figure 16.15, and employ more advanced techniques that are beyond the scope of this book.

The state variable

An algorithm that implements an FSM has an enumerated variable called the *state variable* whose possible values correspond to the possible states of the FSM. The algorithm initializes the state variable to the start state of the machine and gets the string of terminal characters one at a time in a loop. Each character causes a change of state. There are two common implementation techniques:

The two FSM implementation techniques

- Table lookup
- Direct code

They differ in the way that the state variable gets its next value. The table lookup technique stores the state transition table and looks up the next state based on the current state and input character. The direct code technique tests the current state and input character in the code itself and assigns the next state to the state variable directly.

Program 16.1

Program 16.1 implements the FSM of Figure 16.5 with the table lookup technique. Variable FSM is the state transition table shown in Table 16.1. The program classifies each input character as a letter or digit. Since B is the final state, it declares that the input string is a valid identifier if the state on termination of the loop is B.

The program assumes that the user will enter only letters and digits. If the user enters some other character, it will detect the character as a digit. For example, if the user enters `cab#`, the program will detect it as a valid identifier even though it is not. Problem 15, at the end of this chapter, suggests an improved FSM and corresponding implementation.

Program 16.1

Implementation of the FSM of Figure 16.5 with the table lookup technique.

```
program ParseIdent (input, output);
   type
      StateType    = (A, B, C);
      AlphabetType = (Letter, Digit);
   var
      FSM:     array [StateType, AlphabetType] of StateType;
      Ch:      char;
      FSMChar: AlphabetType;
      State:   StateType;
   begin
   FSM [A, Letter] := B;
   FSM [A, Digit]  := C;
   FSM [B, Letter] := B;
   FSM [B, Digit]  := B;
   FSM [C, Letter] := C;
   FSM [C, Digit]  := C;
   State := A;
   write ('Enter a string of letters and digits: ');
   while not eoln (input) do
      begin
      read (Ch);
      if Ch in ['A'..'Z', 'a'..'z'] then
         FSMChar := Letter
      else
         FSMChar := Digit;
      State := FSM [State, FSMChar]
      end;
   if State = B then
      writeln ('The string is a valid identifier.')
   else
      writeln ('Invalid identifier.')
   end.
```

Interactive Input/Output

```
Enter a string of letters and digits: cab3
The string is a valid identifier.
```

Interactive Input/Output

```
Enter a string of letters and digits: 3cab
Invalid identifier.
```

Program 16.2

Program 16.2 illustrates a situation in which a parse of the input is desirable. The Pascal `read` statement requests an integer. If the user of the program types a character, the program crashes.

Converting a string of ASCII characters to a value of type integer or real is one of the most common parsing problems. All numeric input from a keyboard or

Program 16.2

The need for a programmer-designed parse of an integer string.

```
program TestInteger (input, output);
   var
      Num: integer;
   begin
   write ('Enter number: ');
   readln (Num);
   write ('Num = ', Num: 1)
   end.
```

Input/Output

```
Enter number: q
IO error: bad input format
```

The program crashes.

text file must be parsed before it can be processed. That is why text files for numeric input are slower than the equivalent nontext files. Nontext files contain the binary representation of the numeric values ready to be processed.

As this example shows, the Pascal `readln` statement has built into it a parsing algorithm that converts a string of characters to the numeric value. As long as the input is a string of characters that represents a valid number, `readln` will parse them correctly. If not, the program will crash.

Program 16.3

Good commercial software does not allow a program to crash. To prevent crashes in your own programs, you can implement your own parsing algorithm that does not rely on `readln`. In Program 16.3, `ParseNum` allows the user to enter any string of characters. If the string is not a valid integer, `ParseNum` will return false for `Valid` and the program will issue an error message. Otherwise, `Valid` will be true and `Num` will be the correct integer value entered.

The input procedure, `GetLine`, reads the characters from the keyboard into a packed array of characters. It always installs a line feed character as a sentinel, regardless of how many or how few characters the user enters. If the user enters no characters and simply presses the return key, `GetLine` will install the line feed at `Line [1]`.

Procedure `ParseNum` corresponds to the FSM of Figure 16.10(b). The procedure has a local enumerated variable called `State`, whose possible values are I, F, or M corresponding to the states of the FSM. An additional state called Stop is for terminating the loop. The formal parameter, `V`, corresponds to the actual parameter, `Valid`, in the main program. The procedure initializes `V` to true and `State` to the start state, I.

A `repeat` loop simulates the transitions in the finite state machine. This implementation uses the direct code technique. A single `case` statement determines the current state, and a single nested `if` statement within each case determines the next character. Assignment statements in the code change the state variable directly.

In a simplified FSM, there are two ways to stop—either you run out of input or you reach a state with no transitions from it on the next character, in which case the string is not valid. Corresponding to these termination conditions, there are two ways to quit the `repeat` loop—when the input sentinel is reached in a final state or when the string is discovered to be invalid.

The body of a `repeat` loop always executes at least once. Nevertheless, the code executes correctly even if the return key is the first that is pressed. `GetLine`

Program 16.3

A programmer-designed parse of an integer string.

```
program TestInteger (input, output);
   const
      LineLength = 10;
   type
      LineType = packed array [1..LineLength] of char;
   var
      Line:  LineType;
      Num:   integer;
      Valid: boolean;

      {*** Global constant ***}
      LineFeed: char;

procedure GetLine (var L: LineType);
   {  Gets a line of up to LineLength-1 characters from the  }
   {  keyboard.  Inserts a LineFeed after the last character }
   {  entered.                                               }
   var
      I: integer;
   begin
   I := 1;
   while (not eoln (input)) and (I < LineLength) do
      begin
      read (L [I]);
      I := I + 1
      end;
   L [I] := LineFeed
   end;

procedure ParseNum (L: LineType; var V: boolean; var N: integer);
   type
      StateType = (I, F, M, Stop);
   var
      Sign:     integer;
      State:    StateType;
      NextChar: char;
      J:        integer;
```

Program 16.3, continued

```
begin
J := 1;
V := true;
State := I;
repeat
   NextChar := L [J];
   J := J + 1;
   case State of
   I:
      if NextChar = '-' then
         begin
         Sign := -1;
         State := F
         end
      else if NextChar = '+' then
         begin
         Sign := +1;
         State := F
         end
      else if NextChar in ['0'..'9'] then
         begin
         Sign := +1;
         N := ord (NextChar) - ord ('0');
         State := M
         end
      else
         V := false;
   F:
      if NextChar in ['0'..'9'] then
         begin
         N := ord (NextChar) - ord ('0');
         State := M
         end
      else
         V := false;
   M:
      if NextChar in ['0'..'9'] then
         N := 10 * N + (ord (NextChar) - ord ('0'))
      else if NextChar = LineFeed then
         begin
         N := Sign * N;
         State := Stop
         end
      else
         V := false
   end; {case}
until (State = Stop) or not V
end; {procedure ParseNum}
```

Program 16.3, continued

```
begin
LineFeed := chr (10);
write ('Enter number: ');
GetLine (Line);
ParseNum (Line, Valid, Num);
if Valid then
   write ('Num = ', Num: 1)
else
   write ('Invalid entry.')
end. {program TestInteger}
```

Input/Output

```
Enter a number: q
Invalid entry.
```

Input/Output

```
Enter a number: -58
Num = -58
```

installs LineFeed in `Line [1]`. `ParseNum` initializes `State` to I, enters the `repeat` loop, and immediately sets `NextChar` to LineFeed. Then `V` gets false, and the loop terminates correctly.

In addition to determining whether the string is valid, `ParseNum` converts the string of characters to the proper integer value. If the first character is + or a digit, it sets `Sign` to +1. If the first character is `-`, it sets `Sign` to –1. The first digit detected sets `N` to its proper value in state I or F. Its value is maintained correctly in state M each time a succeeding digit is detected. The magnitude is multiplied by the `Sign` when the loop terminates with a valid number.

The computation of the correct integer value is a semantic action, while the state assignment is a syntax action. It is easy with the direct code technique to integrate the semantic processing with the syntactic processing, because there is a distinct place in the syntax code to include the required semantic processing. For example, you know in state I if the character is `-` that `Sign` must be set to –1. It is easy to determine where to include that assignment in the syntax code.

Integrating semantic actions with syntactic actions

If the user enters leading spaces before a legal string of digits, the FSM will declare the string invalid. The next program shows how to correct this deficiency.

Program 16.4

If the parser of a Pascal compiler is analyzing the string

```
Total :=
```

it knows the next nonterminal could be an identifier such as `Amount`, or an integer such as `100`. Since it does not know which token to expect, it calls a finite state machine that can recognize either, as in Figure 16.16.

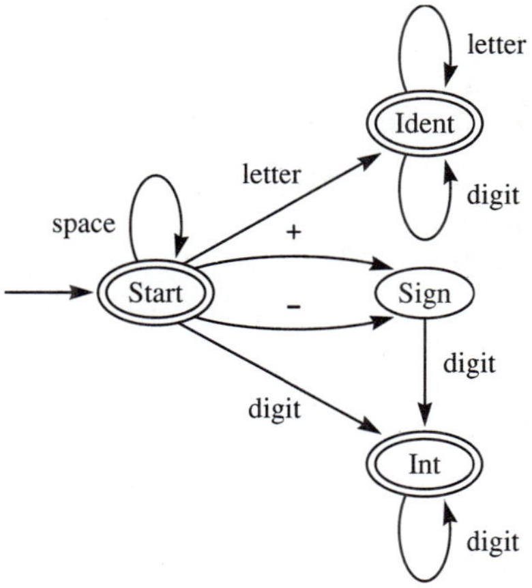

Figure 16.16

The FSM of Program 16.4 to recognize an identifier or an integer.

The state labeled Ident is a final state for detecting the identifier token. Int is the final state for detecting an integer. The transition from Start to Start is on the space character. It allows for leading spaces before either token. If the only characters left to scan are trailing spaces at the end of a line, the FSM procedure will return the empty token. That is why the start state is also a final state.

Program 16.4 is a Pascal implementation of the multiple token recognizer of Figure 16.16. It takes its input from lines of characters in an input file. These characters form a sequence of identifiers, integers, and spaces all concatenated together on each line. Its output is a list that states what kind of tokens were detected and the value of each. The value of an identifier token is simply the first eight characters of the original terminal string. The value of an integer token is its numerical value. The empty token has no value.

A token is defined as a variant record, as shown in Figure 16.17. It has four different structures depending on the value of the tag field named `Key`. Three of the structures correspond to the three kinds of token, and the fourth corresponds to an invalid token. The invalid token serves the same purpose as the variable `V` in Program 16.3, which controlled the termination of the FSM loop.

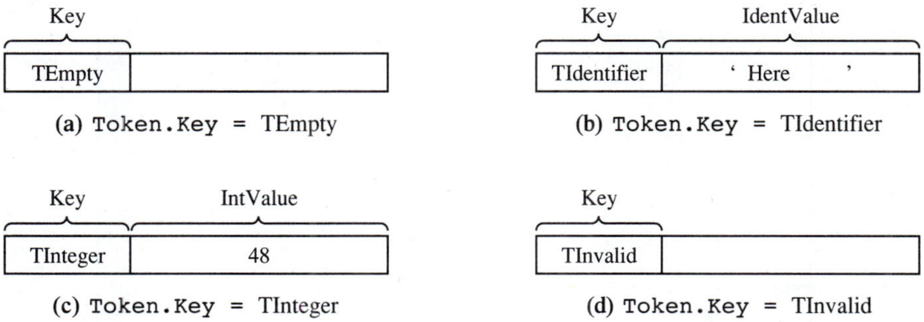

Figure 16.17

The variant record structure of `Token` in Program 16.4.

Program 16.4

A finite state machine that recognizes multiple tokens.

```
program TokenTest (SourceFile, output);
   const
      LineLength = 80;
   type
      IdentType    = packed array [1..8] of char;
      TokenType    = (TIdentifier, TInteger, TEmpty, TInvalid);
      TokenRecType =
         record
         case Key: TokenType of
            TIdentifier: (IdentValue: IdentType);
            TInteger:    (IntValue:   integer);
            TEmpty:      ();
            TInvalid:    ()
         end;
      BufferType =
         record
         Line:  packed array [1..LineLength] of char;
         Index: integer
         end;
   var
      SourceFile: text;
      Token:      TokenRecType;

      {*** Globals ***}
      Buffer:     BufferType;
      LineFeed:   char;

procedure GetLine (var F: text);
   var
      I: integer;
   begin
   {  Assert: eof (F) is false.  }
   I := 1;
   while not eoln (F) and (I < LineLength) do
      begin
      read (F, Buffer.Line [I]);
      I := I + 1
      end;
   Buffer.Line [I] := LineFeed;
   Buffer.Index := 1;
   readln (F)
   {  Assert: eof (F) is true if the line just read was the }
   {  last line in the file.  Otherwise, F is positioned at }
   {  the beginning of the next line.                        }
   end;

procedure AdvanceInput (var Ch: char);
   begin
   Ch := Buffer.Line [Buffer.Index];
   Buffer.Index := Buffer.Index + 1
   end;
```

Program 16.4, continued

```
procedure BackUpInput;
   begin
   Buffer.Index := Buffer.Index - 1
   end;

procedure GetToken (var T: TokenRecType);
   type
      StateType = (SStart, SIdent, SSign, SInteger, SStop);
   var
      State:    StateType;
      NextChar: char;
      Sign:     integer;
      I:        integer;
   begin
   T.Key := TEmpty;
   State := SStart;
   repeat
      AdvanceInput (NextChar);
      case State of
      SStart:
         if NextChar in ['A'..'Z', 'a'..'z'] then
            begin
            T.IdentValue := '          ';
            T.IdentValue [1] := NextChar;
            I := 2;
            State := SIdent
            end
         else if NextChar = '-' then
            begin
            Sign := -1;
            State := SSign
            end
         else if NextChar = '+' then
            begin
            Sign := +1;
            State := SSign
            end
         else if NextChar in ['0'..'9'] then
            begin
            T.IntValue := ord (NextChar) - ord ('0');
            Sign := +1;
            State := SInteger
            end
         else if NextChar = LineFeed then
            State := SStop
         else if NextChar <> ' ' then
            T.Key := TInvalid;
```

Program 16.4, continued

```
   SIdent:
      if NextChar in ['A'..'Z', 'a'..'z', '0'..'9'] then
         begin
         if I <= 8 then
            begin
            T.IdentValue [I] := NextChar;
            I := I + 1
            end;
         end
      else
         begin
         BackUpInput;
         T.Key := TIdentifier;
         State := SStop
         end;
   SSign:
      if NextChar in ['0'..'9'] then
         begin
         T.IntValue := ord (NextChar) - ord ('0');
         State := SInteger
         end
      else
         T.Key := TInvalid;
   SInteger:
      if NextChar in ['0'..'9'] then
         T.IntValue := 10 * T.IntValue + ord (NextChar) - ord ('0')
      else
         begin
         BackUpInput;
         T.Key := TInteger;
         T.IntValue := Sign * T.IntValue;
         State := SStop
         end
   end; {case}
until (State = SStop) or (T.Key = TInvalid)
end; {procedure GetToken}
```

Program 16.4, continued

```
begin
LineFeed := chr (10);
reset (SourceFile);
while not eof (SourceFile) do
   begin
   GetLine (SourceFile);
   repeat
      GetToken (Token);
      case Token.Key of
         TEmpty:      writeln ('Empty token');
         TIdentifier: writeln ('Identifier = ', Token.IdentValue);
         TInteger:    writeln ('Integer    = ', Token.IntValue: 1);
         TInvalid:    writeln ('Syntax error')
      end {case}
   until Token.Key in [TEmpty, TInvalid]
   end
end. {program TokenTest}
```

Input

```
Here   is A47 48B
  C+49 ThisIsLong -50  D16-51
```

Output

```
Identifier = Here
Identifier = is
Identifier = A47
Integer    = 48
Identifier = B
Empty token
Identifier = C
Integer    = 49
Identifier = ThisIsLo
Integer    = -50
Identifier = D16
Integer    = -51
Empty token
```

Program 16.4, continued

Input

```
Here   is A47+ 48B
  C+49

ThisIsLong
```

Output

```
Identifier = Here
Identifier = is
Identifier = A47
Syntax error
Identifier = C
Integer    = 49
Empty token
Empty token
Identifier = ThisIsLo
Empty token
```

Figure 16.18 is a hierarchy diagram that shows the calling relationships. The main program uses the `eof` technique for processing the file. The body of the `while` loop executes once for each line of input. Inside the body, `GetLine` fills an input buffer with the characters of the next line in the text file. `GetToken`, inside a nested `repeat` loop, scans the line of characters until it detects the next token. The nested loop executes once for each token in the current line. `GetToken` calls `AdvanceInput` and `BackUpInput`.

The input buffer and its associated index are global variables. This is typical for large programs whose input comes from a single file. It simplifies the parameter lists of procedures, particularly when many procedures call other procedures.

Although `GetToken` needs to access characters from the input buffer, it does not access the buffer directly. Only procedures `GetLine`, `AdvanceInput`, and `BackUpInput` access the global buffer. The reason for this design is to provide `GetToken` with a more convenient abstract data type of the input stream. As shown in the following explanation of the sample I/O, the FSM sometimes detects a character from the input stream that terminates its call from the main program, yet will be required from the input stream in a subsequent call. Conceptually, `GetToken` must push the character back into the input stream so it will be retrieved on the subsequent call. `BackUpInput` provides that operation on the buffer ADT.

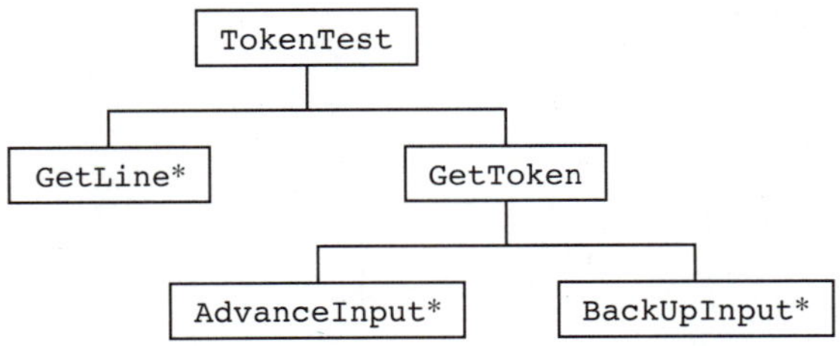

Figure 16.18

The hierarchy diagram of Program 16.4. The asterisk indicates a procedure that accesses the global buffer.

Alan Turing

Alan M. Turing is one of the most enigmatic figures of twentieth century science. Born in London in 1912, he attended Sherborne, an exclusive boarding school, and then studied at King's College in Cambridge. His doctoral dissertation "On the Gaussian Error Function" earned him a fellowship at Cambridge in 1935.

After leaving Cambridge, Turing crossed the Atlantic and studied at Princeton with mathematician Alonzo Church and computer scientist John von Neumann. In 1937, Turing wrote what is considered his most significant contribution to mathematical logic, "On Computable Numbers, with an Application to the *Entscheidungsproblem* [decidability problem]." It is in this work that he developed the theoretical universal computing machine that is now called the Turing machine.

The Turing machine is an abstract mathematical conception of a bare-bones computer. By keeping it pure and abstract, we can assume an infinitely large storage area that can be extended as necessary. This gives theoreticians the power to explore advanced questions in computability theory without being inhibited by the bounds of present technology. The main reason for adopting the Turing machine's conception of computability, however, is that its simplicity, along with its equivalence to actual physical computers, makes it possible to construct elegant mathematical proofs about what can and cannot be computed.

At the onset of World War II in 1939, Turing returned to England where he was hired by the Foreign Office and British Intelligence to work on breaking Germany's secret Enigma Code. The resulting machine, the Colossus (also nicknamed the Eastern Goddess), succeeded in breaking the code and enabled the British to keep up with Germany's military plans. Turing's work during the war was so highly sensitive that it has never been made public, and for his contribution to the war effort, King George VI awarded him the Order of the British Empire. (A few years ago, the award-winning one-man play *Breaking The Code* was performed in London's West End and on Broadway, giving audiences a brief glimpse of Turing's complex character.)

After the war, Turing worked at the National Physical Laboratory in London where he directed the design, construction, and use of the Automatic Computing Engine (ACE), a large electronic digital computer. In 1948, he moved to the University of Manchester where he was the assistant director of the Manchester Automatic Digital Machine (MADAM).

During this period of his research the burning question in Turing's mind was, Can machines think? In 1950, he published "Computing Machinery and Intelligence," an article that earned him the title of father of modern-day artificial intelligence (AI). Turing proposed that computers could be capable of thought, which gave rise to some lively arguments on both sides of the issue. In the article, he described the Turing test, a behavioral test that has an impartial person pose a series of questions to both a computer and a human. The questions would be given to a computer in one room or a human in another without the questioner knowing to which room the conversation was directed. Turing proposed that we acknowledge the machine or program as intelligent if, after a number of blind trials in which there were conversations with both the machine and the human, the questioner could not clearly identify which conversant was which.

Another of Turing's interests was in the area of morphogenesis, the development of pattern and form in living organisms. He published the first part of his theoretical study in 1952, but the rest was unfinished at the time of his death. He died at his home in Wiltshire, England on June 7, 1954 at the age of 42. From the spoon covered with potassium cyanide found near his body, it was concluded that he accidentally took his own life while conducting an experiment.

Current research in cognitive science and artificial intelligence still revolves around Turing's work. He truly helped usher in a new era.

The example input and output shows what happens when the finite state machine is applied to a specific line of input. Here is an explanation of the first sample input of Program 16.4.

The machine starts in the start state and scans the first terminal, `H`. That takes it to the SIdent state. The following terminals, `e`, `r`, and `e`, make transitions to the same state. The next terminal is a space. There is no transition from state SIdent on the terminal space. Since the machine is in the final state for identifiers, it concludes that an identifier has been scanned. It puts the space terminal, which it could not use in this state, back into the input for use as the first terminal for the next token. It then declares that an identifier has been scanned.

The machine starts over in the start state. It uses the leftover space to make a transition to SStart. A few more spaces produce a few more transitions to SStart, after which the `i` and `s` characters produce the recognition of a second identifier, as shown in the sample output. Similarly, `A47` is recognized as an identifier.

For the next token, the initial `4` sends the machine into the SInteger state. The `8` makes the transition to the same state. Now the machine inputs the `B`. There is no transition from state SInteger on the terminal `B`. Since the machine is in the final state for integers, it concludes that an integer has been scanned. It puts the `B` terminal, which it could not use in this state, back into the input for use as the first terminal for the next token. It then declares that an integer has been scanned. Notice that `B` gets detected as an identifier the next time around.

The machine continues recognizing tokens until it gets to the end of the line, at which point it recognizes the empty token. It will recognize the empty token whether or not there are trailing spaces in the input.

The second sample input shows how the machine handles a string of characters that contains a syntax error. After recognizing `Here`, `is`, and `A47`, on the next call the FSM gets the `+` and goes to state SSign. Since the next character is space, and there is no transition from SSign on space, the FSM returns the invalid token.

Like all multiple token recognizers, this machine operates on the following design principle:

A design principle for multiple token recognizers

- You can never fail once you reach a final state. Instead, if the final state does not have a transition from it on the terminal just input, you have recognized a token and should backup the input. The character will then be available as the first terminal for the next token.

The machine handles an empty line (or a line with only spaces) correctly, returning the empty token on the first call. It can use a `repeat` loop even with empty lines because `GetLine` is guaranteed to put at least one character in the buffer, even if it is only the line feed sentinel.

16.4 Code Generation

To *translate* is to transform a string of characters from some input alphabet to another string of characters from some output alphabet. The typical phases in such a translation are lexical analysis, parsing, and code generation. This section consists of a program that translates from one language to another. It illustrates all three phases of a simple automatic translator.

Program 16.5

In Program 16.5, (pp. 828–34), the source and object languages are line oriented, as are assembly languages. The source language has the syntax of Pascal procedure calls, and the object language has the syntax of Pascal assignment statements. An example statement from the input language is

```
set (Time, 15)
```

The corresponding object statement is

```
Time := 15
```

The word `set` is reserved in the source language. The other reserved words are `add`, `sub`, `mul`, `div`, `neg`, and `end`.

`Time` is a user-defined identifier. Identifiers follow the same rules as in the Pascal language, but they are limited to a maximum of eight characters. Integers, such as `15` in the previous example, also follow the Pascal syntax.

The `set` procedure takes two arguments separated by a comma and surrounded by parentheses. The first argument must be an identifier, but the second can be an identifier or an integer constant.

Another example of a translation is

```
mul (TSquared, Time)
```

which is written in the object language as

```
TSquared := TSquared * Time
```

As with the `set` procedure, the first argument of a `mul` procedure call must be an identifier. To translate the `mul` statement, the translator must duplicate its first argument, which appears on both sides of the assignment operator.

The other procedure calls are similar except for `neg`, which takes a single argument and translates it prefixed with a dash character on the right side of the assignment operator. For example, the source statement

```
neg (Alpha)
```

gets translated to

```
Alpha := -Alpha
```

Reserved word `end` is the sentinel for the translator. It generates no code and corresponds to `.END` of Pep/5 assembly language. Any number of spaces can occur anywhere in a source line, except within an identifier or integer. See the end of the program listing for further examples of input and corresponding output.

The translator must not crash if syntax errors occur in the input stream. At the end of the listing there is also a run that shows a source file full of errors. The program generates appropriate error messages to help the user find the bugs in the source program.

Program 16.5

A language translator.

```
program Translate (SourceFile, output);
   const
      LineLength = 80;
   type
      StrType   = packed array [1..9] of char;  {9th is a sentinel ' '}
      MnemType  = (
         MSet, MAdd, MSub, MMul,
         MDiv, MNeg, MEnd, MEmpty);
      ErrorType = (
         NoEnd,   NoFunct, NoLeft,  Bad1st, BadNeg,
         NoComma, Bad2nd,  NoRight, NoError);
      TokenType = (
         TIdentifier, TInteger, TComma, TLeftParen,
         TRightParen, TEmpty,   TInvalid);
      TokenRecType =
         record
         Key:   TokenType;
         Value: StrType
         end;
      CodeType =
         record
         Error:     ErrorType;
         Functn:    MnemType;
         FirstArg:  StrType;
         SecondArg: StrType
         end;
      BufferType =
         record
         Line:  packed array [1..LineLength] of char;
         Index: integer
         end;
   var
      SourceFile: text;
      Terminate:  boolean;

      {*** Global variables ***}
      Buffer: BufferType;
      Code:   CodeType;

      {*** Global constants ***}
      LineFeed:         char;
      LowerMinusUpper:  integer;
      OperatorTable:    array [MAdd..MDiv] of char;
      MnemonTable:      array [MSet..MEmpty] of StrType;

procedure GetLine (var F: text);
   {  Identical to Program 16.4  }

procedure AdvanceInput (var Ch: char);
   {  Identical to Program 16.4  }
```

Program 16.5, continued

```
procedure BackUpInput;
   {  Identical to Program 16.4  }

function LowerCase (Ch: char): char;
   begin
   if Ch in ['A'..'Z'] then
      LowerCase := chr (ord (Ch) + LowerMinusUpper)
   else
      LowerCase := Ch
   end;

procedure InitGlobalConstants;
   begin
   LowerMinusUpper := ord ('a') - ord ('A');
   LineFeed := chr (10);
   MnemonTable [MSet] := 'set      ';
   MnemonTable [MAdd] := 'add      ';
   MnemonTable [MSub] := 'sub      ';
   MnemonTable [MMul] := 'mul      ';
   MnemonTable [MDiv] := 'div      ';
   MnemonTable [MNeg] := 'neg      ';
   MnemonTable [MEnd] := 'end      ';
   OperatorTable [MAdd] := '+';
   OperatorTable [MSub] := '-';
   OperatorTable [MMul] := '*';
   OperatorTable [MDiv] := '/';
   end;

procedure PutError (ENum: ErrorType);
   begin
   write ('Error:  ');
   case ENum of
      NoEnd:   write ('Missing "end" sentinel.');
      NoFunct: write ('Line must begin with function identifier.');
      NoLeft:  write ('Left parenthesis expected after function.');
      Bad1st:  write ('First argument not an identifier.');
      BadNeg:  write ('The argument of "neg" is malformed.');
      NoComma: write ('Comma expected after first arguement.');
      Bad2nd:  write ('Second argument not an identifier or integer.');
      NoRight: write ('Right parenthesis expected after argument.')
   end {case}
   end;
```

Program 16.5, continued

```
procedure LookUpMnemon (Id: StrType; var Mn: MnemType; var Fnd: boolean);
   {  This procedure does a sequential search of MnemonTable.     }
   {  If Id is in the table, Fnd is set true and Mn is set to     }
   {  the enumerated mnemonic type.  Otherwise Fnd is set false.  }
   var
      I:       integer;
      LowerId: StrType;
   begin
   for I := 1 to 9 do
      LowerId [I] := LowerCase (Id [I]);
   MnemonTable [MEmpty] := LowerId;
   Mn := MSet;
   while MnemonTable [Mn] <> LowerId do
      Mn := succ (Mn);
   Fnd := (Mn <> MEmpty)
   end;

procedure GetToken (var T: TokenRecType);
   type
      StateType = (SStart, SIdent, SSign, SInteger, SStop);
   var
      State:    StateType;
      NextChar: char;
      I:        integer;
   begin
   {  A problem for the student.  }
   end;

procedure WriteIdent (W: StrType);
   var
      I: integer;
   begin
   I := 1;
   repeat
      write (W [I]);
      I := I + 1
   until W [I] = ' '  {W has at least one ' ' as sentinel}
   end;
```

Program 16.5, continued

```
procedure GenerateCode;
   begin
   with Code do
      if Error <> NoError then
         PutError (Error)
      else
         case Functn of
         MSet:
            begin
            WriteIdent (FirstArg);
            write (' := ');
            WriteIdent (SecondArg)
            end;
         MAdd, MSub, MMul, MDiv:
            begin
            WriteIdent (FirstArg);
            write (' := ');
            WriteIdent (FirstArg);
            write (' ', OperatorTable [Functn], ' ');
            WriteIdent (SecondArg)
            end;
         MNeg:
            begin
            WriteIdent (FirstArg);
            write (' := -');
            WriteIdent (FirstArg)
            end;
         MEnd, MEmpty:
            {Write nothing}
         end; {case}
   writeln
   end;

procedure ProcessSourceLine (var Term: boolean);
   type
      StateType = (
         SStart,    SFunction,    SOpen,  SFirstOprnd,
         SContinue, SSecondOprnd, SClose);
   var
      Token:    TokenRecType;
      Mnemonic: MnemType;
      Found:    boolean;
      State:    StateType;
```

Program 16.5, continued

```
begin
{  Assert: Term is false and a source line is in }
{  Buffer ready for processing.                  }
Code.Error := NoError;
State := SStart;
repeat
   GetToken (Token);
   case State of
   SStart:
      if Token.Key = TIdentifier then
         begin
         LookUpMnemon (Token.Value, Mnemonic, Found);
         if Found then
            begin
            Code.Functn := Mnemonic;
            if Mnemonic = MEnd then
               State := SClose
            else
               State := SFunction
            end
         else
            Code.Error := NoFunct
         end
      else if Token.Key = TEmpty then
         begin
         Code.Functn := MEmpty;
         State := SClose
         end
      else
         Code.Error := NoFunct;
   SFunction:
      if Token.Key = TLeftParen then
         State := SOpen
      else
         Code.Error := NoLeft;
   SOpen:
      if Token.Key = TIdentifier then
         begin
         Code.FirstArg := Token.Value;
         State := SFirstOprnd
         end
      else
         Code.Error := Bad1st;
```

Program 16.5, continued

```
      SFirstOprnd:
         if Code.Functn = MNeg then
            if Token.Key = TRightParen then
               State := SClose
            else
               Code.Error := BadNeg
         else if Token.Key = TComma then
            State := SContinue
         else
            Code.Error := NoComma;
      SContinue:
         if Token.Key in [TIdentifier, TInteger] then
            begin
            Code.SecondArg := Token.Value;
            State := SSecondOprnd
            end
         else
            Code.Error := Bad2nd;
      SSecondOprnd:
         if Token.Key = TRightParen then
            State := SClose
         else
            Code.Error := NoRight
      end {case}
   until (State = SClose) or (Code.Error <> NoError);
   Term := (Code.Functn = MEnd)
   end; {procedure ProcessSourceLine}

   begin
   InitGlobalConstants;
   reset (SourceFile);
   Terminate := false;
   while not (eof (SourceFile) or Terminate) do
      begin
      GetLine (SourceFile);
      ProcessSourceLine (Terminate);
      GenerateCode
      end;
   if not Terminate then
      PutError (NoEnd)
   end. {program Translate}
```

Input—SourceFile

```
set (Time, 15)
set (Accel, 3)
set (TSquared, Time)
mul (TSquared, Time)
set (Position, TSquared)
mul (Position, Accel)
div (Position, 2)
end
```

Program 16.5, continued

Output

```
Time := 15
Accel := 3
TSquared := Time
TSquared := TSquared * Time
Position := TSquared
Position := Position * Accel
Position := Position / 2
```

Input—`SourceFile`

```
set (Alpha,, 123)
set (Alpha)
sit (Alpha, 123)
set, (Alpha)
MUL (Alpha, Beta
set (123, Alpha)
neg (Alpha, Beta)
```

Output

```
Error:  Second argument not an identifier or integer.
Error:  Comma expected after first arguement.
Error:  Line must begin with function identifier.
Error:  Left parenthesis expected after function.
Error:  Right parenthesis expected after argument.
Error:  First argument not an identifier.
Error:  The argument of "neg" is malformed.
Error:  Missing "end" sentinel.
```

This program is based on a two-stage analysis of the syntax, as shown in Figure 16.15. Instead of using a grammar to specify the parsing problem as indicated in the figure, however, the structure of this source language is simple enough for the parser to be based on an FSM.

Figure 16.19 shows a deterministic FSM that describes the source language. The nonterminals begin with uppercase T and correspond to enumerated values of type `TokenType` in the program. The terminal string `end` is the only identifier that makes the transition from SStart to SClose, the final state. The identifiers that correspond to the other reserved words—`set`, `add`, `sub`, `mul`, `div`, `neg`—make the transition from SStart to SFunction. All other identifiers are invalid when detected in the start state.

The procedures that perform the three phases of the automatic translation are as follows:

The three translation phases of Program 16.5

- Lexical analyzer: `GetToken`
- Parser: `ProcessSourceLine`
- Code generator: `GenerateCode`

The finite state machine in Figure 16.19 is in the parser. The finite state machine for the lexical analyzer is similar to the one in procedure `GetToken` of Program

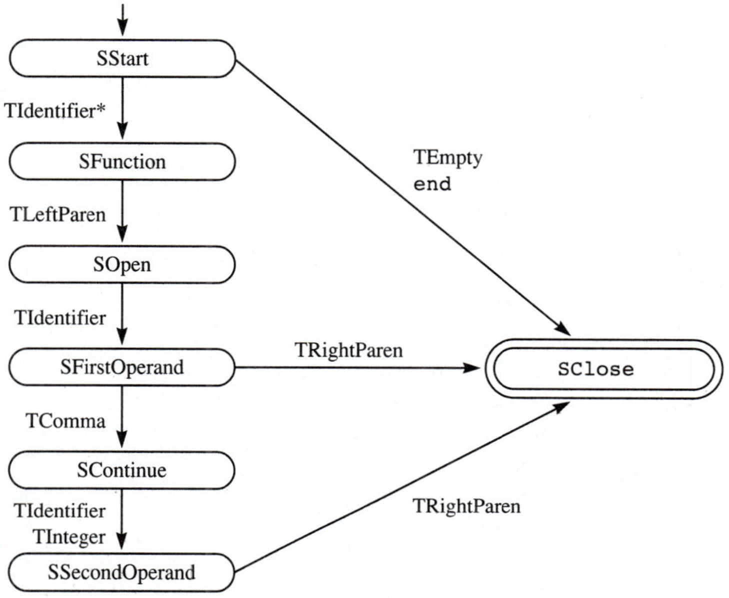

* Note: Includes only the identifiers `set`, `add`, `sub`, `mul`, `div`, `neg`.

Figure 16.19

The FSM for the parser `ProcessSourceLine` of Program 16.5.

16.4 and is left as a problem for the student. Figure 16.20 is a hierarchy diagram that shows the calling structure of all the procedures and functions. An important relationship shown in the diagram is that the parser, `ProcessSourceLine`, is at a higher level of abstraction than the lexical analyzer, `GetToken`.

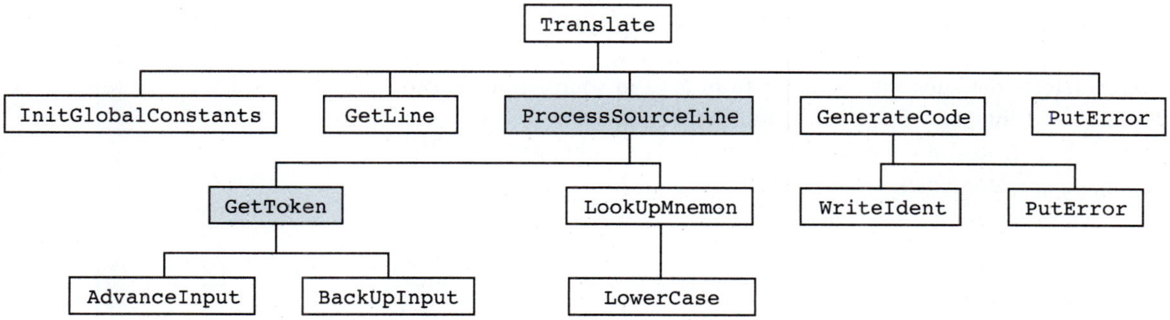

Figure 16.20

The hierarchy diagram of Program 16.5. The parser calls the lexical analyzer, both of which are shaded.

The task of the lexical analyzer, `GetToken`, is to scan the characters from the buffer one at a time in order to recognize an individual token. The task of the parser, `ProcessSourceLine`, is to scan the tokens one at a time in order to recognize a line of source code. It performs the same task as the lexical analyzer but at a higher level of abstraction.

Since both the lexical analyzer and the parser are finite state machines, both are implemented with one `case` statement nested inside a single `repeat` loop. A character is to `GetToken` as a token is to `ProcessSourceLine`. Whereas `AdvanceInput` supplies the next character to `GetToken`, `GetToken` supplies the next token to `ProcessSourceLine`.

Many of the aspects of the translator are identical to the previous program.The input buffer is global and is accessed by `GetToken` via `AdvanceInput` and `BackUpInput`.

A token record is declared in the main program but does not need to have a variant part. The FSM stores the string of characters that represent an integer in a packed array of characters, as it does the string of characters for an identifier. This is possible because the translation never needs the corresponding integer value. It simply reprints the character string in the object statement.

A simplification in the lexical analyzer FSM

Construction of the lexical analyzer FSM and its implementation in `GetToken` is left for a problem at the end of the chapter. One simplification you can make to the `GetToken` code is to not include those final states that have no transitions originating from them. For example, the FSM for the lexical analyzer of Program 16.5 will have a transition from the start state to a final state on `(`. The final state will not have an outgoing transition. If you include the final state for the TLeftParen token and make a transition to it, then the next character after `(` is guaranteed to trigger a termination condition. That character will need to be backed up into the input stream for the next call to `GetToken`.

It is simpler to omit the final state for TLeftParen in the `State` variable enumerated list. If you are in the start state and detect a `(`, you can set the value of `T.Key` to TLeftParen and return immediately. Not only is the code shorter, but it executes faster, since no backup of the following character is required.

Variable `Code` is a global record that stores the information necessary to generate a line of object code. `ProcessSourceLine` expects a reserved word as the first token. Since the reserved words are in the form of identifiers, `GetToken` will return an identifier as the first token of a valid line. `ProcessSourceLine` searches `MnemonTable` to see if the identifier corresponds to a reserved word. If so, it stores the corresponding enumerated value for the instruction mnemonic in `Code`.

As the parser detects the subsequent tokens from a valid source line, it also stores the identifier and integer strings in `Code`. Generating code requires outputting the strings from `Code` along with a few other strings obtained from the global mnemonic and operator tables.

Parser Characteristics

Rather than define the syntax of the source language with the FSM of Figure 16.19, you could define it with a grammar. A formal grammar for the source language would have a simple structure. For example, a production rule for a `set` statement might be

<set-statement> → `set` (<identifier> `,` <argument>)

where <argument> would be defined in another production rule as <identifier> or <integer>. Unlike Pascal, this grammar would contain no recursive definitions.

The simple nature of the source syntax allows the parsing of this language to be based on a deterministic FSM. Parsers for most programming languages cannot be this simple. Although it is common for lexical analyzers to be based on finite state machines, it is rare that a parser can also be based on an FSM. In practice, most languages are too complex for such a technique to be possible.

Parsers are usually not based on an FSM.

Since the production rules of a real grammar invariably contain many recursive definitions, the parsing algorithm itself may contain recursive procedures that reflect the recursion of the grammar. Such an algorithm is called a *recursive descent parser*.

Regardless of the complexity of the source language or the parsing technique of the translator, the relationship of the parser to the lexical analyzer in a translation program is always the same. As illustrated in Program 16.5, the parser is at a higher level of abstraction than the lexical analyzer. The lexical analyzer scans the characters and recognizes tokens, which it passes to the parser. The parser scans the tokens and recognizes a program in the source language.

SUMMARY

The fundamental question of computer science is, What can be automated? The automatic translation of artificial languages is at the heart of computer science. Each artificial language has an alphabet. The closure of a set, T, is the set of all possible strings formed by concatenating elements from T. A language is a subset of the closure of its alphabet. A grammar describes the syntax of a language; it has four parts: a nonterminal alphabet, a terminal alphabet, a set of rules of production, and a start symbol. Derivation is the process by which a grammar specifies a language. To derive a sentence in the language, you begin with the start symbol and substitute production rules until you get a string of terminals. The parsing problem is to determine the substitution sequence to match a given string of terminals. There are over 200 rules of production in the standard Pascal grammar. A context-free grammar is one that restricts the left side of all the production rules to contain a single nonterminal. Although the Pascal grammar is context-free, certain aspects of the language are context-sensitive.

A finite state machine (FSM) also describes the syntax of a language. It consists of a set of states and transitions between the states. Each transition is marked with an input terminal symbol. One state is the start state, and at least one, possibly more, is the final state. A nondeterministic FSM may have more than one transition from a given state on one input terminal symbol. A sentence is valid if, starting at the start state, you can make a sequence of transitions dictated by the symbols in the sentence and end in a final state.

Two software implementation techniques of FSMs are the table lookup technique and the direct code technique. Both techniques contain loops that are controlled by a state variable, which is initialized to the start state. Each execution of the loop corresponds to a transition in the FSM. In the table lookup technique, the transitions are assigned from a two-dimensional transition table. In the direct code technique, the transitions are assigned with selection statements in the body of the loop.

The three translation phases of an automatic translator are the lexical analyzer, the parser, and the code generator. For most high-level languages, the lexical analyzer is based on an FSM and the parser is based on a context-free grammar. The code generator is highly dependent on the nature of the object language.

EXERCISES

Section 16.1

*1. What is the fundamental question of computer science?

2. What is the identity element for the addition operation on integers? What is the identity element for the OR operation on booleans?

3. Derive the following strings with Grammar 16.1 and draw the corresponding syntax tree.

   * (a) `abc123` (b) `a1b2c3` (c) `a321bc`

4. Derive the following strings with Grammar 16.2 and draw the corresponding syntax tree.

   * (a) `-d` (b) `+ddd` (c) `d`

5. Derive the following strings with Grammar 16.3.

   * (a) `abc` (b) `aabbcc`

6. For each of the following strings, state whether it can be derived from the rules of Grammar 16.4. If it can, show a complete derivation and draw the corresponding syntax tree.

   * (a) `a + ( a )` (b) `a * ( + a )` (c) `a * ( a + a )`
   (d) `a * ( a + a ) * a` (e) `a + ( - a )` (f) `( ( ( a ) ) )`

7. For Grammar 16.5, draw the syntax tree for <compound-statement> from the following strings, assuming that S1, S2, and S3 are valid <statement>s and C1 and C2 are valid <expression>s.

   * (a)
```
begin
if C1 then
   S1;
S2
end
```
   (b)
```
begin
if C1 then
   if C2 then
      S1
   else
      S2;
S3
end
```
   (c)
```
begin
if C1 then
   if C2 then
      S1
   else
      S2
else
   S3;
S4
end
```
   (d)
```
begin
S1;
while C1 do
   begin
   if C2 then
      S2;
   S3
   end
end
```

8. For Grammar 16.5, draw the syntax tree for <statement> from the following strings, assuming that `Alpha`, `Beta`, and `Gamma` are valid <identifier>s and `1` and `24` are valid <integer>s.

   * (a) `Alpha := 1`
   (b) `Alpha := Alpha + 1`
   (c) `Alpha := (Beta < 1)`
   (d) `Alpha := ((Beta < 1) or (Gamma > 24))`
   (e) `Alpha (Beta)`
   (f) `Alpha (Beta, 24)`

9. For Grammar 16.5, draw the syntax tree for <program> from the following string, assuming that `Alpha` and `Beta` are valid <identifier>s and `1` and `24` are valid <integer>s.

```
program Alpha;
   var
      Beta: integer;
   begin
   read (Beta);
   if Beta > 24 then
      write (Beta)
   else
      write (Beta + 1)
   end.
```

10. The question this exercise poses is, Can two different grammars produce the same language? Grammars 16.6 and 16.7 are not the same grammar, because they have different nonterminal sets and different production rules. Experiment with these two grammars by deriving some terminal strings. From your experiments, describe the languages produced by these grammars. Is it possible to derive a valid string of terminals in Grammar 16.6 that is not in 16.7 or vice versa? Prove your conjecture.

$N = \{A, B\}$
$T = \{0,1\}$
P = the productions
1. A → 0 B
2. B → 1 0 B
3. B → ε

$S = A$

Grammar 16.6

A grammar for Exercise 10.

$N = \{C\}$
$T = \{0, 1\}$
P = the productions
1. C → C 1 0
2. C → 0

$S = C$

Grammar 16.7

Another grammar for Exercise 10.

Section 16.2

11. For each of the machines described by the state transition tables in Table 16.4, do the following: (1) Draw the state transition diagram. (2) State whether the FSM is deterministic or nondeterministic. (3) Identify any states that are inaccessible. In each machine, W is the start state.

*(a)

Current state	Next state		
	a	b	c
W	Y	Z	X
X	Z	X	
Y		X	
Z	Y	W	X

(b)

Current state	Next state		
	a	b	c
W	X	Z	W
X	Z	W	X
Y	Z	Y	W
Z	W	X	Y

(c)

Current state	Next state		
	a	b	c
W	W		X
X		Z	W
Y	Y	X, Z	Y
Z	Y		X

(d)

Current state	Next state		
	a	b	c
W	X	X	X
X	Y	Y	Y
Y	Z	Z	Z
Z			

Table 16.4

The state transition tables for the finite state machines of Exercise 11.

12. Remove the empty transitions to produce the equivalent machine for each of the finite state machines in Figure 16.21 (p. 840).

13. Draw a deterministic FSM that recognizes strings of 1's and 0's specified by each of the following criteria. Each FSM should reject any characters that are not 0 or 1. * **(a)** The string of three characters, `101`. **(b)** All strings of arbitrary length that end in `101`. For example, the FSM should accept `1101` but reject `1011`. **(c)** All strings of arbitrary length that begin with `101`. For example, the FSM should accept `1010` but reject `0101`. **(d)** All strings of arbitrary length that contain a `101` at least once anywhere. For example, the FSM should accept all the strings mentioned in parts (a), (b), and (c) as well as strings such as `11100001011111100111`.

Section 16.4

14. Design a grammar that describes the language of Program 16.5.

PROBLEMS

Section 16.3

15. Improve Program 16.1 as suggested in the text by defining a third enumeration in `AlphabetType` called Other, which represents a symbol that is neither a letter nor a character.

16. Implement each FSM in Exercise 13 using the table lookup technique of Program 16.1. Classify a character as One, Zero, or Other in the transition table. Take the input from the keyboard.

17. Implement each FSM in Exercise 13 using the direct code technique of Program 16.3. Take the input from the keyboard. Write a procedure called `ParsePat` for parse pattern that corresponds to `ParseNum`. Do not include formal parameter `N` in the procedure.

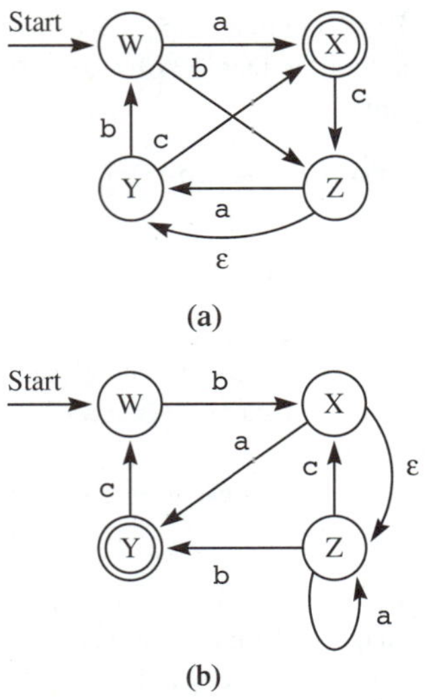

Figure 16.21

The FSMs for Exercise 12.

Section 16.4

18. (a) Draw a state transition diagram for the FSM in procedure `GetToken` of Program 16.5. (b) Complete procedure `GetToken`.

19. Write a limited assembler for Pep/5 assembly language. The source file will contain an assembly language program without symbols with mnemonics `BR`, `DECI`, `LOADA`, `ADDA`, `STOREA`, `DECO`, and `STOP`, dot commands `.BLOCK` and `.END`, and hexadecimal constants. For example, if `SourceFile` contains

```
BR      h#0007,i
.BLOCK  h# 4
DECI    h#0002,d
LOADA   h#0002,d
ADDA    h# 9, i
STOREA  h#0004,d
DECO    h#0004,d
STOP
.END
```

then your assembler should put

```
70 00 07 00 00 00 00 E1 00 02 09 00 02 18 00 09
11 00 04 E9 00 04 00 zz
```

in `ObjFile`. The loader will not accept trailing spaces at the end of an object file line.

Assume the source lines will contain no comments. All addressing modes will be written explicitly, even on the `BR` command. You may assume that any instruction can use any addressing mode. Mnemonics and dot commands can have any mixture of uppercase or lowercase characters. Zero or more spaces can occur anywhere between tokens, except that there must be at least one space immediately after a mnemonic or dot command. If the source file contains one or more errors, print appropriate messages to the screen and suppress the output to `ObjFile`.

(a) Write the top level of the assembler. Model it after `Translate` of Program 16.5. Your procedures `GetLine`, `AdvanceInput`, and `BackUpInput` should be identical to those in program `Translate`. Your main program also should be identical, except that the call to `GenerateCode` should be moved out of the loop and placed just before the end of the program. Rather than generate code after parsing each line, your program will accumulate a list of code records. Then `GenerateCode` will process the entire list of records, outputting the hexadecimal object code to `ObjFile` if there were no errors.

Declare the following types:

```
StrType      = packed array [1..8] of char;
HexNumType   = packed array [1..4] of char;
AddrModeType = (AImmed, ADirect, AIndexed, AStackRel);
TokenType    = (
   TIdentifier, TDotCommand, THexConstant,
   TAddrMode,   TEmpty,      TInvalid);
TokenRecType =
   record
   case Key: TokenType of
      TIdentifier:  (IdentVal: StrType);
      TDotCommand:  (DotVal:   StrType);
      THexConstant: (HexVal:   HexNumType);
      TAddrMode:    (AddrVal:  AddrModeType);
      TEmpty:       ();
      TInvalid:     ()
   end;
```

For the top level test, put a stub in procedure `ProcessSourceLine` that sets `Terminate` in the main program to true regardless of the line that is input to the buffer. Put a `writeln` stub in procedure `GenerateCode`. Test your program twice, once with an empty `SourceFile` and once with some text in `SourceFile`.

(b) Draw the state transition diagram for the FSM of the parser that corresponds to Figure 16.19. Assume that each transition is on one of the tokens listed in part (a).

(c) Complete procedure `ProcessSourceLine` based on your state transition diagram of part (b). Declare the following additional types in your main program.

```
InstrType    = (
   IStop, ILoada, IStorea, IAdda, IBr,
   IDeci, IDeco,  IBlock,  IEnd,  IEmpty);
CodeType =
   record
   Error:       ErrorType;
   Instruction: InstrType;
   OprndSpec:   HexNumType;
   AddrMode:    AddrModeType
   end;
```

Define `ErrorType` as needed, including the value NoError as in Program 16.5. Test your program with a stub in procedure `GetToken` that sets `Key` in the token record to TIdentifier and `IdentVal` to ‘end   ’. Note that this test will not exercise all of your code in the parser.

(d) Complete procedure `GetToken`, which should implement the FSM of Figure 16.22. Note that the transition from SIdent to SHex1 on `#` is only possible if

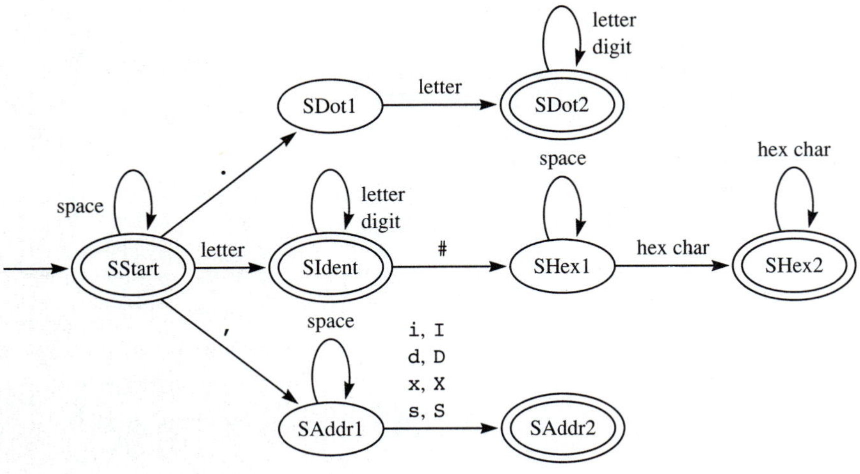

Figure 16.22

The FSM for `GetToken` in Problem 19(d).

`IdentVal` is 'h ' or 'H '. This completes the parsing phase of the assembler. Test it thoroughly with both valid and invalid input before adding the code generation.

(e) Add code generation to your assembler. Declare a global code array in your main program with the following type.

```
CodeArrType = array [1..100] of CodeType
```

Add a statement at the end of `ProcessSourceLine` that appends the code record constructed from the current line to the list of code records stored in the array. Complete procedure `GenerateCode`, which should verify that there are no error records in the array, and should write the hexadecimal code to the object file if there are no error records.

20. Extend the assembler of Problem 19 by including all 32 instructions in the Pep/5 instruction set.

21. Extend the assembler of Problem 19 by checking the addressing mode for each instruction as listed in Table 14.2. If an instruction uses an addressing mode that is not allowable, generate an appropriate error message. Permit the branch instructions to not specify an addressing mode, in which case use immediate addressing as the default mode.

22. Extend the assembler of Problem 19 by producing a listing that shows the object code next to the source line that produced it. Print the source line with the standard spacing conventions and uppercase and lowercase conventions of the Pep/5 assembler.

23. Extend the assembler of Problem 19 by permitting decimal constants prefixed by the string `d#` or `D#`.

24. Extend the assembler of Problem 19 by permitting the dot commands **(a)** `.WORD` and **(b)** `.BYTE`.

25. Extend the assembler of Problem 19 by permitting the `.ASCII` dot command. Assume that all ASCII strings will be delimited by either the `/` character or the `'` character.

26. Extend the assembler of Problem 19 by permitting a source line to contain a comment prefixed by a semicolon. A line may contain only a comment, or a valid instruction followed by a comment. `TokenType` will need to include TSemicolon as a possible value.

LEVEL 4

Operating System

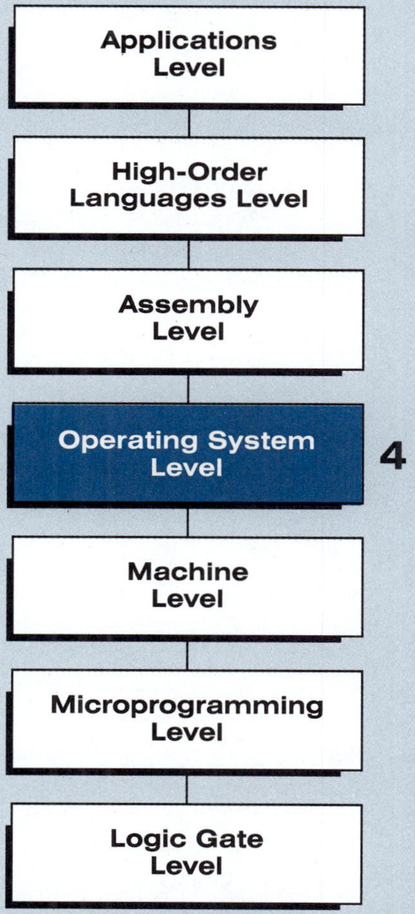

Chapter

17 Process Management

An operating system defines a more abstract machine that is easier to program than the machine at Level 3. Its purpose is to provide a convenient environment for higher-level programming and to allocate the resources of the system efficiently. The operating system level is between the assembly and machine levels. As is the case with abstraction in general, the operating system hides the details of the Level 3 machine from users at higher levels.

The purposes of an operating system

The resources of a typical computer system include CPU time, main memory, and disk memory. This chapter describes how an operating system allocates CPU time. The next chapter will show how it allocates main memory and disk memory.

There are three general categories of operating systems:

Three types of operating systems

- Single-user
- Multiuser
- Real-time

Most personal computers have single-user operating systems. These computers are inexpensive enough for an individual to purchase and to use without sharing it with anyone else. Larger computers, which are almost always owned by an organization rather than an individual, have multiuser operating systems. Such computers usually have only one CPU, but it is sufficiently fast to be able to execute many users' jobs simultaneously. Real-time systems are used in computers that are dedicated to controlling equipment. Their inputs are from sensors and their outputs are the control signals for the equipment. A real-time system is in the computer that controls an automobile engine, for example.

The Pep/5 operating system is a single-user system. It illustrates some of the techniques used to allocate CPU time. However, it does not illustrate the management of main memory or disk memory. The first two sections of this chapter include a complete listing of the Pep/5 operating system.

17.1 Loaders

An important function of an operating system is to manage the jobs that users submit to be executed. In a multiuser system, several users continually submit jobs. The operating system must decide which job to run from a list of pending jobs. After it decides which job to execute next, it must load the appropriate program into main memory and turn control of the CPU over to that program for execution.

The Pep/5 Operating System

Figure 17.1 shows the location of the Pep/5 operating system in main memory. It consists of the system stack and I/O buffer in RAM, the loader at address 0C29, the interrupt service routine at 0C70, and the four machine vectors at 0FF8 through 0FFE. Although the Pep/5 operating system illustrates the operation of a loader, it does not illustrate the process by which the operating system must decide which job to run from a list of pending jobs.

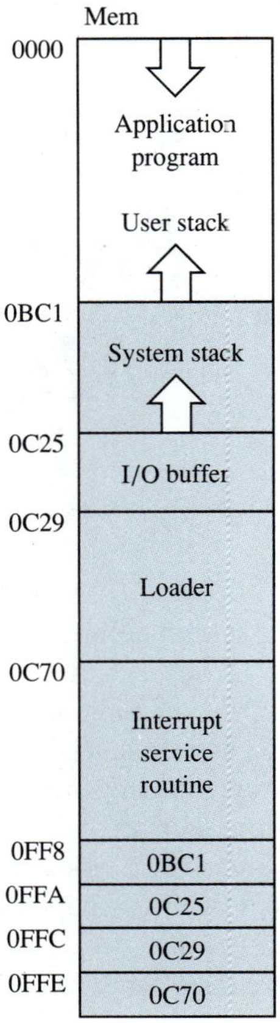

Figure 17.1

A memory map of the Pep/5 system.

The following operating system listing is about 500 lines of assembly language code, including documentation comments. The trend nowadays is to write operating systems in a mixture of a high-order language and the assembly language for the particular computer controlled by the operating system. Typically, 90% of the system is in the high-order language and 10% is in the assembly language. The assembly language portion is reserved for those parts of the operating system that cannot be programmed with the features available in the high-order language or that require an extra measure of efficiency that even an optimizing compiler cannot achieve.

Listing 17.1 shows the beginning of the operating system. Symbols `LineFeed`, `Space`, `True`, and `False` are declared with the `.EQUATE` command, and thus generate no object code. They are used throughout the rest of the program.

Symbols `OsRAM`, `WordBuff`, `ByteBuff`, `WordTemp`, and `ByteTemp` are all defined with the `.BLOCK` command. Normally, `.BLOCK` generates code, and any code generated starts at address 0000 (hex). The listing shows these `.BLOCK` commands generating no code and `OsRAM` starting at 0BC1 instead of at 0000.

The .BURN compiler directive

The reason for this peculiar assembler behavior is the `.BURN` command at 0C29. When you include `.BURN` in a program, the assembler assumes that the program will be burned into ROM. It generates code for those instructions that follow the burn directive but not for those that precede it.

The assembler also assumes that the ROM will be installed at the bottom of memory, leaving the top of memory for the applications programs. It therefore calculates the addresses for the symbol table such that the last byte generated will have the address specified by the burn directive. In this listing, the burn directive indicates that the last byte should be at address 0FFF. Listing 17.9, at the end of the operating system, shows that the last byte, 70 (hex), is indeed at address 0FFF. Since 0FFF (hex) is 4095 (dec), the Pep/5 computer is configured with a total of 4 Kbytes of main memory.

```
               ;**************   Pep/5 Operating System, 4/30/88    **************
               ;
               LineFeed:.EQUATE h#000A     ;ASCII line feed character
               Space:   .EQUATE h#0020     ;ASCII space character
               True:    .EQUATE d#1
               False:   .EQUATE d#0
               ;
               ;*******************   Operating system RAM    *******************
               ;
0BC1           OsRAM:   .BLOCK  d#100      ;System stack area
0C25           WordBuff:.BLOCK  d#1        ;Input/output buffer
0C26           ByteBuff:.BLOCK  d#1        ;Least significant byte of WordBuff
0C27           WordTemp:.BLOCK  d#1        ;Temporary word storage
0C28           ByteTemp:.BLOCK  d#1        ;Least significant byte of TempWord
               ;
               ;*******************   Operating system ROM    *******************
               ;
0C29                    .BURN   h#0FFF     ;Version OS/4.0
```

Listing 17.1

Operating system RAM.

Another feature of Pep/5 is automatic documentation of the operating system version number. The assembler stores the comment from the `.BURN` line and appends it to the object file. When you burn in the object file with the burn utility, the system reads the comment and displays it when you run the simulator. If you ever modify the operating system, you should change the version number in the comment of the `.BURN` command accordingly.

The Pep/5 Loader

Invoking the Pep/5 loader

Listing 17.2 is the Pep/5 loader. To invoke the loader, you select the load option from the simulator. That triggers the following two events:

```
SP := Mem [0FFA]
PC := Mem [0FFC]
```

Since `Mem [0FFA]` contains 0C25, as shown in both Figure 17.1 and Listing 17.9, the stack pointer is initialized to 0C25. Similarly, the program counter is initialized to 0C29, the address of the first instruction of the loader.

The loader begins by clearing the base and index registers to zero. It also clears `WordBuff` to zero. Listing 17.1 shows `WordBuff` declared as a single byte. Since `ByteBuff` is declared as a single byte immediately after `WordBuff`, the program considers `WordBuff` a two-byte buffer with `ByteBuff` its rightmost byte. The `CHARI` instructions all input to `ByteBuff`, but they are followed by a `LOADA` from `WordBuff`. The `LOADA` moves the character just input to the accumulator and guarantees that the leftmost byte of the accumulator is zero.

```
                ;
                ;=======================   System loader   =======================
                ;
                ;LOADER FORMAT RULES
                ;This loader assumes all data in the object file to be loaded is
                ;in the following strict format:  Each hex number representing a
                ;byte must contain exactly two characters, each character in
                ;0..9, A..F, or a..f, and must be followed by exactly one space.
                ;No leading spaces are permitted at the beginning of a line.  No
                ;trailing spaces are permitted at the end of a line. The last two
                ;characters in the file must be lowercase zz, which is used as a
                ;terminating sentinel.  To improve execution speed, this loader
                ;does not trap input errors, and will not function properly
                ;unless the file input format is consistent with these
                ;restrictions!
                ;
0C29   600000 Loader:  LOADB   d#0,i       ;Clear base for memory store
0C2C   0C0000          LOADX   d#0,i       ;Initialize index register
0C2F   150C25          STOREX  WordBuff,d ;Clear input buffer word
                ;
0C32   D10C26 GetChar: CHARI   ByteBuff,d ;Get first hex digit
0C35   090C25          LOADA   WordBuff,d ;Put ASCII in low byte of A
0C38   A0007A          COMPA   c#/z/,i     ;If end of file sentinel, 'z',
0C3B   800C6F          BRZ     StopLoad    ;then exit loader routine
0C3E   A00039          COMPA   c#/9/,i     ;If ASCII <= '9', then assume decimal
0C41   980C47          BRNZ    Shift       ;and right nybble is correct number
0C44   180009          ADDA    d#9,i       ;else convert nybble to correct number
0C47   40     Shift:   ASLA                ;Shift left by four bits, sending the
0C48   40              ASLA                ;number to the most significant
0C49   40              ASLA                ;nybble position in the byte
0C4A   40              ASLA
0C4B   590C28          STBYTA  ByteTemp,d ;Save most significant nybble
0C4E   D10C26          CHARI   ByteBuff,d ;Get second hex digit
0C51   090C25          LOADA   WordBuff,d ;Put second ASCII in low byte of A
0C54   A00039          COMPA   c#/9/,i     ;If ASCII <= '9', then assume decimal
0C57   980C5D          BRNZ    Combine     ;and right nybble is correct number
0C5A   180009          ADDA    d#9,i       ;else convert nybble to correct number
0C5D   28000F Combine: ANDA    h#000F,i    ;Mask out the unwanted left nybble
0C60   190C27          ADDA    WordTemp,d ;Combine both hex digits in binary
0C63   5A0000          STBYTA  h#0000,x    ;Store in Mem [B + X]
0C66   1C0001          ADDX    d#1,i       ;Increment index register
0C69   D10C26          CHARI   ByteBuff,d ;Skip blank or <LF>
0C6C   700C32          BR      GetChar
                ;
0C6F   00     StopLoad:STOP
```

Listing 17.2

The loader.

The loader is in the form of a single loop that inputs a character and compares it with sentinel `z`. If the character is not the sentinel, the program checks to see if it is in `'0'..'9'`. If it is not in that range, the rightmost four bits, called a *nybble* because it is half a byte, is converted to the proper value by adding 9 to it. Note that ASCII `A` is 0100 0001 (bin) so that when 9 is added to it the sum is 0100 1010. The rightmost nybble is the correct bit pattern for hexadecimal digit `A`. It will similarly be correct for hexadecimal digits `B` through `F`. If the character is in `'0'..'9'`, the rightmost nybble is already correct.

Definition of a nybble

The loader shifts the nybble four bits to the left and stores it temporarily in `ByteTemp`. It inputs the second character of the pair, adjusts the nybble similarly, and combines both nybbles into a single byte with the `ADDA` at 0C60. The instruction that places the program byte in memory is `STBYTA` at 0C63. It uses indexed addressing, with the base register 0 and the index register incremented by 1 each time through the loop. The loader terminates with the `STOP` instruction, which returns control to the simulator options.

Programs to be loaded typically are not in the format of hexadecimal ASCII characters. They are already in binary, ready to be loaded. Pep/5 uses ASCII characters for the object file, so you can program directly in machine language and view the object file with a text editor.

Load modules are usually not in ASCII.

Program Termination

The applications programs presented thus far have all terminated with the `STOP` instruction. The `STOP` instruction in a real computer is rarely executed. Rather than generate a `STOP` instruction at the end of a program, a Pascal compiler generates an instruction that returns control to the operating system. If your program ran on a microcomputer, the operating system would set up the screen to wait for you to request another service. If your program ran on a timesharing system, the operating system would continue to process other users' jobs. In no case would the computer itself simply stop.

Since there is only one CPU, it alternates between executing operating system jobs and applications jobs. Figure 17.2 shows a time line of CPU usage when the operating system loads and executes a sequence of jobs. The shaded parts represent that part of the time spent executing the operating system.

Figure 17.2

A time line of CPU usage when the operating system loads and executes a sequence of jobs.

The operating system represents the overhead necessary for doing business. When you shop at a mall, the price you pay for a widget does not reflect just the cost of production and transportation of the widget to the store. It also reflects the salesman's salary, the electricity for the store lighting, the fringe benefits for the store manager, and so on. Similarly, 100% of a computer's resources does not go toward executing user programs. A certain fraction of the resources, in this case CPU time, must be reserved for the operating system.

17.2 Interrupts

When programming in assembly language at Level 5, you may use instructions DECI, DECO, HEXO, and NOP. Table 13.1 showed no such instructions in the Level 3 machine. Instead, when the computer fetches the instructions with these opcodes (11100 through 11111), the hardware executes an interrupt. An *interrupt* is similar to a subroutine jump but more elaborate. The code that executes is called an *interrupt service routine* or *interrupt handler* instead of a subroutine. The operating system returns control to the applications program by executing a return from interrupt instruction, RTI, instead of a return from subroutine instruction, RTS.

The interrupt handler implements the four instructions as if they were part of the Level 3 machine. Remember that one purpose of an operating system is to provide a convenient environment for higher-level programming. The abstract machine provided by the Pep/5 operating system is a more convenient machine because it contains these four additional instructions not present at Level 3.

The Interrupt Mechanism

When an instruction with an unimplemented opcode executes, the following events transpire:

A Pep/5 interrupt

```
Temp              := Mem [0FFA]
Mem [Temp - 1]    := IR {instruction specifier only}
Mem [Temp - 3]    := SP
Mem [Temp - 5]    := PC
Mem [Temp - 7]    := B
Mem [Temp - 9]    := X
Mem [Temp - 11]   := A
Mem [Temp - 12]   := NZVC
SP                := Temp - 12
PC                := Mem [0FFE]
```

Temp represents a temporary value for notational convenience. Mem [0FFA] contains 0C25, the address of the system stack. In the first event, Temp gets 0C25. The next seven events show the CPU pushing the content of all the registers onto the system stack, starting with the instruction specifier of the IR and ending with the NZVC flags. The stack pointer is then modified to point to the new top of the system stack, and the program counter gets the content of Mem [0FFE].

Figure 17.3 shows an example of such an interrupt. The applications program listing contains

```
002D  E9003B DECO    h#003B,d
```

where 002D is the address of the instruction, and E9003B is the object code that triggered the interrupt during execution.

Figure 17.3(a) shows the state of the CPU before the interrupt executes. At Level 3, all unimplemented opcodes correspond to unary instructions. During the

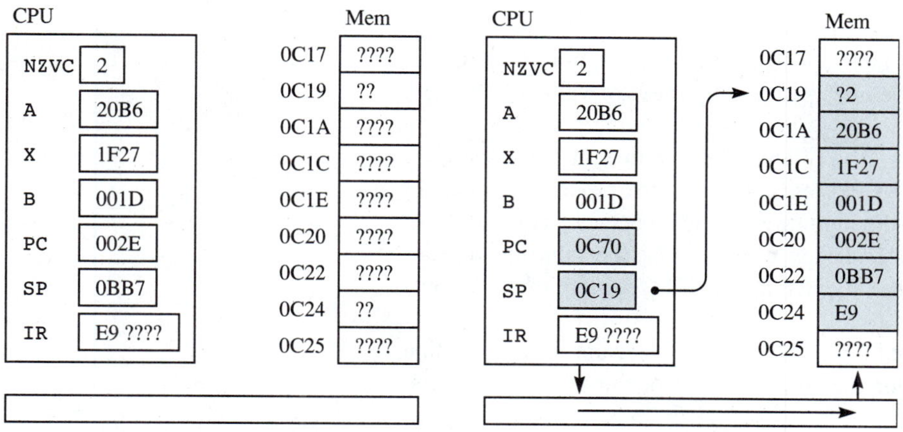

(a) Before the interrupt. **(b)** After the interrupt.

Figure 17.3 An interrupt triggered by the instruction E9003B.

fetch part of the von Neumann execution cycle, the CPU incremented the `PC` by 1, from 002D to 002E. It did not fetch the operand specifier of the `DECO` instruction. The rightmost two bytes of the `IR` are, consequently, undefined.

Figure 17.3(b) shows the state of the computer after the interrupt executes. Only the instruction specifier part of the `IR` is pushed onto the stack. Also note that the four `NZVC` bits are right justified in the byte at `Mem [0C19]`. The left-most nybble of the byte is undefined. `SP` contains 0C19, the new top of the system stack, and `PC` contains `Mem [0FFE]`, which is 0C70, the address of the first instruction of the interrupt handler. Listing 17.9 shows how the operating system sets up the machine vectors at 0FFA and 0FFE with the `.ADDRSS` commands.

The RTI Instruction

The definition of a process

A program during execution is called a *process*. The interrupt mechanism temporarily suspends the process so the operating system can perform a service. The block of information in main memory that contains a copy of the interrupted process' registers is called a *process control block* (PCB). The PCB for this example is stored in `Mem [0C19]` to `Mem [0C24]` as shown in Figure 17.3(b).

The process control block (PCB)

After the operating system performs its service, it must eventually return control of the CPU to the suspended process so the process can complete its execution. In this example, the service performed by the Pep/5 operating system is execution of the `DECO` instruction. It returns control back to the process by executing the return from interrupt instruction, `RTI`.

When `RTI` executes, the following six events occur:

The RTI instruction

```
NZVC := Mem [SP]
A    := Mem [SP + 1]
X    := Mem [SP + 3]
B    := Mem [SP + 5]
PC   := Mem [SP + 7]
SP   := Mem [SP + 9]
```

RTI pops the top 11 bytes off the stack into the NZVC, A, X, B, PC, and SP registers. This reverses the events of the interrupt, except that IR is not popped. The next instruction to execute will be the one specified by the new value of PC. The last register to change is SP.

If the interrupt handler does not modify any of the values in the PCB, RTI will restore the original values in the CPU registers when the process resumes. In particular, the SP will again point to the top of the application stack, as it did at the time of the interrupt. On the other hand, any changes that the interrupt handler makes to the values in the PCB will be reflected in the CPU registers when the process resumes.

Listing 17.3 shows the entry and exit points of the interrupt service routine OldPC and OldIR are the stack addresses of the copies of the PC and IR regis-

```
                 ;
                 ;==================   Interrupt service routine   ==================
                 ;
                 OldPC:   .EQUATE d#7          ;Stack address of PC on interrupt
                 OldIR:   .EQUATE d#11         ;Stack address of IR on interrupt
                 ;
0C70  57000B Intrupt: LDBYTX  OldIR,s          ;X := intrpt IR
0C73  4C              ASRX                     ;Discard addressing mode
0C74  4C              ASRX                     ;Discard addressing mode
0C75  4C              ASRX                     ;Discard register specifier
0C76  2C0003          ANDX    h#0003,i         ;Keep rightmost two bits of opcode
0C79  600000          LOADB   d#0,i            ;B := 0
0C7C  720C7F          BR      JTable,x         ;Branch directly to Opcode routine
                 ;
0C7F  0C91   JTable:  .ADDRSS Opc11100
0C81  0E16            .ADDRSS Opc11101
0C83  0EA9            .ADDRSS Opc11110
0C85  0EF7            .ADDRSS Opc11111
                 ;
                 ;After processing the interrupt, the interrupt handlers branch
                 ;directly to Return or ReturnU.  DECI, DECO and HEXO are all
                 ;three-byte instructions.  The program counter is incremented by
                 ;one byte before the machine interrupt.  It is necessary to
                 ;increment the PC by an additional two bytes here.
                 ;
0C87  0B0007 Return:  LOADA   OldPC,s          ;A := intrpt PC
0C8A  180002          ADDA    d#2,i            ;Increment PC by two
0C8D  130007          STOREA  OldPC,s          ;Restore PC for return
0C90  C8     ReturnU: RTI                      ;Return for unary instructions
```

Listing 17.3

The entry and exit points of the interrupt service routine.

ters stored on the system stack from the interrupt mechanism. Figure 17.4 shows the stack addresses of all the registers.

The code from 0C70 to 0C85 tests the opcode of the instruction that caused the interrupt and branches to the appropriate routine. The first instruction gets the opcode from the copy of the `IR` that was pushed onto the system stack. The next few instructions discard everything but the rightmost two bits, which are sufficient to distinguish the four possible unimplemented opcodes from each other. The jump table contains the starting addresses of the routines for implementing each of the four instructions.

The code from 0C87 to 0C90 sets up the return from the interrupt. The `DECO` instruction from the example of Figure 17.3 should be interpreted as a nonunary instruction. The `PC` should not be restored to its old value of 0C70, since that is the address of the operand specifier of the `DECO` instruction. To make `PC` point to the byte following the operand specifier, the instructions from 0C87 to 0C8D increment the copy of `PC` by two in the PCB. When `RTI` executes, the updated copy of `PC` is restored, and the Level 5 user sees `DECO` as a nonunary instruction.

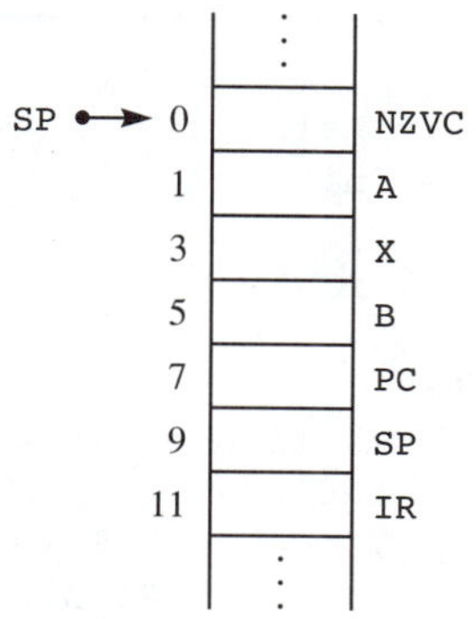

Figure 17.4

The stack addresses of the copies of the CPU registers.

The DECI Interrupt Handler

Listing 17.4 (pp. 855–58) is the interrupt service routine for the `DECI` instruction. It allocates six local variables on the stack—`Total`, `ValAscii`, `IsOvfl`, `IsNeg`, `State`, and `Temp`. Each variable occupies two bytes, so `SUBSP` at 0C91 subtracts 12 from the stack pointer for the allocation. When the routine accesses the value of `NZVC` stored on the stack at the interrupt, its stack address will be 12 greater because of the local variables of this routine. That is why `OldNZVC` equates to 12 instead of 0.

`DECI` must parse the input, converting the string of ASCII characters to the proper bits in two's complement representation. It uses the finite state machine of Figure 17.5. An outline of the logic of the FSM in the `DECI` interrupt handler appears on the next page. `State` has enumerated type with possible values (Init, Sign, Digit).

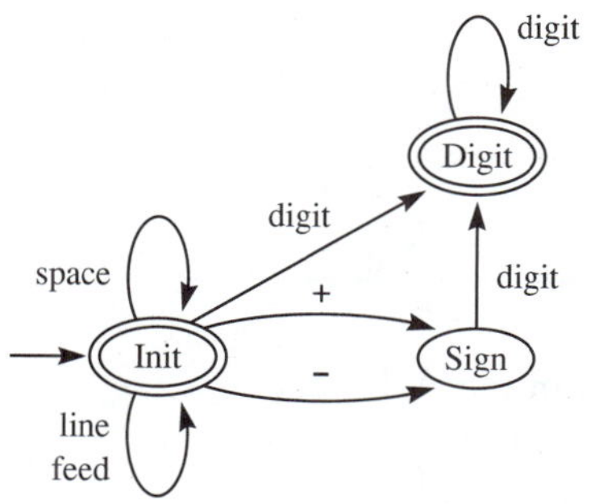

Figure 17.5

The finite state machine in the `DECI` interrupt handler.

The logic of the finite state machine in the DECI interrupt handler

```
begin
IsOvfl := False
State := Init
repeat
   Get AsciiCh
   case State of
   Init:
      if AsciiCh = '+' then
         begin
         IsNeg := False
         State := Sign
         end
      else if AsciiCh = '-' then
         begin
         IsNeg := True
         State := Sign
         end
      else if AsciiCh is a digit then
         begin
         IsNeg := False
         Total := Value (AsciiCh)
         State := Digit
         end
      else if AsciiCh is not <SPACE> or <LF> then
         Exit with DECI error.
   Sign:
      if AsciiCh is a digit then
         begin
         Total := Value (AsciiCh)
         State := Digit
         end
      else
         Exit with DECI error.
   Digit:
      if AsciiCh is a digit then
         begin
         Total := 10 * Total + Value (AsciiCh)
         if overflow then
           IsOvfl := True
         end
      else
         Exit normally.
   end case
until loop exit
```

The routine tests the input string for a value that is out of range. If so, it sets the `V` bit stored in the PCB during the interrupt. When `RTI` returns control to the application, the programmer at Level 5 will be able to test for overflow after executing `DECI`. `IsOvfl` is a boolean flag that indicates the overflow condition. The code from 0C94 to 0CA6 initializes `IsOvfl` to False and the state variable to Init.

Listing 17.4

The interrupt service routine for the DECI instruction.

```
            ;
            ;                          -------------------
            ;----------------------|   Opcode  11100    |----------------------
            ;                          -------------------
            ;The DECI instruction.
            ;Input format:  Any number of leading spaces or line feeds are
            ;allowed, followed by '+', '-', or a digit as the first character,
            ;after which digits are input until the first nondigit is
            ;encountered.  The status flags N, Z, and V are set appropriately
            ;by this DECI routine.  The C status flag is not affected.
            ;
            OldNZVC: .EQUATE d#12       ;Stack address of NZVC on interrupt
            ;
            Total:   .EQUATE d#10       ;Cumulative total of DECI number
            ValAscii:.EQUATE d#8        ;Value (AsciiCh)
            IsOvfl:  .EQUATE d#6        ;Overflow boolean
            IsNeg:   .EQUATE d#4        ;Negative boolean
            State:   .EQUATE d#2        ;State variable
            Temp:    .EQUATE d#0        ;Temporary
            ;
            Init:    .EQUATE d#0        ;Enumerated values for State
            Sign:    .EQUATE d#1
            Digit:   .EQUATE d#2
            ;
0C91  B0000C Opc11100:SUBSP   d#12,i     ;Allocate storage for locals
0C94  080000          LOADA   False,i    ;IsOvfl := False
0C97  130006          STOREA  IsOvfl,s
0C9A  080000          LOADA   Init,i     ;State := Init
0C9D  130002          STOREA  State,s
0CA0  080000          LOADA   d#0,i      ;WordBuff := 0 for input
0CA3  110C25          STOREA  WordBuff,d
0CA6  600000          LOADB   d#0,i      ;B := 0 for case jump
            ;
0CA9  D10C26 Repeat:  CHARI   ByteBuff,d ;Get AsciiCh
0CAC  090C25          LOADA   WordBuff,d ;Set Value (AsciiCh)
0CAF  28000F          ANDA    h#000F,i
0CB2  130008          STOREA  ValAscii,s
0CB5  090C25          LOADA   WordBuff,d ;A contains AsciiCh throughout loop
0CB8  0F0002          LOADX   State,s    ;case State of
0CBB  720CBE          BR      STable,x
            ;
0CBE  0CC4   STable:  .ADDRSS SInit
0CC0  0D27            .ADDRSS SSign
0CC2  0D45            .ADDRSS SDigit
```

Listing 17.4, continued

```
                ;
0CC4  A0002B SInit:    COMPA   c#/+/,i     ;If AsciiCh = '+' then
0CC7  800CCD           BRZ     Plus
0CCA  700CDC           BR      IfMinus
0CCD  0C0000 Plus:     LOADX   False,i     ;IsNeg := False
0CD0  170004           STOREX  IsNeg,s
0CD3  0C0001           LOADX   Sign,i      ;State := Sign
0CD6  170002           STOREX  State,s
0CD9  700CA9           BR      Repeat
                ;
0CDC  A0002D IfMinus:  COMPA   c#/-/,i     ;else if AsciiCh = '-' then
0CDF  800CE5           BRZ     Minus
0CE2  700CF4           BR      IfDigit1
0CE5  0C0001 Minus:    LOADX   True,i      ;IsNeg := True
0CE8  170004           STOREX  IsNeg,s
0CEB  0C0001           LOADX   Sign,i      ;State := Sign
0CEE  170002           STOREX  State,s
0CF1  700CA9           BR      Repeat
                ;
0CF4  A00030 IfDigit1:COMPA    c#/0/,i     ;else if AsciiCh is a digit then
0CF7  780D18           BRN     IfWhite
0CFA  A00039           COMPA   c#/9/,i
0CFD  980D03           BRNZ    Digit1
0D00  700D18           BR      IfWhite
0D03  0C0000 Digit1:   LOADX   False,i     ;IsNeg := False
0D06  170004           STOREX  IsNeg,s
0D09  0F0008           LOADX   ValAscii,s ;Total := Value (AsciiCh)
0D0C  17000A           STOREX  Total,s
0D0F  0C0002           LOADX   Digit,i     ;State := Digit
0D12  170002           STOREX  State,s
0D15  700CA9           BR      Repeat
                ;
0D18  A00020 IfWhite:  COMPA   Space,i     ;else if AsciiCh is not a space
0D1B  800CA9           BRZ     Repeat
0D1E  A0000A           COMPA   LineFeed,i ;or line feed then
0D21  800CA9           BRZ     Repeat
0D24  700DEE           BR      DeciErr     ;exit with DECI error            ;
0D27  A00030 SSign:    COMPA   c#/0/,i     ;If AsciiCh is not a digit then
0D2A  780DEE           BRN     DeciErr
0D2D  A00039           COMPA   c#/9/,i
0D30  980D36           BRNZ    Digit2
0D33  700DEE           BR      DeciErr     ;exit with DECI error
0D36  0F0008 Digit2:   LOADX   ValAscii,s ;else Total := Value (AsciiCh)
0D39  17000A           STOREX  Total,s
0D3C  0C0002           LOADX   Digit,i     ;State := Digit
0D3F  170002           STOREX  State,s
0D42  700CA9           BR      Repeat
```

Listing 17.4, continued

```
                 ;
0D45  A00030 SDigit:  COMPA   c#/0/,i      ;If AsciiCh is not a digit then
0D48  780D99          BRN     DeciNorm
0D4B  A00039          COMPA   c#/9/,i
0D4E  980D54          BRNZ    Digit3
0D51  700D99          BR      DeciNorm     ;exit normally
0D54  0C0001 Digit3:  LOADX   True,i       ;else X := True for later assignments
0D57  0B000A          LOADA   Total,s      ;Multiply Total by 10 as follows:
0D5A  40              ASLA                 ;First, times 2
0D5B  880D61          BRV     Ovfl1        ;If overflow then
0D5E  700D64          BR      L1
0D61  170006 Ovfl1:   STOREX  IsOvfl,s     ;IsOvfl := True
0D64  130000 L1:      STOREA  Temp,s       ;Save 2 * Total in Temp
0D67  40              ASLA                 ;Now, 4 * Total
0D68  880D6E          BRV     Ovfl2        ;If overflow then
0D6B  700D71          BR      L2
0D6E  170006 Ovfl2:   STOREX  IsOvfl,s     ;IsOvfl := True
0D71  40     L2:      ASLA                 ;Now, 8 * Total
0D72  880D78          BRV     Ovfl3        ;If overflow then
0D75  700D7B          BR      L3
0D78  170006 Ovfl3:   STOREX  IsOvfl,s     ;IsOvfl := True
0D7B  1B0000 L3:      ADDA    Temp,s       ;Finally, 8 * Total + 2 * Total
0D7E  880D84          BRV     Ovfl4        ;If overflow then
0D81  700D87          BR      L4
0D84  170006 Ovfl4:   STOREX  IsOvfl,s     ;IsOvfl := True
0D87  1B0008 L4:      ADDA    ValAscii,s   ;A := 10 * Total + ValAscii
0D8A  880D90          BRV     Ovfl5        ;If overflow then
0D8D  700D93          BR      L5
0D90  170006 Ovfl5:   STOREX  IsOvfl,s     ;IsOvfl := True
0D93  13000A L5:      STOREA  Total,s      ;Update Total
0D96  700CA9          BR      Repeat
                 ;
0D99  0B0004 DeciNorm:LOADA   IsNeg,s      ;If IsNeg then
0D9C  A00000          COMPA   False,i
0D9F  800DBB          BRZ     SetNZ
0DA2  0B000A          LOADA   Total,s      ;If not (Total = h#8000) then
0DA5  A08000          COMPA   h#8000,i
0DA8  800DB5          BRZ     L6
0DAB  38              NOTA                 ;Negate Total by taking two's comp
0DAC  180001          ADDA    d#1,i
0DAF  13000A          STOREA  Total,s
0DB2  700DBB          BR      SetNZ
0DB5  080000 L6:      LOADA   False,i      ;else -32768 is a special case
0DB8  130006          STOREA  IsOvfl,s     ;IsOvfl := False
```

Listing 17.4, continued

```
                 ;
0DBB  57000C SetNZ:    LDBYTX  OldNZVC,s   ;Set NZ according to Total result:
0DBE  34000E           ORX     h#000E,i    ;First, initialize NZV to 111
0DC1  0B000A           LOADA   Total,s     ;If Total is not negative then
0DC4  780DCA           BRN     CheckZ
0DC7  2C0007           ANDX    h#0007,i    ;clear N to 0
0DCA  A00000 CheckZ:   COMPA   d#0,i       ;If Total is not zero then
0DCD  800DD3           BRZ     SetV
0DD0  2C000B           ANDX    h#000B,i    ;clear Z to 0
0DD3  0B0006 SetV:     LOADA   IsOvfl,s    ;If not IsOvfl then
0DD6  A00001           COMPA   True,i
0DD9  800DDF           BRZ     StoreFl
0DDC  2C000D           ANDX    h#000D,i    ;clear V to 0
0DDF  5F000C StoreFl:  STBYTX  OldNZVC,s   ;Store the NZVC flags
                 ;
0DE2  A8000A ExitDeci:ADDSP    d#10,i      ;Deallocate all locals except Total
0DE5  B80EFA           JSR     Put         ;Put Total in memory
0DE8  A80002           ADDSP   d#2,i       ;Deallocate Total
0DEB  700C87           BR      Return
                 ;
0DEE  080DFB DeciErr:  LOADA   Msg1,i      ;Push address of message onto stack
0DF1  13FFFE           STOREA  d#-2,s
0DF4  B00002           SUBSP   d#2,i
0DF7  B80FDC           JSR     PrntMsg     ;and print
0DFA  00               STOP                ;Fatal error: program terminates
                 ;
0DFB  455252 Msg1:     .ASCII  /ERROR:  Invalid DECI input/
0E15  00               .BYTE   h#00
```

0CA9 is the start of the FSM loop, identified by the `Repeat` symbol. `ANDA` at 0CAF masks out all but the rightmost four bits of the input character, which leaves the binary value that corresponds to the decimal ASCII digit. For example, ASCII 5 is represented in binary as 0011 0101. The rightmost four bits are 0101, the corresponding binary value of the decimal digit. The accumulator gets the ASCII character at 0CB5 and keeps it throughout the loop. `STable` at 0CBE is a jump table for the `case` statement in the FSM.

The code from 0CC4 to 0D24 is the case for `State` having the value SInit, the start state of the FSM. The assignments are all made via the index register instead of the accumulator, because the accumulator maintains the ASCII character for comparison throughout the loop. For example, the assignment of `IsNeg` to False at 0CCD is implemented by `LOADX` followed by `STOREX` instead of `LOADA` followed by `STOREA`.

The code from 0D27 to 0D42 is the case for `State` having the value SSign, and from 0D45 to 0D96 is the case for `State` having the value SDigit. Pep/5 has no instruction to multiply a value by 10 (dec). This section of code performs the multiply with several left-shift operations. Each ASLA multiplies the value by 2. Three ASLA operations multiply the value by 8, which can be added to the value multiplied by 2 to get the value multiplied by 10. After each ASLA operation and the addition, the routine checks for overflow and sets IsOvfl accordingly.

The code from 0D99 to 0E15 is outside the loop. The algorithm exits the loop under two conditions—normally, or when it has detected an input error. If it exits normally, it checks the IsNeg flag to see if the string of digits was preceded by a negative sign. If it was, the instructions at 0DAB and 0DAC negate the number by taking the two's complement.

The number –32768 (dec), which is 8000 (hex), must be treated as a special case. If the input is -32768, the FSM will set IsOvfl to true when it adds 32760 to 8 at 0D7B. The problem is that 32768 is out of range, even though –32768 is in range. The routine adjusts IsOvfl for this special case at 0DB8.

The code from 0DBB to 0DDF adjusts the copies of the N, Z, and V flags that were stored at the interrupt. ORX at 0DBE sets NZV to 111. Note that the mask is 0E (hex), which is 0000 1110 (bin). Since C is the rightmost bit, it remains unchanged by the OR operation.

LOADA at 0DC1 puts the parsed value into the accumulator, setting the current N, Z, and V bits in the CPU accordingly. The code sets the copies of N and Z in the PCB equal to the current values of N and Z in the CPU. It sets the copy of V in the PCB according to the value of IsOvfl computed earlier in the parse.

The code from 0DE2 to 0DEB sets up a subroutine call to Put in Listing 17.7. Now that the decimal value has been input and parsed, the interrupt handler must store it in memory at the location specified by the operand of the DECI that caused the interrupt. Subroutine Put does precisely that, taking the parsed value as a parameter on the stack.

The code from 0DEE to 0E15 executes when the input string cannot be parsed legally. It prints an error message by calling PrntMsg in Listing 17.9 and terminates the applications program immediately.

The DECO Interrupt Handler

Listing 17.5 is the interrupt service routine for the DECO instruction. This routine outputs the operand of DECO in a format that is equivalent to a Pascal write statement whose format specifier indicates a field width of 1. Since the largest value that can be stored is 32767, the routine will output, at most, five digit characters. It will precede the value by a negative sign if necessary.

The code from 0E16 to 0E19 is a call to function Get in Listing 17.8. It allocates one word for the returned value, called Number. Get determines the addressing mode of the DECO that caused the interrupt and fetches its operand, which it returns in Number. LOADA at 0E1C puts the operand in the accumulator and sets the N bit accordingly. SUBSP at 0E1F allocates two more words on the stack without changing the N bit. The three local variables are now Remain, ChOut, and Place.

Listing 17.5

The interrupt service routine for the DECO instruction.

```
               ;
               ;                ------------------
               ;---------------------|  Opcode  11101  |----------------------
               ;                ------------------
               ;The DECO instruction.
               ;Output format:  If the operand is negative, the algorithm prints
               ;a single '-' followed by the magnitude.  Otherwise it prints the
               ;magnitude without a leading '+'.  It suppresses leading zeros.
               ;
               Number:  .EQUATE d#0        ;Value returned by function Get
               ;
               Remain:  .EQUATE d#0        ;Remainder of number
               ChOut:   .EQUATE d#2        ;Has a character been output yet?
               Place:   .EQUATE d#4        ;Place value of number for division
               ;
0E16  B00002 Opc11101:SUBSP   d#2,i       ;Allocate storage for Number
0E19  B80F81          JSR     Get         ;Get Number from memory
0E1C  0B0000          LOADA   Number,s    ;A := Number
0E1F  B00004          SUBSP   d#4,i       ;Allocate storage for locals
0E22  A00000          COMPA   d#0,i       ;If Oprnd is negative then
0E25  780E2B          BRN     PrntNeg
0E28  700E32          BR      PrntMag
0E2B  D8002D PrntNeg: CHARO   c#/-/,i     ;Print leading '-'
0E2E  38              NOTA                ;and negate Oprnd
0E2F  180001          ADDA    d#1,i
0E32  130000 PrntMag: STOREA  Remain,s    ;Remain := abs (Oprnd)
0E35  080000          LOADA   False,i     ;Initialize CharOut := False
0E38  130002          STOREA  ChOut,s
0E3B  082710          LOADA   d#10000,i   ;Place := 10,000
0E3E  130004          STOREA  Place,s
0E41  B80E71          JSR     Divide      ;Write 10,000's place
0E44  0803E8          LOADA   d#1000,i    ;Place := 1000
0E47  130004          STOREA  Place,s
0E4A  B80E71          JSR     Divide      ;Write 1000's place
0E4D  080064          LOADA   d#100,i     ;Place := 100
0E50  130004          STOREA  Place,s
0E53  B80E71          JSR     Divide      ;Write 100's place
0E56  08000A          LOADA   d#10,i      ;Place := 10
0E59  130004          STOREA  Place,s
0E5C  B80E71          JSR     Divide      ;Write 10's place
0E5F  0B0000          LOADA   Remain,s    ;Always write 1's place
0E62  300030          ORA     h#0030,i    ;Convert decimal to ASCII
0E65  590C26          STBYTA  ByteBuff,d
0E68  D90C26          CHARO   ByteBuff,d
0E6B  A80006          ADDSP   d#6,i       ;Deallocate storage for locals
0E6E  700C87          BR      Return
```

Listing 17.5, continued

```
                 ;
                 ;Subroutine to print the most significant decimal digit of the
                 ;remainder.  It assumes that Place (Place2 here) contains the
                 ;decimal place value.  It updates the remainder.
                 ;
                 Remain2: .EQUATE d#2        ;Stack addresses while executing a
                 ChOut2:  .EQUATE d#4        ;subroutine are greater by two because
                 Place2:  .EQUATE d#6        ;the ret addr is on the stack
                 ;
0E71  0B0002 Divide:   LOADA   Remain2,s   ;A := remainder
0E74  0C0000           LOADX   d#0,i       ;X := 0
0E77  230006 DivLoop:  SUBA    Place2,s    ;Division by repeated subtraction
0E7A  780E86           BRN     WriteNum    ;If remainder is negative, then done
0E7D  1C0001           ADDX    d#1,i       ;X := X + 1
0E80  130002           STOREA  Remain2,s   ;Store new remainder
0E83  700E77           BR      DivLoop
                 ;
0E86  A40000 WriteNum:COMPX    d#0,i       ;If X <> 0 then
0E89  800E95           BRZ     CheckOut
0E8C  080001           LOADA   True,i      ;ChOut := True
0E8F  130004           STOREA  ChOut2,s
0E92  700E9F           BR      PrntDgt     ;and branch to print this digit
0E95  0B0004 CheckOut:LOADA    ChOut2,s    ;else if a previous char was output
0E98  A00001           COMPA   True,i
0E9B  800E9F           BRZ     PrntDgt     ;then branch to print this zero
0E9E  C0               RTS                 ;else return to calling routine
                 ;
0E9F  340030 PrntDgt:  ORX     h#0030,i    ;Convert decimal to ASCII
0EA2  150C25           STOREX  WordBuff,d ;Temporary for output
0EA5  D90C26           CHARO   ByteBuff,d
0EA8  C0               RTS                 ;Return to calling routine
```

The code from 0E22 to 0E2F tests for a negative value. If the operand is negative, the `CHARO` at 0E2B outputs the negative sign, and the following code negates the operand. At 0E32 the accumulator contains the magnitude of the operand, which is stored in `Remain`.

The code from 0E35 to 0E5C writes the 10000's, 1000's, 100's, and 10's place of the magnitude of the operand. To suppress any leading zeros, it initializes `ChOut` to False, which indicates that no digit characters have yet been output.

Subroutine `Divide` outputs the digit character for the place value in `Place` and decreases `Remainder` for the next call. For example, if `Remain` is 24873 before the call to `Divide` at 0E41, then `Divide` will output 2 and leave 4873 in `Remain`. It will also set `ChOut` to True.

Before outputting character 0, `Divide` tests `ChOut` to see if any digit characters have been output yet. If `ChOut` is False, the character is a leading zero and is not output. Otherwise it is an embedded zero and is output. For example, if `Remain` is 761 before the call at 0E41, `Divide` prints nothing and leaves 761 in `Remain` and False in `ChOut`.

The code beginning at 0E5F writes the 1's place regardless of the value of `ChOut`. Thus, a value of zero for the original operand gets output as `0`.

The code from 0E71 to 0EA8 is the subroutine to print the most significant digit of `Remain`. It determines the value to output by repeatedly subtracting `Place` from `Remain`, counting the number of subtractions until `Remain` is less than zero. The effect is to compute the value to output as `Remain` div `Place`.

The HEXO and NOP Interrupt Handlers

Listing 17.6 is the interrupt service routine for the `HEXO` and `NOP` instructions. The `HEXO` interrupt handler is similar in function to the `DECO` interrupt handler. It outputs one word as four hexadecimal characters.

The function call at 0EAC in the `HEXO` interrupt handler is identical to the call at 0E19 in the `DECO` handler. `Get` returns the operand in `Number`, which is then

Listing 17.6

The interrupt service routine for the `HEXO` and `NOP` instructions.

```
                  ;
                  ;                     -------------------
                  ;--------------------|  Opcode  11110    |------------------------
                  ;                     -------------------
                  ;
                  ;The HEXO instruction.
                  ;Output format:  Outputs one word as four hex characters.  Number
                  ;is defined in the DECO interrupt handler.
                  ;
0EA9   B00002 Opc11110:SUBSP   d#2,i         ;Allocate storage for Number
0EAC   B80F81          JSR     Get           ;Get Number from memory
0EAF   0B0000          LOADA   Number,s      ;A := Number
0EB2   A80002          ADDSP   d#2,i         ;Deallocate storage for Number
0EB5   110C27          STOREA  WordTemp,d    ;Save Oprnd
0EB8   510C27          LDBYTA  WordTemp,d    ;Put high order byte in low order A
0EBB   48              ASRA                  ;Shift right four bits
0EBC   48              ASRA
0EBD   48              ASRA
0EBE   48              ASRA
0EBF   B80EDB          JSR     OutputAc      ;Output first hex character
0EC2   510C27          LDBYTA  WordTemp,d    ;Put high order byte in low order A
0EC5   B80EDB          JSR     OutputAc      ;Output second hex character
0EC8   510C28          LDBYTA  ByteTemp,d    ;Put low order byte in low order A
0ECB   48              ASRA                  ;Shift right four bits
0ECC   48              ASRA
0ECD   48              ASRA
0ECE   48              ASRA
0ECF   B80EDB          JSR     OutputAc      ;Output third hex character
0ED2   510C28          LDBYTA  ByteTemp,d    ;Put low order byte in low order A
0ED5   B80EDB          JSR     OutputAc      ;Output fourth hex character
0ED8   700C87          BR      Return
```

Listing 17.6, continued

```
               ;
               ;Subroutine to output in hex the least significant nybble of the
               ;accumulator.
               ;
0EDB   28000F OutputAc:ANDA    h#000F,i    ;Isolate digit value
0EDE   A00009          COMPA   d#9,i       ;If it is not in 0..9 then
0EE1   980EED          BRNZ    PrepNum
0EE4   200009          SUBA    d#9,i       ;convert number to ASCII letter
0EE7   300040          ORA     h#0040,i    ;and prefix ASCII code for letter
0EEA   700EF0          BR      WriteHex
0EED   300030 PrepNum: ORA     h#0030,i    ;else prefix ASCII code for number
0EF0   590C26 WriteHex:STBYTA  ByteBuff,d ;For output
0EF3   D90C26          CHARO   ByteBuff,d
0EF6   C0              RTS
               ;
               ;                     -------------------
               ;----------------------|   Opcode   11111   |----------------------
               ;                     -------------------
               ;The NOP instruction.
               ;
0EF7   700C90 Opc11111:BR      ReturnU     ;Simply return from the interrupt
```

stored in the accumulator. STOREA at 0EB5 puts the operand in WordTemp, declared in Listing 17.1. It is a block of one byte followed by another byte called ByteTemp. In effect, ByteTemp is the rightmost (low order) byte of the word at WordTemp.

For example, if Number is 4CA5 (hex), ByteTemp will have the value A5. LDBYTA at 0EB8 puts the byte at WordTemp into the accumulator. In this example, the rightmost byte of the accumulator would contain 4C. The four ASRA instructions shift the 4 to the rightmost nybble of the accumulator, after which the subroutine from 0EDB to 0EF6 outputs the corresponding hexadecimal character.

The remaining code in the handler from 0EC2 to 0ED8 outputs the remaining three hexadecimal characters from the operand.

The interrupt handler for NOP simply branches back to ReturnU, accomplishing nothing except consuming CPU time while executing the interrupt and RTI. Several problems in this chapter ask you to modify the operating system by changing NOP to some other new instruction. For those problems, you should insert your code to implement the new instruction at 0EF7.

The Put Subroutine

Listing 17.7 is the addressing mode decoder for storing an operand to memory. DECI calls Put after it has parsed the input characters into their proper binary value. The value needs to be stored in memory at a location that depends on the addressing mode specified by the DECI instruction that caused the interrupt. Put

Listing 17.7

The addressing mode decoder for storing an operand to memory.

```
                ;
                ;================   Put/Addressing mode decoder   ================
                ;
                ;Put is a subroutine that DECI calls at the end of its input
                ;processing.  It decodes the addressing mode of the interrupted
                ;instruction, calculates the address of the operand of the
                ;interrupted instruction, and puts the value of Oprnd at that
                ;location in memory.
                ;
                Oprnd:   .EQUATE d#2         ;Value of formal parameter stored
                ;
                OldNZVC4:.EQUATE d#4         ;Stack addresses of the register
                OldA4:   .EQUATE d#5         ;contents while executing this
                OldX4:   .EQUATE d#7         ;routine are greater by four because
                OldB4:   .EQUATE d#9         ;the ret addr and formal parameter
                OldPC4:  .EQUATE d#11        ;are on the stack
                OldSP4:  .EQUATE d#13
                OldIR4:  .EQUATE d#15
                ;
0EFA  53000F Put:        LDBYTA  OldIR4,s    ;A := intrpt IR
0EFD  280003             ANDA    h#0003,i    ;Retain only address mode bits.
0F00  800F48             BRZ     Immed       ;Immediate addressing is invalid
0F03  A00001             COMPA   d#1,i       ;Direct addressing?
0F06  800F22             BRZ     Direct
0F09  A00002             COMPA   d#2,i       ;Indexed addressing?
0F0C  800F32             BRZ     Indexed
                ;
0F0F  0B0002             LOADA   Oprnd,s     ;Stack relative, A := Oprnd
0F12  63000B             LOADB   OldPC4,s    ;B := intrpt PC
0F15  0C0000             LOADX   d#0,i       ;X := 0
0F18  620000             LOADB   h#0000,x    ;B := intrpt OprndSpec
0F1B  6B000D             ADDB    OldSP4,s    ;B := intrpt OprndSpec + intrpt SP
0F1E  120000             STOREA  h#0000,x    ;Store in Mem [OprndSpec + SP]
0F21  C0                 RTS
                ;
0F22  0B0002 Direct:     LOADA   Oprnd,s     ;A := Oprnd
0F25  63000B             LOADB   OldPC4,s    ;B := intrpt PC
0F28  0C0000             LOADX   d#0,i       ;X := 0
0F2B  620000             LOADB   h#0000,x    ;B := intrpt OprndSpec
0F2E  120000             STOREA  h#0000,x    ;Store in Mem [OprndSpec]
0F31  C0                 RTS
```

Listing 17.7, continued

```
                ;
0F32  0B0002 Indexed: LOADA   Oprnd,s     ;A := Oprnd
0F35  63000B          LOADB   OldPC4,s    ;B := intrpt PC
0F38  0C0000          LOADX   d#0,i       ;X := 0
0F3B  620000          LOADB   h#0000,x    ;B := intrpt OprndSpec
0F3E  6B0009          ADDB    OldB4,s     ;B := intrpt OprndSpec + intrpt B
0F41  0F0007          LOADX   OldX4,s     ;X := intrpt X
0F44  120000          STOREA  h#0000,x    ;Store in Mem [OprndSpec + 2*X + B]
0F47  C0              RTS
                ;
0F48  080F55 Immed:   LOADA   Msg2,i      ;Push address of message onto stack
0F4B  13FFFE          STOREA  d#-2,s
0F4E  B00002          SUBSP   d#2,i
0F51  B80FDC          JSR     PrntMsg     ;and print
0F54  00              STOP                ;Fatal error: program terminates
                ;
0F55  455252 Msg2:    .ASCII  /ERROR:  Illegal use of immediate addressing/
0F80  00              .BYTE   h#00
```

must determine what addressing mode DECI specified and use the mode along with DECI's operand specifier to determine where to store the value.

Because the formal parameter and return address are on the stack, the stack addresses are greater by four compared to the addresses shown in Figure 17.4. Figure 17.6 shows the modified stack addresses for this routine.

The code from 0EFA to 0F0C decodes the addressing mode. LDBYTA at 0EFA puts the instruction specifier of the interrupted instruction into the accumulator. The following ANDA masks out all but the rightmost two bits, since 03 (hex) is 0000 0011 (bin). The following BRZ branches if the addressing mode bits are 00, which corresponds to immediate addressing. Otherwise COMPA at 0F03 tests for the addressing mode bits 01 for direct addressing. COMPA at 0F09 similarly tests for indexed addressing.

The code from 0F0F to 0F21 stores the operand on the application stack. LOADA puts the operand value in the accumulator. LOADB at 0F12 fetches the value of the program counter from the PCB. Remember that the Level 3 machine considers all unimplemented instructions to be unary. Therefore, the program counter was incremented by 1 during the von Neumann execution cycle before being saved in the PCB on interrupt. The old PC's current value is therefore the address of the operand specifier of the interrupted instruction. After LOADX clears the index register, LOADB at 0F18 puts the operand specifier of the interrupted instruction into the base register.

ADDB at 0F1B adds the saved value of the application's stack pointer to the content of the base register. The base register now contains the sum of the interrupted instruction's operand specifier and its stack pointer. STOREA at 0F1E puts the operand in the memory location specified by the content of the base register.

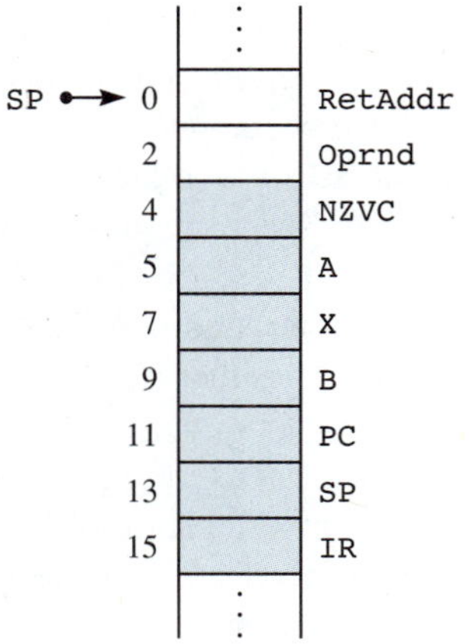

Figure 17.6

The stack addresses of the copies of the CPU registers during execution of Put. The shaded region is the process control block (PCB) of the suspended process.

Architectural Rumblings

The serial computer has been the primary architecture for computers since the 1940s, both in the prevailing abstract model as described by Turing and in the physical machines first used by von Neumann. Despite varying user interfaces, operating systems, and labels on the cabinetry—whether manufactured by Apple, IBM, SUN, DEC, or Atari—chances are that any computer you have ever seen or used is of the same mold.

The classical model of computer architecture contains a random access memory (RAM), a central processing unit (CPU), and input and output (I/O) mechanisms that are interconnected via a wiring pattern designed to shuttle information between components as the machine steps through a program. This model has been very successful in supporting large-scale computing needs and satisfying the individual user.

Despite the remarkable speed of modern computers, some computing tasks are so large in terms of time or space requirements that they can't be accomplished successfully on traditional machines. Consider weather forecasting, for example. Current meteorological models for five-day forecasts involve thousands of data values from a large area of the earth's atmosphere and hundreds of complex equations for modeling the likely interaction of weather systems. The abstract Turing machine could, in principle, compute the weather forecast, as could a personal computer or mainframe. But because some of the computations would take days—even weeks—on a mainframe computer, a five-day forecast computed on one of these machines obviously would have little value.

Many programming problems are solved by networking several computers. For example, an airline reservation system organized by departure date could consist of four computers: one computer for handling same-day departures, another for next-day departures, a third for flights departing in three-to-seven days, and a fourth for flights departing in more than one week. Because all the travel agents who call an airline at 10:15 on a Monday morning would not be booking passengers for the same flight, the load could be distributed over several computers, and each travel agent's request would be processed in a matter of a few seconds.

But clever networking of traditional architectures isn't the only way to perform more computation in less time. For a number of years, researchers have been trying to develop alternative computer architectures. One of the early developments was the improvement of the von Neumann sequential computer with a pipelined machine-code interpreter. In the traditional architecture, the next instruction to be executed usually comes from the next location in memory (except in cases of branching in the flow of control). Pipelining is a technique that allows one part of the machine to carry out the current instruction while another part of the machine decodes the next instruction and prepares it for execution.

Seymour Cray introduced another exciting architectural innovation. Cray observed that as the number of electronic components for large memories increased with customers' demands for bigger and faster machines, the growing distance between components inherently limited the speed of the machine because it had to wait for signals to travel through its miles of wiring. (Even the speed of light is a physical constraint in a large computer.) Yet the heat generated by electronic equipment requires that the circuitry be physically spaced to allow sufficient airflow through the fan-cooled system. Cray's ingenious solution to the predicament was the liquid-cooled computer. To minimize wire length and allow for maximum cooling, he ran refrigeration tubing through the circuits at regular intervals.

But Cray's machines weren't just innovative from the perspective of plumbing. His computer also took advantage of vector processing by using more than one CPU at the same time. This technique, known as parallel processing, allowed certain categories of computations to overlap.

No doubt, there will be other improvements to the traditional single-CPU architecture, and the single-CPU model will survive for some time in both existing and future computers. It is a simple, elegant, and cost-effective design with a large body of programming and maintenance knowledge supporting it. But it is equally clear that traditional architectures will have to begin making room for multiple-CPU machines as we try to solve larger and more complex problems.

The net effect of this code is to implement stack-relative addressing for the interrupted instruction. Why can't you simply use stack-relative addressing with the `STOREA` instruction at 0F1E? Because the current `SP` in the CPU points to the top of the system stack, not to the application stack of the interrupted instruction. Also, the operand specifier of the `STOREA` instruction cannot be the operand specifier of the interrupted instruction. The routine must compute the stack address of the interrupted instruction and store its operand as if it executed stack-relative addressing directly in the hardware. The code simulates stack-relative addressing for the interrupted instruction using indexed addressing with the current CPU registers. As far as the Level 5 user is concerned, the interrupted instruction executed stack-relative addressing.

The code from 0F22 to 0F31 simulates direct addressing similarly. The first four instructions bring the operand specifier of the interrupted instruction into the base register, and `STOREA` puts the operand into memory at the address specified by the operand specifier.

The code from 0F32 to 0F47 simulates indexed addressing. It puts the sum of the operand specifier and the base register from the PCB into the base register, and the index register from the PCB into the index register. Then `STOREA` at 0F44 uses indexed addressing to simulate indexed addressing. Since the copy of the index register from the PCB is in the index register, it is multiplied by two in the hardware as required to compute the address of the operand.

The code from 0F48 to 0F80 is for immediate addressing. Since immediate addressing is illegal with `DECI`, the code issues an error message and terminates the program.

The Get Subroutine

Listing 17.8 is the addressing mode decoder for loading an operand from memory. `DECO` and `HEXO` call function `Get` at the beginning of their routines to fetch the operand. The value needs to be fetched from memory at a location that depends on the addressing mode specified by the instruction that caused the interrupt. `Get` must determine what addressing mode was specified and use the mode along with the operand specifier to determine from where to fetch the value.

For the most part, this code mirrors the code of `Put`. It decodes the addressing mode of the instruction that caused the interrupt and simulates the execution with that addressing mode. The difference is that this function is called at the beginning of `DECO` and `HEXO`, not at the end. Its purpose is to get the operand from memory and pass it to the interrupt handler for further processing, not to put the processed operand into memory. Consequently, the `LOADA` instructions at 0FA2, 0FBF, and 0FD5 replace the `STOREA` instructions at 0F1E, 0F2E, and 0F44, respectively.

Another difference is that immediate addressing is legal with the `DECO` and `HEXO` instructions. The code from 0FA9 to 0FB5 simulates immediate addressing by putting the copy of the program counter from the PCB into the base register and clearing the index register. `LOADA` at 0FAF gets the operand specifier of the interrupted instruction. In immediate addressing, the operand is the operand specifier, so the accumulator contains the operand as desired.

```
              ;
              ;================   Get/Addressing mode decoder   ================
              ;
              ;Get is a function called at the beginning of DECO and HEXO.  It
              ;decodes the addressing mode of the interrupted instruction,
              ;calculates the operand of the interrupted instruction, and
              ;returns its value in Oprnd.  The stack addresses are identical to
              ;those in the Put addressing mode decoder.
              ;
0F81  53000F Get:      LDBYTA  OldIR4,s    ;A := intrpt IR
0F84  280003           ANDA    h#0003,i    ;Retain only address mode bits
0F87  800FA9           BRZ     Immed2      ;Immediate addressing
0F8A  A00001           COMPA   d#1,i       ;Direct addressing?
0F8D  800FB6           BRZ     Direct2
0F90  A00002           COMPA   d#2,i       ;Indexed addressing?
0F93  800FC6           BRZ     Indexed2
              ;
0F96  63000B           LOADB   OldPC4,s    ;Stack relative, B := intrpt PC
0F99  0C0000           LOADX   d#0,i       ;X := 0
0F9C  620000           LOADB   h#0000,x    ;B := intrpt OprndSpec
0F9F  6B000D           ADDB    OldSP4,s    ;B := intrpt OprndSpec + intrpt SP
0FA2  0A0000           LOADA   h#0000,x    ;A := Mem [OprndSpec + SP]
0FA5  130002           STOREA  Oprnd,s
0FA8  C0               RTS
              ;
0FA9  63000B Immed2:   LOADB   OldPC4,s    ;B := intrpt PC
0FAC  0C0000           LOADX   d#0,i       ;X := 0
0FAF  0A0000           LOADA   h#0000,x    ;A := intrpt OprndSpec
0FB2  130002           STOREA  Oprnd,s
0FB5  C0               RTS
              ;
0FB6  63000B Direct2:  LOADB   OldPC4,s    ;B := intrpt PC
0FB9  0C0000           LOADX   d#0,i       ;X := 0
0FBC  620000           LOADB   h#0000,x    ;B := intrpt OprndSpec
0FBF  0A0000           LOADA   h#0000,x    ;A := Mem [OprndSpec]
0FC2  130002           STOREA  Oprnd,s
0FC5  C0               RTS
              ;
0FC6  63000B Indexed2:LOADB    OldPC4,s    ;B := intrpt PC
0FC9  0C0000           LOADX   d#0,i       ;X := 0
0FCC  620000           LOADB   h#0000,x    ;B := intrpt OprndSpec
0FCF  6B0009           ADDB    OldB4,s     ;B := intrpt OprndSpec + intrpt B
0FD2  0F0007           LOADX   OldX4,s     ;X := intrpt X
0FD5  0A0000           LOADA   h#0000,x    ;A := Mem [OprndSpec + 2*X + B]
0FD8  130002           STOREA  Oprnd,s
0FDB  C0               RTS
```

Listing 17.8

The addressing mode decoder for loading from memory.

The Print Subroutine and Machine Vectors

Listing 17.9 includes the subroutine for printing error messages, and the machine vectors. The print subroutine is similar to those in Chapter 15. It assumes that the formal parameter is the address of the message to print and prints the string of characters until it encounters a null byte.

```
                ;
                ;=====================   Print subroutine   =====================
                ;
                ;Prints a line feed character followed by the string of ASCII
                ;bytes until it encounters a null byte (eight zero bits).  Assumes
                ;one parameter, which contains the address of the message.
                ;
                MsgAddr: .EQUATE d#2        ;Address of message to print
                ;
0FDC   D8000A PrntMsg: CHARO   LineFeed,i
0FDF   630002          LOADB   MsgAddr,s   ;B := address of message
0FE2   0C0000          LOADX   d#0,i       ;X := 0
0FE5   080000          LOADA   d#0,i       ;A := 0
0FE8   520000 PrntMore:LDBYTA  h#0000,x    ;Test next char from Mem [B + X]
0FEB   800FF7          BRZ     StopPrnt    ;If null then exit
0FEE   DA0000          CHARO   h#0000,x    ;else print
0FF1   1C0001          ADDX    d#1,i       ;X := X + 1 for next character
0FF4   700FE8          BR      PrntMore
                ;
0FF7   C0      StopPrnt:RTS
                ;
                ;=============   Vectors reserved for machine use   ==============
                ;
0FF8   0BC1            .ADDRSS OsRAM       ;User stack pointer
0FFA   0C25            .ADDRSS WordBuff    ;System stack pointer
0FFC   0C29            .ADDRSS Loader      ;Loader program counter
0FFE   0C70            .ADDRSS Intrupt     ;Interrupt program counter
                ;
1000                   .END
```

Listing 17.9

The print subroutine and machine vectors.

The machine vectors are established with the `.ADDRSS` command. Compare this code with Listing 17.1 and Figure 17.1. The vector at 0FF8 is the address of `OsRAM`, which is the top byte of operating system RAM. The hardware initializes `SP` to this value when the user selects the execute option from the simulator. It is the byte at the bottom of the user stack.

The vector at 0FFA is the address of `WordBuff`. Listing 17.1 shows `WordBuff` as the next byte below the 100-byte block of storage reserved for the system stack. The hardware initializes `SP` to this value when the user selects the load option from the simulator. It also pushes the PCB onto the stack starting from this point when an interrupt occurs.

The vector at 0FFC is the address of the loader, as Listing 17.2 shows. The hardware initializes PC to this value when the user selects the load option. The vector at 0FFE is the address of the interrupt handler, as Listing 17.3 shows. The hardware initializes PC to this value when an interrupt occurs.

17.3 Concurrent Processes

Remember that a process is a program during execution. The previous section showed how the operating system can suspend a process during its execution to provide a service. A time line of CPU activity for a process that uses DECI and DECO would look like Figure 17.7. The shaded regions represent those times that the CPU executes the interrupt service routine. The time line is similar in form to Figure 17.2 except that this figure shows the operating system suspending a process before it terminates, then restarting it when the service is complete.

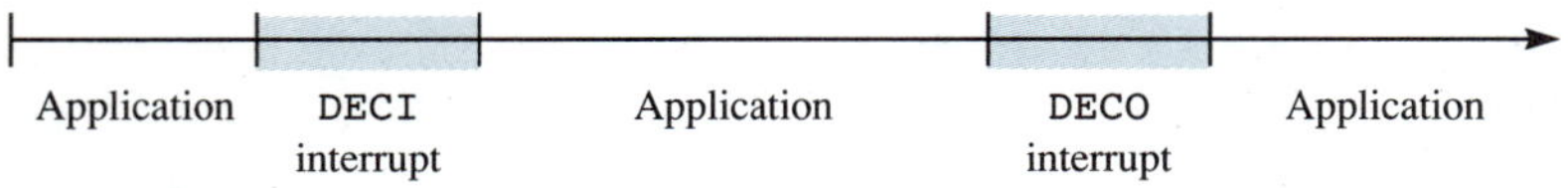

Figure 17.7 A time line of CPU usage when the operating system executes a single program containing DECI and DECO instructions.

The interrupts described in the previous section are called *software interrupts* because the executing process initiates them by the unimplemented opcodes in its listing. They are also called *synchronous interrupts* because each time the process executes, the interrupts always occur at the same time. The interrupts are synchronized with the code and are predictable.

Another way to initiate a synchronous interrupt is to execute an operating system call. A common assembly level mnemonic for an operating system call is SVC, which stands for *supervisor call.* The operand specifier normally acts as a parameter for the system call and tells the system which service the program wants to request. For example, if you want to open a file with the equivalent of reset in Pascal and if the code for reset is 27, you might execute

Supervisor calls

```
SVC d#27
```

Asynchronous Interrupts

Another type of interrupt is the *asynchronous interrupt*, which does not occur at a predictable time during execution. Two common sources of asynchronous interrupts are

Two common asynchronous interrupts

- Time outs
- I/O completions

To see how asynchronous interrupts can occur from time outs, consider a multi-user system, which allows several users to access the computer simultaneously. Since most computers have only one CPU, the operating system must allocate the CPU to each user's job in turn with a technique known as *time sharing*. The operating system allocates a quantum of time called a *time slice*, typically about 100 ms (one tenth of a second), to a job. If the job is not completed within that time (a condition known as *time out*), the operating system suspends the job temporarily and allocates another quantum of CPU time to the next job.

Time outs

To implement time sharing, the hardware must provide an alarm clock that the operating system can set to produce an interrupt after an interval of time.

The reason such an interrupt is unpredictable is that it depends on how busy the system is servicing the requests of its users. If no other job is waiting for the CPU, the system may let your job run longer than the standard time slice. Then if another user suddenly requests a service, the operating system may suspend your process immediately and allocate the CPU to the requesting job. Your process would not be interrupted at the same point as if it timed out after one time slice.

I/O completions

The second common source of asynchronous interrupts is I/O completions. A basic property of I/O devices is their slow speed compared to the processing speed of the CPU. If a running process requests some input from a keyboard, in the fraction of a second that it takes the user to respond, the CPU can execute hundreds of thousands of instructions for another process. Even if the process requests input from a disk file, which is much faster than keyboard input, the CPU could still execute thousands of instructions while waiting for the information to come from the disk.

To keep from wasting CPU time, the operating system can suspend the process that makes an I/O request if it appears that the process will need to wait for the I/O to complete. It can temporarily assign the CPU to a second process with the understanding that when the I/O does complete, the first process may immediately get the CPU back. Since the second process cannot predict when the I/O device will complete the I/O operation for the first process, it cannot know when the operating system might interrupt it to give the CPU back to the first process.

An operating system that can switch back and forth between processes to keep the CPU busy is called a *multiprogramming system*. To implement multiprogramming, the hardware must provide connections for the I/O devices to send interrupt signals to the CPU when the devices complete their I/O operations.

Processes in the Operating System

Multiprogramming

One purpose of an operating system is to allocate the resources of the system efficiently. A multiprogramming time-sharing system allocates CPU time among the jobs in the system. The objective is to keep the CPU as busy as possible executing user jobs instead of being idle waiting for I/O. The operating system tries to be fair in scheduling CPU time so all the jobs will be completed in a reasonable time.

At any given point in time, the operating system must maintain many suspended processes that are waiting their turn for CPU time. It maintains all these processes by allocating a separate PCB for each one, similar to the PCB the interrupt handler maintains in the Pep/5 system. A common practice is to link the process control blocks together with pointers in a linked list called a *queue*. Figure 17.8 shows a queue of process control blocks.

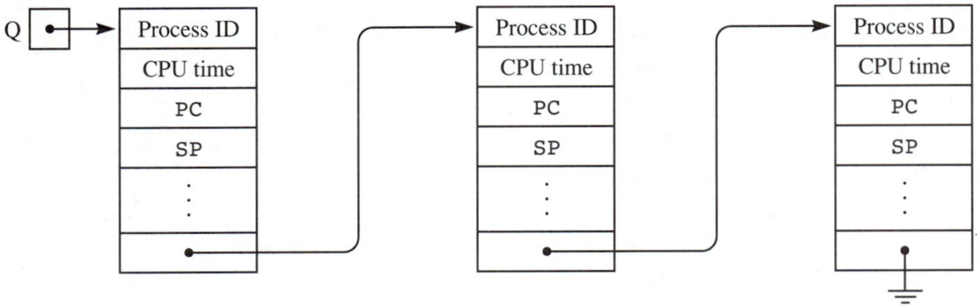

Figure 17.8

A queue of process control blocks.

Each PCB includes copies of all the CPU register values at the time of the process' most recent interrupt. The register set must include a copy of the program counter so the process can continue executing from where it was when the interrupt occurred.

The PCB contains additional information to help the operating system schedule the CPU. An example is a unique process identification number assigned by the system, labeled Process ID in the figure, that serves to reference the process. Suppose a user wants to terminate a process before it completes execution normally and he knows the ID number is 782. He could issue a `KILL (782)` command that would cause the operating system to search through the queue of process control blocks, find the PCB with ID 782, remove it from the queue and deallocate it.

Another example of information stored in the PCB is a record of the total amount of CPU time used so far by the suspended process. If the CPU becomes available and the operating system must decide which of several suspended processes gets the CPU, it can use the recorded time to make a fair decision.

As a job progresses through the system toward completion it passes through several states, as Figure 17.9 shows. The figure is in the form of a state transition diagram and is another example of a finite state machine. Each transition is labeled with the event that causes the change of state.

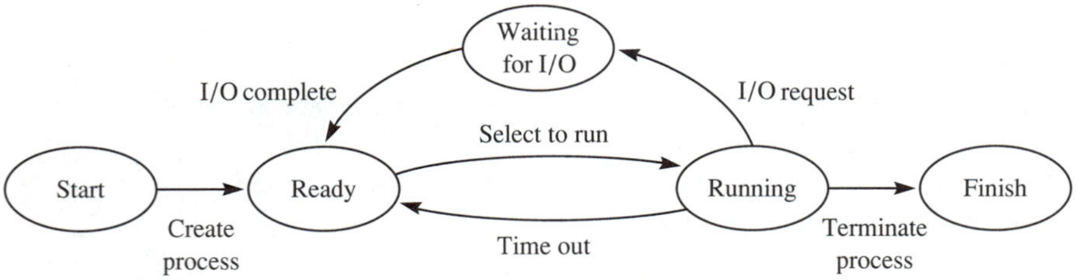

Figure 17.9

The state transition diagram for a job in an operating system.

When a user submits a job for processing, the operating system creates a process for it by allocating a new PCB and attaching it to a queue of processes that are waiting for CPU time. It loads the program into main memory and sets the copy of the `PC` in the PCB to the address of the first instruction of the process. That puts the job in the ready state.

Eventually, the operating system should select the job to receive some processing time. It sets the alarm clock to generate an interrupt after a quantum of time and puts the copies of the registers from the PCB into the CPU. That puts the job in the running state.

Transitions from the running state

While in the running state, three things can happen: (1) The running process may time out if it is still executing when the alarm clock interrupts. If so, the operating system attaches the process' PCB to the ready queue, which puts it back in the ready state. (2) The process may complete its execution normally, in which case the last instruction it executes is a `SVC` to request that the operating system terminate it. (3) The process may need some input, in which case it executes a `SVC` for the request. The operating system would transfer the request to the appropriate I/O device and put the PCB in another queue of processes that are waiting for their I/O operations to complete. That puts the process in the waiting-for-I/O state.

Transition from the waiting for I/O state

While the process is in the waiting-for-I/O state, the I/O device should eventually interrupt the system with the requested input. When that happens, the system puts the input in a buffer in main memory, removes the process' PCB from the waiting-for-I/O queue, and puts it in the ready queue. That puts the process in the ready state, from which it will eventually receive some more CPU time. Then it can access the input from the buffer.

Multiprocessing

As far as the user is concerned, a job simply executes from start to finish. The interruptions are invisible the same way that the `DECI` interrupt is invisible to the assembly language programmer at Level 5. The details at the operating system level are invisible to the users at a higher level of abstraction.

The only perceptible difference to the user is that it will take longer for the program to execute if many jobs are in the system. One way to speed the progress is to attach more than one CPU to the system. Such a configuration is called a *multiprocessing system.* Figure 17.10 shows a multiprocessing system with two processors.

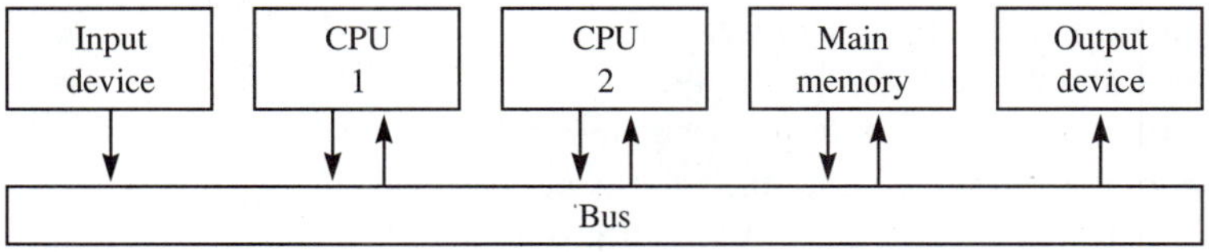

Figure 17.10

Block diagram of a multiprocessing system.

In multiprogramming, the processes appear to be executing concurrently because the CPU switches between them so rapidly. In multiprocessing, the operating system can schedule more than one process to execute concurrently because there is more than one processor.

It would be nice if increasing the number of processors in the system increased the performance proportionally. Unfortunately, that is not usually the case. When you add more processors to the system you place a greater demand on the communication links of the system. For example, if you attach the processors to a common bus, as in Figure 17.10, the bus may limit the performance of the system. If both CPUs request a read from the input device at the same time, one CPU will have to wait. The more processors you add, the more frequently those conflicts will occur.

The communication overhead inherent in a multiprocessor system typically yields a performance curve as in Figure 17.11. The dashed line shows the theoretical maximum benefit of adding processors. On the dashed line, for example, if you double the number of processors you double the performance. In practice, the performance does not increase that much.

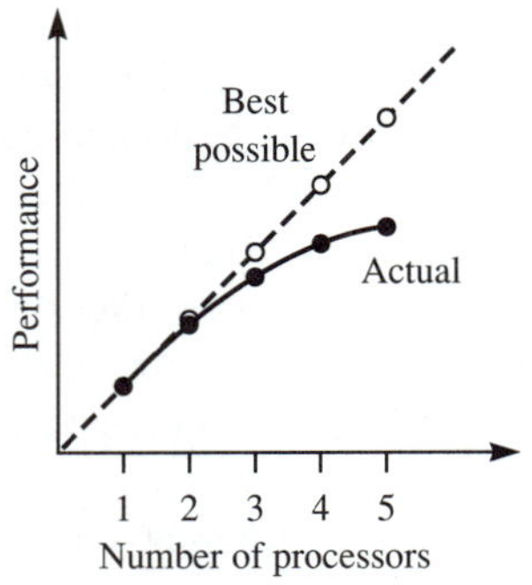

Figure 17.11

The increase in performance by adding processors in a multiprocessing system.

Program 17.1

The processes considered thus far were all independent from each other. Each process belonged to a different user, and there was no interaction between the processes. Under those circumstances, the result of a computation does not depend on when an interrupt occurs. The only effect the interrupt has is to increase the amount of time it takes to execute the process.

Cooperating processes

In practice, processes managed by an operating system frequently need to cooperate with one another to perform their tasks. Program 17.1 describes a situation in which two processes must cooperate to avoid producing incorrect results.

Suppose the operating system must manage an airline's database, with records accessed concurrently by several users. Each flight has a record in the database that contains, among other things, the number of reservations that have been made for that flight. Travel agencies from throughout the city access the system on behalf of prospective passengers. Requests for information from the database are somewhat random, since it is impossible to predict when a given agent will need to access the system.

One day, two different agents have customers who want to make reservations at exactly the same time for the same future flight. The operating system creates a process for each job called P1 and P2. Program 17.1 shows a code fragment from each process. `NumRes` stands for number of reservations. It is an integer variable whose value is in main memory while P1 and P2 progress through the system.

Suppose `NumRes` has the value 47 before either agent makes a reservation for his customer. After both transactions, `NumRes` should have the value 49. At the Pascal level, each process wants to increment `NumRes` by 1 with the assignment statement. If assignment statements are *atomic*, that is, indivisible, then the code fragment at the Pascal level will produce correct results regardless of which pro-

Program 17.1

Concurrent processes at two levels of abstraction.

Pascal Level

Process P1

```
.
.
.
NumRes := NumRes + 1
.
.
.
```

Process P2

```
.
.
.
NumRes := NumRes + 1
.
.
.
```

Assembly Level

Process P1

```
.
.
.
LOADA  NumRes,d
ADDA   d#1,i
STOREA NumRes,d
.
.
.
```

Process P2

```
.
.
.
LOADA  NumRes,d
ADDA   d#1,i
STOREA NumRes,d
.
.
.
```

cess executes its assignment statement first. If P1 executes first, it will make NumRes 48, and P2 will make NumRes 49. If P2 executes first, it will make NumRes 48, and P1 will make NumRes 49. In either case, NumRes gets the correct value of 49.

Nonatomic statements

The problem is that assignment statements at the Pascal level are not atomic. They are compiled to LOADA, ADDA, STOREA, and executed in a system in which an interrupt may occur between any assembly language statement. Table 17.1 is a trace of an execution sequence that shows what can go wrong. A(P1) is the content of P1's accumulator, either in the CPU when P1 is running or in the PCB when P1 is suspended. A(P2) is P2's accumulator.

Table 17.1

A trace of one possible execution sequence of Program 17.1.

Statement executed	A(P1)	A(P2)	NumRes
	?	?	47
(P1) LOADA NumRes	47	?	47
(P1) ADDA d#1, i	48	?	47
(P2) LOADA NumRes, d	48	47	47
(P2) ADDA d#1, i	48	48	47
(P2) STOREA NumRes, d	48	48	48
(P1) STOREA NumRes, d	48	48	48

In this sequence, P1 executes `LOADA`, which puts 47 in its accumulator, then `ADDA`, which increments the accumulator to 48. Then the operating system interrupts P1 and gives P2 some processor time. P2 executes all three of its statements, changing `NumRes` in memory to 48. When P1 eventually resumes, it gives 48 to `NumRes` as well. The net result is that `NumRes` has the value 48 instead of 49, even though each process executed all its statements.

The logical equivalence of multiprogramming and multiprocessing

This problem can occur whether the processes execute in a multiprocessing system with true concurrency or in a multiprogramming system where the concurrency is only apparent. In a multiprocessing system it would be possible for P1 and P2 to execute their `ADDA` instructions at exactly the same time. But if they tried to execute their `STOREA` instructions at exactly the same time, the hardware would force one process to wait while the other wrote the value to memory. From a logical point of view, the problems that can occur are the same whether the concurrency is real or not.

Critical Sections

The basic problem arises because P1 and P2 share that part of main memory that contains the value of `NumRes`. Whenever concurrent processes share a variable, there is always the possibility that the results depend on the timing of the interrupts. To solve the problem, we need a way to ensure that when one process accesses the shared variable, the other process is prevented from accessing it until the first process has completed its access.

Sections of code in two processes that are mutually exclusive are called *critical sections*. For concurrent programs to execute correctly, the software must guarantee that if one process is executing a statement in a critical section, the other process cannot be executing a statement in its critical section. To solve the problem of Program 17.1, we need a way of putting the assignment statements in critical sections so the interleaved execution will not occur at the assembly level.

Entry and exit sections

A critical section requires two additional pieces of code called the *entry section* and the *exit section*. The entry section for P1 is written just before its critical section. Its function is to test whether P2 is executing in its critical section and, if so, to delay somehow the execution of P1's critical section until P2 is finished with its critical section. The exit section for P1 is written just after its critical section. Its function is to alert P2 that P1 is no longer in a critical section, so P2 may enter its critical section.

The code fragment at the Pascal level for each process of the preceding program must be modified as follows:

remainder section
entry section
```
NumRes := NumRes + 1 {the critical section}
```
exit section
remainder section

The remainder sections are all those parts of the code that can execute concurrently with the other process with no ill effects. The critical sections are those parts of the code that must be mutually exclusive.

The following programs show attempts to implement the entry and exit sections that guard the process' access to its critical section. Each program assumes that P1 and P2 have this general form:

Process P1	Process P2
`repeat`	`repeat`
entry section	*entry section*
critical section	*critical section*
exit section	*exit section*
remainder section	*remainder section*
`until Done1`	`until Done2`

`Done1` and `Done2` are local boolean variables (not shared) that are modified somewhere in the remainder sections.

Program 17.2

Program 17.2, our first attempt at designing the entry and exit sections, uses `Turn`, a shared integer variable. The entry section consists of a `while` loop that tests `Turn`, and the exit section consists of an assignment statement that modifies `Turn`. Although the listing does not show it, assume that `Turn` is initialized either to 1 or 2 before the processes enter the `repeat` loops.

Program 17.2

An attempt at programming mutual exclusion.

Process P1

```
repeat
   while Turn <> 1 do
      {nothing}
   critical section
   Turn := 2
   remainder section
until Done1
```

Process P2

```
repeat
   while Turn <> 2 do
      {nothing}
   critical section
   Turn := 1
   remainder section
until Done2
```

The nonatomic nature of the while statement

The body of the `while` loop in the entry section is an empty Pascal statement that generates no code at the assembly level. The code for the entry section of P1 translates to

```
Loop: LOADA Turn
      COMPA d#1
      BRZ   Cont
      BR    Loop
Cont:
```

Suppose `Turn` is initialized to 1 and both processes try to enter their critical sections at the same time. No matter how you interleave the executions of the assembly statements in the entry section, P2 will continually loop until P1 enters its critical section. When P1 finishes its critical section its exit section will set `Turn` to 2, after which P2 will be able to enter its critical section.

This algorithm guarantees that the critical sections are mutually exclusive. P2 can be in its critical section only if `Turn` is 2, during which time P1 cannot be in its critical section, and vice versa. When P2 leaves its critical section it sets `Turn` to 1, which acts as a signal to P1 that it may enter its critical section.

Although the algorithm guarantees mutual exclusion, it has the undesirable property of requiring the processes to strictly alternate their `repeat` loops. The processes communicate through the shared variable `Turn`, which keeps track of whose turn it is to execute a critical section. The user may want P1 to execute its `repeat` loop several times without P2 executing its loop at all. That could never happen with these entry and exit sections.

Program 17.3

To allow a process to execute its `repeat` loops unrestrained by the execution of the other process (except for the mutual exclusion requirement), Program 17.3 uses two shared boolean variables, `Enter1` and `Enter2`. Assume that `Enter1` and `Enter2` are both initialized to false.

Process P1

```
repeat
   Enter1 := true
   while Enter 2 do
      {nothing}
   critical section
   Enter1 := false
   remainder section
until Done1
```

Process P2

```
repeat
   Enter2 := true
   while Enter1 do
      {nothing}
   critical section
   Enter2 := false
   remainder section
until Done2
```

Program 17.3

Another attempt at programming mutual exclusion.

If P2 is in its remainder section, `Enter2` must be false. Then P1 can execute its `repeat` loop as often as it likes. It simply sets `Enter1` to true, tests `Enter2` once in the `while` loop, executes its critical section, sets `Enter1` to false, and executes its remainder section. It can repeat the sequence as long as it likes. Similarly, P2 can loop repeatedly if P1 is in its remainder section.

This implementation guarantees mutual exclusion. When P1 sets `Enter1` to true, it is signaling P2 that it is trying to enter a critical section. If P2 has just a little earlier fetched `Enter1` with

```
LOADA Enter1,d
```

in its `while` test, P2 will not immediately know of P1's intentions. P2 may be executing its critical section already. However, if P2 is in its critical section, `Enter2` must be true, and P1's `while` loop will keep it from entering its critical section at the same time. When P2 finally exits, it sets `Enter2` to false, which allows P1 into its critical section.

The problems that confront the designer of cooperating processes can be quite subtle and unexpected. This algorithm is a case in point. Although it guarantees mutual exclusion and does not constrain the `repeat` loop execution as in the previous program, it nevertheless has a serious bug.

Table 17.2 shows a trace where P1 sets `Enter1` to true, then experiences an interrupt. P2 sets `Enter2` to true, then begins executing its `while` loop. The `while` loop will continue executing until P2 times out and P1 resumes, because `Enter1` is true. But P1 will also loop indefinitely because `Enter2` is true.

Table 17.2

A trace of Program 17.3 that produces deadlock.

Statement executed	`Enter1`	`Enter2`
	false	false
(P1) `Enter1 := true;`	true	false
(P2) `Enter2 := true;`	true	true
(P2) `while Enter1 do`	true	true
(P1) `while Enter2 do`	true	true

P1 and P2 are in a state in which each one wants to enter a critical section. P1 cannot enter until P2 enters, executes its critical section, and sets `Enter2` to false. But P2 cannot enter until P1 enters, executes its critical section, and sets `Enter1` to false. Each process is waiting for an event that will never occur, a condition called *deadlock*. Deadlocks, like endless loops, are conditions to avoid.

Definition of deadlock

Program 17.4

We need a solution that guarantees mutual exclusion, allows the outer `repeat` loops of each process to execute without restraint, and avoids deadlock. Program 17.4, an implementation of Peterson's algorithm, combines features from Programs 17.2 and 17.3 to achieve all these objectives. The basic idea is that `Enter1` and `Enter2` provide the mutual exclusion as in Program 17.3, and `Turn` allows one of the processes to enter its critical section even if both processes try to enter at the same time. `Enter1` and `Enter2` initially are false, and `Turn` initially can be 1 or 2.

Proof that Peterson's algorithm guarantees mutual exclusion

To see that mutual exclusion is guaranteed, consider the situation if P1 and P2 were both executing their critical sections simultaneously. `Enter1` and `Enter2` would both be true. In P1, the `while` test would imply that `Turn` has the value 1, since `Enter2` is true. But in P2, the `while` test would imply that `Turn` has the value 2, since `Enter1` is true. This contradiction implies that P1 and P2 cannot execute their critical sections simultaneously.

Process P1

```
repeat
   Enter1 := true
   Turn := 2
   while Enter2 and (Turn = 2) do
      {nothing}
   critical section
   Enter1 := false;
   remainder section
until Done1
```

Process P2

```
repeat
   Enter2 := true
   Turn := 1
   while Enter1 and (Turn = 1) do
      {nothing}
   critical section
   Enter2 := false
   remainder section
until Done2
```

Program 17.4

Peterson's algorithm for mutual exclusion.

But what if P1 and P2 try to enter their critical sections at about the same time? Is there some interleaving of the executions in the entry section that will permit them to both execute their critical sections simultaneously? No there is not, even though the `while` test with the AND operation is not atomic at the assembly level. There are two ways that P1 can get past the `while` test into its critical section—if `Enter2` is false or if `Turn` is 1. If either of these conditions holds, P1 can enter regardless of the other condition.

Suppose that P1 gets past the `while` test because when it gets the value of `Enter2` with

```
LOADA Enter2,d
```

`Enter2` has the value false. That can only happen when P2 is in its remainder section. Even if P1 is interrupted after it loads the value of `Enter2`, and P2 then sets `Enter2` to true and `Turn` to 1, P2 will not be able to enter its critical section because P1 has set `Enter1` to true and `Turn` is now 1.

Suppose that P1 gets past the `while` test because when it gets the value of `Turn` with

```
LOADA Turn,d
```

`Turn` has the value 1. Since the previous instruction in P1 set `Turn` to 2, that can only happen if P1 was interrupted between its previous instruction and the `while` test, and P2 set `Turn` to 1. But then, P2 again will be prevented from getting past its `while` loop into its critical section because P1 has set `Enter1` to true and `Turn` now has the value 1.

Proof that Peterson's algorithm avoids deadlock

To see that deadlock cannot occur, assume that both processes are deadlocked, both executing their `while` loops concurrently (in a multiprocessing system) or during alternate time slices (in a multiprogramming system). The `while` test in P1 implies that `Turn` must have the value 2, but the test in P2 implies that `Turn` must have the value 1. This contradiction shows that both processes cannot be looping together.

Suppose both processes try to set `Turn` at the same time with

```
STOREA Turn,d
```

In a multiprogramming system, P1's assignment to `Turn` will occur either before or after P2's assignment because they must execute in different time slices. In a multiprocessing system, if both processes try to store a value to `Turn` in main memory at exactly the same time, the hardware will force one of the processes to wait while the other executes its `STOREA`. In either system, the process that stores to `Turn` first will enter its critical section, and deadlock will not occur.

Semaphores

Although Program 17.4 solves the critical section problem while avoiding deadlock, it does have an undesirable inefficiency. The mechanism that prevents a process from entering its critical section is a `while` loop. The loop's only purpose is to stall the process until it is interrupted, allowing time for the other process to finish executing its critical section. Such a loop is called a *spin lock* because the process is locked out of its critical section by spinning around the loop.

Spin locks

Spin locks are a waste of CPU time, especially if the process is executing in a multiprogramming system and has just been allocated a new time slice. It would be more efficient if the CPU were allocated to another process that could use the time to perform useful work. *Semaphores* are shared variables that some operating systems provide for concurrent programming. They enable the programmer to implement critical sections without spin locks.

A semaphore is an integer variable whose value can only be modified by an operating system call. The three operations on semaphore `S` are

The three operations on a semaphore

- `Init (S)`
- `Wait (S)`
- `Signal (S)`

where `Init`, `Wait`, and `Signal` are procedures provided by the operating system. At the assembly level, the procedures would be invoked by a `SVC` with the appropriate operand specifier. A semaphore is another example of an ADT with operations whose meanings are known to the programmer but whose implementations are hidden at a lower level of abstraction. (`Wait (S)` and `Signal (S)` are frequently written `P (S)` and `V (S)` respectively.)

Each semaphore, `S`, has associated with it a queue of process control blocks, called `SQueue`, that represents suspended processes. The meanings of the operations are

Init (S)

```
S := 1
SQueue := an empty list of process control blocks
```

Wait (S)

```
S := S - 1
if S < 0 then
    Suspend this process by adding it to SQueue
```

Signal (S)

```
S := S + 1
if S <= 0 then
    Transfer a process from SQueue to the ready queue
```

An important characteristic of each operation is that the operating system guarantees them to be atomic. For example, it is impossible for two processes to execute `Signal (S)` simultaneously with `S` incremented only by 1 as `NumRes` was in Program 17.1. The assembly level statements for the assignments will never be interleaved.

Figure 17.12 is the state transition diagram for a job in an operating system that provides semaphores. A process in the waiting-for-`S` state is suspended, its PCB in `SQueue`, in the same way that a process in the ready state is suspended, its PCB in the ready queue. Such a process is blocked from running, since it must make a transition to the ready state before it can run.

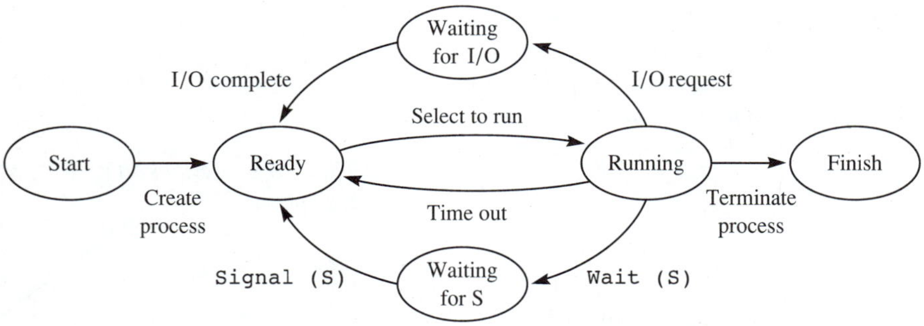

Figure 17.12

The state transition diagram for a job in an operating system that provides a semaphore.

If a running process executes `Wait (S)` when `S` is greater than 0, then `Wait (S)` simply decrements `S` by 1 and the process continues executing. A running process makes a transition to the waiting-for-`S` state by executing `Wait (S)` when `S` is less than or equal to 0. If a running process executes `Signal (S)` when `S` is greater than or equal to 0, it simply increments `S` by 1 and continues executing. A running process that executes `Signal (S)` when `S` is less than 0 causes some other process that is waiting for `S` to be selected by the operating system and placed in the ready state. The process that executed `Signal (S)` continues to run.

The meaning of a negative semaphore value

From the definitions of `Wait` and `Signal`, it follows that a negative value of `S` means one or more processes are blocked in `SQueue`. Furthermore, the magnitude of `S` is the number of processes blocked. For example, if the value of `S` is –3, then three processes are blocked in `SQueue`.

If more than one process is blocked when `Signal (S)` executes, the operating system tries to be fair in selecting the process to transfer to the ready state. A common strategy is to use *first in, first out* (FIFO) scheduling so the process that was blocked for the longest period of time gets sent to the ready state. FIFO is the characteristic that distinguishes a queue from a stack, which is a *last in, first out* (LIFO) list.

Figure 17.12 shows only one semaphore wait state. In a system that provides semaphores, the programmer can declare as many different semaphores as she likes. The operating system will maintain a queue of blocked processes for each one.

Program 17.5

Critical sections are trivial to program if the operating system provides semaphores. Program 17.5 assumes that `MutEx` is a semaphore initialized to 1 with `Init (MutEx)`.

Process P1	Process P2
`repeat`	`repeat`
`Wait (MutEx)`	`Wait (MutEx)`
critical section	*critical section*
`Signal (MutEx)`	`Signal (MutEx)`
remainder section	*remainder section*
`until Done1`	`until Done2`

Program 17.5

Critical sections with a semaphore.

The first process to execute `Wait (MutEx)` will change `MutEx` from 1 to 0 and enter its critical section. If the other process executes `Wait (MutEx)` in the meantime, it will change `MutEx` from 0 to –1, and the operating system will immediately block it. When the first process eventually leaves its critical section it will execute `Signal (MutEx)`, which will put the other process in the ready state.

Since the operating system guarantees that `Wait` and `Signal` are atomic, the programmer need not worry about interleaving within the entry and exit sections. Also, time is not wasted on spin locks, since the system immediately puts the second process on the wait queue for `MutEx`. Of course, hiding the details does not eliminate them. The operating system designer must use the features of the hardware, along with algorithmic reasoning such as that employed in the previous programs, to provide the semaphores. Semaphores satisfy both goals of the operating system—to provide a convenient environment for higher-level programming and to allocate the resources of the system efficiently.

17.4 Deadlocks

Program 17.3 showed how concurrent processing can produce a deadlock between two processes that share a variable in main memory. The deadlock phenomenon can occur when processes share other resources as well. Resources that an operating system must manage include printers, tape drives, and disk files. Sharing any of these resources among concurrent processes can lead to deadlock.

As an example of a deadlock with these resources, suppose process P1 requests the computer's single magnetic tape drive for data input. The operating system allocates the tape drive to P1, which holds it until it does not need the drive any longer. P2 may then request input from a disk file, which the operating system opens and allocates to that process.

Now suppose P1 needs to read from the same disk file P2 is accessing. It requests access, but the operating system cannot grant the request because the file is already open for P2. The operating system blocks P1 until the file becomes available. If P2 requests the tape drive, the operating system will block it as well until P1 releases the drive.

In this case, the processes are in a state of deadlock. P1 cannot proceed until P2 relinquishes the disk file, and P2 cannot proceed until P1 relinquishes the tape drive. Both are waiting for an event that will never happen, suspended by the operating system.

Resource Allocation Graphs

To manage its resources effectively, the operating system needs a way to detect possible deadlocks. It does so with a structure called a *resource allocation graph.* A resource allocation graph is a visual depiction of the processes and resources in the system that shows which resources are allocated to which processes and which processes are blocked by a request on which resources.

Figure 17.13 shows the resource allocation graph for the state in which P1 and P2 are deadlocked over the tape drive and disk file. Processes and resources are nodes in the graph, with processes in circles and resources as solid dots inside boxes. There are two types of edges, allocation edges (al) and request edges (req).

An *allocation edge* from a resource to a process means the resource is allocated to the process. In the figure, the edge labeled al from the tape drive to P1 means the operating system has allocated the tape drive to process P1. A *request edge* from a process to a resource means the process is blocked, waiting for the resource. The edge labeled req from P2 to the tape drive means P2 is blocked waiting for the tape drive.

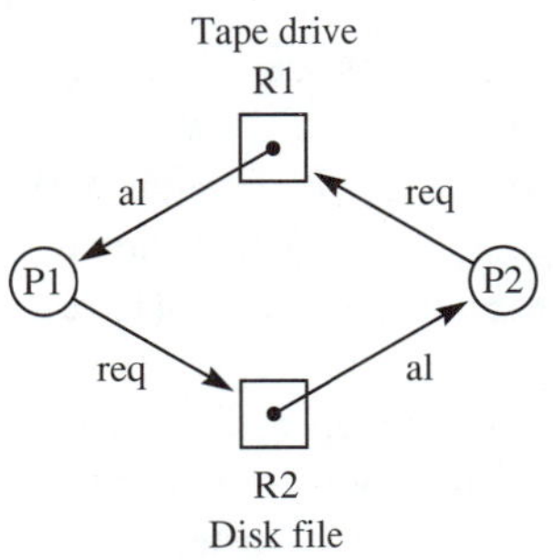

Figure 17.13

A resource allocation graph with a deadlock cycle.

The deadlock is evident from the fact that the edges describe a closed path from P1 to R2 to P2 to R1 and back to P1. Such a closed path in a graph is called a *cycle*. A cycle in a resource allocation graph means that a process is blocked on a resource because it is allocated to another process that is blocked on another

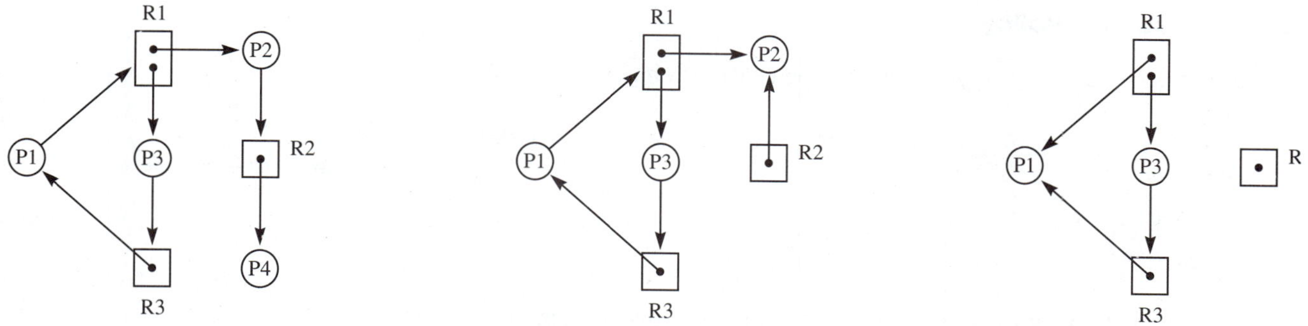

(a) Initial state. (b) P4 completes. (c) P2 completes.

Figure 17.14

A resource allocation graph with a cycle but with no deadlock.

resource, and so on, with the last resource allocated to the first process. If the cycle cannot be broken, there is a deadlock.

Sometimes the resources in a class are indistinguishable from each other. A process may request one resource from the class and not care which particular resource it gets because they are all equivalent. An example is a group of identical tape drives or identical laser printers. If a process needs a laser printer and it does not care which one, the operating system can allocate any printer that is free.

A resource allocation graph represents a class of n identical resources with n solid dots inside the rectangular box. When the operating system allocates a resource from the class, the allocation edge starts from one of the dots that represents the individual resource. A request edge, however, points to the box because the requesting process does not care which resource within the class it gets.

Figure 17.14(a) shows a situation in which both resources in class R1 are allocated. P1 has a request outstanding for one of those resources and does not care which resource it gets.

Even though this graph has cycle (P1, R1, P3, R3, P1), it does not represent a deadlock because the cycle can be broken. Any process in a resource allocation graph that has no request edge from it is not blocked. P4 is not blocked in this figure, and you can assume it will eventually complete, releasing R2. The operating system will grant P2's request for R2 changing the request edge from P2 to R2, to an allocate edge from R2 to P2, as Figure 17.14(b) shows.

Now P2 can use R2 and R1 and run to completion, eventually releasing those resources. When P2 releases an R1 resource, the operating system can allocate the resource to P1, yielding Figure 17.14(c). P1 can run to completion since it has all the resources it needs, after which P3 can complete also. All the processes can complete, so there is no deadlock.

You must consider the direction of the edges when looking for a cycle. You may be tempted to consider (R1, P1, R2, P2, R1) a cycle in Figure 17.15, but it is not. There is no edge from R2 to P2, or from P2 to R1. A cycle is a necessary but not sufficient condition for a deadlock. In this figure, there is no cycle and, therefore, no deadlock.

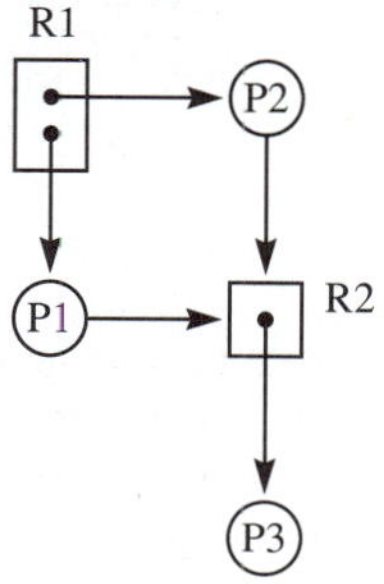

Figure 17.15

A resource allocation graph with no cycle and, therefore, no deadlock.

Deadlock Policy

An operating system may employ one of three general techniques for dealing with deadlock:

Three deadlock policies

- Prevent
- Detect and recover
- Ignore

Several different policies may be found in a given operating system. The system may use one policy for one set of resources and another policy for another set.

The prevent policy

The prevention policy employs techniques to ensure that deadlock will not occur. One technique is to require that a job request and be granted once, at the beginning of execution, all the resources it will need to run to completion. The deadlock of Figure 17.13 could not have occurred if P1 had been granted R1 and R2 simultaneously. A deadlock cycle can only be set up if a process is granted a resource and later requests another resource to complete the cycle.

The detect and recover policy

The detect and recover policy allows deadlocks to occur. With it, the operating system periodically executes a program to detect a deadlock cycle in the system. If the operating system discovers a deadlock, it takes away one of the resources held by a process in the cycle. Since the process has partially executed, the operating system usually must terminate the process, unless the state of the resource can be reconstructed later when it is granted to the process.

All these policies have a cost. The prevention policy puts a constraint on the user, particularly if the resources required depend on the input and cannot be known in advance. The detect and recover policy requires CPU time for the detection and recovery algorithms, time that could be spent on user jobs.

The ignore policy

The third policy is to ignore deadlocks. This policy is effective if the costs of the other policies are considered too great, the probability of deadlock is small, or the occurrence of deadlock is inconsequential. For example, a time-shared system may be shut down periodically for routine maintenance, at which time all jobs, including any that are deadlocked will be removed.

SUMMARY

The goals of an operating system are to provide a convenient environment for higher-level programming and to allocate the resources of the system efficiently. One important function of an operating system is to manage the jobs that users submit to be executed. A loader is that part of the operating system that places a job into main memory for execution. After the job finishes executing, it turns control of the CPU back to the operating system, which can then load another applications program.

An interrupt service routine performs processing for a job, hiding the lower-level details from the programmer. When an interrupt occurs, the running job's process control block (PCB) is stored while the operating system services the interrupt. The PCB consists of the state of the process: copies of the program counter, the status bits, and the contents of all the CPU registers. To resume the job, the operating system places the PCB back into the

CPU. An interrupt functions in the same fashion as a procedure call, except that an interrupt is initiated by the operating system, not by the applications programmer's code.

A process is a program during execution. In a multiprogramming system, one CPU switches between several processes. In a multiprocessing system, there is more than one CPU. Both multiprogramming and multiprocessing systems maintain concurrently executing processes. To execute cooperating processes concurrently, the operating system must be able to guarantee mutual exclusion of critical sections and avoid deadlock. Peterson's algorithm fills both these requirements. A semaphore is an integer variable provided by the operating system. Its operations include `Wait` and `Signal`, each of which is atomic, or indivisible. Semaphores can also be used to fill the mutual exclusion and deadlock requirements.

The deadlock phenomenon can also occur when processes share resources managed by the operating system. A resource allocation graph consists of nodes representing resources and processes, and edges between the nodes representing resource allocations and requests. If the resource allocation graph contains a cycle that cannot be broken, a deadlock has occurred.

EXERCISES

Section 17.1

1. What are the two purposes of an operating system?

2. The loader in Listing 17.2 executes with the following input:

```
09 00 11 19 00 13 31 00 15 59 00 10 D9 00 10 00
00 00 05 00 03 00 30 zz
```

Assume the loop from 0C32 to 0C6C is executing for the ninth time. State the values in the following registers as four hexadecimal digits.

* (a) `A` after `LOADA` at 0C35
* (b) `A` before `ASLA` at 0C47
* (c) `A` after `ASLA` at 0C4A

(d) `A` after `LOADA` at 0C51

(e) `A` after `ANDA` at 0C5D

(f) `A` after `ADDA` at 0C60

(g) `X` after `ADDX` at 0C66

3. Do Exercise 2 for the thirteenth execution of the loop.

Section 17.2

4. The following program executes, generating an interrupt for `DECI`.

```
0000  700005          BR       Main        ;Branch around data
0003  0000   Num:     .BLOCK   d#2
             LineFeed:.EQUATE  h#000A      ;ASCII line feed
             ;
0005  E10003 Main:    DECI     Num,d
0008  E90003          DECO     Num,d       ;Interpret as dec
000B  D8000A          CHARO    LineFeed,i
000E  F10003          HEXO     Num,d       ;Interpret as hex
0011  00              STOP
0012                  .END
```

For Listing 17.3, the entry to and exit from the interrupt service routine, state the values in the following registers as four hexadecimal digits.

- *(a) `X` after `LDBYTX` at 0C70
- *(b) `X` after `ANDX` at 0C76
- (c) `PC` after `BR` at 0C7C
- (d) `A` after `LOADA` at 0C87
- (e) `PC` after `RTI` at 0C90

*5. Do Exercise 4 for the `DECO` instruction.

*6. Do Exercise 4 for the `HEXO` instruction.

7. The program in Exercise 4 runs with an input of `37`. For Listing 17.4, the `DECI` interrupt handler, state the values in registers (a–h) as four hexadecimal digits and answer the question in (i).

- *(a) `A` after `ANDA` at 0CAF the first time it executes
- *(b) `A` after `ANDA` at 0CAF the second time it executes
- *(c) `X` after `LOADX` at 0CB8 the first time it executes
- (d) `X` after `LOADX` at 0CB8 the second time it executes
- (e) `PC` after `BR` at 0CBB the first time it executes
- (f) `PC` after `BR` at 0CBB the second time it executes
- (g) `A` after `LOADA` at 0DC1
- (h) `X` before `STBYTX` at 0DDF assuming the carry bit is zero before the interrupt
- (i) What statement executes just before `LOADA` at 0D99?

*8. Do Exercise 7 with an input of `-295`.

9. The program in Exercise 4 runs with an input of `37`. For Listing 17.5, the `DECO` interrupt handler, state the values in the following registers as four hexadecimal digits.

- *(a) `A` after `LOADA` at 0E1C
- *(b) `A` before `STOREA` at 0E32

In the following parts, assume subroutine `Divide` is called from `JSR` at 0E53.

- *(c) `A` after `LOADA` at 0E71
- (d) `X` before `COMPX` at 0E86
- (e) `A` after `LOADA` at 0E95

In the following parts, assume subroutine `Divide` is called from `JSR` at 0E5C.

- (f) `A` after `LOADA` at 0E71
- (g) `X` before `COMPX` at 0E86
- (h) `X` after `ORX` at 0E9F

*10. Do Exercise 9 with an input of `-2068`.

11. The program in Exercise 4 runs with an input of `950`. For Listing 17.6, the `HEXO` interrupt handler, state the values in registers (a–g) as four hexadecimal digits and answer the questions in (h).

- *(a) `A` after `LOADA` at 0EAF
- *(b) `A` after `LDBYTA` at 0EB8
- *(c) `A` after `ASRA` at 0EBE

State the values in the same manner for `A` after `ANDA` at 0EDB called from `JSR`

- (d) at 0EBF
- (e) at 0EC5
- (f) at 0ECF
- (g) at 0ED5
- (h) How many times does `ORA` at 0EE7 execute? What are the values in `A` after each execution of `ORA`?

*12. Do Exercise 11 with an input of `-2108`.

13. The following program executes, generating an interrupt for the `DECO` at 000F.

```
0000  70000F                BR       Main
0003  0049    I:            .WORD    d#73
0005  001F    Num:          .WORD    d#31          ;Num [2]
0007  0036                  .WORD    d#54          ;Num [3]
0009  0014                  .WORD    d#20          ;Num [4]
              ;------- procedure -------
              Value:        .EQUATE d#2            ;formal parameter
000B  EB0002  Proc:         DECO     Value,s       ;write (Value: 1)
000E  C0                    RTS                    ;pop RetAddr
              ;------- main program -------
000F  E80026  Main:         DECO     d#38,i        ;write (38: 1)
0012  E90003                DECO     I,d           ;write (I: 1)
0015  08002E                LOADA    d#46,i        ;call by value
0018  13FFFE                STOREA   d#-2,s
001B  B00002                SUBSP    d#2,i         ;push parameter
001E  B8000B                JSR      Proc          ;push RetAddr
0021  A80002                ADDSP    d#2,i         ;pop parameter
0024  60FFFC                LOADB    d#-4,i
0027  0C0003                LOADX    d#3,i
002A  EA0005                DECO     Num,x         ;write (Num [3]: 1)
002D  00                    STOP
002E                        .END
```

For Listing 17.8, the `Get` function that contains the addressing mode decoder, state the values in the following registers as four hexadecimal digits.

* **(a)** `A` after `LDBYTA` at 0F81 * **(b)** `A` after `ANDA` at 0F84
(c) `B` after `LOADB` at 0FA9 **(d)** `A` after `LOADA` at 0FAF

14. The program of Exercise 13 executes, generating an interrupt for the `DECO` at 0012. For Listing 17.8, the `Get` function that contains the addressing mode decoder, state the values in the following registers as four hexadecimal digits.

* **(a)** `A` after `LDBYTA` at 0F81 * **(b)** `A` after `ANDA` at 0F84
(c) `B` after `LOADB` at 0FB6 **(d)** `B` after `LOADB` at 0FBC
(e) `A` after `LOADA` at 0FBF

15. The program of Exercise 13 executes, generating an interrupt for the `DECO` at 000B. For Listing 17.8, the `Get` function that contains the addressing mode decoder, state the values in the following registers as four hexadecimal digits assuming the user `SP` is initialized to 0BC1 as usual.

* **(a)** `A` after `LDBYTA` at 0F81 * **(b)** `A` after `ANDA` at 0F84
(c) `B` after `LOADB` at 0F96 **(d)** `B` after `LOADB` at 0F9C
(e) `B` after `ADDB` at 0F9F **(f)** `A` after `LOADA` at 0FA2

16. The program of Exercise 13 executes, generating an interrupt for the `DECO` at 002A. For Listing 17.8, the `Get` function that contains the addressing mode decoder, state the values in the following registers as four hexadecimal digits.

* **(a)** `A` after `LDBYTA` at 0F81 * **(b)** `A` after `ANDA` at 0F84
(c) `B` after `LOADB` at 0FC6 **(d)** `B` after `LOADB` at 0FCC
(e) `B` after `ADDB` at 0FCF **(f)** `X` after `LOADX` at 0FD2
(g) `A` after `LOADA` at 0FD5.

Section 17.3

17. A short notation for the interleaved execution sequence in Table 17.1 is 112221, which represents statements executed by P1, P1, P2, P2, P2, P1 in Program 17.1. **(a)** How many different execution sequences are possible? List each possible sequence in the short notation. For each sequence, state whether `NumRes` has the correct value. **(b)** What percent of the total number of possible sequences produce an incorrect value? **(c)** Would you expect that percentage to be approximately the probability of an incorrect value when the program runs? Explain.

18. The following attempt to implement critical sections is similar to Program 17.3 except for the order of the statements in the entry section.

Process P1

```
repeat
   while Enter2 do
      {nothing}
   Enter1 := true
   critical section
   Enter1 := false
   remainder section
until Done1
```

Process P2

```
repeat
   while Enter1 do
      {nothing}
   Enter2 := true
   critical section
   Enter2 := false
   remainder section
until Done2
```

* **(a)** Does the algorithm guarantee mutual exclusion? If not, show an execution sequence that lets both processes in their critical sections simultaneously. **(b)** Does the algorithm prevent deadlock? If not, show an execution sequence that deadlocks P1 and P2.

19. Show from the definitions of `Wait` and `Signal` that the magnitude of `S` is the number of processes blocked.

20. Let I represent an execution of `Init (S)`, W of `Wait (S)`, and S of `Signal (S)`. Then, for example, IWWS represents the sequence of calls `Init (S)`, `Wait (S)`, `Wait (S)`, and `Signal (S)` by some processes in an operating system. For each of the following sequences of calls, state the value of `S` and the number of processes blocked after the last call in the sequence.

* **(a)** IW **(b)** IS **(c)** ISSSW
(d) IWWWS **(e)** ISWWW

21. Suppose three concurrent processes execute the following code:

Process P1

```
repeat
   Wait (MutEx)
   critical section
   Signal (MutEx)
   remainder section
until Done1
```

Process P2

```
repeat
   Wait (MutEx)
   critical section
   Signal (MutEx)
   remainder section
until Done2
```

Process P3

```
repeat
   Wait (MutEx)
   critical section
   Signal (MutEx)
   remainder section
until Done3
```

Explain how the code guarantees mutual exclusion of all three critical sections.

22. Suppose `S` and `T` are two semaphores initialized with `Init (S)` and `Init (T)`. Consider the following code fragment of two concurrent processes:

Process P1	Process P2
`Wait (S)`	`Wait (T)`
`Wait (T)`	`Wait (S)`
critical section	*critical section*
`Signal (S)`	`Signal (T)`
`Signal (T)`	`Signal (S)`
remainder section	*remainder section*

* **(a)** Does the algorithm guarantee mutual exclusion? If not, show an execution sequence that lets both processes in their critical sections simultaneously. **(b)** Does the algorithm prevent deadlock? If not, show an execution sequence that deadlocks P1 and P2.

23. Consider the code fragment of two concurrent processes:

Process P1	Process P2
Statement 1	*Statement 4*
Statement 2	*Statement 5*
Statement 3	*Statement 6*

Modify the code fragment to guarantee that Statement 5 occurs before Statement 2. Use a semaphore.

24. Each code fragment contains a bug in the entry or exit section. For each fragment, state whether mutual exclusion still holds. If not, show an execution sequence that violates it. State whether deadlock can occur. If so, show an execution sequence that produces it.

***(a)**

Process P1
```
repeat
   Wait (MutEx)
   critical section
   Signal (MutEx)
   remainder section
until Done1
```

Process P2
```
repeat
   Signal (MutEx)
   critical section
   Wait (MutEx)
   remainder section
until Done2
```

(b)

Process P1
```
repeat
   Signal (MutEx)
   critical section
   Wait (MutEx)
   remainder section
until Done1
```

Process P2
```
repeat
   Signal (MutEx)
   critical section
   Wait (MutEx)
   remainder section
until Done2
```

(c)

Process P1

```
repeat
   Wait (MutEx)
   critical section
   Signal (MutEx)
   remainder section
until Done1
```

Process P2

```
repeat
   Wait (MutEx)
   critical section
   Wait (MutEx)
   remainder section
until Done2
```

(d)

Process P1

```
repeat
   Wait (MutEx)
   critical section
   Signal (MutEx)
   remainder section
until Done1
```

Process P2

```
repeat
   Wait (MutEx)
   critical section
   remainder section
until Done2
```

Section 17.4

25. An operating system has processes P1, P2, P3, P4 and resources R1 (one resource), R2 (one resource), R3 (two resources), R4 (three resources). The notation (1, 1), (2, 2), (1, 2) means that P1 requests R1, then P2 requests R2, then P1 requests R2. Note that the first two requests produce allocation edges on the resource allocation graph, but the third request produces a request edge on the graph because R2 is already allocated to P2.

    Draw the resource allocation graph after each sequence of requests. State whether the graph contains a cycle. If it does, state whether it is a deadlock cycle.

   * **(a)** (1, 1), (2, 2), (1, 2), (2, 1)
   * **(b)** (1, 4), (2, 4), (3, 4), (4, 4)
   (c) (3, 3), (4, 3), (2, 2), (3, 2), (2, 3)
   (d) (1, 2), (1, 3), (1, 4), (2, 2), (2, 3), (2, 4)
   (e) (2, 1), (1, 2), (2, 3), (3, 3), (2, 2), (1, 3)
   (f) (2, 1), (1, 2), (2, 3), (3, 3), (2, 2), (1, 3), (3, 1)
   (g) (1, 4), (2, 3), (3, 3), (2, 1), (3, 4), (1, 3), (4, 4), (3, 1), (2, 4)

PROBLEMS

Section 17.2

26. Implement a new unary instruction in place of `NOP` called `ASL2` that does two left shifts on the accumulator. `V` should remain unchanged, but `N` and `Z` should correlate with the new value in the accumulator, and `C` should be the carry from the second shift. Write a program that tests all the features of the new instruction.

27. Implement a new nonunary instruction in place of `NOP` called `ASLMANY` whose operand is the number of times the accumulator is shifted left. Allow all four address-

ing modes by using `Get` in Listing 17.8. `V` should remain unchanged, but `N` and `Z` should correlate with the value in the accumulator, and `C` should be the carry from the last shift. Write a program that tests all the features of the new instruction.

28. Implement a new nonunary instruction in place of `NOP` called `MULA` that multiplies the operand by the accumulator and puts the result in the accumulator. Allow all four addressing modes by using `Get` in Listing 17.8. `V` and `C` should remain unchanged, but `N` and `Z` should correlate with the value in the accumulator. Write a program that tests all the features of the new instruction.

29. The discussion following Program 15.16 (see pp. 764–65) proposed a new addressing mode called stack-relative deferred. Implement a new nonunary instruction in place of `NOP` called `STASRD`, which means store accumulator with stack-relative deferred addressing. Test it by replacing

```
LOADB    Per,s
LOADX    d#0,i
STOREA   d#0,x
```

in Program 15.16 with

```
STASRD Per,i
```

You must include the addressing mode specifier for the assembler, even though your interrupt handler will ignore the addressing mode bits.

30. Implement a new unary instruction in place of `NOP` called `HEXOB` that outputs the content of the base register in hexadecimal. Write a program that tests all the features of the new instruction.

31. Implement a new nonunary instruction in place of `NOP` called `BOOLOUT`, which means boolean output. It should output `false` if the operand is zero and `true` otherwise. Allow all four addressing modes by using `Get` in Listing 17.8. Write a program that tests all the features of the new instruction.

32. Implement a new unary instruction in place of `NOP` called `STACKADD`. It should replace the two topmost items on the stack with their sum. For example, the code fragment

```
LOADA     d#5,i     ;Push 5
STOREA    d#-2,s
LOADA     d#9,i     ;Push 9
STOREA    d#-4,s
SUBSP     d#4,i
STACKADD            ;Add 5 + 9
DECO      d#0,s     ;Output top of stack
ADDSP     d#2,i     ;Pop the sum
```

should output the sum of 5 and 9.

Chapter

18

Storage Management

The purpose of an operating system is to provide a convenient environment for higher-level programming and to allocate the resources of the system efficiently. The previous chapter showed how the operating system allocates CPU time to the processes in the system. This chapter shows how it allocates space. The two primary classes of storage space are main memory and peripheral memory. Disk memory is the most common peripheral storage and is the type described here. The chapter concludes with a description of several commercial operating systems.

Two primary classes of storage space

18.1 Memory Allocation

Normally, programs that are not executing reside in a disk file. To execute, a program needs main memory space and CPU time. The operating system allocates space by loading the program from disk into main memory. It allocates time by setting the program counter to the address of the first instruction loaded into main memory.

The first two sections of this chapter describe five techniques for allocating main memory space:

Main memory allocation techniques

- Uniprogramming
- Fixed-partition multiprogramming
- Variable-partition multiprogramming
- Paging
- Virtual memory

The techniques are listed in order of increasing complexity. Each improves on the previous technique by solving a performance problem. A sixth technique, segmentation, is common but is beyond the scope of this book.

Uniprogramming

The simplest memory allocation technique is *uniprogramming,* exemplified by the Pep/5 operating system. The operating system resides at one end of memory, and the application resides at the other end. The system executes only one job at a time.

Since every job will be loaded at the same place, the translators can generate object code accordingly. For example, the Pep/5 assembler computes the symbols for the symbol table assuming the first byte will be loaded at address 0000 (hex). Or, if the program contains a burn directive, it assumes the last byte will be loaded at the address at the bottom of memory.

Advantages of uniprogramming

Uniprogramming has its advantages and disadvantages. Its main advantage comes from its size. The system can be small, simple to design, and therefore, relatively bug-free. It also executes with little overhead. Once an application is loaded, that application is guaranteed 100% of the processor's time, since no other process will interrupt it. Uniprocessing systems are appropriate for microcomputers.

Disadvantages of uniprogramming

The primary disadvantages are the inefficient use of CPU time and the inflexibility of job scheduling. Compared to main memory, disk memory has long access time. If the application executes a read from disk, the CPU will remain idle while waiting for the disk to deliver the input. The time could better be used executing another user's job. You can tolerate some waste of CPU time in a microcomputer, but in a computer that costs an organization hundreds of thousands of dollars you cannot, especially in a multiuser system in which other processes are executing concurrently.

Even in a single-user system, the inflexibility of job scheduling can be a nuisance. The user may want to start up two programs and switch back and forth between them without quitting either one. For example, you may want to run a word processor for a while, switch to a drawing program to create an illustration for your document, then switch back to the word processor where you left off to continue the text.

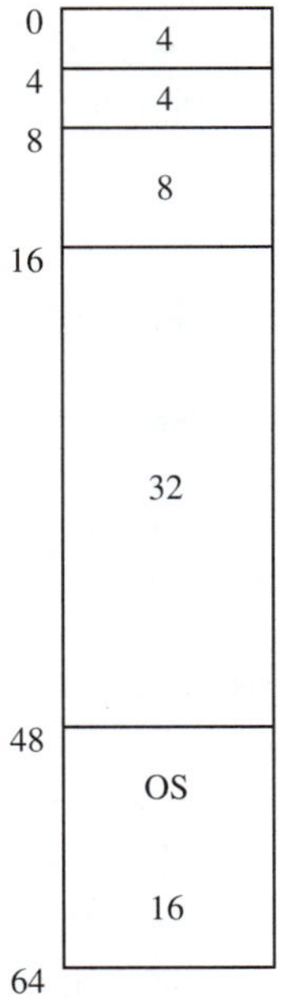

Figure 18.1

Fixed partitions in a 64-Kbyte main memory. Partition sizes and addresses are in Kbytes. The operating system occupies the bottom 16 Kbytes.

Fixed-Partition Multiprogramming

Multiprogramming solves the problem of inefficient CPU usage by allowing more than one application to run concurrently. To switch between two processes, the operating system loads both applications into main memory. When the running process is suspended, the operating system stores its PCB and gives the CPU to the other process.

To implement multiprogramming, the operating system needs to partition main memory into different regions for storing the different processes while they execute. In a fixed-partition scheme, it subdivides memory into several regions whose sizes and locations do not change with time. Figure 18.1 shows one possible subdivision in a fixed-partition multiprogramming system with 64 Kbytes of main memory. The operating system occupies 16 Kbytes at the bottom of memory. It assumes the jobs will not all be the same size, so it partitions the remaining 48 Kbytes into two 4-Kbyte regions, one 8-Kbyte region, and one 32-Kbyte region.

The address problem

A problem with providing different regions of memory for different processes is that the memory references in the object code must be adjusted accordingly. Suppose an assembly language programmer writes an application that is 20 Kbytes long, and the operating system loads it into the 32-Kbyte partition. If the assembler assumes that the object code will be loaded starting at address zero, all the memory references will be wrong.

For example, suppose the first few lines of code are

```
0000  700005          BR      AbsVal
0003  0000   Number:  .BLOCK  d#2
0005  E10003 AbsVal:  DECI    Number,d
```

The assembler has computed the value of symbol `AbsVal` to be 0005, because `BR` is a three-byte instruction and `Number` occupies two bytes. The problem is that `BR` branches to 0005, the address of the code for the process in the first partition. Not only would this process work incorrectly, it may destroy some data in the other process. The operating system needs to protect processes from unauthorized tampering by other concurrent processes.

There are several approaches to this problem. The operating system could require the assembly language programmer to decide where in memory to load the application. The assembler would need a directive that allows the programmer to specify the address of the first byte of object code. A common designation for such a directive is `.ORG`, which means origin. In this example, the starting address of the 32-Kbyte partition is 16K or 8000 (hex). The first few lines of the listing would be modified as follows:

```
                      .ORG    h#8000
8000  708005          BR      AbsVal
8003  0000   Number:  .BLOCK  d#2
8005  E18003 AbsVal:  DECI    Number,d
```

The net effect is to add 8000 to all the memory references in the application code.

If a compiler generates the object code for an application, the programmer has no concept of memory addresses. The translator would need to cooperate with the operating system to generate the correct memory references in the object code.

Logical Addresses

Requiring the programmer or the compiler to specify in advance where the object code will be loaded has several drawbacks. An applications programmer should not have to worry about partition sizes and locations. That information is not relevant to the programmer. The scheme defeats the purpose of the operating system to provide a convenient environment for higher-level programming.

It also defeats the purpose of allocating the resources of the system efficiently. Suppose the programmer specifies a 3-Kbyte program to be loaded in the second

4-Kbyte partition at address 4K and sets the `.ORG` directive accordingly. During the course of events, the job may be waiting to be loaded while another job occupies that partition, even though the first 4-Kbyte partition is free. The unused memory represents an inefficient allocation of a resource.

To alleviate these problems, the operating system can let the programmer or compiler generate the object code as if it will be loaded at address zero. An address generated under this assumption is called a *logical address*. If the program is loaded into a partition whose address is not zero, the operating system must translate logical addresses to *physical addresses*.

The folowing equation depicts the relation between the physical address, logical address, and address of the first byte of the partition in which the program is loaded.

Logical address versus physical address

Physical address = logical address + partition address

An example is the previous code fragment, in which the logical address of `Number` is 0003 and the physical address is 8003.

Two address-translation techniques are possible. The operating system could provide a software utility that adds the partition address to all the memory references in the object code. The translator would need to specify those parts of the object code that need adjusting, since the utility cannot tell by inspection of the raw object code which parts are memory references.

Operation of base and bound registers

Another technique depends on the availability of specialized hardware called base and bound registers. The *base register* solves the address-translation problem. The *bound register* solves the protection problem. Figure 18.2 shows how base and bound registers work with the previous example.

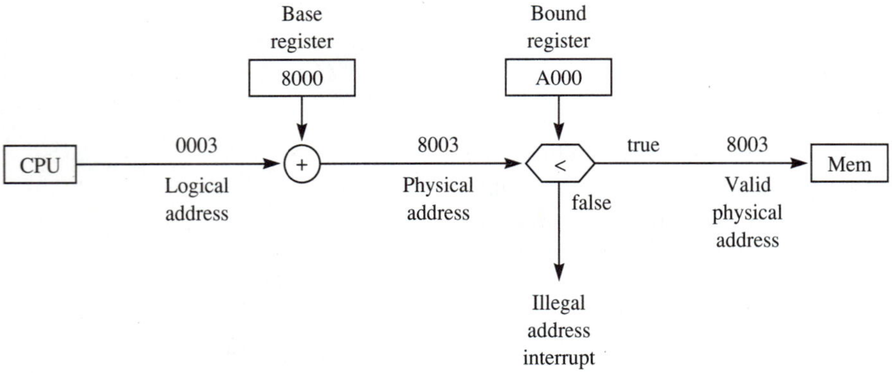

Figure 18.2

Transformation of a logical address to a physical address with base and bound registers.

The operating system loads the object program with unmodified logical addresses into the partition at 8000. It loads the base register with a value of 8000 and the bound register with a value of A000 (hex) = 48K, the address of the upper bound of the partition in which the program is loaded. It turns the CPU over to the process by setting the program counter to 0000, the logical address of the first instruction.

Whenever the CPU issues a memory read request, the hardware adds the content of the base register to the address supplied by the CPU to form the physical address. It compares the physical address to the content of the bound register. If the physical address is less than the bound register, the hardware completes the memory access. Otherwise it generates an illegal-address interrupt that the operating system must service. The bound register prevents a process from invading another process's memory partition.

The first memory read request in this example will be from the fetch part of the von Neumann execution cycle. The CPU will request a fetch of the instruction from 0000, which the hardware will translate to a fetch from 8000. Figure 18.2 shows the translation of logical address, 0003, from the `DECI` operand specifier. (Actually, at a lower level of abstraction, it is the operand of the `STOREA` instruction at 0F31 in the `DECI` interrupt handler.)

To switch to another process, the operating system sets the base register to the address of the partition where the process has been loaded and the bound register to the address of the next-higher partition. When it restores the CPU registers (including the program counter) from the PCB, the process will continue executing from where it was suspended.

Scheduling problems with fixed partitions

Consider some of the problems that confront the operating system when it must schedule jobs to occupy the fixed partitions. Assume all the partitions in Figure 18.1 are occupied except the 32-Kbyte partition. If a 4-Kbyte job requests execution, should the system put it in the 32-Kbyte partition or should it wait until a smaller partition becomes available? Suppose it starts the job in the 32-Kbyte partition, and then a 4-Kbyte process terminates. If a 32-Kbyte job now enters the system, it cannot be loaded. In retrospect, it would have been better to not schedule the small job in the large partition. Then the large job could use the large partition as soon as it requested execution, and the small job could be loaded soon anyway. Since the operating system cannot predict when a process will terminate or when a job will request execution, it cannot achieve the optimum schedule.

Another problem is how the operating system should set up the partitions in the first place. In Figure 18.1, if a 16-Kbyte job and a 32-Kbyte job request execution at the same time, only one can be loaded, even though a total of 48 Kbytes is available in user memory. On the other hand, if the operating system sets up user memory in two large partitions, and six or eight 4-KByte jobs request execution, all but two will be delayed. Again the optimum partition cannot be established because the operating system cannot predict the future.

Variable-Partition Multiprogramming

To alleviate the inefficiencies inherent in fixed-partition scheduling, the operating system can maintain partitions with variable boundaries. The idea is to establish a partition only when a job is loaded into memory. The size of the partition can exactly match the size of the job so more memory will be available to jobs as they enter the system.

When a job stops execution, the region of memory that it occupied becomes available for other jobs. A region of memory that is available for use by incoming jobs is called a *hole*. Holes are filled when the operating system allocates them to subsequent jobs. As in the fixed-partition scheme, the operating system attempts to schedule the jobs to maintain the largest number of processes in memory at any given point in time.

Figure 18.3 shows an example of a 48-Kbyte region of available memory before any jobs are scheduled. Table 18.1 is a hypothetical sequence of job requests for the user memory in Figure 18.3. The table also indicates when a job stops executing, thereby releasing its memory for another job to use.

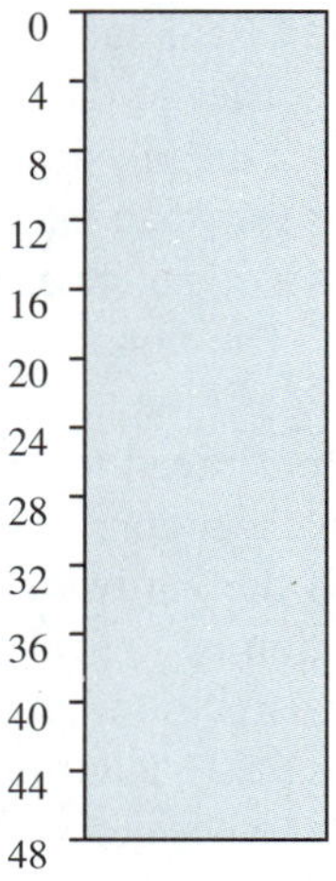

Figure 18.3

The initial available user memory. Addresses are in Kbytes.

Figure 18.4 illustrates the scheduling process. The question that must be resolved is the selection criterion for determining which hole to fill when a new job requests some memory. Figure 18.4 uses what is called the *best-fit algorithm*. Of all the holes that are larger than the memory required for the job, the operating system selects the smallest. That is, the system selects the hole that the job fits the best.

When J1 requests 12 Kbytes, there is only one hole from which to allocate memory, the initial hole in Figure 18.3. The system gives the first 12 Kbytes to J1, leaving a 36-Kbyte hole. When J2 requests 8 Kbytes, the system gives the first part of the smaller hole to it, and similarly for J3, J4, and J5. The result is the memory allocation in Figure 18.4(a).

Figure 18.4(b) shows the allocation when J1 stops executing, relinquishing its 12 Kbytes and creating a second hole at the top of main memory. When J6 requests a 4-Kbyte region, the operating system has the option of allocating memory for it from either hole. According to the best-fit algorithm, the system selects the 8-Kbyte hole rather than the 12-Kbyte hole, because the smaller hole is a better fit. Figure 18.4(c) shows the result.

Job	Size	Action
J1	12	Start
J2	8	Start
J3	12	Start
J4	4	Start
J5	4	Start
J1	12	Stop
J6	4	Start
J5	4	Stop
J7	8	Start
J8	8	Start

Table 18.1

A job execution sequence for a variable-partition multiprogramming system. Job size is in Kbytes.

Figure 18.4(d) shows the allocation after J5 stops, and (e) shows it after the system allocates memory from the top hole to J7. There are now three small holes scattered throughout memory. This phenomenon is called *fragmentation*. Even though J8 wants 8 Kbytes and available memory totals 12 Kbytes, J8 cannot run because the memory is not contiguous.

When confronted with a request that cannot be satisfied because of fragmented memory, the operating system could simply wait for enough processes to complete until a large enough hole becomes available. In this example, the request is so small that any job to complete will free enough memory for J8 to be loaded.

In a crowded system running many small jobs with a large request outstanding, the request may be pending for a long time before allocation. In such a case, the operating system may take time to move some processes to make a large enough hole to satisfy the request. This operation is called *compaction*.

Figure 18.5(a) shows the most straightforward compaction technique. The operating system shifts the processes up in memory, eliminating all the holes between them. Another possible compaction scheme is to move only enough processes to create a hole big enough to satisfy the request. In Figure 18.5(b), the system shifts only J6, leaving a large enough hole to load J8.

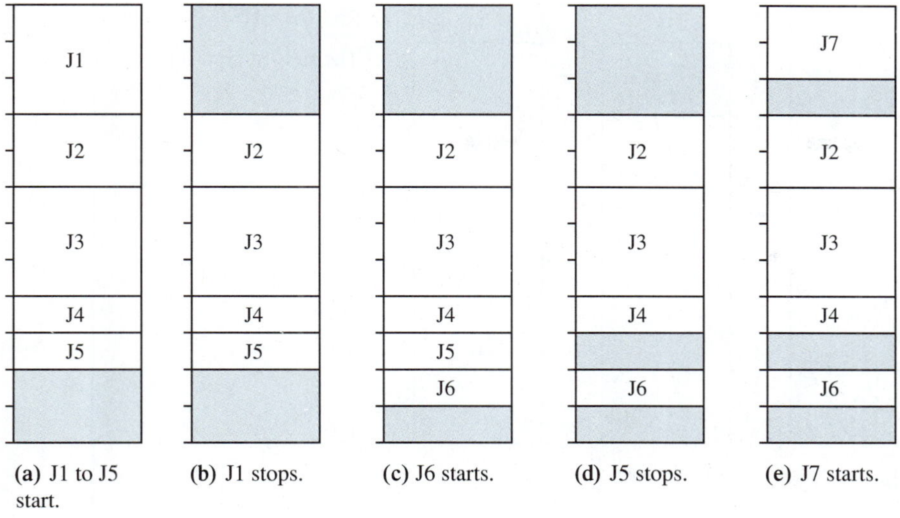

Figure 18.4

The best-fit algorithm.

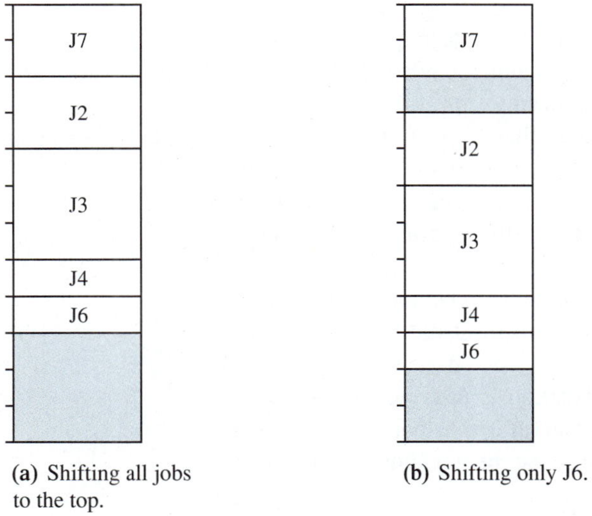

Figure 18.5

Compacting main memory.

The idea behind the best-fit algorithm is to minimize fragmentation by using the smallest hole possible, leaving the larger holes available for future scheduling. Another scheduling technique that may not appear as reasonable is the *first-fit algorithm*. Rather than search for the smallest possible hole, this algorithm begins its search from the top of main memory, allocating memory from the first hole that can accommodate the request. Figure 18.6 is a trace of the first-fit algorithm for the request sequence of Table 18.1.

Figure 18.6(a) and (b) are identical to the best-fit algorithm of Figure 18.4. In Figure 18.6(c), J6 requests a 4-Kbyte partition. Rather than allocate from the

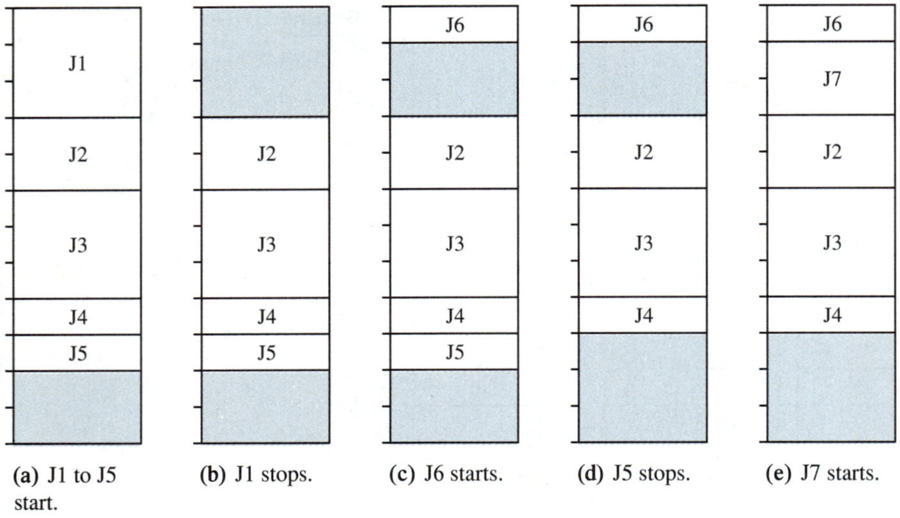

Figure 18.6

The first-fit algorithm.

smaller hole at the bottom of memory, the first-fit algorithm finds the hole at the top of memory first, from which it allocates storage for J6.

Figure 18.6(d) shows J5 terminating. In (e), the 8-Kbyte request from J7 is filled by the first available hole, which is between J6 and J2. When J8 requests 8 Kbytes, a hole is available, and the system does not need to compact memory.

First fit versus best fit

One example does not prove that first fit is better than best fit. In fact, you can devise a sequence of requests and releases that will require compaction under the first-fit algorithm before best fit. The question is, What happens on the average? It turns out that in practice, neither algorithm is substantially superior to the other in terms of memory utilization.

The reason first-fit works so well is that storage tends to be allocated from the top of main memory. Therefore, large holes tend to form at the bottom of main memory. That is what happened in Figure 18.6.

Regardless of the allocation strategy, fragmentation is unavoidable in a variable-partition system. Noncontiguous holes represent an inefficient allocation of a resource. Even though unusable memory regions can be reclaimed with compaction, that is a time-consuming procedure.

Paging

The idea behind paging

Paging is an ingenious idea to alleviate the fragmentation problem. Rather than coalesce several small holes to form one big hole for the program, in paging you fragment the program to fit the holes. Programs are no longer contiguous, but broken up and scattered throughout main memory.

Figure 18.7 shows three jobs executing in a paged system. Each job is subdivided into pages, and main memory is subdivided into frames that are the same size as the pages. The figure shows the first 12 Kbytes of a 64-Kbyte memory with

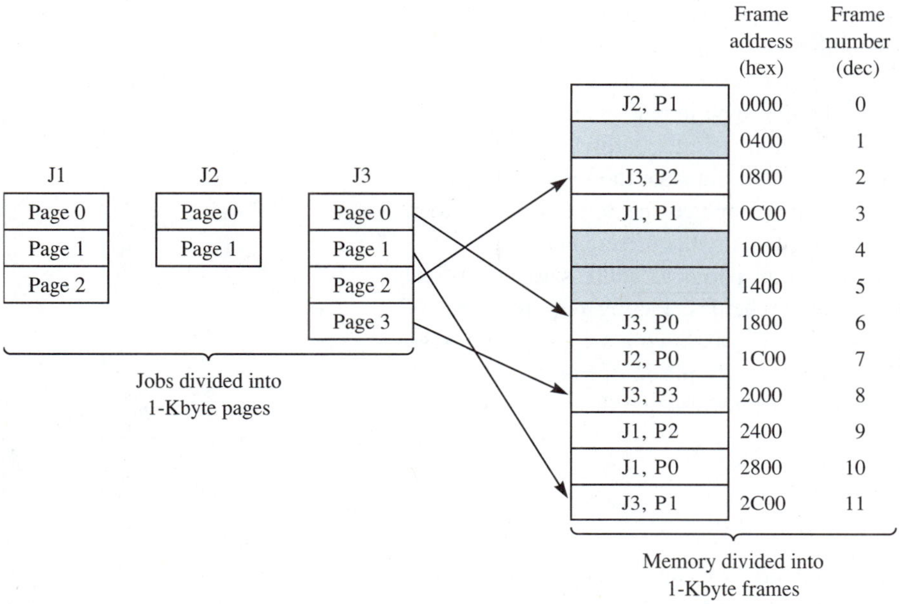

Figure 18.7

A paging system.

1-Kbyte frames. The page size is always a power of 2, in practice usually 512, 1024, or 2048 bytes.

The code for job J3 is distributed to four noncontiguous frames in main memory. J3, P0 in the frame at 1800 represents page 0 of job J3. The second page is at 2C00, and the third and fourth pages are at 0800 and 2000 respectively. Jobs J1 and J2 are similarly scattered throughout memory. If job J4 comes along and needs 3 Kbytes of memory, the operating system can distribute its pages to 0400, 1000, and 1400. The system does not need to compact memory to allocate it to the incoming job.

As with the previous multiprogramming memory management techniques, the applications programs in paging assume logical addresses. The operating system must convert logical addresses to physical addresses during execution.

Figure 18.8 shows the relationship between a logical address and a physical address in the paged system of the previous figure. Since a page contains 1 Kbyte, which is 2^{10}, the rightmost 10 bits of a logical address is the offset from the top of the page. The leftmost 6 bits are the page number.

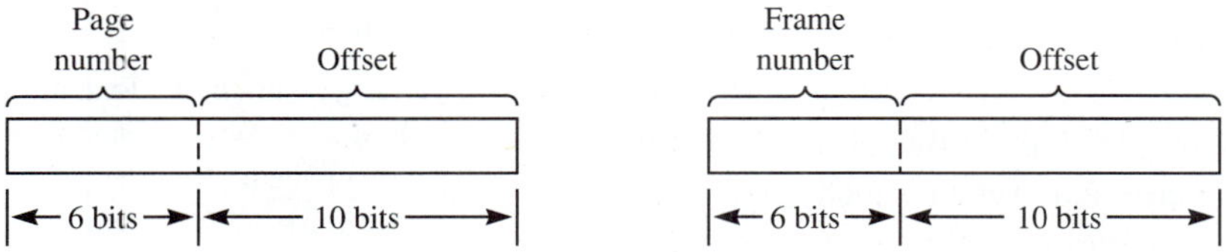

(a) Logical address.

(b) Physical address.

Figure 18.8

The logical and physical addresses in a paging system.

For example, consider the address 058F, which is 0000 0101 1000 1111 in binary. The leftmost 6 bits are 0000 01, which means that the address corresponds to a memory location in page number 1. Since 01 1000 1111 is 399 (dec), the logical address represents the 399th byte from the first byte in page number 1.

Referring to Figure 18.7, the physical address of this byte is the 399th byte from the first byte in the frame at address 2C00. To translate the logical address to the physical address, the operating system must replace the 6-bit page number, 0000 01, with the 6-bit frame number, 0010 11, leaving the offset unchanged.

One base register was enough to transform a logical address to a physical address in the previous memory management schemes. Paging requires a set of frame numbers, however, one for each page of the job. Such a set is called a *page table*. Figure 18.9 shows the page table associated with job J3 of Figure 18.7. Each entry in the page table is the frame number that must replace the page number in the logical address.

Suppose job J3 executes the statement

```
LDBYTA h#058F,d
```

which causes the CPU to request a memory read from logical address 058F. The operating system extracts the first 6 bits, 0000 01, and uses them as an address in the page table, a special-purpose hardware memory that stores the frame numbers for the job. The frame number from the page table replaces the page number in the logical address to produce the physical address.

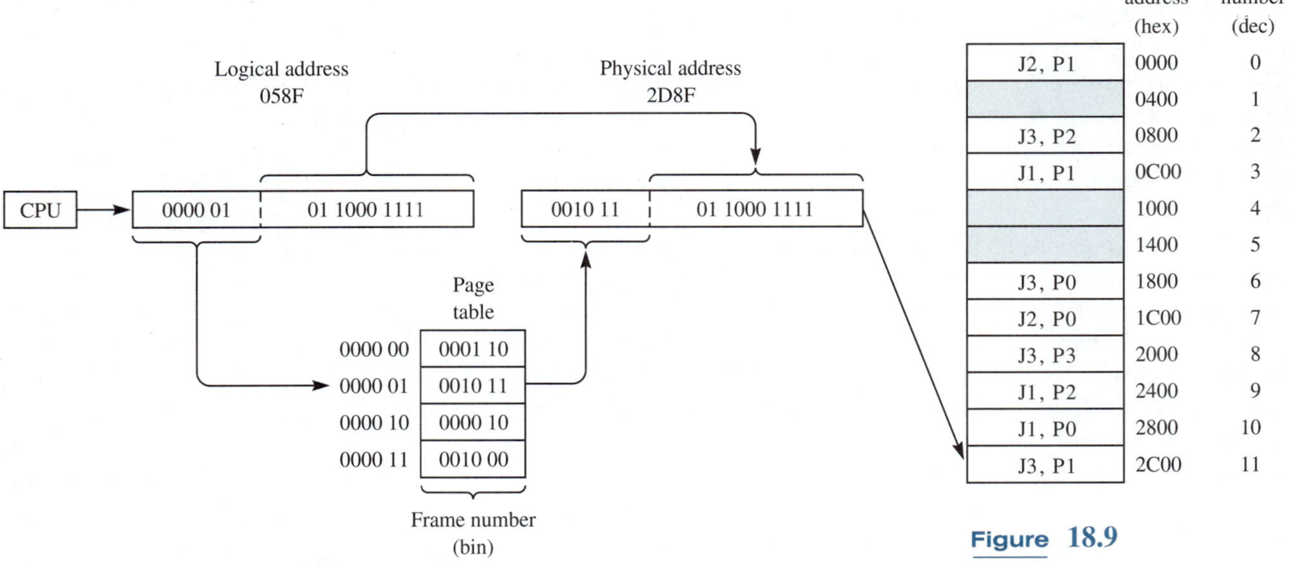

Figure 18.9

Transformation of a logical address to a physical address with a page table.

The byte is read from physical location 2D8F, even though the CPU issued a request for a read from location 058F. The program executes under the illusion that it has been loaded into a contiguous memory region starting at address 0000. The operating system perpetrates the illusion by maintaining a page table for each process loaded into memory. It is the ultimate scam. A process is continually interrupted in time and scattered through space without being aware of either indignity.

It is important to note that paging does not eliminate fragmentation altogether. It is rare that a job's size will be an exact multiple of the page size for the system. In that case, the last page will contain some unused memory, as Figure 18.10 shows for job J3. The unused memory at the end of the last page in a job is called *internal fragmentation* in contrast to the external fragmentation that is visible to the operating system in the variable-partition scheme.

The smaller the page size, the less the internal fragmentation, on the average. Unfortunately, there is a tradeoff. The smaller the page size, the greater the number of frames for a given main memory size and, therefore, the longer the page table. Since every reference to memory includes an access from a page table, the page tables usually are designed with the fastest possible circuitry. Such circuitry is expensive, so the page tables must be small to minimize the cost.

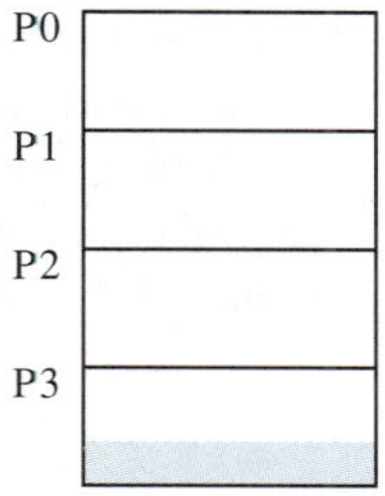

Figure 18.10

Internal fragmentation.

18.2 Virtual Memory

It may seem unlikely that you could improve on the memory utilization of a paged system, but the paging concept can be carried one step further. Consider the structure of a large program, say one that would fill 50 pages. To execute the program, is it really necessary for all 50 pages to be loaded into main memory at the same time?

Large Program Behavior

Most large programs consist of dozens of procedures, some of which may never execute. For example, procedures that are responsible for processing some input error condition will not execute if the input has no errors. Other procedures, such as those that initialize data, may execute only once and never be needed during the remainder of the execution.

A common control structure in any large program is the loop. As the body of a loop executes repeatedly, only that code in the loop need reside in main memory. Any code that is far from the loop (from an execution point of view) does not need to be in memory.

A program may also contain large regions of data that are never accessed. For example, if you declare an array of records in Pascal without knowing how many records will be encountered when the program runs, you allocate more than you would reasonably expect to have. Pages that consist of unaccessed records never need to be loaded.

These considerations of the typical large program show that it may be feasible to have only the active pages of the program loaded in memory. The active pages are those that contain code that is repeatedly executing and data that is repeatedly being accessed.

The set of active pages is called the *working set.* As the program progresses, new pages will enter the working set and old ones will leave. For example, at the beginning of execution the pages that contain initialization procedures will be in the working set. Later, the working set will include the pages that contain the processing procedures and not the initialization procedures.

The working set

Virtual Memory

Remember that the programmer at a higher level of abstraction is under the illusion that the program executes in contiguous memory with logical addresses beginning at zero. Suppose the system can be designed to load only a few pages at a time from the executing job while still maintaining the illusion. It then becomes possible for the programmer to write a program that is too large to fit in main memory, but that will execute nonetheless. The user sees not the limited physically installed memory, but a virtual memory that is limited only by the virtual addresses.

For example, a Pep/5 address contains 16 bits. It is, therefore, theoretically possible to access 2^{16} bytes (64 Kbytes) of memory. However, only 4 Kbytes of memory are installed. The applications program starts at 0000 and cannot contain more than about 3000 (dec) bytes without running into the operating system. It is common for a system to contain less memory than that permitted by the number of address bits. That situation allows the owner to upgrade the system at a later date by purchasing additional memory.

Suppose the Pep/5 computer has a virtual memory operating system. The program's physical memory is limited to 3000 bytes, but the programmer still could execute a 64-Kbyte program. The operating system loads the pages from disk into the memory frames as needed to execute the program. When a page needs to be loaded because it contains a statement to execute or some data to access, the operating system removes a page that is no longer active and replaces it with the one that needs to be loaded. The programmer sees the program execute in a 64-Kbyte virtual address space, even though the physical address space is 3000 bytes.

Figure 18.11 shows how paging can be extended to implement a virtual memory system. It shows three jobs in the system, J1 with 10 pages, J2 with 2 pages, and J3 with 4 pages. Notice that physical memory contains only eight frames, but J1 can execute even though it is larger than physical memory. The special hardware required by the operating system includes a page table for each job and one frame table with an entry for each frame. To keep the illustration simple, frame numbers are given in decimal.

The page tables function to transform logical addresses to physical addresses, as in Figure 18.9. In a virtual memory system, however, some of the pages may not be loaded as the job is running. Each page table contains one extra bit per page that tells the operating system whether the page is loaded. The bit is 1 if the page is loaded and 0 if it is not. The figure shows 1 as Y for yes, and 0 as N for no.

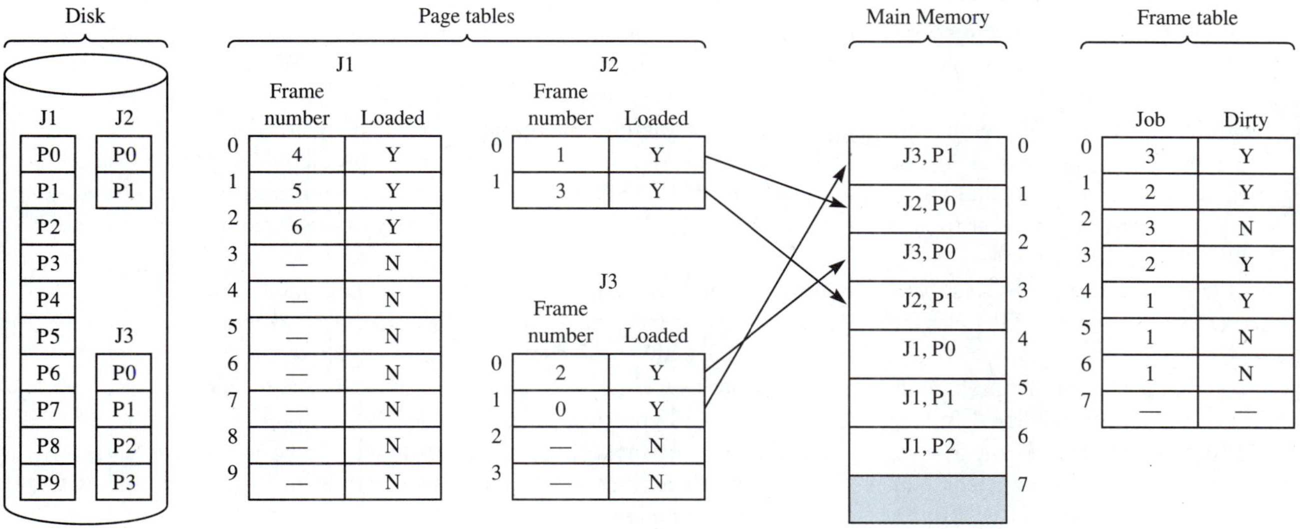

Figure 18.11

An implementation of virtual memory.

The frame table is needed to help the operating system allocate frames from main memory to the various jobs. The first entry is the job allocated to that frame. The second entry is a bit called the *dirty bit*, whose function will be explained shortly.

Demand Paging

Figure 18.11 shows that jobs J1 and J3 do not have all their pages loaded into main memory. Suppose J3 is executing some code in page P1, loaded into frame 0. It will shortly execute a `LOADA` instruction whose operand is in P2. How will the operating system know that J3 is going to need P2 loaded into memory? Since the system cannot predict the future, it cannot know until J3 actually executes the `LOADA`.

Page faults

In the course of translating the logical address to a physical address, the hardware accesses the page table for J3 to determine the frame number of the physical address. Since the loaded bit says N, an interrupt called a *page fault* occurs. The operating system intervenes to service the interrupt.

When a page fault occurs, the operating system searches the frame table to determine if there are any empty frames in the system. Figure 18.11 shows that frame 7 is available, so the operating system can load P2 into that frame. It updates the frame table to show that frame 7 contains a page from J3. It updates the page table for J3 to show that P2 is in frame 7, and sets the loaded bit to Y.

When the operating system returns from the interrupt, it sets the program counter to the address of the instruction that caused the page fault. That is, it restarts the instruction. This time, when the hardware accesses the page table for J3

Parallel Processing

One of the most active research areas in computer science today is parallel computer architectures. Traditional sequential-architecture machines process programs one step at a time. But parallel-architecture machines are constructed with many semiautonomous CPUs that work simultaneously to solve a large problem. Each CPU has its own private memory area and receives a portion of the problem to solve; the subproblems, then, are solved in parallel. Compared to sequential architecture, parallel architecture theoretically reduces the time required to execute a large program by a factor of the number of processors in its system.

There are many large computing problems that the new parallel architecture can solve, but each different problem requires different architecture. For example, in an artificial intelligence search problem—such as finding a path through a maze—it is important that the CPUs be able to communicate with each other. Because the search is over as soon as any one processor finds a path through the maze, there is no need for the other processors to continue working. A communications network connecting all the processors is needed so that the successful processor can tell the others to stop execution.

Other computing problems require that all possible solutions be explored. In this case, some processors may arrive at their conclusions early, while others may need much more time. Ideally, the early-finishing processors should record their results and then make themselves available to help the other processors. The processors still working could assign portions of their tasks to the early-finishing processors, completing the entire search more quickly.

One of the parallel architectures introduced during the mid-1980s and still under development is based on the hypercube concept. Recognizing that individual processors often need to share data and communicate synchronized messages, the basic hypercube concept is to distribute the multiple processors in such a way that their interconnectivity is maximized.

The Connection Machine, a working parallel system developed by W. D. Willis, has 64,000 processors. The power of the Connection Machine does not come from the cleverness of the individual processors, but from the behavior of the system as a whole. Each processor has a small area of local memory on which to operate, and performs the same operations as the other processors but on different data. Depending on the problem being solved, the communications network among the nodes can be dynamically reconfigured.

Parallel architecture raises an important question for software systems designers and mathematicians interested in the theory of algorithms: What good is parallelism if you can't represent the problems you wish to solve? For many problems—especially large-scale, open-ended problems in industry, science, and business—the extent to which parallel processing can be exploited is not yet clear. It would not be efficient to use a parallel computer for a sequentially oriented problem because most of the CPUs would remain idle. For example, to swap the contents of two variables using Pascal, the code would look like the following:

The Connection Machine.

```
Temp := x;   {Save the
   value of x in Temp.}
x := y;      {Assign the
   value of y to x.}
y := Temp;   {Assign the
   original value of x
   to y.}
```

Because these three statements must be executed in strict time sequence for the desired swap to occur, the problem cannot be conceivably transformed so that the statements can be executed in parallel. Other problems, such as those involving maximization of a collection of independent variables, are more suited to parallel processing.

Roughly stated, a problem is amenable to parallel processing if it can be broken down into a number of largely independent subproblems, each assignable to its own CPU and memory area. The research into which problems can be solved best, if at all, on which particular computer architectures is only just beginning. Young computer scientists can expect to help define this emerging field.

an interrupt will not occur, and the operand of the LOADA instruction will be brought into the accumulator.

So when does the operating system load a page into main memory? The answer is, simply, when the program demands it. In the previous example, J3 demanded via the page fault interrupt mechanism that P2 be loaded. The difference between paging and demand paging is that demand paging brings pages into main memory only on demand. If a page is never demanded, it will never be loaded.

Page Replacement

When J3 demanded that P2 be loaded, the operating system had no problem because there was an empty frame in main memory. Suppose, however, that a job demands a page when all the frames are filled. In that case, the operating system must select a page that was previously loaded and replace it, freeing its frame for the demanded page.

The replaced page may subsequently be loaded again, perhaps into a different frame. To ensure that the page is reloaded in the same state that it was in when it was replaced, the operating system may need to save its state by writing the page to disk when the page is replaced. On the other hand, it may not be necessary to write the page to the disk when it is replaced.

Deciding whether the state of the replaced page needs to be updated on disk

In Figure 18.11, J1 has 10 pages stored on disk, 3 of which have been loaded into main memory. When J1 executes instructions such as LOADA and ASLA, the effect is to not change the state of a page in main memory. LOADA issues a memory read and places the operand in the accumulator. ASLA changes the accumulator, an action that involves neither a memory read nor a memory write. Neither instruction issues a memory write.

But when J1 executes an instruction such as STOREA, the instruction changes the state of the page in main memory. STOREA puts the content of the accumulator in the operand, issuing a memory write in the process. If the operand is in P0 in frame 4, P0's state will change in main memory. Page P0 on disk will no longer be an exact copy of the current P0 in main memory. If no store instruction ever executes, the image of the page on disk will be an exact replica of the page in main memory.

When the operating system selects a page for replacement during a page fault, it does not need to write the page back to disk if the disk image is still a replica of the page in memory. To help the operating system decide whether the write is necessary, the hardware contains a special bit, called the dirty bit, in the frame table.

The dirty bit

When a page is first loaded into an empty frame the operating system sets the dirty bit to 0, indicated by N in Figure 18.11. If a store instruction ever issues a write to memory, the hardware sets the dirty bit for that frame to 1, indicated by Y in the figure. Such a page is said to be dirty because it has been altered from its original clean state. If a page is selected for replacement, the operating system inspects the dirty bit to see if it must write the page back to disk before overwriting the frame with the new page.

Page-Replacement Algorithms

The operating system has two memory management tasks in a demand paged system. It must allocate frames to jobs, and it must select a page for replacement when a page fault occurs and all the frames are full.

Frame allocation strategy

A reasonable allocation strategy for frames is to assume that a large job will need more frames than a small job. The system can allocate frames proportionally. If J1 is twice as big as J2, it gets twice as many frames in which to execute.

Page-replacement strategies

Given that a job has a fixed number of frames in which to execute, how does the operating system decide which page to replace when a page fault occurs and all the job's frames are full? Two possible page-replacement algorithms are *first in, first out* (FIFO) and *least-recently used* (LRU).

Figure 18.12 shows the behavior of the FIFO page-replacement algorithm in a system that has allocated three frames to a job. As a job executes, the CPU sends a continuous stream of read and write requests to main memory. The first group of bits in each address is the page number, as Figures 18.8 and 18.9 show. The page references are the sequence of page numbers that the executing job generates.

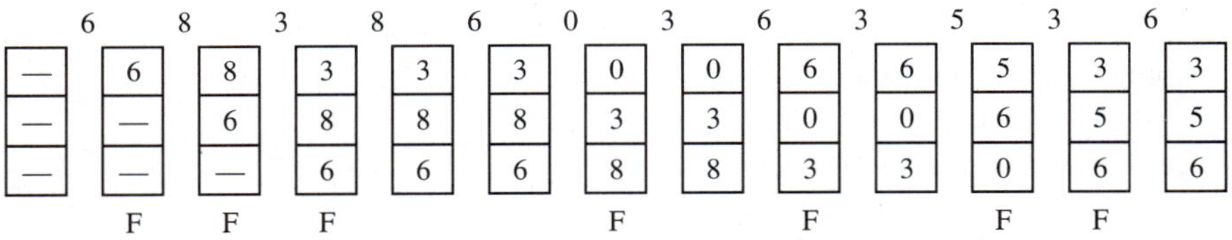

Figure 18.12

The FIFO page-replacement algorithm with three frames.

Figure 18.12 shows three empty frames available before the first request. When the job demands P6, a page fault is generated, indicated by F in the figure, and P6 is loaded into a frame.

When the job demands P8, another page fault is generated and P8 is loaded into an empty frame. The boxes do not represent particular page frames. The figure shows P6 shifting to a lower box to accommodate P8. In the computer, P6 does not shift to another frame.

The reference to P3 causes another page fault, but the following reference to P8 does not, because P8 is still in the set of loaded pages. Similarly, the reference to P6 does not produce a page fault.

The reference to P0 triggers a page fault interrupt that must be serviced by selecting a replacement page. The FIFO algorithm replaces the page that was the first to enter the set. Since the figure shifts the pages down to accommodate a new page, the first page in is the one at the bottom, P6. The operating system replaces P6 with P0.

The given sequence of 12 page references produces 7 page faults when the job has three frames. If the job has more frames, the same sequence of page references should generate fewer page faults. Figure 18.13 shows the FIFO algorithm with the same page reference sequence but with four frames. As expected, the sequence generates fewer page faults.

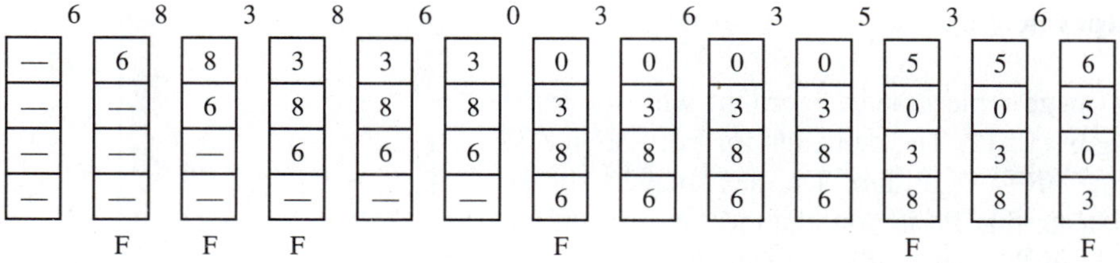

Page references

Loaded pages

Page fault

Figure 18.13

The FIFO page-replacement algorithm with four frames.

In general, you would expect the number of page faults to decrease with an increase in the number of frames, as Figure 18.14(a) shows, and as the two previous examples illustrate. Early in the development of demand paging systems, however, a curious phenomenon was discovered in which a given page reference sequence with the FIFO page-replacement algorithm actually produced more page faults with a greater number of frames.

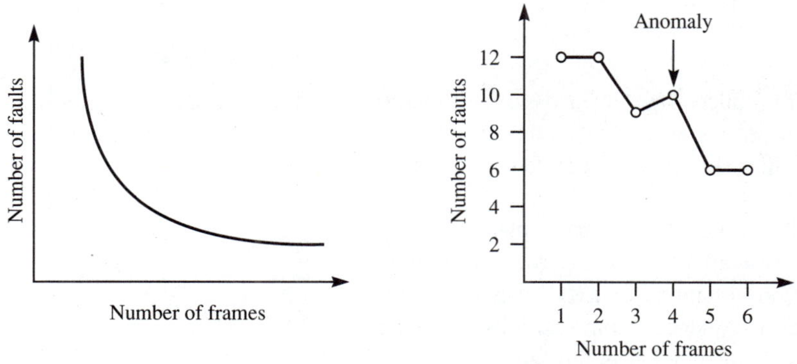

(a) The expected effect of more frames on the number of page faults.

(b) Belady's anomaly with the FIFO replacement algorithm.

Figure 18.14

The effect of more frames on the number of page faults.

A page reference sequence with this property is

0, 1, 2, 3, 0, 1, 4, 0, 1, 2, 3, 4

Figure 18.14(b) is a plot of the number of page faults versus the number of frames for this sequence. It turns out that more page faults are generated with four frames than with three frames. This phenomenon is called *Belady's anomaly,* after L. A. Belady, who discovered it.

The FIFO algorithm selects the page that has been in the set of frames the longest. That may appear to be a reasonable criterion. As the job executes it will enter into new regions of code and data, so pages from the old region will no longer be needed. The oldest page is the one replaced.

On further reflection, however, it may be better to consider not how long a page has been in the set of frames, but how long it has been since a page was last referenced. The idea behind LRU is that a page referenced recently in the past is more likely to be referenced in the near future than a page that has not been referenced as recently.

Figure 18.15 illustrates the LRU page-replacement algorithm with the same sequence of page references as in Figure 18.12. The demands for P6, P8, and P3 produce a state identical to that of the FIFO algorithm. The next request for P8 brings that page to the top box to indicate that P8 is now the most-recently used. The following request for P6 brings it to the top, shifting down P8 and P3. The boxes maintain the pages in order of previous use, with the least-recently used page at the bottom.

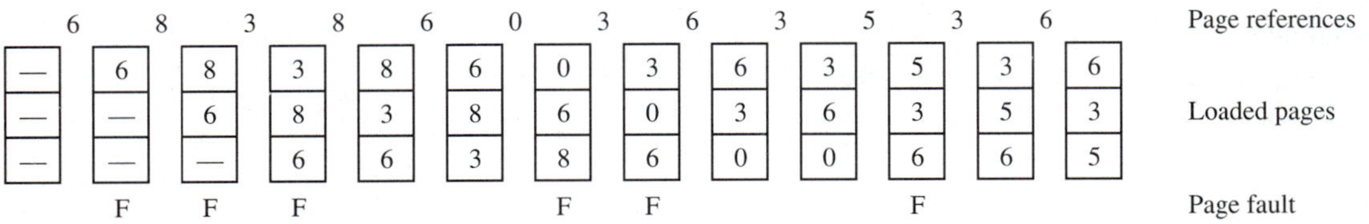

Figure 18.15

The LRU page-replacement algorithm with three frames.

For this sequence, the LRU algorithm produced one fewer page fault than the FIFO algorithm did. One example does not prove that LRU is better than FIFO. It is possible to construct a sequence for which FIFO produces fewer faults than LRU.

In practice, operating systems have their own unique page-replacement algorithms that depend on the hardware features available on the particular computer. Most page replacement algorithms are approximations to LRU, which generally works better than FIFO with the page request sequences from real jobs. An indication that LRU is better from a theoretical point of view is the fact that Belady's anomaly cannot occur with LRU replacement.

The sequences of page references in the previous examples only illustrate the page-replacement algorithms and are not realistic. For a demand paging system to be effective, the page fault rate needs to be kept to less than about one fault per 100,000 memory references.

A properly designed virtual memory system based on demand paging satisfies both goals of an operating system. It offers a convenient environment for higher-level programming because the programmer can develop code without being restricted by the limits of physical memory. It also allocates the memory efficiently, because a job's pages are loaded only if needed.

18.3 File Management

The operating system is also responsible for maintaining the collection of files on disk. A file is an abstract data type (ADT). To the user of the system, a file contains a sequence of data and can be manipulated either by a program or by operating system commands. Common operations on files include

Common operations on files

- Create a new file.
- Delete a file.
- Rename a file.
- Open a file for reading (reset).
- Read the next data item from the file.

The operating system makes the connection between the logical organization of the file as seen by a programmer at Level 6 or Level 5, and the physical organization on the disk itself.

Disk Drives

Figure 18.16 shows the physical characteristics of a disk drive. Part (a) shows a hard disk drive that consists of several platters coated with magnetic recording material. They are attached to a central *spindle* that rotates at a typical speed of 3600 revolutions per minute. Adjacent to each disk surface is a *read/write head* attached to an *arm*. The arm can move the heads in a radial direction across the surface of the platters.

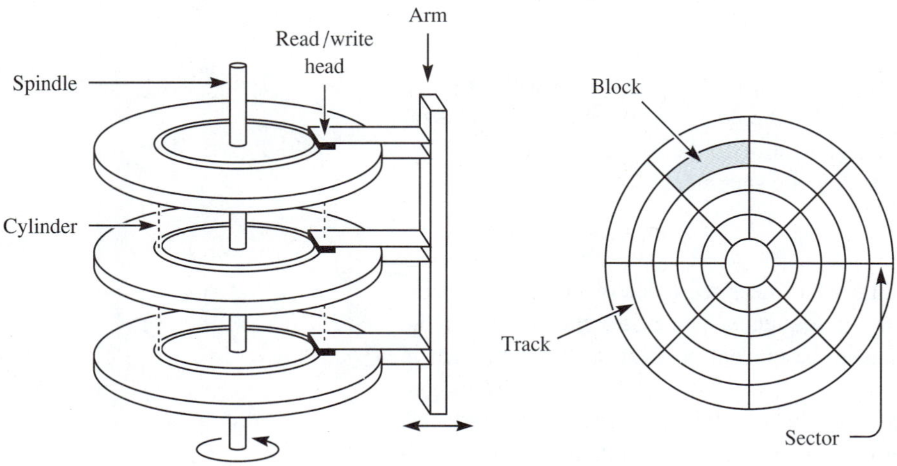

(a) A hard disk drive. **(b)** A single disk.

Figure 18.16 The physical characteristics of a disk drive.

Figure 18.16(b) shows a single disk. With the arm in a fixed position, the area under a read/write head sweeps out a ring as the disk rotates. Each ring is a *track* that stores a sequence of bits. Tracks are divided into *sectors*. A *block* is one sector of one track of one surface. A *cylinder* is the set of tracks on all the surfaces at a fixed arm position. A *block address* consists of three numbers—a cylinder number, a surface number, and a sector number.

Floppy disks

Floppy disks are similar to hard disks except that the platter is flexible. In a floppy disk drive, the read/write heads are in physical contact with the surface of the disk. In a hard disk drive, the read/write heads float just above the surface on a small cushion of air. A *head crash* in a hard disk is a mechanical failure in which the heads scrape the surface, damaging the recording material.

Reading a block from a disk

Reading the information from a given block is a four-step process: (1) The arm must move the heads to the designated cylinder. (2) The electronic circuitry must select the read/write head on the designated surface. (3) A period of time must elapse for the designated block to reach the read/write head. (4) The entire block must pass beneath the head to be read. Step 2 is an electronic function, which occurs in negligible time compared to the other three steps.

Associated with the three mechanical steps are the following times:

Contributions to the disk access time

- Seek time
- Latency
- Transmission time

Seek time is the time it takes the arm to move to the designated cylinder. *Latency* is the time it takes the block to reach the head once the head is in place. *Transmission time* is the time it takes the block to pass beneath the head. The time it takes to access a block is the sum of these three times.

File Abstraction

The user at a high level of abstraction does not want to be bothered with physical tracks and sectors. The operating system hides the details of the physical organization and presents the file with a logical organization to the user as an ADT.

For example, in Pacal when you execute the statement

```
read (SomeFile, Data1)
```

you have a logical image of `SomeFile` as a linear sequence of items with a current position maintained somewhere in the sequence. The `read` statement gets the item at the current position and advances the current position to the next item in the sequence.

Physically, the items in the file may be on different tracks and surfaces. Furthermore, there is no physical current position that is maintained by the hardware. The logical behavior of the read statement is due to the operating system software.

Allocation Techniques

The remainder of this section describes three memory-allocation techniques at the physical level—contiguous, linked, and indexed. Each technique requires the operating system to maintain a directory that records the physical location of the files. The directory is itself stored on the disk, along with the files.

If each file were small enough to fit in a single block, the file system would be simple to maintain. The directory would simply contain a list of the files on the disk. Each entry in the directory would have the name of the file and the address of the block in which the file was stored.

Contiguous allocation

If a file is too big to fit in a single block, the operating system must allocate several blocks for it. With *contiguous allocation,* the operating system matches the physical organization of the file to the logical organization by laying out the file sequentially on adjacent blocks of one track.

If the file is too big to fit on a single track, the system continues it on a second track. On a single-sided floppy disk, the second track would be adjacent to the first track on the same surface. On a double-sided floppy or a hard disk, the second track would be on the same cylinder as the first track. If the file is too big to fit on a single cylinder, the file would continue on an adjacent cylinder.

Figure 18.17 is a schematic diagram of contiguous allocation. Each row of eight blocks represents one track divided into eight sectors, as in Figure 18.16(b). The single number above each block is the block address, an abbreviation for the three numbers required to specify the address. Block 0 contains the directory.

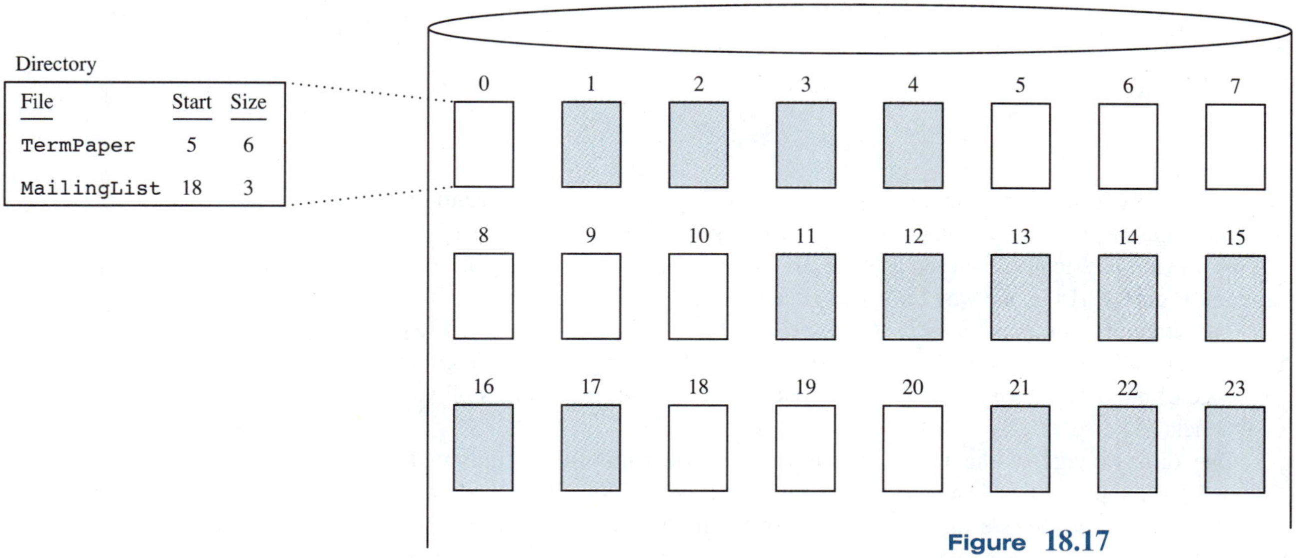

Figure 18.17

Contiguous allocation on a disk.

The directory lists the name of each file, its starting address, and its size. The file `TermPaper` starts at block 5 and contains six blocks. Its last three blocks are continued on a second track. Why wouldn't the system allocate blocks 1 through 6 for this file? The configuration in the figure could arise if another file previously occupied blocks 1 through 4, then was deleted from the disk by the user.

The pattern of occupied and unoccupied disk memory in Figure 18.17 looks suspiciously like the pattern of occupied and unoccupied main memory in Figures 18.4 and 18.6. In fact, the memory management issues are the same. As files are created and deleted they become fragmented. It may be impossible to create a new file because many small holes are scattered throughout the disk. To make room for the new file, the operating system supplies a disk compaction utility that shifts the files on the disk to make one large hole, as in Figure 18.5.

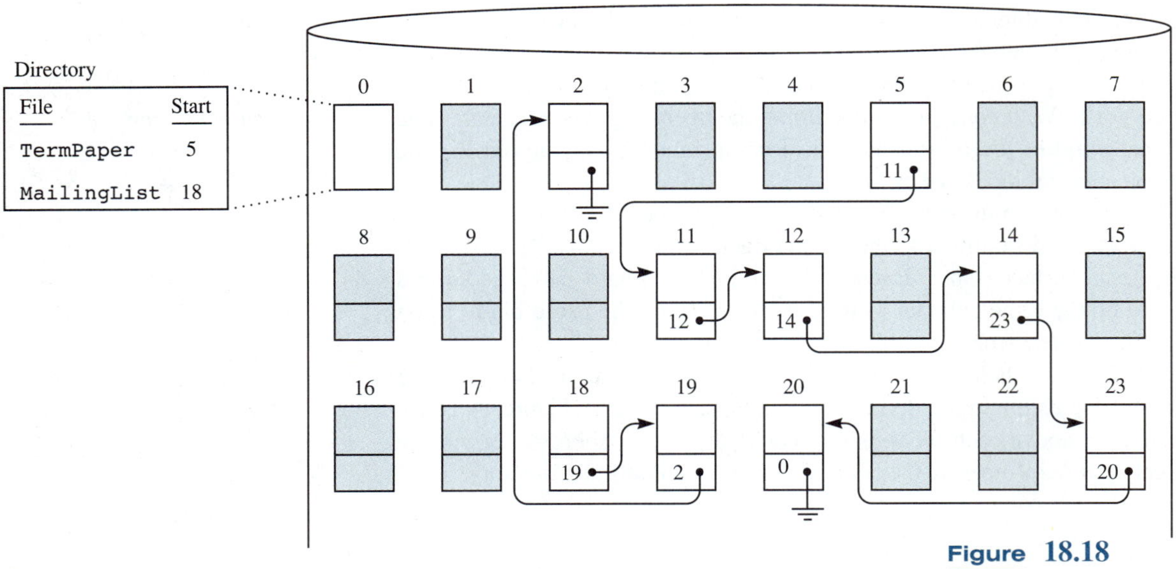

Figure 18.18

Linked allocation on a disk.

As with main memory, the compaction operation on disk is time-consuming. To eliminate the need for compaction, the operating system can store the file in blocks that are physically scattered throughout the disk. The linked allocation technique of Figure 18.18 is one way the system can maintain the file.

Linked allocation

The directory contains the address of the first block of the file. The last few bytes of each block are reserved for the address of the following block. The entire sequence of blocks forms a linked list. The link field in the last block has a nil value that acts like a sentinel.

One disadvantage of the linked technique is its susceptibility to failure. In Figure 18.18, suppose that just one byte in the link field of block 10 is damaged, either by a hardware failure or by a software bug. The operating system can still access the first three blocks of the file, but it will have no way of knowing where the last three blocks are.

Indexed allocation

The indexed allocation technique in Figure 18.19 collects all the addresses into a single list called an *index* in the directory. Now if a single byte in address 10 in the index is damaged, the operating system will lose track of only one block.

Contiguous allocation does have one major advantage over noncontiguous allocation, namely speed. If a file is contained on one cylinder, you only need to wait for one seek and one latency period to begin the access. You can read the entire file at a speed that is limited only by the transmission time. Even if the file is not all on one cylinder, after you read the first cylinder you only need to wait for a short seek to an adjacent cylinder.

With the blocks of one file scattered throughout the disk, you must endure a seek time and a latency time to access each block. Even with noncontiguous allo-

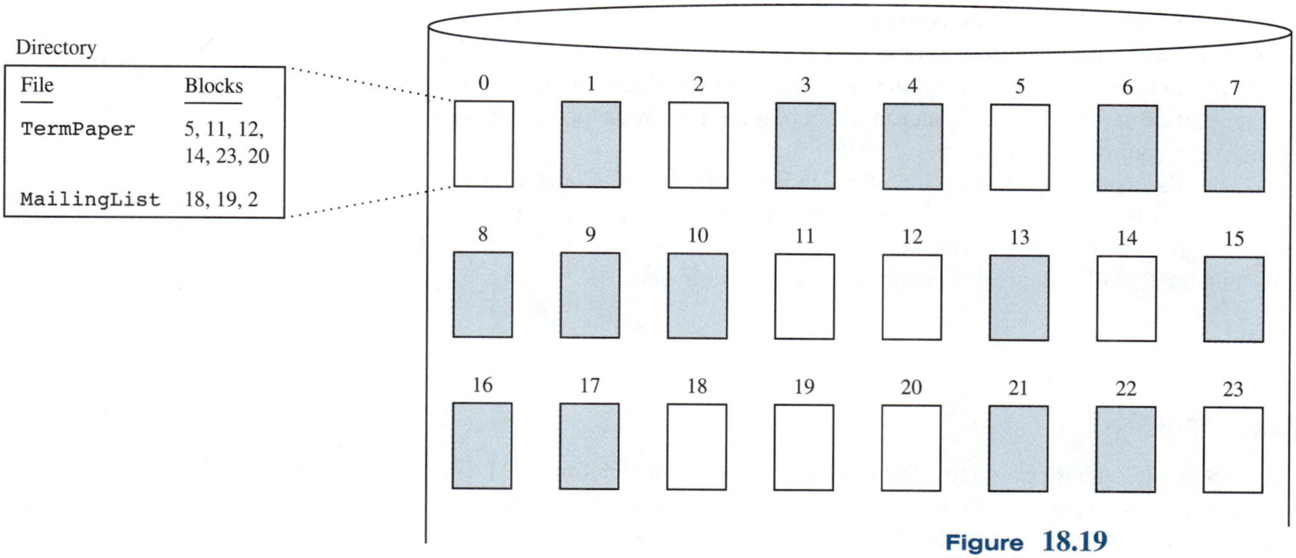

Figure 18.19

Indexed allocation on a disk.

cation, it is sometimes worthwhile to periodically reorganize the physical layout of the files to make their blocks contiguous.

18.4 Some Typical Operating Systems

The concepts described in Chapters 17 and 18 are some of the basic issues in operating system design. Commercial systems are more complex than these descriptions might indicate. This section presents three commercial operating systems—MS-DOS, MacOS, and UNIX—and shows how they use the concepts that were just presented. The chances are that you are now using one of these popular operating systems.

MS-DOS

MS-DOS stands for Microsoft Disk Operating System, which was designed by the Microsoft Corporation for the IBM PC microcomputer. It is a single-user system that is designed specifically for the Intel 80 series microprocessors, including 8088, 80286, and others.

MS-DOS main memory

The memory map of MS-DOS is similar to that of Pep/5. Pep/5 has 4 Kbytes of installed memory with the application at the top of memory and the operating system at the bottom of the 4-Kbyte region. A Pep/5 address is 16 bits, so the maximum possible memory size is 2^{16}, which is 64 Kbytes. An 8088 address is 20 bits, so the maximum possible memory size is 2^{20}, which is 1024 Kbytes or 1 Mbyte. The user memory is in the top 640 Kbytes at address 00000 to 9FFFF. The region from A0000 on is reserved for the operating system.

Unlike Pep/5, most of the operating system is not in ROM but on disk. All MS-DOS disks reserve sector 1, track 0, side 0 for the boot record. The first four bytes of the boot record are a machine language branch instruction to the loader in a later part of the record. The loader in the boot record loads the operating system, which then controls the computer.

MS-DOS disk files

The file system uses a variation of the index technique. The operating system maintains a file directory and a file allocation table. Several adjacent sectors of the disk are grouped to make a cluster. The directory contains the starting cluster of the file, and the file allocation table contains the cluster numbers.

MacOS

MacOS graphics emphasis

MacOS is the operating system designed by Apple Computer for its Macintosh series of microcomputers. Like MS-DOS, the system was designed to run on a particular microprocessor, in this case the Motorola 68000 series.

The distinguishing characteristic of MacOS is its graphical user interface. The entire operating system is designed to present the user with a visual, as opposed to textual, framework in which to execute applications programs. Figure 18.20 shows two sample screen images.

Figure 18.20(a) is called the desktop because its appearance is similar to the top of a desk. In the same way that an office worker's desktop contains overlapping pages of paper, the screen image contains overlapping windows that can be arranged and sized as the user sees fit.

Instead of typing commands to the operating system, the user (Level 7) selects commands with a mouse from a standard menu bar at the top of the screen. All applications are designed to follow the same user interface. Figure 18.20(b) is a screen image of the MacDraw application used to create the figures in this book. Note the same style window and menu bar as in the desktop of (a). Once the user knows how to manipulate windows and make menu selections with the mouse, learning how to use a new application requires only a minimal amount of training.

Levels of abstraction within MacOS

The operating system (Level 4) provides the applications programmer (Level 6 or 5) with an environment that makes it convenient to implement the graphical interface. Two levels of abstraction within MacOS are the Toolbox routines at the higher level and the QuickDraw routines at the lower level. An example of a QuickDraw routine is a procedure that draws an image of a single line as a set of pixels on the screen. A Toolbox routine, for example, is a procedure to draw a window. The window-drawing procedure calls the line drawing procedure, among others, at the lower level of abstraction to draw the window.

The Toolbox and QuickDraw routines are contained in ROM beginning at address 400000 (hex). As in the Pep/5 system, the top of memory is RAM for both the user and the operating system. Also similar to Pep/5 is the mechanism for calling an operating system routine with an unimplemented opcode. Opcode 1010 (bin) is not implemented in the 68000 instruction set and therefore generates a synchronous interrupt. The first Kbyte of memory is reserved for the interrupt vectors to the Toolbox routines, corresponding to the Pep/5 vectors for the starting addresses of the loader and interrupt handler.

Figure 18.20

The Macintosh operating system.

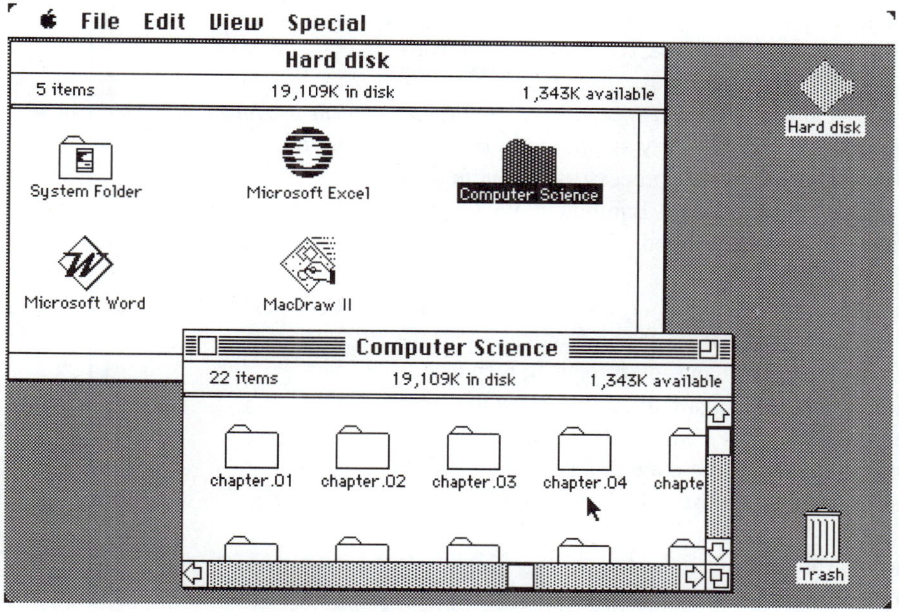

(a) The desktop screen.

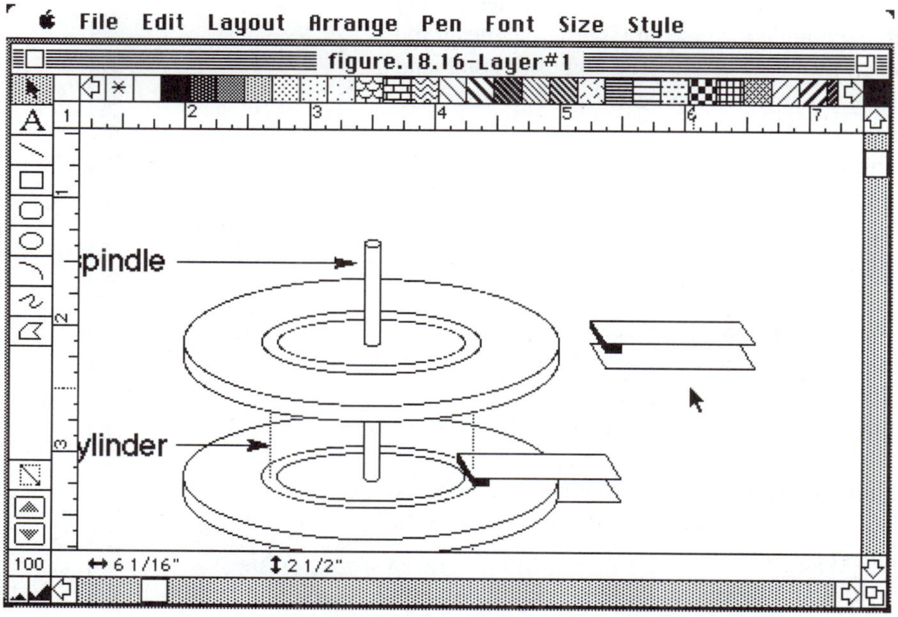

(b) An application screen.

UNIX

Ken Thompson developed UNIX at Bell Laboratories in 1969 to control a PDP-7 computer. Dennis Ritchie later helped him expand the operating system and move it to several different computers. It was not originally designed to be a commercial operating system, but a system for internal use by the programmers at Bell Labs.

Its popularity soon spread, first throughout the company, then to several universities, notably the University of California at Berkeley. AT&T, the parent company of Bell Labs, eventually marketed UNIX to other companies.

The machine independence of UNIX

UNIX differs from MS-DOS and MacOS in several respects. It is a multiuser timesharing system, not a single-user system. Although it was originally designed for a specific computer, it now runs on many different processors, including the Intel 80 series, the Motorola 68000 series, and the Digital Equipment VAX series. The version of UNIX described here is one developed at the University of California at Berkeley for the VAX computer.

Command processes

When you log in, the system creates a command interpreter process, which immediately prompts you for input. As with MS-DOS, you communicate with the operating system by typing a command to the command interpreter. In response to a command request, the command interpreter creates a child process for the command that immediately enters the ready state. The command interpreter process goes into a wait state. After the child process receives enough CPU time to complete the command, it signals the waiting parent process, which then continues and issues another prompt.

If you do not want the command interpreter to wait for the child process, you can simply type the ampersand character, `&`, after your command. The command interpreter and its child process will both go to the ready state and will execute concurrently. For example, suppose you have a large program that takes a long time to compile. You want the system to compile the program, but in the meantime you want to do some word processing. You simply issue the compiler command followed by `&`, and you can immediately do your word processing while your program compiles concurrently in the background.

Virtual memory on VAX UNIX

The VAX version of UNIX is a virtual memory system based on demand paging. Memory frame size on the VAX is 512 bytes. The hardware supplies a dirty bit for each frame. The operating system, however, prefers a page size of 1024 bytes, so it uses two frames per page. The page-replacement algorithm is a variation of LRU.

The UNIX file system

The UNIX file system is based on the indexed technique. The operating system maintains the global file directory for every file in the system. Each file also has its individual directory called an *inode,* for index node. Each inode contains the name and type of the file and 15 pointers to other disk blocks. Only the first 12 pointers point to blocks that contain data.

If the file is too big to fit into 12 blocks, the thirteenth pointer points to a block of pointers. Each pointer in the block of pointers in turn points to a data block. This block of pointers is called a *single indirect block.*

If the file is too big to fit into the first 12 blocks plus all the blocks pointed to by the pointers in the single indirect block, the fourteenth pointer in the inode points to a double indirect block. Each pointer in the double indirect block points to a single indirect block. This concept is analogous to the indirect addressing mode for main memory as described in Section 15.3, but it is applied to disk addresses.

The fifteenth pointer in the inode could point to a triple indirect block, but it is not used on the VAX. Without it, a file can be as large as 4 Gbytes (four billion bytes) anyway, which is large enough for most purposes.

SUMMARY

The operating system allocates time in the form of CPU utilization and space in the form of main memory and disk allocation. Five techniques for allocation of main memory are uniprogramming, fixed-partition multiprogramming, variable-partition multiprogramming, paging, and virtual memory. With uniprogramming, only one job executes at a time from start to finish, and the job has the entire main memory to itself. Fixed-partition multiprogramming allows several jobs to execute concurrently and requires the operating system to determine the partition sizes in memory before executing any jobs. Variable-partition multiprogramming alleviates the inefficiencies inherent in fixed-partition multiprogramming by allowing the partition sizes to vary depending on the job requirements. The best-fit and first-fit algorithms are two different strategies to cope with the fragmentation problem of variable-partition multiprogramming.

Paging alleviates fragmentation by fragmenting the program to fit the memory holes. Programs are no longer contiguous but broken up and scattered throughout main memory. Jobs are divided into equal-sized pages and main memory is divided into frames of the same size. Logical addresses as seen by the programmer are converted to physical addresses with the help of a page table. The page table contains the frame number for each page that is stored in main memory.

Demand paging, also called virtual memory, postpones page loading into memory until the job demands the page. The entire program does not need to reside in main memory to execute. Instead, only its active pages, called the working set, are loaded. A page fault occurs when a page is referenced but has not yet been loaded into memory. First in, first out (FIFO) and least recently used (LRU) are two algorithms for determining which page to swap out of main memory when a frame is needed for a new page. You would normally expect the number of faults to decrease with increasing number of memory frames. But Belady's anomaly shows that it is possible for an increase in the number of frames to produce an increase in the number of faults with the FIFO replacement algorithm.

Three contributions to disk access time are seek time, which is the time it takes for the arm to move to the designated cylinder; latency, which is the time it takes for the block to rotate to the head once the head is in place; and transmission time, which is the time it takes for the block to pass underneath the head. Three techniques of disk management are contiguous, linked, and indexed. The problem of fragmentation occurs with disk memory, as it does with main memory.

EXERCISES

Section 18.1

1. Using the format of Table 18.1, devise a job execution sequence for which the first-fit algorithm would require compaction before the best-fit algorithm. Sketch the fragmentation in main memory just before compaction is required for each algorithm.

*2. Figure 18.9 shows how a page table in a paging system performs the same transformation of the logical address as the base register does in a multiprogramming system. The equivalent job of the bound register is not shown in the figure. **(a)** To protect other process' memory space from unauthorized access, would a paging system require a table of bound values, one for each page, or would a single bound register suffice? Explain. **(b)** Modify Figure 18.9 to include main memory protection from other processes.

3. Suppose the page size in a paging system is 512 bytes. **(a)** If most of the files are large, that is, much greater than 512 bytes, what do you suppose is the average internal fragmentation (in bytes of unused space) for each file? Explain your reasoning. **(b)** How would your answer to part (a) change if most of the files were much smaller than 512 bytes? **(c)** How would your answer to part (b) change if you express the fragmentation in terms of the percent of unused space instead of the number of unused bytes?

Section 18.2

4. A computer has 12-bit addresses and a main memory that is divided into 16 frames. Memory management uses demand paging. ***(a)** How many bytes is virtual memory? **(b)** How many bytes are in each page? **(c)** How many bits are in the offset of a logical and physical address? **(d)** What is the maximum number of entries in a job's page table?

5. Answer Exercise 4 for a computer with n-bit addresses and a memory divided into 2^k frames.

*6. For which pages in Figure 18.11 is the image on disk an exact replica of the page in main memory?

7. Verify the data of Figure 18.14(b), which shows Belady's anomaly, for the sequence of page references given in the text. Display the content of the frames in the format of Figure 18.12.

*8. Devise a sequence of 12 page references for which the FIFO page-replacement algorithm is better than the LRU algorithm.

9. Plot the graph of Figure 18.14(b) for the page reference sequence in Figure 18.12 using the FIFO page-replacement algorithm. On the same graph, plot the data for the LRU algorithm.

*10. If the operating system could predict the future, it could select the replacement page such that the next page fault is delayed as long as possible. Such an algorithm is called OPT, the optimum page-replacement algorithm. It is a useful theoretical algorithm because it represents the best you could possibly do. When designers measure the performance of their page-replacement algorithms, they try to get as close as possible to the performance of OPT. How many page faults does OPT produce for the sequence of Figures 18.12 and 18.15? How does that compare with FIFO and LRU?

Section 18.3

11. Suppose a disk rotates at 3600 revolutions per minute and has each surface divided into 16 sectors. ***(a)** What is the maximum possible latency time? Under what circumstance will that occur? **(b)** What is the minimum possible latency time? Under what circumstance will that occur? **(c)** From (a) and (b), what will be the average latency time? **(d)** What is the transmission time for one block?

Section 18.4

12. Suppose a file system uses the indexed technique of the VAX UNIX operating system. Each block has enough storage for 64 bytes of data or 16 block addresses. The inode has eight pointers, six of which point to data blocks, one of which points to a single indirect block, and one of which points to a double indirect block. What is the maximum number of data blocks a file can contain?

LEVEL 1

Logic Gate

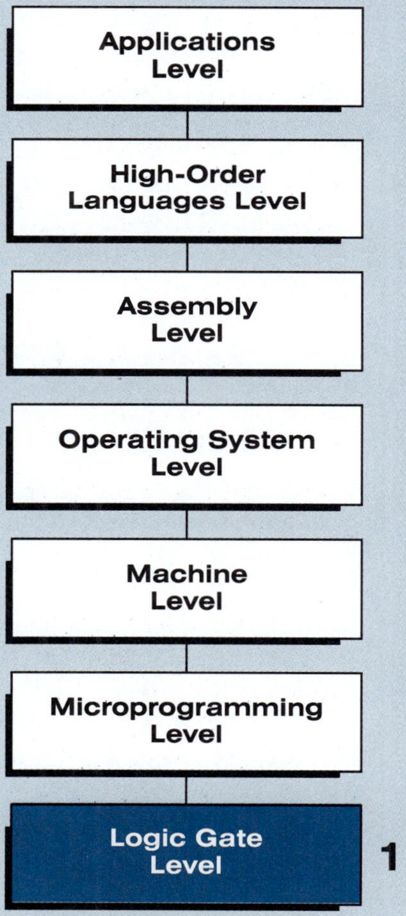

Chapter

19

Combinational Networks

Finally we come to the lowest level in our description of the typical computer system. Each level of abstraction hides the details that are unnecessary for the user at the next-higher level. The details at Level 1 are hidden from the user at Level 3, the machine level. Remember that the user at Level 3 sees a von Neumann machine whose language is machine language. The job of the designer at Level 1 is to construct the Level 3 machine. These last two chapters will describe the language and design principles at Level 1 that are required to construct a von Neumann machine.

Omitting Level 2

The figures in this book have consistently shown the microprogramming level between the machine level and the logic gate level. Some designers choose to omit the microprogramming level in their machines and construct the Level 3 machine directly from Level 1. Others choose to design their systems with a microprogramming level.

What are the advantages and disadvantages of each design approach? The same as we encountered at Levels 7, 6, and 5. Suppose you need to design an application for a user at Level 7. Would you rather write it in Pascal at Level 6 and compile it to a lower level or write it directly in Pep/5 assembly language at Level 5? Since Pascal is at a higher level of abstraction, one Pascal statement can do the work of many Pep/5 statements. The Pascal program would be much shorter than the equivalent Pep/5 program. It would, therefore, be easier to design and debug. But it would require a compiler for translation to a lower level. Furthermore, a good assembly language programmer can usually produce shorter, faster code than the object code from even an optimizing compiler. Though the program would execute faster, it would be difficult to design and debug; it would thus be more costly to develop.

The tradeoff at Levels 7, 6, and 5 is development cost versus execution speed. The same tradeoff applies at Levels 3, 2, and 1. Generally systems that include Level 2 are simpler and less costly than those that omit it. But they usually execute more slowly than if they were built directly from Level 1.

The 370, VAX, and 68000 families described in Chapter 14 are all microprogrammed. The 8086 processor is not. A recent design trend is to build simple but fast von Neumann machines with small instruction sets, called *reduced instruction set computers* (RISC). An important characteristic of a RISC machine is its omission of Level 2.

Space does not permit a description of Level 2 in this book. Two levels that are interesting but also not included here are the levels below the logic gate level, as shown in Figure 19.1.

At the electronic device level (Level 0), designers connect transistors, resistors, and capacitors to make an individual logic gate at Level 1. At the physics level (Level –1), applied physicists construct the transistors that the electrical engineer can use to construct the gates that the computer architect can use to construct the von Neumann machine. There is no level below physics, the most fundamental of all the sciences.

The languages at Levels 0 and –1 are the set of mathematical equations that model the behavior of the objects at that level. You may be familiar with some of them. At Level 0 they include Ohm's law, Kirchoff's rules, and the voltage versus current characteristics of electronic devices. At Level –1 they include Coulomb's law, Newton's laws, and some laws from quantum mechanics. At all the levels, from the calculus for relational databases at Level 7 to Newton's laws at Level –1, formal mathematics is the tool for modeling the behavior of the system.

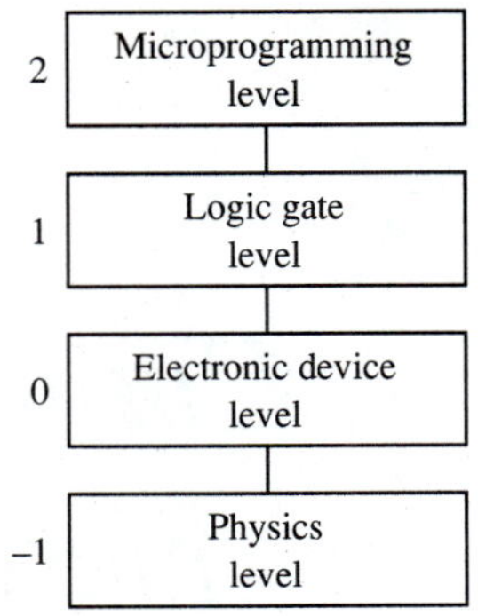

Figure 19.1

The levels below the logic gate level.

19.1 Boolean Algebra and Logic Gates

A *circuit* is a collection of devices that are physically connected by wires to form a *network* or *net*. The two basic types of nets at Level 1 are combinational and sequential. You can visualize either type of network as a rectangular block called a *black box* with a fixed number of input lines and a fixed number of output lines. Figure 19.2 shows a three-input, two-output network.

Each line can carry a signal whose value is either 1 or 0. Electrically, a 1 signal is a small voltage, usually about 5 volts, and a 0 signal is 0 volts. The network is designed to detect and produce only those binary values.

You should recognize Figure 19.2 as one more manifestation of the input, processing, output structure that is present at all levels of the computer system. The network performs the processing that transforms the input to the output.

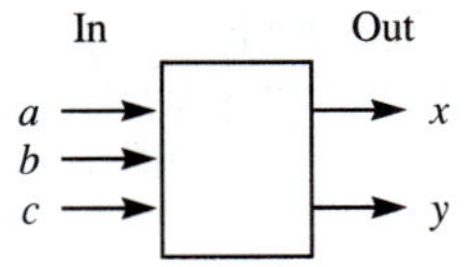

Figure 19.2

The black box representation of a network.

Combinational Networks

With a *combinational network,* the input determines the output. For example, in Figure 19.2 if you put in $a = 1$, $b = 0$, $c = 1$ (abbreviated $abc = 101$) today and get out $xy = 01$, then if you put in $abc = 101$ tomorrow you will get out $xy = 01$ again. Mathematically x and y are functions of a, b, and c. That is, $x = x(a, b, c)$ and $y = y(a, b, c)$.

This behavior is not characteristic of a sequential net. It may be possible for you to put $abc = 101$ into a sequential net and get out $xy = 01$ at one moment, but $xy = 11$ a few microseconds later. The next chapter shows how this seemingly useless behavior comes about and how it is, in fact, indispensable for building computers.

The three most common methods for describing the behavior of a combinational net are

- Truth tables
- Boolean algebraic expressions
- Logic diagrams

The remainder of this section describes those representations.

a	*b*	*c*	*x*	*y*
0	0	0	0	0
0	0	1	1	0
0	1	0	0	0
0	1	1	1	1
1	0	0	0	1
1	0	1	0	0
1	1	0	0	0
1	1	1	0	0

Table 19.1

The truth table for a three-input, two-output combinational net.

Truth Tables

Of these three methods of representing a combinational net, truth tables are at a higher level of abstraction than algebraic expressions or logic diagrams. A truth table specifies what the combinational net does, not how it does it. A truth table simply lists the output for every possible combination of input values (hence the name, combinational net).

Example 19.1 Table 19.1 is the truth table for a three-input, two-output combinational net. Since there are three inputs and each input can have one of two possible values, the table has $2^3 = 8$ entries. In general, the truth table for an n-input combinational net will have 2^n entries. ■

Example 19.2 Another example of a combinational net specified by a truth table is Table 19.2. It is a four-input network with 16 entries in its truth table. ■

a	*b*	*c*	*d*	*x*	*y*
0	0	0	0	0	0
0	0	0	1	0	0
0	0	1	0	0	0
0	0	1	1	0	0
0	1	0	0	0	1
0	1	0	1	1	1
0	1	1	0	0	0
0	1	1	1	1	0
1	0	0	0	0	0
1	0	0	1	0	0
1	0	1	0	0	0
1	0	1	1	0	0
1	1	0	0	0	1
1	1	0	1	1	1
1	1	1	0	0	0
1	1	1	1	1	0

Table 19.2

The truth table for a three-input, two-output combinational net.

The black box schematic of Figure 19.2 is particularly appropriate for the truth table representation of a combinational net. You cannot see inside a box that is painted black. Similarly, you cannot see how a network produces a function that is defined by a truth table.

Boolean Algebra

An algebraic expression written according to the laws of boolean algebra specifies not only what a combinational net does, but how it does it. Boolean algebra is similar in some respects to the algebra for real numbers that you are familiar with, but it is different in other respects. The four basic operations for real algebra are addition, subtraction, multiplication, and division. Boolean algebra has three basic operations—OR, denoted +; AND, denoted ·; and complement, denoted ′. AND and OR are binary operations, and complement is a unary operation.

The 10 fundamental properties of boolean algebra are

Ten fundamental properties of boolean algebra

$x + y = y + x$	$x \cdot y = y \cdot x$	commutative
$(x + y) + z = x + (y + z)$	$(x \cdot y) \cdot z = x \cdot (y \cdot z)$	associative
$x + (y \cdot z) = (x + y) \cdot (x + z)$	$x \cdot (y + z) = (x \cdot y) + (x \cdot z)$	distributive
$x + 0 = x$	$x \cdot 1 = x$	identity
$x + (x') = 1$	$x \cdot (x') = 0$	complement

where x, y, and z are boolean variables. As with real algebra, the notation is infix with parentheses to denote which of several operations to perform first. To simplify expressions with many parentheses, the boolean operations have the precedence structure shown in Table 19.3. Using the precedence rules, the distributive properties are

Precedence	Operator
Highest	Complement
	AND
Lowest	OR

Table 19.3

Precedence of the boolean operators.

$$x + y \cdot z = (x + y) \cdot (x + z) \qquad x \cdot (y + z) = x \cdot y + x \cdot z$$

and the complement properties are

$$x + x' = 1 \qquad x \cdot x' = 0$$

The distributive law

A striking difference between the properties of real algebra and boolean algebra is the distributive law. With real numbers, multiplication distributes over addition. For example,

$$2 \cdot (3 + 4) = 2 \cdot 3 + 2 \cdot 4$$

But addition does not distribute over multiplication. It is not true that

$$2 + 3 \cdot 4 = (2 + 3) \cdot (2 + 4)$$

In boolean algebra, however, where + represents OR and $\cdot$ represents AND, OR does distribute over AND.

Duality

The laws of boolean algebra have a symmetry that the laws of real algebra do not have. Each boolean property has a *dual* property. To obtain the dual expression,

- Exchange + and $\cdot$
- Exchange 1 and 0

The two forms of the distributive law are an example of dual expressions. In the distributive property

$$x + (y \cdot z) = (x + y) \cdot (x + z)$$

if you exchange the + and $\cdot$ operators you get

$$x \cdot (y + z) = (x \cdot y) + (x \cdot z)$$

which is the other distributive property. Each fundamental property of boolean algebra has a corresponding dual property.

The associative law

The associative properties also permit simplification of expressions. Since the order in which you perform two OR operations is immaterial, you can write

$$(x + y) + z$$

without parentheses as

$$x + y + z$$

The same is true for the AND operation.

Boolean Algebra Theorems

Since boolean algebra has a different mathematical structure from the real algebra with which you are familiar, the theorems of boolean algebra may appear unusual at first. The theorems proved from the 10 basic properties of boolean algebra, which will be discussed next, are useful in the analysis and design of combinational nets.

The *idempotent property* states that

The idempotent property

$$x + x = x$$

Proving this theorem requires a sequence of substitution steps, each of which is based on one of the 10 basic properties of boolean algebra.

$$\begin{aligned} x + x &= (x + x) \cdot 1 && \text{identity} \\ &= (x + x) \cdot (x + x') && \text{complement} \\ &= x + (x \cdot x') && \text{distributive} \\ &= x + 0 && \text{complement} \\ &= x && \text{identity} \end{aligned}$$

The dual property is

$$x \cdot x = x$$

The proof of the dual theorem requires exactly the same sequence of steps, with each substitution based on the dual of the corresponding step in the original proof.

$$\begin{aligned} x \cdot x &= (x \cdot x) + 0 && \text{identity} \\ &= (x \cdot x) + (x \cdot x') && \text{complement} \\ &= x \cdot (x + x') && \text{distributive} \\ &= x \cdot 1 && \text{complement} \\ &= x && \text{identity} \end{aligned}$$

Using duality to assert a theorem

The proofs of the idempotent properties illustrate an important application of duality in boolean algebra. Once you prove a theorem, you can assert immediately that its dual must also be true. Since each of the 10 basic properties has a dual, the corresponding proof will be identical in structure to the original proof, but with each step based on the dual of the original step.

Two other useful theorems and their duals are

Two useful theorems, including the absorption properties

$$x + 1 = 1 \qquad x \cdot 0 = 0$$
$$x + x \cdot y = x \qquad x \cdot (x + y) = x$$

The last pair of theorems are called the *absorption properties* because y is absorbed into x. Proofs of these theorems are left for the exercises at the end of the chapter.

Proving Complements

The complement of x is x'. To prove that some expression, y, is the complement of some other expression, z, you must show that y and z obey the same complement properties

$$y + z = 1 \qquad y \cdot z = 0$$

that x and x' obey.

An example of proving complements is *De Morgan's law,* which states that

$$(a \cdot b)' = a' + b'$$

De Morgan's law

To show that the complement of $a \cdot b$ is $a' + b'$, you must show that

$$(a \cdot b) + (a' + b') = 1 \qquad (a \cdot b) \cdot (a' + b') = 0$$

The first part of the proof is

$(a \cdot b) + (a' + b')$	$= (a' + b') + (a \cdot b)$	commutative
	$= [(a' + b') + a] \cdot [(a' + b') + b]$	distributive
	$= [b' + (a + a')] \cdot [a' + (b + b')]$	commutative, associative
	$= [b' + 1] \cdot [a' + 1]$	complement
	$= 1 \cdot 1$	theorem, $x + 1 = 1$
	$= 1$	identity

and the second part of the proof is

$(a \cdot b) \cdot (a' + b')$	$= (a \cdot b) \cdot a' + (a \cdot b) \cdot b'$	distributive
	$= (a \cdot a') \cdot b + (b \cdot b') \cdot a$	commutative, associative
	$= 0 \cdot b + 0 \cdot a$	complement
	$= 0 + 0$	theorem $x \cdot 0 = 0$
	$= 0$	identity

The second De Morgan's law,

$$(a + b)' = a' \cdot b'$$

follows immediately from duality.

De Morgan's laws generalize to more than one variable. For three variables, the laws are

$$(a \cdot b \cdot c)' = a' + b' + c' \qquad (a + b + c)' = a' \cdot b' \cdot c'$$

De Morgan's law for three variables

Proofs of the general theorems for more than two variables are left for an exercise at the end of the chapter.

The complement of x'

Another complement theorem is $(x')' = x$. That the complement of x' is x follows because

$x' + x$	$= x + x'$	commutative
	$= 1$	complement

and

$$
\begin{aligned}
x' \cdot x &= x \cdot x' && \text{commutative} \\
&= 0 && \text{complement}
\end{aligned}
$$

The complement of 1

Yet another complement theorem is $1' = 0$. That 1 is the complement of 0 follows because

$$1 + 0 = 1 \qquad \text{identity with } x = 1$$

and

$$
\begin{aligned}
1 \cdot 0 &= 0 \cdot 1 && \text{commutative} \\
&= 0 && \text{identity with } x = 0
\end{aligned}
$$

The dual theorem, $0' = 1$, follows immediately.

Logic Diagrams

The third representation of a combinational net is an interconnection of logic gates. This representation corresponds most closely to the hardware, since the lines that connect the gates in a logic diagram represent physical wires that connect physical devices on a circuit board or in an integrated circuit.

Each boolean operation is represented by a gate symbol, shown in Figure 19.3. The AND and OR gates have two input lines, labeled *a* and *b*. The inverter has one input line, corresponding to the fact that the complement is a unary operation. The output is x. Also shown in the figure are the corresponding boolean expression and truth table for each gate.

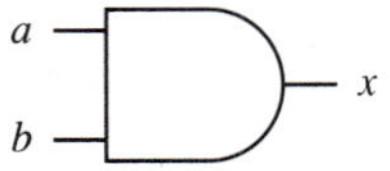

$x = a \cdot b$

a	b	x
0	0	0
0	1	0
1	0	0
1	1	1

(a) AND gate.

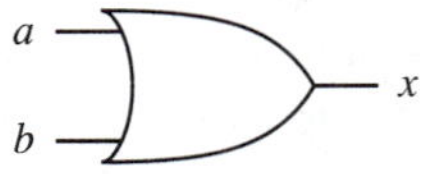

$x = a + b$

a	b	x
0	0	0
0	1	1
1	0	1
1	1	1

(b) OR gate.

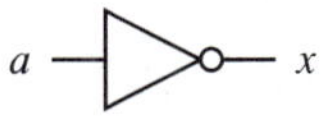

$x = a'$

a	x
0	1
1	0

(c) Inverter.

Figure 19.3
The three basic logic gates.

Any boolean function can be written with only the AND, OR, and complement operations. It follows that to construct any combinational net you only need the three basic gates of Figure 19.3. In practice several other gates are common. Figure 19.4 shows three of them.

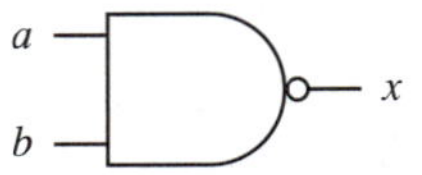

$x = (a \cdot b)'$

a	b	x
0	0	1
0	1	1
1	0	1
1	1	0

(a) NAND gate.

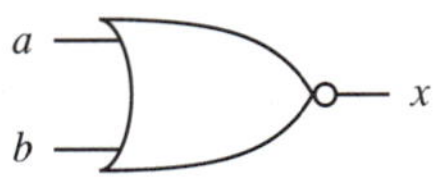

$x = (a + b)'$

a	b	x
0	0	1
0	1	0
1	0	0
1	1	0

(b) NOR gate.

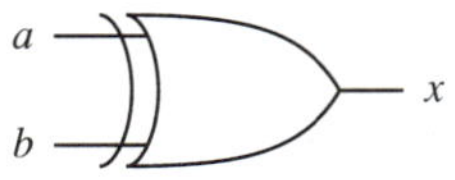

$x = a \oplus b$

a	b	x
0	0	0
0	1	1
1	0	1
1	1	0

(c) XOR gate.

Figure 19.4

Three common logic gates.

The NAND gate (Not AND) is equivalent to an AND gate followed by an inverter, as shown in Figure 19.5. Similarly, a NOR gate (Not OR) is equivalent to an OR gate followed by an inverter. Electronically it is frequently easier to build a NAND gate than to build an AND gate. In fact, an AND gate is often built as a NAND gate followed by an inverter. NOR gates are also more common than OR gates.

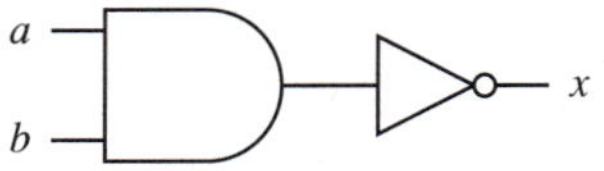

(a) AND inverter.

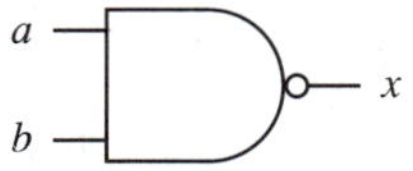

(b) NAND.

Figure 19.5 (left)

Two equivalent combinational nets.

XOR stands for *exclusive* OR in contrast to OR, which is sometimes called *inclusive* OR. The output of an OR gate is 1 if either or both of its inputs are 1. The output of an XOR gate is 1 if either of its inputs is 1 exclusive of the other input. Its output is 0 if both inputs are 1. The algebraic symbol for the XOR operation is $\oplus$.

The AND and OR gates are also manufactured with more than two inputs. Figure 19.6 shows a three-input AND gate and its truth table. The output of an AND gate is 1 only if all of its inputs are 1. The output of an OR gate is 0 only if all of its inputs are 0.

$x = a \cdot b \cdot c$

a	b	c	x
0	0	0	0
0	0	1	0
0	1	0	0
0	1	1	0
1	0	0	0
1	0	1	0
1	1	0	0
1	1	1	1

Figure 19.6

The three-input AND gate.

Alternate Representations

You may have recognized the similarity of the truth tables for the AND, OR, and inverter gates and the truth tables for the AND, OR, and NOT operations in Pascal's boolean expressions. The truth tables are identical, with NOT corresponding to the inverter and Pascal's true and false values corresponding to boolean algebra's 1 and 0 respectively.

The mathematical structure of boolean algebra is important because it applies not only to combinational nets but to statement logic as well. Pascal uses statement logic to determine the truth of a condition contained in `if` and loop statements. A recent group of programming languages important in artificial intelligence makes even more extensive use of statement logic. Programs written in these languages simulate human reasoning by a technique called *logic programming*. That entire discipline is based on boolean algebra.

Statement logic interpretation

Another interpretation of boolean algebra is a description of operations on sets. If you interpret a boolean variable as a set, the OR operation as set union, the AND operation as set intersection, the complement operation as set complement, 0 as the empty set, and 1 as the universal set, then all the properties and theorems of boolean algebra hold for sets.

Set theory interpretation

Example 19.3 The theorem

$$x + 1 = 1$$

states that the union of the universal set with any other set is the universal set. ■

Example 19.4 Figure 19.7 shows the set theory interpretation of an absorption property

$$x + x \cdot y = x$$

with a Venn diagram. Figure 19.7(a) shows set x. The intersection of x and y, shown in (b), is the set of elements in both x and y. The union of that set with x is shown in (c). The fact that the region in (a) is the same as the region in (c) illustrates the absorption property. ■

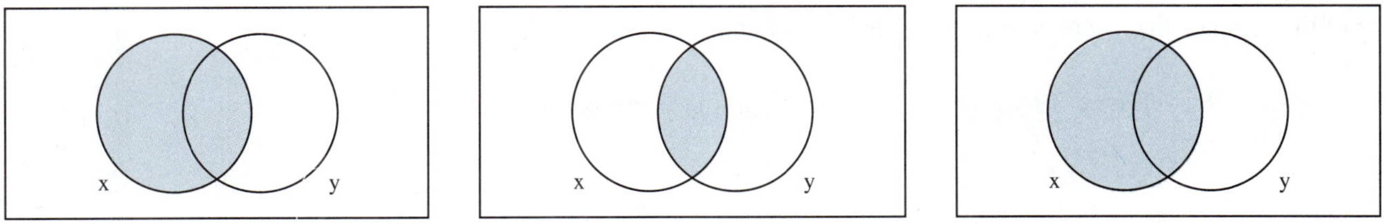

(a) x (b) $x \cdot y$ (c) $x + x \cdot y$

Figure 19.7

The set theory interpretation of an absorption property.

The interpretation of boolean algebra as a description of combinational nets and as the basis of statement logic illustrates that it is the mathematical basis of a large part of computer science. The fact that it also describes set theory shows its importance in other areas of mathematics as well.

19.2 Combinational Analysis

Every boolean expression has a corresponding logic diagram, and every logic diagram has a corresponding boolean expression. In mathematical terminology, there is a one-to-one correspondence between the two. A given truth table, however, can have several corresponding implementations. Figure 19.8 shows a truth table with several corresponding boolean expressions and logic diagrams.

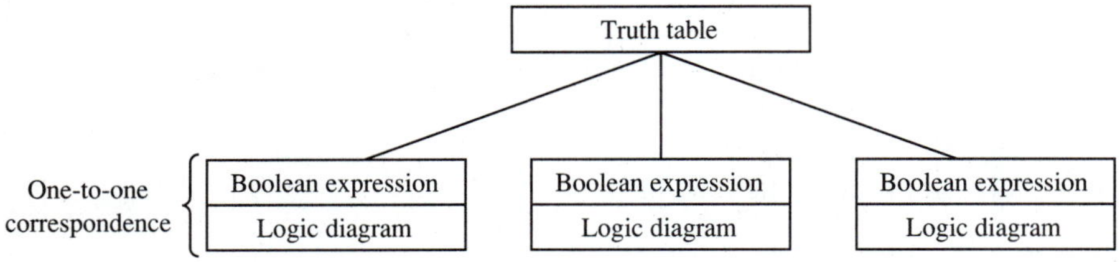

Figure 19.8

Several implementations of a given truth table.

This section shows the correspondence among the three representations of a combinational net.

Boolean Expressions and Logic Diagrams

A boolean expression consists of one or more variables combined with the AND, OR, and invert operations. The number of inputs to the network equals the number of variables. This section and the next concentrate on networks with one output. The last section of this chapter considers networks with more than one output.

To draw the logic diagram from a given boolean expression, draw an AND gate for each AND operation, an OR gate for each OR operation, and an inverter for each complement operation. Connect the output of one gate to the input of another according to the expression. The output of the combinational net is the output of the one gate that is not connected to the input of another.

Example 19.5 Figure 19.9 shows the logic diagram corresponding to the boolean expression

$$a + b' \cdot c$$

From now on, we will omit the AND operator symbol and write the boolean expression as

$$a + b'c$$

The output of each gate is labeled with its corresponding expression. ■

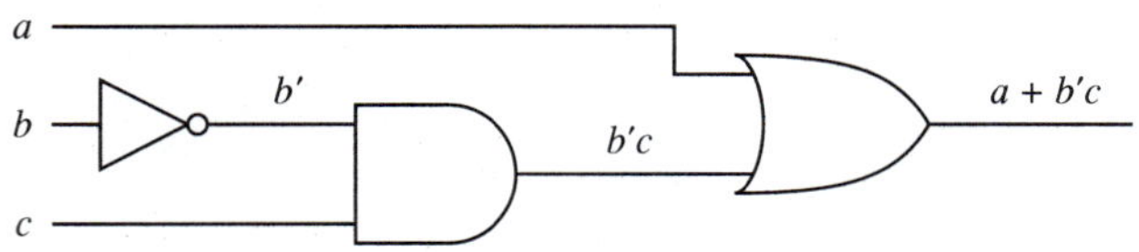

Figure 19.9

The logic diagram for the boolean expression $a + b'c$.

When the expression has parentheses, you must construct the subdiagram within the parentheses first.

Example 19.6 Figure 19.10 is the logic diagram for the three-variable expression

$((ab + bc')a)'$

You first form *ab* with one AND gate, then *bc'* with another AND gate. The output of those two are ORed and then ANDed with *a*. Since the entire expression is complemented, an inverter is the last gate. ■

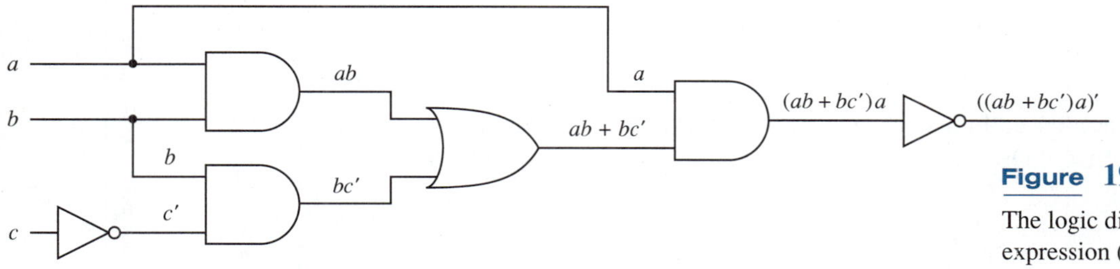

Figure 19.10

The logic diagram for the boolean expression $((ab + bc')a)'$.

Properties of an electrical junction

Figure 19.10 shows two junctions as small black dots where two wires are physically connected. Recall that the physical signal supplied by variable *a* is a voltage. When the signal from input *a* reaches the junction, it does not act like water in a river that encounters a fork in its path. In the river analogy, some of the water takes one path and some takes the other. In a logic diagram it does not happen that part of the signal goes to the input of one AND gate and part goes to the other gate. The full signal from *a* is duplicated at the inputs at both gates.

For those who know some physics, the reason for this behavior is that voltage is a measure of electric potential. The wires have low resistance, which from Ohm's law means there is negligible potential change along a wire. So the voltage along any wires that are physically connected is constant. The full voltage signal is, therefore, available at any point regardless of the junction. (For those who do not know some physics, this may be an incentive to learn!)

The signal from any variable can be duplicated with a junction. The complement of any variable can be produced by an inverter, which can, in turn, also be duplicated by a junction. Rather than show variable-duplicating junctions and variable inverters, they are often omitted from the logic diagram. It is assumed that any variable or its complement is available as input to any gate.

Example 19.7 Figure 19.11 shows an abbreviated version of Figure 19.10 that takes advantage of this assumption. It also recognizes that an AND gate followed by an inverter is equivalent to a NAND gate. ■

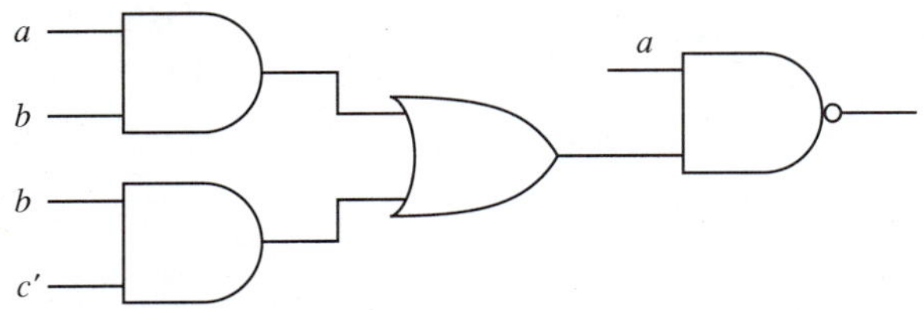

Figure 19.11

An abbreviated version of Figure 19.10.

A disadvantage of this abbreviated diagram is that the three-input nature of the network is not as evident as it is in Figure 19.10.

Example 19.8 Figure 19.12 shows the logic diagram for the four-input boolean expression

$(a'bc \oplus c + a + d)'$

We will assume the precedence of the exclusive OR operator to be less than that of AND and greater than that of OR. ■

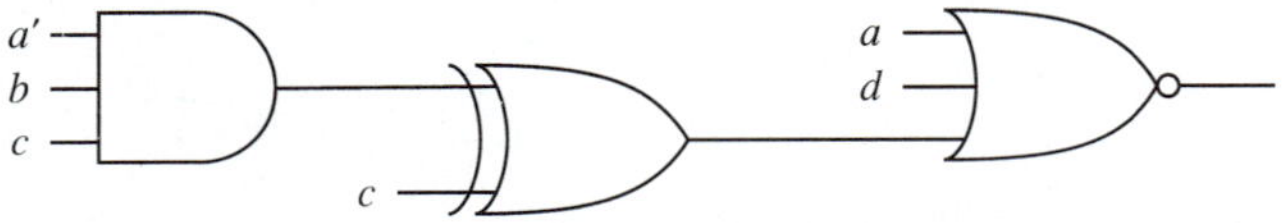

Figure 19.12

The logic diagram for the boolean expression $(a'bc \oplus c + a + d)'$

To write the boolean expression from a given logic diagram, simply label the output of each gate with the appropriate subexpression. If you were given the logic diagram of Figure 19.12 without the boolean expression, you would start by labeling the output of the AND gate as $a'bc$. The output of the XOR gate would be labeled $a'bc \oplus c$, which when passed through the NOR gate produces the full boolean expression.

Truth Tables and Boolean Expressions

One method for constructing a boolean expression from a truth table is to write the expression without parentheses as an OR of several AND terms. Each AND term corresponds to a 1 in the truth table.

Example 19.9 The truth table for $a \oplus b$ has two 1's. The corresponding boolean expression is

$a \oplus b = a'b + ab'$

If a is 0 and b is 1, the first AND term will be 1. If a is 1 and b is 0, the second AND term will be 1. In either case the OR of the two terms will be 1. Furthermore, any other combination of values for a and b will make both AND terms 0, and the boolean expression 0. ■

Example 19.10 Table 19.1 shows x is 1 when $abc = 001$ and $abc = 011$; x is 0 for all other combinations of abc. A corresponding boolean expression is

$$x = a'b'c + a'bc$$

The first AND term, $a'b'c$, is 1 if and only if $abc = 001$. The second is 1 if and only if $abc = 011$. So the OR of the two terms will be 0 except under either of those conditions, duplicating the truth table. ■

Example 19.11 An example with four variables is the truth table for x in Table 19.2. A corresponding expression is

$$x = a'bc'd + a'bcd + abc'd + abcd$$

which gives 1 for the four combinations of a, b, c, and d that have 1 in the truth table. ■

The dual technique is to write an expression as the AND of several OR terms. Each OR term corresponds to a 0 in the truth table.

Example 19.12 The expression from Table 19.4 is

$$x = (a + b' + c')(a' + b' + c)$$

If $abc = 011$, the first OR term is 0. If $abc = 110$, the second OR term is 0. Under either of these conditions, the AND of the OR terms is 0. All other combinations of abc will make both OR terms 1, and the expression 1. ■

a	b	c	x
0	0	0	1
0	0	1	1
0	1	0	1
0	1	1	0
1	0	0	1
1	0	1	1
1	1	0	0
1	1	1	1

Table 19.4

A three-variable truth table.

Given a boolean expression, the most straightforward way to construct the corresponding truth table is to evaluate the expression for all possible combinations of the variables.

Example 19.13 To construct the truth table for

$$x(a, b) = (a \oplus b)' + a'$$

requires the evaluation of

$$x(0, 0) = (0 \oplus 0)' + 0' = 1$$
$$x(0, 1) = (0 \oplus 1)' + 0' = 1$$
$$x(1, 0) = (1 \oplus 0)' + 1' = 0$$
$$x(1, 1) = (1 \oplus 1)' + 1' = 1$$

This example requires the evaluation of all four possible combinations of the two variables *a* and *b*. ▪

If the expression contains more than two variables, sometimes it is easier to convert the boolean expression into an OR of AND terms using the properties and theorems of boolean algebra. The truth table can then be written by inspection.

Example 19.14 The expression in Figure 19.12 reduces to

$x = (a'bc \oplus c + a + d)'$	given
$= (a'bcc' + (a'bc)'c + a + d)'$	definition of $\oplus$
$= ((a'bc)'c + a + d)'$	$cc' = 0$
$= ((a + b' + c')c + a + d)'$	De Morgan
$= (ac + b'c + a + d)'$	distributive
$= (ac)'(b'c)'a'd'$	De Morgan
$= (a' + c')(b + c')a'd'$	De Morgan
$= (a' + a'c')(b + c')d'$	distributive
$= (a'b + a'c' + a'bc' + a'c')d'$	distributive
$= (a'b + a'c' + a'bc')d'$	$y + y = y$
$= a'bd' + a'c'd' + a'bc'd'$	distributive

The truth table has 16 entries. By inspection, insert a 1 where *abd* = 010 (two places), *acd* = 000 (two places), and *abcd* = 0100 (one place). All other entries are 0. The result is Table 19.5. It has three 1's instead of five because *abcd* = 0100 is also one of the places where *abd* = 010 and where *acd* = 000.

This technique saves you from evaluating the original expression 16 times. Actually, that task may not be as difficult as it first appears. With a little thought, you can reason from the original expression that when *d* is 1, the expression inside the parentheses must be 1, and its inverse must be 0 regardless of the values of *a*, *b*, and *c*. Similarly, the expression must be 0 when *a* is 1. That leaves you with only the four evaluations where *ad* = 00. ▪

a	*b*	*c*	*d*	*x*
0	0	0	0	1
0	0	0	1	0
0	0	1	0	0
0	0	1	1	0
0	1	0	0	1
0	1	0	1	0
0	1	1	0	1
0	1	1	1	0
1	0	0	0	0
1	0	0	1	0
1	0	1	0	0
1	0	1	1	0
1	1	0	0	0
1	1	0	1	0
1	1	1	0	0
1	1	1	1	0

Table 19.5

The truth table for the expression in Figure 19.12.

Two-Level Networks

The fact that every boolean expression can be transformed to an OR of AND terms has an important practical effect on the processing speed of the combinational net. When you change a signal at the input of a gate, the output does not respond instantly. Instead, there is a time delay during which the signal works its way through the internal electronic components of the gate. The time it takes for the output of a gate to respond to a change in its input is called the *gate delay*. Different manufacturing processes produce gates with different gate delays. To produce gates with short gate delays is more expensive, and the gates require more power to operate than gates with longer delays. A typical gate delay is 10 ns (nanoseconds), although the delay varies widely depending on the device technology.

Gate delays

Physical limits on processing speed

Ten billionths of a second may not seem like a long time to wait for the output, but in a circuit with a long string of gates that must do its processing in a loop, the time can be significant. By way of comparison, consider the fact that the signal travels through the wires at approximately the speed of light, which is 3.0×10^8 m/s (meters per second). That is 30 cm, or about a foot, in 1 ns. In 10 ns, the time of a typical gate delay, the signal can travel through 3 m of wire. This is such a long distance compared to the size of an integrated circuit or circuit board that the gate delay is, for all practical purposes, responsible for the limit on a network's processing speed.

Example 19.15 Consider the circuit of Figure 19.12. If the gate delay is 10 ns, a change in b requires 10 ns to propagate through the AND gate, 10 ns to propagate through the XOR gate, and another 10 ns to propagate through the NOR gate. That is a total of 30 ns of propagation time. (We will ignore the propagation delay through any inverters.)

Now consider that we used boolean algebra to write the expression for this circuit as an OR of AND terms:

$$x = (a'bc \oplus c + a + d)'$$
$$= a'bd' + a'c'd' + a'bc'd'$$

Figure 19.13 shows the corresponding circuit. It is called a two-level network because a change in the input requires only two gate delays to propagate to the output. ■

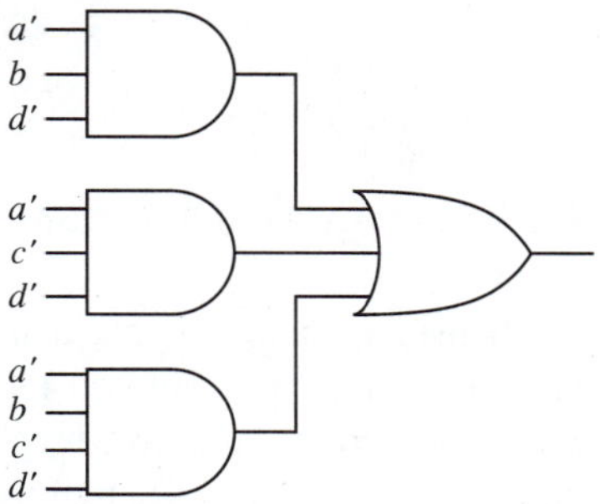

Figure 19.13

The two-level AND-OR network equivalent to the network of Figure 19.12.

Reducing the processing time from 30 ns to 20 ns is a 33% improvement in speed, which is significant. Since any boolean expression can be transformed to an OR of AND terms, which corresponds to a two-level AND-OR network, it follows that any function can be implemented with a combinational net with a processing time of two gate delays at most.

The same principle applies to the dual. It is always possible to transform a boolean expression to an AND of OR terms, which corresponds to a two-level OR-AND network. Such a network has a processing time of two gate delays at most. To obtain the boolean expression as an AND of OR terms, you can first obtain the complement as an OR of AND terms, then use De Morgan's law.

Example 19.16 Figure 19.14 is the two-level OR-AND network of Table 19.4 for the expression

$$x = (a + b' + c')(a' + b' + c)$$

Recall that each OR term corresponds to a 0 in the truth table. ■

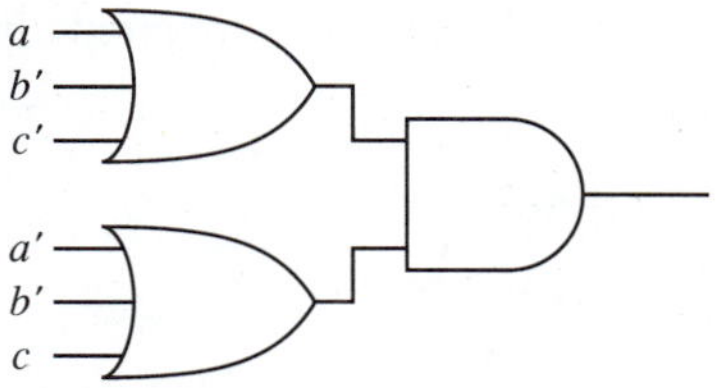

Figure 19.14

The two-level OR-AND network of Table 19.4.

Example 19.17 The expression from Figure 19.9 is

$$x = a + b'c$$

To transform this expression into an AND of OR terms, first write its complement as

$$\begin{aligned} x' &= (a + b'c)' \\ &= a'(b'c)' \\ &= a'(b + c') \\ &= a'b + a'c' \end{aligned}$$

which is an OR of AND terms. Now use De Morgan's law to write x as

$$\begin{aligned} x &= (x')' \\ &= (a'b + a'c')' \\ &= (a'b)'(a'c')' \\ &= (a + b')(a + c) \end{aligned}$$

which is an AND of OR terms. ■

It usually happens that a network with three or more levels requires fewer gates than the equivalent two-level net. Since a gate occupies physical space in an integrated circuit, the two-level net achieves its faster processing time at the expense of the extra space required for the additional gates.

The fundamental space/time tradeoff

This is yet another example of the space/time tradeoff in computer science. It is remarkable that the same space/time principle is manifest from software at the highest level of abstraction to hardware at the lowest level. It is truly a fundamental principle.

The Ubiquitous NAND

The expression $(abc)'$ represents a three-input NAND gate. De Morgan's law states that

$$(abc)' = a' + b' + c'$$

You can visualize the second expression as the output of an OR gate that inverts each input before performing the OR operation. Logic diagrams occasionally draw the NAND gate as an inverted input NOR, as in Figure 19.15(a).

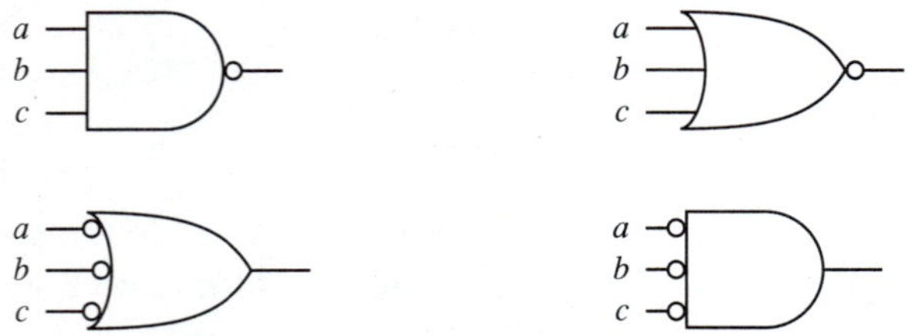

(a) A NAND gate as an inverted input OR gate.

(b) A NOR gate as an inverted input AND gate.

Figure 19.15

Equivalent gates.

The dual concept follows from the dual expressions

$$(a + b + c)' = a'b'c'$$

A NOR gate is equivalent to an AND gate that inverts its inputs as in Figure 19.15(b).

Carrying this idea one step further to two-level networks, consider the equivalence of

$$abc + def = [(abc)'(def)']'$$

which again follows from De Morgan's law. The first expression represents a two-level AND-OR network, while the second represents a two-level NAND-NAND network. Figure 19.16 shows the equivalent circuits.

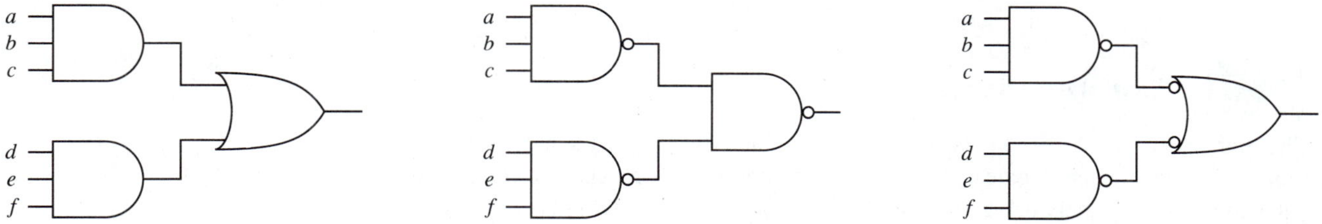

(a) An AND-OR net. **(b)** The equivalent NAND-NAND net. **(c)** The same NAND-NAND net as in part (b).

Figure 19.16

An AND-OR net and its equivalent NAND-NAND net.

Figure 19.16(a) shows an AND-OR net with two AND gates and one OR. You can make the equivalent circuit entirely out of NAND gates, as shown in (b). Part (c) shows the same network as (b) but with the last NAND drawn as an inverted-input OR. This drawing style makes it apparent that the complement following the AND operation cancels the complement preceding the OR operation. The shape of the gate symbols becomes similar to those in the AND-OR net, which helps to convey the meaning of the network.

Not only can you replace an arbitrary AND-OR network entirely with NAND gates, you can also construct an inverter from a NAND gate by connecting the NAND inputs together, as shown in Figure 19.17. Since the NAND produces $(ab)'$ with input a and b, if you force $b = a$ the gate will produce $(a \cdot a)' = a'$, the complement of a.

Conceptually, you can construct any combinational net from only NAND gates. Furthermore, NAND gates are usually easier to manufacture than either AND or OR gates. Consequently, the NAND gate is by far the most common gate found in integrated circuits.

Of course, the same principle applies to the dual network. De Morgan's law for two-level networks is

$$(a + b + c)\,(d + e + f) = [(a + b + c)' + (d + e + f)']'$$

which shows that an OR-AND network is equivalent to a NOR-NOR network. Figure 19.18 is the dual network of Figure 19.16.

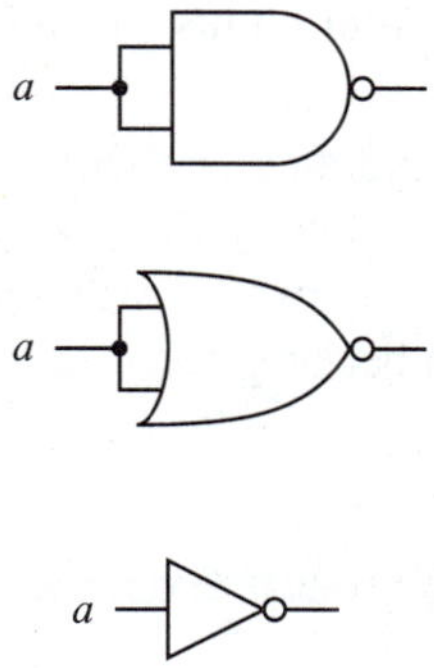

Figure 19.17

Three equivalent circuits.

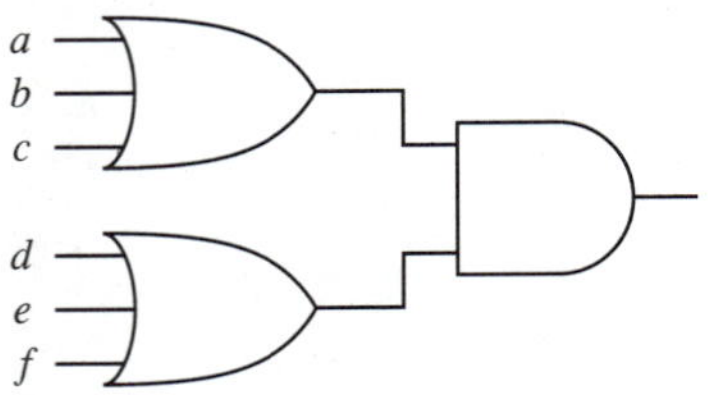

(a) An OR-AND net.

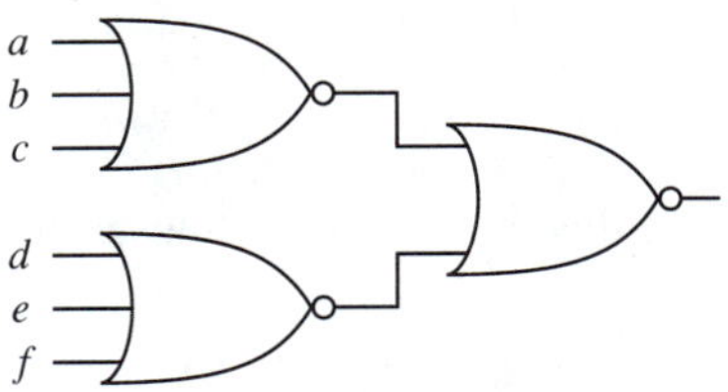

(b) The equivalent NOR-NOR net.

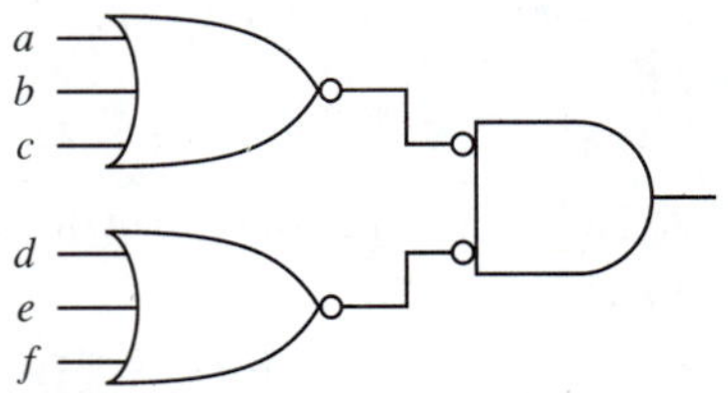

(c) The same NOR-NOR net as in part (b).

Figure 19.18

An OR-AND net and its equivalent NOR-NOR net.

The same reasoning that applies to NAND networks also applies to NOR networks. Any combinational net can be written as a two-level OR-AND net, which can be written as NOR-NOR. Connecting the inputs of a NOR makes an inverter. You can conceptually construct any combinational network with only NOR gates.

19.3 Combinational Design

The high speed of two-level networks gives them an advantage over networks with more than two levels of gates. Sometimes it is possible to reduce the number of gates in a two-level network and retain the processing speed of two gate delays.

Example 19.18 The boolean expression for the logic diagram in Figure 19.13 is

$$x(a, b, c, d) = a'bd' + a'c'd' + a'bc'd'$$

which can be simplified using the absorption property to

$$\begin{aligned} x(a, b, c, d) &= a'bd' + (a'c'd') + (a'c'd')b \\ &= a'bd' + a'c'd' \end{aligned}$$

This expression also corresponds to a two-level network, but it requires only two three-input AND gates and a two-input OR gate compared to three AND gates, one of which has four inputs, and a three-input OR gate. ■

Minimizing the number of gates in a two-level network is not always straightforward with boolean algebra. This section presents a graphical method for designing two-level networks with three or four variables that contain the minimum possible number of gates.

Canonical Expressions

The previous section showed that any boolean expression can be transformed to a two-level OR of AND terms. To minimize the two-level network, it is desirable to first make each AND term contain all input variables exactly once. Such an AND term is called a *minterm*. It is always possible to transform an OR of AND terms into an OR of minterms.

Minterms

Example 19.19 Consider the boolean expression

$$x(a, b, c) = abc + a'bc + ab$$

The first two AND terms are minterms because they contain all three variables, but the last is not. The transformation is

$$\begin{aligned} x &= abc + a'bc + ab \\ &= abc + a'bc + ab(c + c') \\ &= abc + a'bc + abc + abc' \\ &= abc + a'bc + abc' \end{aligned}$$

The last expression is called a *canonical expression* because it is an OR of minterms in which no two identical minterms appear. ■

The definition of a canonical expression

A canonical expression is directly related to the truth table because each minterm in the expression represents a 1 in the truth table. A convenient shorthand notation for a canonical expression and its corresponding truth table is called *sigma notation*, which consists of the uppercase Greek letter sigma (Σ) followed by a list of decimal numbers that specify the rows in the truth table that contain 1's. The uppercase sigma represents the OR operation. It is understood that all the rows not listed contain 0's.

Example 19.20 In the previous example, since the canonical expression for x has three minterms, its truth table has three 1's. Table 19.6 shows the truth table for this function. It labels each row with the decimal number equivalent of the binary number abc. The corresponding sigma notation for this function is

$$x(a, b, c) = \Sigma(3, 6, 7)$$

since rows 3, 6, and 7 contain 1's. ■

Row (dec)	*a*	*b*	*c*	*x*
0	0	0	0	0
1	0	0	1	0
2	0	1	0	0
3	0	1	1	1
4	1	0	0	0
5	1	0	1	0
6	1	1	0	1
7	1	1	1	1

Table 19.6

The truth table for a canonical expression.

The dual canonical expression is an AND of OR terms, each of which contains all variables once, with no OR terms duplicated. The corresponding notation for this canonical expression contains the list of 0's in the truth table. The uppercase Greek letter pi (Π), which represents the AND operation, is used instead of sigma.

Example 19.21 The dual canonical expression for the previous example is

$$x(a, b, c) = (a + b + c)\ (a + b + c')\ (a + b' + c)(a' + b + c)\ (a' + b + c')$$

which is written in pi notation as

$$x(a, b, c) = \Pi(0, 1, 2, 4, 5)$$

since these are the five rows that contain 0's in the truth table. ■

Circuits and Chips: The Evolution of Electronics Manufacturing

Almost everyone is aware of the microelectronics revolution of the last several decades. Improvements in the price-performance ratio of computers have made it possible to buy a fast portable or laptop computer for $1000 today; in 1960, a machine of equivalent computational capacity was affordable only for the wealthiest businesses, occupied a large room, and took much longer to run programs.

Before 1951, clunky electromechanical relays, which depended on physical motion to implement switching, were used in computers. The UNIVAC I, completed in June 1951, was the first general-purpose computer to use vacuum tubes. Although vacuum tubes were much faster than the relays, they tended to burn out frequently. In 1948, the solid state transistor was invented at Bell Labs. Because it was smaller, lighter, and more reliable than the vacuum tube, by 1959 it had replaced the vacuum tube in most CPUs.

When transistors first moved from the research lab into regular production, they looked like a pencil-eraser-sized dot of plastic with a few pin-length wires sticking out. Each transistor acted like a simple switch; it either allowed electricity to flow from its input wire to its output wire or it inhibited the flow depending on the state of the control wire. Complex circuits could be constructed by assembling a number of transistors, cascading their interdependently switched signals to implement the logical behavior required for the application at hand.

Researchers soon found that a wafer of silicon could house a number of circuits laid out adjacent to one another. Silicon is a semiconducting material that adopts a well-differentiated charged or uncharged state. The pieces of silicon changed state rapidly on demand by varying the electrical characteristics of their interconnections. Between 1965 and 1970, small pieces of silicon replaced transistors in CPUs, and by the mid-1970s, silicon chips that contained an entire CPU, called microprocessors, were being produced.

The chip manufacturing process requires extremely precise engineering, as well as attention to cleanliness—workers have to wear surgical-quality scrub masks and gowns and work in atmospherically filtered rooms in order to prevent impurities from contaminating a chip. The technique of photolithography makes possible a hands-free manufacturing process in which precise engineering tolerances can be attained largely automatically in circuits so tiny that they can only be seen with a microscope. Photolithography involves a process similar to hobby photography. In photography, exposure to light changes the physiochemical structure of film so that prints can be made by shining light back through the negative onto photographic paper. For circuit printing, light is shone through a negative called a mask. The mask blocks exposure of most of the surface, allowing light to strike only the chemicals where the conductive circuit is to be etched. Subsequent chemical baths prepare the chip to have other layers sandwiched on top, which leads to the construction of three-dimensional integrated chips.

Circuits within the individual layers may be connected with circuits on other levels by vertical conduits. This is the technique that allows us to have an entire CPU on a single chip. The complexity of activity now supported within a chip has led to the curious *pin-out problem:* the centipede-like chips, with their 16 or so wire-like pins, have barely enough channels to communicate with the other chips in the computer, so bottlenecks occur while the 16 pins transmit information in or out. Unfortunately, it is physically impossible to attach many more pins to such a tiny chip.

Because a misprinted circuit can make a whole chip useless, manufacturers obviously need to minimize waste. To do so, they have turned to other current manufacturing techniques, including computer-aided design (CAD), which can help them optimize circuit layout, by minimizing path length and channel crosstalk while maximizing chip density. With millions of electronic switches now necessary per chip, humans need computers to help manage the task of designing tomorrow's even more complex computers.

Example 19.22 Using the sigma notation, x and y from Table 19.1 are

$$x(a, b, c) = \Sigma(1, 3)$$
$$y(a, b, c) = \Sigma(3, 4)$$

Functions x and y from Table 19.2 are

$$x(a, b, c, d) = \Sigma(5, 7, 13, 15)$$
$$y(a, b, c, d) = \Sigma(4, 5, 12, 13)$$

This is a more compact notation than the canonical boolean expressions or the truth tables. ■

The remainder of this section will assume that the function to be minimized has been transformed to its unique canonical expression, or that its truth table has been given or determined.

Three-Variable Karnaugh Maps

Distance between minterms

Minimization of two-level networks is based on the concept of distance. The *distance* between two minterms is the number of places in which they differ.

Example 19.23 Consider the canonical expression for x,

$$x(a, b, c) = a'bc + abc + abc'$$

You can minimize it algebraically as follows:

$$\begin{aligned} x(a, b, c) &= a'bc + abc + abc' \\ &= a'bc + abc + abc + abc' \\ &= (a' + a)bc + ab(c + c') \\ &= bc + ab \end{aligned}$$

In this example, the distance between $a'bc$ and abc is 1 because a' and a are the only variables that differ. Variables b and c are the same in both. The distance between minterms $a'bc$ and abc' is 2 because a' and c in $a'bc$ differ from a and c' in abc'. ■

The key to minimization is recognizing those minterms that differ by one variable. In the previous example, the first and second minterms differ by 1, as do the second and third. To minimize to the fullest, we had to duplicate the second minterm so it could be combined with both the first and third minterms. A *Karnaugh map* is a truth table arranged so that adjacent entries represent minterms that differ by 1.

a \ bc	00	01	11	10
0	0	0	1	0
1	0	0	1	1

Figure 19.19

A Karnaugh map for a function of three variables.

Example 19.24 Figure 19.19 shows the Karnaugh map for the previous example. The rows and columns are arranged so that abc = 011 differs by 1 from abc = 111, and abc = 111 differs by 1 from abc = 110. The bottom row contains the truth table entries for which $a = 1$, the two right columns contain entries for which $b = 1$, and the two middle columns entries for which $c = 1$.

Figure 19.20 shows the minimization process. Empty cells are assumed to contain 0's, which are omitted to reduce clutter in the diagram. Grouping two adjacent 1's with an oval represents combining two minterms that differ by one variable. The 1 in the cell for $abc = 111$ is covered by two ovals because minterm abc had to be duplicated to minimize to the fullest. ■

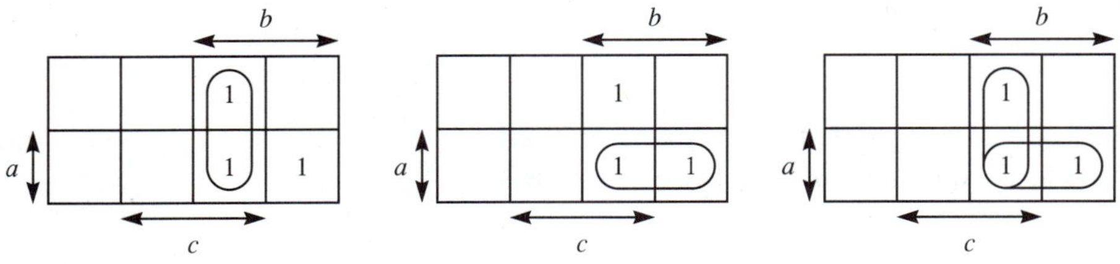

(a) $a'bc + abc = bc$ (b) $abc + abc' = ab$ (c) $x = bc + ab$

Figure 19.20 Minimizing a function of three variables.

The general minimization procedure is to first write the 1's from the truth table in the form of a Karnaugh map. Then determine by visual inspection the best set of ovals that will cover all the 1's. Each oval represents an AND term in the minimized expression. Given the optimum set of ovals that cover the 1's, you finally write the corresponding AND terms, one for each oval.

Example 19.25 Figure 19.21 illustrates the last step in the previous example for the two 1's covered by the oval in Figure 19.20(a). Given the oval in the third column of the Karnaugh map, the problem is to write the corresponding AND term. If you visualize the region for b as the last two columns and the region for c as the middle two columns, you can see that the third column is the intersection of those two regions as if the Karnaugh map were a Venn diagram. Therefore, the AND term for that oval is bc. ■

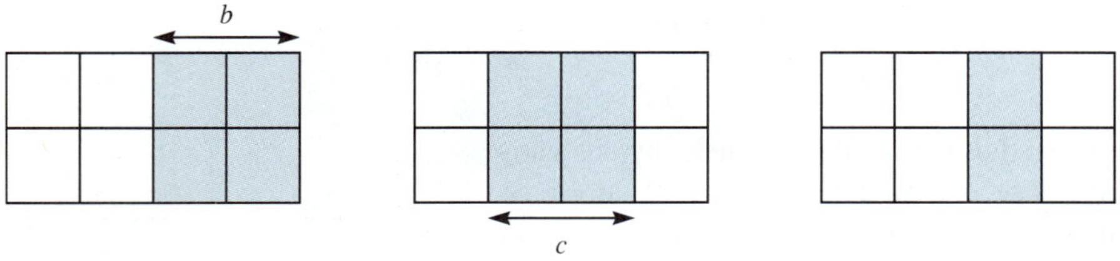

(a) Region b. (b) Region c. (c) Region bc.

Figure 19.21 The intersection of two regions for the 1's of Figure 19.20(a).

When the original truth table is given in sigma notation, use the decimal labels of Figure 19.22 to insert 1's in the Karnaugh map.

Example 19.26 Suppose the function of the previous example was originally given in sigma notation as

$$x(a, b, c) = a'bc + abc' + abc$$
$$= \Sigma(3, 6, 7)$$

For example, $a'bc$ is 1 when

$$abc = 011 \text{ (bin)}$$
$$= 3 \text{ (dec)}$$

So for this minterm, you would insert 1 in the cell labeled 3 in Figure 19.22. You would also insert 1's in the cells labeled 6 and 7, then proceed to minimize the function. ■

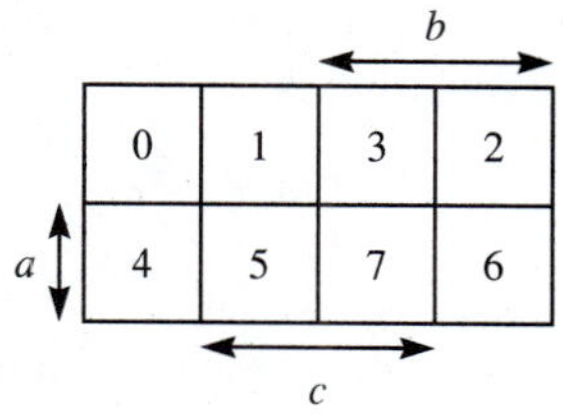

Figure 19.22

Decimal labels for the minterms in the Karnaugh map.

A strategy for minimizing

The minimization procedure requires you to determine the best set of ovals that will cover all the 1's in the Karnaugh map. "Best" means the set that corresponds to a two-level network with the least number of gates and the least number of inputs per gate. The number of ovals equals the number of AND gates. The more 1's an oval covers, the smaller the number of inputs to the corresponding AND gate. It follows that you want the smallest number of ovals, with each oval as large as possible such that the ovals cover all the 1's and no 0's. It is permissible for a 1 to be covered by several ovals. The next few examples show the general strategy.

Example 19.27 Figure 19.23 shows the minimization of

$$x(a, b, c) = \Sigma(4, 6)$$

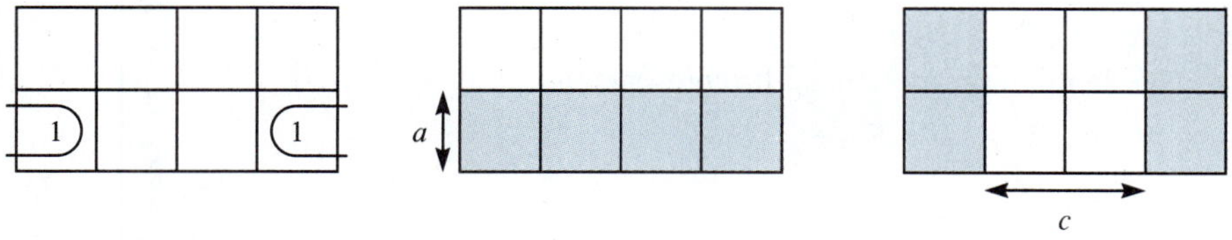

(a) Minimization with two corner minterms.

(b) Region a.

(c) Region c'.

Figure 19.23

The minimized expression ac'.

It may appear that cells 4 and 6 are not adjacent, but in fact they are. Cells 4 and 6 represent minterms $ab'c'$ and abc', which differ by one variable. Cells 0 and 2 are adjacent by the same reasoning. You should think of the Karnaugh map as being able to wrap around so that its left and right sides are adjacent. The single oval in Figure 19.23(a) is drawn as two open-ended half ovals to convey this property of the Karnaugh map.

This example also illustrates complement regions. Figure 19.23(c) shows the region that corresponds to c', those Karnaugh map cells for which $c = 0$. The intersection of regions a and c' is the region corresponding to cells 4 and 6. The minimized expression is

$$x(a, b, c) = \Sigma(4, 6)$$
$$= ac'$$

which requires a single two-input AND gate with no OR gate. ■

Example 19.28 Figure 19.24 shows a common minimization mistake. To minimize

$$x(a, b, c) = \Sigma(0, 1, 5, 7)$$

you may be tempted to first group minterms 1 and 5 as in Figure 19.24(a). That is a bad first choice because minterm 1 is adjacent to both 0 and 5, and minterm 5 is adjacent to both 1 and 7. On the other hand, minterm 0 is only adjacent to 1. To cover 0 with the largest possible oval you must group it with 1. Similarly, minterm 7 is only adjacent to 5. To cover 7 with the largest possible oval you must group it with 5.

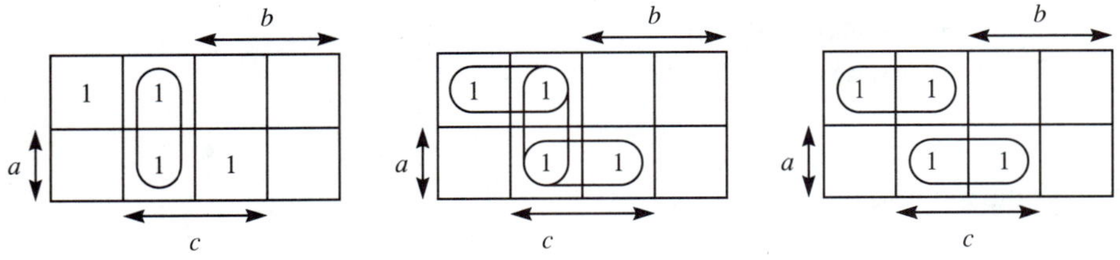

(a) A bad strategy.

(b) The result of the bad strategy.

(c) The correct minimization.

Figure 19.24 The result of a bad first choice.

Figure 19.24(b) shows the result of these minterm groupings. It represents the expression

$$x(a, b, c) = \Sigma(0, 1, 5, 7)$$
$$= a'b' + b'c + ac$$

which requires three two-input AND gates and a three-input OR gate. But the grouping of the first choice is not necessary. Figure 19.24(c) shows the correct minimization, which represents

$$x(a, b, c) = \Sigma(0, 1, 5, 7)$$
$$= a'b' + ac$$

This implementation requires only two two-input AND gates and a two-input OR gate. ■

The rule of thumb that the previous example teaches us is to start a grouping with minterms that have only one nearest neighbor. Since their neighbors must be grouped with them in any event, you may be spared an unnecessary grouping of their neighbors.

Another common mistake is failing to recognize a large grouping of 1's, as the following example illustrates.

Example 19.29 Figure 19.25(a) shows the minimization of a three-variable function as

$$x(a, b, c) = \Sigma(0, 2, 4, 6, 7)$$
$$= b'c' + bc' + ab$$

which requires three two-input AND gates and one three-input OR gate. Figure 19.25(b) shows the correct minimization as

$$x(a, b, c) = c' + ab$$

which requires only one two-input AND gate and a two-input OR gate. ■

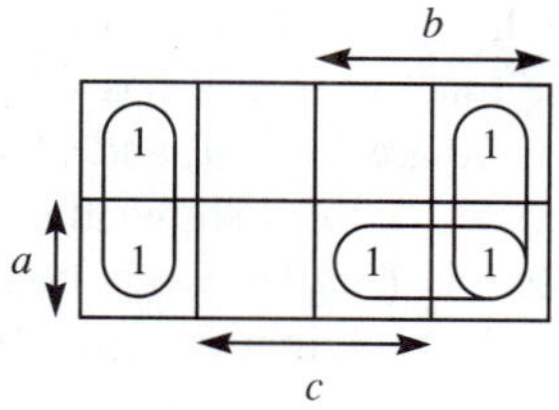

(a) An incorrect minimization.

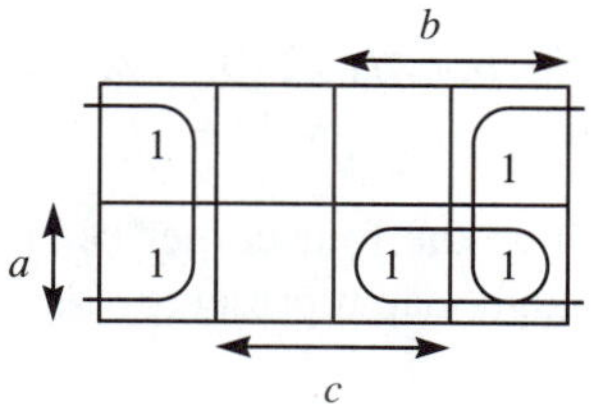

(b) The correct minimization.

Figure 19.25

Failing to recognize a large grouping.

In a three-variable problem, a grouping of four 1's corresponds to an AND term of only one variable. Since the number of 1's in a group must correspond to an intersection of regions for *a, b,* and *c* and their complements, the number of 1's in a group must be a power of 2. For example, an oval can cover one, two, or four 1's but never three or five.

Four-Variable Karnaugh Maps

Minimization of a four-variable network follows the same procedure as a three-variable network, except that the Karnaugh map has twice as many entries. Figure 19.26(a) shows the arrangement of cells. Not only are minterms 0 adjacent to 2 and 4 adjacent to 6, but minterm 12 is adjacent to 14, and 8 to 10. Also, cells on the top row are adjacent to the corresponding cells on the bottom row. Minterm 0 is adjacent to 8, 1 to 9, 3 to 11, and 2 to 10.

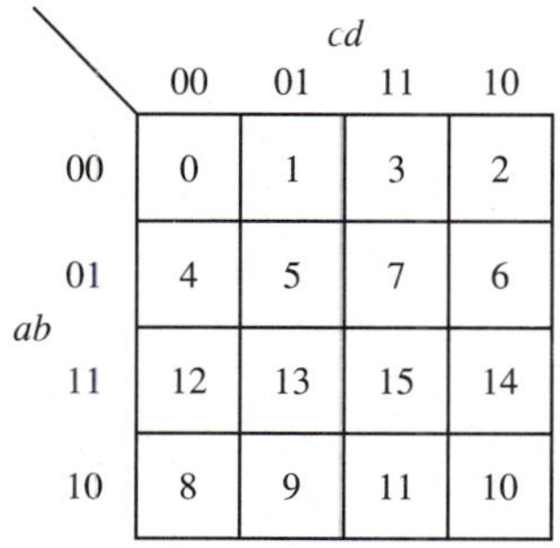

(a) Decimal labels for the minterms in the Karnaugh map.

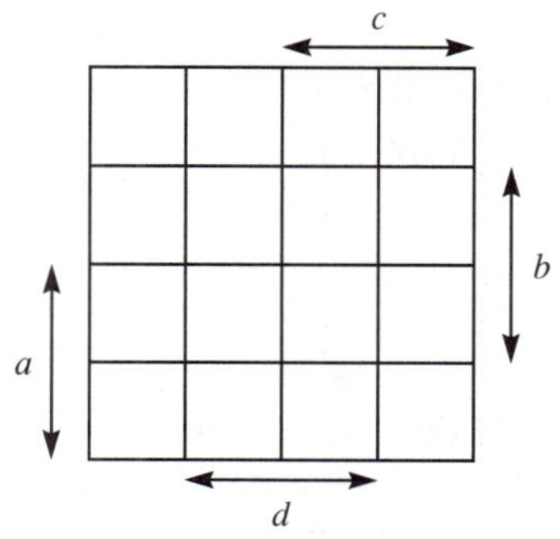

(b) The regions where the variables are 1.

Figure 19.26

The Karnaugh map for a function of four variables.

Each cell in a three-variable Karnaugh map has three adjacent cells. In a four-variable map, each cell has four adjacent cells. For example, the cells adjacent to minterm 10 are 2, 8, 11, and 14. Those adjacent to 4 are 0, 5, 6, and 12.

Figure 19.26(b) shows the regions of the truth table where the variables are 1. Variable a is 1 in the two bottom rows, and b is 1 in the two middle rows. Variable c is 1 in the two right columns, and d is 1in the two middle columns.

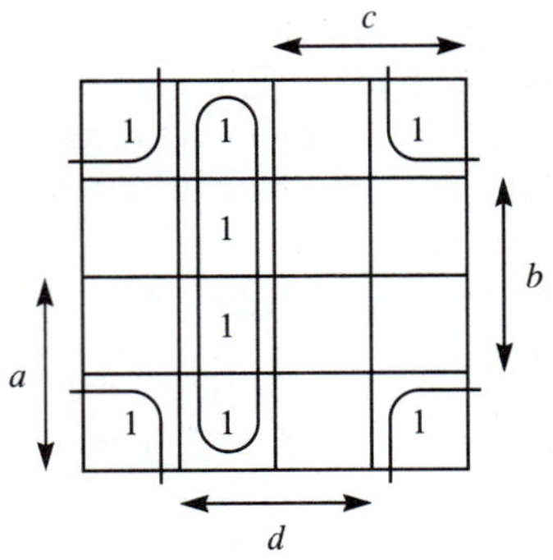

Figure 19.27

Minimizing a function of four variables.

Example 19.30 Figure 19.27 shows the minimization

$$x(a, b, c, d) = \Sigma(0, 1, 2, 5, 8, 9, 10, 13)$$
$$= c'd + b'd'$$

Note that the four corner cells can be grouped as $b'd'$. The second column of the Karnaugh map represents $c'd$. ■

Example 19.31 Figure 19.28 shows the minimization

$$x(a, b, c, d) = \Sigma(0, 1, 2, 5, 8, 9, 10)$$
$$= a'c'd + b'c' + b'd'$$

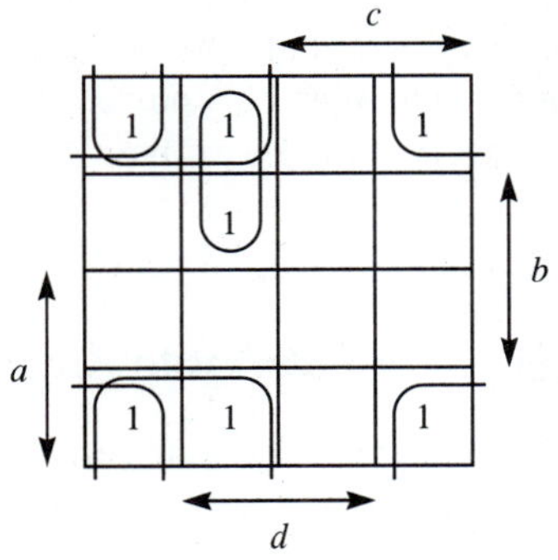

Figure 19.28

The expression of Figure 19.27 with one less minterm.

Even though it differs from the previous example by the omission of a single term, the minimization is much different.

Minterm 5 has only one adjacent 1, so it is grouped first by our rule of thumb with minterm 1. The AND term for this group is $a'c'd$, which you can determine by visualizing the intersection of the top two rows (a'), the left two columns (c'), and the middle two columns (d).

Covering minterm 9 with the largest oval requires you to group it with minterms 0, 1, and 8, not just 8. The AND term for this group is $b'c'$, which you can determine by visualizing the intersection of the top and bottom rows (b') with the left two columns (c').

The remaining uncovered 1's are minterms 2 and 10, which are grouped with 0 and 8 as before. ■

Example 19.32 Figure 19.29 shows that the minimization may not be unique. Two valid minimizations of this function are

$$x(a, b, c, d) = \Sigma(0, 4, 7, 8, 12, 13, 15)$$
$$= c'd' + bcd + abc'$$
$$= c'd' + bcd + abd$$

The first 1 you should group is minterm 7, since it has only one adjacent 1. Minterm 0 must be grouped with 4, 8, and 12, since there is no other possible group for it. That leaves minterm 13, which can be grouped with either 12 or 15. ■

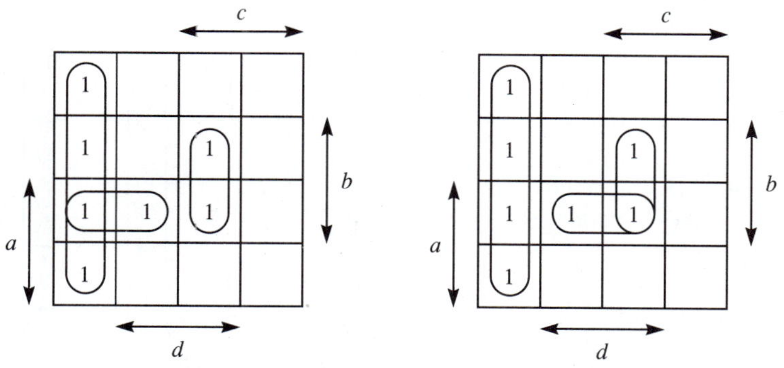

(a) One possible minimization. (b) A different minimization.

Figure 19.29

Two different correct minimizations.

Minimizing a four-variable function is not always straightforward. Sometimes you must simply experiment with several groupings in order to determine the true minimum.

Example 19.33 Figure 19.30 shows such a problem. The function is

$$\Sigma(0, 1, 2, 3, 5, 6, 7, 8, 9, 12, 13, 14)$$

Figure 19.30(a) is the result of the following reasoning. Consider minterm 12. The largest group it belongs to is the group of four corresponding to ac′. Similarly, the largest group minterm 6 belongs to is the group of four, $a'c$. Given these two groupings, you can group minterm 5 in $c'd$, minterm 0 in $a'b'$, and minterm 14 in bcd'. The expression

$$ac' + a'c + c'd + a'b' + bcd'$$

is plausible because none of the groupings looks redundant. You cannot remove any oval without uncovering a 1.

Given the selection of the first two groups, the remaining three groups are the best choices possible. The problem is in the selection of the second group.

Figure 19.30(b) is the result of the following reasoning. Group minterm 12 with ac' as before. Now consider minterm 14. You must group it with either 12 or 6. Since 12 is covered, group 14 with 6. Group the remaining minterms—0, 1, 2, 3, 5, 7—most efficiently, as in Figure 19.30(b). The resulting expression,

$$ac' + a'd + a'b' + bcd'$$

requires one fewer AND gate than Figure 19.30(a).

This is a tricky problem because in general you should cover a 1 with the largest possible group. That general rule does not apply in this problem, however. Once you determine the group ac', you should not place minterm 6 in the largest possible group.

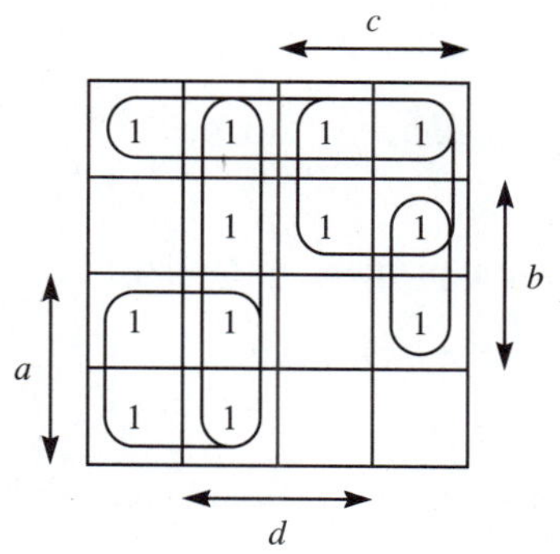

(a) A plausible but incorrect minimization.

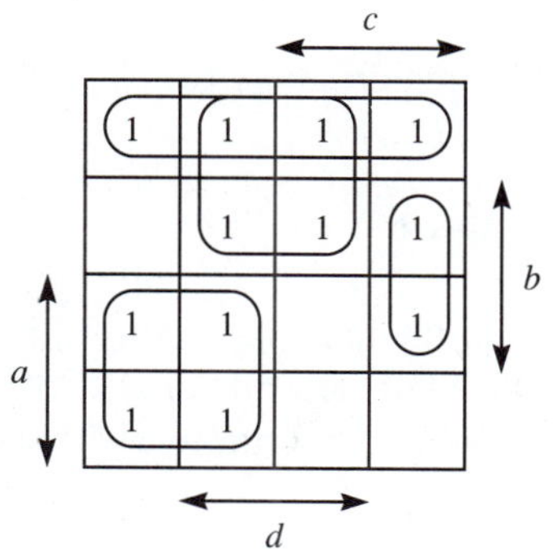

(b) A correct minimization.

Figure 19.30

A complicated minimization problem.

Figure 19.31 shows that this solution is not unique. It begins by grouping minterm 6 in $a'c$, then minterm 14 with 12. The result is

$$a'c + b'c' + c'd + abd'$$

■

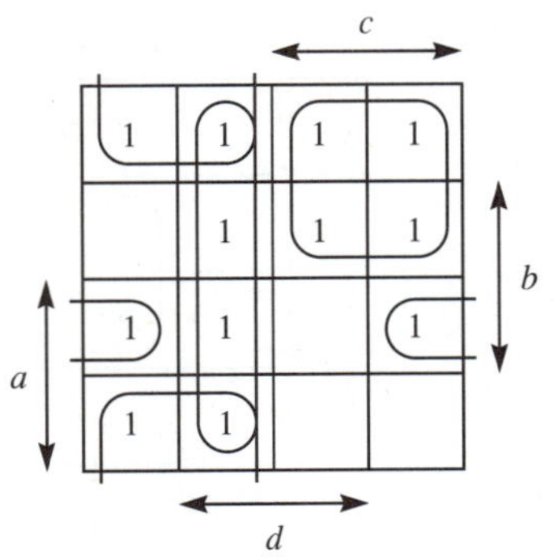

Figure 19.31

Another correct minimization of the function of Figure 19.30.

How do you know which minterms and groupings to consider when confronted with a complicated Karnaugh map? It simply takes practice, reasoning, and a little experimentation.

Dual Karnaugh Maps

To minimize a function in an AND of OR terms, minimize the complement of the function in the OR of AND terms, and use De Morgan's law.

Example 19.34 Figure 19.32 shows the minimization of the complement of the function in Figure 19.20. The original function is

$$x(a, b, c) = \Sigma(3, 6, 7)$$
$$= \Pi(0, 1, 2, 4, 5)$$

Its complement, minimized as shown in the figure, is

$$x'(a, b, c) = \Sigma(0, 1, 2, 4, 5)$$
$$= b' + a'c'$$

The original function in the minimized AND of OR terms form is

$$x(a, b, c) = (x'(a, b, c))'$$
$$= (b' + a'c')'$$
$$= b(a + c)$$

which requires only two gates, compared to three with the minimized OR of AND expression,

$$x(a, b, c) = bc + ab$$

■

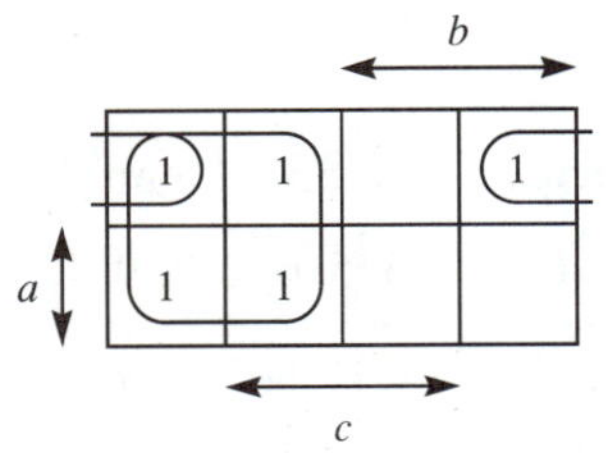

Figure 19.32

The complement of the function in Figure 19.20.

In the previous example, it pays to implement the function with a two-level NOR-NOR network instead of a NAND-NAND network. In general, you must minimize both forms to determine which requires fewer gates.

Don't-Care Conditions

Sometimes a combinational network is designed to process only some of the input combinations. The other combinations are not ever expected to be present in the input. These combinations are called *don't-care conditions* because you do not care what the output is if those conditions would ever appear.

Don't-care conditions give you extra flexibility in the minimization process. You can arbitrarily design the net to produce either 0 or 1 when a don't-care condition is present. By selectively choosing some don't-care conditions to produce 1 and others to produce 0, you can improve the minimization.

Example 19.35 Figure 19.33(a) shows minimization of

$$x(a, b, c) = \Sigma(2, 4, 6)$$
$$= bc' + ac'$$

without don't-care conditions. Now suppose that instead of requiring minterms 0 and 7 to produce 0, the problem specifies that those minterms can produce either 0 or 1. The notation for this specification is

$$x(a, b, c) = \Sigma(2, 4, 6) + \mathrm{d}(0, 7)$$

where d preceding the minterm labels stands for a don't-care condition. Figure 19.33(b) shows × in the Karnaugh map cells for don't-care conditions.

When you minimize with don't-care conditions you are free to cover or not cover a cell with an ×. An × acts like a wild card in that you can treat it as a 0 or a 1 as you like. In this problem, if you treat minterm 0 as a 1, and 7 as a 0, the minimization is

$$x(a, b, c) = \Sigma(2, 4, 6) + \mathrm{d}(0, 7)$$
$$= \Sigma(0, 2, 4, 6)$$
$$= c'$$

The function without don't-care conditions requires two AND gates and one OR gate, while this function requires no AND or OR gates. ■

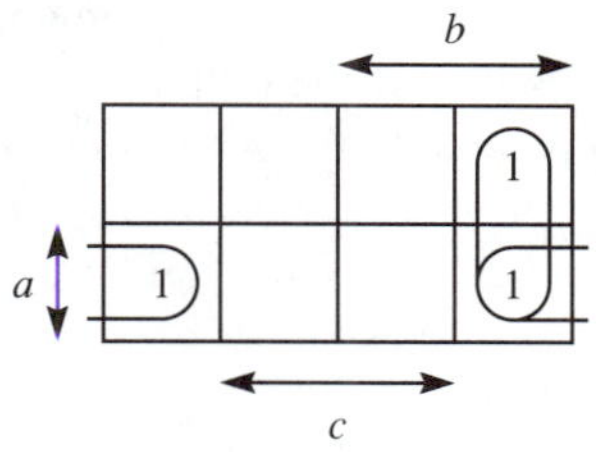

(a) Minimizing a function without don't-care conditions.

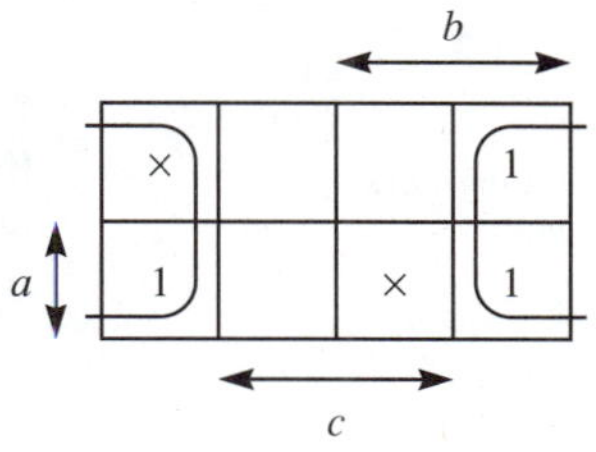

(b) Minimizing the same function with don't-care conditions.

Figure 19.33

Don't-care conditions.

19.4 Combinational Devices

This section describes some combinational devices that are commonly used in computer design. Each device can be specified as a black box with a corresponding truth table to define how the outputs depend on the inputs. Since all devices in this section are combinational, they can be implemented with two-level AND-OR networks. Some implementations shown here trade off processing time for less space, that is, fewer gates, and have more than two levels.

Viewpoints

Several of the following devices have an input line called *enable*. The enable line acts like the on/off switch of an appliance. If the enable line is 0, the output lines are all 0's regardless of the values of the input lines. The device is turned off, or disabled. If the enable line is 1, the output lines depend on the input lines according to the function that specifies the device. The device is turned on, or enabled.

An AND gate can implement the enable property as shown in Figure 19.34(a). Line a is one of the outputs from the combinational net (not shown in the figure), which is input to the AND gate. The other input to the AND gate is the enable line.

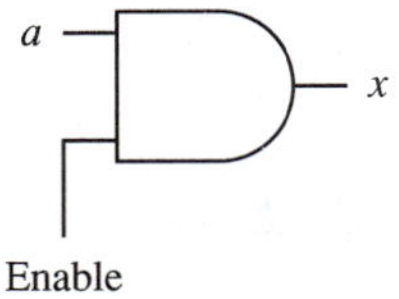

(a) Logic diagram of enable gate.

Enable = 1	
a	x
0	0
1	1

(b) Truth table with the device turned on.

Enable = 0	
a	x
0	0
1	0

(c) Truth table with the device turned off.

Figure 19.34

AND input as an enable.

When the enable line is 1,

$$\begin{aligned} x &= a \cdot (\text{enable}) \\ &= a \cdot 1 \\ &= a \end{aligned}$$

and the output equals the input as in Figure 19.34(b). When the enable line is 0,

$$\begin{aligned} x &= a \cdot (\text{enable}) \\ &= a \cdot 0 \\ &= 0 \end{aligned}$$

regardless of the input as in Figure 19.34(c).

Implementing the enable property does not require a new "enable gate." It only requires that you adopt a different viewpoint of the familiar AND gate. You can think of input a as a data line and enable as a control line. The enable controls the data by either letting it pass through the gate unchanged or preventing it from being output.

Another useful gate is the *selective inverter.* For input, it has a data line and an invert line. If the invert line is 1, the output is the complement of the data line. If the invert line is 0, the data passes through to the output unchanged.

Figure 19.35(a) shows that the selective inverter is an XOR gate considered with a different viewpoint than it was previously. When the invert line is 1,

$$\begin{aligned} x &= a \oplus (\text{invert}) \\ &= a' \cdot (\text{invert}) + a \cdot (\text{invert})' \\ &= a' \cdot 1 + a \cdot 1' \\ &= a' \end{aligned}$$

and the output equals the complement of the data input, as in Figure 19.35(b).

When the invert line is 0,

$$\begin{aligned} x &= a \oplus (\text{invert}) \\ &= a' \cdot (\text{invert}) + a \cdot (\text{invert})' \\ &= a' \cdot 0 + a \cdot 0' \\ &= a \end{aligned}$$

and the data passes through the gate unchanged.

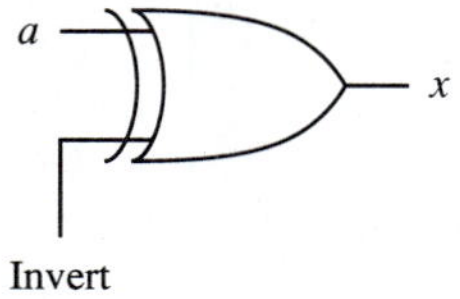

(a) Logic diagram of the selective inverter.

Invert = 1	
a	*x*
0	1
1	0

(b) Truth table with the inverter turned on.

Invert = 0	
a	*x*
0	0
1	1

(c) Truth table with the inverter turned off.

Figure 19.35

XOR input as a selective invert.

Multiplexer

A *multiplexer* is a device that selects one of several data inputs to be routed to a single data output. A set of control lines determine the particular data input to be passed through.

Figure 19.36(a) shows the block diagram of an eight-input multiplexer. D0 to D7 are the data input lines, and S2 to S0 are the select control lines. F is the single data output line.

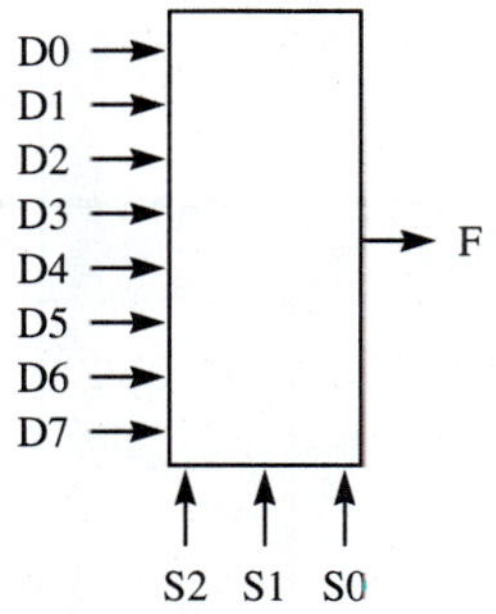

(a) Block diagram.

S2	S1	S0	F
0	0	0	D0
0	0	1	D1
0	1	0	D2
0	1	1	D3
1	0	0	D4
1	0	1	D5
1	1	0	D6
1	1	1	D7

(b) Truth table.

Figure 19.36

The eight-input multiplexer.

Since this device has 11 inputs, a complete truth table would require $2^{11} = 2048$ entries. Figure 19.36(b) shows an abbreviated truth table. The second entry shows that the output is D1 when the select lines are 001. That is, if D1 is 1,

F is 1, and if D1 is 0, F is 0, regardless of the other values of D0 and D2 through D7.

Since n select lines can select one of 2^n data lines, the number of data inputs of a multiplexer is a power of 2. Figure 19.37 shows the implementation of a four-input multiplexer, which contains four data lines, D0 through D3, and two select lines, S1 and S0

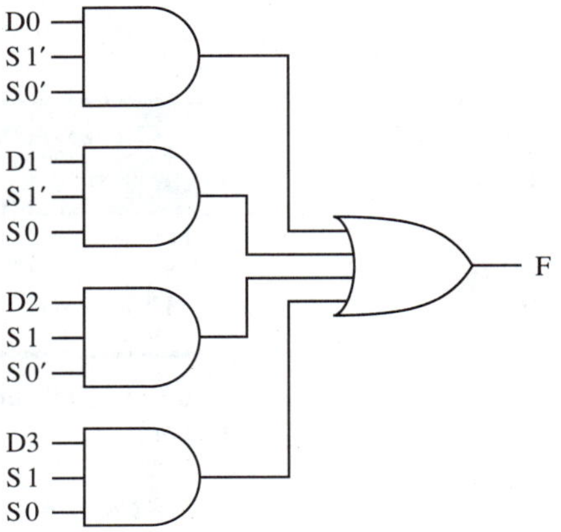

Figure 19.37

Implementation of a four-input multiplexer.

An example of where a multiplexer might be used is in the implementation of the `STORER` instruction in Pep/5. This instruction puts the contents of one of two registers from the CPU into memory via the bus. The CPU could do that with a two-input multiplexer that would make the selection. The select line would come from the register specifier bit, the inputs would come from the A and X registers, and the output would go to the bus.

Binary Decoder

A *decoder* is a device that takes a binary number as input and sets one of several data output lines to 1 and the rest to 0. The data line that is set to 1 depends on the value of the binary number that is input.

Figure 19.38(a) shows the block diagram of a 2 × 4 binary decoder. S1 S0 is the two-bit binary number input and D0 through D3 are the four outputs, one of which will be 1. Part (b) is the truth table.

Since an n-bit number can have 2^n values, the number of data outputs of a decoder is a power of 2. Figure 19.39 shows the implementation of a 2 × 4 decoder. Some other possible sizes are 3 × 8 and 4 × 16.

Some decoders are designed with an enable input. Figure 19.40 is a block diagram of a 2 × 4 decoder with enable. When the enable line is 1, the device operates normally as in Figure 19.38(b). When the enable line is 0, all the outputs are 0. To implement a decoder with enable requires an extra input for each AND gate. The details are left for an exercise at the end of the chapter.

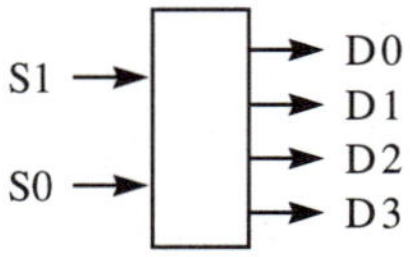

(a) Block diagram.

S1	S0	D0	D1	D2	D3
0	0	1	0	0	0
0	1	0	1	0	0
1	0	0	0	1	0
1	1	0	0	0	1

(b) Truth table.

Figure 19.38

The 2 × 4 binary decoder.

An example of where a decoder might be used is in the CPU of Pep/5. When the execute part of the von Neumann cycle begins, the instruction is in the instruction register (`IR`). The first five bits are the opcode, which signifies one of the 32 instructions to execute. The CPU would have these five bits connected to a 5×32 binary decoder. Each output line from the decoder would trigger the circuitry for executing one of the instructions in the instruction set.

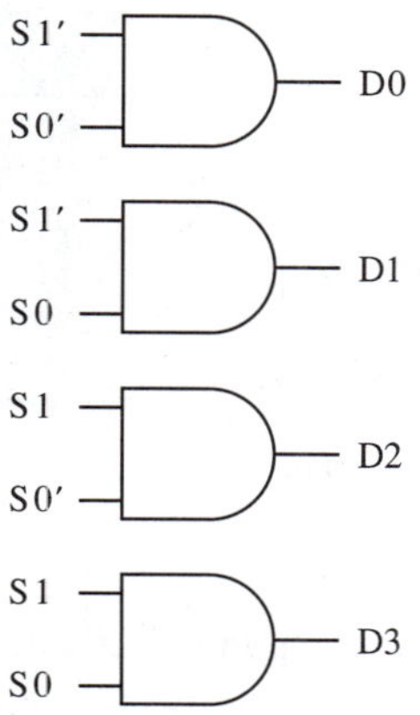

Figure 19.39

Implementation of a 2×4 binary decoder.

Demultiplexer

A multiplexer routes one of several data input values to a single output line. A *demultiplexer* does just the opposite. It routes a single input value to one of several output lines.

Figure 19.41(a) is the block diagram of a four-output demultiplexer. Part (b) is the truth table. If S1 S0 is 01, all the output lines are 0 except D1, which has the same value as the data input line.

This truth table is similar to Figure 19.38(b), the truth table for a decoder. In fact, a demultiplexer is nothing more than a decoder with enable. The data input line, D, is connected to the enable. If D is 0 the decoder is disabled, and the data output line selected by S1 S0 is 0. If D is 1, the decoder is enabled, and the data output line selected is 1. In either case, the selected output line has the same value as the data input line. This is another example of considering a combinational device from a different viewpoint to obtain a useful operation.

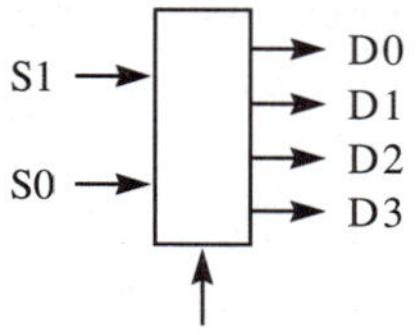

Figure 19.40

A 2×4 binary decoder with enable.

Adder

Consider the binary addition

```
         1011
ADD      0011
C = 0    1110
```

The sum of the least significant bits (LSBs) is 1 plus 1, which is 0 with a carry of 1 to the next column. To add the LSBs of two numbers requires the *half adder* of

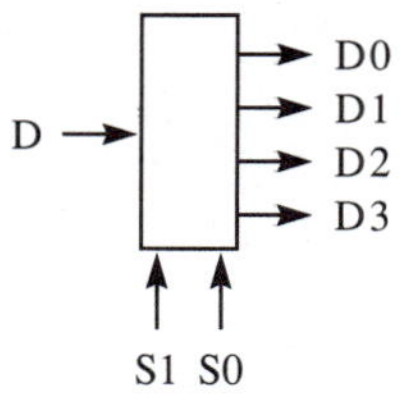

(a) Block diagram.

S1	S0	D0	D1	D2	D3
0	0	D	0	0	0
0	1	0	D	0	0
1	0	0	0	D	0
1	1	0	0	0	D

(b) Truth table.

Figure 19.41

The four-output demultiplexer.

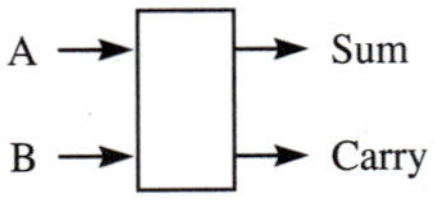

(a) Block diagram.

A	B	Sum	Carry
0	0	0	0
0	1	1	0
1	0	1	0
1	1	0	1

(b) Truth table.

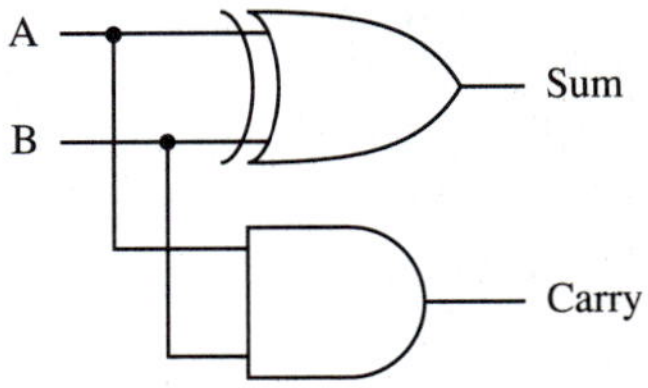

(c) Implementation.

Figure 19.42

The half adder.

Figure 19.42(a). In the figure, A represents the LSB of the first number, and B the LSB of the second number. One output is Sum, 0 in this example, and the other is Carry, 1 in this example. Part (b) shows the truth table. The sum is identical to the XOR function and the carry is identical to the AND function. Part (c) is a straightforward implementation.

To find the sum in the column next to the LSB requires a combinational net with three inputs, Cin, A, and B. Cin is the carry input, which comes from the carry of the LSB. A and B are the bits from the first and second numbers. The outputs are Sum and Cout, the carry output which goes to Cin of the full adder for the next column. Figure 19.43(a) is the block diagram of the network, called a *full adder.* Figure 19.43(b) is the truth table. If the sum of the three inputs is odd, Sum is 1. If the sum of the three inputs is greater than 1, Cout is 1.

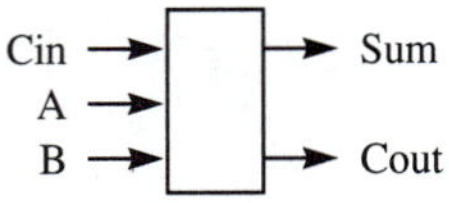

(a) Block diagram.

A	B	Cin	Sum	Cout
0	0	0	0	0
0	0	1	1	0
0	1	0	1	0
0	1	1	0	1
1	0	0	1	0
1	0	1	0	1
1	1	0	0	1
1	1	1	1	1

(b) Truth table.

Figure 19.43

The full adder.

Figure 19.44 shows an implementation of the full adder that uses two half adders and an OR gate. The first half adder adds A and B. The second half adder adds the sum from the first half adder to Cin. The full adder sum is the sum from the second half adder. If either the first or second half adder has a carry, the full adder has a carry out.

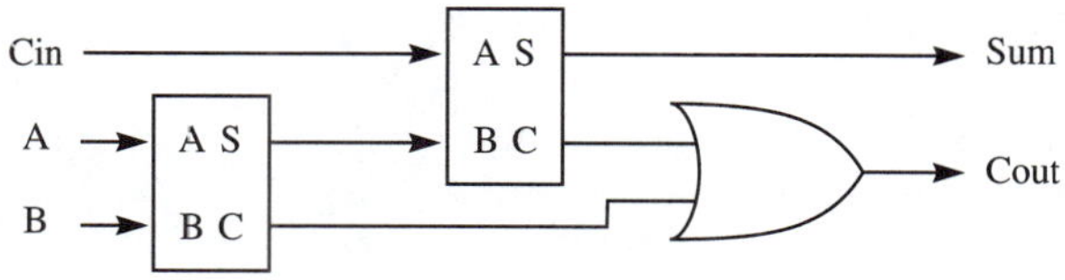

Figure 19.44

An implementation of the full adder with two half adders.

To add the two four-bit numbers requires an eight-input network, shown in Figure 19.45. A3 A2 A1 A0 are the four bits of the first number, with A0 the LSB. B3 through B0 are the same for the second number. S3 S2 S1 S0 is the four-bit sum, with C the carry bit.

An implementation of the four-bit adder could use one half adder for the LSB and three full adders, one for each of the remaining columns in the addition. That implementation is called a *ripple-carry adder,* because a carry that originates from the LSB must propagate, or ripple through, the columns to the left. Implementation details are left for an exercise at the end of the chapter.

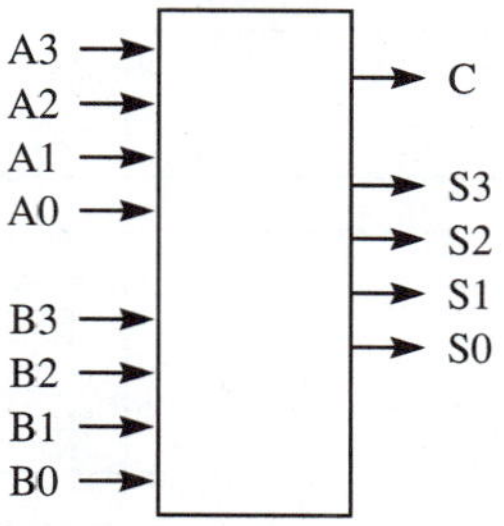

Figure 19.45

The block diagram of a four-bit adder.

Arithmetic Logic Unit

The Pep/5 instructions that perform processing include `ADDR`, `ANDR`, and `ORR`. The addition is an arithmetic operation, while AND and OR are logical operations. The CPU typically contains a single combinational net called the *arithmetic logic unit* (ALU) that performs these operations.

Figure 19.46(a) is the block diagram of a one-bit ALU. Cin, A, and B are data inputs. S1 and S0 are control inputs that specify which operation the ALU will perform. The two outputs are F and Cout.

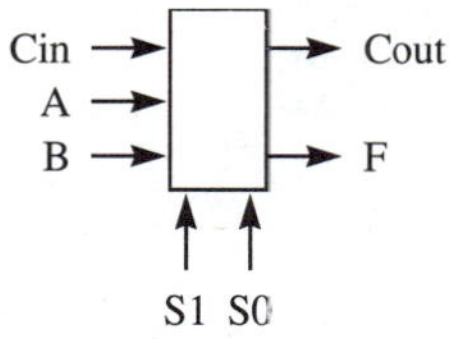

(a) Block diagram.

S1	S0	F	Cout
0	0	$A \cdot B$	0
0	1	$A + B$	0
1	0	A	0
1	1	A plus B plus Cin	C

(b) Truth table.

Figure 19.46

A one-bit ALU.

The truth table in Figure 19.46(b) shows that if S1 S0 is 00, output F is the AND of A and B. If S1 S0 is 01, F is the OR of A and B; and if S1 S0 is 10, F is simply A regardless of the value of B. In these three cases, F does not depend on the value of Cin. If S1 S0 is 11, F is the full adder sum of A, B, and Cin, and Cout is the full adder carry out.

Figure 19.47 shows an implementation of this one-bit ALU. The full adder is similar to Figure 19.43 except that it contains an enable input. When E is 0, Cout and Sum are 0 regardless of Cin, A, and B. When E is 1, the full adder operates normally. D0, D1, and D2 are connected to the enable lines for A • B, A + B, and A respectively in the logic unit.

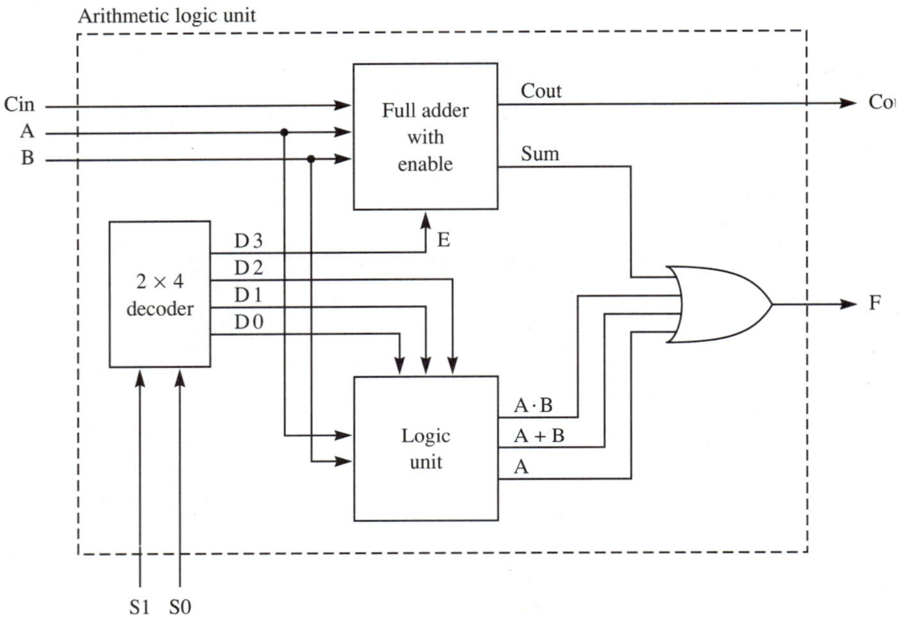

Figure 19.47

An implementation of a one-bit ALU.

For a given value of S1 S0, one of the decoder outputs will be 1 and the others will be 0. The output that is 1 will enable one of the four lines into the OR gate. The other three lines into the OR gate will come from disabled circuits, and hence, will be zero. The value of the one enabled line will pass through the OR gate to the output, unaffected by the other three lines. Implementation details of the adder and logic unit are left for an exercise at the end of the chapter.

In the same way that a set of $n - 1$ full adders and a half adder can be connected to form a ripple carry adder for an n-bit number, a set of n one-bit ALUs can be connected to form an n-bit ALU. Figure 19.48 is the block diagram for a four-bit ALU. Its implementation from a set of four one-bit ALUs is left for an exercise.

In practice, ALUs are more complex than the one shown here. A typical ALU might contain five select lines for a total of $2^5 = 32$ operations, half of which are arithmetic and half logical. The concept and implementation approach of this ALU, however, is similar to the real thing.

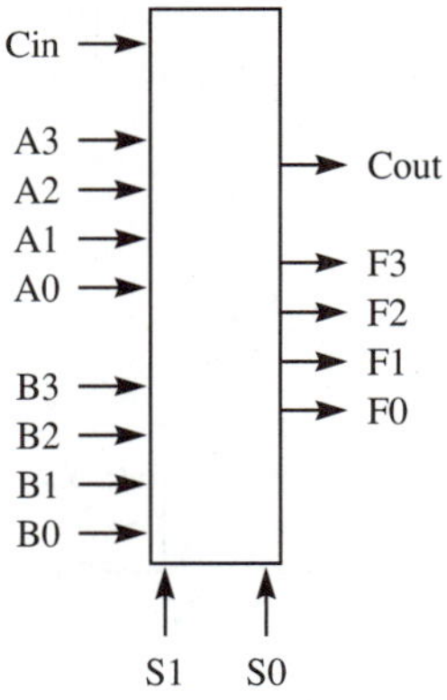

Figure 19.48

The block diagram of a four-bit ALU.

Abstraction at Level 1

Abstract data types (ADTs) are an important design tool at Level 6. The idea is that you should understand the behavior of an ADT by knowing what the functions and procedures that operate on the ADT do, not necessarily how they do it. Once an operation has been implemented, you can free your mind of the implementation details and concentrate on solving the problem at a higher level of abstraction.

The same principle operates at the hardware level. Each combinational device in this section has a block diagram and a truth table that describes its function. The block diagram is to hardware what an ADT is to software. It is an abstraction that specifies the input and output while hiding the implementation details.

The block diagram as an ADT

Higher levels of abstraction in the hardware are obtained by constructing devices defined by block diagrams whose implementation is an interconnection of blocks at a lower level of abstraction. Figure 19.43 is a perfect example. This full adder block is implemented with the half adder blocks in Figure 19.44.

The highest level of abstraction for the hardware is the block diagram of the Pep/5 computer we have seen repeatedly. The four blocks—input device, CPU, main memory, and output device—are connected by the bus. At a slightly lower level of abstraction you see the registers in the CPU. Each register is depicted as a block. The next chapter will show an implementation of a register as an interconnection of blocks at a lower level of abstraction.

SUMMARY

In a combinational network, the input determines the output. Three representations of a combinational network are truth tables, boolean algebraic expressions, and logic diagrams. Of the three representations, truth tables are at the highest level of abstraction. They specify the function of a network without specifying its implementation. A truth table lists the output for all possible combinations of the input, hence the name "combinational network."

The three basic operations of boolean algebra are AND, OR, and NOT. The ten fundamental properties of boolean algebra consist of five laws—commutative, associative, distributive, identity, and complement—and their duals, from which useful boolean theorems may be proved. An important theorem is De Morgan's law, which shows how to take the NOT of the AND or OR of several terms.

A boolean expression corresponds to a logic diagram, which in turn corresponds to a connection of electronic gates. Three common gates are NAND (AND followed by NOT), NOR (OR followed by NOT), and XOR (exclusive OR). Two-level networks minimize processing time, but may require more gates than an equivalent multilevel network. This is another manifestation of the fundamental space/time tradeoff. Karnaugh maps help minimize the number of gates needed to implement a two-level combinational network.

Combinational devices include the multiplexer, the decoder, the demultiplexer, the adder, and the arithmetic logic unit (ALU). A multiplexer selects one of several data inputs to be routed to a single data output. A decoder takes a binary number as input and sets one of several data output lines to 1 and the rest to 0. A demultiplexer routes one of several data input values to a single output line, and is logically equivalent to a decoder with an enable line. A half adder adds two bits, and a full adder adds three bits, one of which is the previous carry. An ALU performs both arithmetic and logic functions.

EXERCISES

Section 19.1

1. *(a) Prove that $x + 1 = 1$ with boolean algebra. Give a reason for each step in your proof. Hint: Expand the 1 on the left with the complement property and then use the idempotent property. **(b)** Show the dual proof of part (a).

2. **(a)** Prove with boolean algebra the absorption property, $x + x \cdot y = x$. Give a reason for each step in your proof. **(b)** Show the dual proof of part (a).

*3. Prove De Morgan's law, $(a + b)' = a' \cdot b'$, by giving the dual of the proof in the text. Give a reason for each step in your proof.

4. **(a)** Prove the general form of De Morgan's law,

$$(a_1 \cdot a_2 \cdot \cdots \cdot a_n)' = a_1{}' + a_2{}' + \cdots + a_n{}' \qquad \text{where } n \geq 2$$

from De Morgan's law for two variables using mathematical induction. **(b)** Show the dual proof of part (a).

5. *(a) Prove with boolean algebra that $(x + y) \cdot (x' + y) = y$. Give a reason for each step in your proof. **(b)** Show the dual proof of part (a).

6. **(a)** Prove with boolean algebra that $(x + y) + (y \cdot x') = x + y$. Give a reason for each step in your proof. **(b)** Show the dual proof of part (a).

7. *(a) Draw a three-input OR gate, its boolean expression, and its truth table, as in Figure 19.6. **(b)** Do part (a) for the three-input NAND gate. **(c)** Do part (a) for the three-input NOR gate.

8. For each of the following boolean properties or theorems, state the set theory interpretation.

   *(a) $x + 0 = x$ **(b)** $x \cdot 1 = x$ **(c)** $x + x' = 1$ **(d)** $x \cdot x' = 0$
   (e) $x \cdot x = x$ **(f)** $x + x = x$ **(g)** $x \cdot 0 = 0$

9. *(a) Show the associative property for the OR operation using Venn diagrams with x, y, and z overlapping regions. Sketch the following regions to show that region (3) is the same as region (6).

   (1) $(x + y)$ (2) z (3) $(x + y) + z$
   (4) x (5) $(y + z)$ (6) $x + (y + z)$

   (b) Do the dual of part (a).

10. **(a)** Show the distributive property using Venn diagrams with x, y, and z overlapping regions. Sketch the following regions to show that region (3) is the same as region (6).

    (1) x (2) $y \cdot z$ (3) $x + y \cdot z$
    (4) $(x + y)$ (5) $(x + z)$ (6) $(x + y) \cdot (x + z)$

    (b) Do the dual of part (a).

11. **(a)** Show De Morgan's law using Venn diagrams with a, b, and c overlapping regions. Sketch the following regions to show that region (2) is the same as region (5).

    (1) $a \cdot b$ (2) $(a \cdot b)'$ (3) a' (4) b' (5) $a' + b'$

    (b) Do the dual of part (a).

12. Although a boolean variable for a combinational net can have only two values, 1 or 0, boolean algebra can describe a system where a variable can have one of four possible values—0, 1, A, or B. Such a system corresponds to the description of subsets of $\{a, b\}$ where $1 = \{a, b\}$ (the universal set), $A = \{a\}$, $B = \{b\}$, and $0 = \{\ \}$ (the empty set). The truth tables for two-input AND and OR operations have 16 entries instead of 4, and the truth table for the complement has 4 entries instead of 2. Construct the truth table for the following:

*(a) AND (b) OR (c) the complement

13. The exclusive NOR gate, written XNOR, is equivalent to an XOR followed by an inverter. *(a) Draw the symbol for a two-input XNOR gate. (b) Construct its truth table. (c) The XNOR is also called a comparitor. Why?

Section 19.2

14. Draw the nonabbreviated logic diagram for the following boolean expressions.

*(a) $((a')')'$ (b) $(((a')')')'$
*(c) $a'b + ab'$ (d) $ab + a'b'$
(e) $ab + ab' + a'b$ (f) $((ab \oplus b')' + a'b)'$
(g) $(a'bc + a)b$ (h) $(ab'c)'(ac)'$
(i) $((ab)'(b'c)' + a'b'c')'$ (j) $(a \oplus b + b' \oplus c')'$
(k) $(abc)' + (a'b'c')'$ (l) $(a + b)(a' + c)(b' + c')$
(m) $(a \oplus b) \oplus c + ab'c$ (n) $(((a + b)' + c)' + d)'$
(o) $(ab' + b'c + cd)'$ (p) $((a + b')(b' + c)(c + d))'$
(q) $(((ab)'c)'d)'$ (r) $(((a \oplus b)' \oplus c)' \oplus d)'$

15. Draw the abbreviated logic diagram for the boolean expressions of Exercise 14.

16. Construct the truth tables for the boolean expressions of Exercise 14.

17. Write the boolean expressions for the logic diagrams of Figure 19.49 (p. 964).

18. Write the boolean expression as the OR of AND terms for the following:

*(a) function *y* in Table 19.1
(b) function *y* in Table 19.2,
(c) function x in Table 19.4
(d) the NAND gate in Figure 19.4(a)
(e) the XOR gate in Figure 19.4(c)

19. Write the boolean expression as the AND of OR terms for the following:

*(a) function *y* in Table 19.1
(b) function *x* in Table 19.4
(c) the NOR gate in Figure 19.4(b)
(d) the XOR gate in Figure 19.4(c)

20. Use the properties and theorems of boolean algebra to reduce the following expressions to an OR of AND terms without parentheses. The expressions may not be unique. Construct the truth table, which will be unique, by inspection of your final expression.

*(a) $(a'b + ab')'$ (b) $(ab + a'b')'$
(c) $(ab + ab' + a'b)'$ *(d) $(ab \oplus b')' + ab$
(e) $(a'bc + a)b$ (f) $(ab'c)'(ac)'$

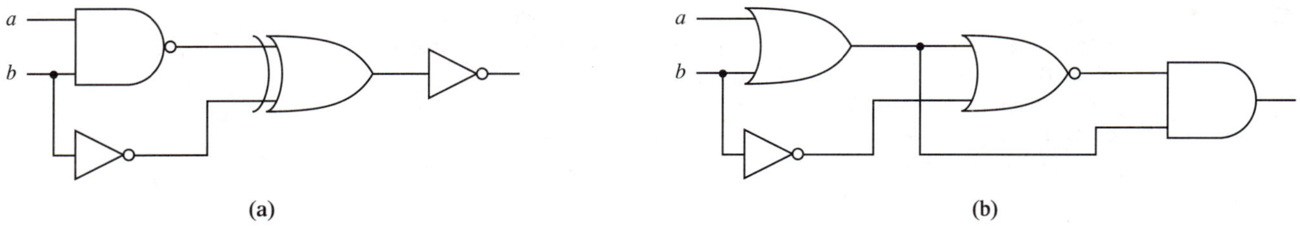

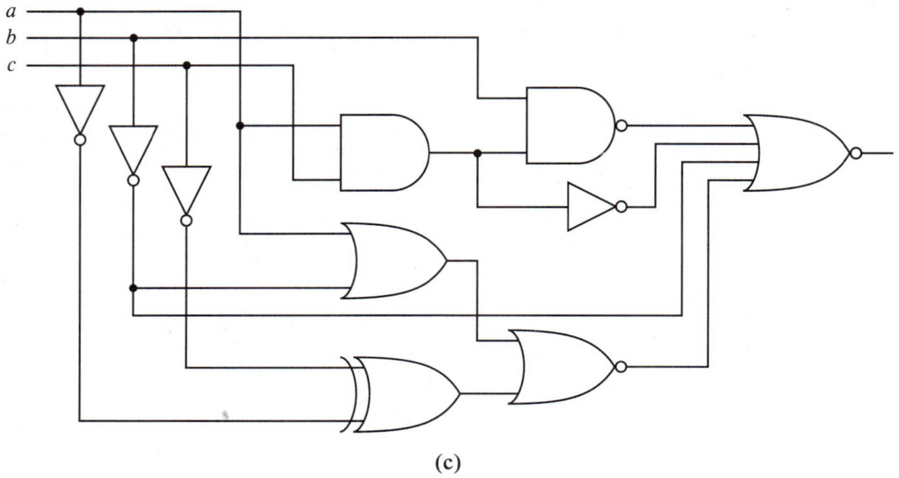

Figure 19.49

The logic diagrams for Exercise 17.

(g) $(a \oplus b) \oplus c$ **(h)** $a \oplus (b \oplus c)$
(i) $(a + b)(a' + c)(b' + c')$ **(j)** $((a + b)' + c)'$

*__21.__ Construct two-level networks for the expressions of Exercise 20 using only NAND gates.

22. Use the properties and theorems of boolean algebra to reduce the following expressions to an AND of OR terms without parentheses. The expressions may not be unique. Construct the truth table, which will be unique, by inspection of your final expression.

(a) $a'b + ab'$ *__(b)__ $ab + a'b'$
(c) $ab + ab' + a'b$ **(d)** $((ab \oplus b')' + ab)'$
(e) $(a'bc + a)b$ **(f)** $(ab'c)'(ac)'$
(g) $(a \oplus b) \oplus c$ **(h)** $a \oplus (b \oplus c)$
(i) $((a + b)(a' + c)(b' + c'))'$ **(j)** $(a + b)' + c$

*__23.__ Construct a two-level network for the expressions of Exercise 22 using only NOR gates.

24. Draw the logic diagram of a two-level network that produces the XOR function using the following:

*__(a)__ only NAND gates **(b)** only NOR gates

25. State whether each gate in Figure 19.50 is the following:

(1) an AND gate (2) an OR gate
(3) a NAND gate (4) a NOR gate

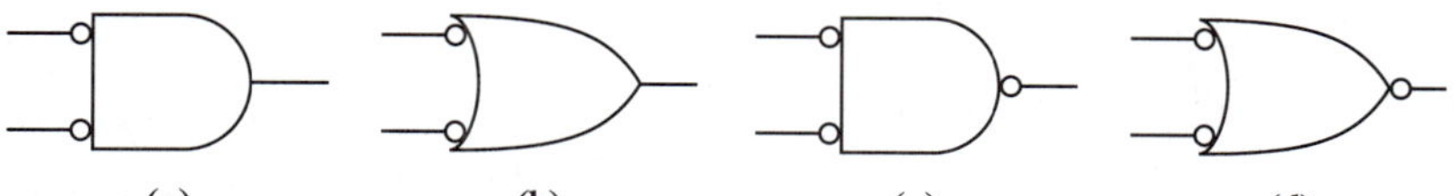

Figure 19.50

The gates for Exercise 25.

Section 19.3

*26. Write each function of Exercise 20 with the sigma notation.

*27. Write each function of Exercise 22 with the pi notation.

28. In Table 19.1, find the minimum OR of AND expression for the following:

*(a) $x(a, b, c)$ (b) $y(a, b, c)$

Draw the minimized two-level network for each expression with only NAND gates.

29. In Table 19.1, find the minimum AND of OR expression for the following:

*(a) $x(a, b, c)$ (b) $y(a, b, c)$

Draw the minimized two-level network for each expression with only NOR gates.

30. Use a Karnaugh map to find the minimum OR of AND expression for $x(a, b, c)$.

*(a) $\Sigma(0, 4, 5, 7)$ (b) $\Sigma(2, 3, 4, 6, 7)$ (c) $\Sigma(0, 3, 5, 6)$
(d) $\Sigma(0, 1, 2, 3, 4, 6)$ (e) $\Sigma(1, 2, 3, 4, 5)$ (f) $\Sigma(1, 2, 3, 4, 5, 6, 7)$
(g) $\Sigma(0, 1, 2, 4, 6)$ (h) $\Sigma(1, 4, 6, 7)$ (i) $\Sigma(2, 3, 4, 5, 6)$
(j) $\Sigma(0, 2, 5)$

*31. Write each expression of Exercise 30 in pi notation, and find its minimum AND of OR expression.

32. Use a Karnaugh map to find the minimum OR of AND expression for $x(a, b, c, d)$.

*(a) $\Sigma(2, 3, 4, 5, 10, 12, 13)$ (b) $\Sigma(1, 5, 6, 7, 9, 12, 13, 15)$
(c) $\Sigma(0, 1, 2, 4, 6, 8, 10)$ (d) $\Sigma(7)$
(e) $\Sigma(2, 4, 5, 11, 13, 15)$ (f) $\Sigma(1, 2, 4, 5, 6, 7, 12, 15)$
(g) $\Sigma(1, 7, 10, 12)$ (h) $\Sigma(0, 2, 3, 4, 5, 6, 8, 10, 11, 13)$
(i) $\Sigma(0, 1, 2, 3, 4, 5, 6, 10, 11, 13, 14, 15)$
(j) $\Sigma(0, 1, 2, 3, 4, 5, 6, 7, 8, 9, 10, 11, 12, 13, 14)$

*33. Write each expression of Exercise 32 in pi notation, and find its minimum AND of OR expression.

34. Use a Karnaugh map to find the minimum OR of AND expression for $x(a, b, c)$ with don't-care conditions.

*(a) $\Sigma(0, 6) + d(1, 3, 7)$ (b) $\Sigma(5) + d(0, 2, 4, 6)$
(c) $\Sigma(1, 3) + d(0, 2, 4, 6)$ (d) $\Sigma(0, 5, 7) + d(3, 4)$
(e) $\Sigma(1, 7) + d(2, 4)$ (f) $\Sigma(4, 5, 6) + d(1, 2, 3, 7)$

35. Use a Karnaugh map to find the minimum OR of AND expression for $x(a, b, c, d)$ with don't-care conditions.

*(a) $\Sigma(5, 6) + d(2, 7, 9, 13, 14, 15)$
(b) $\Sigma(0, 3, 14) + d(2, 4, 7, 8, 10, 11, 13, 15)$
(c) $\Sigma(3, 4, 5, 10) + d(2, 11, 13, 15)$

(d) $\Sigma(5, 6, 12, 15) + d(0, 4, 10, 14)$
(e) $\Sigma(1, 6, 9, 12) + d(0, 2, 3, 4, 5, 7, 14, 15)$
(f) $\Sigma(0, 2, 3, 4) + d(8, 9, 10, 11, 13, 14, 15)$
(g) $\Sigma(2, 3, 10) + d(0, 4, 6, 7, 8, 9, 12, 14, 15)$

36. **(a)** A Karnaugh map for three variables has minterms 0 adjacent to 2, and 4 adjacent to 6. Copy Figure 19.22, cut out the Karnaugh map, and tape it in the shape of a cylinder so that adjacent minterms are physically adjacent. **(b)** For adjacent minterms to be physically adjacent in a four-variable Karnaugh map requires a three-dimensional *torus* (shaped like a doughnut). Construct a torus from clay or some other suitable material and inscribe or write on it the cells and their decimal labels of Figure 19.26(a). For example, the cell with 2 should be physically adjacent to the cells with 0, 3, 6, and 10.

Section 19.4

37. Using the viewpoint that one of the lines is a data line and the other is a control line, explain the operation of each of the following two-input gates.

*(a) OR
(b) NAND
(c) NOR
(d) XNOR

See Exercise 13 for the definition of XNOR.

38. Draw a nonabbreviated logic diagram of an eight-input multiplexer.

***39.** Construct a 16-input multiplexer from five four-input multiplexers. Draw the 16-input multiplexer as a large block with 16 data lines labeled D0 through D15 and 4 select lines labeled S3 through S0. Inside the large block, draw each four-input multiplexer as a small block with data lines D0 through D3 and select lines S1 and S0. Show the connections to the small blocks from the outside lines and the connections between the blocks to implement the big multiplexer. Explain the operation of your circuit.

40. Do Exercise 39 with two eight-input multiplexers and any other gates you need.

41. *(a) Draw a nonabbreviated logic diagram of a 3×8 binary decoder. (b) Draw a nonabbreviated logic diagram of a 2×4 binary decoder with an enable input.

42. Construct a 4×16 binary decoder without an enable input from five 2×4 binary decoders with enable inputs. Use the drawing guidelines of Exercise 39 to label your external and internal lines. Explain the operation of your circuit.

43. Construct a 4×16 binary decoder without an enable input from two 3×8 binary decoders with enable inputs plus any other gates you need. Use the drawing guidelines of Exercise 39 to label your external and internal lines. Explain the operation of your circuit.

44. Implement the 2×4 binary decoder with an enable input, as shown in Figure 19.40. Draw a nonabbreviated diagram of your circuit.

45. *(a) Draw the implementation of the full adder in Figure 19.44 showing the AND and XOR gates of the half adders. ***(b)** What is the maximum number of gate delays from input to output? **(c)** Design minimized two-level networks for Sum and Cout from the truth table of Figure 19.43(b). **(d)** Compute the percentage change in the number of gates and in the processing time for the design of part (c) compared to part (a). How do your results illustrate the space/time tradeoff?

46. *(a) Implement the four-bit adder of Figure 19.45 as a ripple-carry adder with one half adder and three full adders. **(b)** Draw the circuit with the individual XOR, AND, and OR gates of the half adders. *(c) What is the maximum number of gate delays from input to output? Consider an XOR gate as requiring one gate delay. This problem requires some thought. Assume that all eight inputs are presented at the same time, even though the carry will ripple through the circuit.

47. Construct an eight-bit ripple-carry adder with one half adder and seven full adders. Assume that the adder is for a CPU that uses two's complement binary representation for storing negative numbers, with the first bit as the sign bit. Implement four additional outputs for `NZVC`, as in the Pep/5 computer but with only an 8-bit sum instead of 16. `N` should be 1 if the number is negative. `Z` should be 1 if the eight bits of the sum are all 0's. `V` should be 1 if there is an overflow, which will happen if the carry into the sign bit is different from the carry out from the sign bit. `C` should be 1 if there is a carry out from the sign bit.

48. Draw the logic diagram of the one-bit ALU in Figure 19.47 showing all the gates and inverters in the decoder, logic unit, and adder with enable. What is the maximum number of gate delays from input to output not counting delays through the inverters?

***49.** Implement the four-bit ALU of Figure 19.48 with four one-bit ALUs.

50. Implement a four-bit ASL shifter with select line S. The input is A3 A2 A1 A0, which represents a four-bit number with A0 the LSB and A3 the sign bit. The output is B3 B2 B1 B0 and C, the carry bit. If S is 1, the output is the ASL of the input. If S is 0, the output is the same as the input, and C is 0.

51. Do Exercise 50 for a four-bit ASR shifter.

Chapter

20

Sequential Networks

The previous chapter discussed combinational devices, which are commonly used in computer design. As useful as these devices are, however, it is impossible to build even the smallest computers as an interconnection of combinational nets. In all the combinational devices that were mentioned, the output depends only on the input. When the input changes, it is only a matter of a few gate delays before that change is reflected in the output.

The distinguishing characteristic of sequential networks

The state of the network is the characteristic that distinguishes a sequential net from a combinational net. A sequential net can remember what state it is in. It has memory, in other words. The output of a sequential net depends not only on the input but on the state as well.

This chapter will show how to construct the basic sequential elements and how to connect them to form useful blocks at successively higher levels of abstraction. It concludes with a description of how these blocks might be connected to build a Pep/5 computer.

20.1 Latches and Clocked Flip-Flops

Sequential devices are constructed from the same gates described in the previous chapter, but with a different type of connection called *feedback*. In combinational nets and the boolean expressions that describe them, the output of each gate goes to the input of a previously unconnected gate. A feedback connection, however, forms a loop or cycle where the output of one or more gates "feeds back" to the input of a previous gate of the network.

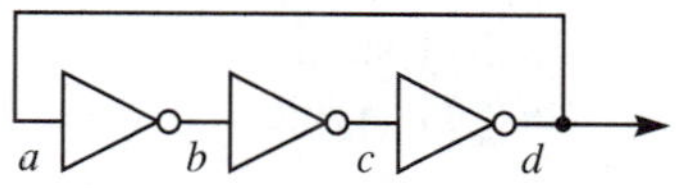

(a) An unstable network.

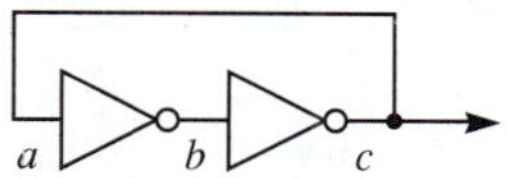

(b) A stable network.

Figure 20.1

Simple feedback circuits.

Figure 20.1 shows two simple circuits with feedback connections. Part (a) is a string of three inverters fed back to the input of the first inverter. To analyze the behavior of this circuit, suppose that point *d* has a value of 1. Since *d* is connected to *a* with the feedback loop, point *a* must also have a value of 1. One gate delay later, point *b* must have a value of 0. (Though we previously ignored the delay through an inverter for simplicity, we must take it into account with this circuit.)

One more gate delay later, point *c* will have a value of 1, and after a third gate delay, *d* will have a value of 0.

The problem now is that we started our analysis assuming point *d* has a value of 1. It will now change to 0, and three gate delays later it will become 1 again. The circuit will oscillate, with the values at each point in the circuit switching back and forth between 1 and 0 every few gate delays. A state that remains constant only for a duration of a few gate delays is called an *unstable state*.

Unstable states

In Figure 20.1(b), if you assume point *c* has a value of 1, then point *a* will be 1, *b* will be 0, and *c* will be 1, which is consistent with the first assumption. Such a state is stable. The points at all parts of the circuit will retain their values indefinitely.

Stable states

Another possible stable state is for points *c* and *a* to have a value of 0 and *b* to have a value of 1. If you construct this circuit, which state will it have? Will point *c* be 0 or 1?

Like all electrical devices, gates require a source of electrical power and must be turned on to operate. If you construct the circuit of Figure 20.1(b) and turn it on, its state will be established at random. About half the time when you turn on the circuit, point *c* will be 0, and about half the time it will be 1. The circuit will remain indefinitely in the state that is established when the power is turned on.

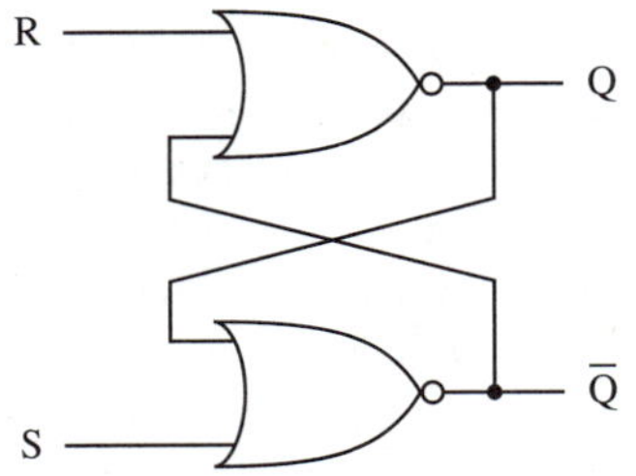

Figure 20.2

The SR latch.

The SR Latch

To be useful, a sequential device needs a mechanism for setting its state. Such a device is the *SR latch* of Figure 20.2. Its two inputs are S and R and its two outputs are Q and $\overline{Q}$ (pronounced *Q bar*). The feedback connections are from Q to the input of the bottom NOR and from $\overline{Q}$ to the input of the top NOR.

To see the possibility of a stable state, suppose S and R are both 0, and Q is also 0. The two inputs to the bottom gate are both 0, which makes $\overline{Q}$ 1. The two inputs to the top NOR are 0 (from R) and 1 (from $\overline{Q}$). Thus, the output of the top NOR is 0, which is consistent with our first assumption about Q. So the stable state is $Q\overline{Q} = 01$ when SR = 00.

Starting with this stable state, consider what happens if you change input S to 1. Table 20.1 summarizes the sequence of events. T_g stands for a time interval of one gate delay, typically 10 ns.

Table 20.1

Changing S to 1 in the SR latch.

Time	S	R	Q	$\overline{Q}$	Stability
Initial	0	0	0	1	Stable
0	1	0	0	1	Unstable
T_g	1	0	0	0	Unstable
$2T_g$	1	0	1	0	Stable

At time 0, S changes to 1. That makes the two inputs to the bottom gate 1 (from S) and 0 (from Q). One gate delay later the effect of that change propagates to $\bar{Q}$, which becomes 0. Now the two inputs to the top gate are 0 (from R) and 0 (from $\bar{Q}$). After another gate delay, the output of the top gate becomes 1. Now the input to the bottom gate is 1 (from S) and 1 (from Q). That makes the output of the bottom gate 0.

The output of the bottom gate was already 0, however, so it does not change. Since a trace through the feedback connections shows consistent values, this last state is stable. The two intermediate states in Table 20.1 are unstable because they last for only a few gate delays.

What happens if you change S back to 0? Table 20.2 shows the sequence of events. The two inputs to the bottom gate are 0 (from S) and 1 (from Q). That makes the output of the bottom gate 0. Since it was already 0, no other changes propagate through the circuit, and the state is stable.

Table 20.2

Changing S back to 0 in the SR latch.

Time	S	R	Q	$\bar{Q}$	Stability
Initial	1	0	1	0	Stable
0	0	0	1	0	Stable

Tables 20.1 and 20.2 show that $\bar{Q}$ is always the complement of Q when the SR latch is in a stable state. The bar is another common notation for the complement and is equivalent to the prime notation used in the previous chapter.

Compare the first state of Table 20.1 with the last state of Table 20.2. In both cases the inputs are SR = 00, but in the first case the output is Q = 0 and in the second Q = 1. The output depends not only on the input, but also on the state of the latch.

The effect of changing S to 1, then back to 0 was to set the state to Q = 1. If the latch begins in the state Q = 1 with SR = 00, a similar analysis shows that changing R to 1, then back to 0 will reset the state to Q = 0. S stands for set, and R stands for reset.

An SR latch is analogous to a light switch on a wall. Changing S to 1 and back to 0 is like flipping the switch up to turn the light on. Changing R to 1 and back to 0 is like flipping the switch down. If the switch is already up and you try flipping it up, nothing changes. The switch stays up. Similarly, if Q is already 1 and you change S to 1 and back to 0, the state does not change. Q stays 1.

The normal input condition for the SR latch

The normal input condition for the SR latch is SR = 00. To set or reset the latch, you change S or R to 1, then back to 0. Normally, S and R are not 1 simultaneously. If S and R are both 1, Q and $\bar{Q}$ will both be 0, and $\bar{Q}$ will not be the complement of Q. Furthermore, if you change SR = 11 to SR = 00 simultaneously, the state of the latch is unpredictable. About half the time it will return to $Q\bar{Q}$ = 01 and half the time to $Q\bar{Q}$ = 10. In practice, SR = 11 should not occur.

A *timing diagram* is a graphical representation of the behavior of a sequential circuit. Figure 20.3 is a timing diagram that shows the change in outputs Q and $\overline{Q}$ as inputs S and R change. The horizontal axis is time, and the vertical axis is the electrical voltage that represents 1 when it is high and 0 when it is low.

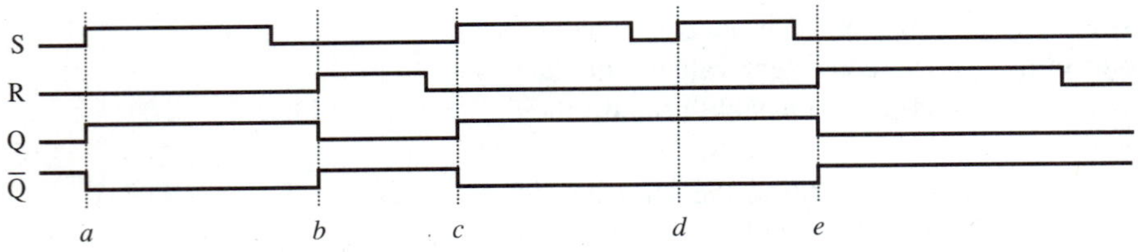

Figure 20.3

A timing diagram for the SR latch.

The timing diagram shows the initial state as Q = 0. When S goes to 1 at time *a*, it immediately sets Q to 1 and $\overline{Q}$ to 0. The diagram shows the transitions occurring simultaneously. As shown in our previous analysis, $\overline{Q}$ will change one gate delay after S changes, and Q will change one gate delay later than that. The timing diagram assumes that the time scale is too large to show a time interval as short as a gate delay.

When S goes back to 0, the state does not change. When R goes to 1 at time *b*, it resets Q to 0. When S goes to 1 again at time *c*, it sets Q to 1. At time *d*, the 0-to-1 transition of S does not change the state of the latch, because Q is already 1. At all points of the diagram, $\overline{Q}$ is the inverse of Q.

Figure 20.3 also shows the transitions as instantaneous. Nothing in nature occurs in zero time. If you magnify the time scale, the transitions will show a more gradual change with a finite slope at every point. You can think of the simultaneous and instantaneous transitions in the timing diagram as a high level of abstraction that hides the details of the gate delays and gradual slopes at a lower level of abstraction.

The Clocked SR Flip-Flop

Computer circuits consist of combinational and sequential networks with many devices. Each sequential device is like an SR latch, which is in one of two states. As the machine executes its von Neumann cycle, the states of all the sequential devices change with time. To control this large collection of devices in an orderly fashion, the machine maintains a clock and requires all the devices to change their states at the same time. The clock generates a sequence of pulses, as in Figure 20.4. CP stands for *clock pulse*.

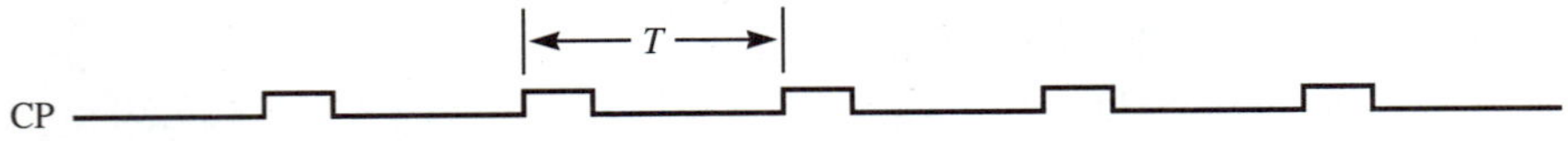

Figure 20.4

A sequence of clock pulses.

Every sequential device has a CP input in addition to its other inputs. The device is designed to respond to its inputs only during a clock pulse. The time between pulses, indicated by T in the figure, is the period of the clock. The shorter the period, the more frequently the devices will change their states and the faster the network will compute.

Figure 20.5 is an SR latch with a clock input, called a *flip-flop*. It consists of the same pair of NOR gates with feedback that were shown in Figure 20.2. But instead of the SR inputs going directly into the NOR gates, they go through two AND gates that act as an enable. Figure 20.5(a) is the block diagram, and Figure 20.5(b) is an implementation. Notice that the convention for the block diagram has S opposite from Q at the top of the block, while the implementation has S opposite $\overline{Q}$.

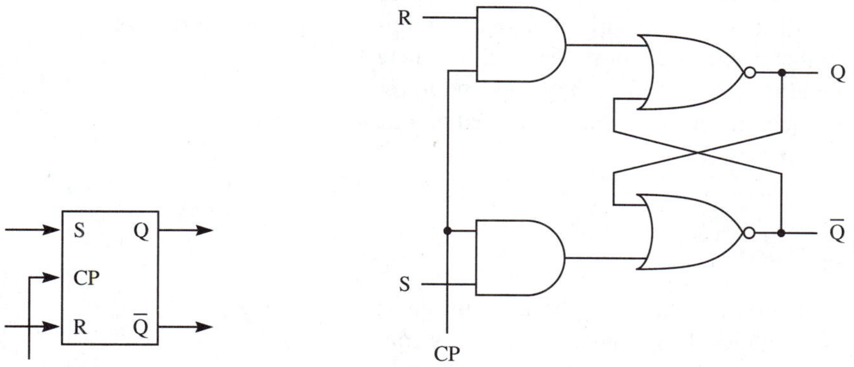

(a) Block diagram.

(b) Implementation.

Figure 20.5

The clocked SR flip-flop.

During the time that CP is low, the inputs to the NOR gates will be 0 regardless of the values of S and R. When there are inputs of 0 into the NOR gates, it means that the latch will not change its state. During the time that CP is high, the values of S and R pass through the enable gates unchanged. The device behaves as the SR latch of Figure 20.2. The AND gates shield the NOR gates from the effect of S and R except during the time that CP is high. Figure 20.6 is a timing diagram that shows the behavior of the device. $\overline{Q}$ is always the complement of Q and is not shown in the figure.

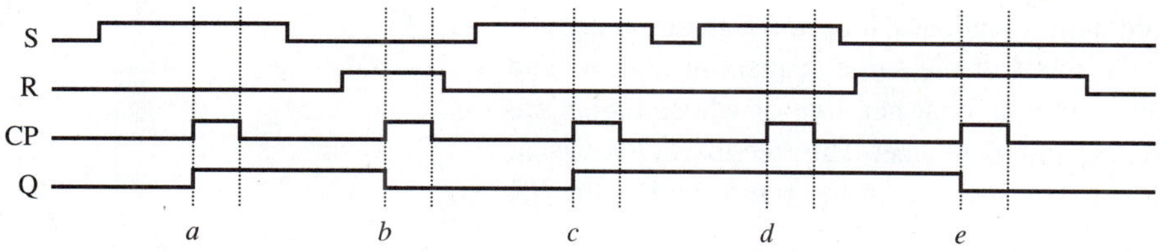

Figure 20.6

A timing diagram of the clocked SR flip-flop.

When S goes to 1, that change does not affect Q because the clock is still low. At time *a* when the clock goes high, CP allows SR = 10 to pass through the AND gates and set the latch to Q = 1. A little later when the clock goes low, CP disables the SR input from the latch. When R goes to 1 before time *b*, it cannot affect the state of the latch. Only at time *b*, when CP goes high again, can R reset the latch.

It would be physically possible to let S and R make several transitions during a single time interval when the clock is high, but that does not happen in practice. The idea is to design the circuit to set up the SR input for the desired transition and wait for the next clock pulse. When the clock pulse arrives, the state may change according to the values of S and R. After the clock goes low, the circuit prepares the SR values for the next pulse.

Digitizing the time axis

The evenly spaced clock pulses force any change in state to occur only at evenly spaced time intervals. The S and R inputs of Figure 20.6 are identical to those of Figure 20.3, but the corresponding state changes in Q have been smoothed out by the clock. The effect of a clock is to make time (the horizontal axis of a timing diagram) digital in the same way that the electrical circuitry makes the voltage signal (vertical axis) digital. Just as a signal must be either high or low and never anything in between, a state change of a sequential device must occur at either one clock pulse or another—never between two pulses.

The Master-Slave SR Flip-Flop

The clocked flip-flop of Figure 20.5 is called *level sensitive* because the latch responds to CP only when the clock is at a high level. Although the device is constrained to follow the clock as desired, it has a serious practical deficiency, illustrated in Figure 20.7.

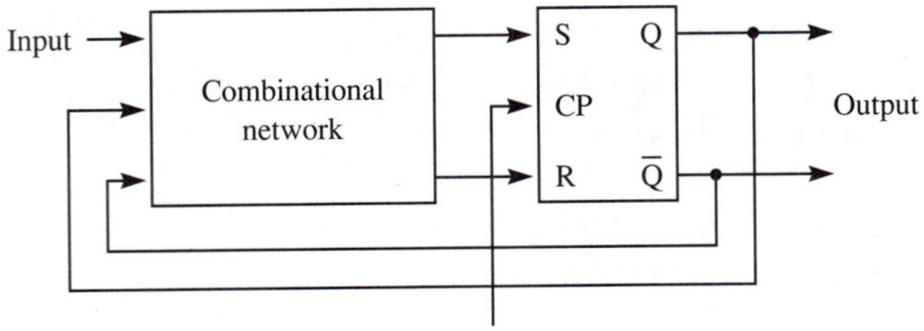

Figure 20.7

A possible interconnection of an SR device.

The figure shows a possible interconnection of an SR device. It is common for the output of a sequential device to contain a feedback loop through some combinational net that eventually leads to the input of the same sequential device. The figure shows a three-input, two-output combinational net, two of whose inputs are feedback from the output of the SR sequential device. This feedback loop is in addition to the feedback of the NOR gates not shown in the figure within the SR block.

Consider what might happen if the SR flip-flop were level sensitive. Suppose SR is 10, $Q\overline{Q}$ is 01, and the clock is low. Since the clock disables SR from the NOR latch, S cannot set Q to 1. Now suppose the clock goes high. After a few gate delays SR will set Q to 1.

Now imagine that the change in $Q\overline{Q}$, after propagating through the combinational net with the same external input, makes SR = 01. If CP is still high, the clock will allow the value of SR to reset Q to 0 after a few more gate delays. Unfortunately, a value of 01 for $Q\overline{Q}$ will propagate through the combinational net again and change SR to 10.

Possibility of an unstable state with feedback

You should recognize this situation as unstable. Every few gate delays the feedback connection from the sequential device forces the SR flip-flop to change its state as long as the clock is high. The state may change hundreds of times while the clock is high. When the clock eventually goes low at the end of its pulse, it would be impossible to predict exactly what state the flip-flop would be in.

Since feedback connections through combinational nets are necessary for the construction of computer circuits, we need a sequential device that is not only constrained to change its state during a clock pulse but is also immune from further changes through the feedback connection. The device needs to be sensitive to its input for an extremely short period of time—so short that no matter how fast the feedback propagates through the combinational net and changes SR, that change cannot again affect the state of the flip-flop.

Two design solutions to the instability problem from feedback

Two common techniques for designing such devices are edge-triggered and master-slave. *Edge-triggered* flip-flops are not designed to be sensitive to their inputs when the clock is at a high level, but rather when the clock is making a transition from a low level to a high level. The implementation of an edge-triggered flip-flop is more difficult to understand than the implementation of a master-slave flip-flop and will not be considered here. It is enough to say that both types of flip-flops solve the same problem arising from feedback connections.

Operation of the master-slave circuit

Figure 20.8 shows an implementation of the *master-slave* SR flip-flop. Both the master and the slave are level-sensitive, clocked SR flip-flops. The $\overline{Q}$ output of the master ($\overline{Q2}$) connects to the R input of the slave (R2), and the Q output of the master (Q2) connects to the S input of the slave (S2). CP connects to the enable of the master, and the complement of CP connects to the enable of the slave. The block diagram of a master-slave flip-flop is identical to the block diagram of the level-sensitive flip-flop.

Since the master is an SR flip-flop, Q2 and $\overline{Q2}$ will always be the complement of each other. Since Q2 is connected to S2 of the slave and $\overline{Q2}$ is connected to R2 of the slave, when the slave is clocked the slave will either be set or reset depending on the state of the master. If the master is in state Q2 = 1, the master will set the slave to Q = 1 also. If the master is in state Q2 = 0, it will reset the slave to Q = 0. The reason for the master-slave terminology is that the slave obediently takes the state of the master when the slave is clocked.

The *threshold* of a gate is the value of the input signal that causes the output to change. For the master-slave circuit to function properly, the inverter and the enable gates of the master must be designed with special threshold values. The

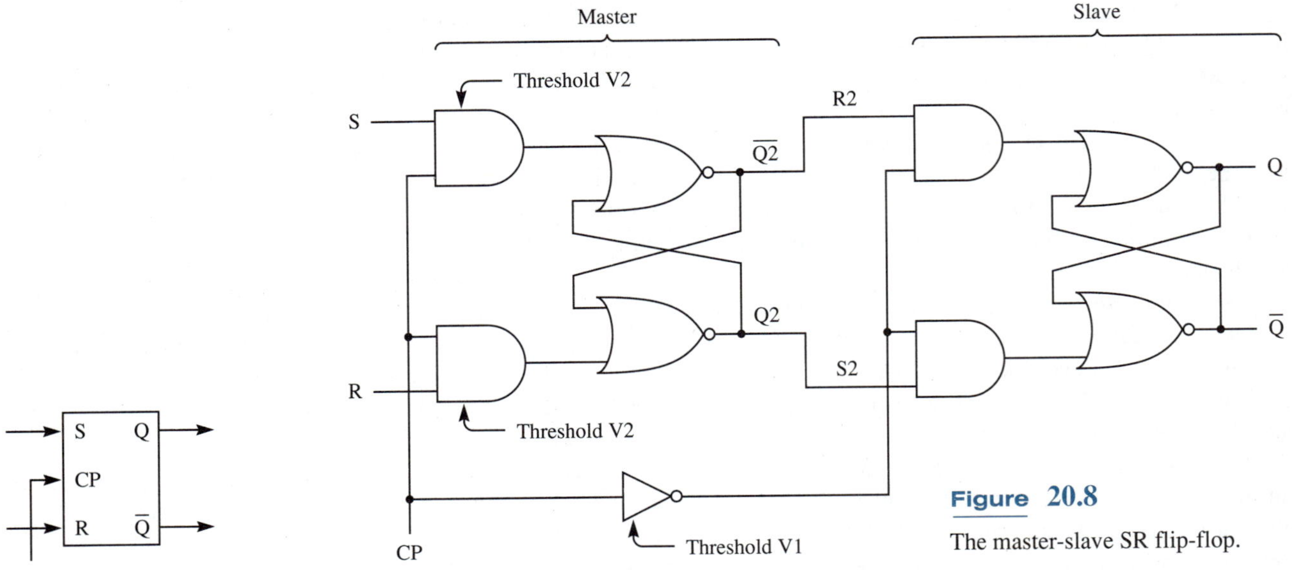

(a) Block diagram.

(b) Implementation.

Figure 20.8

The master-slave SR flip-flop.

threshold of the inverter, V1, must be less than the threshold of the master enable gates, V2.

Figure 20.9 shows V1 and V2 on a magnified timing diagram of CP during one clock pulse. The clock does not make an instantaneous transition from a low to high value. Instead, it gradually increases first to value V1 at time t_1, then to value V2 at time t_2 on the way to its high level. On the way down it passes through value V2 at time t_3, then V1 at time t_4.

Before the pulse begins its upward transition, the master is disabled from the input. Regardless of the value of SR, the master will remain in its established state. The inverter ensures that the slave input is connected to the master because the slave inputs are enabled. The slave must be in the same state as the master.

As the clock signal rises and falls, passing through times t_1, t_2, t_3, and t_4, the effect of the circuit is as follows:

- t_1: Isolate slave from master.
- t_2: Connect master to input.
- t_3: Isolate master from input.
- t_4: Connect slave to master.

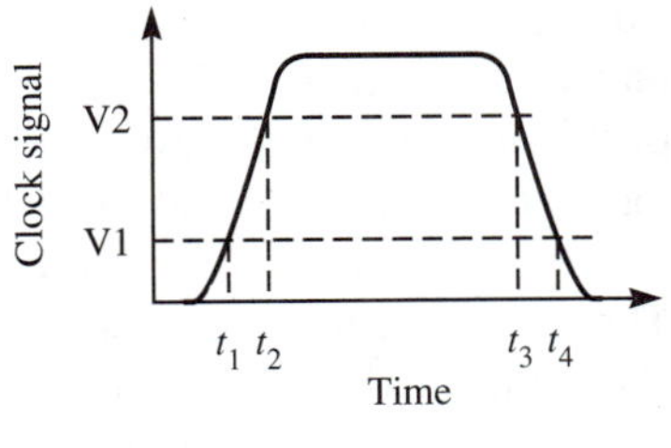

Figure 20.9

Timing detail of a single clock pulse.

At time t_1 the signal reaches the threshold of the inverter, which makes the output of the inverter change from 1 to 0. A 0 to the enable gates of the slave shields the slave from any further effects of S2 and R2. Whatever state the slave was in at time t_1, it will remain in that state as long as CP is above the threshold value V1.

At time t_2 the signal reaches the threshold of the master enable gates, which makes the master sensitive to the SR inputs. If SR is 10 the input will set the master to Q2 = 1. If SR is 01 the input will reset the master to Q2 = 0. If SR is 00 the master will not change its state. However, if the master does change its state its new state will not affect the slave, since the slave was isolated from the master at time t_1.

Consider how this arrangement protects the flip-flop from the feedback connection of Figure 20.7. The feedback is based on the $Q\bar{Q}$ output of the slave, which does not change as a result of the input to the master. The fact that V1 is less than V2 ensures that the slave will be isolated from the master before the master becomes sensitive to the input. Even if the gate delay through the combinational net were zero, the feedback would not affect the state of the slave.

When CP makes its high-to-low transition, the clock reaches value V2 at time t_3. V2 is the threshold of the enable gates for the master, so now the master becomes insensitive to the input. Since V2 is greater than V1 the slave is still isolated from the effect of the master.

At time t_4, the clock signal becomes less than the threshold of the inverter. The output of the inverter changes from 0 to 1, connecting the slave to the master. Whatever state the master was in is forced on the slave. The slave may change its state. If there is feedback from the output of the slave to the input of the master, it will not affect the master since the master was isolated from the input at time t_3.

The decompression chamber analogy

A rough analogy of the operation of a master-slave circuit is a decompression chamber in a spacecraft. Inside the craft, the astronauts do not need to wear spacesuits. To go for a space walk outside the craft an astronaut dons a spacesuit and approaches the decompression chamber, which has two doors that are initially closed.

The astronaut opens the inner door, which connects the chamber with the craft, and steps inside the chamber. She closes the inner door, isolating the chamber from the craft, and opens the outer door, connecting the chamber with outer space. She exits the outer door, closing it behind her. At no time are both doors open at the same time. If they were, the craft would loose all its air to outer space.

Similarly, the master-slave circuit has two doors—one to isolate or connect the master to the input, and one to isolate or connect the slave to the master. At no time are both doors open, with the master connected to the input and the slave connected to the master. If they were, a feedback loop might cause an unstable state in the circuit.

Figure 20.10 is a timing diagram of the behavior of a master-slave SR flip-flop. A change occurs in Q, the state of the slave latch, at time t_4, when the slave is connected to the master. That is during the high-to-low transition of CP.

Since a flip-flop is not combinational, a truth table is not sufficient to characterize its behavior. Instead, flip-flops have *characteristic tables* that specify the

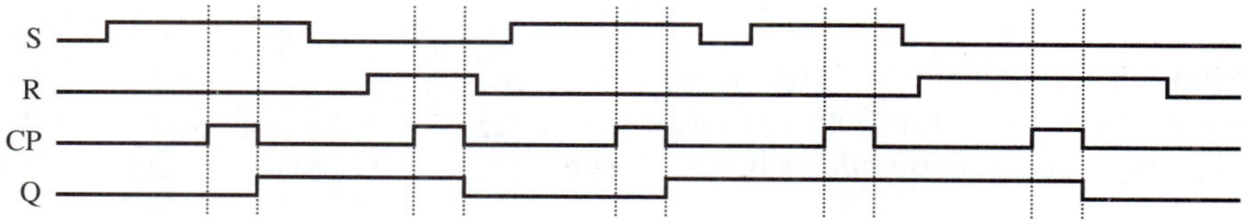

Figure 20.10

A timing diagram of the master-slave SR flip-flop.

Table 20.3

The characteristic table for the SR flip-flop.

S(*t*)	R(*t*)	Q(*t*)	Q (*t* + 1)	Condition
0	0	0	0	No change
0	0	1	1	
0	1	0	0	Reset
0	1	1	0	
1	0	0	1	Set
1	0	1	1	
1	1	0	–	Not defined
1	1	1	–	

state of the device after one clock pulse for a given input and initial state. Table 20.3 is the characteristic table for the SR flip-flop.

S(*t*) and R(*t*) are the inputs at time *t* before a clock pulse. Q(*t*) is the state of the flip-flop before a clock pulse, and Q(*t* + 1) is the state after the pulse. The table shows that if SR is 00 the device does not change its state when clocked. If SR is 01 the device resets to Q = 0, and if it is 10 the device sets to Q = 1. It is impossible to predict what the state would be if SR = 11 when clocked.

The characteristic table is, in essence, a state transition table similar to Table 16.1 for a finite state machine. An SR flip-flop is a finite state machine with two possible states, Q = 0 and Q = 1. As with any finite state machine, its behavior can be characterized by a state transition diagram. Figure 20.11 is the state transition diagram for an SR flip-flop.

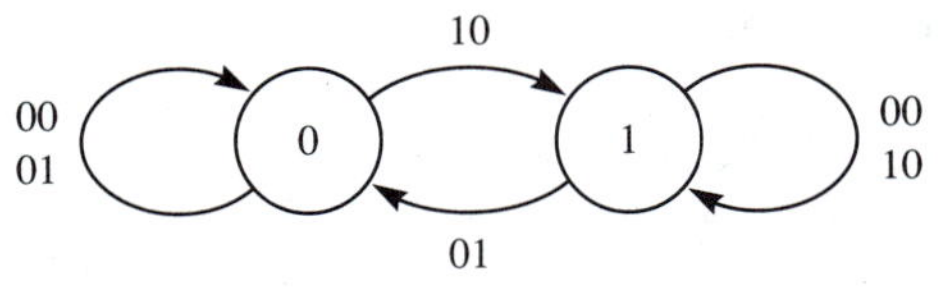

Figure 20.11

The state transition diagram for an SR flip-flop.

Circles denote the states of the machine with the value of Q inside the circle. Transitions are labeled with the values of SR that produce the given transition. For example, the transition from Q = 0 to Q = 1 is labeled with SR = 10.

The Basic Flip-Flops

The SR flip-flop is one of four basic flip-flops common in computer design. The other three are the JK, D, and T flip-flops. These three flip-flops can all be constructed from the SR flip-flop. The following is a description of each device with its characteristic table and implementation. The state transition diagrams are left for the exercises at the end of the chapter.

The *JK flip-flop* resolves the undefined transition in the SR flip-flop. The J input acts like S, setting the device, and the K input acts like R, resetting the device. But when JK = 11 the condition is called the *toggle condition*. Table 20.4 is the characteristic table for the JK flip-flop.

J(*t*)	K(*t*)	Q(*t*)	Q (*t* + 1)	Condition
0	0	0	0	No change
0	0	1	1	
0	1	0	0	Reset
0	1	1	0	
1	0	0	1	Set
1	0	1	1	
1	1	0	1	Toggle
1	1	1	0	

Table 20.4

The characteristic table for the JK flip-flop.

Toggling means switching from one state to the other. In the toggle condition, if the initial state is 0 the final state will be 1, and if the initial state is 1 the final state will be 0.

Figure 20.12 shows a block diagram of the JK flip-flop and an implementation with an SR flip-flop and two AND gates.

To understand the implementation, consider the four possibilities for JK. If JK is 00, SR will be 00 because the AND of 0 with any value is 0. The SR flip-flop, therefore, will not change its state when clocked.

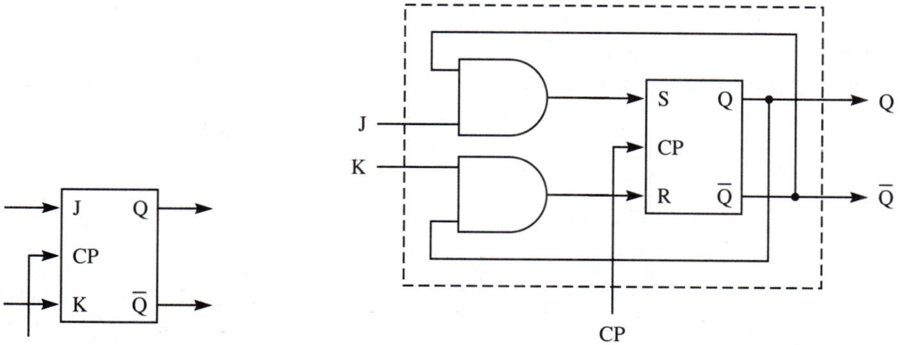

(a) Block diagram.

(b) Implementation.

Figure 20.12

The JK flip-flop.

If JK is 10, R must be 0. On one hand, if Q is 0, $\bar{Q}$ will be 1 and SR will be 10,the set condition. The flip-flop will change its state to Q = 1. On the other hand, if Q is 1, $\bar{Q}$ will be 0 and SR will be 00, the no-change condition. The flip-flop will remain in state Q = 1. In either case the final state will be Q = 1, which it should be with JK in the set condition.

Similarly, if JK is 01 the final state will be Q = 0, which it should be with JK in the reset condition.

If JK is 11, Q connects directly to R, and $\bar{Q}$ connects directly to S. If Q is 1, SR will be 01 and the SR flip-flop will be reset to Q = 0. If Q is 0, SR will be 10 and the SR flip-flop will be set to Q = 1. In either case the flip-flop will toggle.

The *D flip-flop* is a *data* flip-flop. It has only one input, D, besides the clock. Table 20.5 is the characteristic table of the D flip-flop.

Table 20.5

The characteristic table for the D flip-flop.

D(*t*)	Q(*t*)	Q(*t* + 1)	Condition
0	0	0	Delay
0	1	0	
1	0	1	Delay
1	1	1	

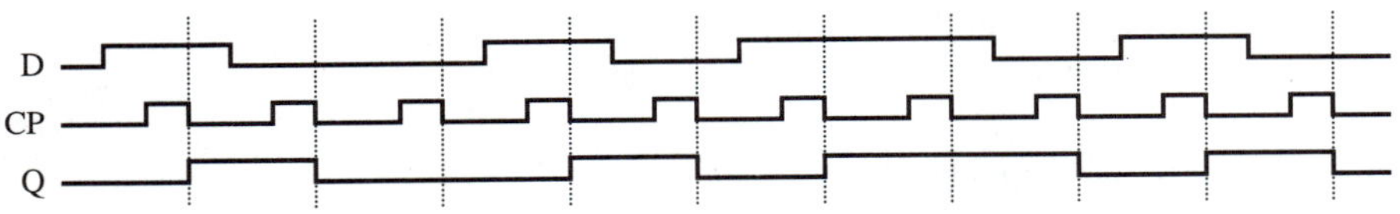

Figure 20.13

A timing diagram of the D flip-flop.

The table shows that Q(*t* + 1) is independent of Q(*t*). It depends only on the value of D at time *t*. The D flip-flop stores the data until the next clock pulse. Figure 20.13 shows a timing diagram for the D flip-flop. This flip-flop is also called a *delay* flip-flop because on the timing diagram, the shape of Q is identical to that of D except for a time delay.

Figure 20.14 shows the block diagram and implementation of the D flip-flop. The implementation requires a single inverter in addition to the SR flip-flop. This

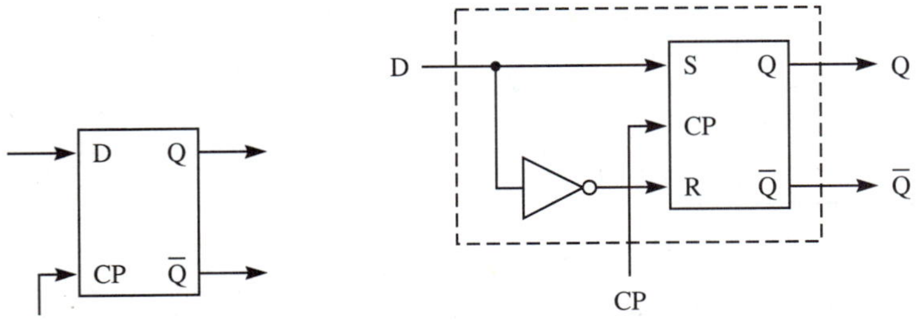

(a) Block diagram.

(b) Implementation.

Figure 20.14

The D flip-flop.

T(*t*)	Q(*t*)	Q(*t* + 1)	Condition
0	0	0	No change
0	1	1	
1	0	1	Toggle
1	1	0	

Table 20.6

The characteristic table for the T flip-flop.

implementation has no feedback connections from Q or $\overline{Q}$ as the JK implementation does because the next state does not depend on the current state.

The *T flip-flop* is a *toggle* flip-flop. Like the D flip-flop it has only one input, T, besides the clock. Table 20.6 is the characteristic table of the T flip-flop.

The T input acts like a control line that specifies a selective toggle. If T is 0 the flip-flop does not change its state, and if T is 1 the flip-flop toggles. Figure 20.15 shows the block diagram and implementation of the T flip-flop.

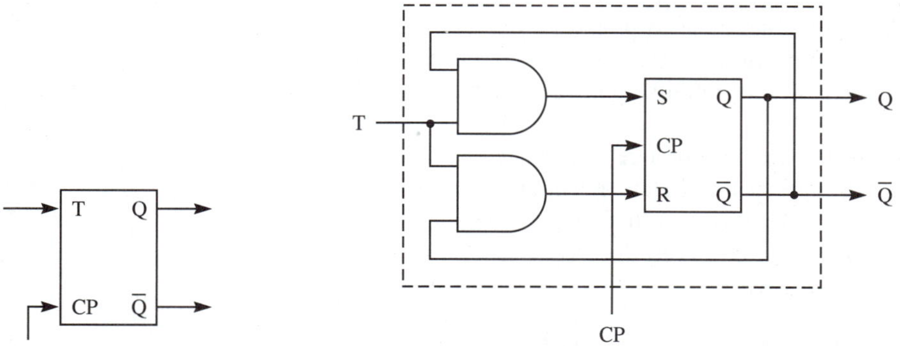

(a) Block diagram. (b) Implementation.

Figure 20.15

The T flip-flop.

The implementation is identical to that of the JK flip-flop with J and K constrained to have the same values. If T is 0, SR is 00 and Q does not change. If T is 1, SR has the complement values of $Q\overline{Q}$ and Q toggles.

20.2 Sequential Analysis

A sequential circuit consists of an interconnection of gates and flip-flops. Conceptually, you can group all the gates together into a combinational net and all the flip-flops together in a group of *state registers*, as in Figure 20.16. This is a generalization of Figure 20.7, which contained only one state register and whose output required no additional gates from the combinational net.

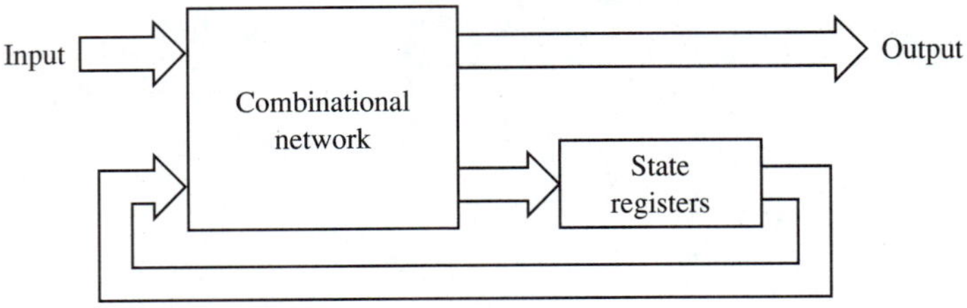

Figure 20.16

A general sequential network.

The solid arrows in Figure 20.16 represent one or more connecting lines. The input and output lines are the external connections to the environment of the circuit. The lines from the combinational net to the state registers are the input lines to SR, JK, D, or T flip-flops. The feedback lines are from the flip-flops' Q and $\bar{Q}$ outputs to the combinational net. The figure assumes a common clock line (not shown) to each flip-flop in the group of state registers.

Between clock pulses, the combinational part of the circuit produces its output from the external input and the state of the circuit, that is, the states of the individual flip-flops. The amount of time it takes to produce the combinational output and the state register input depends on how many gate levels are in the net. The CP period is adjusted to be long enough to allow the input to propagate through the combinational net to the output before the next clock pulse. All the state registers are edge-triggered or master-slave to protect against multiple propagations through the feedback loop.

As in Figure 20.11, you can describe the behavior of a general sequential network with a state transition diagram or its corresponding state transition table. The difference is that Figure 20.11 is for a single device with two possible states, whereas Figure 20.16 is for n flip-flops. Since each flip-flop has two possible states, the sequential network has a total of 2^n states.

The difference between analysis and design at the hardware level is the same as the difference at the software level. Figure 20.17 illustrates the difference. In analysis, the input and sequential network are given and the output is to be determined. In design, the input and desired output are given and the sequential network is to be determined.

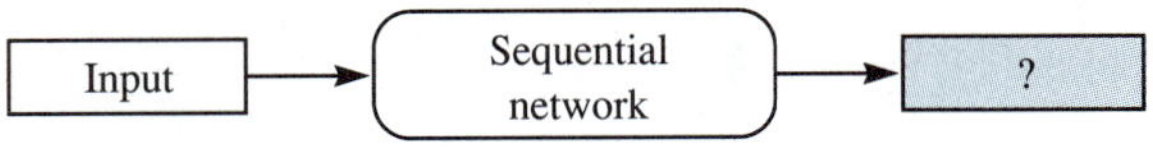

(a) Analysis—The input and sequential network are given. The output is to be determined.

(b) Design—The input and desired output are given. The sequential network is to be determined.

Figure 20.17

The difference between analysis and design.

This section shows how to determine the output from a given sequential circuit and input stream. The general approach is to construct the state transition table and transition diagram from the circuit. From them you can easily determine the output stream for any given input stream.

Example 20.1 Suppose the circuit of Figure 20.18 is given. The state registers are the two D flip-flops labeled FFA and FFB. The combinational net is the group of three AND gates. The inputs are X1 and X2, and the single output is Y. The feedback loop consists of the line from Q of FFA, labeled A, and the two lines from Q and $\bar{Q}$ of FFB labeled B and $\bar{B}$. The input to FFA is labeled DA, and the input to FFB is labeled DB.

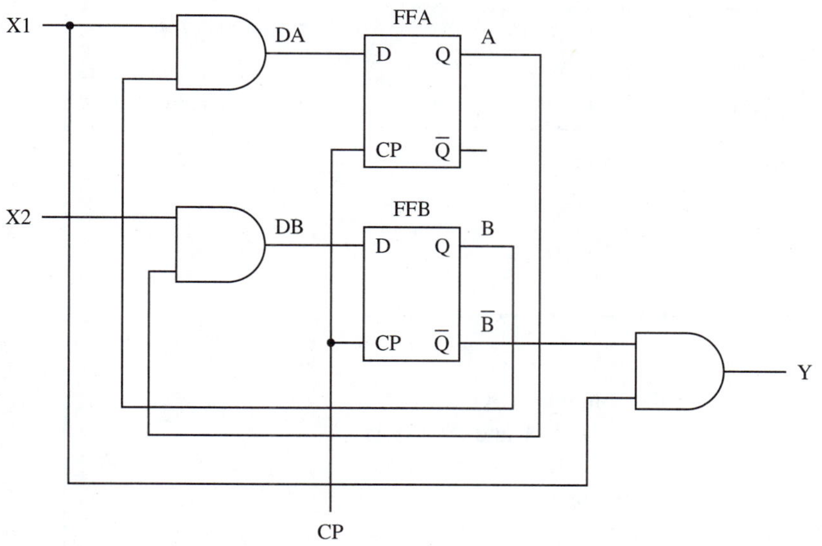

Figure 20.18

The circuit for analysis in Example 20.1.

Since there are two flip-flops, there are four possible states,

AB = 00
AB = 01
AB = 10
AB = 11

where, for example, AB = 01 means that Q = 0 in FFA and Q = 1 in FFB. Since there are two inputs, there are four possible input combinations,

X1 X2 = 00
X1 X2 = 01
X1 X2 = 10
X1 X2 = 11

Here is the problem. You are given a current state, AB, and a current input, X1 X2. (a) What is the current output? (b) What will be the next state after a clock pulse occurs? Since there are four states, and with each state there are four possible input combinations, you must answer these questions 16 times.

For D flip-flops, $Q(t+1) = D(t)$. The state at time $t + 1$ is equal to the D input at time t. From the circuit you know that

$$\begin{aligned} A(t+1) &= X1\ B(t) \\ B(t+1) &= X2\ A(t) \\ Y(t) &= X1\ \overline{B}(t) \end{aligned}$$

Table 20.7 is the state transition table from these relationships.

Table 20.7

The state transition table for the circuit of Figure 20.18.

Present state		Next state, present output (AB, Y)			
		Input X1 X2			
A	B	00	01	10	11
0	0	00, 0	00, 0	00, 1	00, 1
0	1	00, 0	00, 0	10, 0	10, 0
1	0	00, 0	01, 0	00, 1	01, 1
1	1	00, 0	01, 0	10, 0	11, 0

For example, consider the row for AB = 10 under the column for X1 X2 = 01. Since X1 is 0 and $B(t)$ is 0, $A(t + 1)$ also must be 0. Since X2 is 1 and $A(t)$ is 1, $B(t + 1)$ also must be 1. Therefore, the next state is AB = 01. The present output (before the transition) is 0 because it is the AND of X1 and $\overline{B}$, and X1 is 0.

Figure 20.19 is the state transition diagram from the table. The states in the circles are the values of AB. The transitions are labeled with input/present output, where input is the value of X1 X2. Again, the present output is the output before the transition, not after the transition.

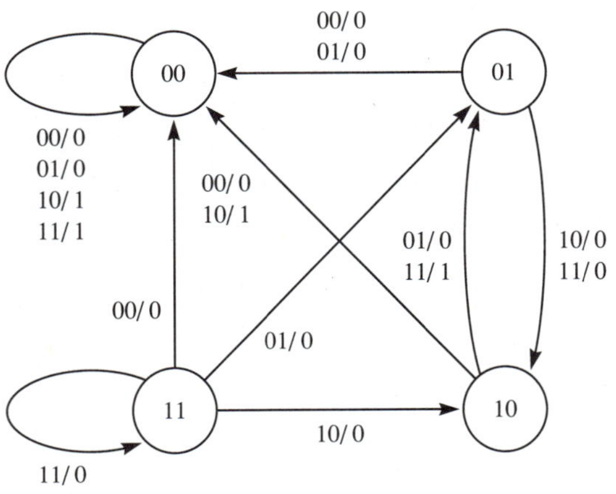

Figure 20.19

The state transition diagram for the circuit of Figure 20.18.

It is usually much easier to visualize the behavior of the circuit from the diagram than from the table. For example, from Figure 20.19 you can easily see that once you enter state 00 you can never leave it.

To determine the output from a given input stream, assume that you start in state AB = 11 and input the following values of X1 X2:

11, 01, 10, 10, 11

From the diagram you will make transitions to the states:

11, 11, 01, 10, 00, 00

and will generate the following output:

0, 0, 0, 1, 1 ■

The analysis is similar for sequential circuits containing other flip-flops or even mixtures of different types of flip-flops. Using your knowledge of combinational nets, you would simply determine the input of each flip-flop for all possible combinations of inputs and states. Then, from the characteristic table of each flip-flop, you would determine what the next state will be. In general, if there are *m* inputs and *n* flip-flops, you will need to analyze $2^m 2^n$ transitions.

The output sequence for the previous example assumed that the flip-flops were both in their Q = 1 state. A legitimate question is, How do the flip-flops get in their start states? In practice, most flip-flops are constructed with two additional inputs, called *preset* and *clear*. These inputs are *asynchronous;* that is, they do not depend on the clock pulse to function. Figure 20.20 shows the block diagram of an SR flip-flop with asynchronous preset and clear inputs.

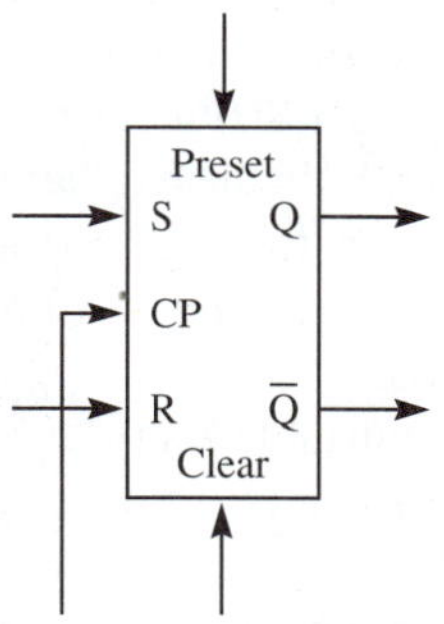

Figure 20.20

The block diagram of an SR flip-flop with asynchronous preset and clear.

In normal operation, both preset and clear lines are 0. To initialize the flip-flop to Q = 1, send preset to 1 and back to 0. To initialize the flip-flop to Q = 0, send clear to 1 and back to 0. You do not need to send a clock pulse while either input is high for it to function. Implementation of the asynchronous preset and clear is left as an exercise at the end of the chapter.

20.3 Sequential Design

With sequential design the behavior of the circuit is given, frequently in the form of a state transition diagram, and the implementation of the circuit with a minimum number of gates is to be determined. Also given in the problem formulation is the type of flip-flop to be used for the state registers in the sequential circuit.

Excitation Tables

Characteristic tables are useful in sequential analysis but not as useful in sequential design. The analysis problem asks what the next state is for a given state and input, a question answered by the characteristic table. The design problem asks what input is required for a given initial state and final state, a question answered by the *excitation table*. Table 20.8 shows the excitation tables for the four basic flip-flop types.

Table 20.8(a) is the excitation table for the SR flip-flop. The first table entry is for the transition from Q = 0 to Q = 0. There are two possible inputs that permit this transition, namely SR = 00 and SR = 01. An SR value of 00 specifies the no change condition. An SR value of 01 specifies the reset condition. Either of these conditions will cause the flip-flop to make the transition from Q = 0 to Q = 0.

The × in the entry under R(*t*) is a don't-care value. As long as S is 0, you do not care what the value of R is. The transition will be from Q = 0 to Q = 0 regardless of the value of R.

The second entry in the table is for the transition from Q = 0 to Q = 1. The only way to force this transition is to input 10 for SR, the set condition. Similarly, the third entry is for the transition from Q = 1 to Q = 0, which can only occur with a value of 01 for SR.

The last entry is for the transition from Q = 1 to Q = 1. The two possible input conditions that permit this transition are SR = 00, the no change condition, and SR = 10, the set condition. Regardless of the value of S, if R is 0 the transition will occur. The × under S(*t*) indicates the don't-care condition for S.

Table 20.8(b) is the excitation table for the JK flip-flop. The first table entry is for the transition from Q = 0 to Q = 0. Using the same reasoning as with the SR flip-flop, the transition will occur if JK is 00 or 01; hence the don't-care condition under K(*t*).

The second table entry also has a don't-care condition. The transition from Q = 0 to Q = 1 can occur under two conditions. JK can be either 10, the set condition, or 11, the toggle condition. Both allow Q to change from 0 to 1.

The excitation tables for D in Table 20.8(c) and T in Table 20.8(d) do not have don't-care values for the input.

Sequential Design

The design procedure has three steps. First, from the state transition diagram tabulate the transitions of the circuit. For each combination of present state and input, list the next state and the present output. Then, from the excitation tables list the necessary flip-flop input conditions to cause the transitions.

Second, transfer the entries for each flip-flop input to a Karnaugh map. It helps to prevent mistakes if you look ahead in your tabulation of the first table and list the entries in the same order as a Karnaugh map. Design the combinational part of the sequential circuit by minimizing the expressions from the Karnaugh map.

Third, draw the minimized combinational circuit. Each flip-flop input will come from a combinational net two gate-levels deep at most.

Example 20.2 This example illustrates the design procedure. The problem is to implement the state transition diagram of Figure 20.21 with SR flip-flops. As in Figure 20.19, the transitions are labeled with the input values, X1 X2, and the present output, Y. The values in the state circles are the Q values of the first SR flip-flop, FFA, and the second SR flip-flop, FFB.

This machine has only three input combinations and four states, for a total of 12 transitions. The input combinations are 01, 11, and 10. Since the combination 00 is not expected to occur, you can treat it as a don't-care condition to help with the minimization.

Q(*t*)	Q(*t* + 1)	S(*t*)	R(*t*)
0	0	0	×
0	1	1	0
1	0	0	1
1	1	×	0

(a) The SR flip-flop.

Q(*t*)	Q(*t* + 1)	J(*t*)	K(*t*)
0	0	0	×
0	1	1	×
1	0	×	1
1	1	×	0

(b) The JK flip-flop.

Q(*t*)	Q(*t* + 1)	D(*t*)
0	0	0
0	1	1
1	0	0
1	1	1

(c) The D flip-flop.

Q(*t*)	Q(*t* + 1)	T(*t*)
0	0	0
0	1	1
1	0	1
1	1	0

(d) The T flip-flop.

Table 20.8

Excitation tables for the four basic flip-flops.

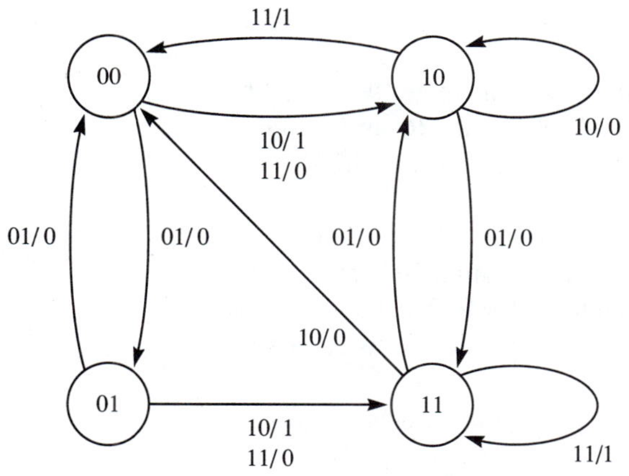

Figure 20.21

The state transition diagram for the design problem of Example 20.2.

To implement a finite state machine with eight states, you need three flip-flops. To implement a machine with five to seven states also requires three flip-flops, but some of the states are not expected to occur and can be treated as don't-care states.

Table 20.9 is the first step in the design process. The four columns on the left are all the possible combinations of present state and input. The middle three

Present state		Input		Next state		Present output	Flip-flop input conditions			
							FFA		FFB	
A	B	X1	X2	A	B	Y	SA	RA	SB	RB
0	0	0	1	0	1	0	0	×	1	0
0	1	0	1	0	0	0	0	×	0	1
1	1	0	1	1	0	0	×	0	0	1
1	0	0	1	1	1	0	×	0	1	0
0	0	1	1	1	0	0	1	0	0	×
0	1	1	1	1	1	0	1	0	×	0
1	1	1	1	1	1	1	×	0	×	0
1	0	1	1	0	0	1	0	1	0	×
0	0	1	0	1	0	1	1	0	0	×
0	1	1	0	1	1	1	1	0	×	0
1	1	1	0	0	0	0	0	1	0	1
1	0	1	0	1	0	0	×	0	0	×

Table 20.9

The design table for the state transition diagram of Figure 20.21.

columns are a simple tabulation of the next state and present output from Figure 20.21.

The four columns on the right come from the fact that there are two SR flip-flops, each with two inputs. SA is the S input of FFA, RA is the R input of FFA, and so on. The flip-flop input conditions that produce the given transition come from the excitation table for the SR flip-flop, Table 20.8(a).

For example, consider the first line for the transition from AB = 00 to AB = 01. The transition for FFA is from Q = 0 to Q = 0. The excitation table shows that transition is caused by a 0 for S and a don't-care condition for R. The transition for FFB is from Q = 0 to Q = 1. The excitation table shows that transition is caused by 10 for SR.

The next step is to consider that each flip-flop input is a function of four variables—the present state, AB, and the input, X1 X2. To design the combinational net requires a four-variable Karnaugh map for each flip-flop input. Figure 20.22 shows the Karnaugh maps from Table 20.9. The map for input SA, Figure 20.22(a) shows the row values for the state AB and the column values for the input X1 X2.

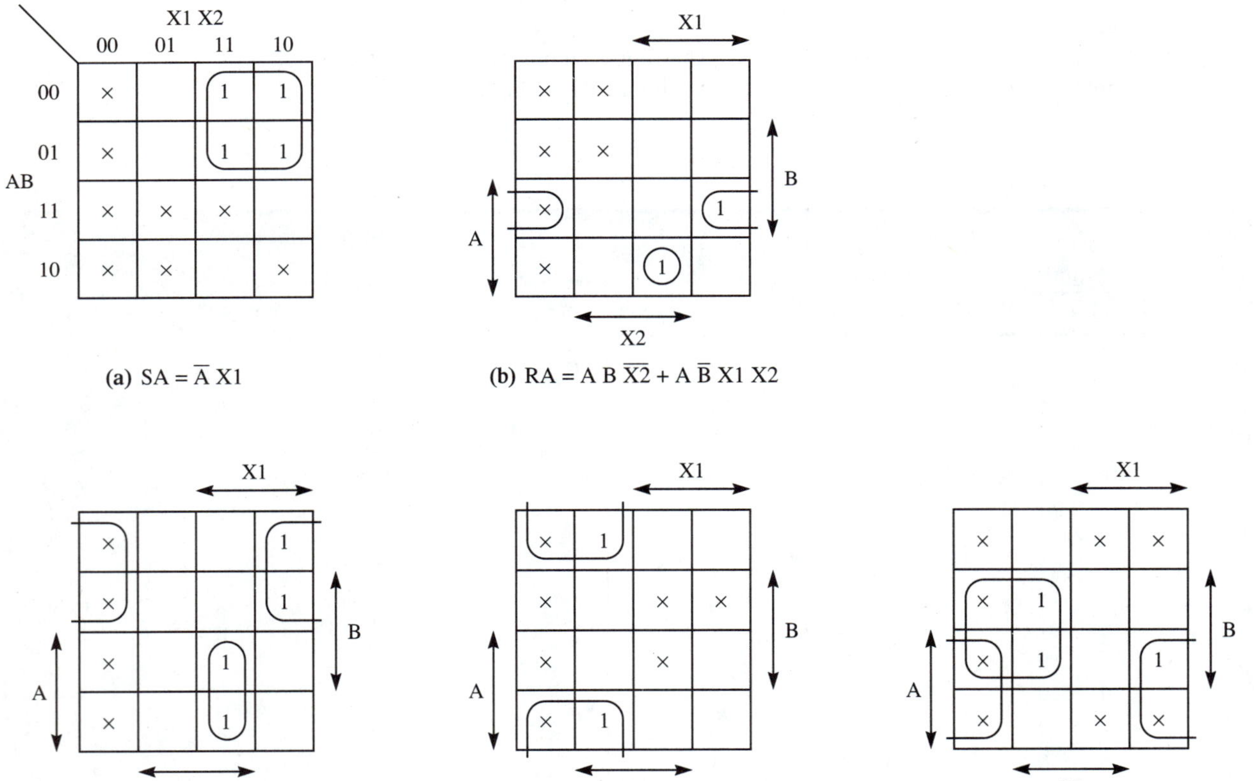

(a) SA = $\overline{A}$ X1

(b) RA = A B $\overline{X2}$ + A $\overline{B}$ X1 X2

(c) Y = $\overline{A}$ $\overline{X2}$ + A X1 X2

(d) SB = $\overline{B}$ $\overline{X1}$

(e) RB = B $\overline{X1}$ + A $\overline{X2}$

Figure 20.22

The Karnaugh maps for Example 20.2.

Note that the combination X1 X2 = 00, the first column in the Karnaugh maps, is a don't-care condition.

The output, Y, is also a function of the present state and input and requires a Karnaugh map for minimization. Shown below each Karnaugh map is the corresponding minimized expression.

Figure 20.23 is the resulting sequential network. Rather than show the feedback connections explicitly, the diagram is in abbreviated form. ■

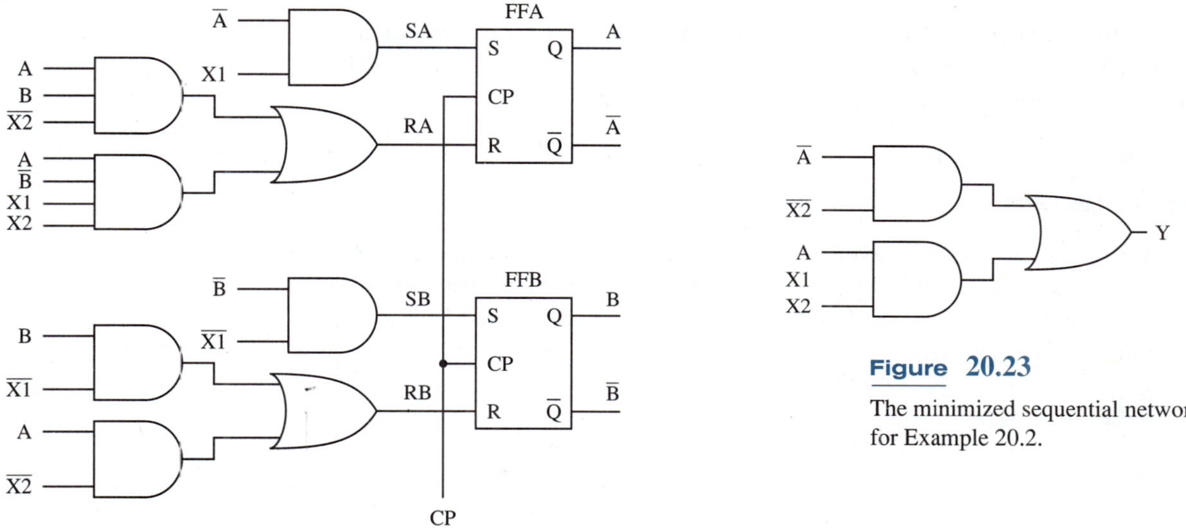

Figure 20.23

The minimized sequential network for Example 20.2.

The design procedure illustrated by Example 20.2 had two flip-flops and two inputs, for a total of four variables in the Karnaugh map. Four-variables maps would also be required for a design with three flip-flops and one input, or one flip-flop and three inputs. The procedure for one flip-flop and two inputs, or two flip-flops and one input would be identical except that three-variable Karnaugh maps would suffice for the minimization.

Some sequential circuits require minimization of a combinational net with more than four variables. Karnaugh maps cannot conveniently handle a problem of that size. Systematic procedures exist to deal with these larger problems but are beyond the scope of this book.

20.4 Constructing a Level 3 Machine

This final section shows the connection between the combinational and sequential networks at Level 1 and the machine at Level 3. It describes how hardware devices can be connected to form black boxes at successively higher levels of abstraction to eventually construct the Pep/5 computer. Figure 20.24 is a block diagram of Pep/5.

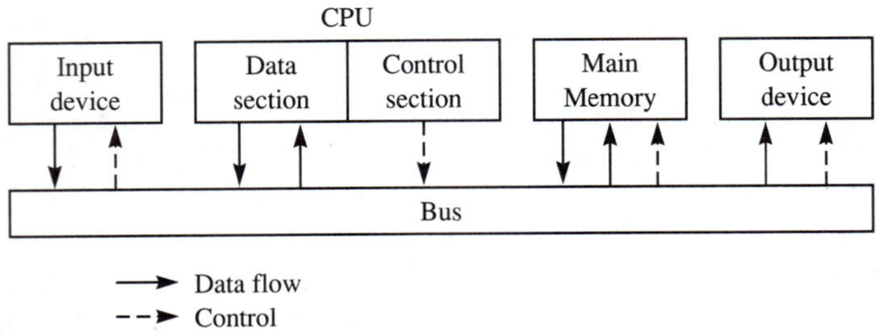

Figure 20.24
Block diagram of the Pep/5 computer.

The figure shows the CPU divided into a data section and a control section. The *data section* receives and sends data from load and store instructions. The *control section* issues the control signals to the other components of the computer.

Registers

A basic building block of the Level 3 machine is the register. You are familiar with the 16-bit registers in the Pep/5 CPU. The instruction set includes instructions to manipulate the register contents. Figure 20.25 shows a block diagram and implementation of a 4-bit register.

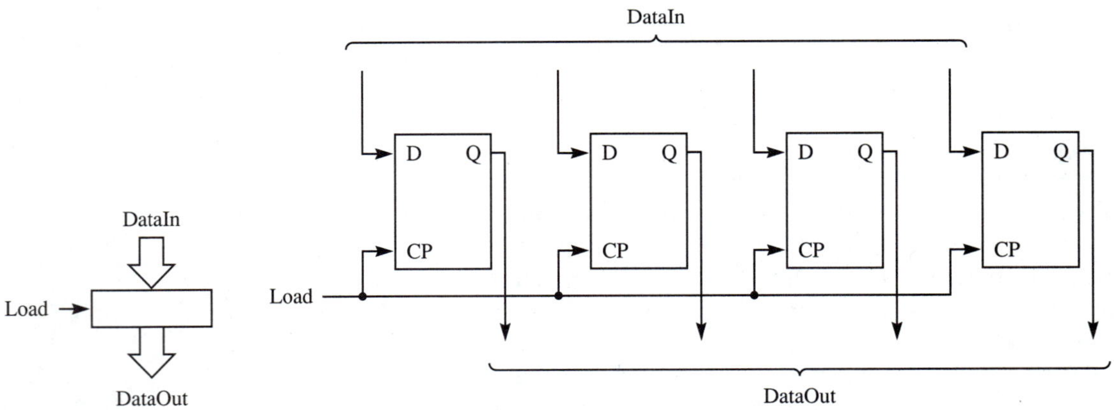

(a) Block diagram.

(b) Implementation with D flip-flops.

Figure 20.25
A 4-bit register.

The register has four data inputs, four data outputs, and a control input that is labeled Load. The block diagram shows the four data lines as a single wide arrow. The implementation shows the data lines individually.

The register is simply an array of D flip-flops. Each data input line connects to the D input of a flip-flop. Each data output line connects to the Q output of a flip-flop. The load input connects to the clock inputs of all the flip-flops.

The register operates by presenting the values you wish to load into the register on the data input lines. You then clock them into the register by sending the load signal to 1 and back to 0. All four values will be loaded simultaneously into the register. If each flip-flop is a master-slave device, the output will appear when the slave is connected to the master at time t_3 of Figure 20.9.

Each D flip-flop is a bit in the register. An 8-bit register would have 8 flip-flops and a 16-bit register would have 16 flip-flops. The number of flip-flops would not affect the speed of the load operation, since the load into each flip-flop occurs simultaneously. The block diagram of Figure 20.25(a) is the same regardless of the number of bits in the register.

Main Memory

Conceptually, main memory is simply an array of registers. Each register is a cell with an address in main memory. Figure 20.26 is the block diagram and implementation of a tiny main memory with only four cells. The sequential devices are shaded to distinguish them from the combinational devices.

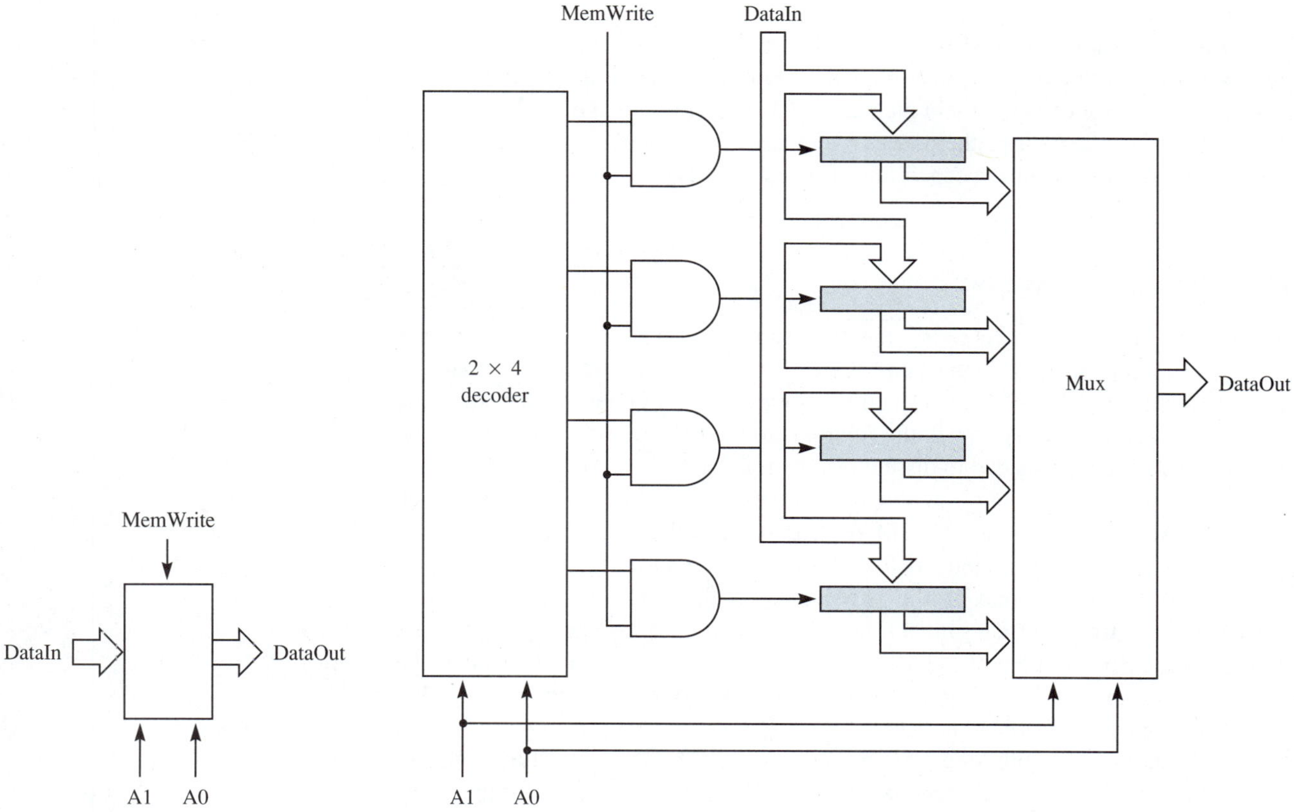

(a) Block diagram.

(b) Implementation with a set of registers.

Figure 20.26

Main memory.

The memory device has a set of data input lines and a set of data output lines. You cannot tell from the figure how many bits are in each register. The number of data lines in the wide arrows equals the number of bits in each register. Pep/5 memory has eight bits in each cell.

Each cell has an address, which ranges from 0 to 3 because of the two address lines. To read the content of a memory cell, set A1 A0 to the address of the cell you wish to access, and DataOut will provide the value.

Reading a value from memory

In the implementation, Mux is a four-input multiplexer. Actually, it is *n* four-input multiplexers, where *n* is the number of data lines. A1 A0 specifies which of the four inputs is routed to the single output. For example, if A1 A0 is 01 then the content of the second register from the top will be routed to DataOut.

To store a value to memory, first you set A1 A0 to the address of the cell you wish to receive the value and then you clock it into memory by sending MemWrite to 1 and back to 0. As long as MemWrite is 0, the output of each AND gate will be 0 and none of the load lines will be activated. The 2×4 decoder enables only one of the AND gates, the one specified by the address A1 A0. When you send MemWrite to 1, DataIn will be clocked into only that register specified by the address.

Writing a value to memory

If each register contained 8 bits, this circuit would be a 4×8 memory device with a total of 32 bits. In practice, memory devices are much larger than 32 bits. The maximum size of Pep/5 main memory is $64K \times 8$, for a total of 512 Kbits. The 64K comes from 2^{16}, since there are 16 address lines in Pep/5. That size is well within current manufacturing capabilities for a single device.

The Data Section

The CPU is divided into two parts—the data section and the control section. Figure 20.27 is the data section of the Pep/5 CPU. The bus on the left of the figure is the bus of Figure 20.24 to which main memory and the I/O devices are attached. The control section, not shown in the figure, is to the right of the data section. The sequential devices are shaded to distinguish them from the combinational devices.

Each wide arrow in the figure represents eight data lines. Each register—ALatch, BLatch, MARA, MARB, and MBR—has eight bits. Each multiplexer—AMux, ALUMux, and MBRMux—is a two-input multiplexer whose single control line routes one of the two inputs to the single output. A 0 on a multiplexer control line routes the left input to the output. A 1 routes the right input to the output. For example, if the MBRMux control line is 0, MBRMux routes the content of the bus to the MBR. Similarly, if the AMux control line is 0, AMux routes the content of MBR to the ALU.

The data flow is a big loop, starting with the 32 8-bit registers at the top, and proceeding to ALatch and BLatch via ABus and BBus, through AMux to the ALU, through ALUMux, and finally back to the bank of 32 registers via CBus. Data from main memory can be injected into the loop from MBR, the *memory buffer register*. MAR is the *memory address register*, a 16-bit register divided into two 8-bit registers labeled MARA (the most significant byte) and MARB (the least significant byte).

The memory buffer register and memory address register

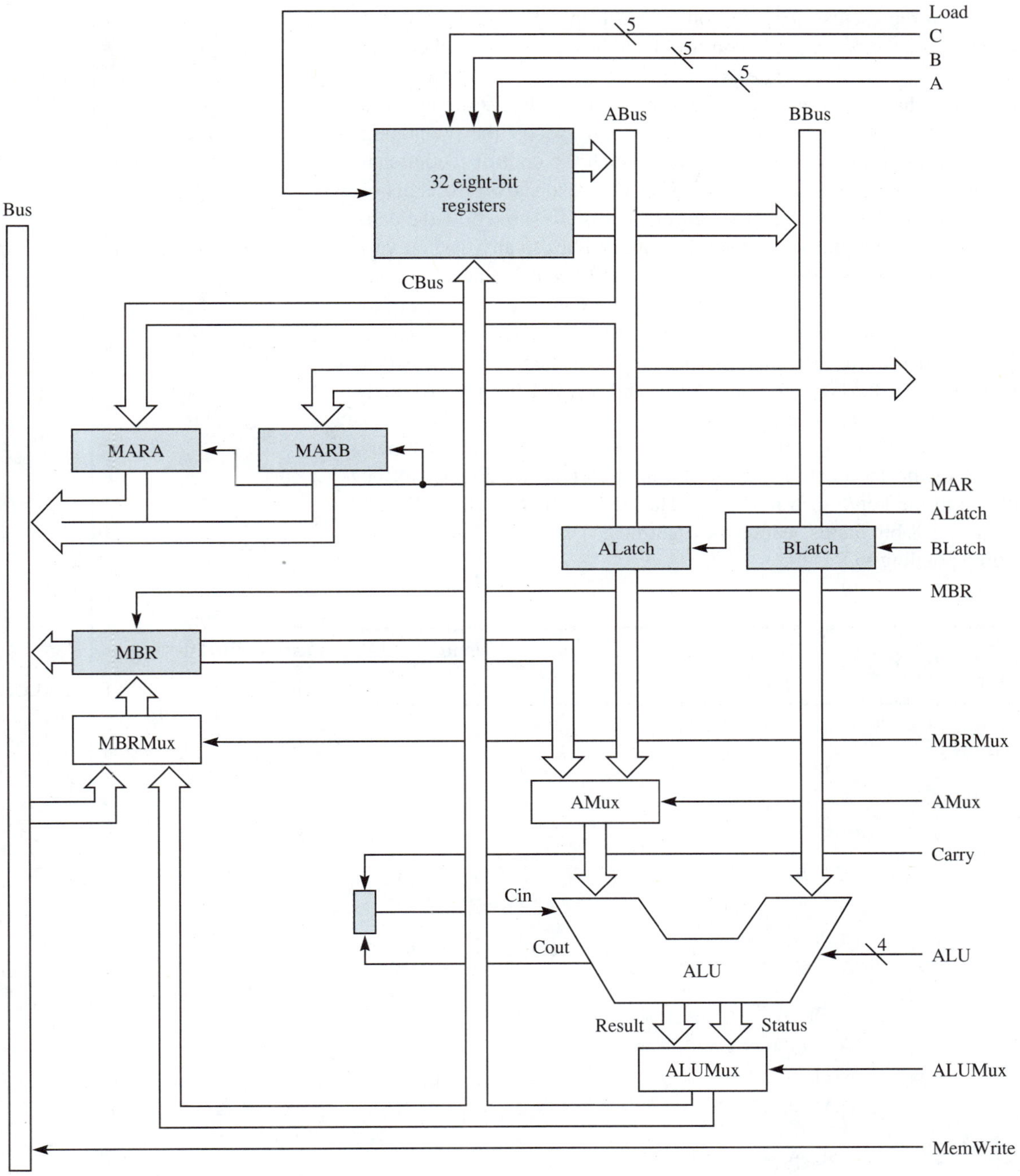

Figure 20.27

The data section of the Pep/5 CPU. The control section, not shown, is to the right.

A line with a slash represents more than one control line. The number by the slash is the number of lines. For example, control line C has five wires and control line ALU has four.

The control section has 29 output lines and 8 input lines. The 29 output lines control the flow of data around the data section loop and specify the processing that is to occur. The 8 input lines come from BBus, which the control section can test for certain conditions. It is beyond the scope of this book to show the details of how the control section generates the proper control signals. To show how the data section works, we will assume that we can set the control lines to any desired values at any time. The following is a description of how the 29 control lines function.

Control lines A and B select two registers from the bank of 32 registers to place on ABus and BBus respectively. Control lines ALatch and BLatch can be pulsed to clock the values from ABus and BBus into the latches. If AMux is 0 it routes the contents of MBR through the multiplexer, and if it is 1 it routes ALatch. BLatch is always the other input to the ALU.

The four ALU control lines specify which of 16 functions the ALU will perform. Table 20.10 lists the 16 functions, most of which correspond directly to the operations available in the Pep/5 instruction set. The ALU outputs an 8-bit Result and simultaneously an 8-bit Status value, the rightmost 4 bits of which are the NZVC values corresponding to Result.

Table 20.10

The 16 functions of the Pep/5 ALU.

ALU control	Result	Status			
		N	Z	V	C
0000	A	N	Z	0	0
0001	A + Cin	N	Z	V	C
0010	A + B	N	Z	V	C
0011	A + B + Cin	N	Z	V	C
0100	A − B	N	Z	V	C
0101	A − B − Cin	N	Z	V	C
0110	A AND B	N	Z	0	0
0111	A AND B AND Cin	N	Z	0	0
1000	A OR B	N	Z	0	0
1001	A OR B OR Cin	N	Z	0	0
1010	NOT A	N	Z	0	0
1011	NOT A + Cin	N	Z	V	C
1100	ASL A	N	Z	V	C
1101	ROL A	N	Z	0	C
1110	ASR A	N	Z	0	C
1111	ROR A	N	Z	0	C

Computer Networks

Networking refers to getting two or more computers to communicate with each other. The local-area network (LAN) is becoming increasingly popular in small businesses or within office work groups. Rather than buying five stand-alone computers, each with its own hard disk, it may be cheaper to buy one machine with a large hard disk and four workstations, even though the network cabling and software may cost up to a couple of hundred dollars per workstation. The machine with the disk is designated as the server from which the other machines can retrieve programs and data, and on which they may save information. Before genuine networking arrived on the scene, either every machine had to have its own printer attached or you had to rely on the SneakerNet—saving the data on a floppy disk and hand-carrying it over to a machine that did have a printer attached. Today networked machines can each be connected directly to a central printer. If you consider the added savings of only having to buy one printer, in addition to the convenience of each machine being able to send output directly to a printer, the savings really start to add up.

However, the advantages of LANs are not strictly monetary: data sharing can be helpful—even necessary—if you want to give each member of your work group access to the same information. For applications like inventory management, it's critical that sales terminals all debit the same file of stock on hand as customers make purchases; otherwise the clerk at terminal A might sell the same last three widgets as the clerk at terminal B.

Getting a LAN up and running is not quite as simple as plugging in the cables and loading a networking program. A business typically needs to designate a network administrator to smooth out the details of connecting the machines. There are also security issues to be considered. Data sharing can be a disadvantage if your system allows sales clerks to access the payroll files and grant themselves a raise! Thus, most networking systems allow the network administrator to assign passwords to individual users—the passwords allow the users to gain access only to the information they need.

Wide-area networks (WANs) are used to connect computers not located in the same building, or even in the same city. High-speed dedicated data lines or satellite connections may be used to link computers separated by great distances. Electronic mail (E-mail) is sent over WANs. WANs also support remote log-in services, which allow you to log in to a supercomputer at another location, transfer a program over from your microcomputer, run the program, and receive the results electronically.

Network topologies, the way in which the components are connected, vary according to the physical distances involved and the performance characteristics expected by the users. LANs used within a small office environment may have a star topology in which a server is located in the middle and the remote workstations are each connected to it. In this configuration, the workstations are not directly connected to each other. Although conceptually simple, this design has a few drawbacks. The server can only handle one request at a time, so remote machines may have to wait sometimes for another workstation's request to be serviced first. Also, if the server breaks down, the remote stations are dead in the water, at least as far as network communications goes.

In response to these problems, more sophisticated topologies such as the ring have been devised. In a ring topology, the computers in the network are connected in a loop, and each machine is weighted equally in terms of network control. When one machine initiates a request for a service from another one, the message is transmitted around the ring in both directions simultaneously. The message is sent in a packet labeled with the destination machine's name, and each machine along the way examines the packet, looking to see if the message is addressed to it. If one machine in the loop breaks down, the message will still reach its destination the other way around the loop. If both messages get through, the one that arrives later is discarded. Of course, topologies like the ring require more sophisticated software to ensure that messages sent from more than one machine at the same time are staggered in such a way as to guarantee that they get through in a timely fashion. But the convenience of bypassing SneakerNet systems makes it worth investing in a more complex network.

The Carry control line is the clock input to a 1-bit register (a single D flip-flop) whose input is the carry output from the ALU. The output from the register is the carry input to the ALU. The register stores the carry from one ALU operation to be used as input for a subsequent ALU operation.

Example 20.3 To perform a 16-bit addition you would input the low-order bytes into the ALU, select an ALU control of 0010 (bin), and pulse the Carry control line to save the carry output. Then you would input the high-order bytes into the ALU and select an ALU control of 0011 (bin), which adds A, B, and Cin. Since the carry was saved from the low-order computation, it is available as input for the high-order computation. ■

A value of 0 for ALUMux routes Result through the multiplexer. A value of 1 routes Status. To put the output from ALUMux into one of the 32 registers, select the desired register with the value of C, and clock it in by sending Load to 1 and back to 0.

Memory Access

Reading a value from memory

To read a value from memory, the address of the desired cell must be loaded into MAR, the memory address register. A Pep/5 address is 16 bits, assumed to be in two of the 8-bit registers in the register bank. To get the address into MAR, select it with the A and B lines, then clock it into MARA and MARB by pulsing the MAR control line.

The address from MAR travels along the bus to main memory. As in Figure 20.26(b), the memory device uses the address from the bus to select one of 64K cells to send to DataOut. The information from DataOut is placed on the bus. The CPU gets the data by clocking it into MBR, the memory buffer register.

To get the data into MBR, set MBRMux to 0, which routes the data from the data lines on the bus to the output of the multiplexer. Then pulse the MBR control line to clock the data into MBR.

If you want to load the data from MBR into one of the 32 registers, send it through AMux by setting the AMux control line to 0, and through the ALU by setting the ALU control lines to 0000 (bin), which gives Result the value of the left input of the ALU. Set the ALUMux control line to 0, and clock Result into the desired register specified by C.

Writing a value to memory

To write a value to memory, the address must be loaded into MAR as with a memory read. Then, assuming that the value to write is also in one of the 32 registers, you must transfer it to MBR. Connect the desired register to ABus, and pulse ALatch. Set AMux to 1, ALU to 0, ALUMux to 0, MBRMux to 1, and clock the value into the memory buffer register by pulsing the MBR control line.

Now that the address and data value are on the bus, pulse MemWrite. MemWrite is a control signal that travels on the bus to the memory device of Figure 20.26(b). DataIn as well as the address lines are connected to the bus. When MemWrite is pulsed, it clocks DataIn into the memory cell specified by the value on the address line.

The Level 1 Registers

Figure 20.28 shows the 32 8-bit registers, addressed from 0 to 31. Figure 20.28(a) looks familiar. It shows the seven registers visible to the programmer at the machine level. Each 16-bit register is divided into two 8-bit registers. That division is invisible to the machine level programmer.

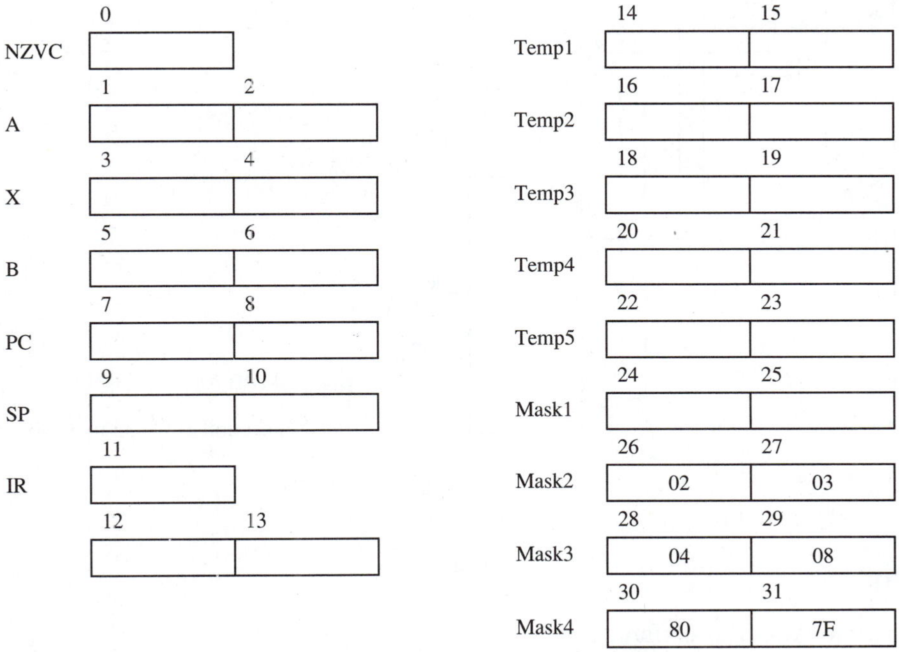

(a) The registers visible at Level 3.

(b) The registers not visible at Level 3.

Figure 20.28

The 32 8-bit registers in the data section.

Figure 20.28(b) shows the remaining registers, which are not visible to the machine level programmer. Registers 14 through 23 comprise a group of registers for storing temporary values. Registers 24 through 31 are read-only registers that contain fixed values. They are similar to ROM in that if you select one of them with C and pulse the Load control line, the value in the register will not change. Their constant values are given in hexadecimal.

Figure 20.29 shows the interconnection of the 32 registers. The sequential devices are shaded to distinguish them from the combinational devices.

The input follows the same organization as a main memory device. The five control lines from C make one decoder output line 1 and the rest 0. CBus is connected to each of the 32 registers. When you pulse the Load control line, the value on CBus is clocked into one of the registers.

The output is also organized like a memory device, except that the data output from each register encounters a junction that sends the data to two multiplexers instead of just one. Any two registers can be simultaneously connected to ABus and BBus. It is even possible to put the same register on both busses.

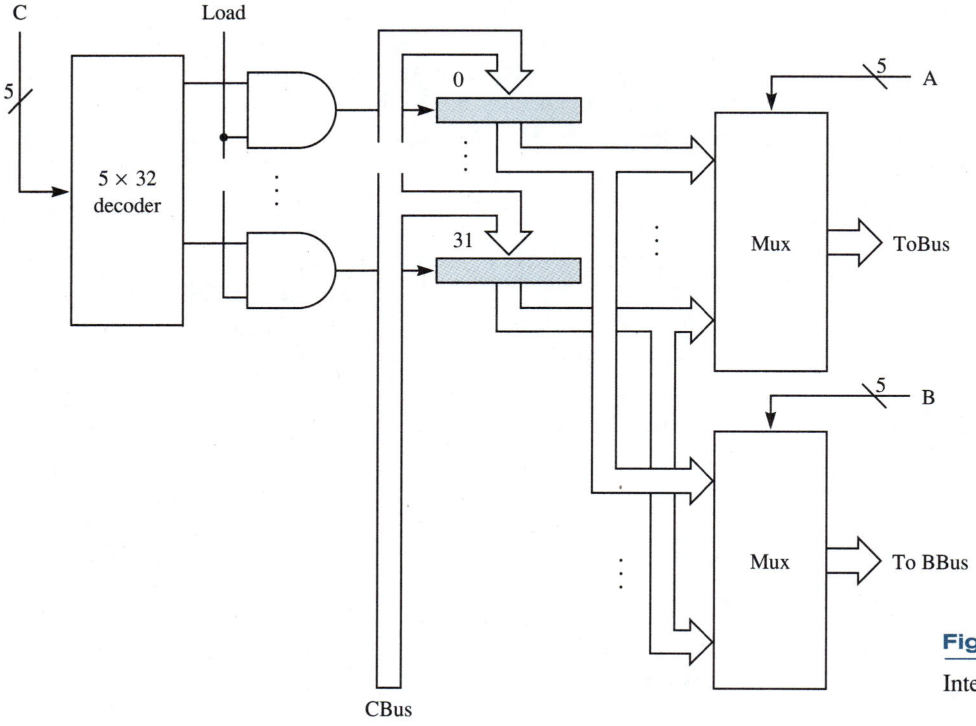

Figure 20.29

Interconnection of the 32 registers.

The Arithmetic Logic Unit

Table 20.10 shows the operations that the ALU can perform. Listed with each operation are the values of the corresponding NZVC bits, which are the rightmost 4 bits of the 8-bit status output. Figure 20.30 shows how some of the status bits are derived.

The computation unit inside the ALU performs the 16 functions, the first 6 of which are arithmetic functions and the last 10 of which are logical functions. The unit could be implemented as eight stages of a 1-bit ALU, each of which is similar to the one of Figure 19.47 but with four select lines instead of just two.

The leftmost 4 bits of the Status output are always 0. The N bit is 1 when the Result is negative. Since Pep/5 uses two's complement binary representation, N is simply a copy of the sign bit. The Z bit is 1 if Result is 0, so it is simply the NOR of all eight Result lines.

The values of the V and C bits are sometimes not applicable, particularly with the logical operations. Table 20.10 shows that in those cases the ALU output makes them 0 regardless of the value of Result. For example, with an ALU control value of 6, which is A AND B, N and Z are affected but V and C are 0. Figure 20.30 shows that V and C are produced by the computation unit whose details are not shown. (See Exercise 19.47 for the implementation of the V bit with addition.) Cout from the ALU and C from the Status output are identical.

The functions that the ALU can perform at Level 1 correspond closely with the operations of Pep/5's instruction set at Level 3. The primary difference is that

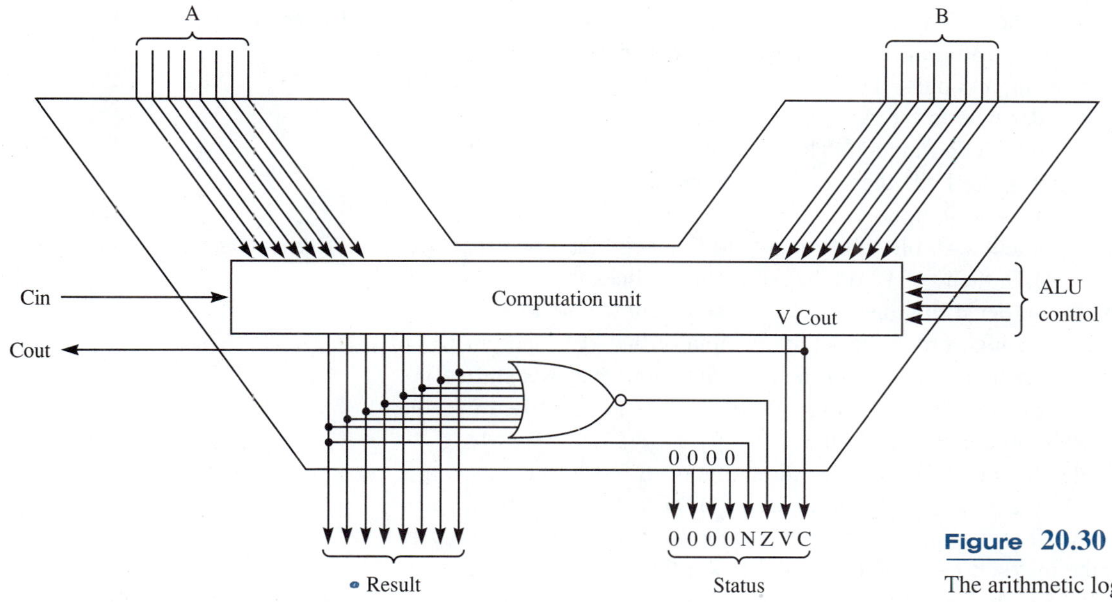

Figure 20.30

The arithmetic logic unit.

the ALU operates on 8-bit quantities while the instructions operate on both 8- and 16-bit quantities. To perform a 16-bit operation at Level 1 requires two 8-bit operations, as indicated in Example 20.3.

Figure 20.31 shows the ALU shift and rotate functions at Level 1. The rotate functions are useful for implementing 16-bit shifts at Level 3. ASR shifts each bit to the right, duplicates the sign bit and shifts the least significant bit to Cout. ASR ignores Cin. ROR rotates each bit to the right and is identical to ASR except that the most significant bit comes from Cin. ROL rotates each bit to the left, taking the least significant bit from Cin and sending the most significant bit to Cout. ROL is the inverse operation of ROR. ASL shifts each bit to the left, taking a zero as the least significant bit and sending the most significant bit to Cout. ASL and ASR are the familiar arithmetic operations illustrated in Figures 12.13 and 12.14.

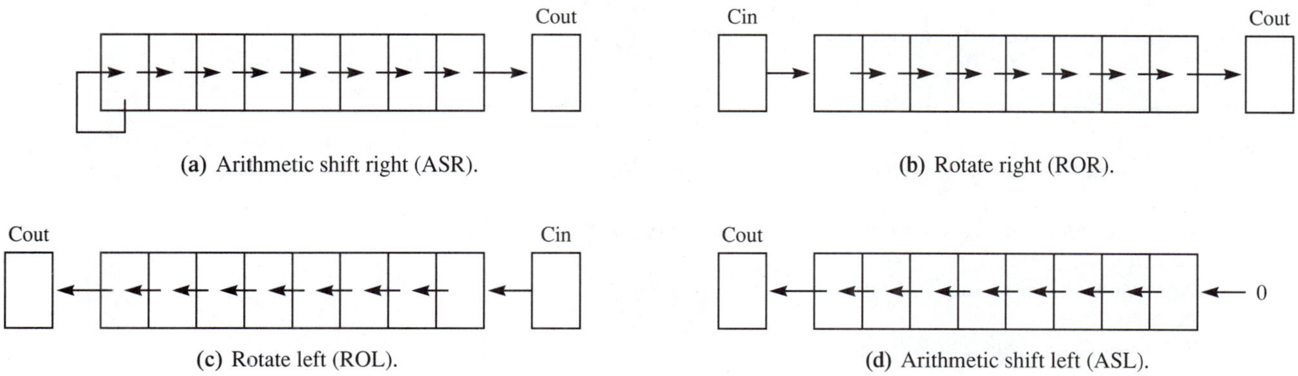

Figure 20.31

The ALU shift and rotate functions at Level 1.

Implementing a 16-bit ASR

To implement a 16-bit ASR you would first send the high-order byte to the A input of the ALU, then put 14 on the ALU control lines to select the ASR function, store the high-order result, and pulse the Carry control line to save Cout. Then you would send the low-order byte to the A input of the ALU and put 15 on the ALU control lines to select the ROR function. The carry that was shifted out from the low-order bit of the high-order byte, therefore, would be shifted into the high-order bit of the low-order byte as desired.

Implementing a 16-bit ASL

Similarly, to implement a 16-bit ASL you would first send the low-order byte to the A input of the ALU, then put 12 on the ALU control lines to select the ASL function, store the low-order result, and pulse the Carry control line to save Cout. Then you would send the high-order byte to the A input of the ALU and put 13 on the ALU control lines to select the ROL function. The carry that was shifted out from the high-order bit of the low-order byte, therefore, would be shifted into the low-order bit of the high-order byte as desired.

Note from Table 20.10 that the ASL function affects all four status bits, while ROL, ASR, and ROR affect only N, Z, and C, with a 0 for V. V is 0 for these functions because an overflow is impossible with a right shift or a rotate. Compare Table 20.10 with the instruction set of Table 14.2 to see the similarity of the status bits affected at Level 5 with the Status output of the ALU.

The von Neumann Cycle

Section 13.3 listed a pseudocode description of the von Neumann execution cycle that contained the following code fragment for incrementing the program counter:

```
if the instruction is unary then
   PC := PC + 1
else
   PC := PC + 3
```

A more detailed description of the von Neumann cycle at a lower level of abstraction follows. At this level of abstraction, we see that the control section always increments PC by 1. If, after inspecting the instruction specifier the control section determines that the instruction is nonunary, it increments PC by 1 twice more.

Pseudocode description of the von Neumann execution cycle

```
repeat
   Fetch the instruction specifier from the address as specified by PC
   PC := PC + 1
   if the opcode of the instruction specifier indicates a nonunary instruction then
      begin
      Fetch the high-order byte of the operand specifier as specified by PC
      PC := PC + 1
      Fetch the low-order byte of the operand specifier as specified by PC
      PC := PC + 1
      end
   Execute the instruction fetched
until (the stop instruction executes) or (an illegal operation is attempted)
```

The control section sends control signals to the data section to implement the von Neumann cycle. What follows is the control sequence to fetch a unary instruction and to increment `PC` by 1. Not shown is the method by which the control section determines whether the instruction is unary. The necessary control signals to fetch the operand specifier if it is not unary are not shown either.

Each line consists of a set of control signals that are input into the combinational devices, followed by a clock pulse into a register. The combinational signals, denoted by the assignment operators, must be set up for a long enough period of time to let the data reach the register before being clocked into the register. Comments are enclosed in braces.

The control sequence for the fetch and increment part of the von Neumann cycle for a unary instruction

```
{  Transfer PC to MAR and fetch instruction specifier. }
1. A:=7, B:=8, MAR
2. MBRMux:=0, MBR
3. AMux:=0, ALU:=0, ALUMux:=0, C:=11, Load

{  Add one to PC, low-order byte first. }
4. A:=8, B:=25, ALatch, BLatch
5. AMux:=1, ALU:=2, ALUMux:=0, C:=8, Carry, Load
6. A:=7, ALatch
7. AMux:=1, ALU:=1, ALUMux:=0, C:=7, Load
```

Lines 1–3 fetch the instruction specifier. Line 1 puts register 7 on ABus and register 8 on BBus. Figure 20.28 shows registers 7 and 8 to be the two halves of the program counter. The MAR pulse on line 1 clocks `PC` into the memory address register (MAR).

The address in MAR goes along the bus to main memory, which puts the content of the cell specified by MAR on the data lines of the bus. Line 2 sets MBRMux to 0, which routes the data from the bus to the output of the multiplexer. The MBR pulse on line 2 clocks the instruction specifier into the memory buffer register.

Line 3 sends the instruction specifier from MBR into the instruction register, `IR`, as follows. It sets AMux to 0, which routes the MBR to the output of the multiplexer. Next, it sets ALU to 0, which passes the data through the ALU unchanged. It sets ALUMux to 0, which routes Result through the multiplexer. Then it sets C to 11, which specifies the instruction register (Figure 20.28). Finally, it pulses Load, which clocks the content of the MBR into the instruction register.

In line 3, the control section must not set up the combinational signals and pulse Load at the same time. It must wait for the content of MBR to propagate through the two multiplexers and the ALU before it pulses Load. The control section designer must count the number of gate delays through those combinational nets to figure how long to wait before clocking the data in.

Lines 4–7 increment `PC` by 1. Line 4 puts the low-order byte of `PC` on ABus and constant 1 on BBus, and clocks them into ALatch and BLatch.

In line 5, AMux selects ALatch to pass through the multiplexer. A value of 2 for ALU selects the A + B function of the arithmetic logic unit. Since the low-order byte of PC has been loaded into the ALatch and 1 has been loaded into the BLatch, the ALU adds 1 to the low-order byte of PC. A value of 0 for ALUMux sends the sum through the multiplexer, and a value of 8 for C puts the sum back into the low-order byte of PC. The Carry pulse saves the carry output from the low-order addition. Both the Carry and Load clock pulses must wait long enough for the data to flow through the combinational devices specified by the other control signals in line 5, before triggering the loads into their registers.

If the original low-order byte of PC is 1111 1111 (bin), then adding 1 will cause a carry to the high-order byte. Line 6 brings the high order byte of PC to ALatch. Line 7 Selects the A + Cin function for the ALU, adding the saved carry to the high-order byte of the PC. The control section puts 7 on the C line to load the result of the addition back to the high-order byte of the PC.

Although the details of the control section are not shown, you can imagine how it would test the instruction just fetched to determine if it is unary. The control section would set B to 11 to put the instruction specifier on BBus, which it then could test. If the instruction fetched was not unary, the control section must fetch the operand specifier, incrementing PC accordingly. The control sequence to fetch the operand specifier and increment PC is left for an exercise at the end of the chapter.

After fetching an instruction, whether unary or not, the control section tests the instruction specifier to determine which of the 32 instructions to execute. The control signals to execute the instruction will depend not only on the opcode, but on the register specifier and addressing mode as well. Recall that the relation between the operand (Oprnd) and the operand specifier (OprndSpec) for each addressing mode is

Relation between the operand and operand specifier for the four Pep/5 addressing modes

- Immediate Addressing:
  `Oprnd = OprndSpec`
- Direct Addressing:
  `Oprnd = Mem [OprndSpec]`
- Indexed Addressing:
  ```
  if byte instruction then
     Oprnd = Mem [B + X + OprndSpec]
  else
     Oprnd = Mem [B + 2*X + OprndSpec]
  ```
- Stack-Relative Addressing:
  `Oprnd = Mem [SP + OprndSpec]`

The quantity in square brackets is a memory address. To execute the instruction, the control section must provide control signals to the data section to compute the memory address. For example, to execute a byte instruction that uses the indexed addressing mode, the control section must perform a 16-bit addition of the contents of B (registers 5 and 6), X (registers 3 and 4), and OprndSpec (registers 12 and 13). The result of this addition is then loaded into MAR in preparation for a memory read in case of a LOAD instruction or memory write in case of a STORE instruction.

The control sequence to implement the first part of the von Neumann execution cycle looks suspiciously like a program in some low-level programming language. The job of control section designers is to devise a circuit that, in effect, programs the data section to implement the instructions at Level 3, the machine level. The language at Level 1 is a specification of the binary signals to input into the combinational nets and the clock pulses to input into the state registers.

The next few examples show the control sequence necessary to execute some representative instructions. Each example assumes that the instruction has been fetched and `PC` incremented accordingly. The control sequences are called programs to emphasize their similarity to programs at higher levels of abstraction. Each statement in the program is written on a separate, numbered line and consists of a set of combinational signals to route data through some multiplexer or to select some function for the ALU, followed by one or two clock pulses to load some registers. Keep in mind that a program at this level of abstraction (Level 1) consists of the control signals necessary to implement just one instruction at the higher level of abstraction (Level 3).

Program 20.1

Program 20.1 shows the control sequence to execute the instruction

```
STBYTA There,d
```

Since the instruction specifies direct addressing, the control section transfers the operand specifier, which we will assume is already in the instruction register, to the memory address register. Then it transfers the least significant byte of the accumulator to the memory buffer register to be clocked into memory.

Line 1 transfers the operand specifier into MAR. Line 2 latches the least significant byte into ALatch, and line 3 latches it into MBR. Line 4 clocks the data into the operand.

The store instructions do not affect the status bits at the machine level. Consequently, the control section does not tamper with register 0.

```
{  Transfer OprndSpec to MAR. }
1. A:=12, B:=13, MAR

{  Transfer low-order byte of accumulator to MBR. }
2. A:=2, ALatch
3. AMux:=1, ALU:=0, ALUMux:=0, MBRMux:=1, MBR

{  Write MBR to memory. }
4. MemWrite
```

Program 20.1

The control sequence for `STBYTA` with direct addressing.

Program 20.2

In Program 20.2, the control sequence for

```
STOREA There,d
```

has more register transfers than the preceding program. The control sequence must write two bytes to memory, and it must add 1 to the address of the first byte to compute the address of the second byte.

Lines 1–3 transfer the operand specifier to the memory address register and the high-order byte of the accumulator to the memory buffer register. Lines 4–6 add 1 to the operand specifier and put the sum in temporary registers 14 and 15. The remaining lines transfer the incremented operand specifier to the memory address register, the low-order byte of the accumulator to the memory buffer register, and complete the store to memory.

Line 4 shows how several processing steps can occur in parallel if they do not conflict. Rather than pulse MemWrite first and then ALatch and BLatch, they can be pulsed simultaneously. The data flow from ABus and BBus into ALatch and BLatch does not conflict with the data flow from MBR over the bus to main memory. Performing these steps in parallel speeds up the execution of the statement.

```
 {  Transfer OprndSpec to MAR. }
 1. A:=12, B:=13, MAR

 {  Transfer high-order byte of accumulator to MBR. }
 2. A:=1, ALatch
 3. AMux:=1, ALU:=0, ALUMux:=0, MBRMux:=1, MBR

 {  Write MBR to memory.                              }
 {  Add one to low-order OprndSpec and put it in reg 15. }
 {  Put high-order incremented OprndSpec in reg 14.      }
 4. A:=13, B:=25, ALatch, BLatch, MemWrite
 5. AMux:=1, ALU:=2, ALUMux:=0, C:=15, Carry, Load
 6. A:=12, ALatch
 7. AMux:=1, ALU:=1, ALUMux:=0, C:=14, Load

 {  Transfer incremented OprndSpec to MAR. }
 8. A:=14, B:=15, MAR

 {  Transfer low-order byte of accumulator to MBR. }
 9. A:=2, ALatch
10. AMux:=1, ALU:=0, ALUMux:=0, MBRMux:=1, MBR

 {  Write MBR to memory. }
11. MemWrite
```

Program 20.2

The control sequence for STOREA with direct addressing.

Program 20.3

Program 20.3 shows the control sequence to execute the unary instruction

```
ASRX
```

This instruction differs from the previous ones because status bits N, Z, and C are affected. The control sequence must change them accordingly for the machine level programmer without changing the V bit. The main idea is to perform an ASR on the high-order byte followed by a ROR on the low-order byte as shown in Figures 20.31(a) and (b).

```
 {  Perform ASR on the high-order byte of X.   }
 {  Transfer the high-order Status to reg 14. }
 1. A:=3, ALatch
 2. AMux:=1, ALU:=14, ALUMux:=0, C:=3, Carry, Load
 3. AMux:=1, ALU:=14, ALUMux:=1, C:=14, Load

 {  Perform ROR on the low-order byte of X.  }
 {  Transfer the low-order Status to reg 15. }
 {  Save the low-order carry.                }
 4. A:=4, ALatch
 5. AMux:=1, ALU:=15, ALUMux:=0, C:=4, Load
 6. AMux:=1, ALU:=15, ALUMux:=1, C:=15, Carry, Load

 {  Zero out all machine-level status bits except V. }
 7. A:=0, B:=26, ALatch, BLatch
 8. AMux:=1, ALU:=6, ALUMux:=0, C:=0, Load

 {  Put low-order carry in machine level C. }
 9. A:=0, B:=24, ALatch, BLatch
10. AMux:=1, ALU:=9, ALUMux:=0, C:=0, Load

 {  Transfer NHigh to reg 16 and put in machine level N.}
11. A:=14, B:=29, ALatch, BLatch
12. AMux:=1, ALU:=6, ALUMux:=0, C:=16, Load
13. A:=0, B:=16, ALatch, BLatch
14. AMux:=1, ALU:=8, ALUMux:=0, C:=0, Load

 {  Extract ZHigh and ZLow in reg 14 and send to }
 {  machine level Z.                             }
15. A:=14, B:=15, ALatch, BLatch
16. AMux:=1, ALU:=6, ALUMux:=0, C:=14, Load
17. A:=14, B:=28, ALatch, BLatch
18. AMux:=1, ALU:=6, ALUMux:=0, C:=14, Load
19. A:=0, B:=14, ALatch, BLatch
20. AMux:=1, ALU:=8, ALUMux:=0, C:=0, Load
```

Program 20.3

The control sequence for ASRX.

Let NHigh be the N bit from the Status output for the high-order byte and NLow be the N bit from the Status output for the low-order byte. Define ZHigh, ZLow, CHigh, and CLow similarly. Then the machine-level `NZVC` bits must be computed as

- Machine level `N` = NHigh
- Machine level `Z` = ZHigh AND ZLow
- Machine level `V` unchanged
- Machine level `C` = CLow

In addition, the high-order bit of the low-order byte must be CHigh. The following is a description of the control sequence to perform these computations.

Lines 1–3 perform the eight-bit ASR on the high-order byte of the index register and put the resulting Status in temporary register 14. Lines 4–6 do the same for the low-order byte, saving its Status in register 15.

Lines 7 and 8 zero out all the machine-level status bits except `V`. Register 26 contains the binary mask 0000 0010, and a value of 6 for ALU selects the AND operation. Since the rightmost four bits of the machine-level status register are `NZVC`, all bits other than `V` will be masked out and the value of `V` will remain unchanged.

Lines 9 and 10 put the low-order carry in the machine level `C`. Line 9 latches the machine-level status bits into ALatch and all 0's into BLatch. Line 10 selects the A OR B OR Cin function for the ALU. Since B is 0, the effect is A OR Cin, so that the low-order C is ORed into the status bit field without changing any other bit values.

Lines 11–14 transfer NHigh to the machine level `N` via temporary register 16. Line 11 puts the high-order status bits, which were saved in temporary register 14, into ALatch and binary mask 0000 1000 into BLatch. Line 12 selects the A AND B function to extract NHigh and puts it in temporary register 16. Lines 13 and 14 OR this quantity with the machine-level status bits, which installs NHigh.

Lines 15–20 compute the machine-level `Z` bit. Lines 15 and 16 AND the high- and low-level status bits, which were saved in registers 14 and 15, and save the result in temporary register 14. Lines 17 and 18 AND this temporary value with binary mask 0000 0100, which makes all the bit positions 0 except for the `Z` bit. Lines 19 and 20 install `Z` with the same technique that lines 13 and 14 used to install `N`.

The Control Section

The examples just presented illustrate the fundamental nature of a von Neumann computer. The data section is a sequential network with state registers and combinational networks. It is a big finite state machine. Input to the data section consists of data from main memory and control signals from the control section. Output from the data section is also sent to main memory and the control section (via BBus). Each time the control section sends a clock pulse to a state register the machine makes a transition to a different state.

The finite state machine nature of the data section

The number of states is huge but finite. The Pep/5 data section has 37 eight-bit registers and a one-bit carry register for a total of 297 bits of storage, or 2^{297} states. With 8 inputs from the bus and 29 control inputs from the control section, the number of transitions from each state is 2^{37}. The total number of transitions is 2^{297} times 2^{37}, or 2^{334}. The number 2^{334} is greater than the number of atoms that are thought to be in the universe—and Pep/5 is a tiny computer!

Two approaches to the design of the control section

As you recall, control section designers can take two approaches. They can choose to construct the control section directly with sequential networks, or they can devise a microprogramming level between the machine level and the logic gate level.

The microprogramming design of the control section

The second approach imposes structure on the control section that otherwise would not be present. The idea is to force the processing to take place in regular, structured clock cycles. Each clock cycle is subdivided into several subcycles. The various registers in the data section can only be loaded on specific, predetermined subcycles within the cycle.

For example, the control section that controls the data section of Figure 20.27 might divide the clock cycle into three subcycles. The first subcycle could be reserved for clocking data from the register bank into the MAR or ALatch and BLatch, the second for clocking data into the MBR, and the third for clocking data into the register bank. The programming language for such a control section would consist of a set of microprogramming statements, each of which would specify the operations to take place during a complete cycle, with the dataflow starting from the bank of 32 eight-bit registers and ending there as well.

One microprogramming statement, therefore, would do the job of several control sequence statements from our sample programs. For example, one microprogramming statement could do the job of the two control sequences

```
7. A:=0, B:=26, ALatch, BLatch
8. AMux:=1, ALU:=6, ALUMux:=0, C:=0, Load
```

from Program 20.3. With a microprogramming level, the design of a set of Level 2 instructions is based on a common dataflow pattern.

The space/time tradeoff

This is another example of the fundamental space/time tradeoff. Standardizing the Level 2 instruction set on one pattern of control sequences simplifies the design and requires less space on the chip to implement. Simplicity of design also translates directly to low development cost. However, such standardization inevitably means that some desired control sequences cannot be implemented efficiently. This translates to slower execution speed than would otherwise be possible.

Simplifications in the Model

The Pep/5 data section illustrates the basic organizational idea behind all real von Neumann machines. Of course, many simplifications were made to keep the machine easy to understand.

Probably the biggest simplification was the interface of the CPU and main memory with the bus. The Pep/5 model has DataOut of the memory device connected directly to the bus. In the data section, the input of MBRMux is also connected directly to the bus, as is the output of MBR. Such a configuration would be impossible in a real machine because the output of MBR could conflict with DataOut of the memory device.

The control signal to write data to main memory via the bus is also grossly simplified. In a real system, read and write signals are required and must follow complex timing constraints. Nevertheless, the basic organizational principles that were presented are truly representative of a real von Neumann machine.

The Big Picture

Now consider the big picture from Level 7 all the way down to Level 1. Suppose a user is entering data in a database system with an application at Level 7. She wants to enter a numerical value, so she types it and executes an enter command. What lies behind such a seemingly innocuous action?

A Pascal programmer wrote the database system, including the procedure to input the numerical value. The Pascal program was compiled to assembly language, which in turn was assembled into machine language. A compiler designer wrote the compiler and an assembler designer wrote the assembler. The compiler and assembler, being automatic translators, both contain a lexical analysis phase, a parsing phase, and a code generating phase. The lexical analysis phase is based on finite state machines.

The Pascal programmer also used a finite state machine in the numerical input procedure. The compiler translated each Pascal statement in that procedure to many assembly language statements. The assembler, however, translated each assembly language statement into one machine language statement. So the code to process the user's enter command was expanded into many Pascal commands, each of which was expanded into many machine level commands.

Each machine level command in turn was translated into the control section signals to fetch the instruction and to execute it. Each control signal is input to a multiplexer or some other combinational device, or it is a pulse to clock a value into a state register. The sequential circuits are governed by the laws of finite state machines.

Each register is an array of flip-flops, and each flip-flop is a pair of latches designed with the master-slave principle. Each latch is a pair of NOR gates with simple cross-coupled feedback connections. Each combinational part of the data section is an interconnection of only a few different types of gates. The behavior of each gate is governed by the laws of boolean algebra. Ultimately, the user's enter command translates into electrical signals that flow through the individual gates.

The user's enter command may be interrupted by the operating system if it is executing in a multiprogramming system. The enter command may generate a page fault, in which case the operating system may need to execute a page replacement algorithm to determine the page to copy back to disk.

Of course, all these events happen without the user getting any hint of what is going on at the lower levels of the system. Design inefficiencies at any level can tangibly slow the processing to the extent that the user may curse the computer.

Remember that the design of the entire system from Level 7 to Level 1 is constrained by the fundamental space/time tradeoff.

The connection between one signal flowing through a single gate in some multiplexer at Level 1 and the user executing an enter command at Level 7 may seem remote, but it does exist. Literally millions of gates must cooperate to perform a task for the user. So many devices can be organized into a useful machine only by structuring the system into successive levels of abstraction.

Levels of abstraction

It is remarkable that each level of abstraction consists of a few simple concepts. At Level 1, either the NAND or NOR gate is sufficient to construct any combinational circuit. There are only four basic types of flip-flops, all of which can be produced from the SR flip-flop. The simple von Neumann cycle is the controlling force at Level 3 behind the operation of the machine. At Level 4, a process is a running program that can be interrupted by storing its process control block. Assembly language at Level 5 is a simple one-to-one translation to machine language. A high-order language at Level 6 is a one-to-many translation to a lower-level language.

The concept of a finite state machine permeates the entire level structure. A Pascal flowchart is a finite state machine. Finite state machines are the basis of lexical analysis for automatic translators, and they also describe sequential circuits. The process control block stores the state of a process.

Finite state machines

All sciences have simplicity and structure as their goals. In the natural sciences, the endeavor is to discover those laws of nature that explain the most phenomena with the fewest number of mathematical laws or concepts. Paradoxically, computer scientists have also discovered that simplicity is the key to harnessing complexity. It is possible to construct a machine as complicated as a computer only because of the simple concepts that govern its behavior at every level of abstraction.

Simplicity is the key to harnessing complexity.

SUMMARY

A sequential network, constructed from logic gates with feedback loops, can remember its state. The three basic sequential devices are the SR flip-flop (set, reset), the JK flip-flop, the D flip-flop (data or delay), and the T flip-flop (toggle). The S input to the SR flip-flop sets the state to 1, and the R input resets the state to 0. The input condition SR = 11 is undefined. The JK inputs correspond to SR, except that the input condition JK = 11 is defined and toggles the state. The D input transfers directly to the state. If the T input is 1, the state toggles; otherwise it remains unchanged. Each of these flip-flops may be constructed as master-slave devices to solve the instability problem that external feedback would produce.

A general sequential network consists of a combinational network whose output feeds into a set of state registers. The output from the state registers feeds back to the input of the combinational network. A sequential network can be characterized by a state transition diagram, which is a manifestation of a finite state machine. When you analyze a sequential network, you are given the input and the sequential network, and you determine the output.

When you design a sequential network, you are given the input and the desired output and you determine the sequential network. Excitation tables aid the design process. An excitation table for a flip-flop consists of the four possible state changes of the device—0 to 0, 0 to 1, 1 to 0, and 1 to 1—and the input conditions necessary to produce the change. The design process consists of tabulating the input conditions necessary to produce the given state transition diagram, and then designing the combinational network to produce those input conditions.

A register is a sequence of D flip-flops. Main memory is (conceptually) a large set of registers. A CPU is divided into a data section and a control section. The data section consists of a bank of registers, some of which are visible to the machine level programmer; an arithmetic logic unit; a memory address register; a memory buffer register; and various multiplexers and latches to control the flow of data around a data loop. The control section supplies the control signals to the data section to implement the instructions in the machine level instruction set.

EXERCISES

Section 20.1

*1. Under what circumstances will a string of an arbitrary number of inverters with a feedback loop, as in Figure 20.1, produce a stable network?

2. Construct tables analogous to Table 20.1 and 20.2 to show that changing R to 1 and back to 0 resets the SR latch to Q = 0 if it starts in state Q = 1.

3. Define the following points in Figure 20.8. (1) A is the output of the top master AND gate. (2) B is the output of the bottom master AND gate. (3) C is the output of the inverter. (4) D is the output of the top slave AND gate. (5) E is the output of the bottom slave AND gate.

   Suppose SR = 10 and Q = 0 before the arrival of a clock pulse. Construct a table that shows the values of A, B, C, D, E, R2, S2, Q, and $\bar{Q}$ during each of the following intervals of Figure 20.9, assuming zero gate delay.

   *(a) before t_1 *(b) between t_1 and t_2 (c) between t_2 and t_3
   (d) between t_3 and t_4 (e) after t_4

4. Do Exercise 3 with SR = 01 and Q = 1 before the arrival of the clock pulse.

5. Draw the state transition diagram, as in Figure 20.11, for the following flip-flops.

   (a) JK *(b) D (c) T

6. Draw the timing diagram of Figure 20.13 for the toggle flip-flop with the D input replaced by T.

7. This section showed how the JK, D, and T flip-flops can be constructed from the SR flip-flop and a few gates. In fact, any flip-flop can be constructed from any other with the help of a few gates. Construct the following flip-flops from a JK flip-flop.

   *(a) D (b) T

   Construct the following flip-flops from a D flip-flop.

   (c) SR (d) JK (e) T

   Construct the following flip-flops from a T flip-flop.

   (f) SR (g) JK (h) D

Section 20.2

8. *(a) Modify Figure 20.8, the implementation of the SR master-slave flip-flop, to provide an asynchronous clear input, as in Figure 20.20. When Clear is 0, the device should operate normally. When Clear is 1, both the master state, Q2, and the slave state, Q, should be forced to 0. **(b)** Modify Figure 20.8 to provide an asynchronous preset. **(c)** Modify Figure 20.8 to provide both an asynchronous clear and preset.

9. Draw the circuit and the state transition diagram for a sequential net with two JK flip-flops, FFA and FFB, and two inputs, X1 and X2, with flip-flop inputs

   $J1 = X1\,B \qquad J2 = X1\,\overline{A}$

   $K1 = X2 + X1\,A\,\overline{B} \qquad K2 = X2 + X1\,A$

   There is no output other than the flip-flop states.

10. Draw the circuit and the state transition diagram for a sequential net with one JK flip-flop, FFA; one T flip-flop, FFB; and one input, X, with flip-flop inputs

    $J = X \oplus B \qquad T = X \oplus A$

    $K = \overline{X}\,B$

    and output

    $Z = A\,B$

11. Draw the circuit and the state transition diagram for a sequential net with two SR flip-flops, FFA and FFB; two inputs, X1 and X2, with flip-flop inputs

    $SA = X1 \qquad SB = \overline{X1}\,X2\,\overline{A}$

    $RA = \overline{X1}\,X2 \qquad RB = X1\,A + X2$

    and output

    $Z = X1\,\overline{X2}\,\overline{A}\,B$

Section 20.3

12. Design the sequential circuit of Example 20.2 using the following flip-flops.

    *(a) D (b) T

13. Figure 20.32 is a state transition diagram for a sequential net with three flip-flops and one input. It counts up in binary when the input is 0 and remains in the same state when the input is 1. Design the circuit and draw the circuit diagram using the following flip-flops.

    (a) JK (b) SR (c) D (d) T

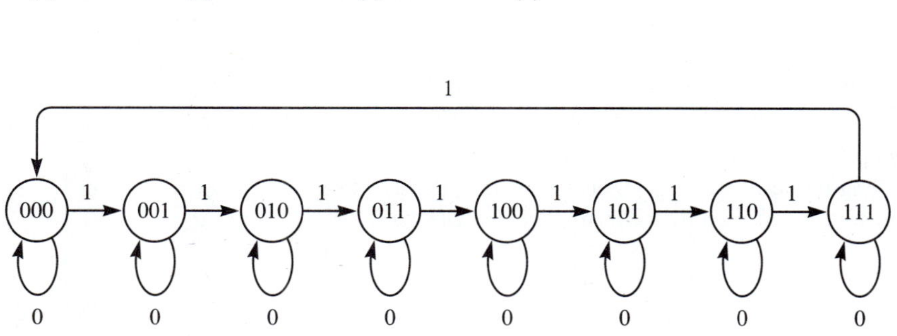

Figure 20.32

The state transition diagram for Exercise 13.

14. Figure 20.33 is a state transition diagram for a sequential net with three flip-flops and one input. It counts up in binary when the input is 1 and counts down when the input is 0. Design the circuit and draw the circuit diagram using the following flip-flops.

   * (a) JK (b) SR (c) D (d) T

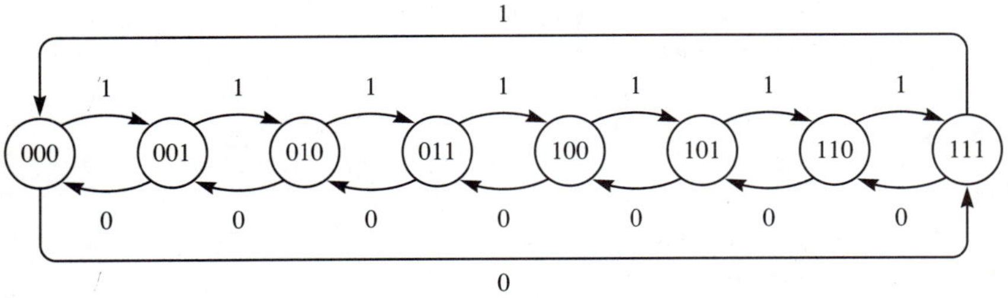

Figure 20.33

The state transition diagram for Exercise 14.

15. Figure 20.34 is a state transition diagram for a sequential net with two flip-flops and two inputs. It counts up in binary when the input is 01, down in binary when the input is 10, and does not change state when the input is 00. An input of 11 will never occur and can be treated as a don't-care condition. Design the circuit and draw the circuit diagram using the following flip-flops.

   (a) JK (b) SR (c) D (d) T

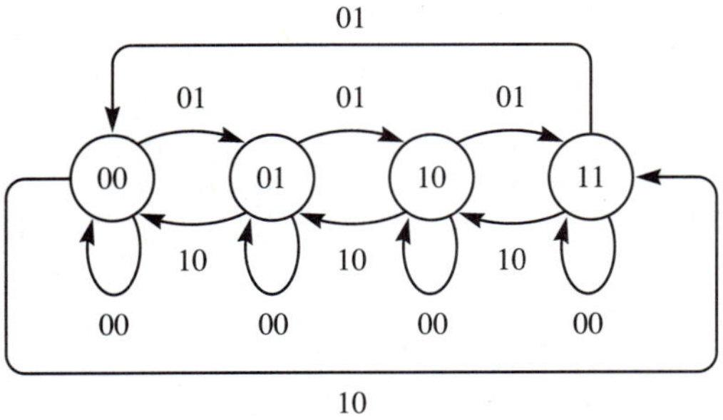

Figure 20.34

The state transition diagram for Exercise 15.

Section 20.4

16. Write the control sequence for the von Neumann cycle to fetch the operand specifier and increment `PC` accordingly. Assume that the instruction specifier has already been fetched, and the control section has already determined that the instruction is nonunary.

17. Write the control sequence to execute each of the following instructions. Assume that the instruction has been fetched, including the instruction specifier if nonunary. Refer to Table 14.2 to determine which status bits are affected by the instruction and change them accordingly.

*(a) `LDBYTA Num,i`	(b) `LDBYTA Num,d`	(c) `LDBYTA Num,x`
(d) `LDBYTA Num,s`	(e) `LOADX Num,i`	(f) `ADDX Num,i`
(g) `ANDA Num,i`	(h) `NOTA`	(i) `ASLA`
(j) `LOADB Num,i`	(k) `BR There`	(l) `ADDSP Num,i`
(m) `JSR There`	(n) `RTS`	(o) `RTI`

18. Write the control sequence to execute the instruction

```
HEXO Num,i
```

Assume that the instruction has been fetched. Remember that this instruction has an unimplemented opcode. You may wish to review the interrupt service routines in Chapter 17 (see pp. 850–51).

* **19.** In Program 20.3, could the Carry just as easily be clocked on instruction 5 instead of instruction 6? Explain.

20. A sequential net has six state registers and three input lines. **(a)** How many states does it have? **(b)** How many transitions from each state does it have? **(c)** How many total transitions does it have?

21. Design an 11-input, 9-output combinational shifter that might be used in the computation unit of the Pep/5 ALU. It should have 8 data inputs, a Cin input, 2 select line inputs, 8 data outputs, and a Cout output. Select line values of 00, 01, 10, and 11 should select the ASL, ROL, ASR, and ROR functions respectively, which are defined in Figure 20.31.

APPENDIX

Pep/5 Architecture

This appendix summarizes the architecture of the Pep/5 computer.

	0	1	2	3	4	5	6	7	8	9	A	B	C	D	E	F
0_	0	1	2	3	4	5	6	7	8	9	10	11	12	13	14	15
1_	16	17	18	19	20	21	22	23	24	25	26	27	28	29	30	31
2_	32	33	34	35	36	37	38	39	40	41	42	43	44	45	46	47
3_	48	49	50	51	52	53	54	55	56	57	58	59	60	61	62	63
4_	64	65	66	67	68	69	70	71	72	73	74	75	76	77	78	79
5_	80	81	82	83	84	85	86	87	88	89	90	91	92	93	94	95
6_	96	97	98	99	100	101	102	103	104	105	106	107	108	109	110	111
7_	112	113	114	115	116	117	118	119	120	121	122	123	124	125	126	127
8_	128	129	130	131	132	133	134	135	136	137	138	139	140	141	142	143
9_	144	145	146	147	148	149	150	151	152	153	154	155	156	157	158	159
A_	160	161	162	163	164	165	166	167	168	169	170	171	172	173	174	175
B_	176	177	178	179	180	181	182	183	184	185	186	187	188	189	190	191
C_	192	193	194	195	196	197	198	199	200	201	202	203	204	205	206	207
D_	208	209	210	211	212	213	214	215	216	217	218	219	220	221	222	223
E_	224	225	226	227	228	229	230	231	232	233	234	235	236	237	238	239
F_	240	241	242	243	244	245	246	247	248	249	250	251	252	253	254	255

Figure A.1

The hexadecimal conversion chart.

Hexadecimal	Binary	Hexadecimal	Binary	Hexadecimal	Binary	Hexadecimal	Binary
0	0000	4	0100	8	1000	C	1100
1	0001	5	0101	9	1001	D	1101
2	0010	6	0110	A	1010	E	1110
3	0011	7	0111	B	1011	F	1111

Figure A.2

The relation between hexadecimal and binary.

Char	Bin	Hex	Char	Bin	Hex	Char	Bin	Hex	Char	Bin	Hex
NUL	000 0000	00	SP	010 0000	20	@	100 0000	40	`	110 0000	60
SOH	000 0001	01	!	010 0001	21	A	100 0001	41	a	110 0001	61
STX	000 0010	02	"	010 0010	22	B	100 0010	42	b	110 0010	62
ETX	000 0011	03	#	010 0011	23	C	100 0011	43	c	110 0011	63
EOT	000 0100	04	$	010 0100	24	D	100 0100	44	d	110 0100	64
ENQ	000 0101	05	%	010 0101	25	E	100 0101	45	e	110 0101	65
ACK	000 0110	06	&	010 0110	26	F	100 0110	46	f	110 0110	66
BEL	000 0111	07	'	010 0111	27	G	100 0111	47	g	110 0111	67
BS	000 1000	08	(	010 1000	28	H	100 1000	48	h	110 1000	68
HT	000 1001	09	)	010 1001	29	I	100 1001	49	i	110 1001	69
LF	000 1010	0A	*	010 1010	2A	J	100 1010	4A	j	110 1010	6A
VT	000 1011	0B	+	010 1011	2B	K	100 1011	4B	k	110 1011	6B
FF	000 1100	0C	,	010 1100	2C	L	100 1100	4C	l	110 1100	6C
CR	000 1101	0D	-	010 1101	2D	M	100 1101	4D	m	110 1101	6D
SO	000 1110	0E	.	010 1110	2E	N	100 1110	4E	n	110 1110	6E
SI	000 1111	0F	/	010 1111	2F	O	100 1111	4F	o	110 1111	6F
DLE	001 0000	10	0	011 0000	30	P	101 0000	50	p	111 0000	70
DC1	001 0001	11	1	011 0001	31	Q	101 0001	51	q	111 0001	71
DC2	001 0010	12	2	011 0010	32	R	101 0010	52	r	111 0010	72
DC3	001 0011	13	3	011 0011	33	S	101 0011	53	s	111 0011	73
DC4	001 0100	14	4	011 0100	34	T	101 0100	54	t	111 0100	74
NAK	001 0101	15	5	011 0101	35	U	101 0101	55	u	111 0101	75
SYN	001 0110	16	6	011 0110	36	V	101 0110	56	v	111 0110	76
ETB	001 0111	17	7	011 0111	37	W	101 0111	57	w	111 0111	77
CAN	001 1000	18	8	011 1000	38	X	101 1000	58	x	111 1000	78
EM	001 1001	19	9	011 1001	39	Y	101 1001	59	y	111 1001	79
SUB	001 1010	1A	:	011 1010	3A	Z	101 1010	5A	z	111 1010	7A
ESC	001 1011	1B	;	011 1011	3B	[	101 1011	5B	{	111 1011	7B
FS	001 1100	1C	<	011 1100	3C	\	101 1100	5C	|	111 1100	7C
GS	001 1101	1D	=	011 1101	3D	]	101 1101	5D	}	111 1101	7D
RS	001 1110	1E	>	011 1110	3E	^	101 1110	5E	~	111 1110	7E
US	001 1111	1F	?	011 1111	3F	_	101 1111	5F	DEL	111 1111	7F

Abbreviations for Control Characters

NUL null, or all zeros
SOH start of heading
STX start of text
ETX end of text

EOT end of transmission
ENQ enquiry
ACK acknowledge
BEL bell

BS backspace
HT horizontal tabulation
LF line feed
VT vertical tabulation

FF form feed
CR carriage return
SO shift out
SI shift in

DLE data link escape
DC1 device control 1
DC2 device control 2
DC3 device control 3

DC4 device control 4
NAK negative acknowledge
SYN synchronous idle
ETB end of transmission block

CAN cancel
EM end of medium
SUB substitute
ESC escape

FS file separator
GS group separator
RS record separator
US unit separator

SP space
DEL delete

Figure A.3

The American Standard Code for Information Interchange (ASCII).

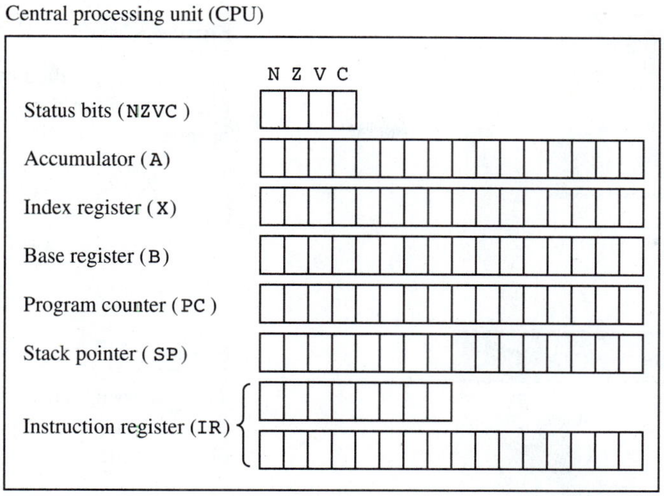

Figure A.4

The central processing unit of the Pep/5 computer.

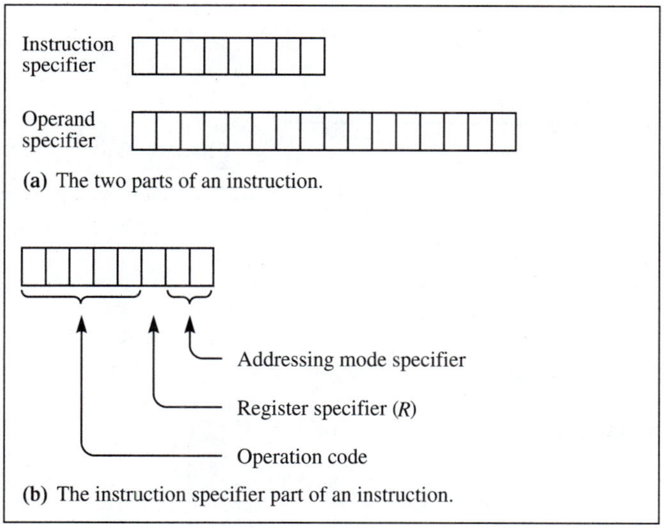

Figure A.5

The Pep/5 instruction format.

Register specifier	Register specified (*R*)
0	Accumulator (A)
1	Index register (X)

Figure A.6

The register specified by the register specifier part of the opcode.

Addr. mode specifier	Addr. mode specified
00	Immediate (i)
01	Direct (d)
10	Indexed (x)
11	Stack relative (s)

Figure A.7

The addressing mode specified by the addressing mode specifier part of the opcode.

- Immediate addressing:
  `Oprnd = OprndSpec`
- Direct addressing:
  `Oprnd = Mem [OprndSpec]`
- Indexed addressing:
  ```
  if byte instruction then
     Oprnd = Mem [B + X + OprndSpec]
  else
     Oprnd = Mem [B + 2*X + OprndSpec]
  ```
- Stack-relative addressing:
  `Oprnd = Mem [SP + OprndSpec]`

Figure A.8

The relationship between the operand and the operand specifier.

Opcode	Mnemonic	Meaning	Addr. modes	Status bits
00000	STOP	stop execution	*U*	
00001	LOAD*R*	*R* := Oprnd	idxs	NZ
00010	STORE*R*	Oprnd := *R*	dxs	
00011	ADD*R*	*R* := *R* + Oprnd	idxs	NZVC
00100	SUB*R*	*R* := *R* - Oprnd	idxs	NZVC
00101	AND*R*	*R* := *R* AND Oprnd	idxs	NZ
00110	OR*R*	*R* := *R* OR Oprnd	idxs	NZ
00111	NOT*R*	*R* := NOT *R*	*U*	NZ
01000	ASL*R*	C := most significant bit; *R* := arithmetic shift left *R*	*U*	NZVC
01001	ASR*R*	C := least significant bit; *R* := arithmetic shift right *R*	*U*	NZC
01010	LDBYT*R*	*R* := byte Oprnd	idxs	NZ
01011	STBYT*R*	byte Oprnd := *R*	dxs	
01100	LOADB	B := Oprnd	idxs	NZ
01101	ADDB	B := B + Oprnd	idxs	NZVC
01110	BR	PC := Oprnd	ix	
01111	BRN	if N=1 then PC := Oprnd	ix	
10000	BRZ	if Z=1 then PC := Oprnd	ix	
10001	BRV	if V=1 then PC := Oprnd	ix	
10010	BRC	if C=1 then PC := Oprnd	ix	
10011	BRNZ	if N=1 or Z=1 then PC := Oprnd	ix	
10100	COMP*R*	*R* - Oprnd	idxs	NZVC
10101	ADDSP	SP := SP + Oprnd	i	NZVC
10110	SUBSP	SP := SP - Oprnd	i	NZVC
10111	JSR	SP := Sp - 2; Mem [SP] := PC; PC := Oprnd	ix	
11000	RTS	PC := Mem [SP]; SP := SP + 2	*U*	
11001	RTI	not used at Level 5	*U*	
11010	CHARI	byte Oprnd := input	dxs	
11011	CHARO	output := byte Oprnd	idxs	
11100	DECI	Oprnd := input	dxs	NZV
11101	DECO	output := Oprnd	idxs	
11110	HEXO	output := Oprnd	idxs	
11111	NOP	no operation	*U*	

Figure A.9

The Pep/5 instruction set at Level 5.

`.ADDRSS`	the address of a symbol
`.ASCII`	a string of ASCII bytes
`.BLOCK`	a block of bytes
`.BURN`	initiate ROM burn
`.BYTE`	a byte value
`.END`	the sentinel for the assembler
`.EQUATE`	equate a symbol to a constant value
`.WORD`	a word value

Figure A.10

The eight pseudo-ops of Pep/5 assembly language.

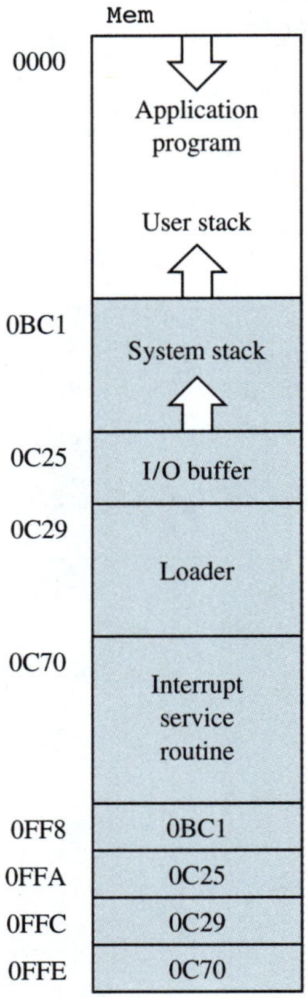

Figure A.11

A memory map of the Pep/5 system.

```
Temp               := Mem [0FFA]
Mem [Temp - 1]     := IR {instruction specifier only}
Mem [Temp - 3]     := SP
Mem [Temp - 5]     := PC
Mem [Temp - 7]     := B
Mem [Temp - 9]     := X
Mem [Temp - 11]    := A
Mem [Temp - 12]    := NZVC
SP                 := Temp - 12
PC                 := Mem [0FFE]
```

Figure A.12

An interrupt.

```
NZVC := Mem [SP]
A    := Mem [SP + 1]
X    := Mem [SP + 3]
B    := Mem [SP + 5]
PC   := Mem [SP + 7]
SP   := Mem [SP + 9]
```

Figure A.13

A return from interrupt, `RTI`.

```
SP := Mem [0FFA]
PC := Mem [0FFC]
```

Figure A.14

The load option.

```
SP := Mem [0FF8]
PC := 0000
```

Figure A.15

The execute option.

Solutions to Selected Exercises

Chapter 12

1.

(a)	(b)	(c)	(d)
267	2102	10101	2433
270	2110	10110	2434
271	2111	10111	2440
272	2112	11000	2441
273	2120	11001	2442
274	2121	11010	2443
275	2122	11011	2444
276	2200	11100	3000
277	2201	11101	3001
300	2202	11110	3002
301	2210	11111	3003

3. **(a)** 18 **(b)** 6 **(c)** 11 **(d)** 8 **(e)** 31 **(f)** 85

5. **(a)** 11001 **(b)** 10000 **(c)** 1 **(d)** 1110 **(e)** 101 **(f)** 101001

7. **(a)** 3 **(b)** 7

8. **(a)** C = 0, 111 0100 **(b)** C = 1, 001 0000 **(c)** C = 1, 111 1110 **(d)** C = 1, 000 0000

12. **(a)** $7 \times 8^4 + 0 \times 8^3 + 1 \times 8^2 + 4 \times 8^1 + 6 \times 8^0$

13. **(a)** $2 \times 10^2 + 9 \times 10^0 + 4 \times 10^{-1} + 5 \times 10^{-2} + 8 \times 10^{-3}$

15. **(a)** 011 0001 **(b)** 110 0101 **(c)** 000 0000 **(d)** 100 0000 **(e)** 111 1111 **(f)** 111 1110

17. **(a)** 29 **(b)** –43 **(c)** –4 **(d)** 1 **(e)** –64 **(f)** –63

19. **(a)** C = 0, V = 0, 011 1001 **(b)** C = 1, V = 0, 000 0110 **(c)** C = 1, V = 1, 001 1001 **(d)** C = 1, V = 0, 101 0110 **(e)** C = 0, V = 1, 100 0001 **(f)** C = 0, V = 0, 111 0100

21. **(a)** From 10 to 01 in binary or –2 to 1 in decimal **(b)** From 100 to 011 in binary or –4 to 3 in decimal

22. **(a)** 010 1000 **(b)** 000 0101 **(c)** 110 1110 **(d)** 101 1111 **(e)** 010 0100, 001 0101

24. ASL operation:

(a) 24 (dec) = 001 1000 (bin), ASL 001 1000 = 011 0000 (bin) = 48 (dec), C = 0, V = 0
(b) 37 (dec) = 010 0101 (bin), ASL 010 0101 = 100 1010 (bin) = –54 (dec), C = 0, V = 1
(c) –26 (dec) = 110 0110 (bin), ASL 110 0110 = 100 1100 (bin) = –52 (dec), C = 1, V = 0
(d) 1 (dec) = 000 0001 (bin), ASL 000 0001 = 000 0010 (bin) = 2 (dec), C = 0, V = 0
(e) 0 (dec) = 0000 0000 (bin), ASL 000 0000 = 000 0000 (bin) = 0 (dec), C = 0, V = 0
(f) –1 (dec) = 111 1111 (bin), ASL 111 1111 = 111 1110 (bin) = –2 (dec), C = 1, V = 0

ASR operation:

(a) 24 (dec) = 001 1000 (bin), ASR 001 1000 = 000 1100 (bin) = 12 (dec), C = 0
(b) 37 (dec) = 010 0101 (bin), ASR 010 0101 = 001 0010 (bin) = 18 (dec), C = 1
(c) –26 (dec) = 110 0110 (bin), ASR 110 0110 = 111 0011 (bin) = –13 (dec), C = 0
(d) 1 (dec) = 000 0001 (bin), ASR 000 0001 = 000 0000 (bin) = 0 (dec), C = 1
(e) 0 (dec) = 0000 0000 (bin), ASR 000 0000 = 000 0000 (bin) = 0 (dec), C = 0
(f) –1 (dec) = 111 1111 (bin), ASR 111 1111 = 111 1111 (bin) = –1 (dec), C = 1

26. **(a)** 3AB7, 3AB8, 3AB9, 3ABA, 3ABB, 3ABC

27. **(a)** 11,615 (dec)

28. **(a)** 68CF

30. **(a)** –35 **(b)** 47 **(c)** –64

32. **(a)** 65 (hex) **(b)** 3F (hex) **(c)** 7F (hex)

34. Have a nice day!

36. 101 0000 110 0001 111 10001 010 0000 010 0100 011 0000 010 1110 011 1001 011 0010

40. **(a)** An octal digit represents three bits.

Chapter 13

1. (a) 4096 bytes (b) 2048 words (c) 32,768 bits (d) 108 bits (e) About 300 times bigger

3. **For the 54F82C instruction:** (a) Opcode is 01010 (b) Loads a byte from memory into a CPU register (c) 1 (d) Specifies the index register (e) 00 (f) Specifies immediate addressing (g) F82C **For the 3223D0 instruction:** (a) Opcode is 00110 (b) ORs the operand to a register in the CPU (c) 0 (d) Specifies the accumulator (e) 10 (f) Specifies indexed addressing (g) 23D0

5.

	A	X	Mem [0A3F]	Mem [0A41]
(a)	FF00	FE20	FF00	103D
(b)	1900	FE20	FF00	103D
(c)	19AC	FE20	FF00	1020
(d)	19AC	FE20	FF00	FE20
(e)	18AC	FE20	FF00	103D
(f)	19AC	EDE3	FF00	103D
(g)	1900	FE20	FF00	103D
(h)	FFAC	FE20	FF00	103D
(i)	19AC	01DF	FF00	103D

7. `Joy`

9. (a) `M`

Chapter 14

1. (a) `LOADA h#0D4E,i` (b) `ASRA` (c) `STOREA h#014B,d`

3. (a) 40 (b) D3000F (c) 7A01E6

5. (a) 42 65 61 72 (b) F8 (c) 03 16

7. `mug`

10.
```
129
0081
-2
FFFE
```

12. (a)
```
109
28013
FE38
&
```

13.

Symbol	Value
`Here`	`0003`
`There`	`0005`

Output

`9`

15.

Symbol	Value
`This`	`0000`

Output

`F100`

18. The compiler uses its symbol table to store the type of each variable. Whenever it encounters an expression or assignment statement, it consults the symbol table to verify that the types are compatible.

Chapter 15

1. (a)

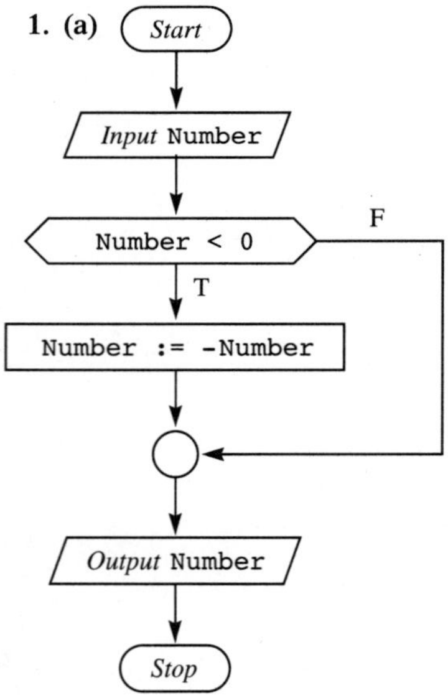

3. Because the current value of `I` will be in the accumulator regardless of whether control came from the `STOREA` at 008 or from the `BR` at the bottom of the loop. Before the `BR` at the bottom of the loop, the accumulator was used to increment `I`, thus its current value will still be in the accumulator when `COMPA` executes.

6.

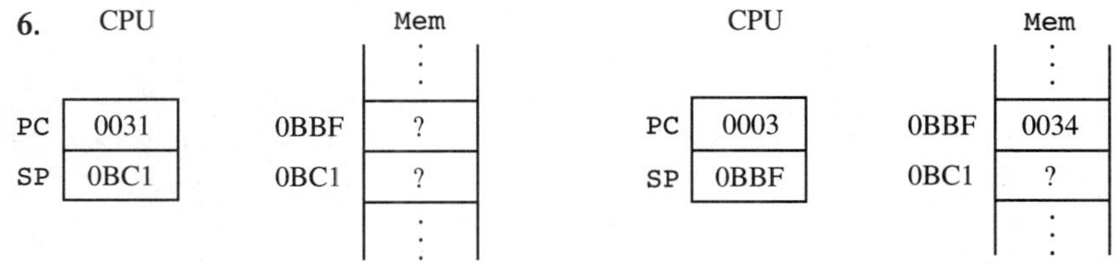

8. The branch address is calculated as

$$
\begin{aligned}
\texttt{Oprnd} &= \text{Mem}\,[\text{B} + 2 \times \text{X} + \text{OprndSpec}] \\
&= \text{Mem}\,[-2 + 0 + 0020\ (\text{hex})] \\
&= \text{Mem}\,[001\text{E}] \\
&= 00
\end{aligned}
$$

Of course, the 00 was intended to be interpreted as the first byte of the operand of an instruction. However, the von Neumann cycle blindly interprets it as the `STOP` instruction.

10.

```
                Tiger:    .EQUATE d#0
                Lion:     .EQUATE d#1
                Bear:     .EQUATE d#2
                ;
0000  0000      Animal:   .BLOCK  d#2
                ;
0002  080001              LOADA   Lion,i        ;Animal := Lion
0005  110000              STOREA  Animal,d
0008                      .END
```

14.

```
                True:     .EQUATE h#FFFF
                False:    .EQUATE h#0000
                Mask:     .EQUATE h#FFFE
                ;
0000  0000      P:        .BLOCK  d#2
0002  0000      Q:        .BLOCK  d#2
                ;
0004  090000              LOADA   P,d           ;(a) P and Q
0007  290002              ANDA    Q,d
                ;
000A  090000              LOADA   P,d           ;(d) ord (P)
000D  28FFFE              ANDA    Mask,i
0010                      .END
```

15. **(a)** Hint: The object code cannot simply generate an `ANDA` instruction. For example, if `P` has value 0002 (hex) and `Q` has value 0004 (hex), they both represent true, but the AND of their values is 0000 (hex), which represents false. You must `LOADA` followed by `BRZ` to test for a false value. **(d)** To compute `ord (P)` requires a `BRZ` also.

16.
```
0000  0000    Pref1:    .BLOCK   d#2
0002  0000    Pref2:    .BLOCK   d#2
              ;
0004  090000            LOADA    Pref1,d      ;(a) Pref1 + Pref2
0007  310002            ORA      Pref2,d
              ;
000A  090000            LOADA    Pref1,d      ;(d) Pref1 <= Pref2
000D  0D0002            LOADX    Pref2,d
0010  4C      Loop:     ASRX                  ;Check for 1 in Pref2
0011  90001E            BRC      Prf2Has1     ;If so, branch
0014  48                ASRA                  ;Pref2 has 0, so check Pref1
0015  90002B            BRC      SetFalse     ;Pref2 has 0, Pref1 has 1
0018  800025            BRZ      SetTrue      ;Exit with True if done
001B  700010            BR       Loop
001E  48      Prf2Has1:ASRA                   ;Ignore C
001F  800025            BRZ      SetTrue      ;Exit with True if done
0022  700010            BR       Loop
0025  080001 SetTrue:  LOADA    True,i
0028  70002E            BR       Continue
002B  080000 SetFalse:LOADA    False,i
002E  F8      Continue:NOP
```

18.
```
              EmplNum: .EQUATE d#0
              Name:    .EQUATE d#2
              Salary:  .EQUATE d#17
              ;
0000  0000    P:       .BLOCK   d#2
              ;
0002  610000           LOADB    P,d         ;Load P into base register
0005  680002           ADDB     Name,i      ;Advance P to start of Name
0008  0C0006           LOADX    d#6,i       ;Corresponds to Pascal index
000B  DA0000           CHARO    d#0,x
```

Chapter 16

1. The fundamental question of computer science is, What can be automated?

3. (a)

<identifier> ⇒ <identifier> <digit>
⇒ <identifier> 3
⇒ <identifier> <digit> 3
⇒ <identifier> 2 3
⇒ <identifier> <digit> 2 3
⇒ <identifier> 1 2 3
⇒ <identifier> <letter> 1 2 3
⇒ <identifier> c 1 2 3
⇒ <identifier> <letter> c 1 2 3
⇒ <identifier> b c 1 2 3
⇒ <letter> b c 1 2 3
⇒ a b c 1 2 3

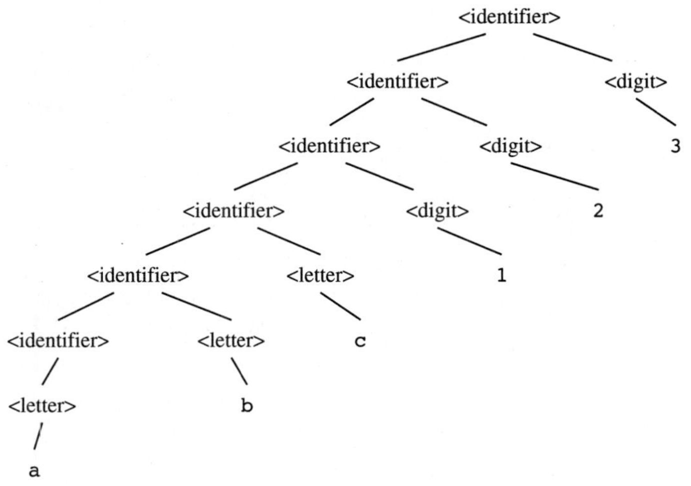

4. **(a)** I ⇒ FM ⇒ - M ⇒ - `d`

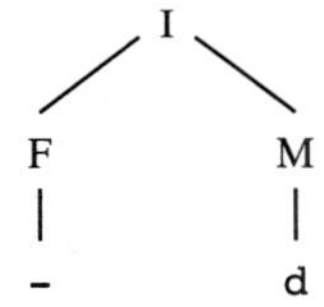

5. **(a)** A ⇒ `a b` C ⇒ `a b c`

6. **(a)** It can be derived as follows:

E ⇒ E + T
⇒ E + F
⇒ E + (E)
⇒ E + (T)
⇒ E + (F)
⇒ E + (a)
⇒ T + (a)
⇒ F + (a)
⇒ a + (a)

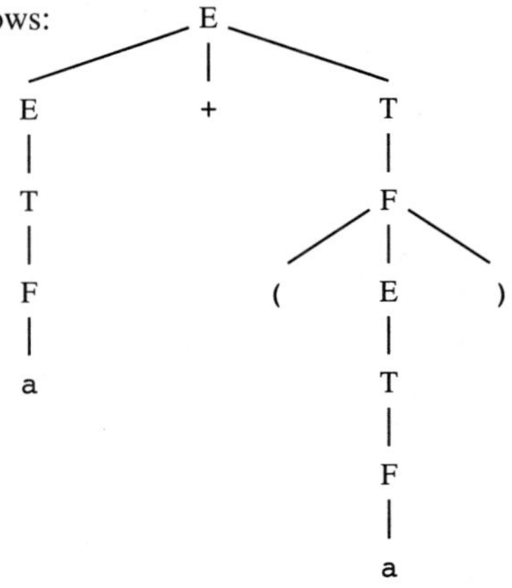

7. **(a)**

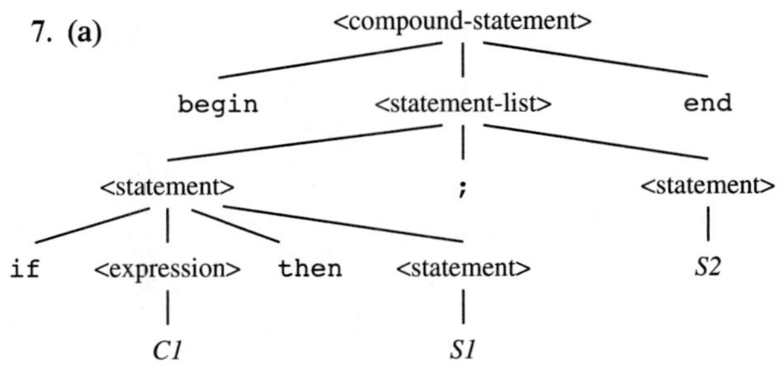

8. **(a)**

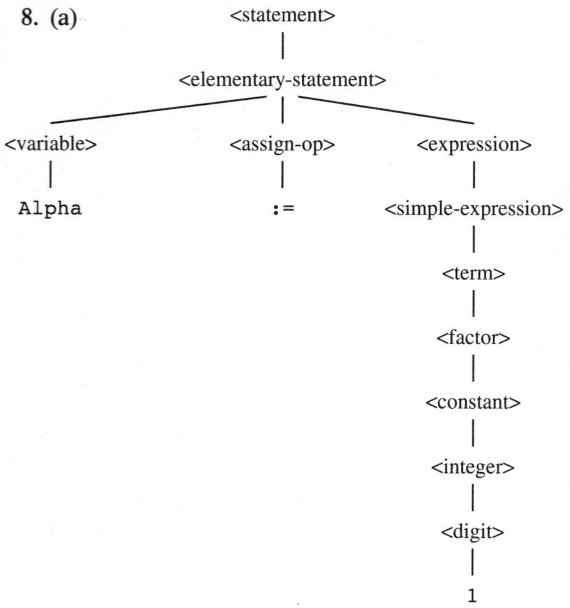

11. **(a)** The machine is deterministic. There are no inaccessible states.

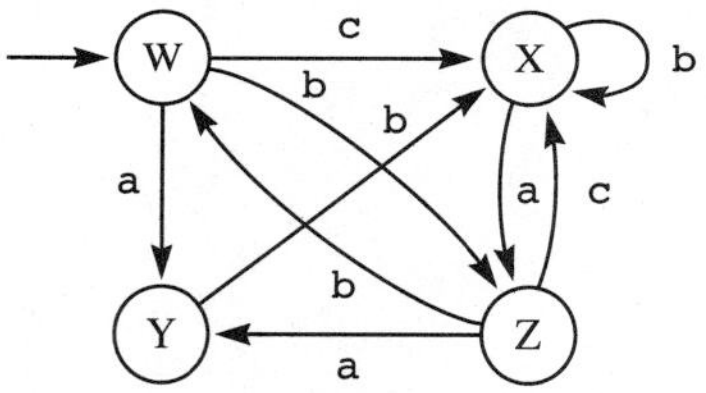

13. **(a)**

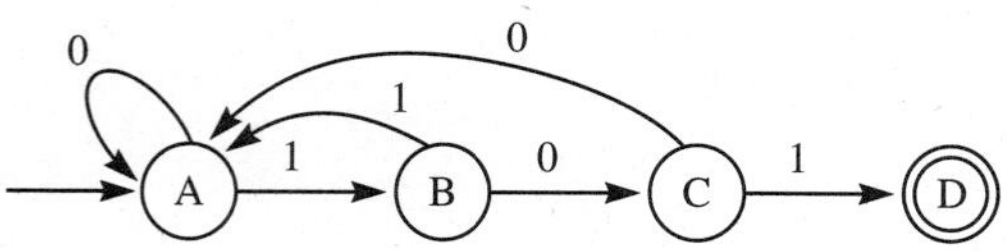

Chapter 17

2. **(a)** 0031 (hex), which is the ASCII code for `1` in the ninth byte, `15` **(b)** 0031 **(c)** 0062

4. **(a)** 00E1, the opcode of the interrupted instruction **(b)** 0000 (hex), since the rightmost two bits of the `DECI` opcode are 00 (bin)

5. **(a)** 00E9, the opcode of the interrupted instruction **(b)** 0001 (hex), since the rightmost two bits of the `DECO` opcode are 01 (bin)

6. (a) 00F1, the opcode of the interrupted instruction (b) 0002 (hex), since the rightmost two bits of the `HEXO` opcode are 10 (bin)

7. (a) The instruction changes the accumulator from 0033, the ASCII value of `3`, to 0003 by masking the left nybble. (b) 0007, the numeric value of the second character in `37` (c) 0000, the value of `Init`, the start state

8. Hint: The first character input is the ASCII hyphen character.

9. (a) 0025 (hex), which is 37 (dec) (b) 0025, not negated since it was already nonnegative (c) The JSR from 0E53 is for writing the 100's place. The accumulator still contains 0025, which is 37 (dec), since 37 mod 100 is 37.

10. Hint: –2068 (dec) = F7EC (hex), which is 0814 (hex) when you take its two's complement.

11. (a) 03B6 (hex), which is 950 (dec) (b) 0303; the second hexadecimal 0 is the important one. (c) 0030, now the last hexadecimal 0 is the important one, since the subroutine will output it.

12. Hint: –2108 (dec) = F7C4 (hex)

13. (a) 00E8, since E8 is the opcode of the interrupted instruction (b) 0000 (hex), since the rightmost two bits of the `DECI` opcode are 00 (bin), specifying immediate addressing

14. (a) 00E9, since E9 is the opcode of the interrupted instruction (b) 0001 (hex), since the rightmost two bits of the `DECO` opcode are 01 (bin), specifying direct addressing

15. (a) 00EB, since EB is the opcode of the interrupted instruction (b) 0003 (hex), since the rightmost two bits of the `DECO` opcode are 11 (bin), specifying stack relative addressing

16. (a) 00EA, since EA is the opcode of the interrupted instruction (b) 0002 (hex), since the rightmost two bits of the `DECI` opcode are 10 (bin), specifying indexed addressing

18. (a) The algorithm no longer guarantees mutual exclusion. Suppose P1 and P2 are both in their remainder sections with `Enter1` and `Enter2` both false. P1 could execute its `while` loop test and be interrupted, after which P2 could execute its `while` loop test. They could then assign their respective Enter variables to true and enter their critical sections sumultaneously.

20. (a) S = 0, and there are no blocked processes.

22. (a) The algorithm does guarantee mutual exclusion. If you remove the `T` semaphore altogether, you get the algorithm of Program 17.5, which guarantees mutual exclusion, regardless of any other code present in the algorithm.

24. (a) Mutual exclusion is no longer guaranteed. Can you find a trace that allows P1 and P2 to enter their critical sections simultaneously? Deadlock, however, cannot occur.

25. (a) Contains a deadlock cycle

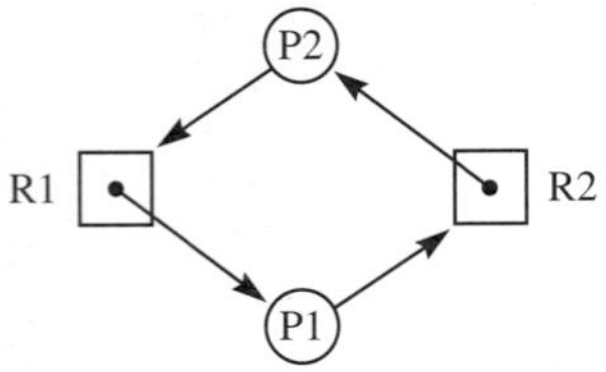

(b) Does not contain a cycle, and therefore does not have a deadlock

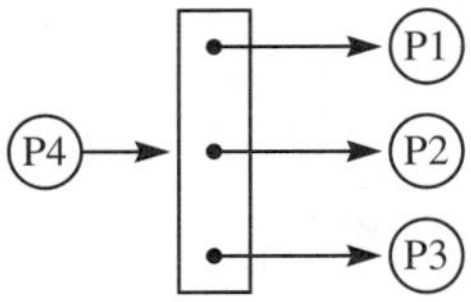

Chapter 18

2. A single bound register would suffice because only one process at a time can execute. If a user process tries to access a memory location outside its logical address space, the hardware must interrupt the access before the page table since there is no such page in main memory. Can you show this modification to Figure 18.9? How many bound values must the operating system keep track of: one for each process, one for each page in the page table, or one for each main memory frame?

4. (a) 2^{12} or 4098 bytes

6. Those that have a dirty bit value of N, namely, the ones in frames 2, 5, and 6

8. The start of one page reference sequence for a job that has three frames allocated is 1, 2, 3, 1, 4, 2, . . . , which has four faults for FIFO and five for LRU. Can you complete the sequence in such a way that FIFO is better in this special case?

10. It produces five faults compared to seven for FIFO and six for LRU. You should trace the algorithm to verify this figure.

11. (a) Hint: The worst case occurs when the start of the block has just rotated past the read/write head when the head has reached the track. Thus, it is the time for the disk to make one complete revolution. You can calculate it from the RPM number.

Chapter 19

1. (a)

$x + 1 = x + (x + x')$	complement
$= (x + x) + x'$	associative
$= x + x'$	idempotent
$= 1$	complement

3. To show that the complement of $a + b$ is $a'b'$, you must show that

$$(a + b) \cdot (a' \cdot b') = 0 \qquad (a + b) + (a' \cdot b') = 1$$

The first part of the proof is

$$\begin{aligned}
(a+b)\cdot(a'\cdot b') &= (a'\cdot b')\cdot(a+b) && \text{commutative}\\
&= [(a'\cdot b')\cdot \mathrm{a}\,] + [(a'\cdot b')\cdot b] && \text{distributive}\\
&= [(a'\cdot a)\cdot b\,'] + [a'\cdot(b\cdot b')] && \text{commutative, associative}\\
&= [0\cdot b'\,] + [a'\cdot 0] && \text{complement}\\
&= 0+0 && \text{theorem } x\cdot 0 = 0\\
&= 0 && \text{identity}
\end{aligned}$$

Can you complete the second part?

5. **(a)** Hint:

$$\begin{aligned}
(x+y)\cdot(x'+y) &= (y+x)\cdot(y+x') && \text{commutative}\\
&= y + (x\cdot x') && \text{distributive}
\end{aligned}$$

7. **(a)**

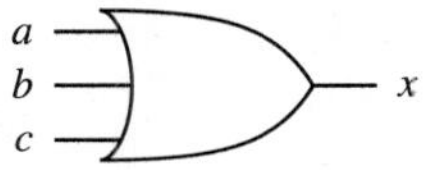

$x = a + b + c$

a	b	c	x
0	0	0	0
0	0	1	1
0	1	0	1
0	1	1	1
1	0	0	1
1	0	1	1
1	1	0	1
1	1	1	1

8. **(a)** The union of any set with the empty set is the set itself.

9. **(a)**

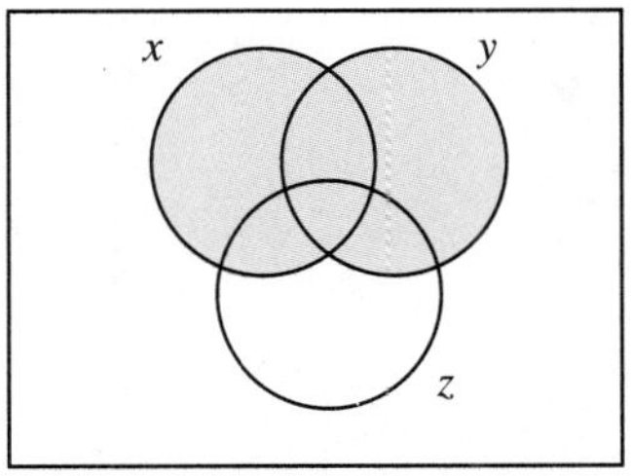

(1) $(x + y)$

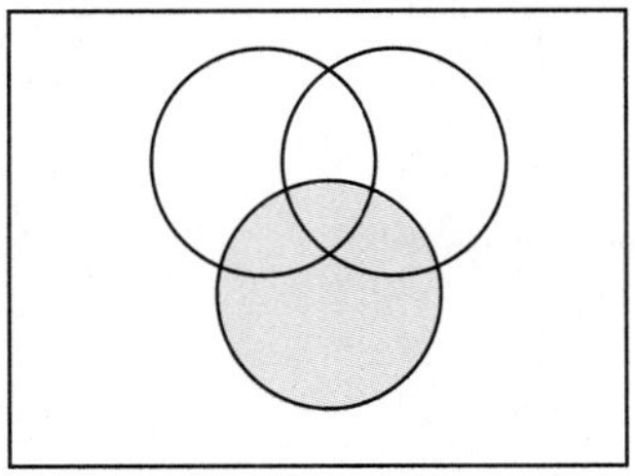

(2) z

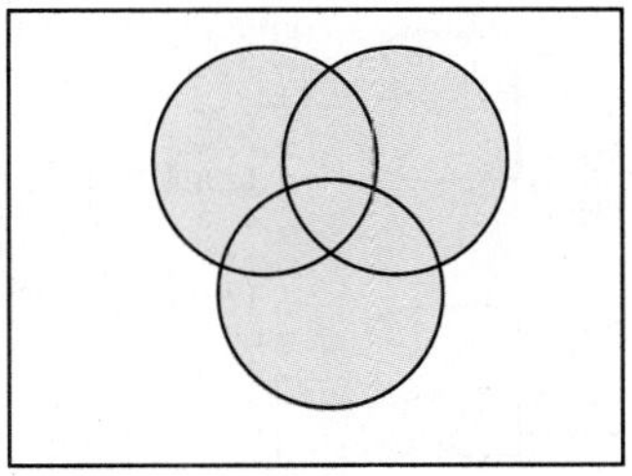

(3) $(x + y)+z$

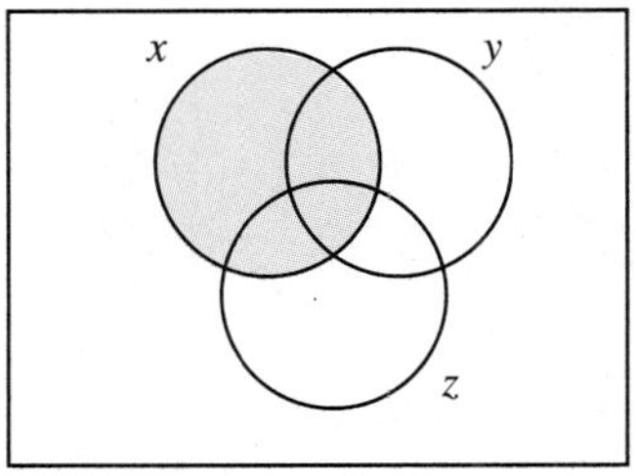

(4) x

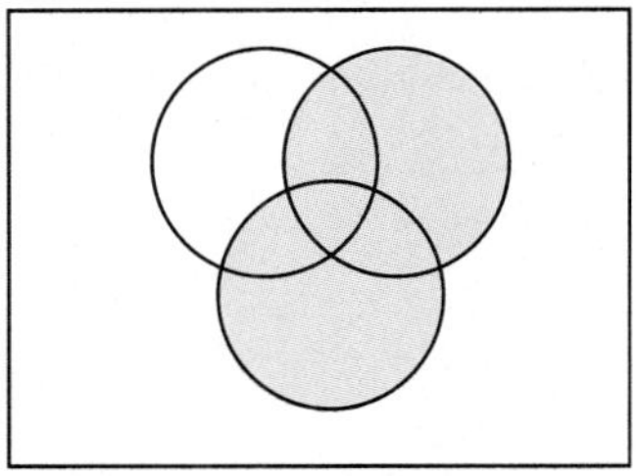

(5) $(y + z)$

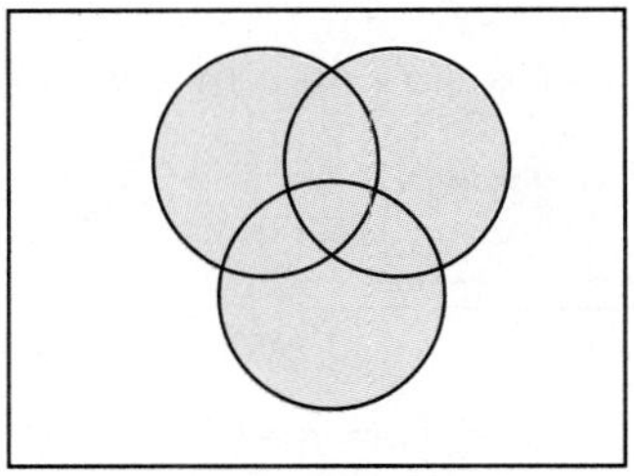

(6) $x + (y + z)$

12. (a)

x	y	x AND y
0	0	0
0	A	0
0	B	0
0	1	0
A	0	0
A	A	A
A	B	0
A	1	A
B	0	0
B	A	0
B	B	B
B	1	B
1	0	0
1	A	A
1	B	B
1	1	1

13. (a)

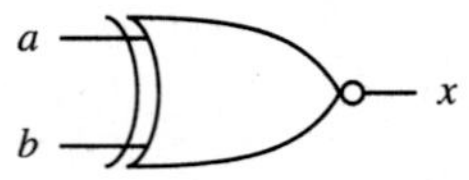

14. (a)

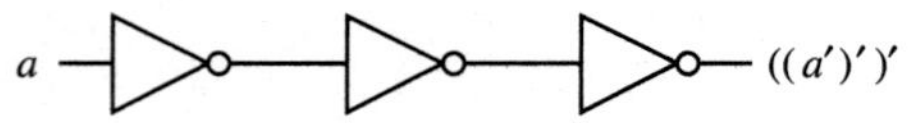

(c)

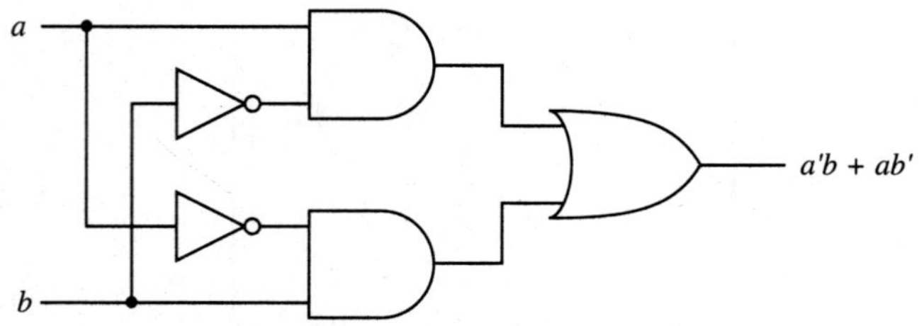

18. (a) $y(a, b, c) = a'bc + ab'c'$

19. (a) $y(a, b, c) = (a + b + c)(a + b + c')(a + b' + c)(a' + b + c')(a' + b' + c)(a' + b' + c')$

20. (a) $ab + a'b'$ (d) $a'b + ab$

a	b	20(a)	20(d)
0	0	1	0
0	1	0	1
1	0	0	0
1	1	1	1

21. (a)

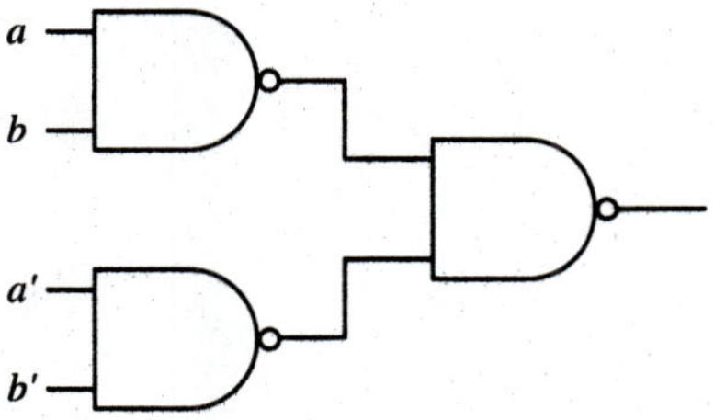

(d)

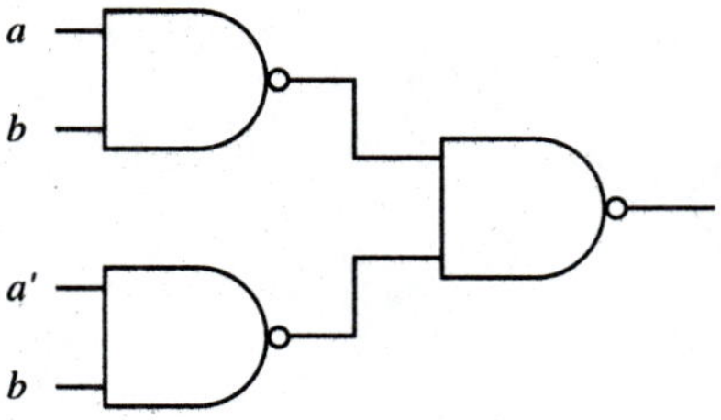

22. (b) $(a' + b)(a + b')$

a	*b*	
0	0	1
0	1	0
1	0	0
1	1	1

23. (b)

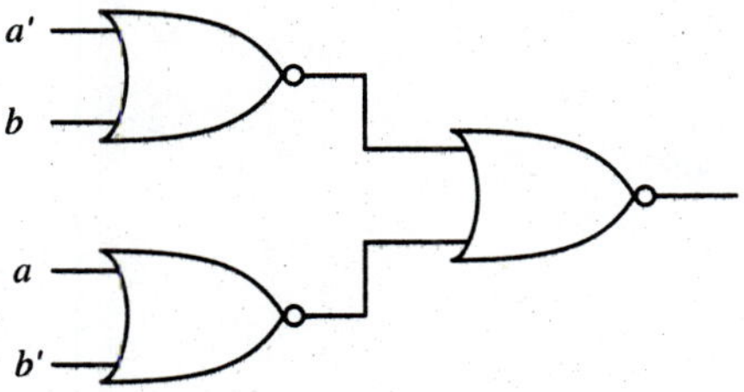

24. (a)

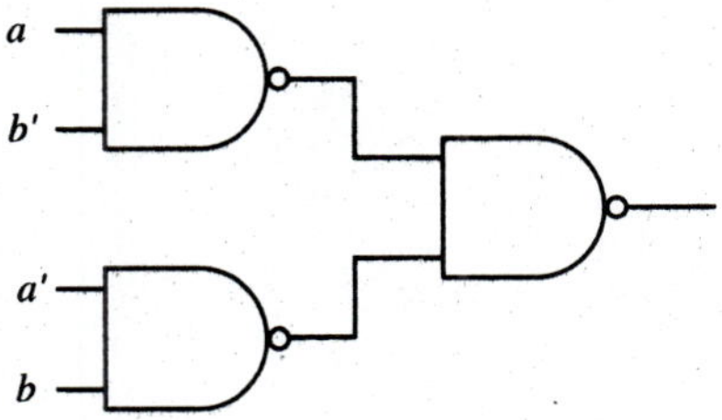

26. (a) $\Sigma(0, 3)$ **(d)** $\Sigma(1, 2, 3)$

27. (b) $\Pi(1, 2)$

28. (a) $x = a'c$

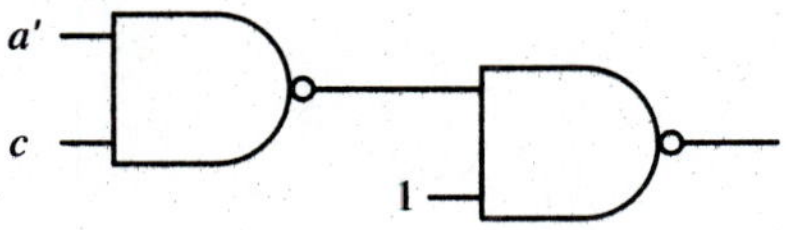

29. **(a)** $x = (a')(c)$

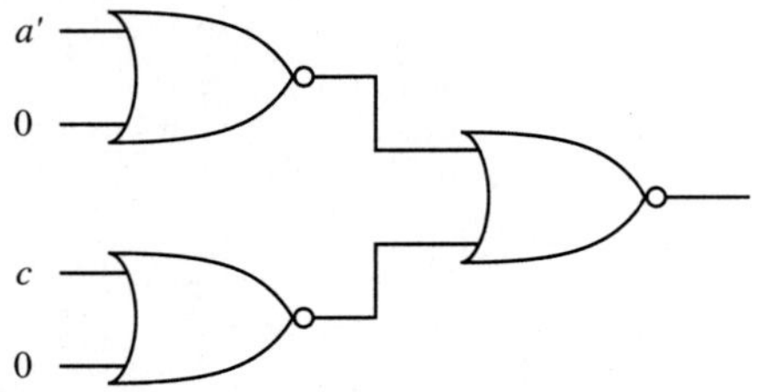

30. **(a)** $x(a, b, c) = ac + b'c'$

31. **(a)** $x(a, b, c) = \Pi(1, 2, 3, 6) = (a + c')(b' + c)$

32. **(a)** $x(a, b, c, d) = bc' + a'b'c + b'cd'$

33. **(a)** $\Pi(0, 1, 6, 7, 8, 9, 11, 14, 15)$, $x(a, b, c, d) = (b + c)(b' + c')(a' + c' + d')$ or $x(a, b, c, d) = (b + c)(b' + c')(a' + b + d')$

34. **(a)** $x(a, b, c) = a'b' + ab$

35. **(a)** $x(a, b, c, d) = bc + bd$

37. **(a)** The control line acts as an enable that passes the data through unchanged when it is 0. When the control line is 1, it disables the output, which is set to 1 regardless of the data input.

39.

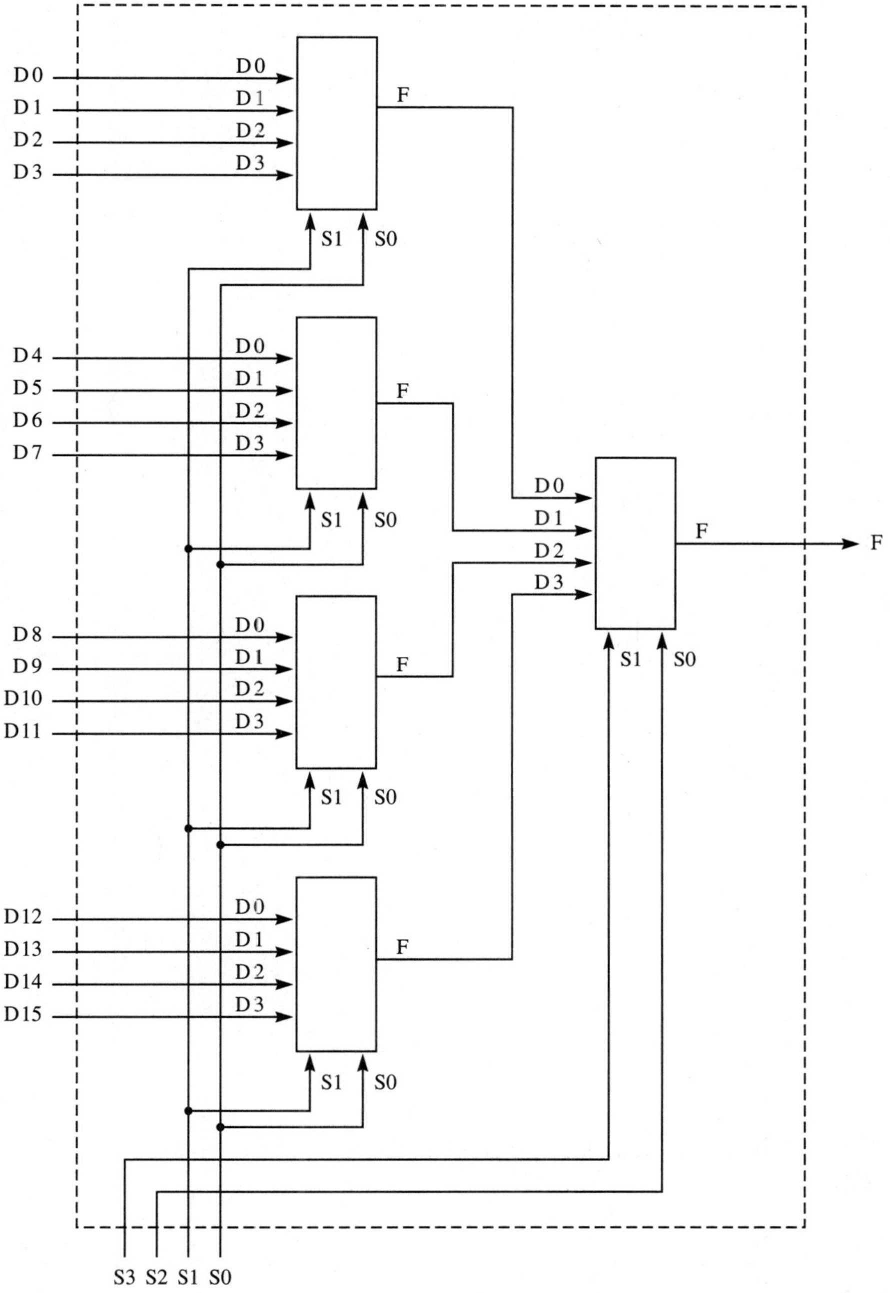

D0
D1
D2
D3
D0
D1
D2
D3
F
S1
S0
D4
D5
D6
D7
D0
D1
D2
D3
F
S1
S0
D8
D9
D10
D11
D0
D1
D2
D3
F
S1
S0
D12
D13
D14
D15
D0
D1
D2
D3
F
S1
S0
D0
D1
D2
D3
F
S1
S0
F
S3 S2 S1 S0

41. **(a)**

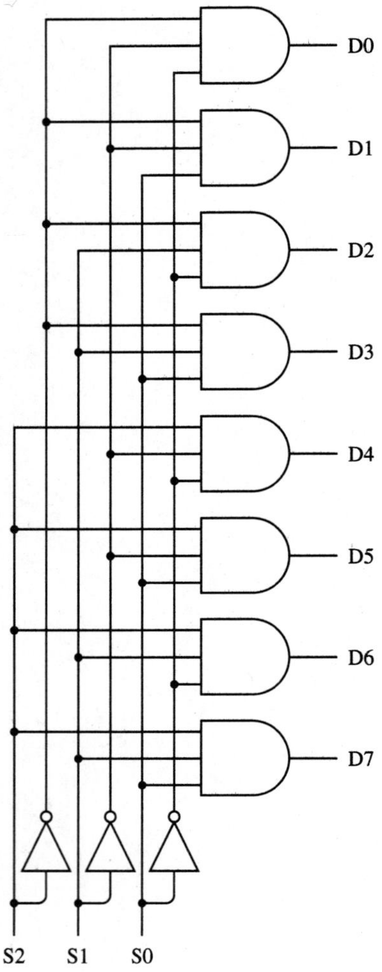

45. **(a)**

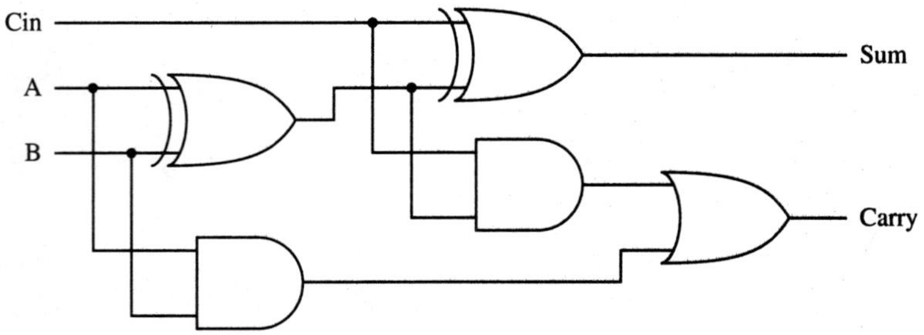

(b) Maximum of three gate delays

46. (a)

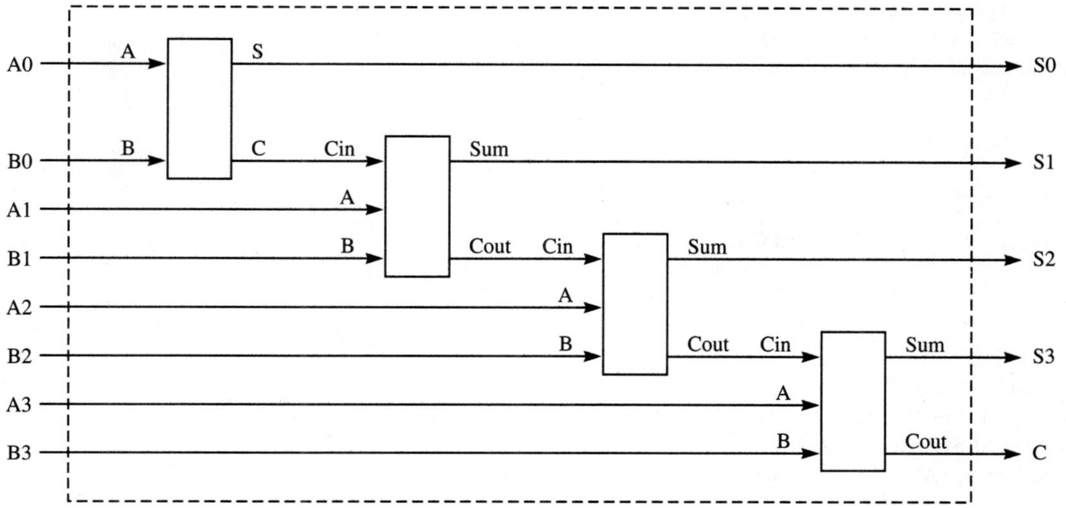

(c) Hint: If you look at the figure of part (a) and use the fact that a full adder has three gate delays and a half adder has one gate delay, you might conclude that the total gate delay is 10. However, it is less than that.

49. Hint: The construction will be identical to the four-bit adder in Exercise 46(a), but with additional inputs for the select lines.

Chapter 20

1. The network will be stable if there are an even number of inverters.

3.

	A	B	C	D	E	R2	S2	Q	$\overline{Q}$
(a)	0	0	1	1	0	1	0	0	1
(b)	0	0	0	0	0	1	0	0	1

5. (b)

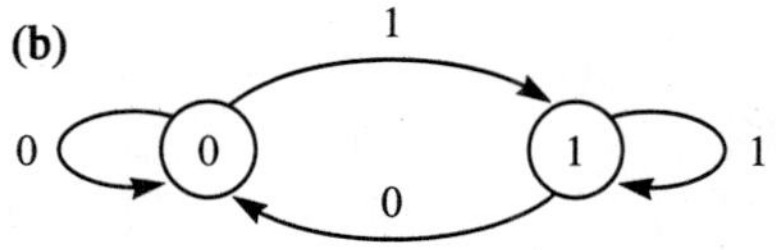

7. (a)

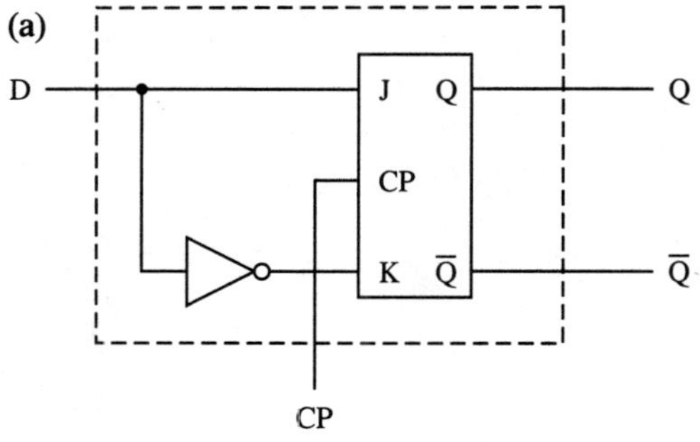

8. (a) Hint: To force the master and slave to 0, the Clear input should (1) force the slave to be connected to the master regardless of the output of the inverter, and (2) force the master to the Q = 0 state. To implement (2), consider the possibility of adding a third input line to one of the master NOR gates and/or a third input line to one of the master AND gates.

12. (a) $DA = A\,\overline{X1} + \overline{A}\,X1 + A\,B\,\overline{X2} + B\,X1\,X2$

$DB = \overline{B}\,\overline{X1} + B\,X1\,X2 + \overline{A}\,B\,X1$

14. (a) $JA = \overline{B}\,\overline{C}\,X + B\,C\,X$ $\quad KA = \overline{B}\,\overline{C}\,X + B\,C\,X$

$JB = \overline{C}\,\overline{X} + C\,X$ $\quad KB = \overline{C}\,\overline{X} + C\,X$

$JC = 1$ $\quad KC = 1$

17. (a) Note that the N and Z bits are affected.

```
{  Zero out the N and Z bits.  }
1. A:=0, B:=27, ALatch, BLatch
2. AMux:=1, ALU:=6, ALUMux:=0, C:=0, Load

{  Transfer OprndSpec to low-order A.  }
3. A:=13, ALatch
4. AMux:=1, ALU:=0, ALUMux:=0, C:=2, Load

{  Store status bits in Templ.  }
5. ALU:=0, ALUMux:=1, C:=14, Load

{  Extract N and OR with machine-level N. }
6. A:=14, B:=29, ALatch, BLatch
7. AMux:=1, ALU:=6, ALUMux:=0, C:=15, Load
8. A:=0, B:=15, ALatch, BLatch
9. AMux:=1, ALU:=8, ALUMux:=0, C:=0, Load

{  Extract Z and OR with machine-level Z. }
10. A:=14, B:=28, ALatch, BLatch
11. AMux:=1, ALU:=6, ALUMux:=0, C:=15, Load
12. A:=0, B:=15, ALatch, BLatch
13. AMux:=1, ALU:=8, ALUMux:=0, C:=0, Load
```

19. Hint: Since instruction 5 saves `Result` and instruction 6 saves `Status`, it may appear that `Carry` could be clocked on either. However, it cannot. If `Carry` is clocked on instruction 5, `Status` will be incorrect. Explain.

Index